METAX

Antoine Cossé

Fantagraphics Books ● Seattle, Washington

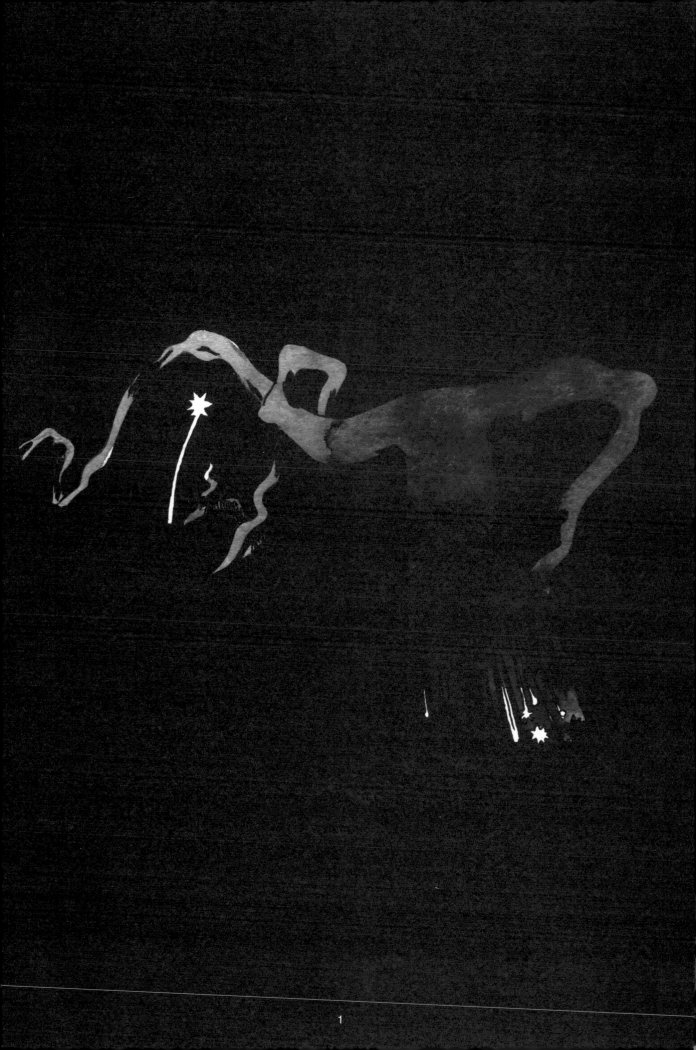

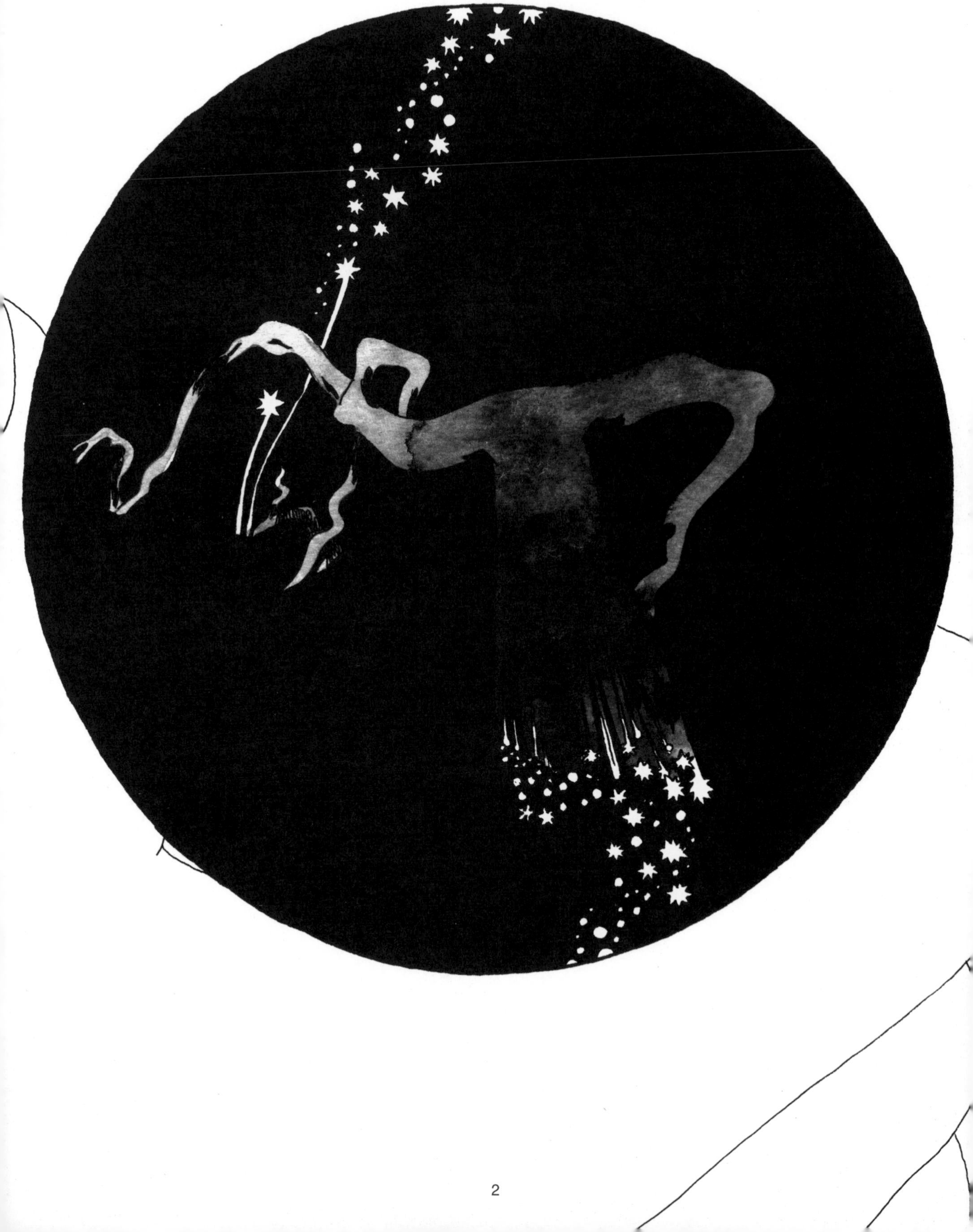

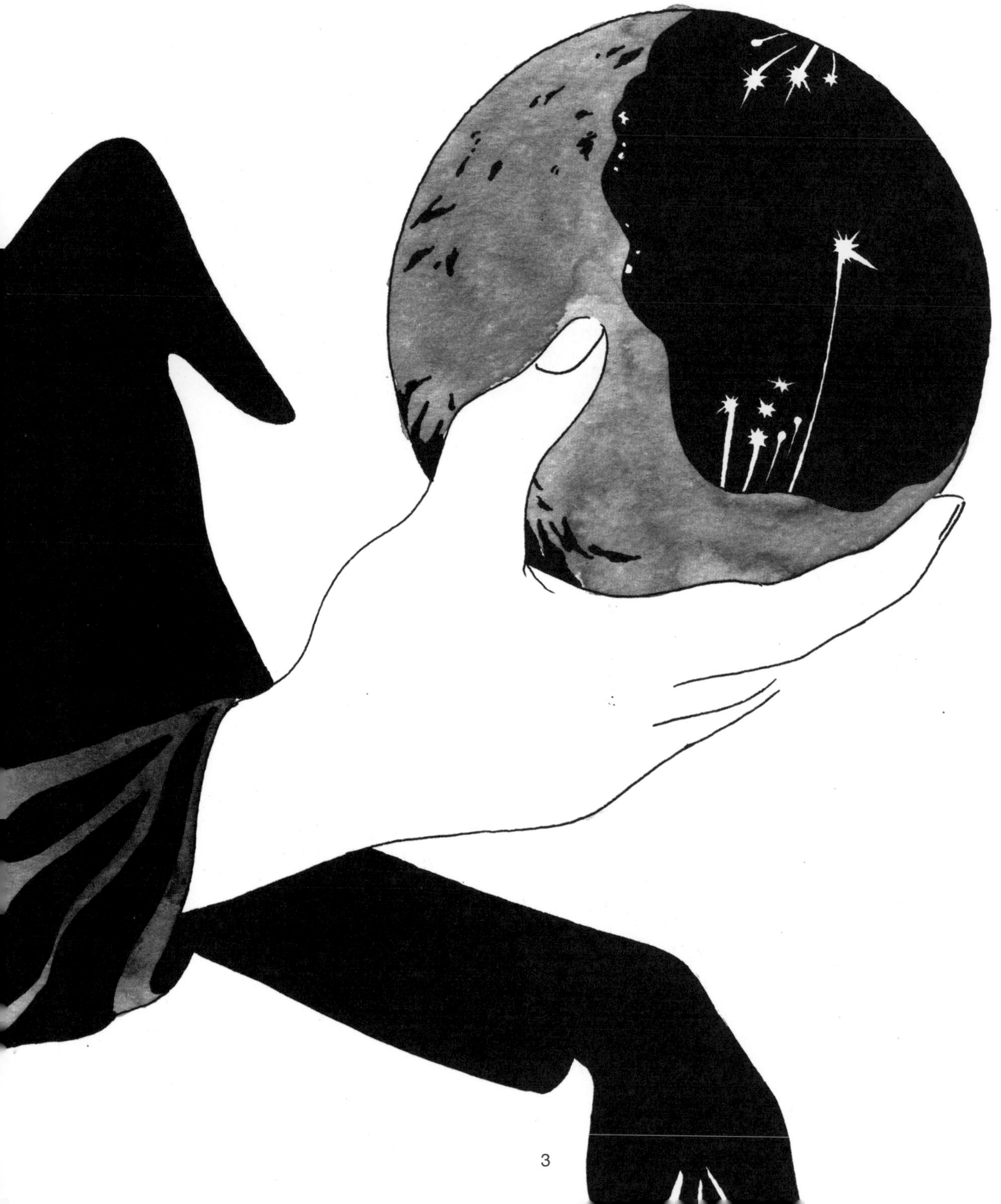

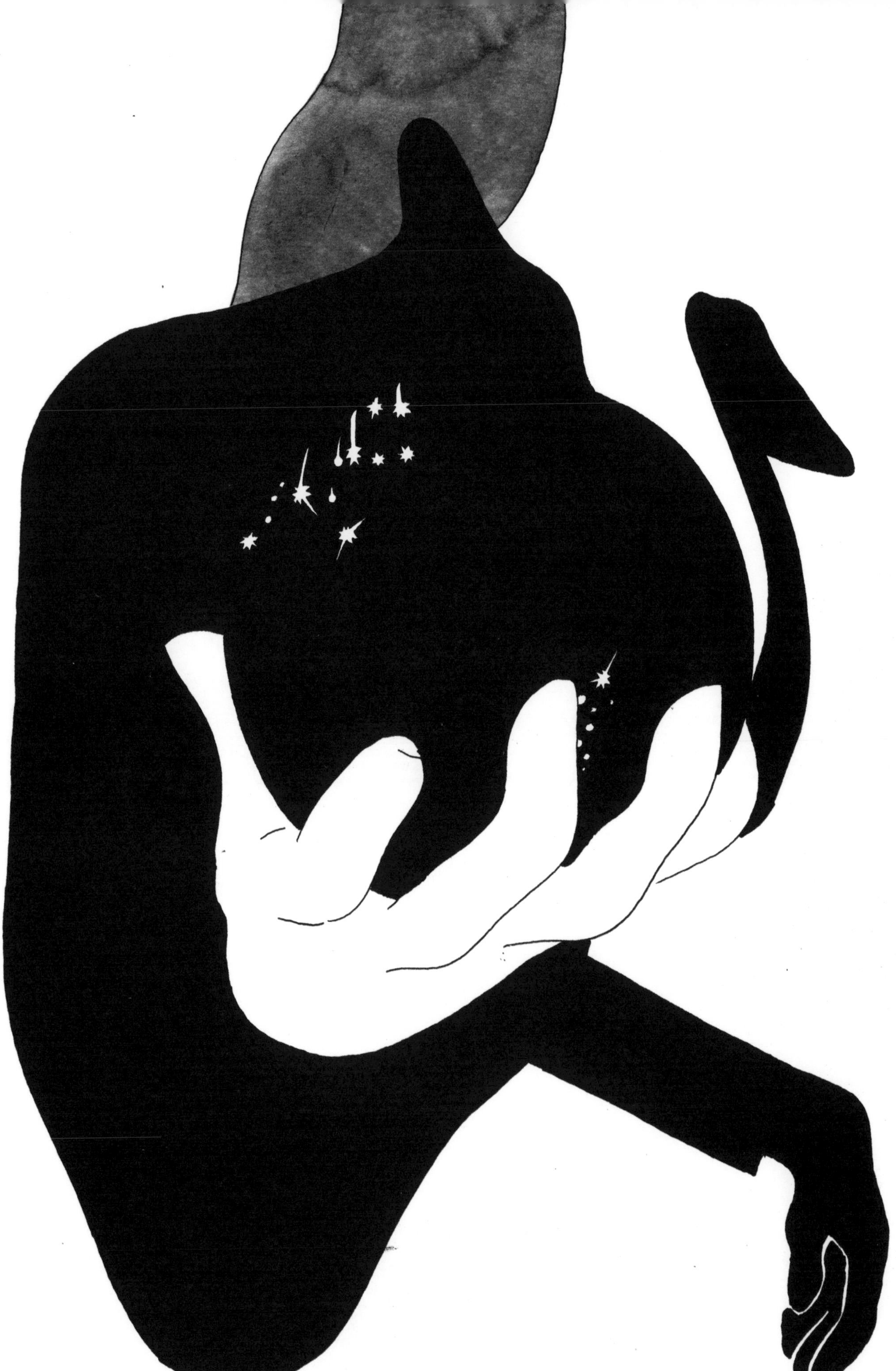

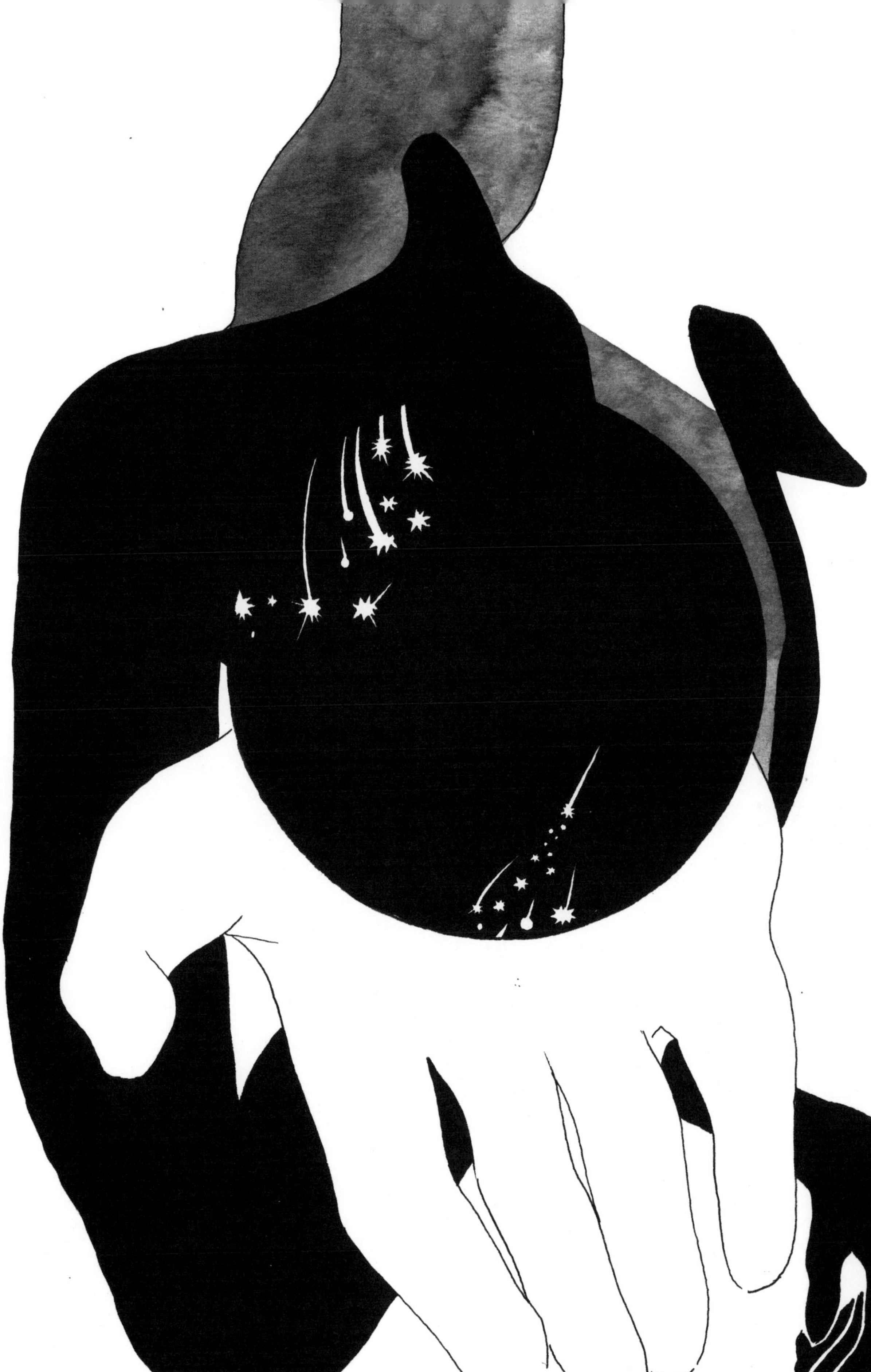

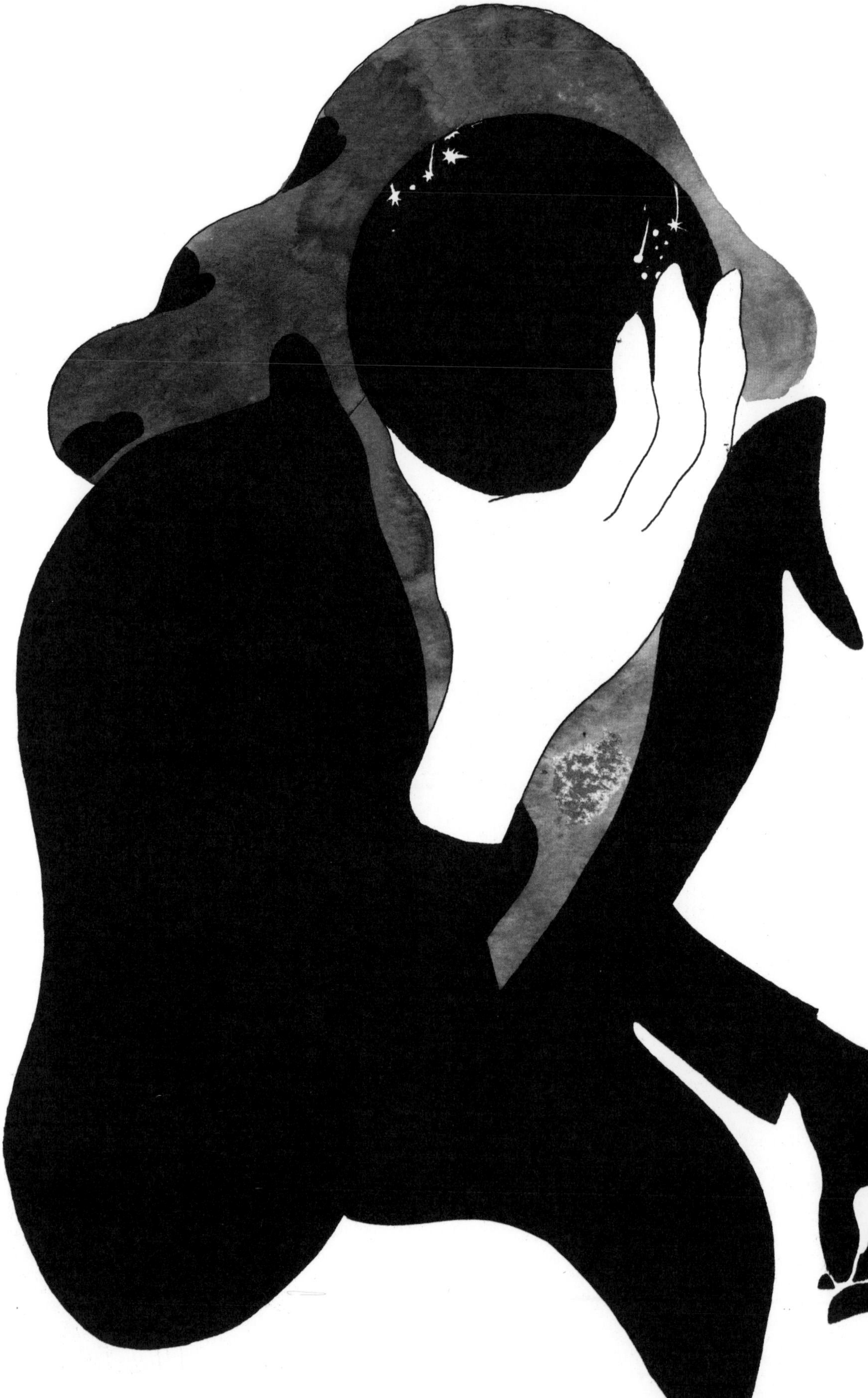

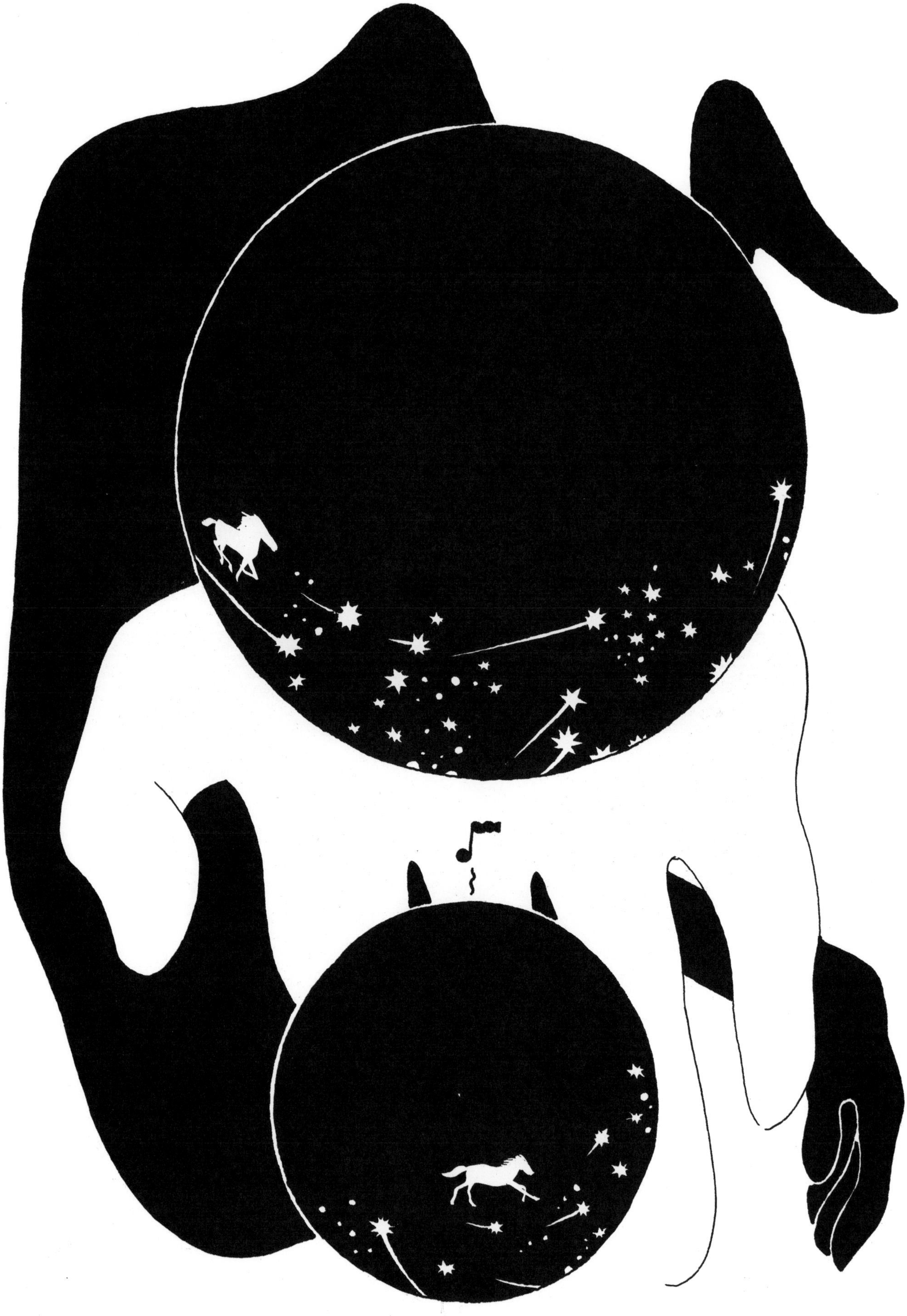

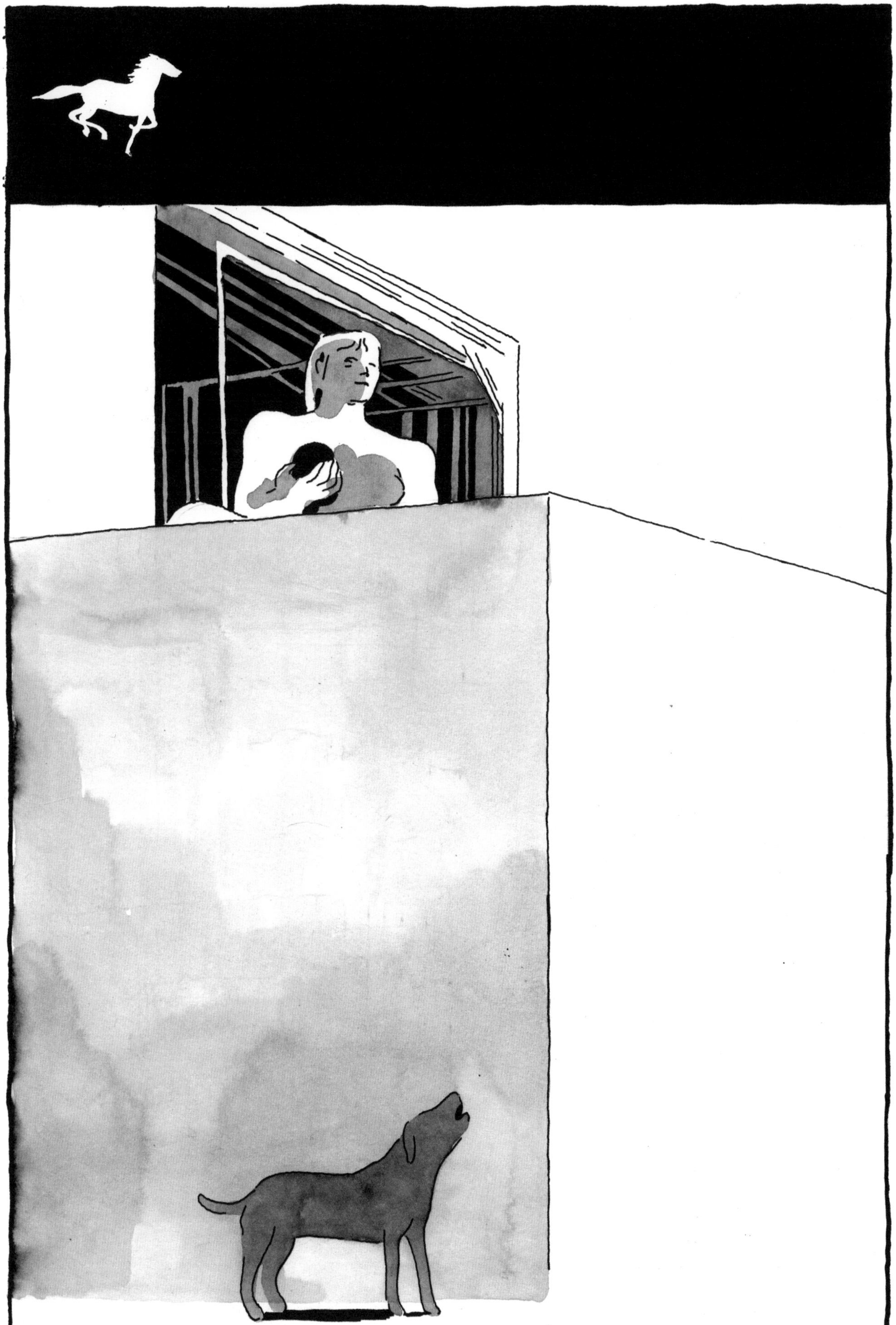

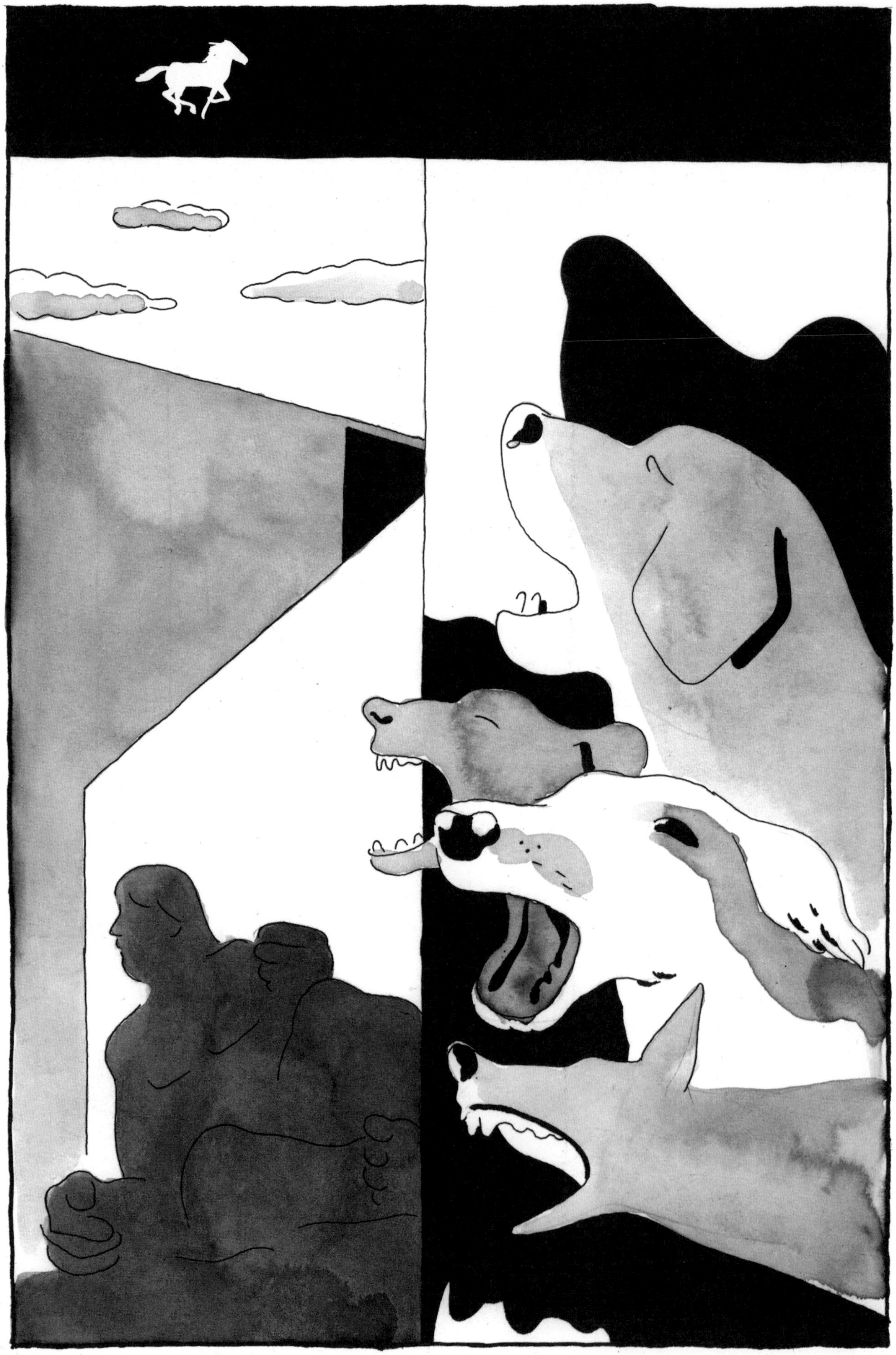

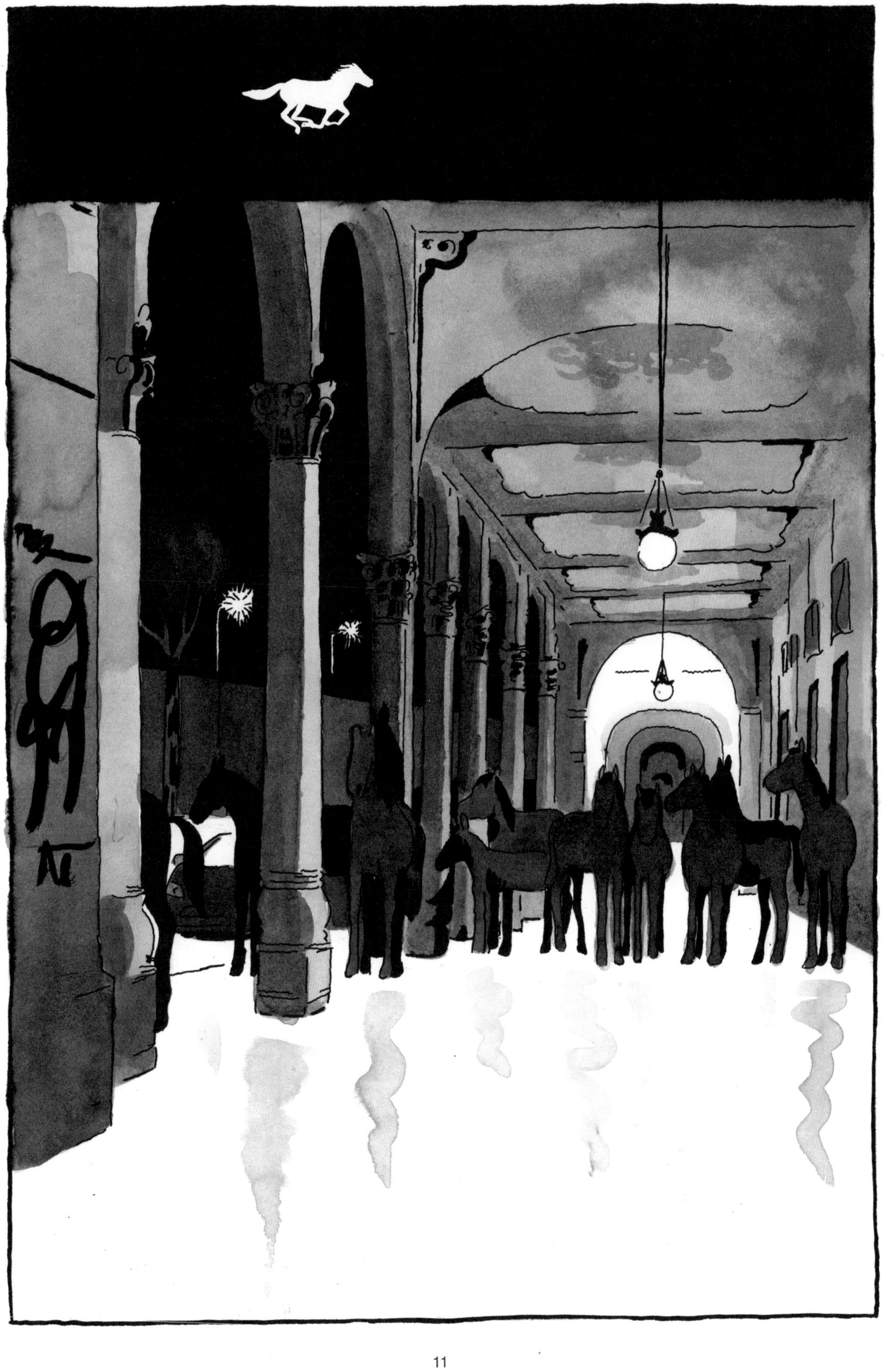

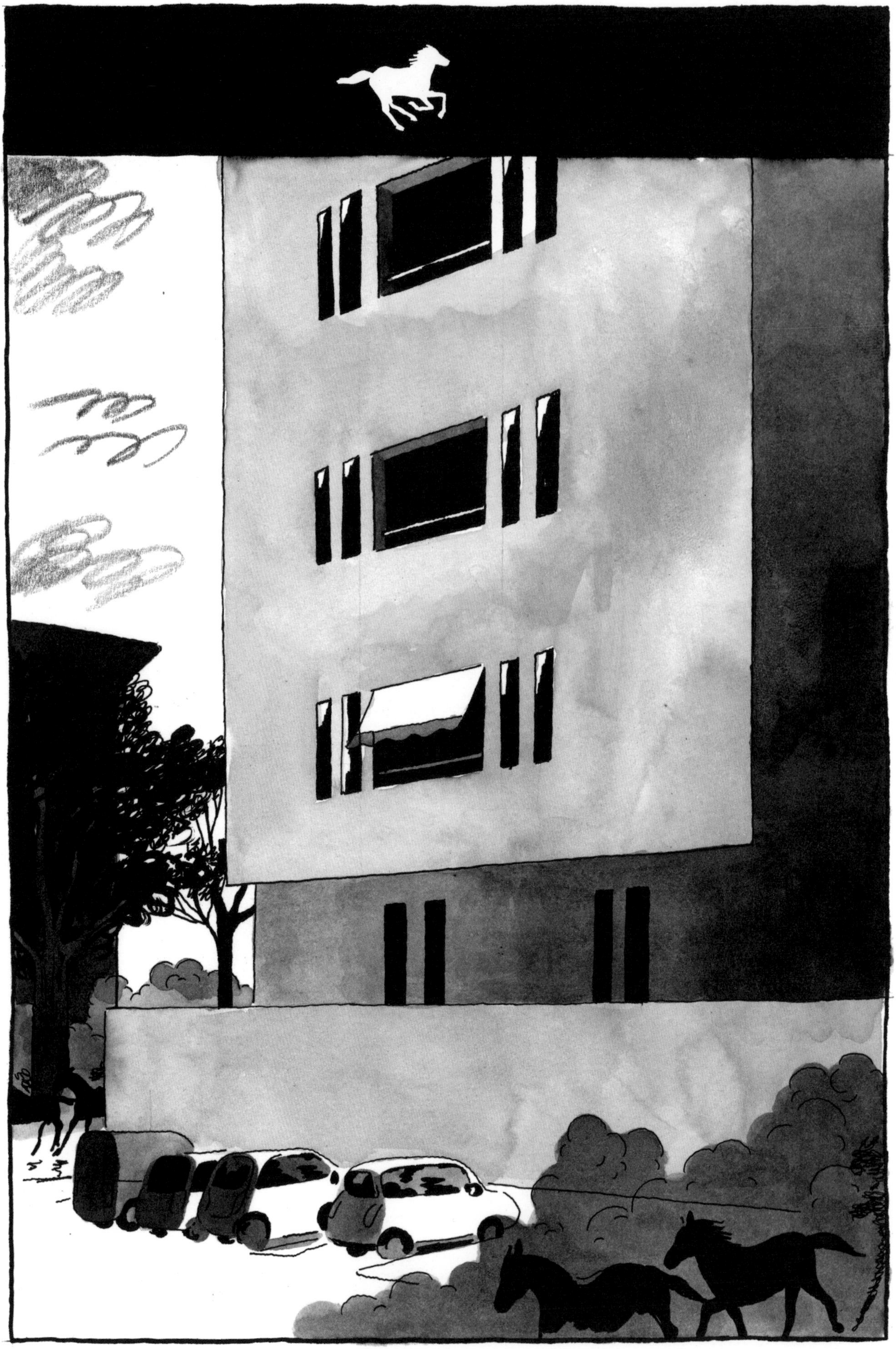

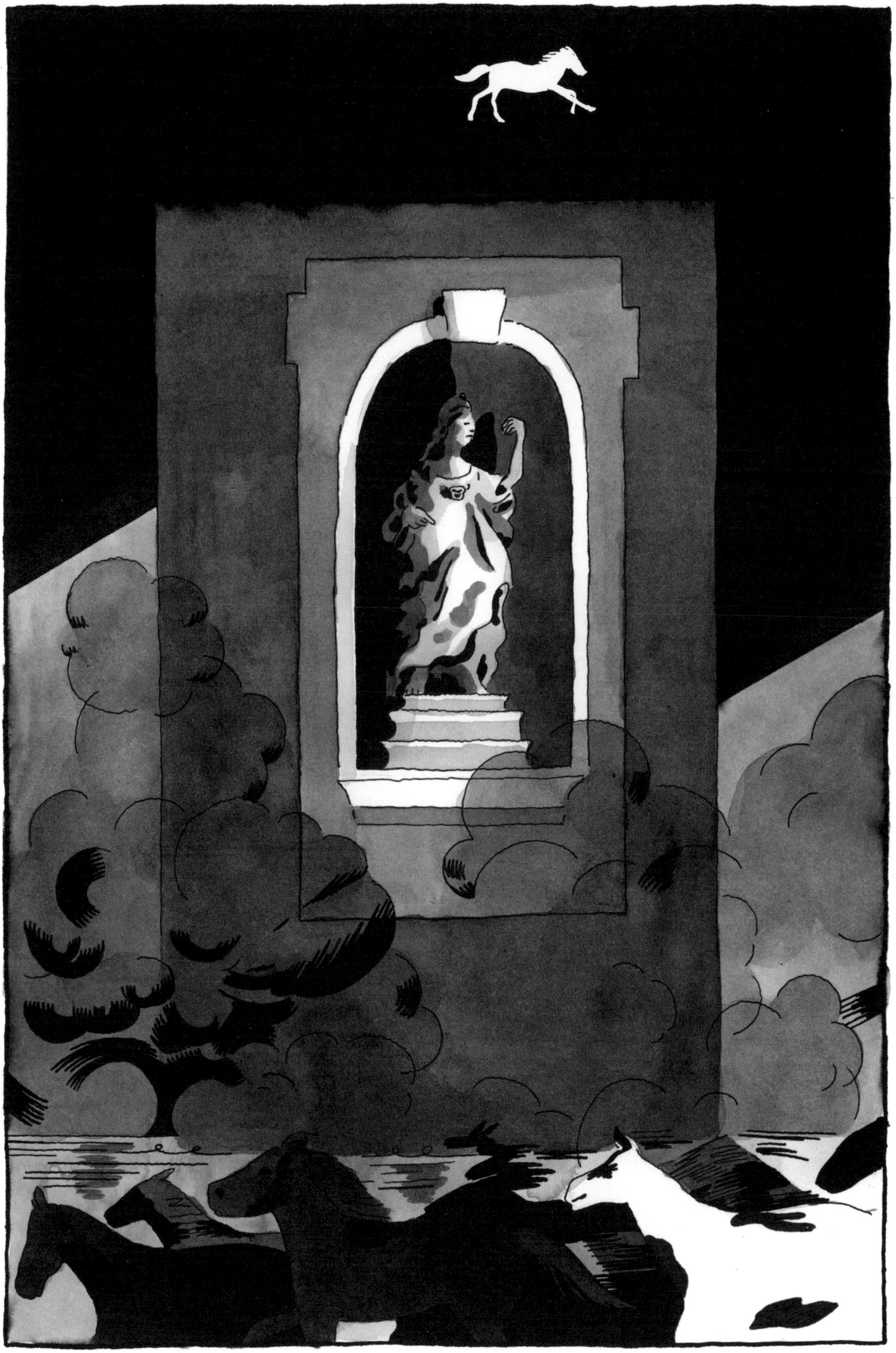

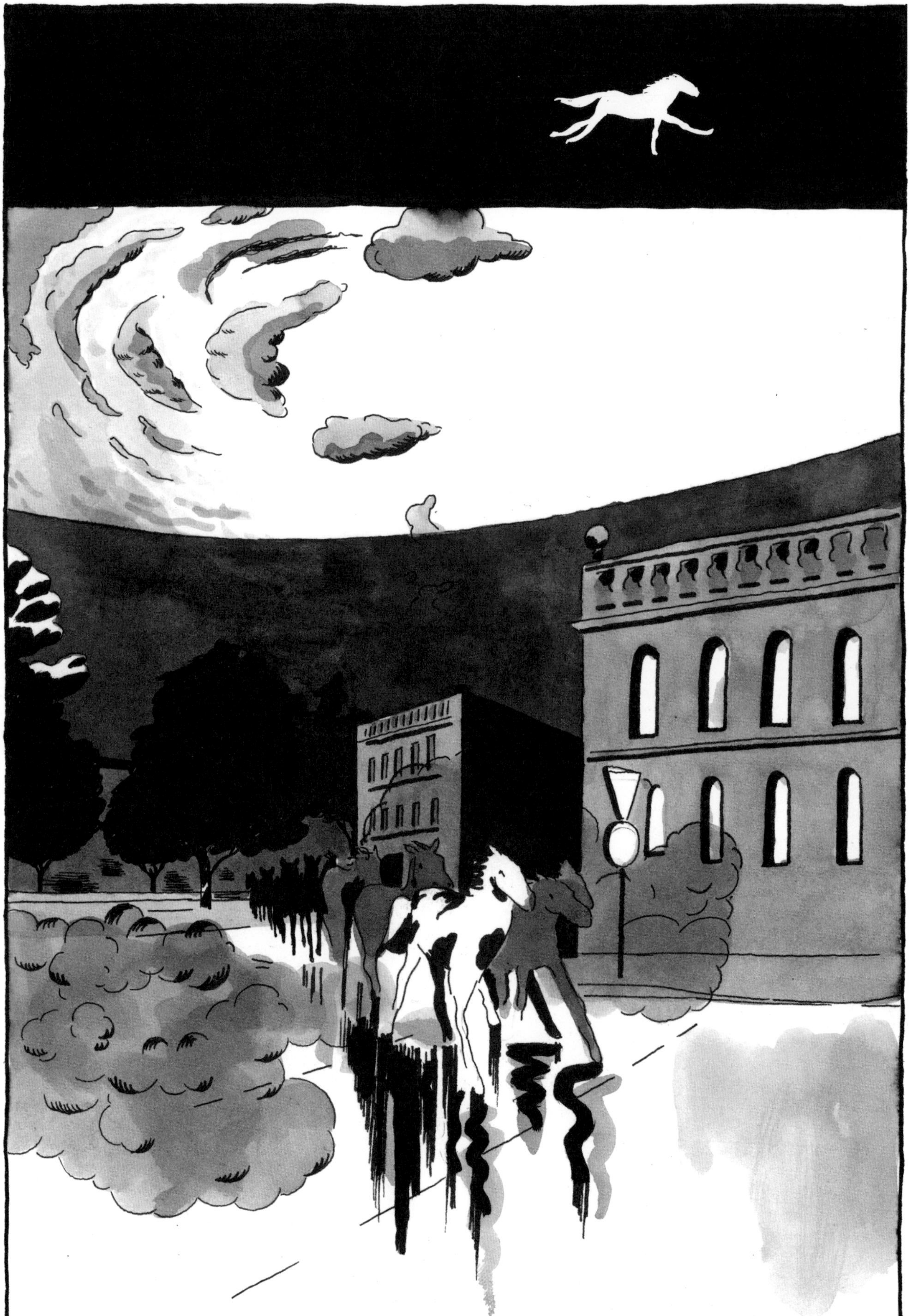

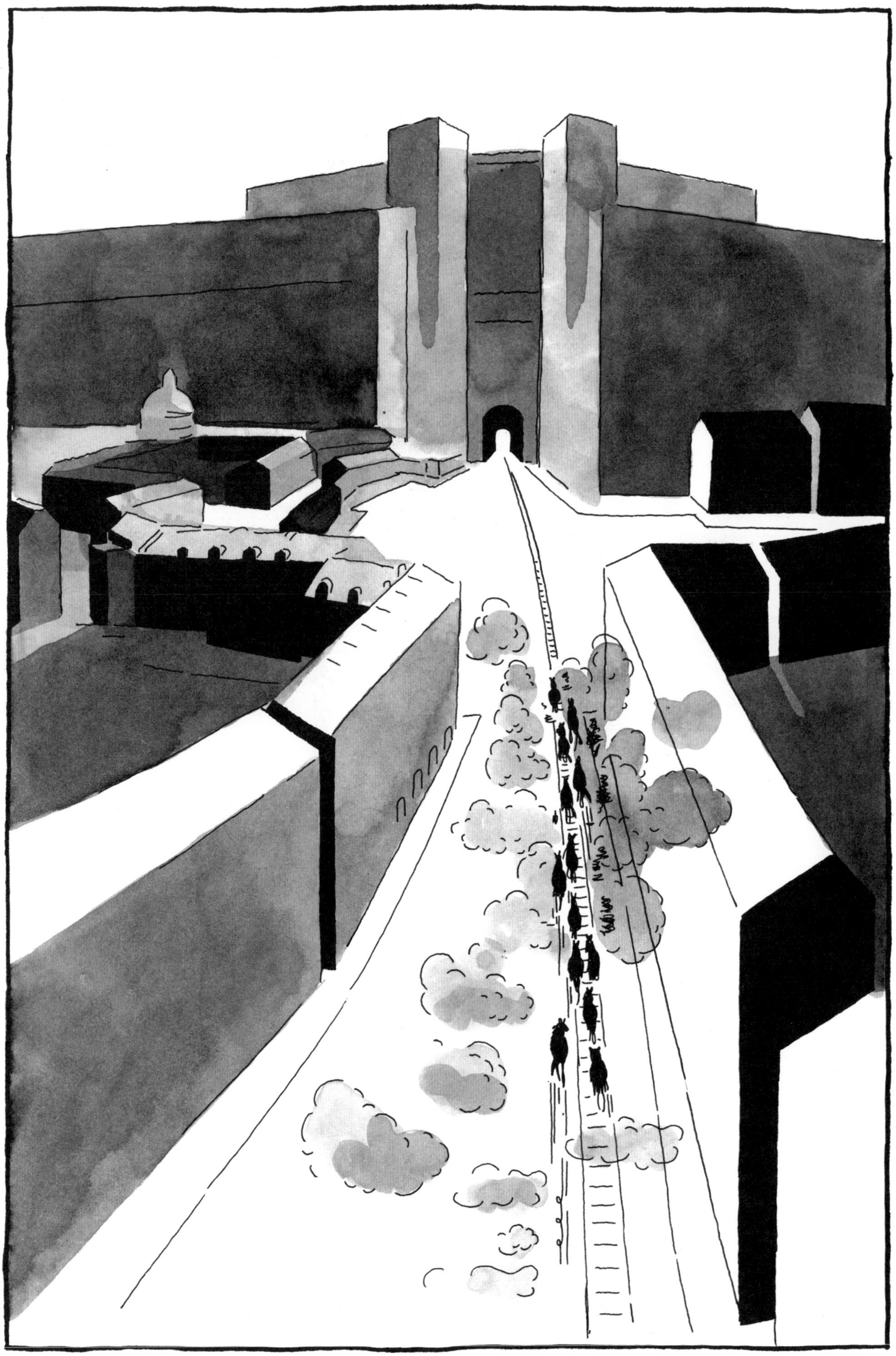

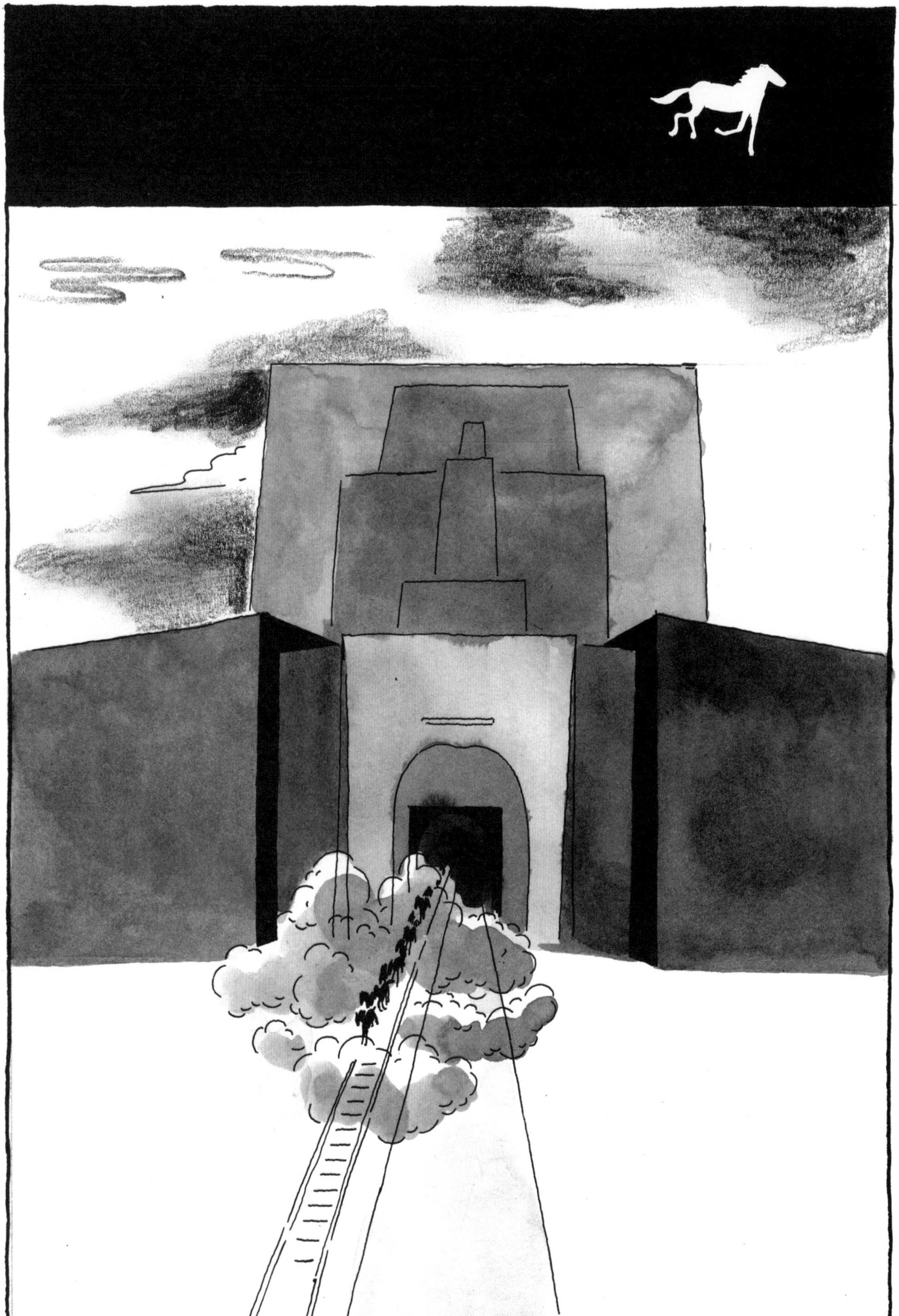

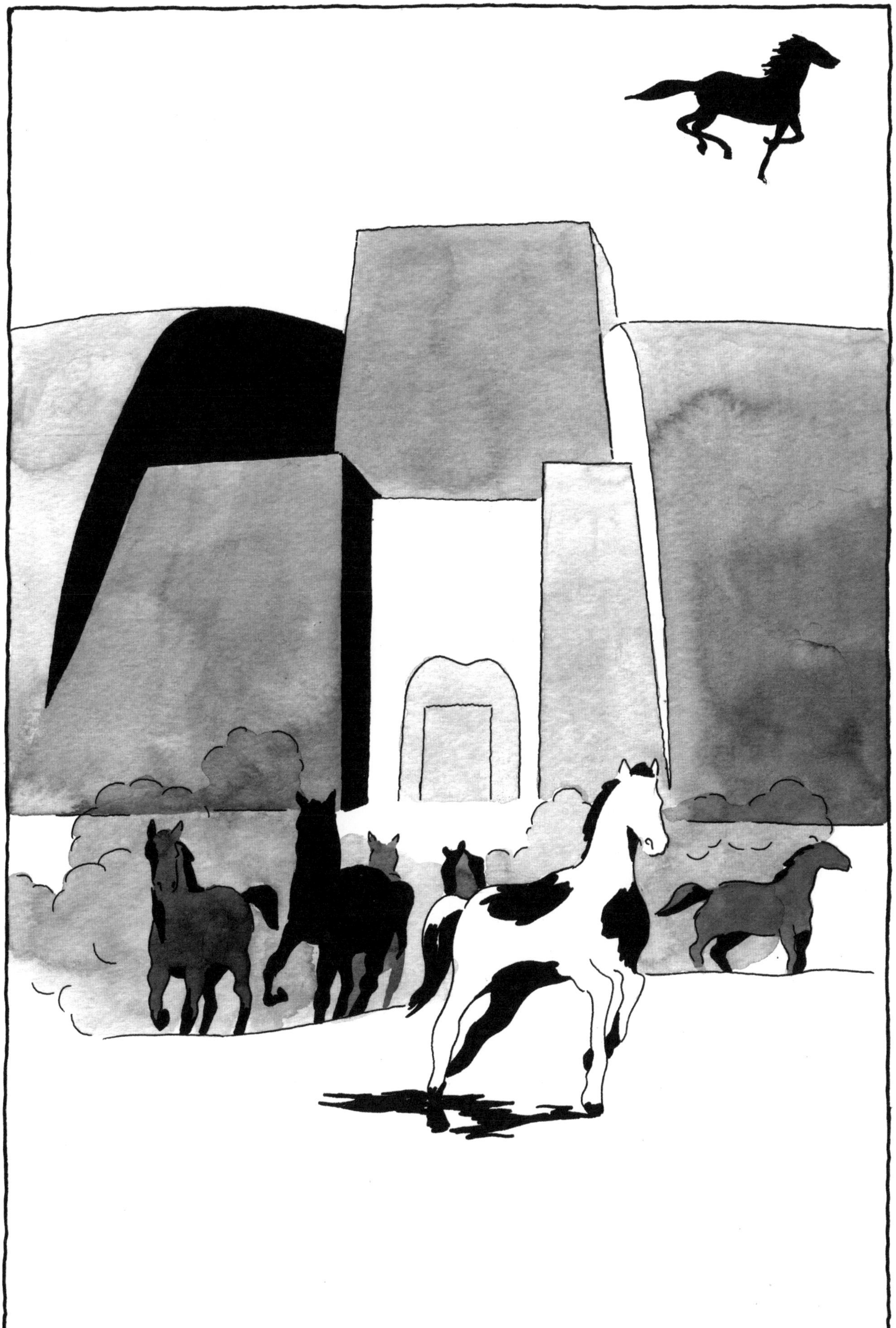

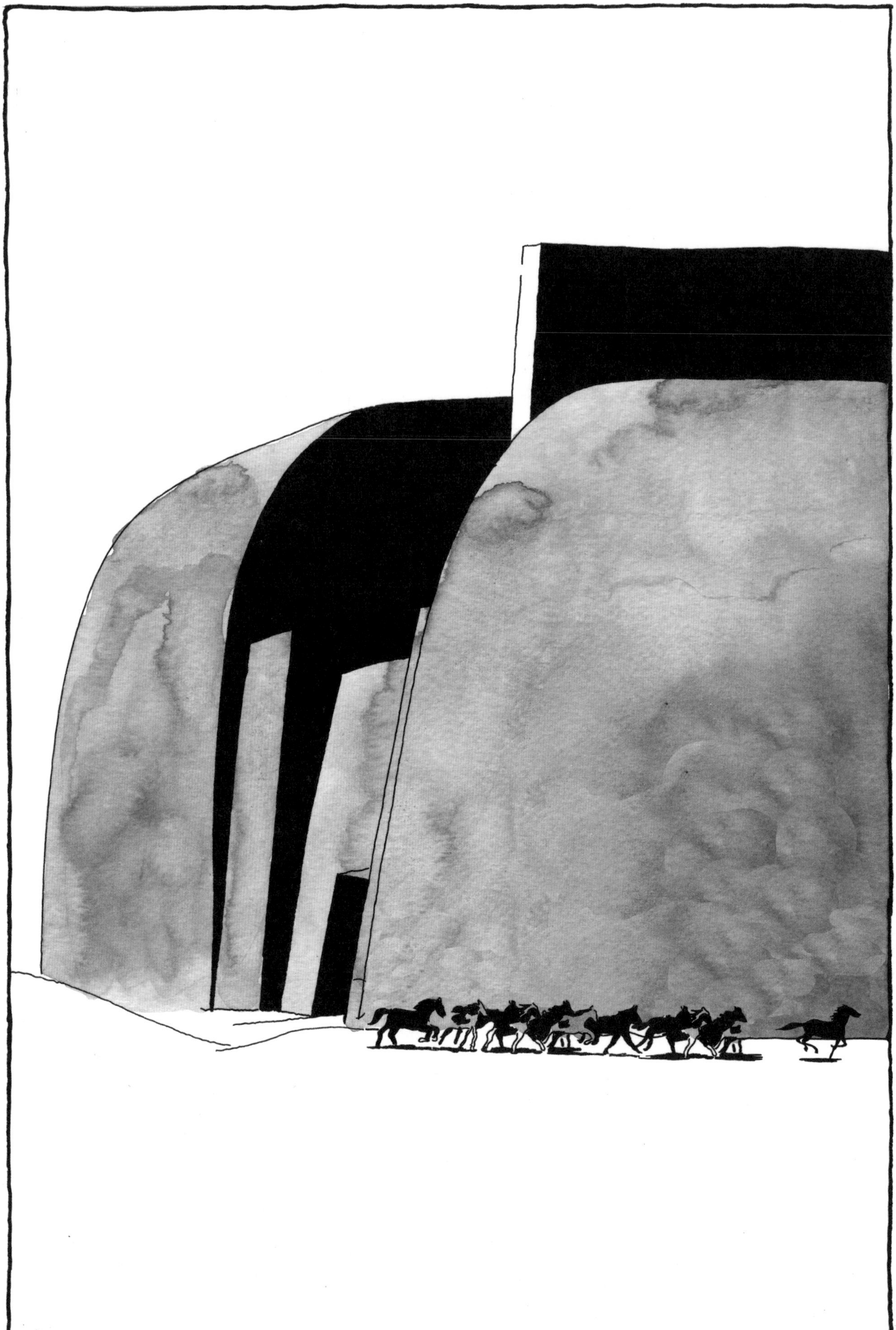

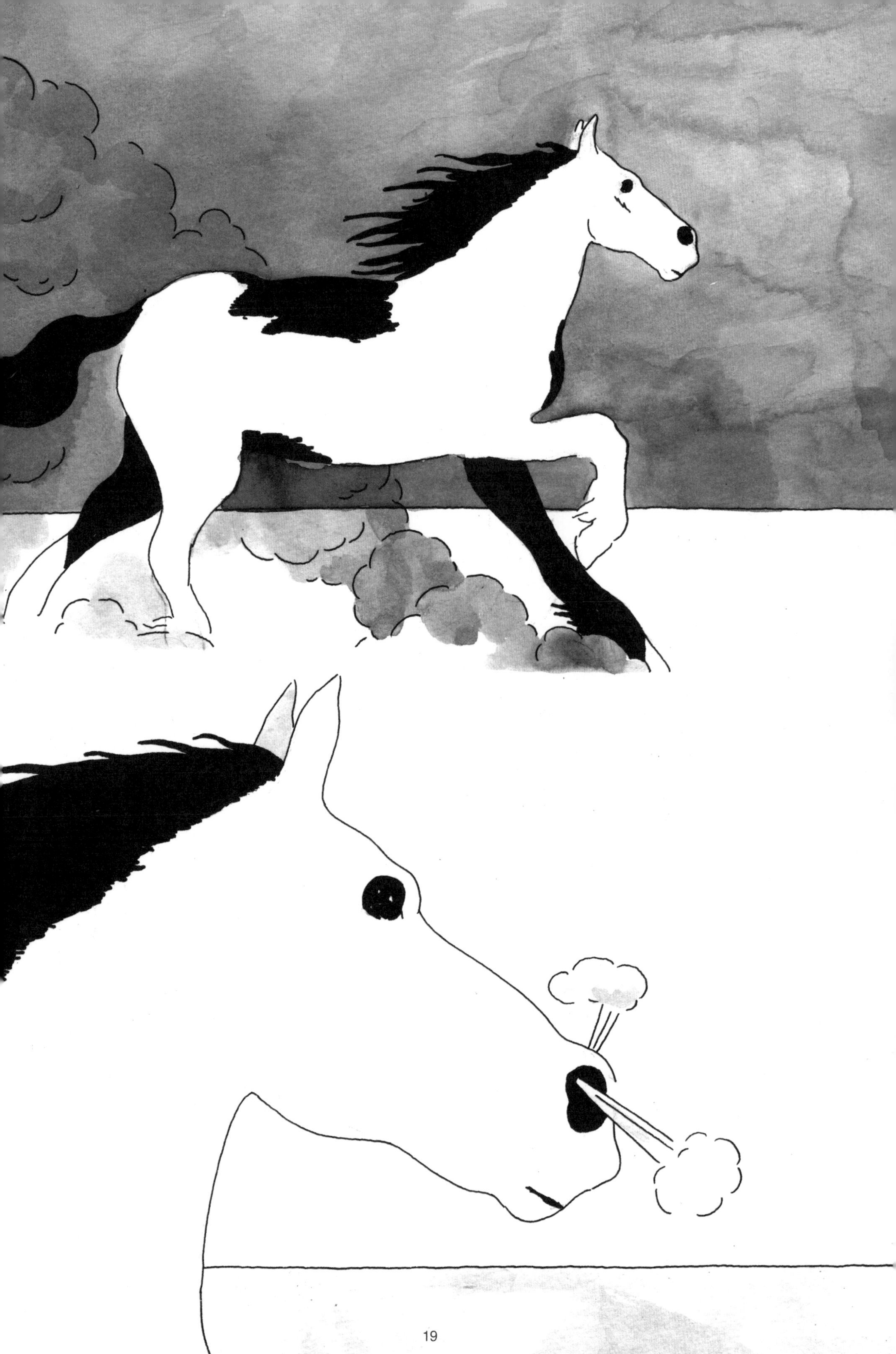

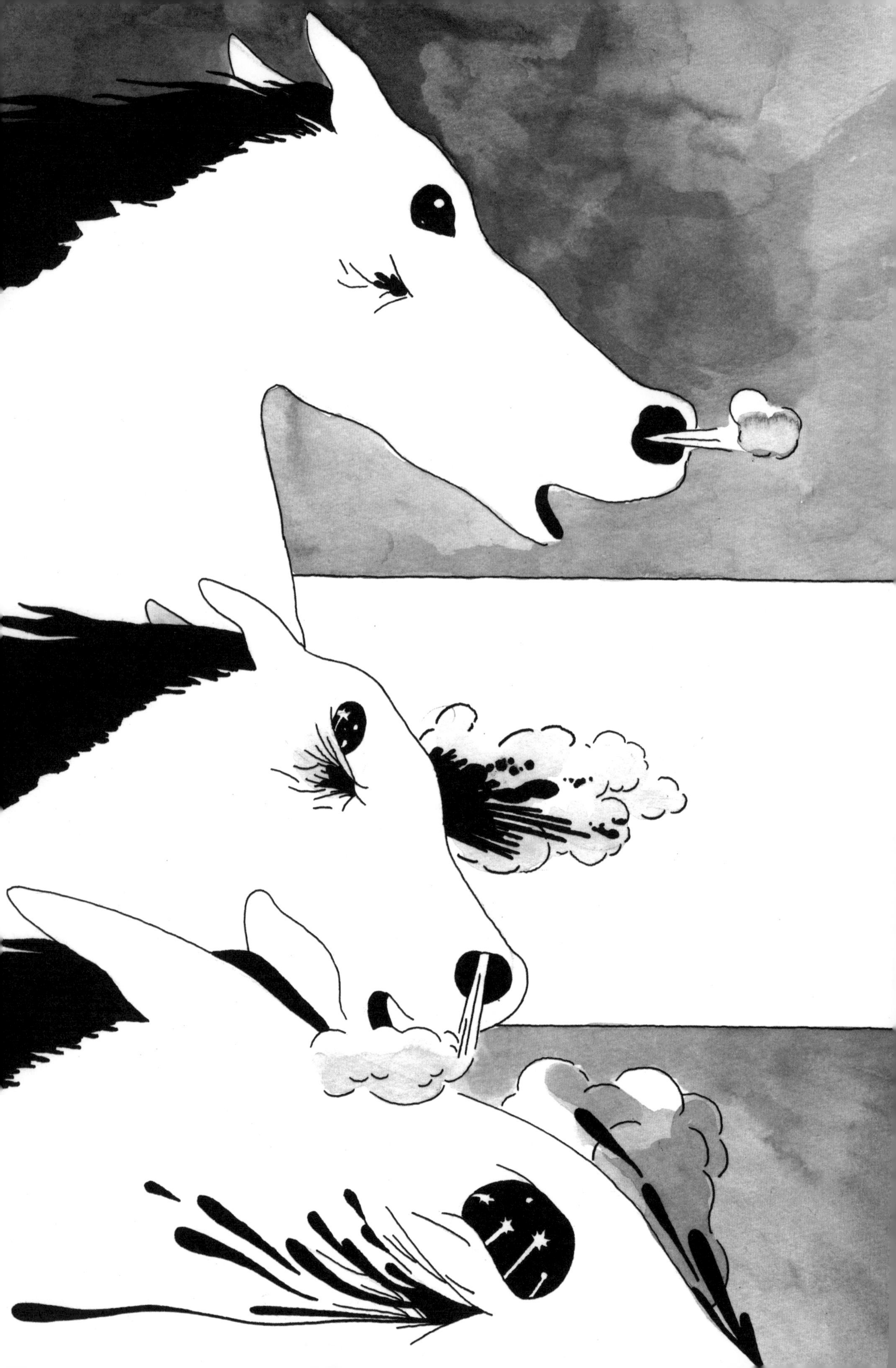

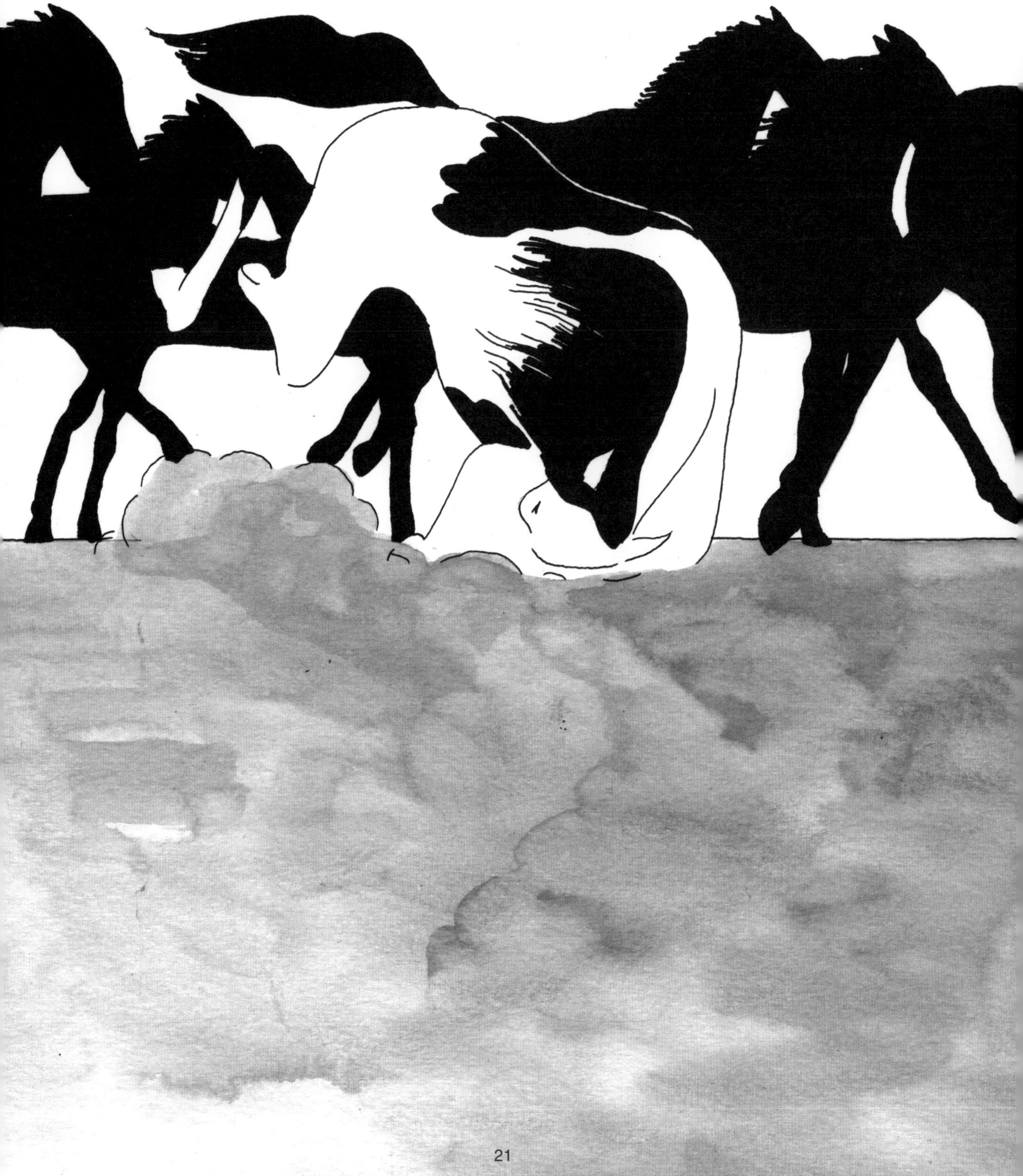

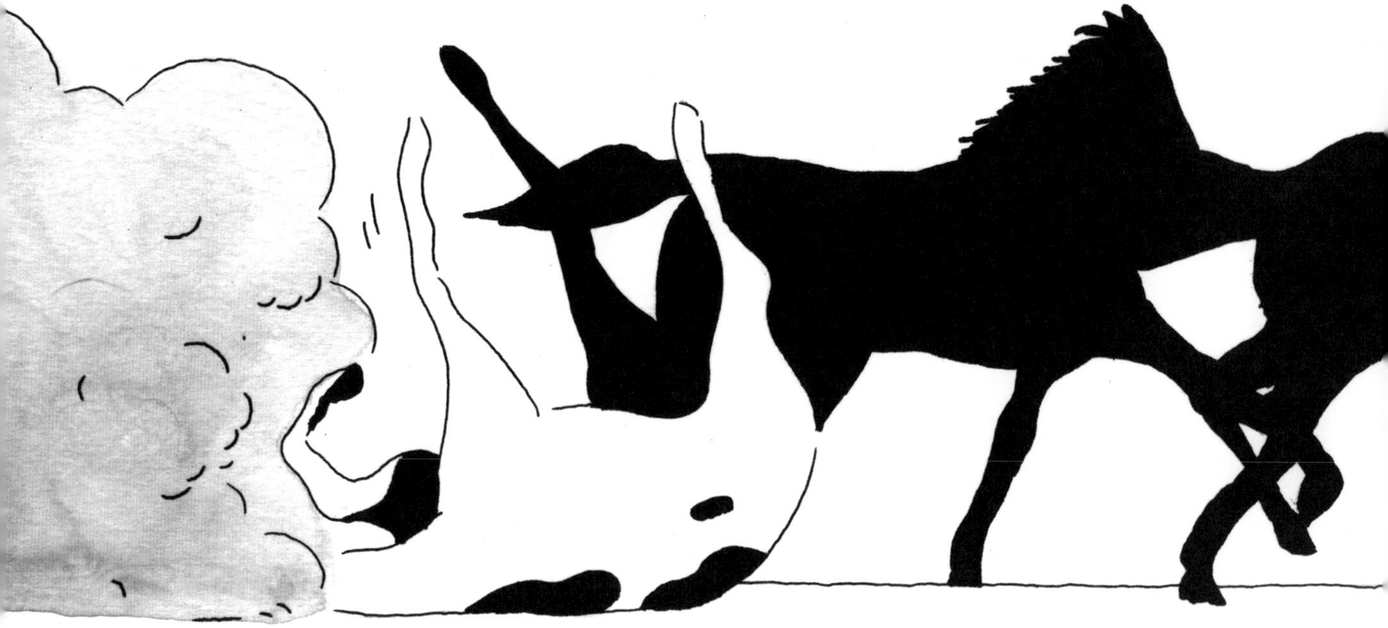

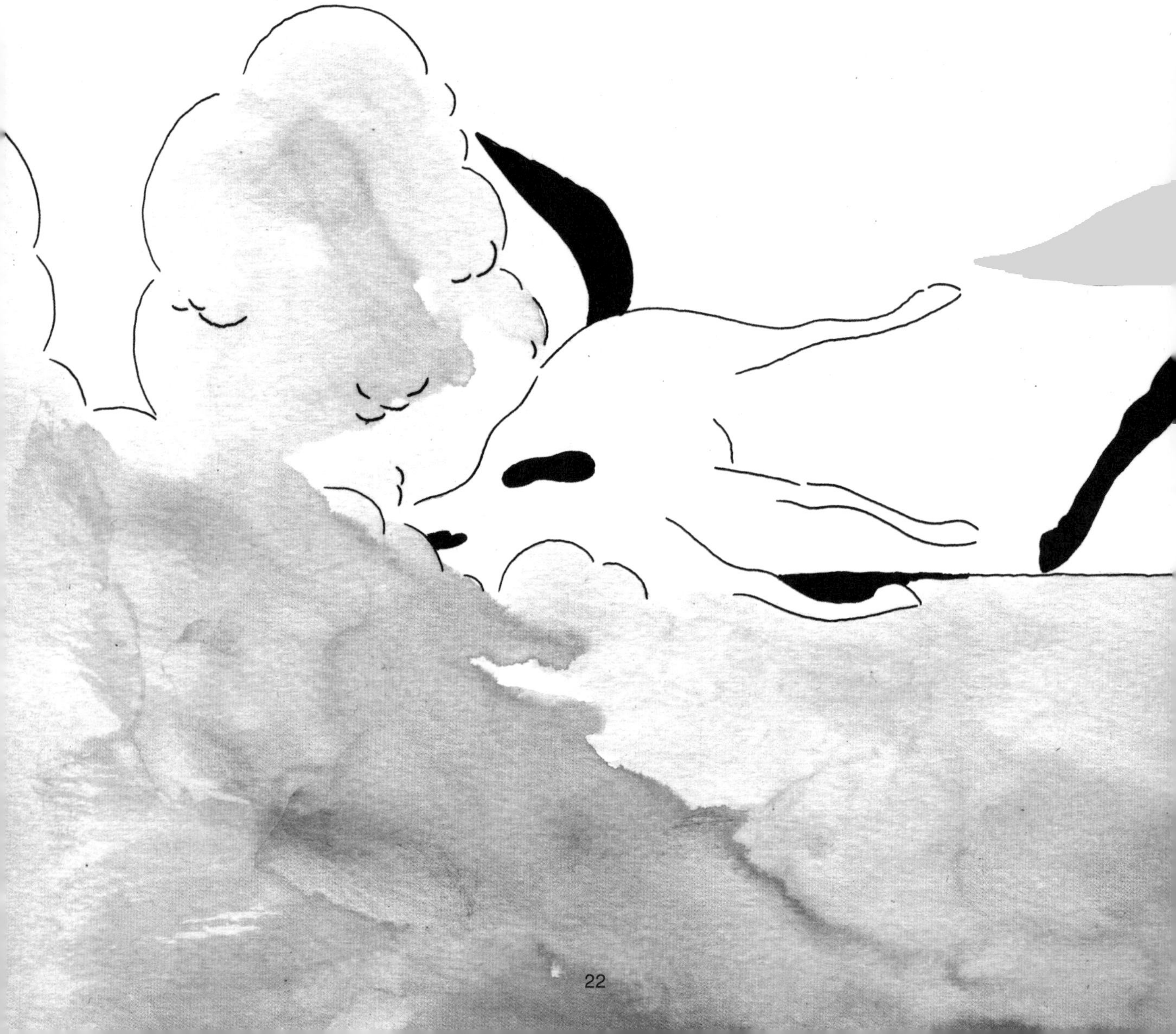

Ronin City.

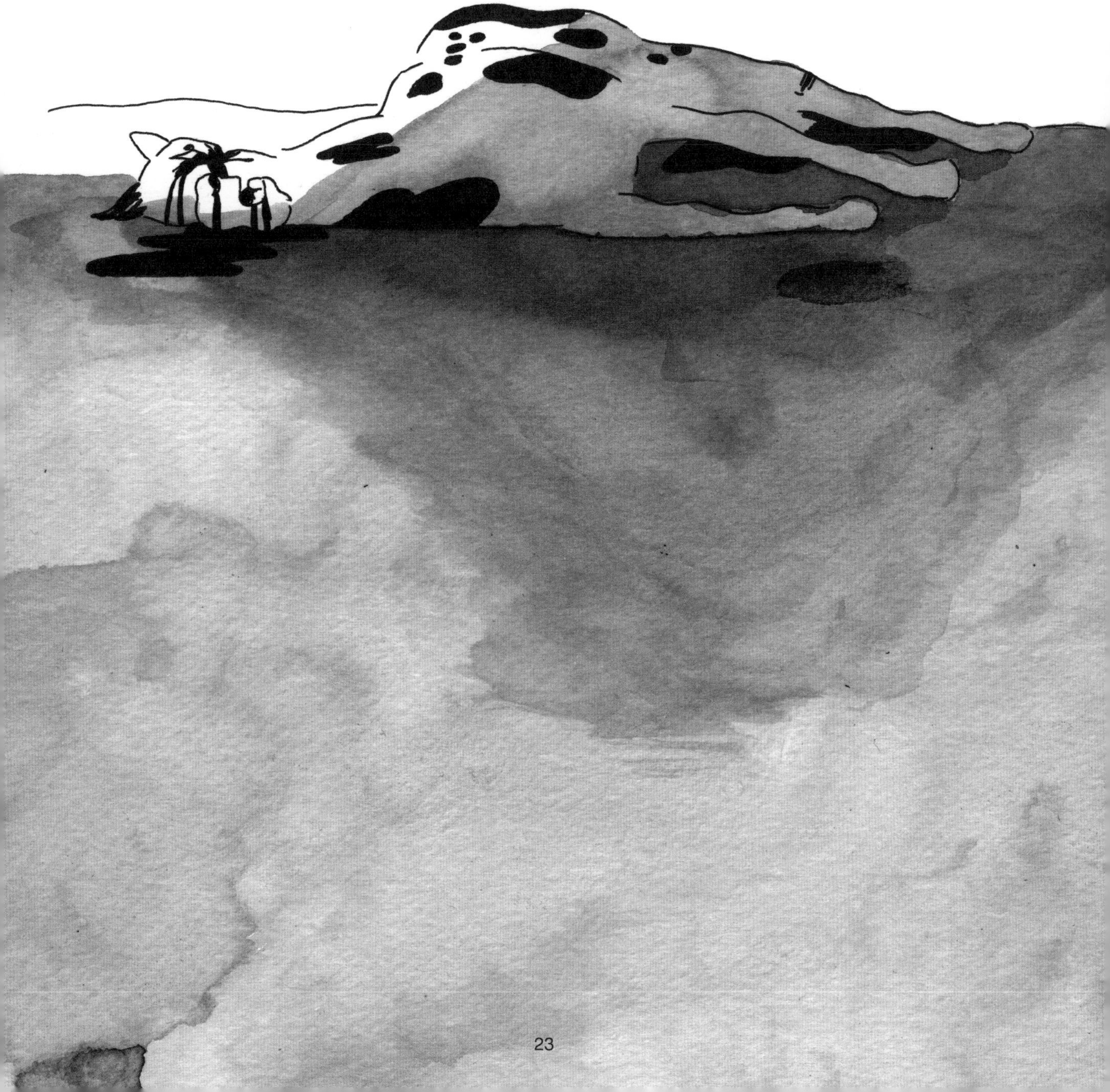

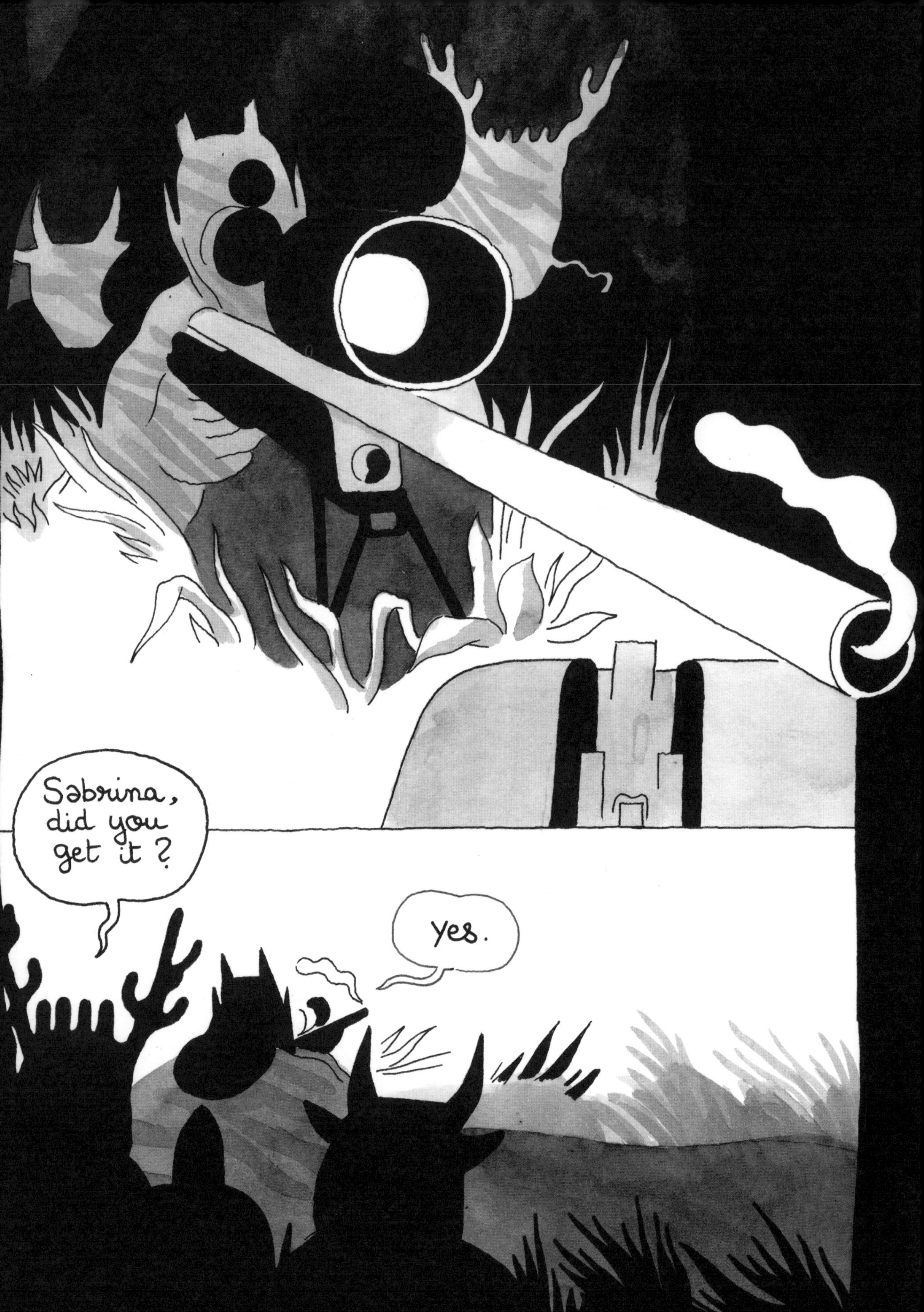
Sabrina, did you get it ?
yes.

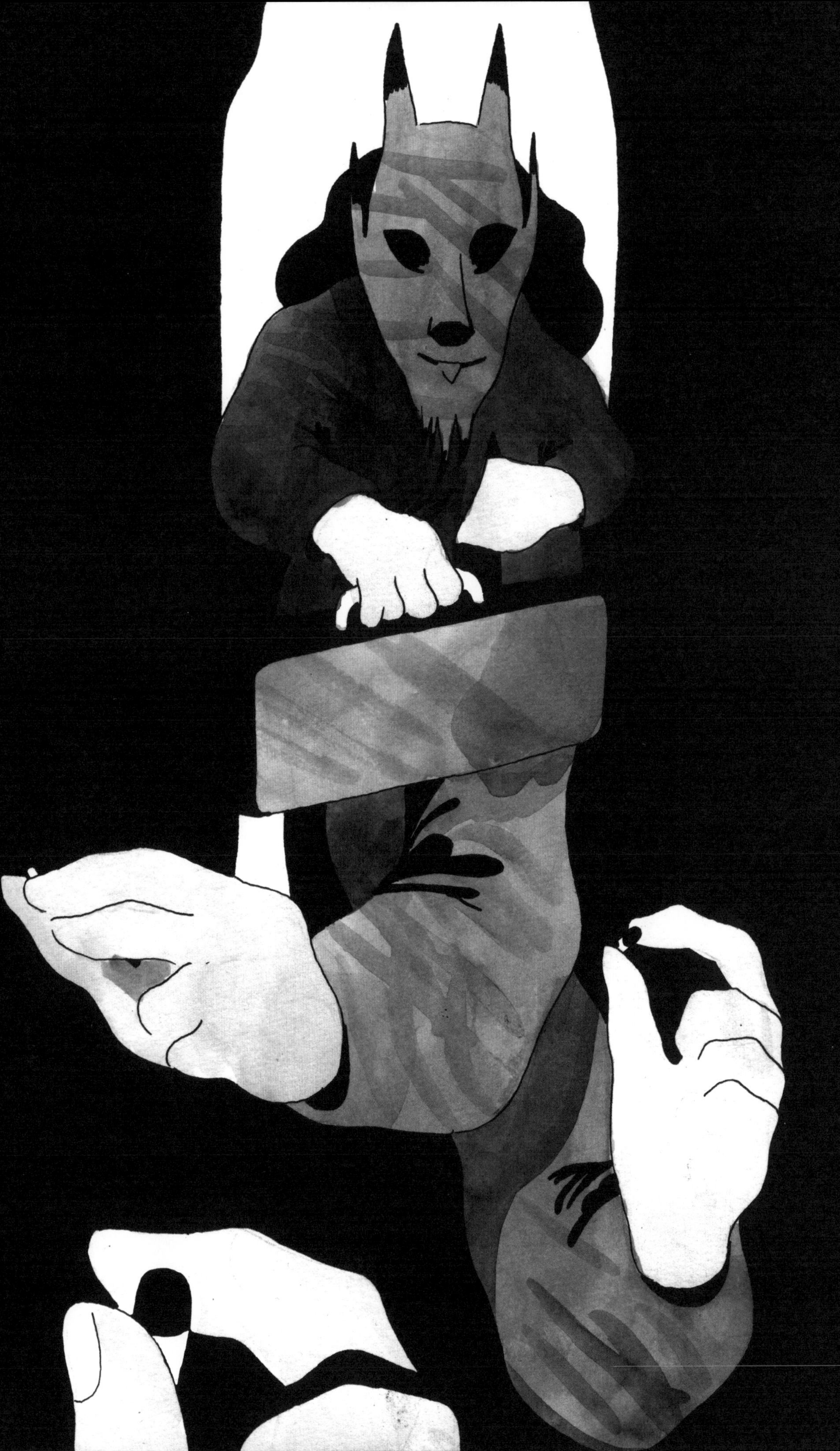

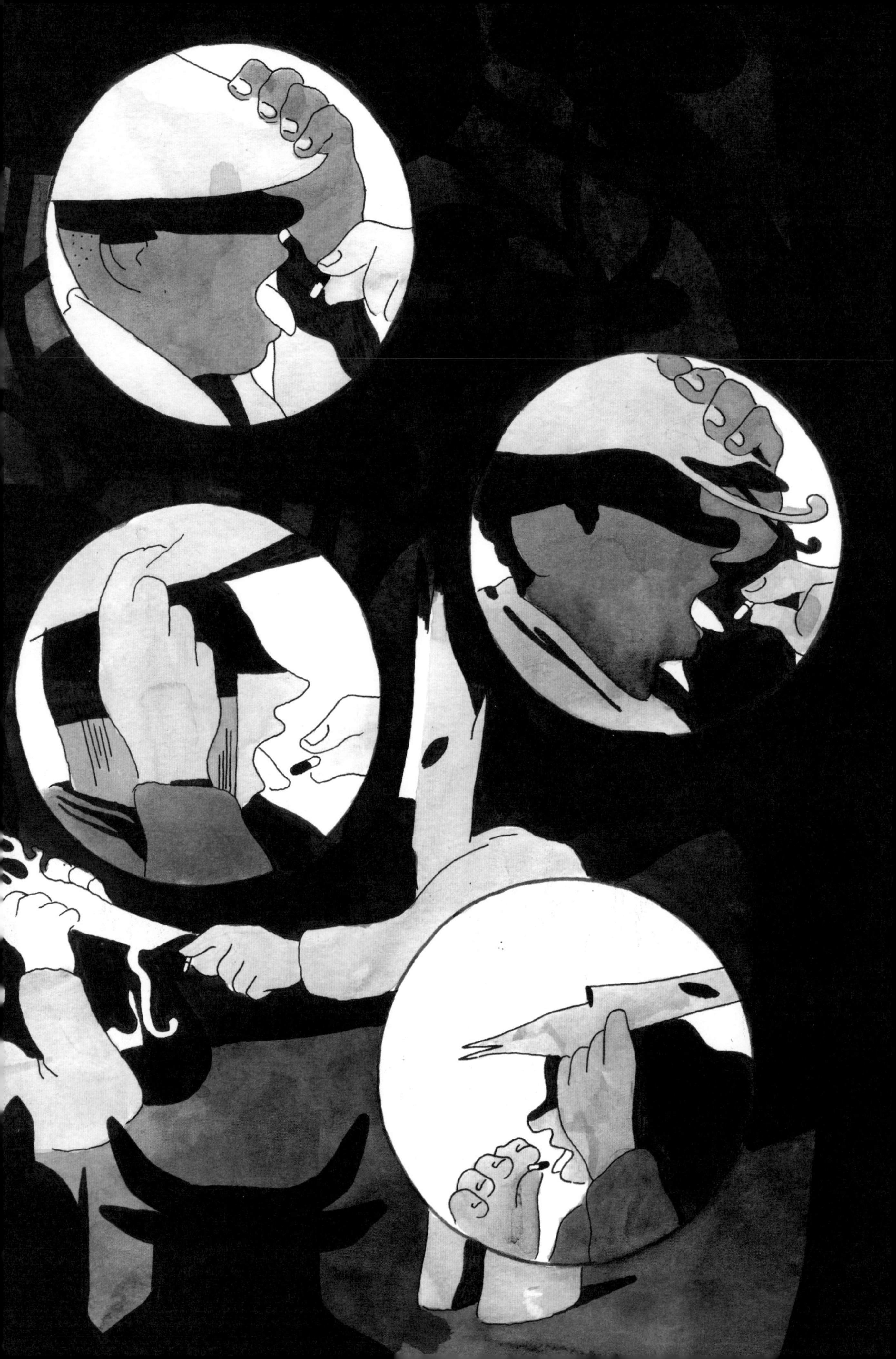

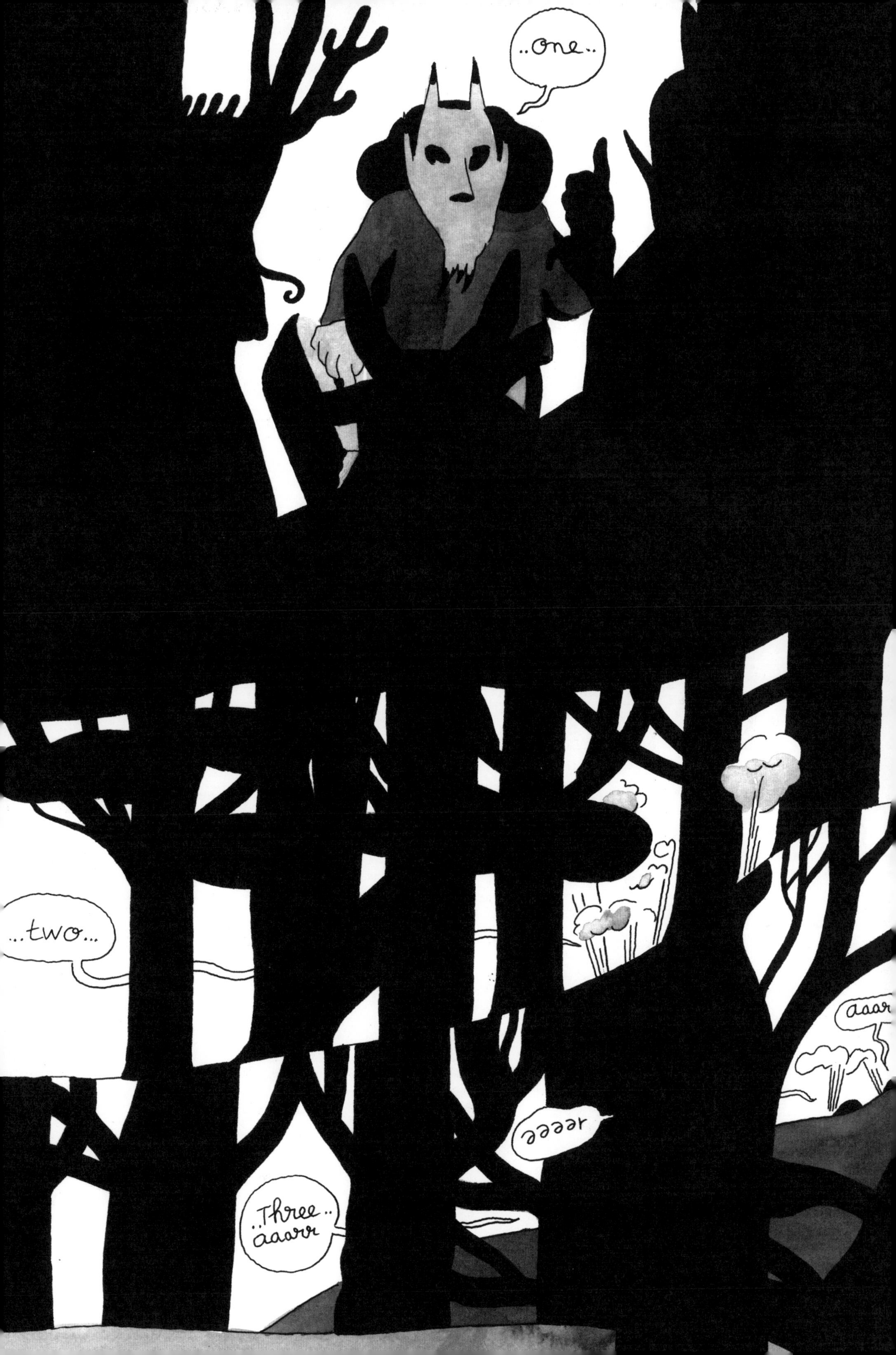
..one..
...two...
aaar
..Three..
aaarr

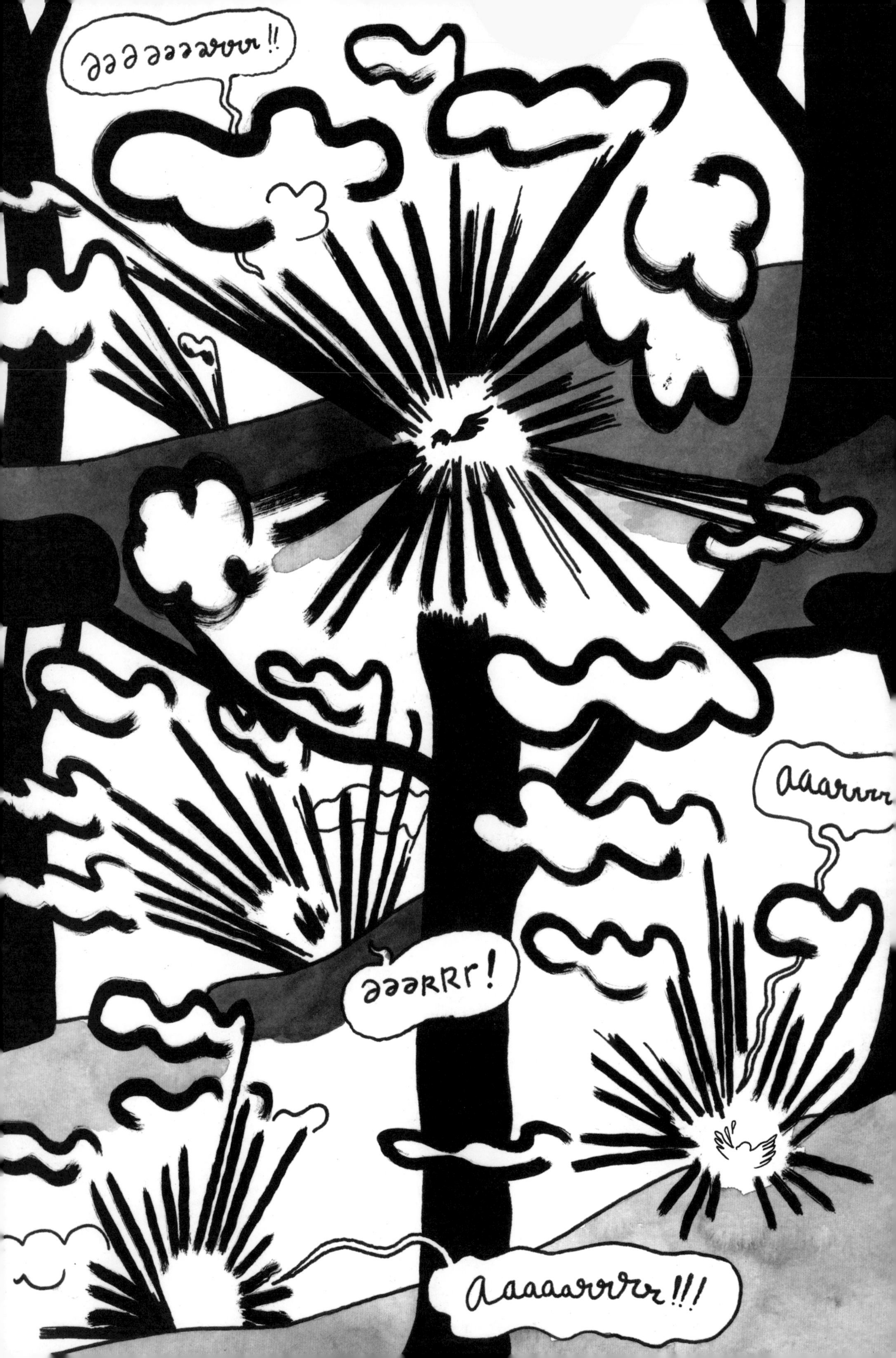

əəəəəəarrrr!!
aaarrrr
əəəRRr!
Aaaaarrrrr!!!

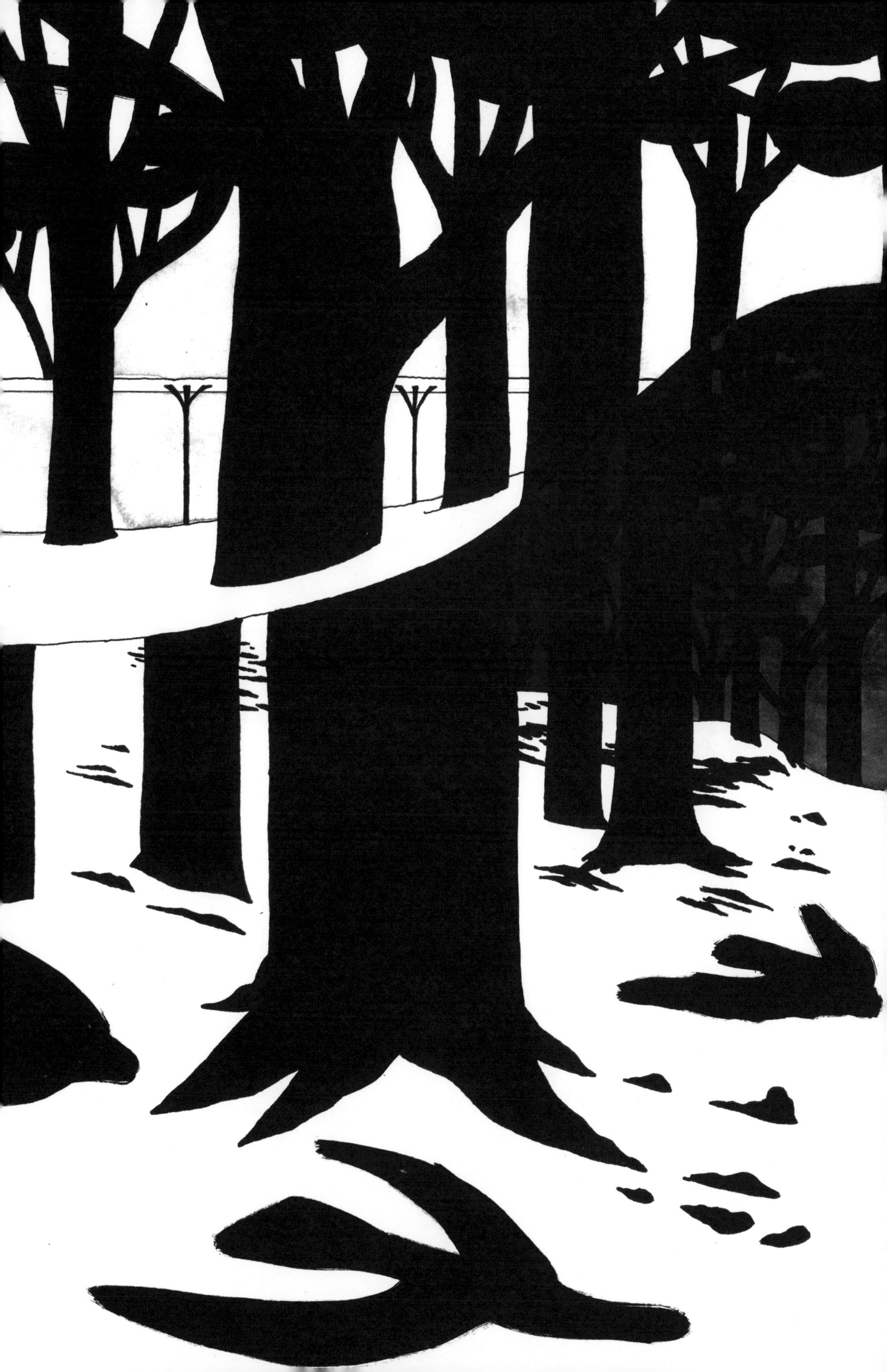

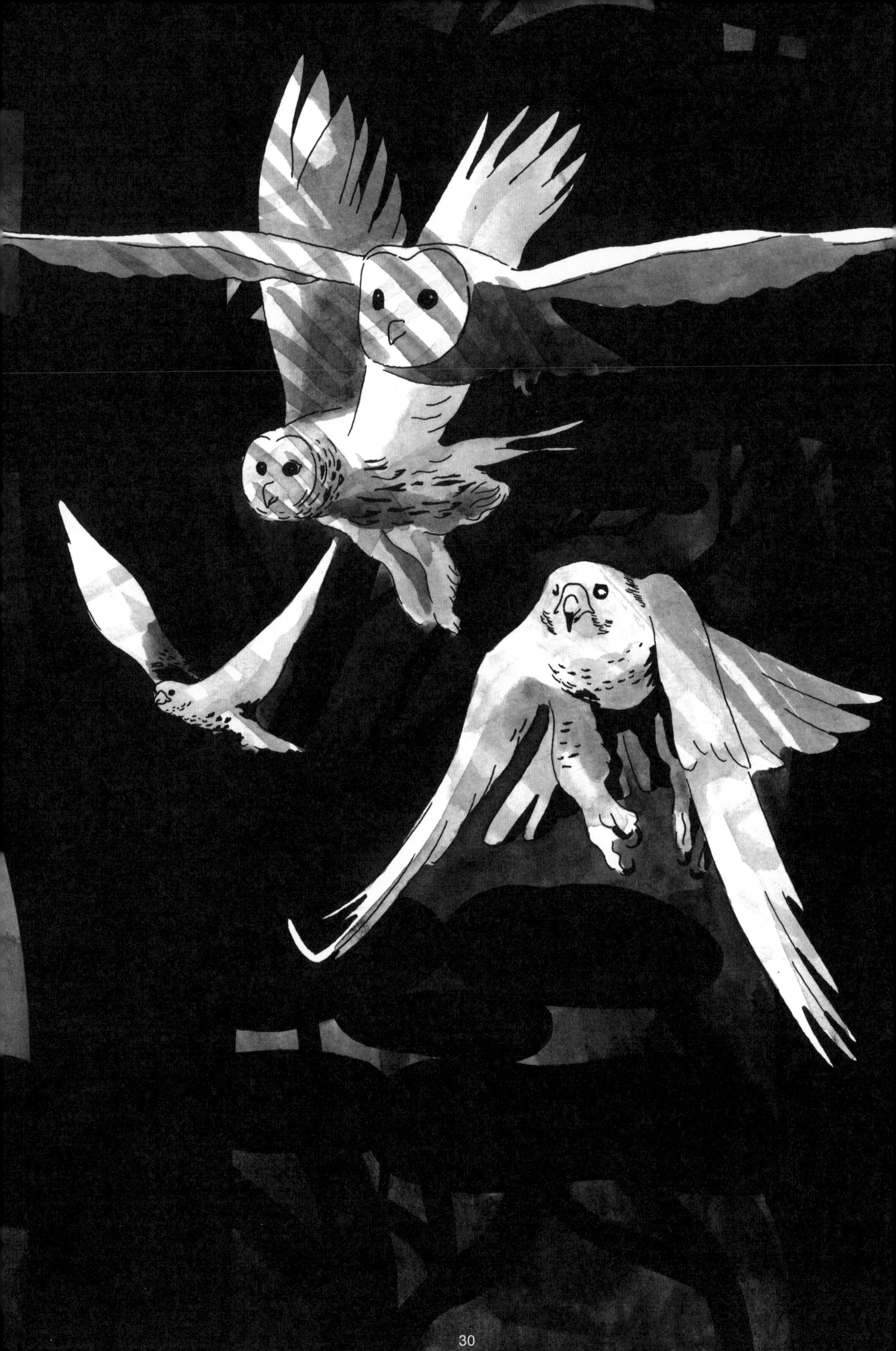

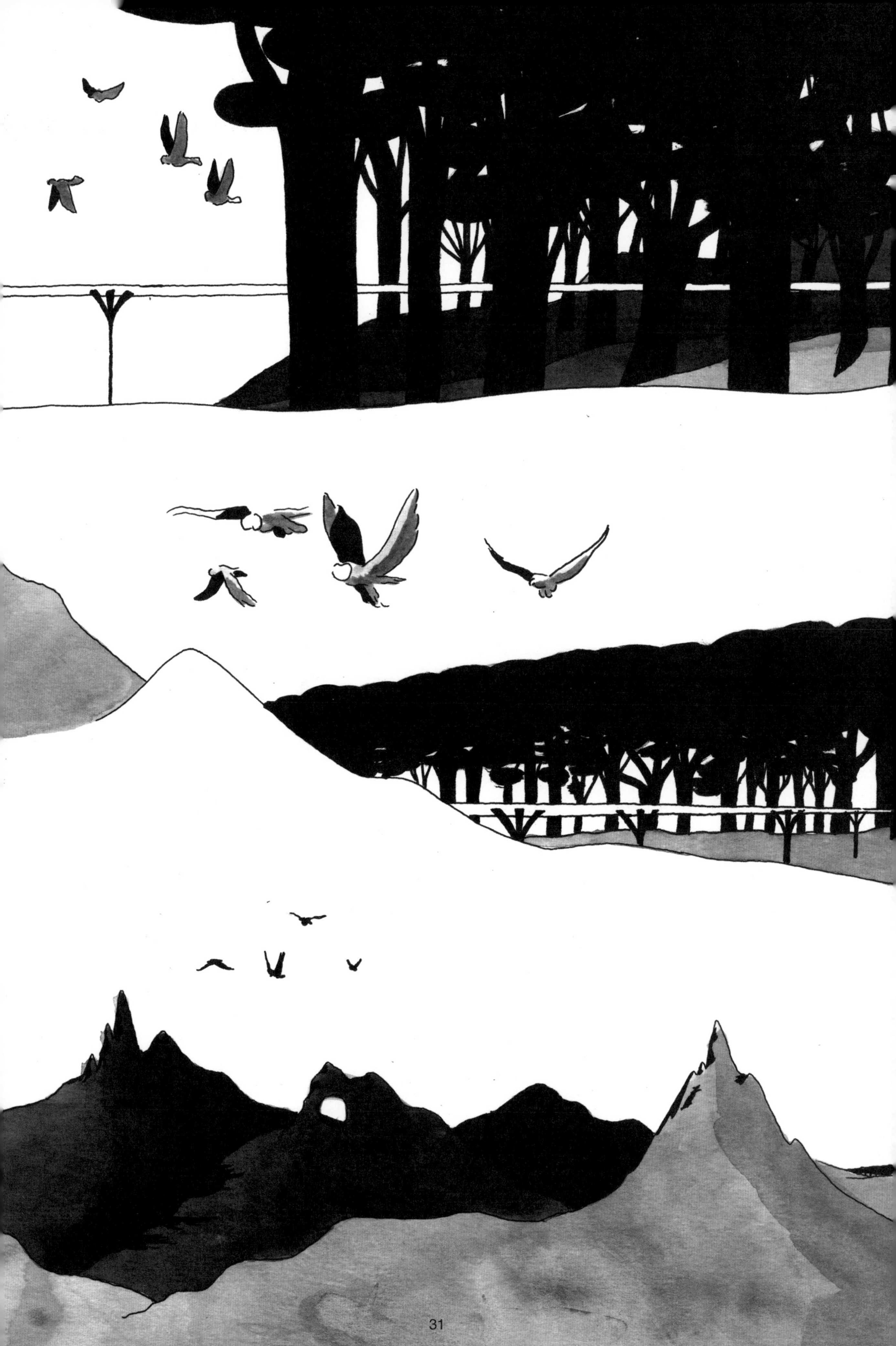

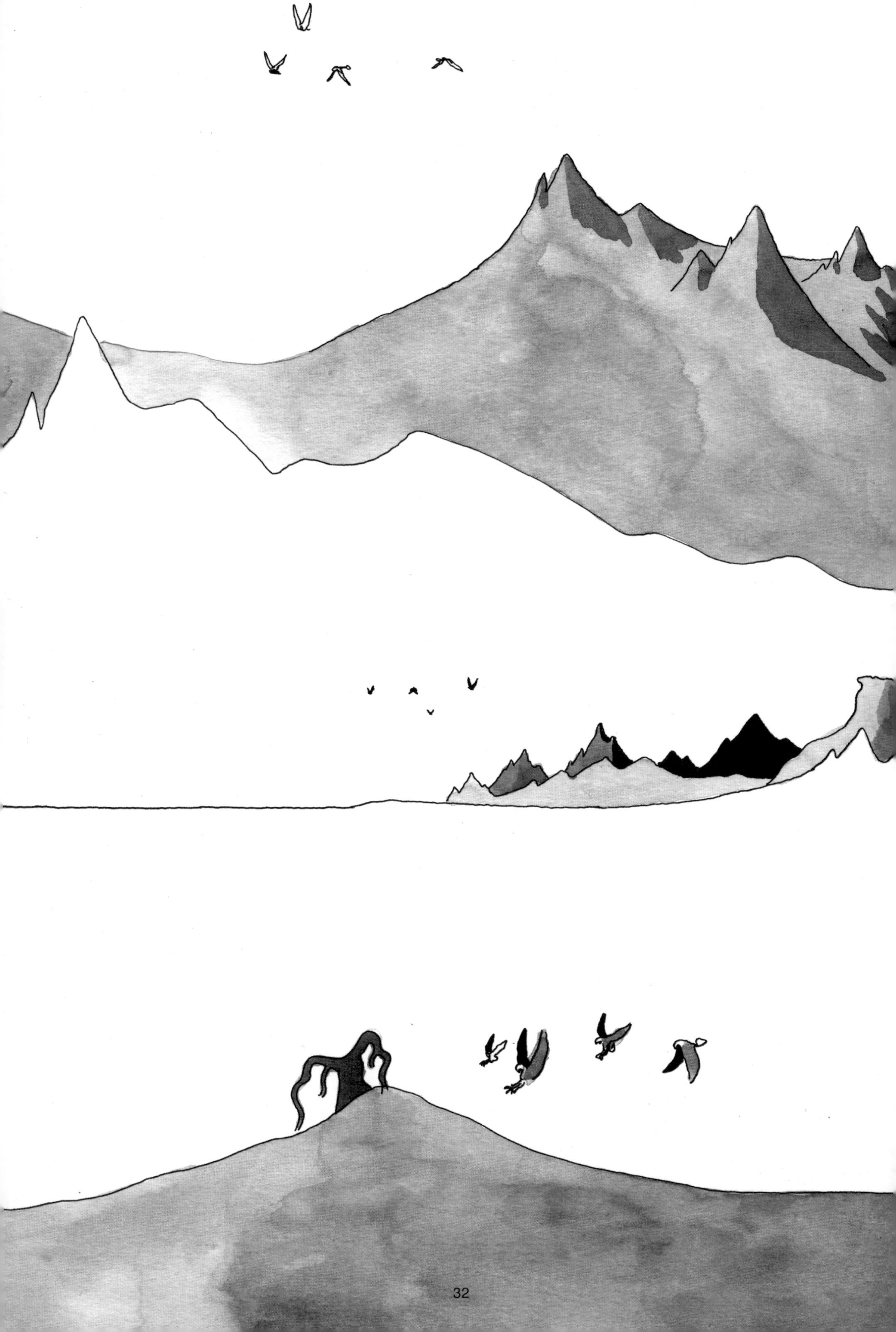

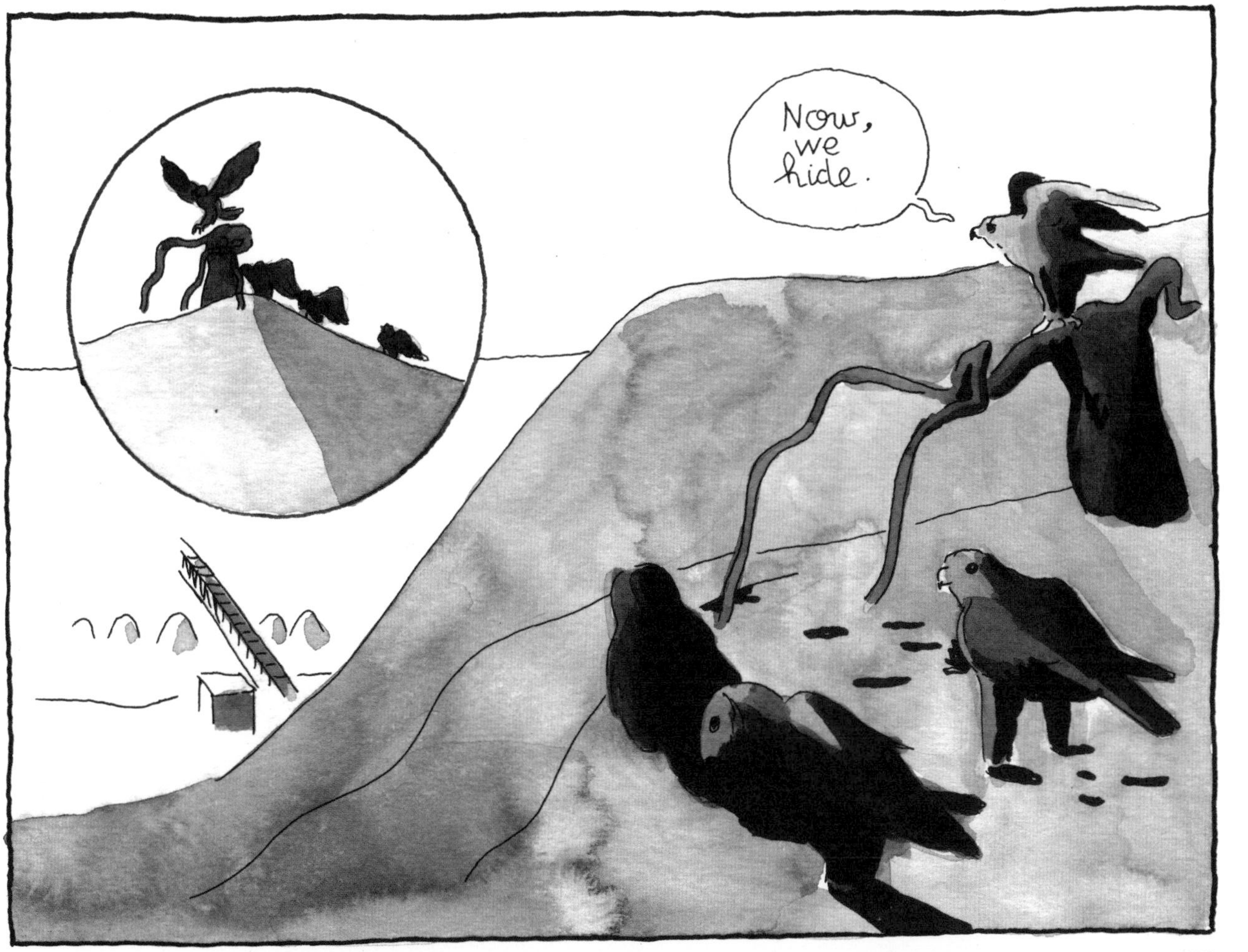
Now, we hide.

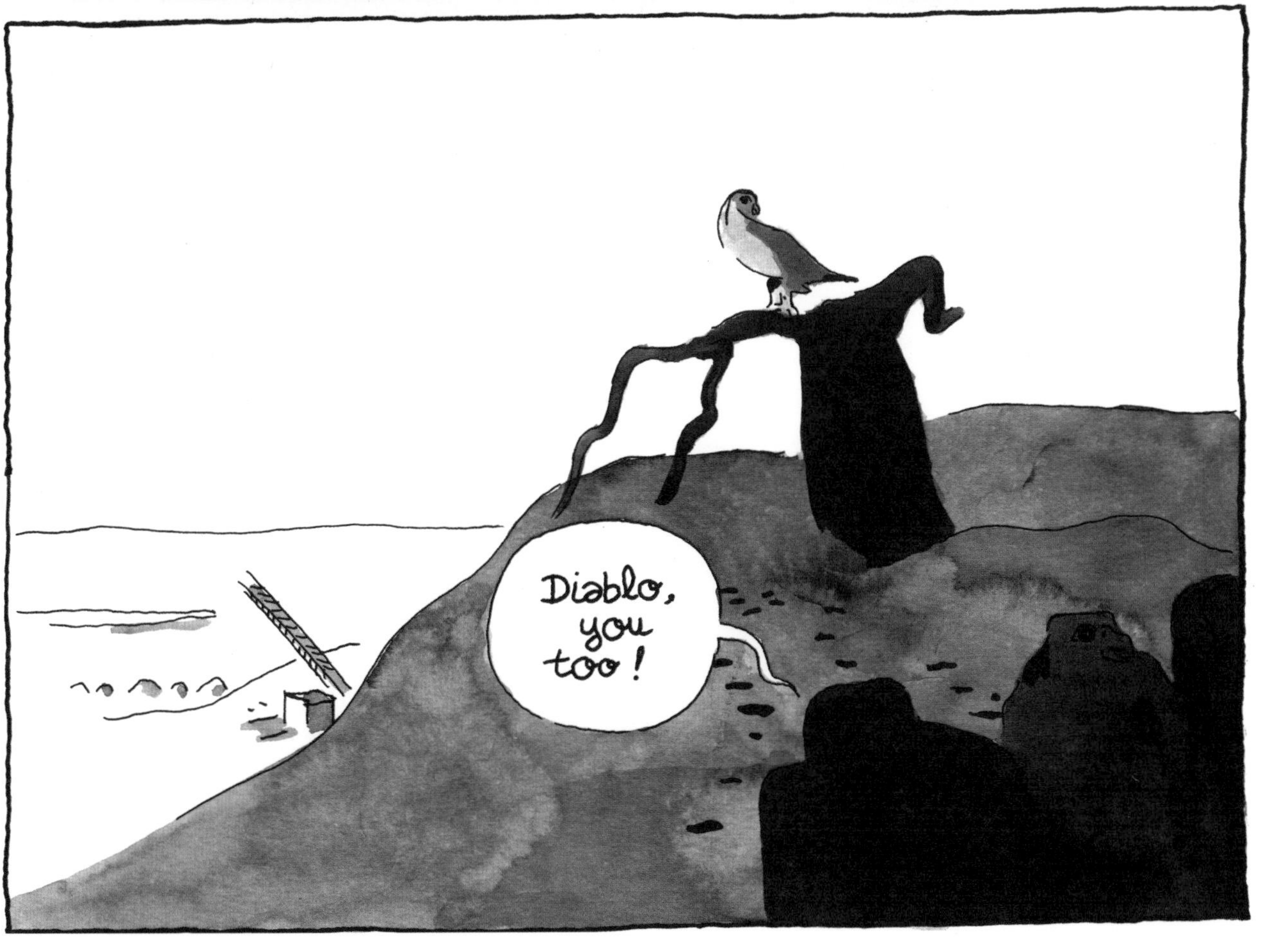
Diablo, you too!

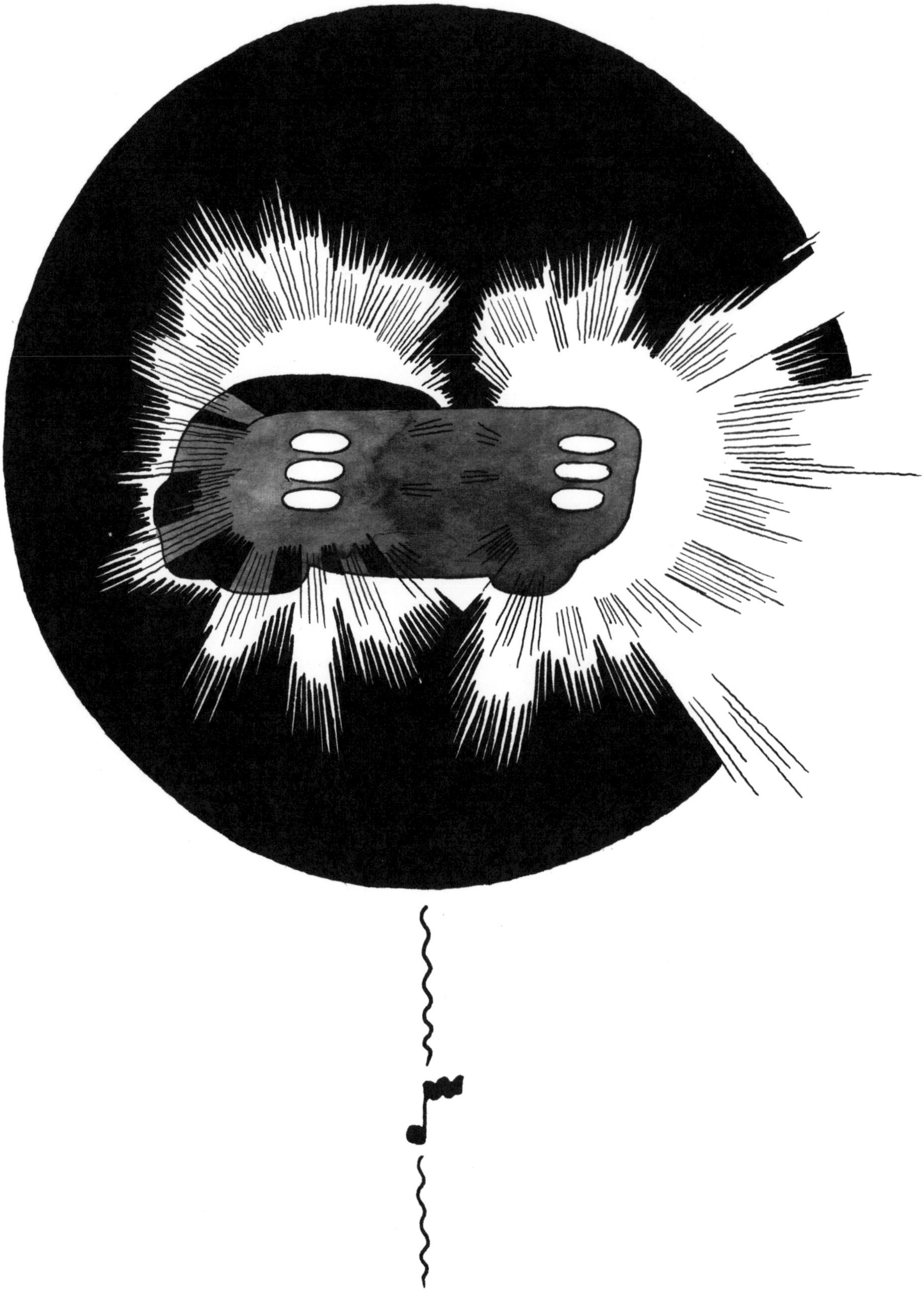

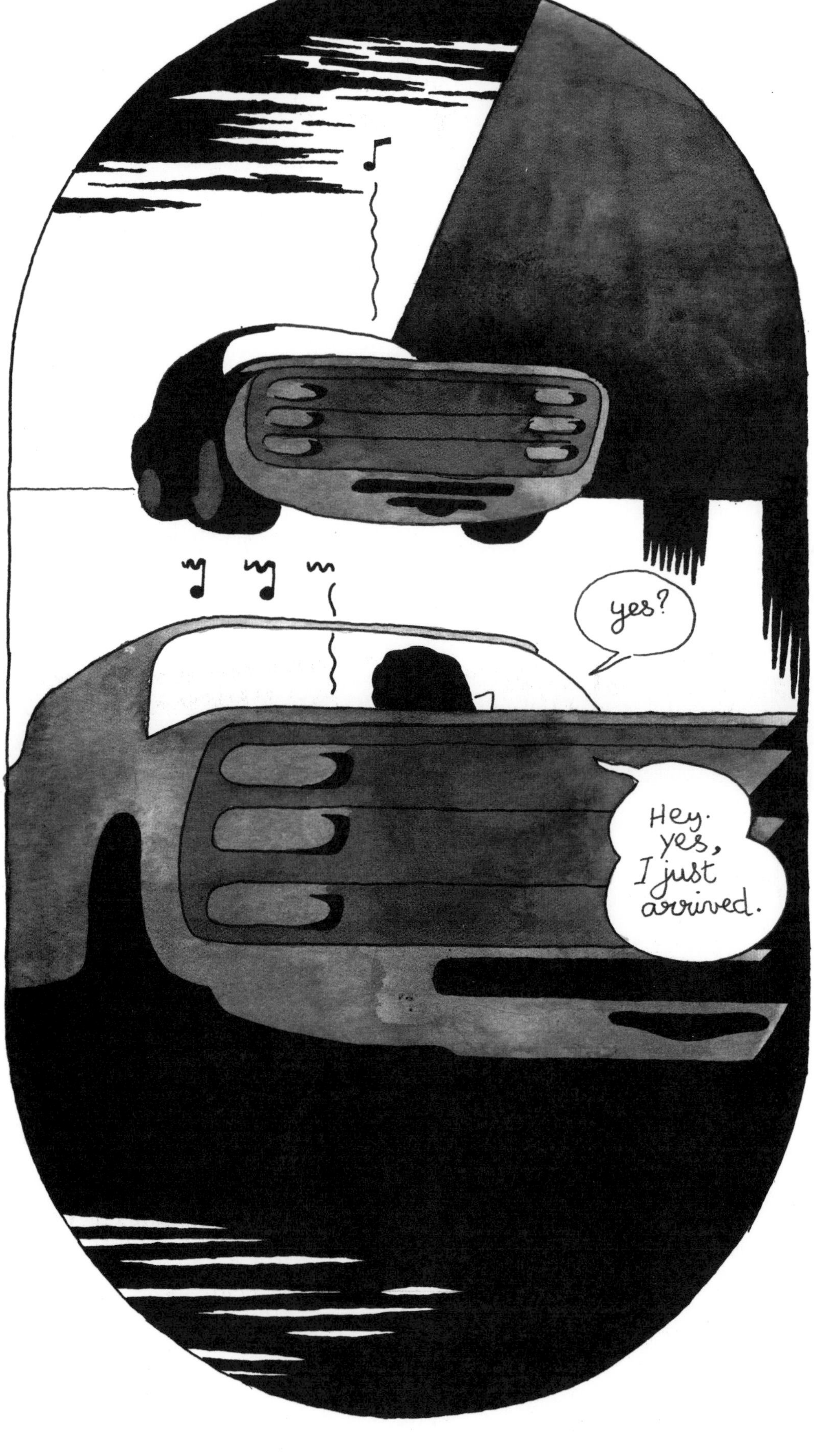
yes?
Hey. yes, I just arrived.

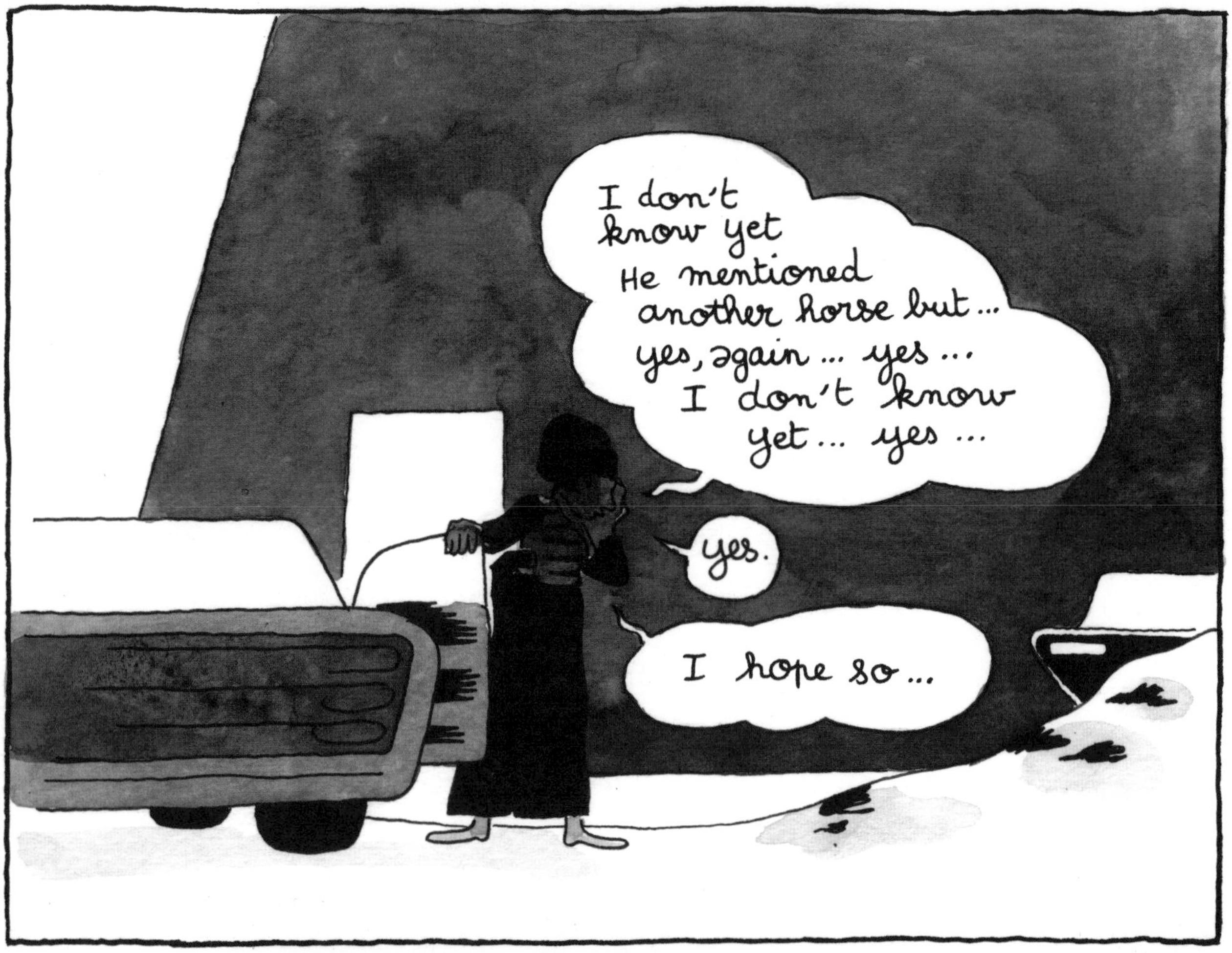
I don't know yet
He mentioned another horse but...
yes, again ... yes ...
I don't know yet... yes ...
yes.
I hope so...

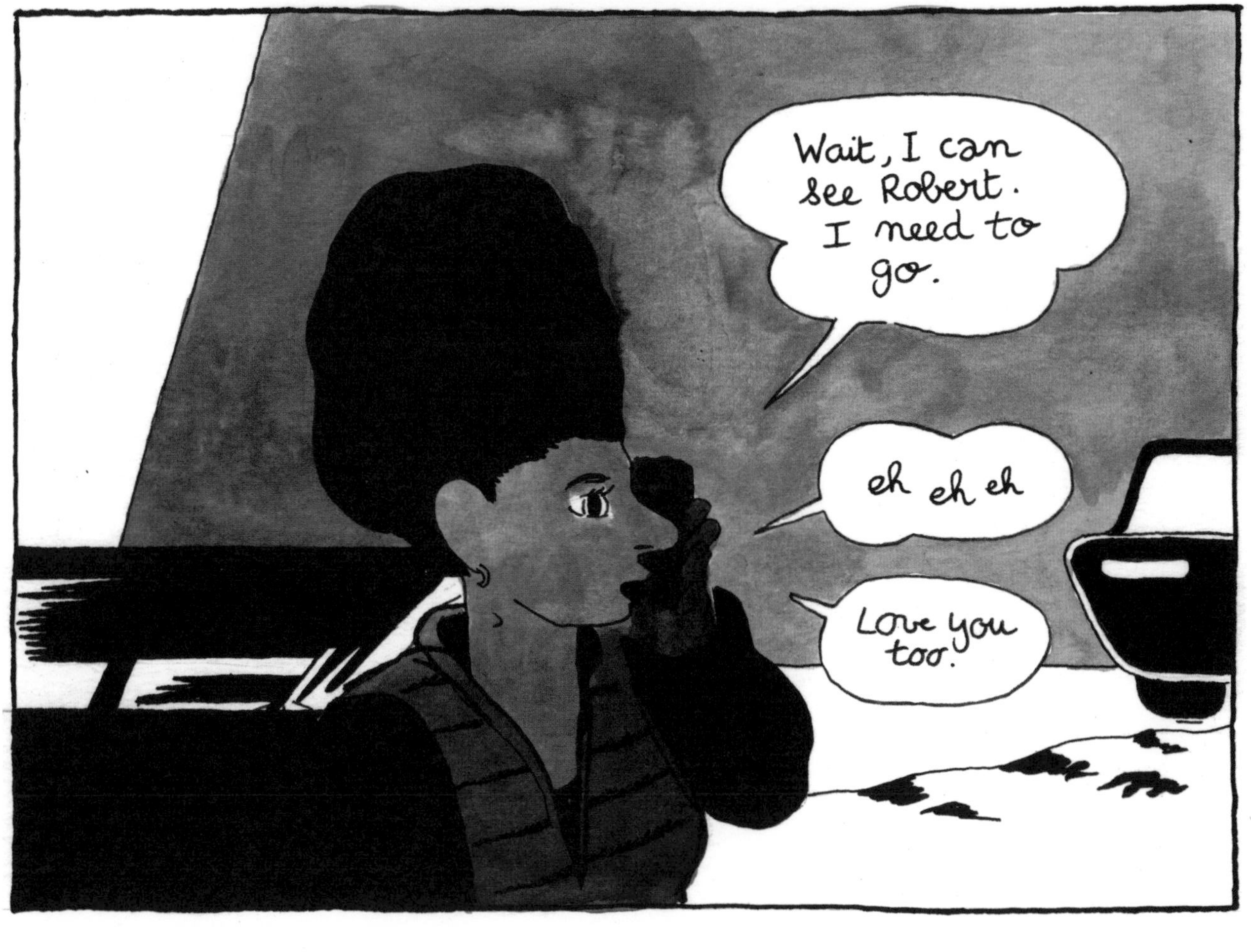
Wait, I can see Robert. I need to go.
eh eh eh
Love you too.

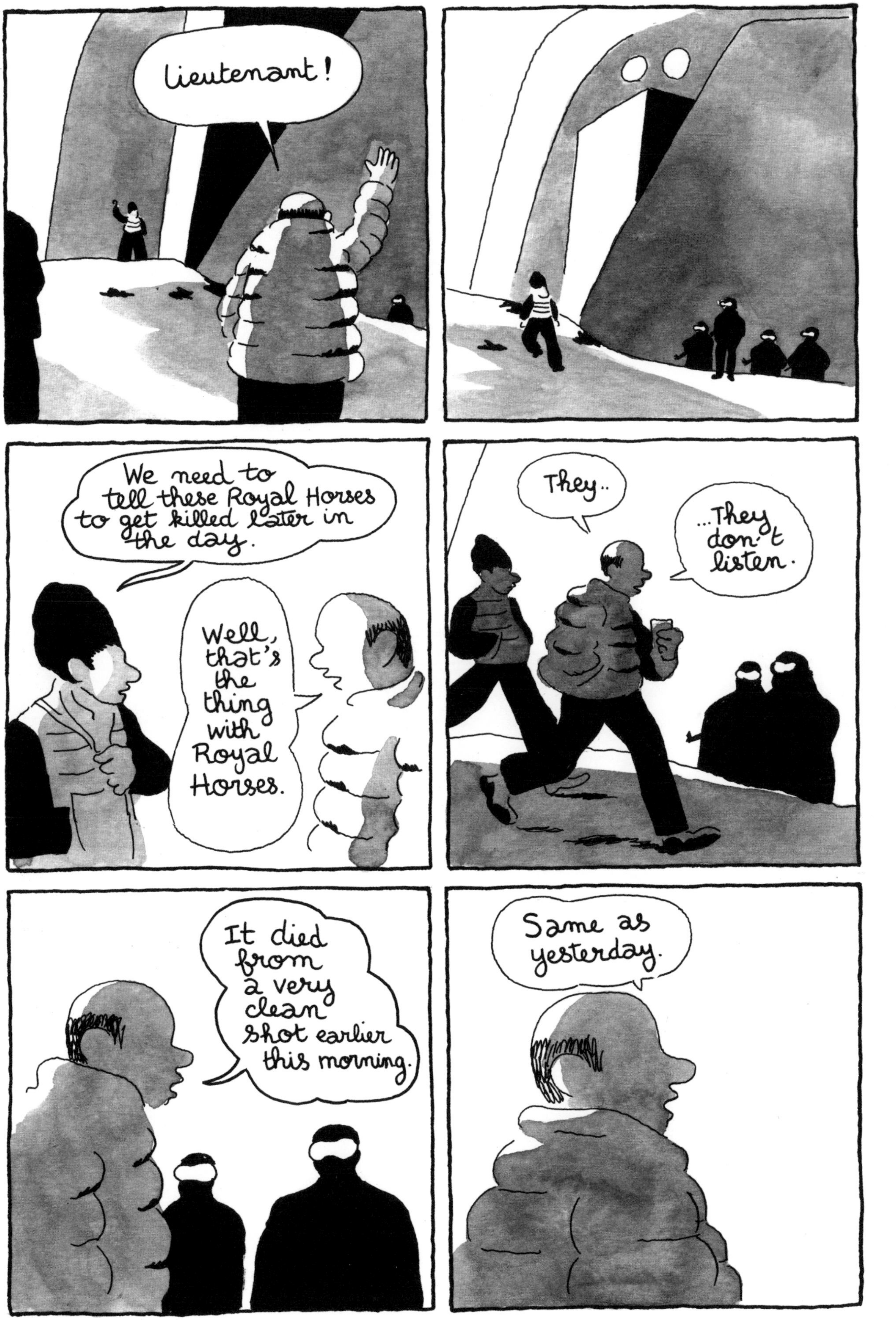

Lieutenant!
We need to tell these Royal Horses to get killed later in the day.
Well, that's the thing with Royal Horses.
They..
...They don't listen.
It died from a very clean shot earlier this morning.
Same as yesterday.

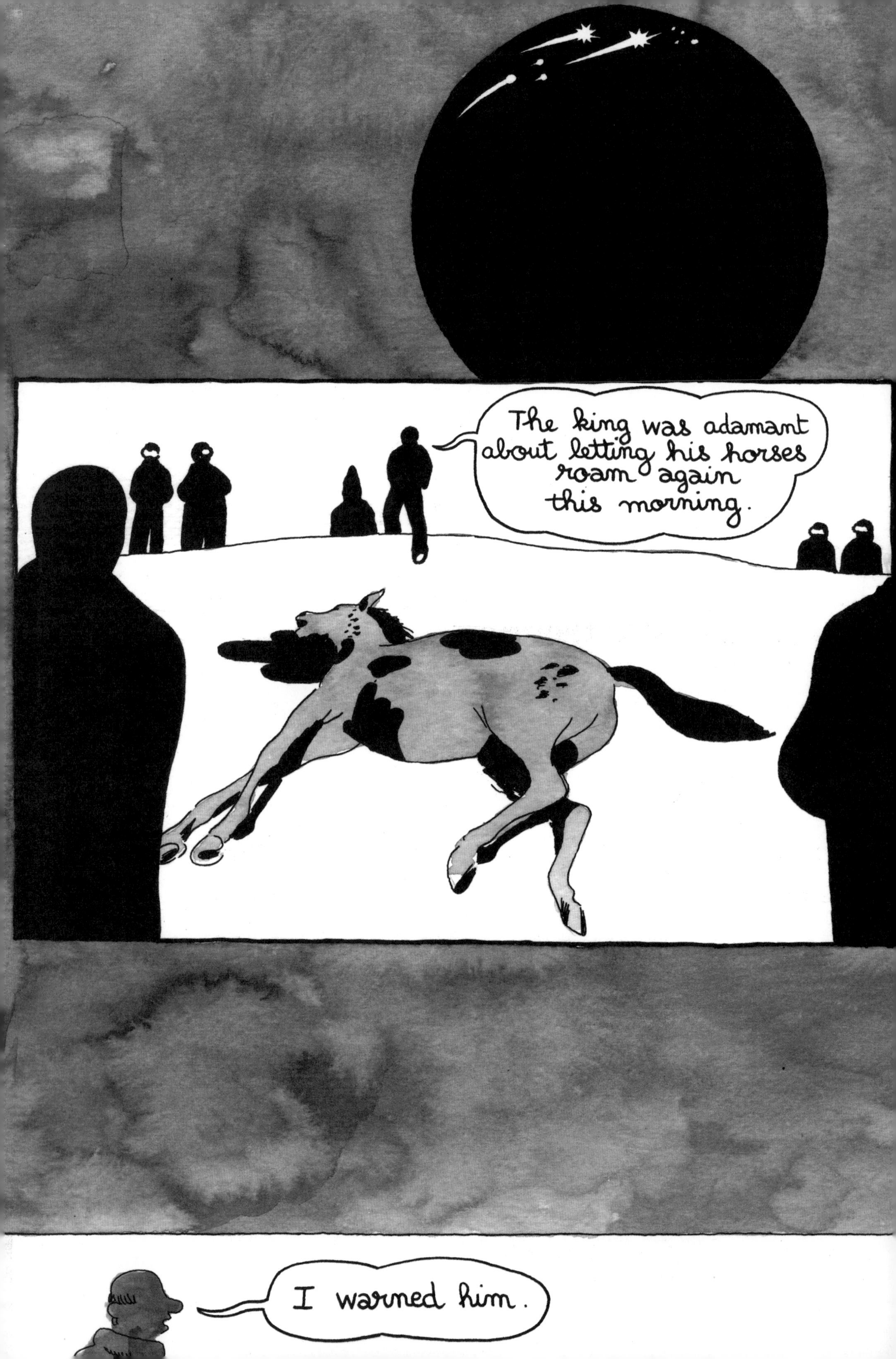
The king was adamant about letting his horses roam again this morning.
I warned him.

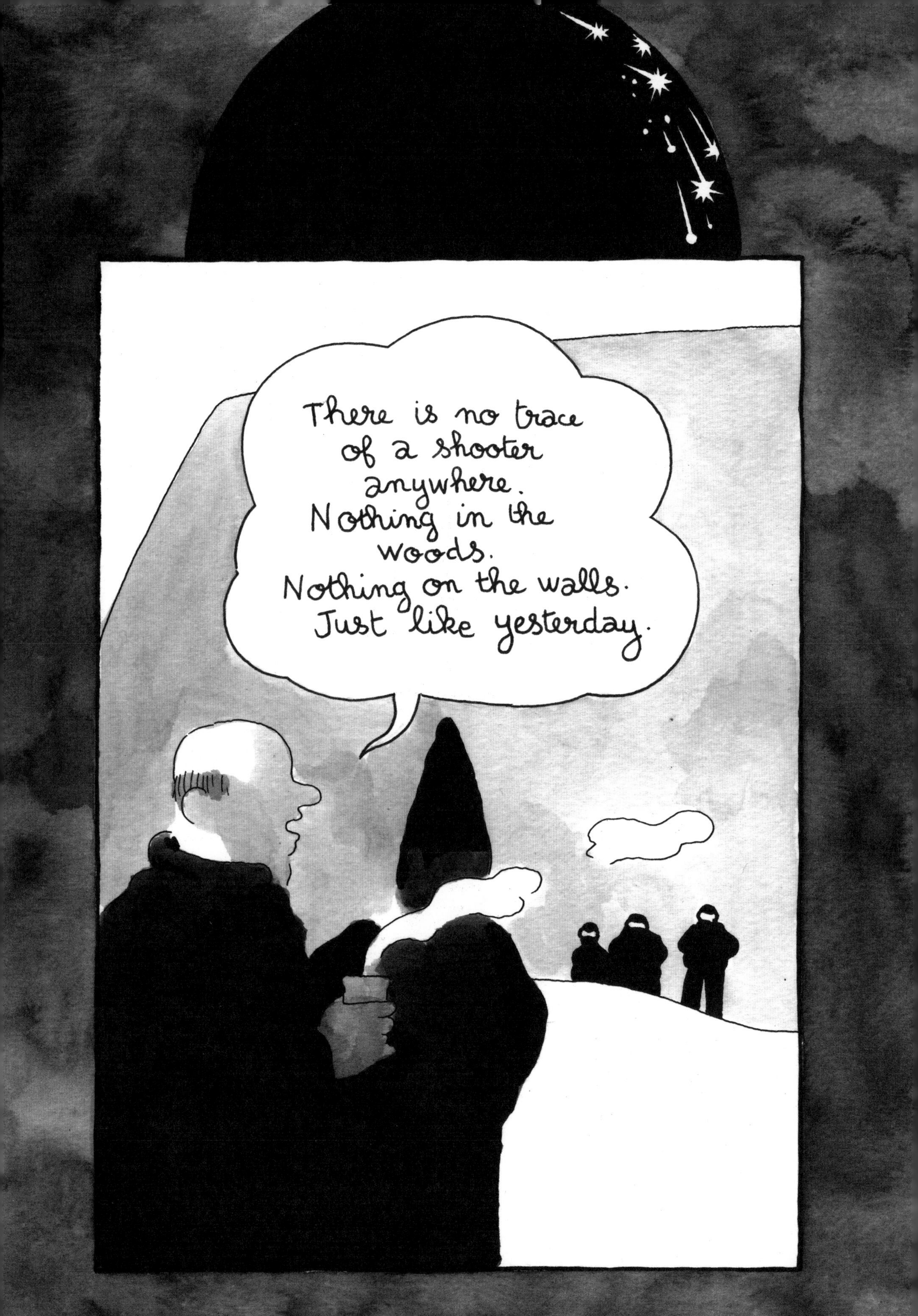
There is no trace of a shooter anywhere. Nothing in the woods. Nothing on the walls. Just like yesterday.

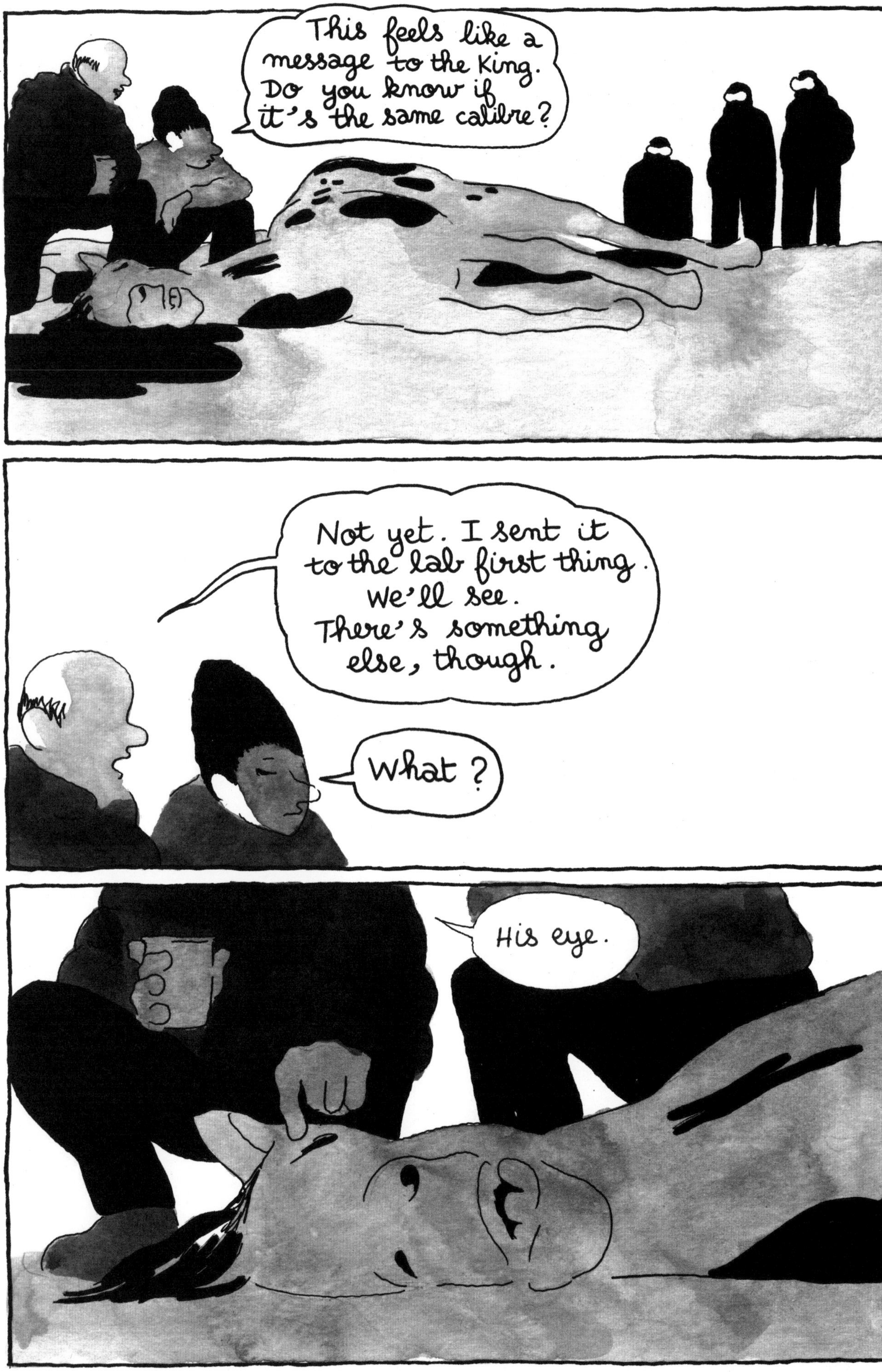
This feels like a message to the King. Do you know if it's the same calibre?
Not yet. I sent it to the lab first thing. We'll see. There's something else, though.
What?
His eye.

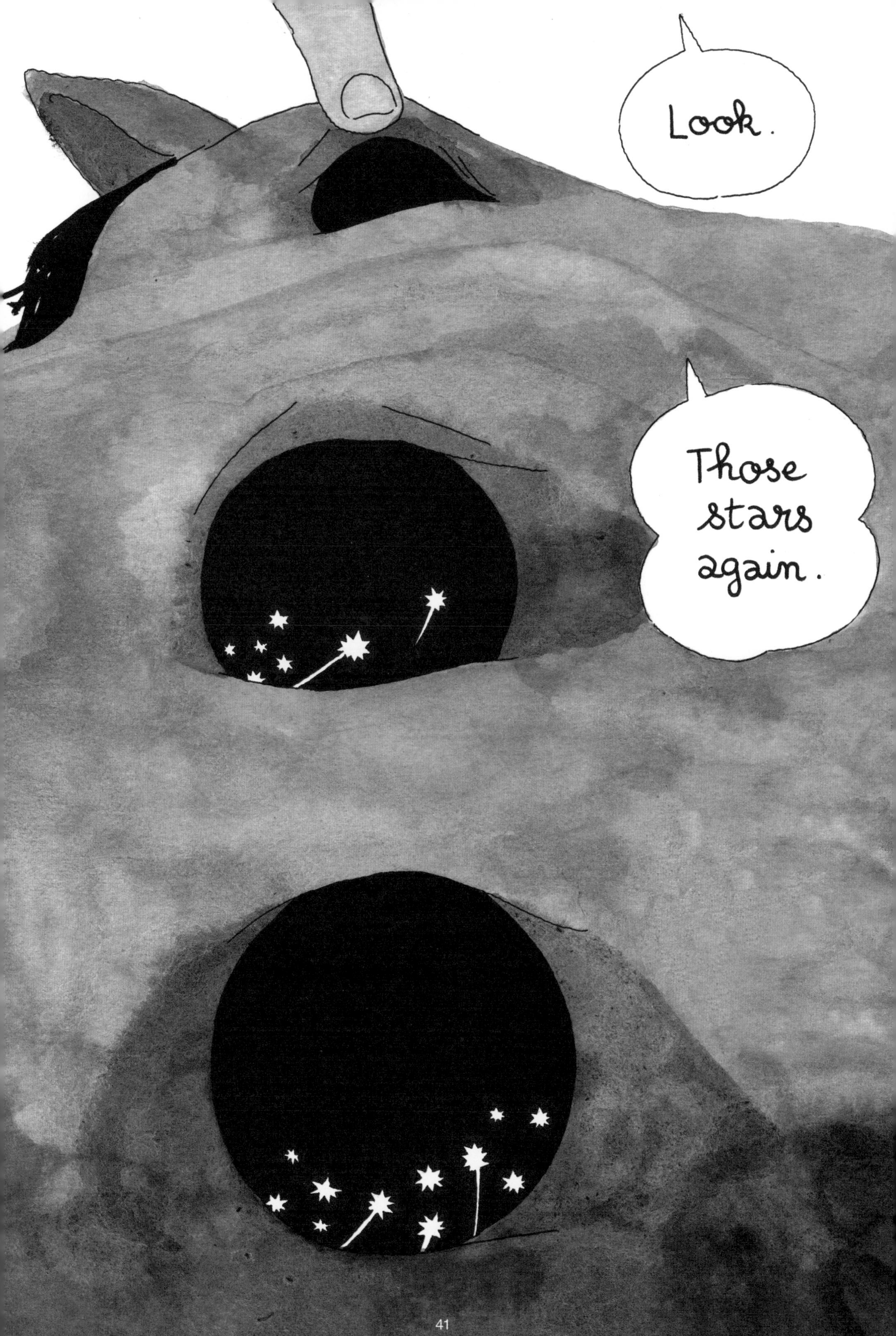
Look.
Those stars again.

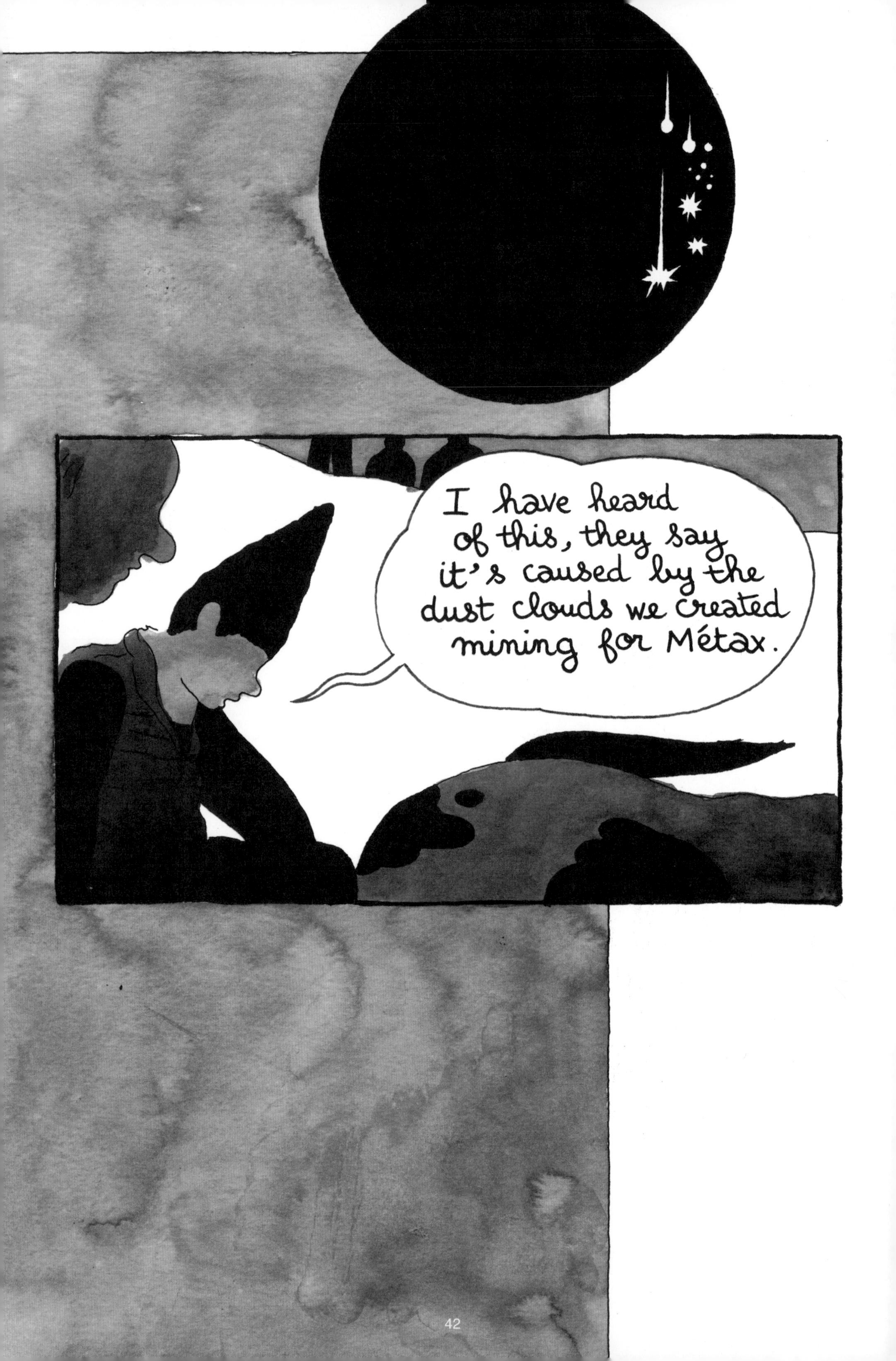
I have heard of this, they say it's caused by the dust clouds we created mining for Métax.

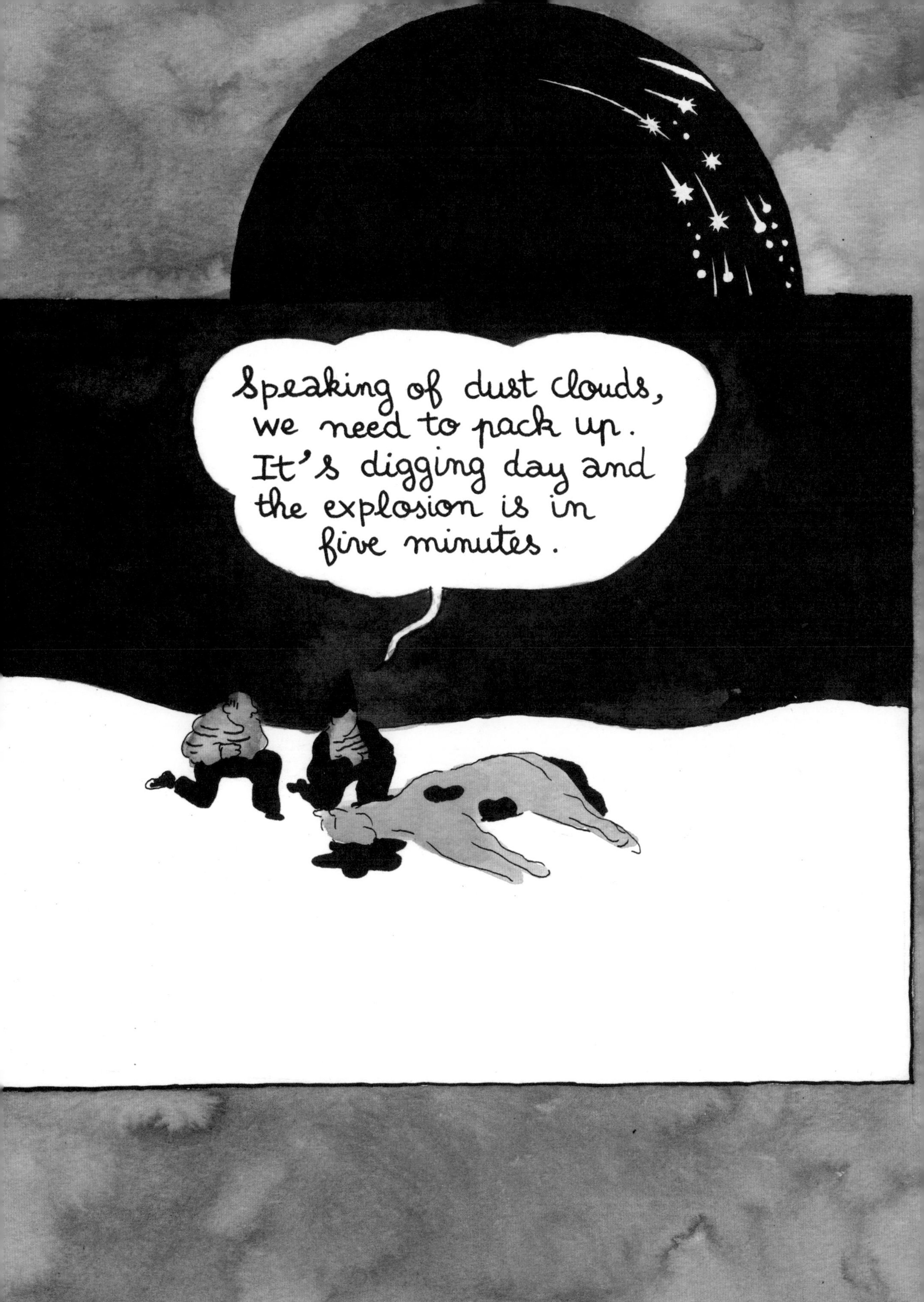
Speaking of dust clouds, we need to pack up. It's digging day and the explosion is in five minutes.

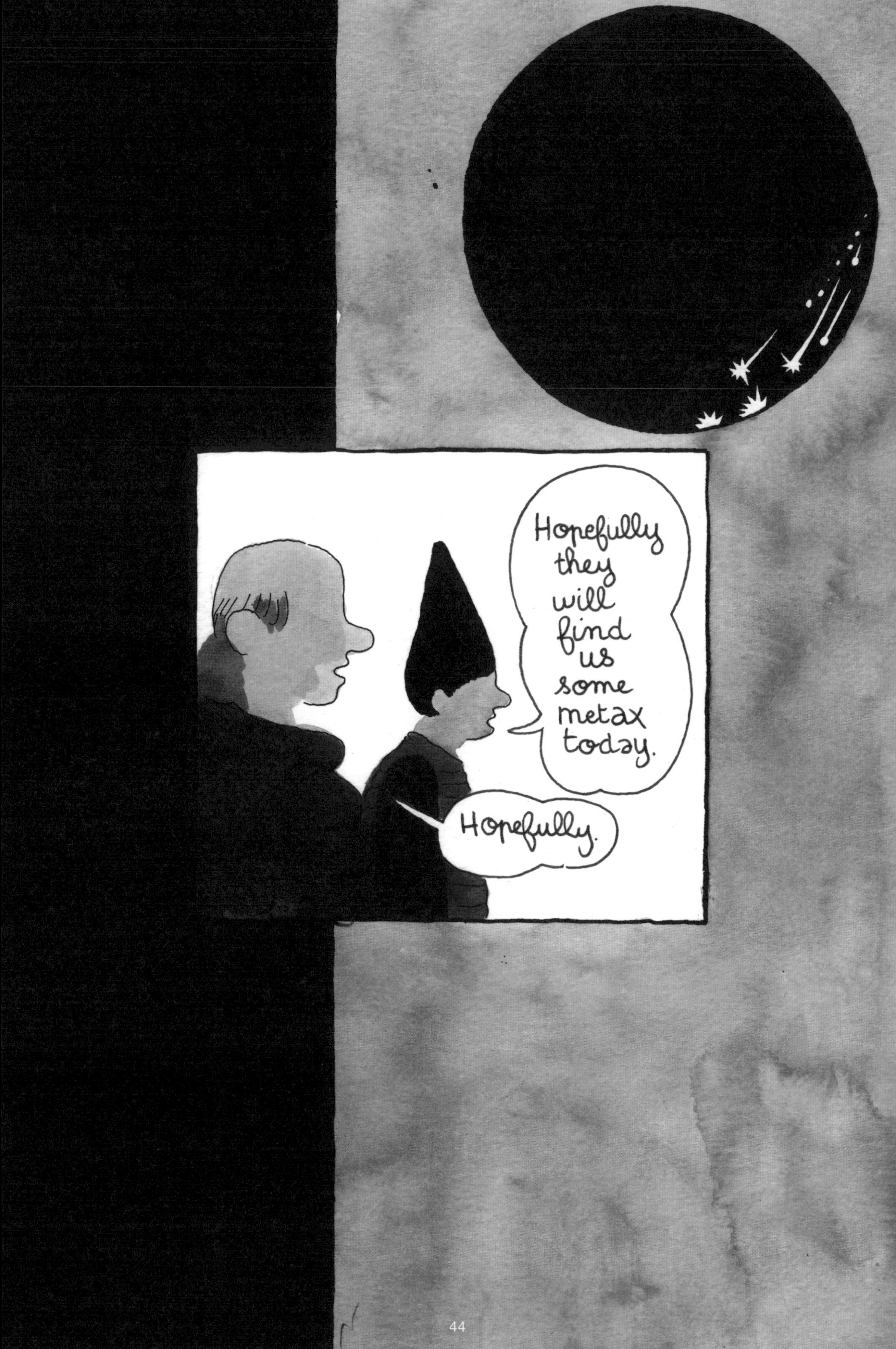
Hopefully they will find us some metax today.
Hopefully.

10

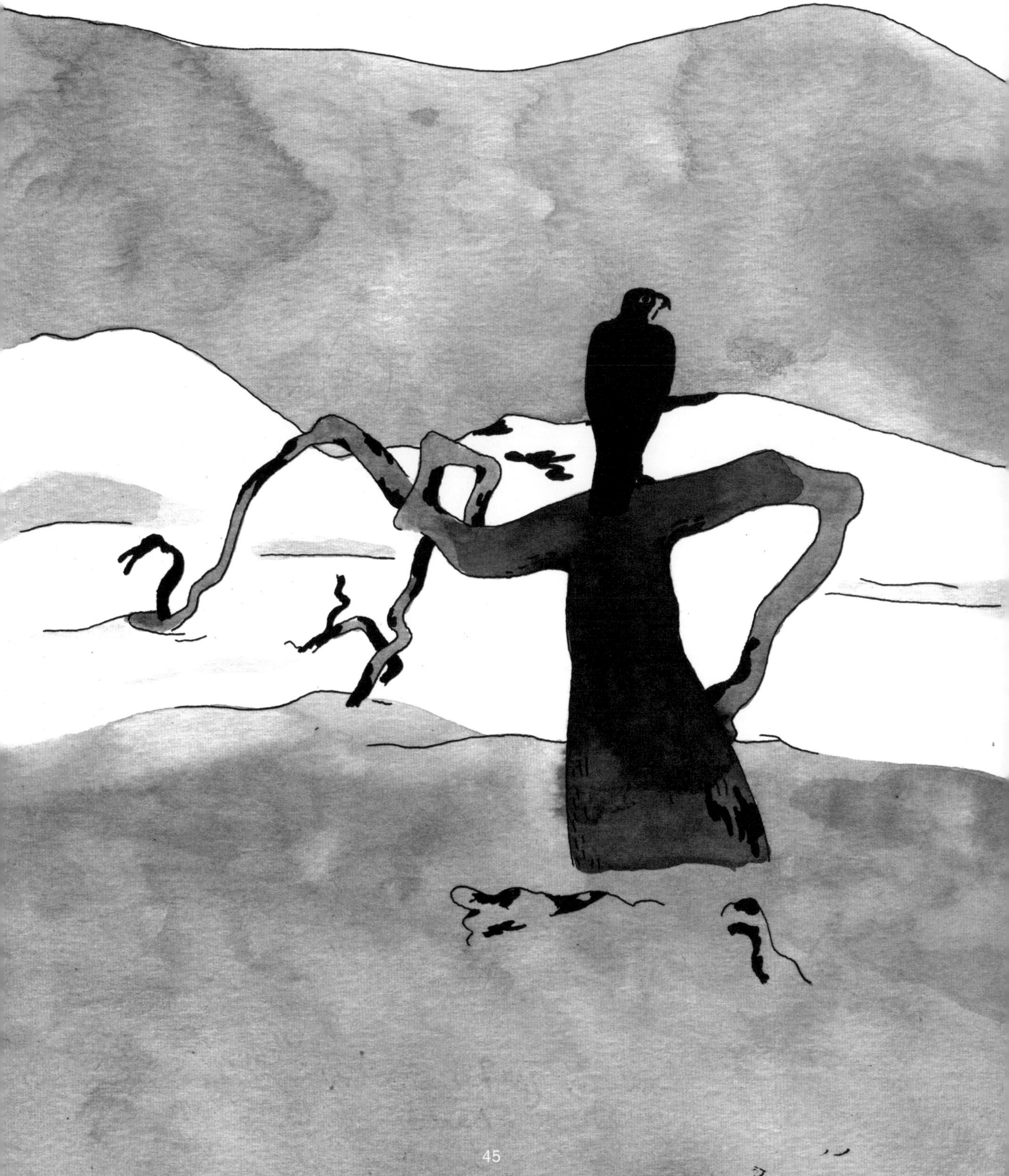

9

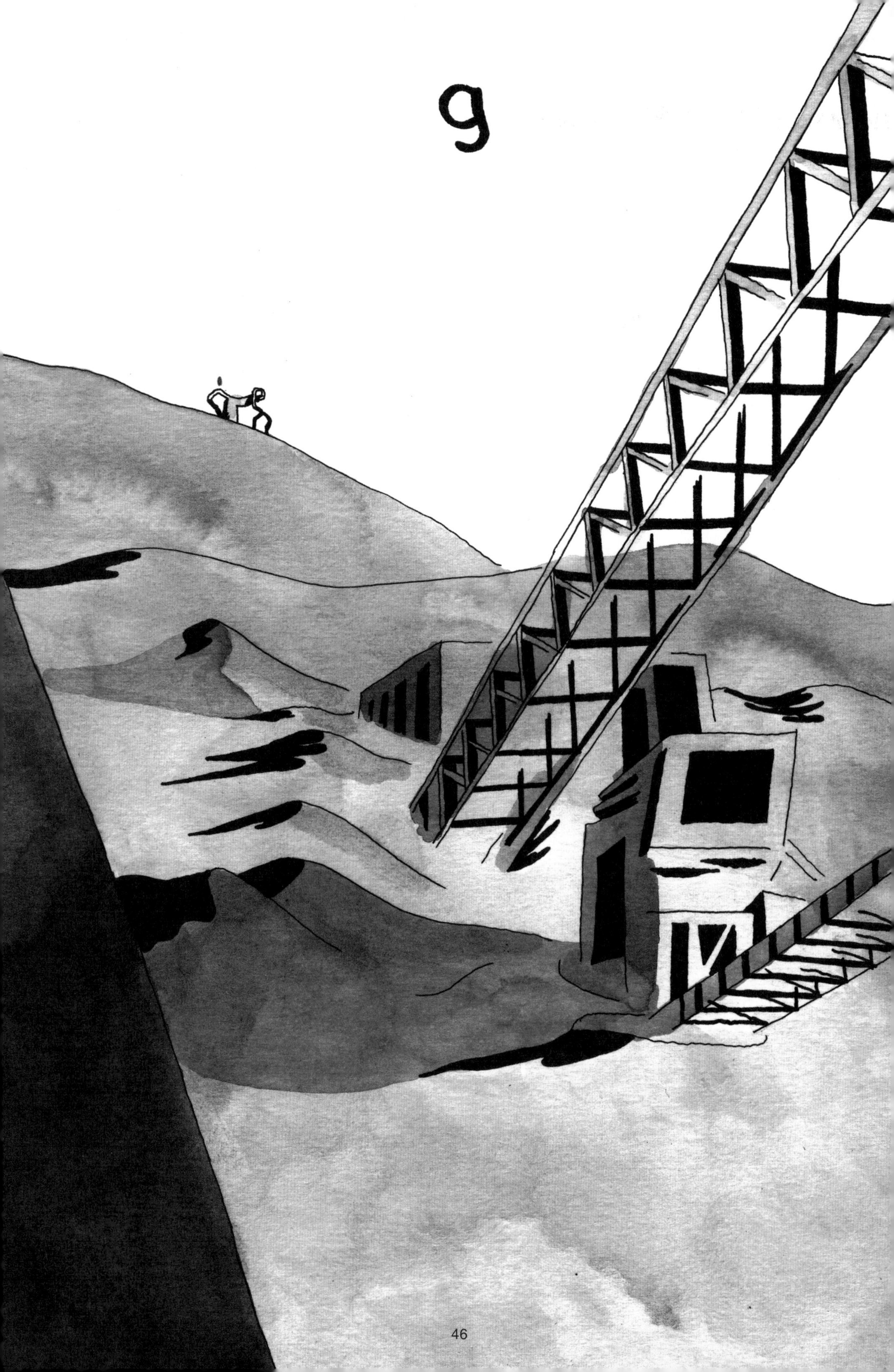

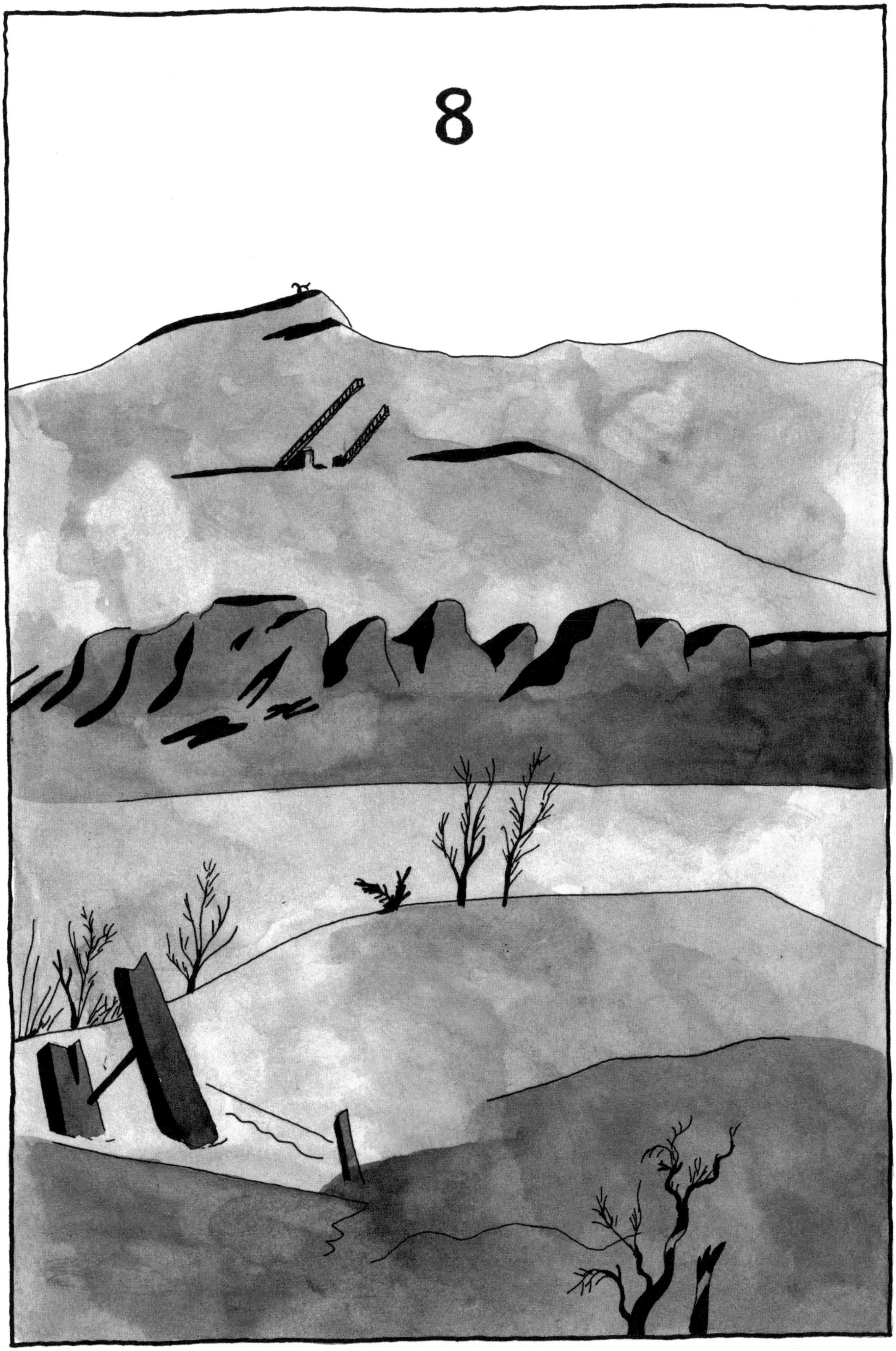
8

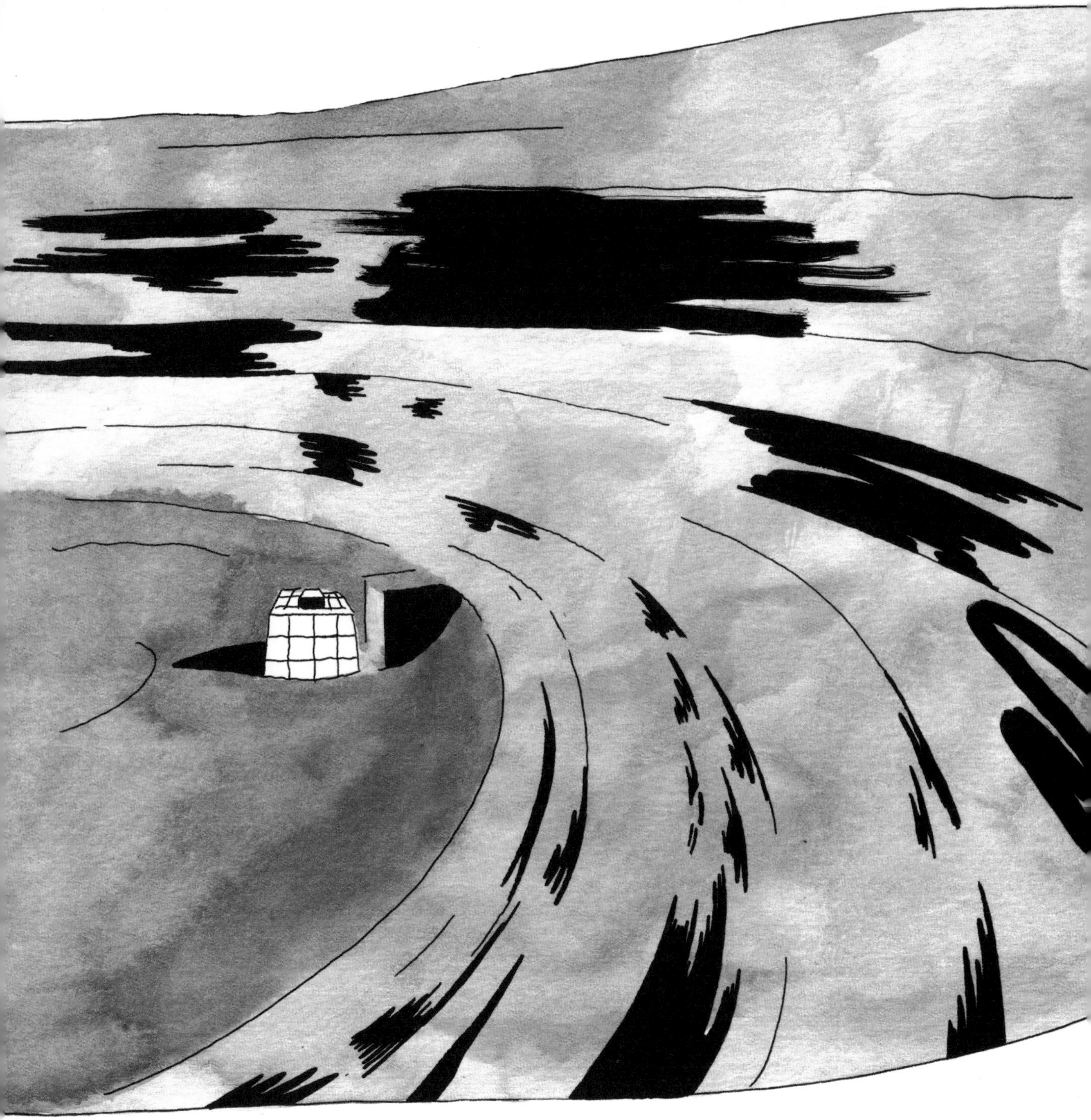

7

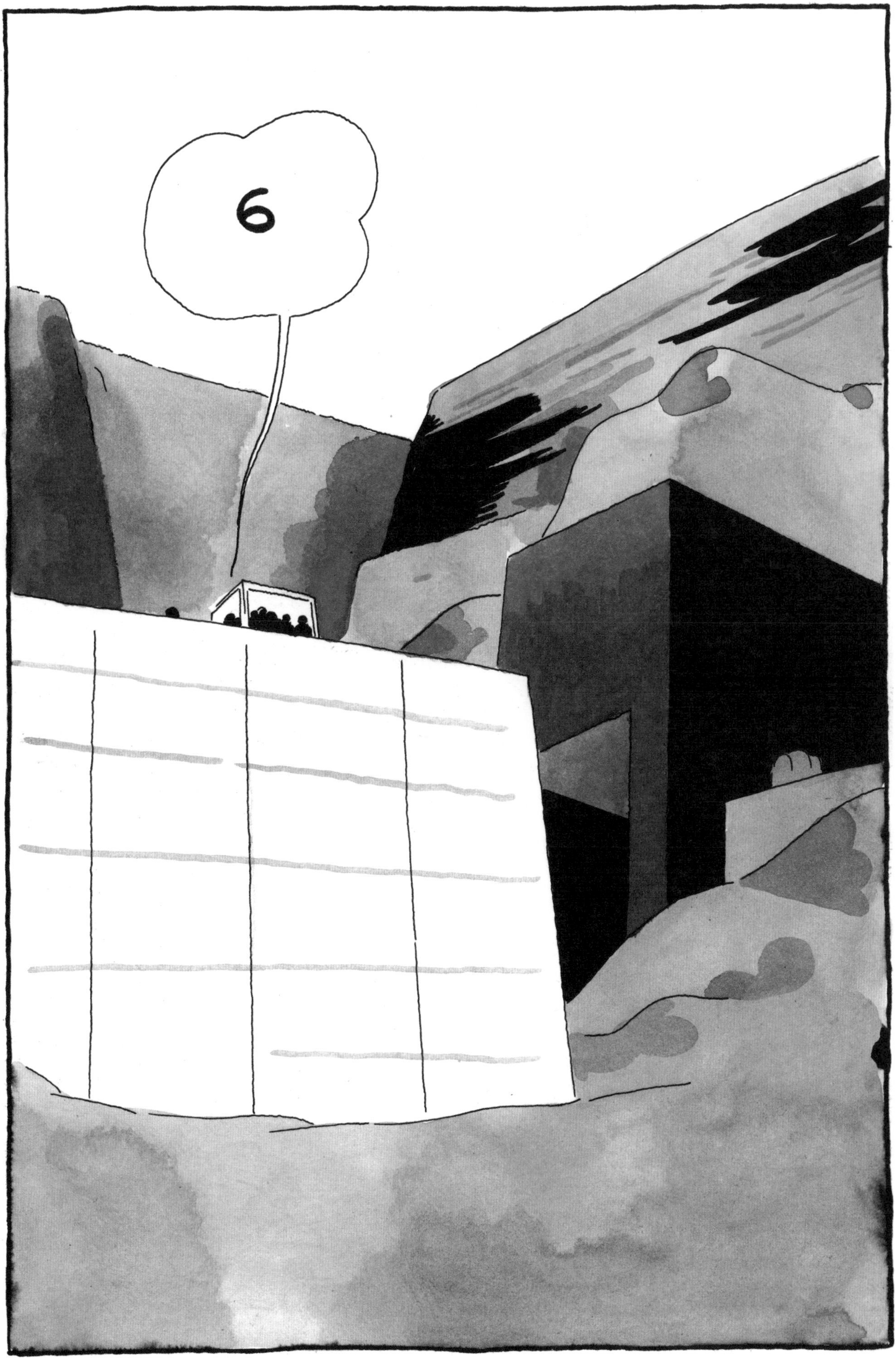
6

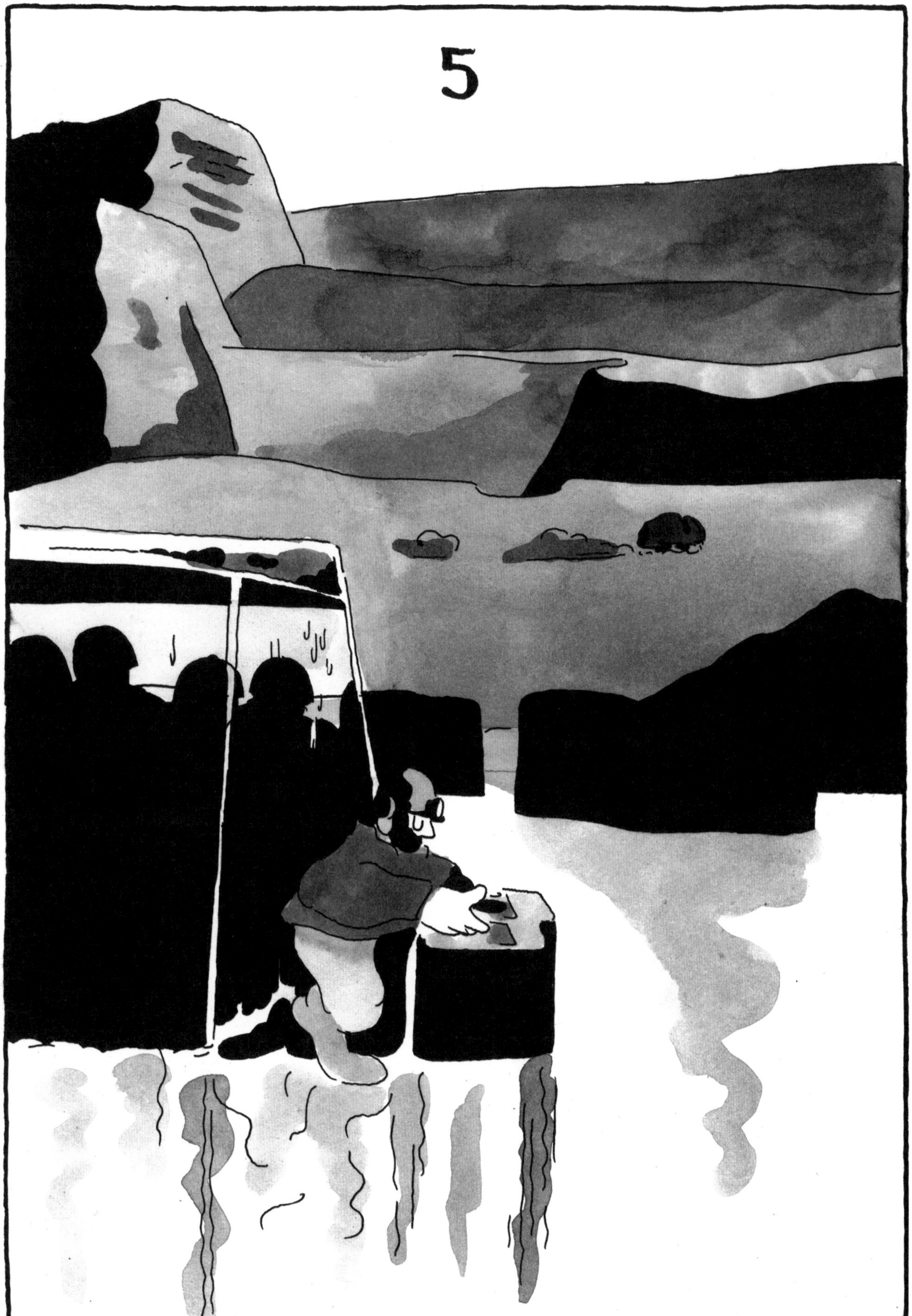
5

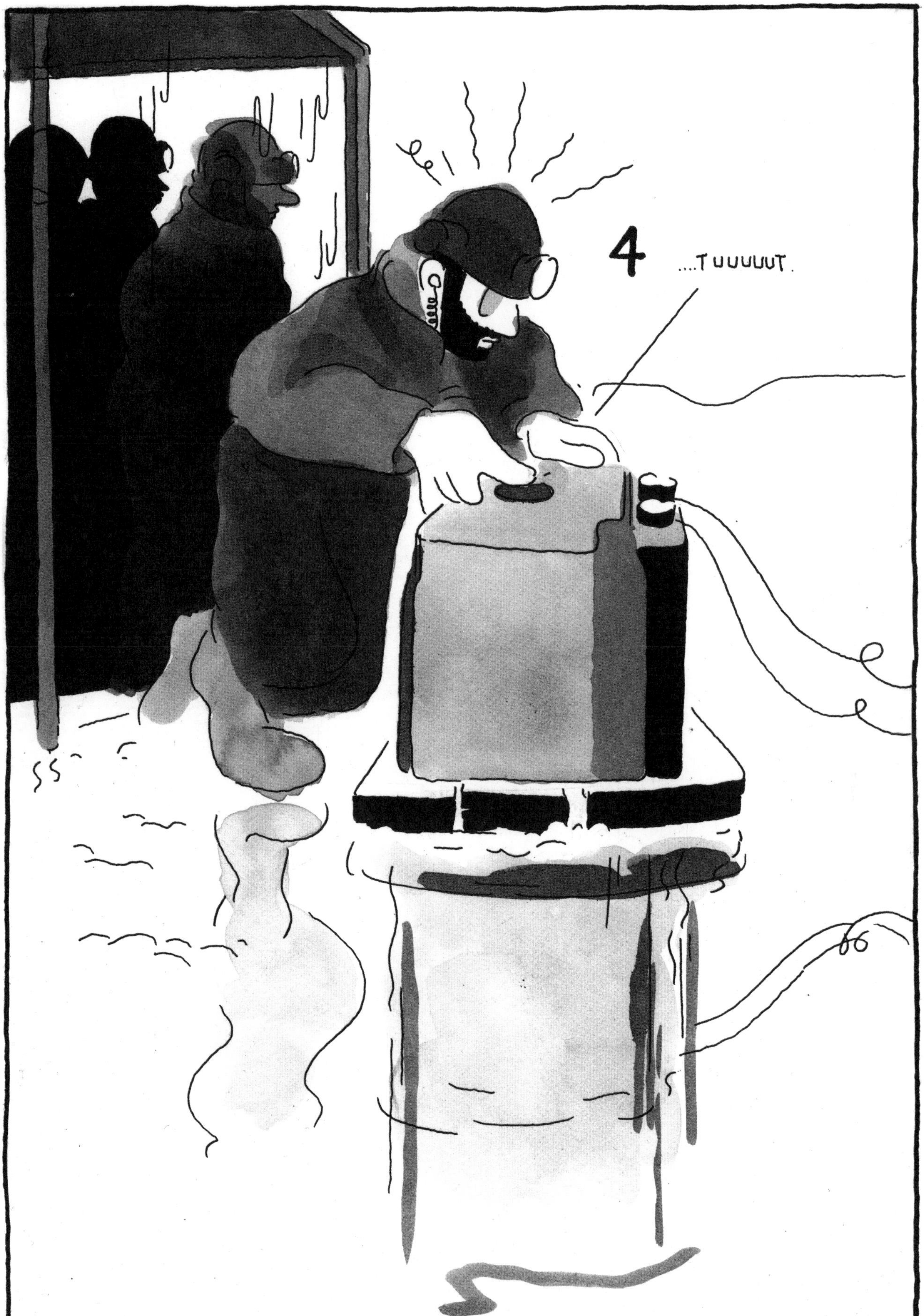
4
....TUUUUUT.

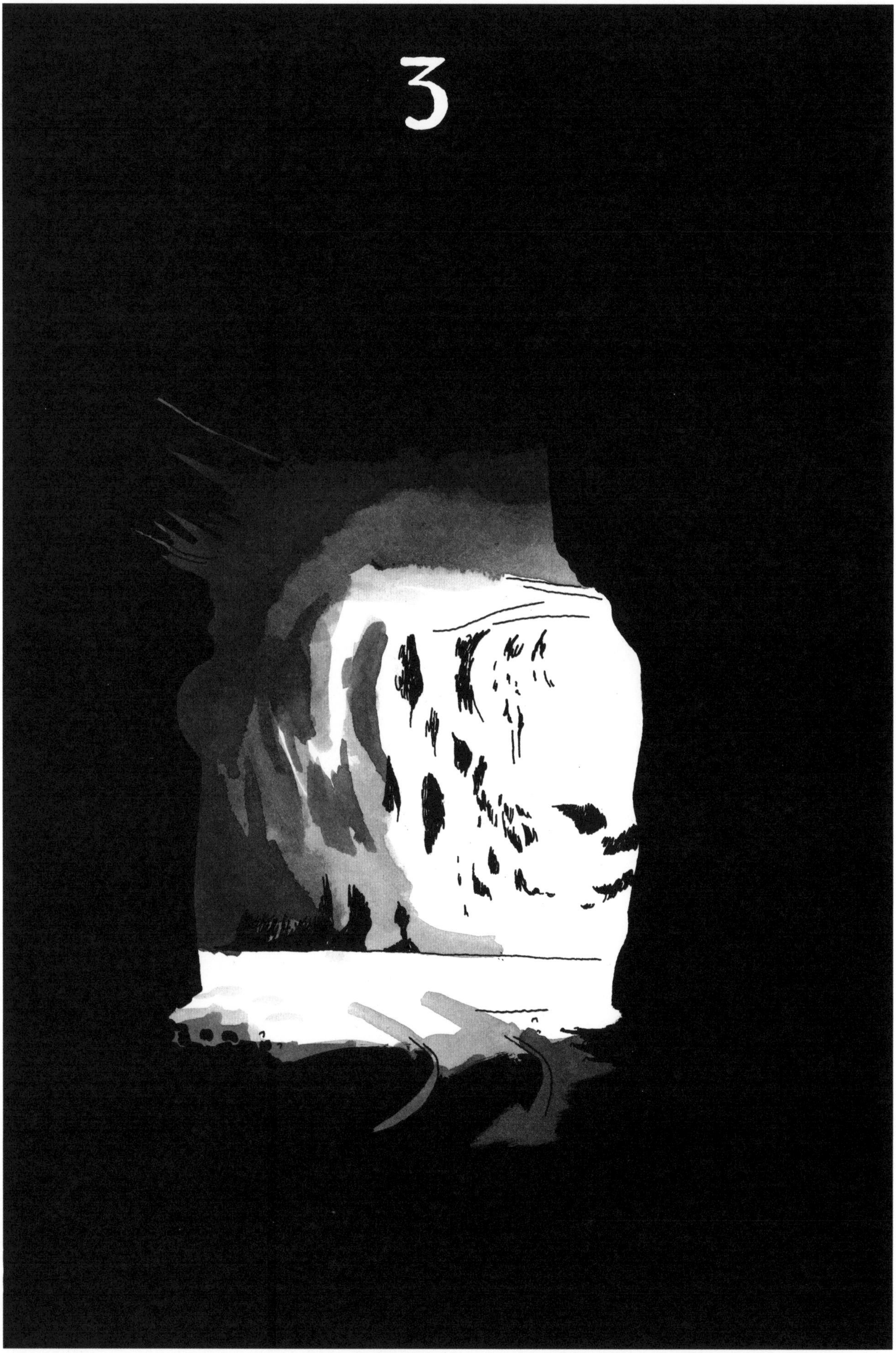
3

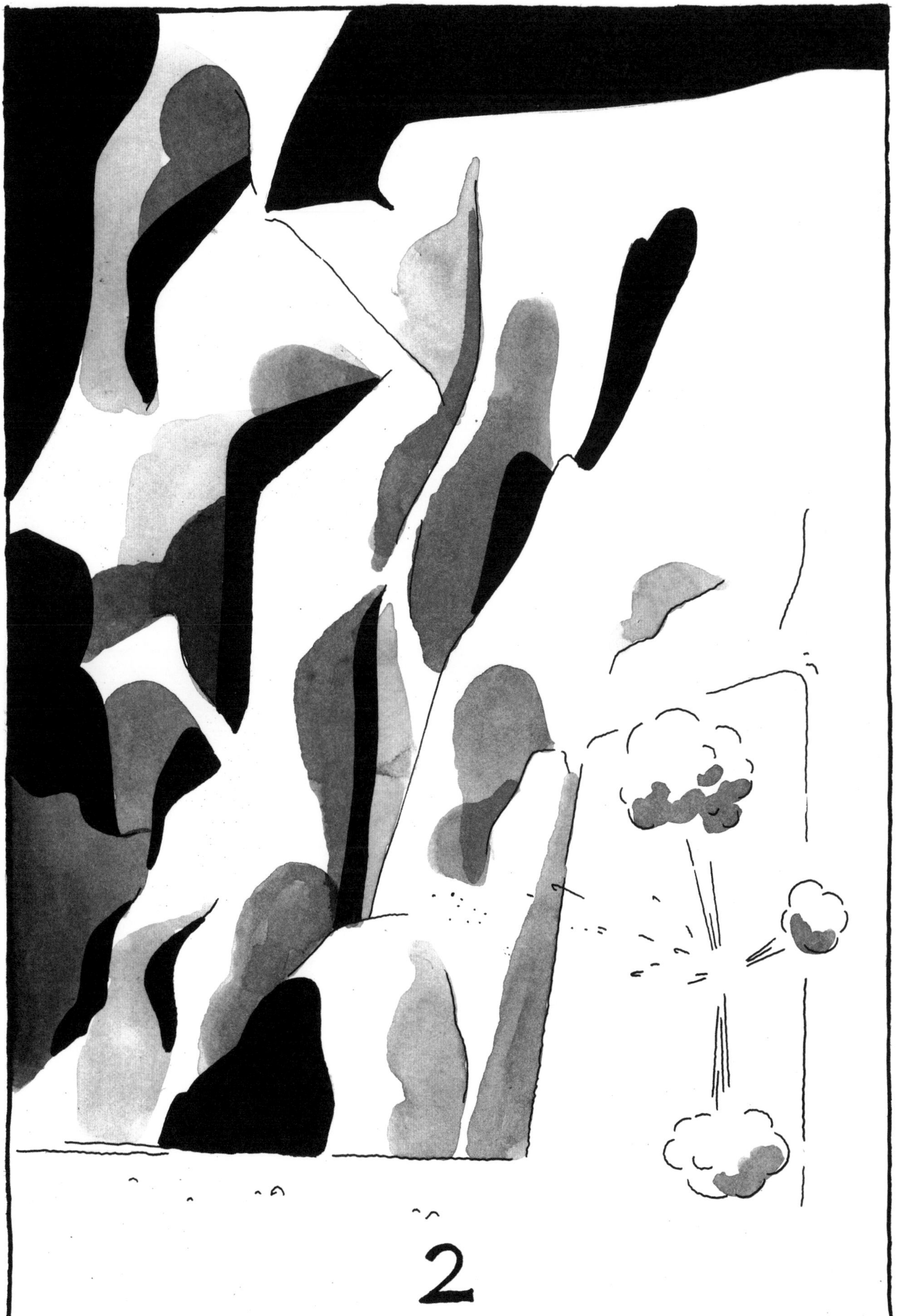
2

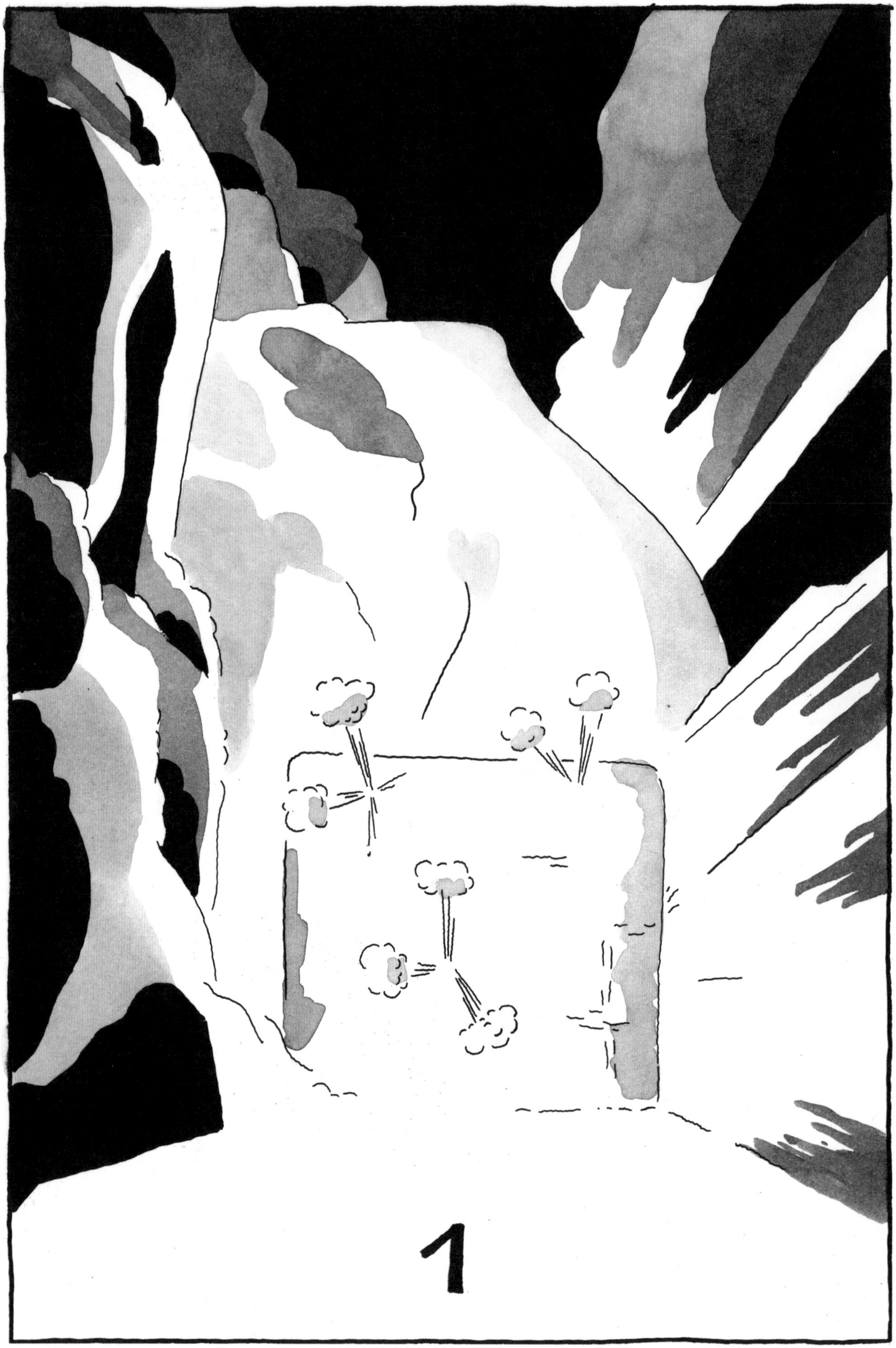
1

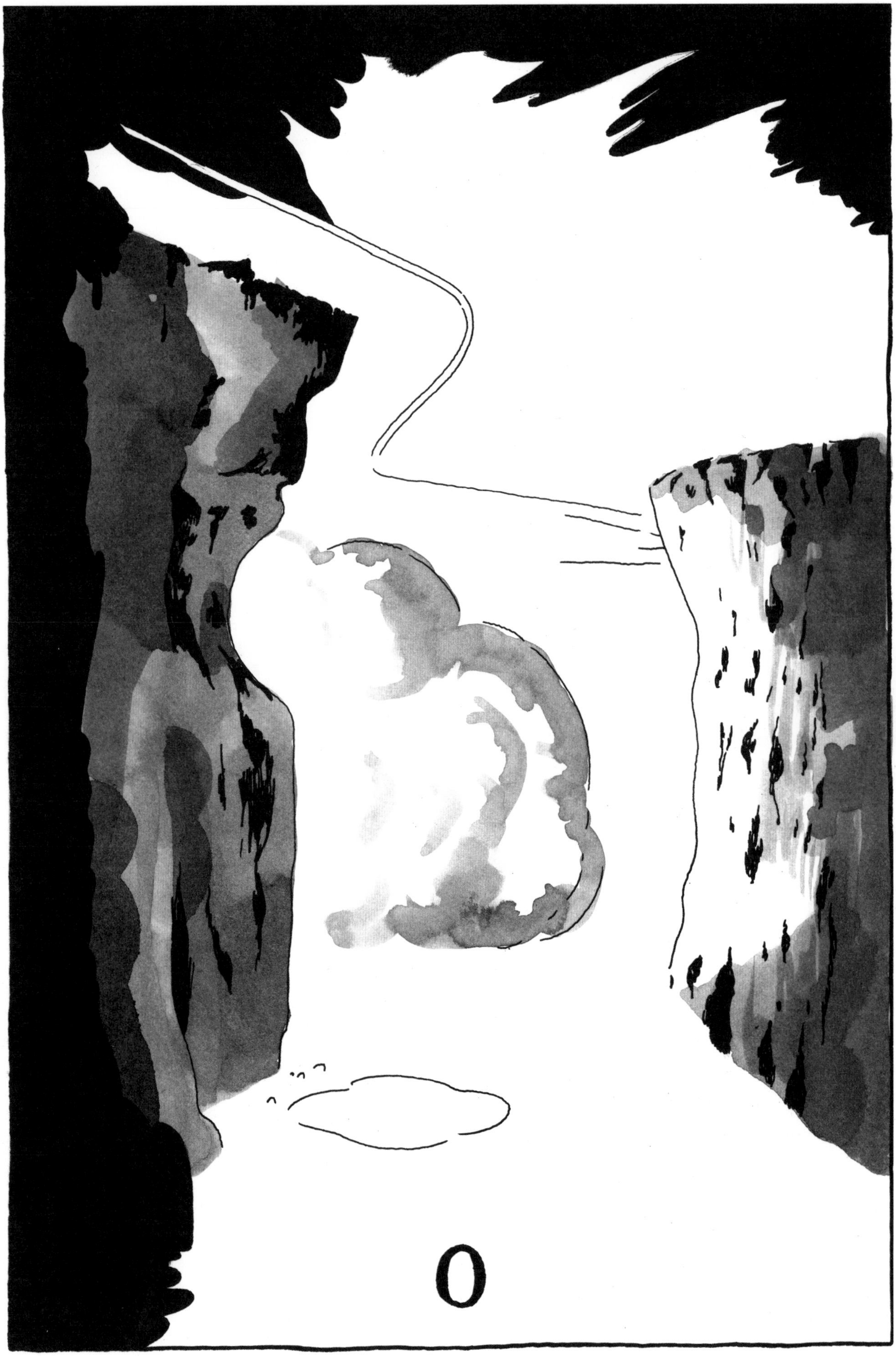
O

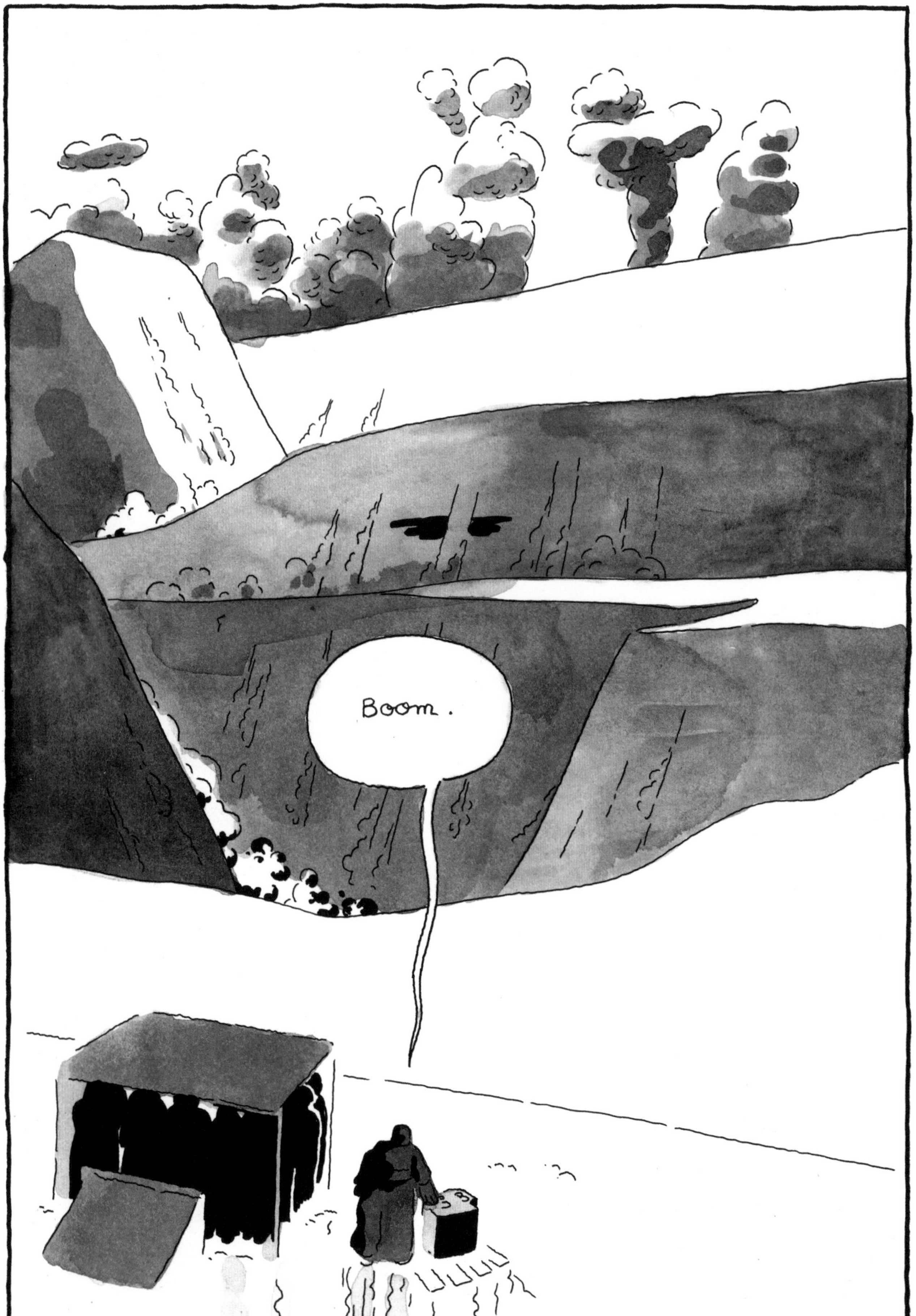
Boom.

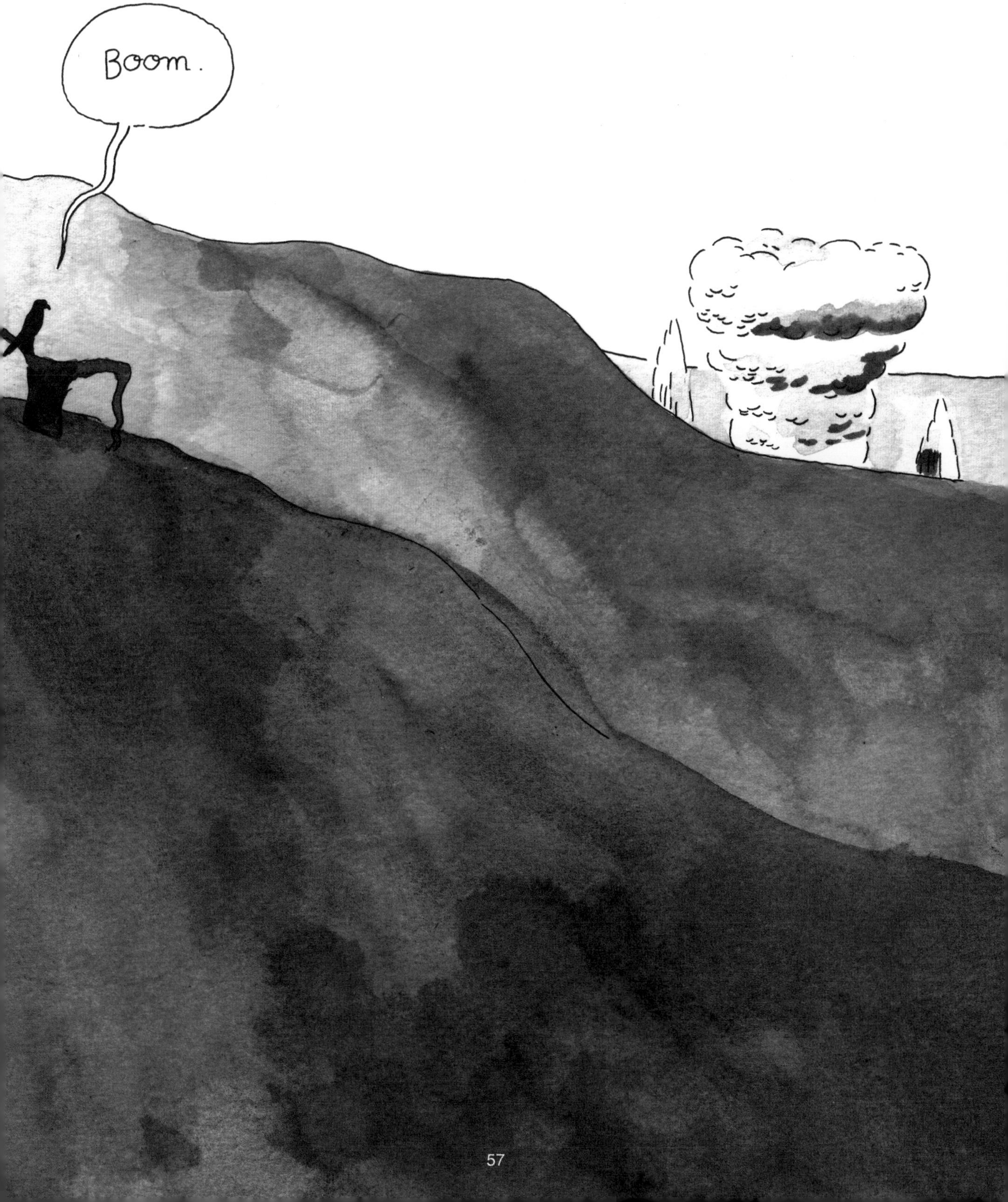
Boom.

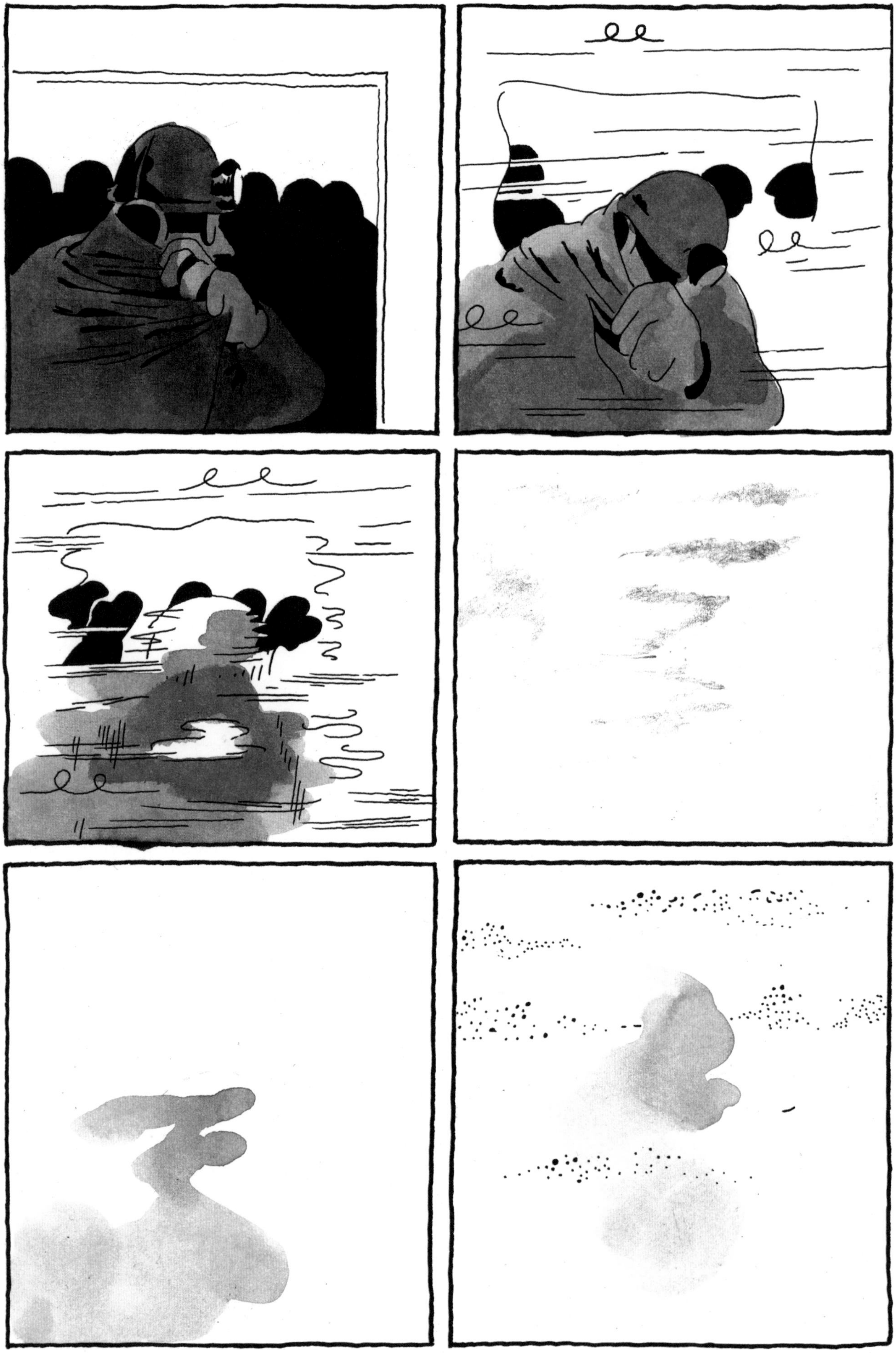

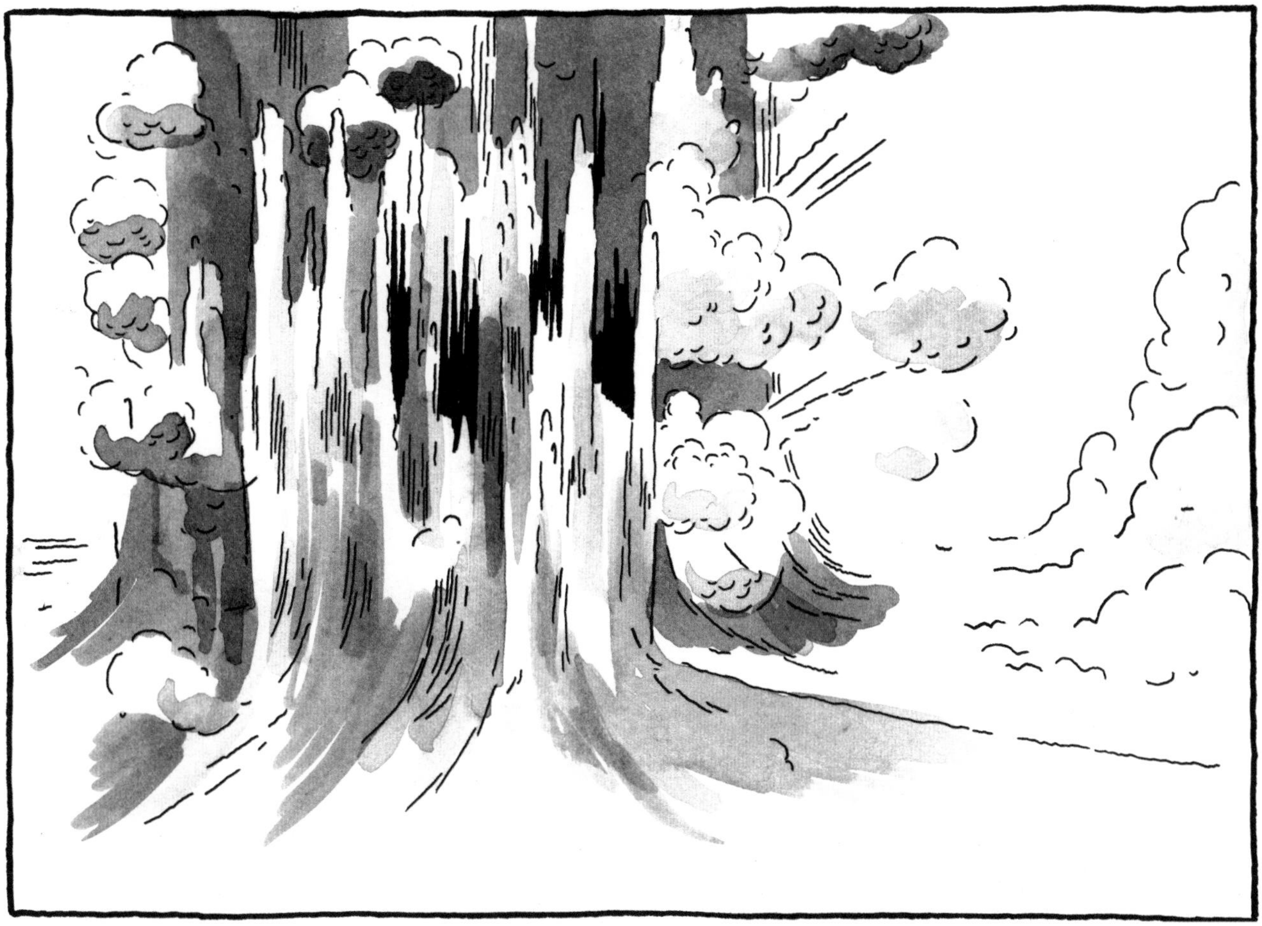

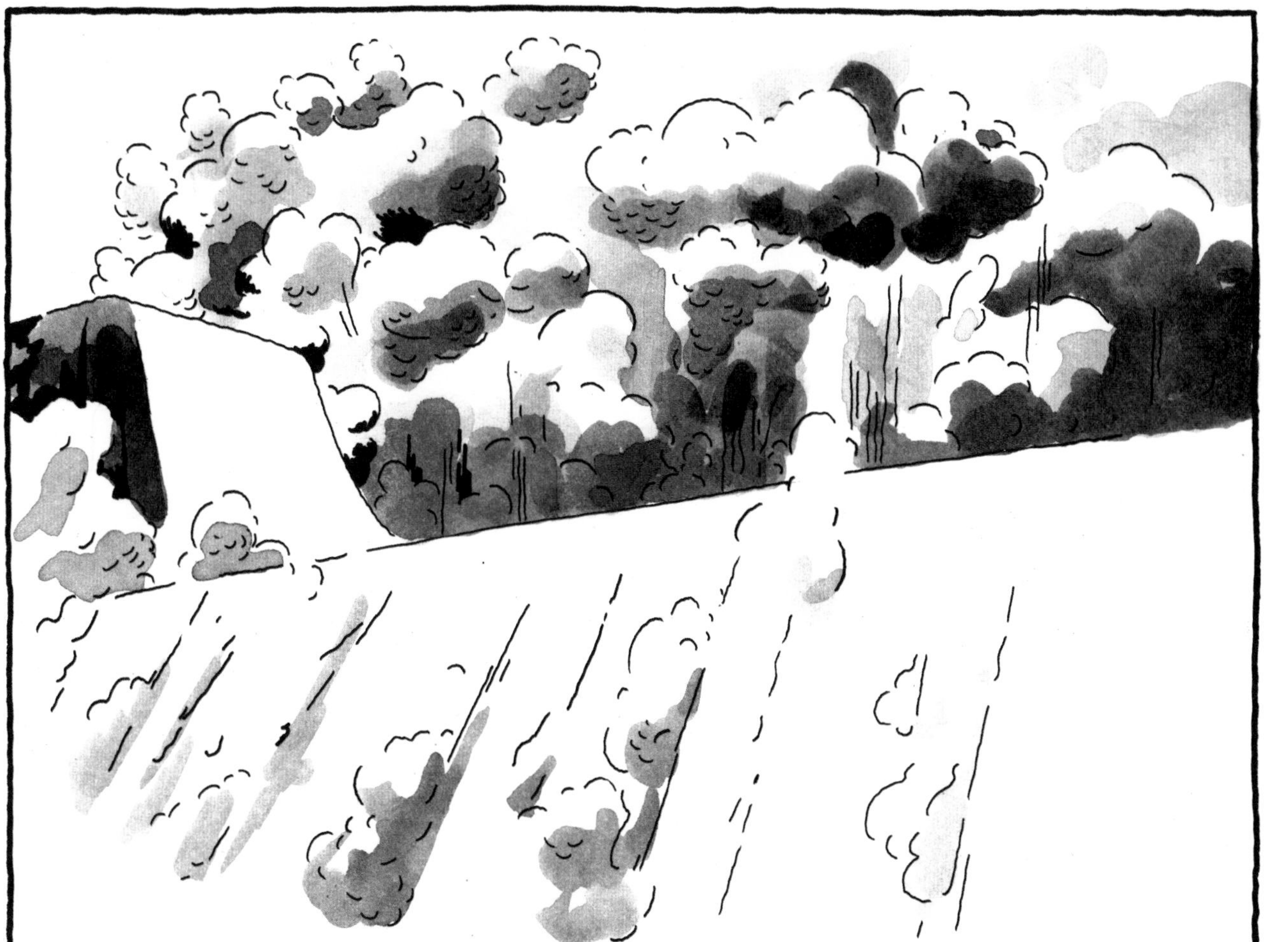

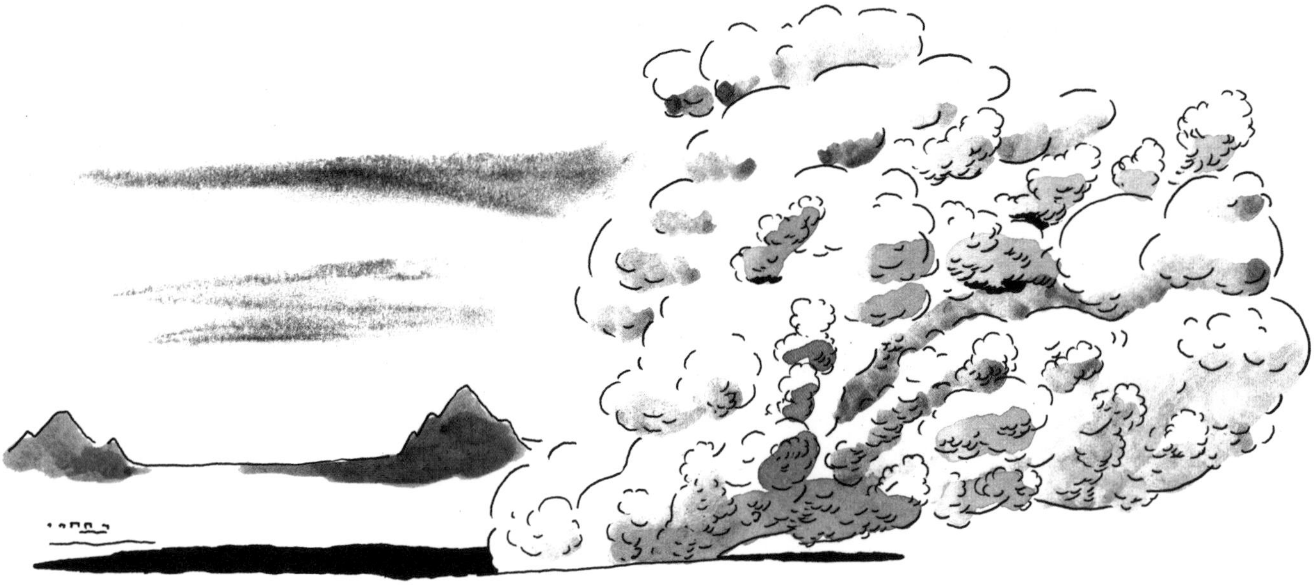

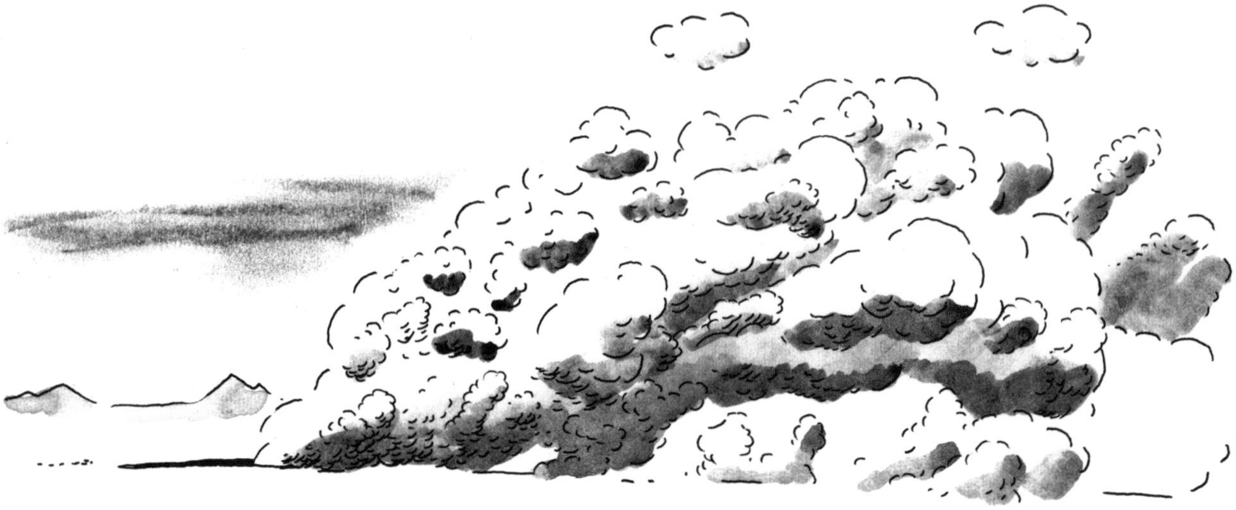

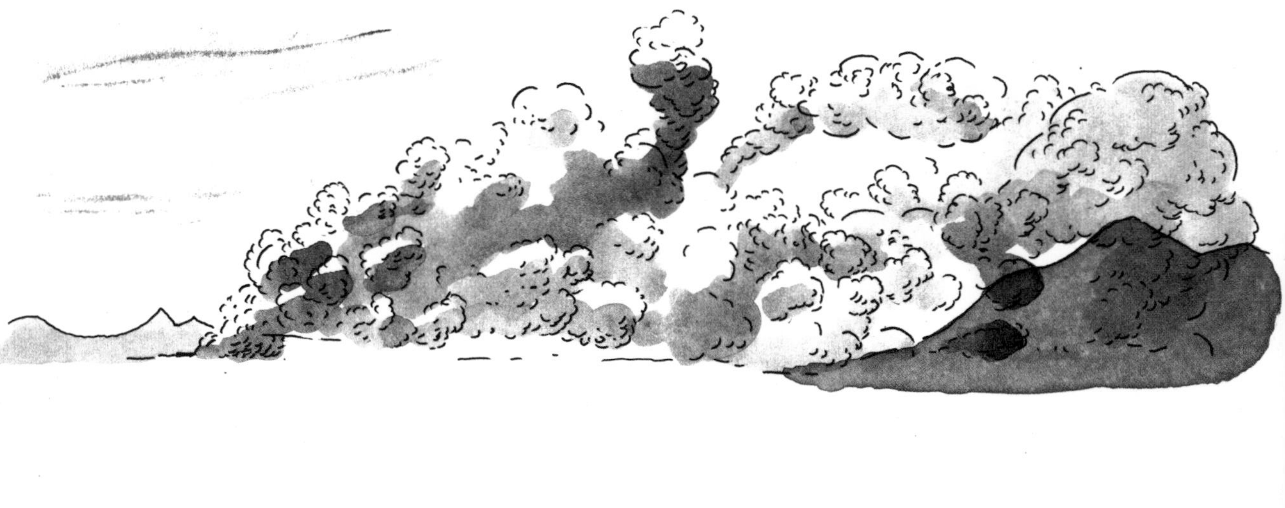

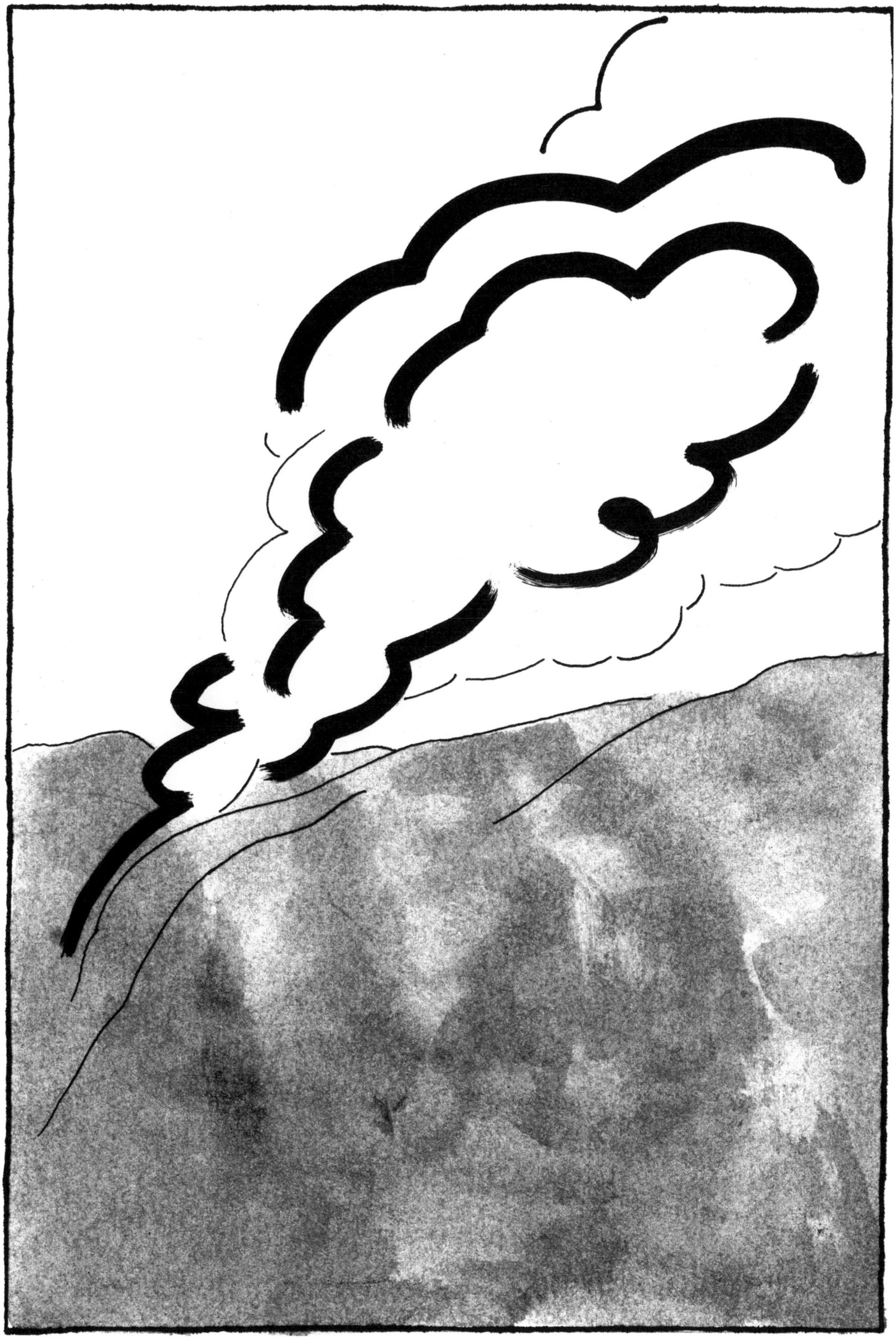

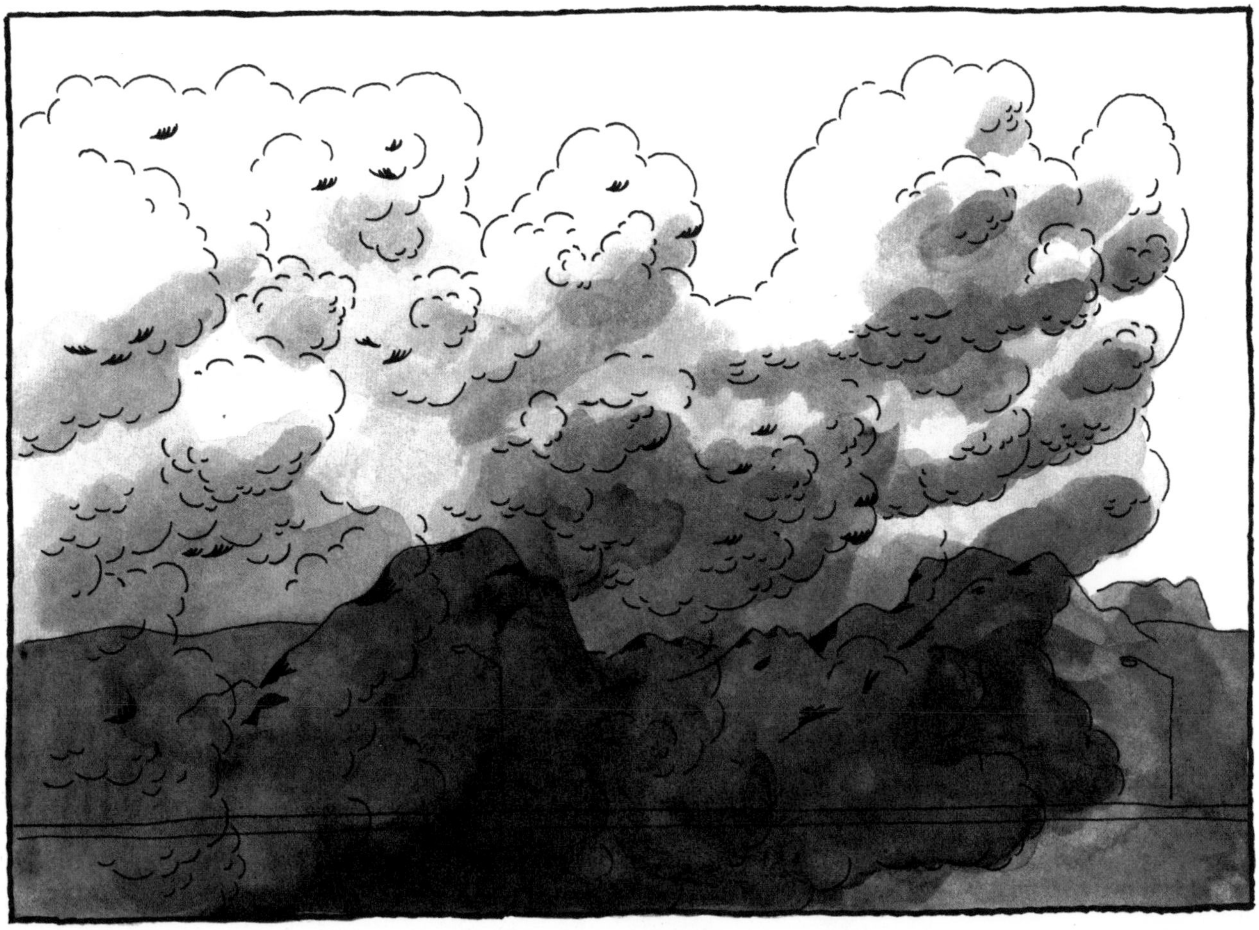

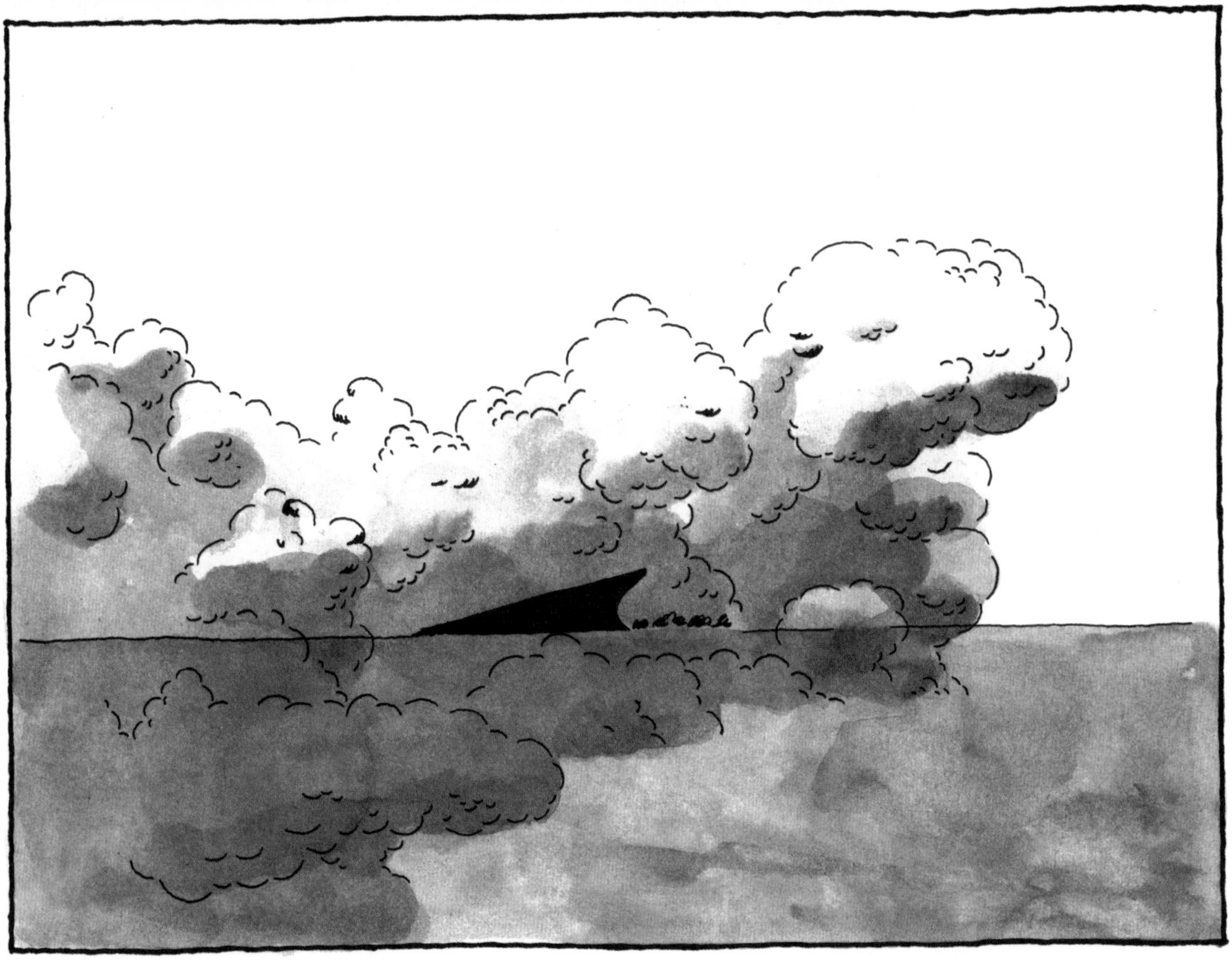

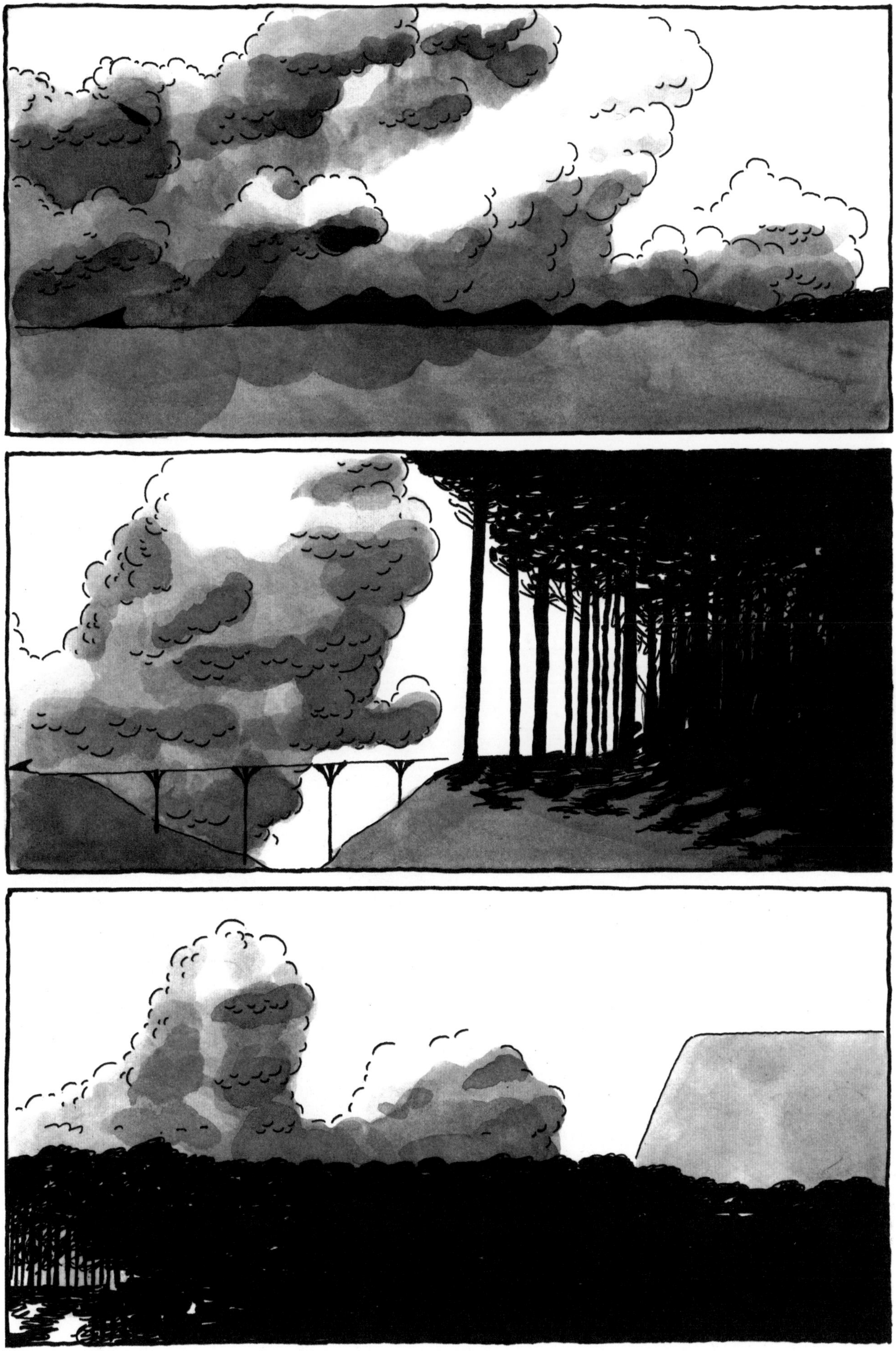

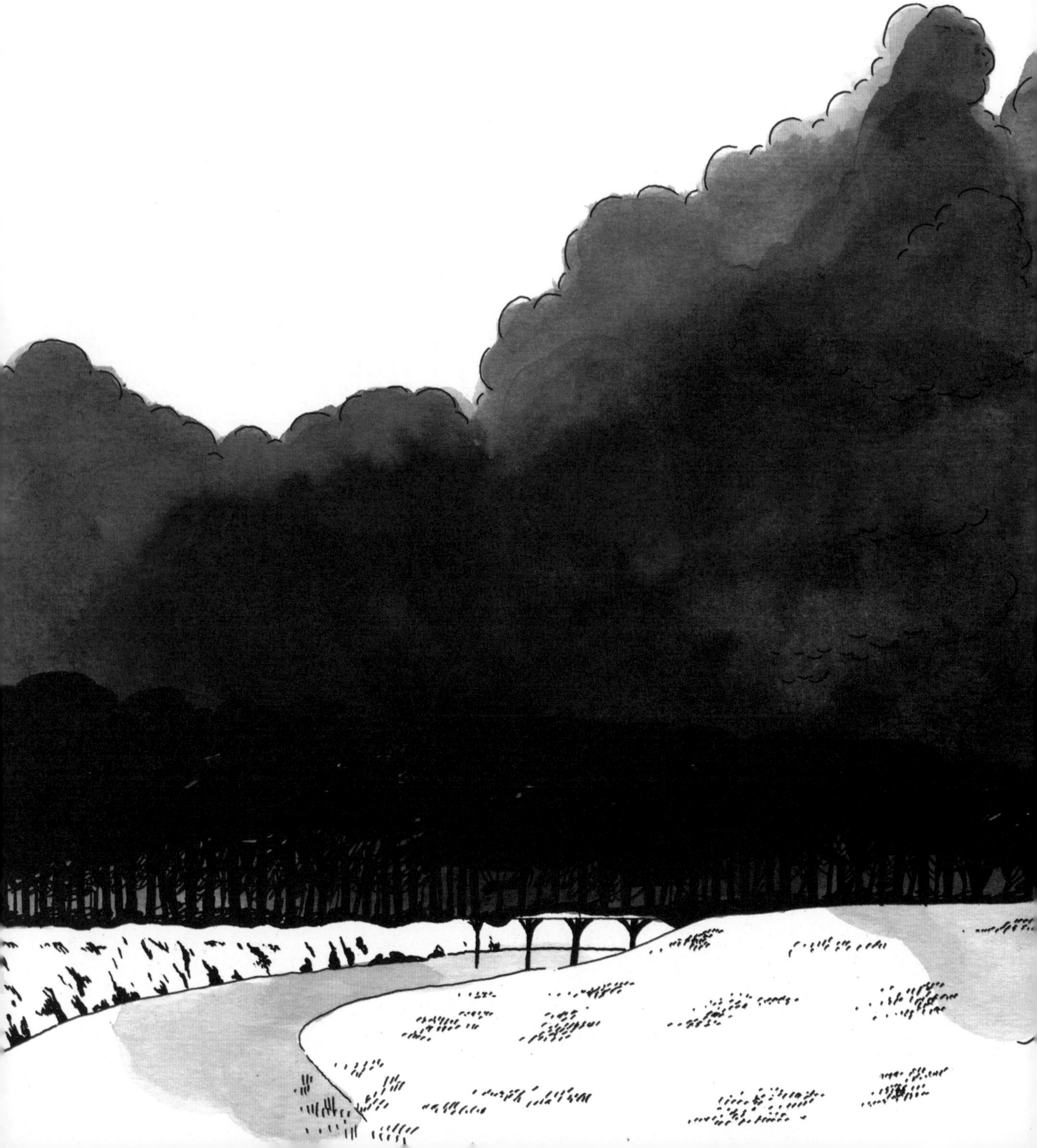

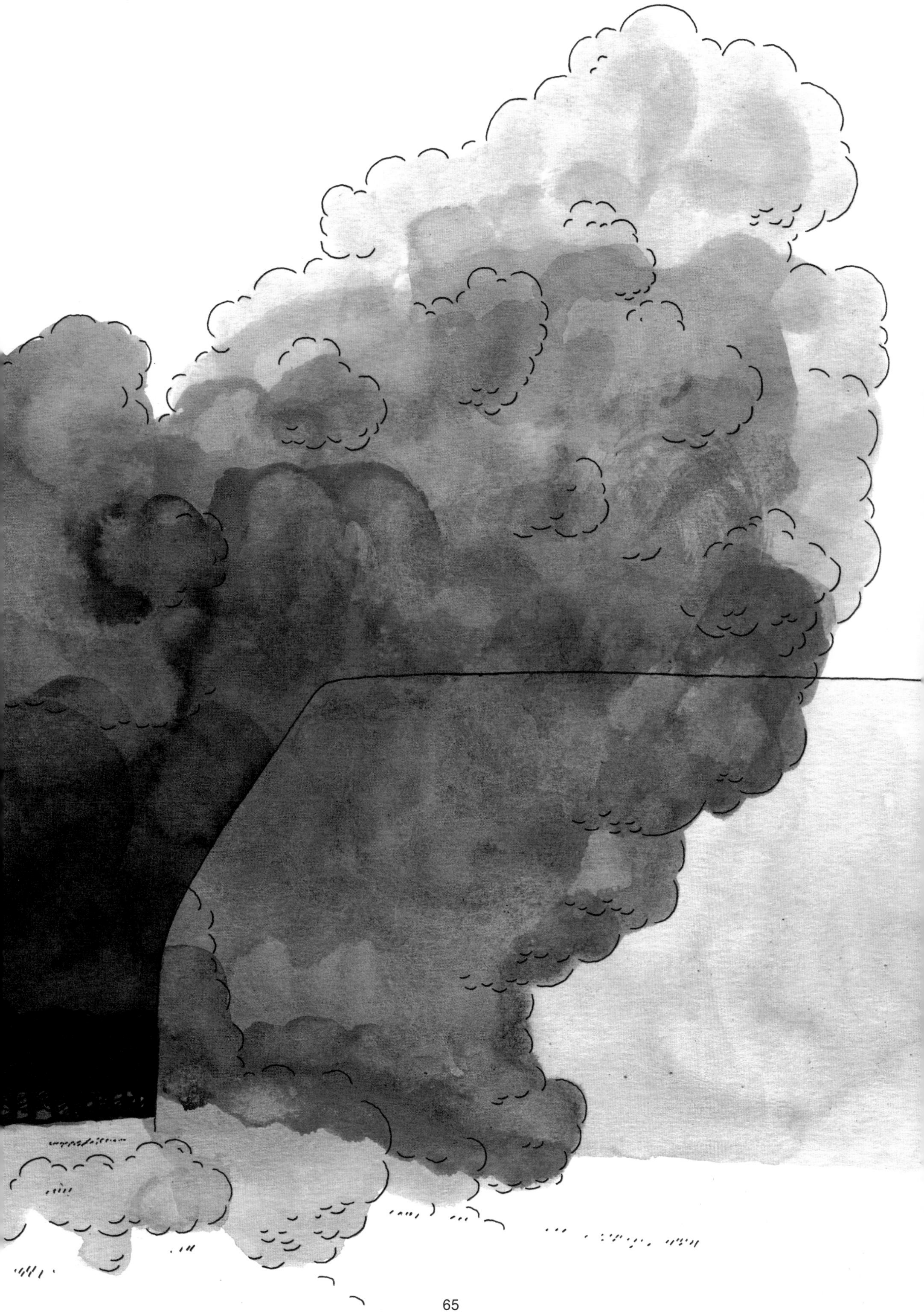

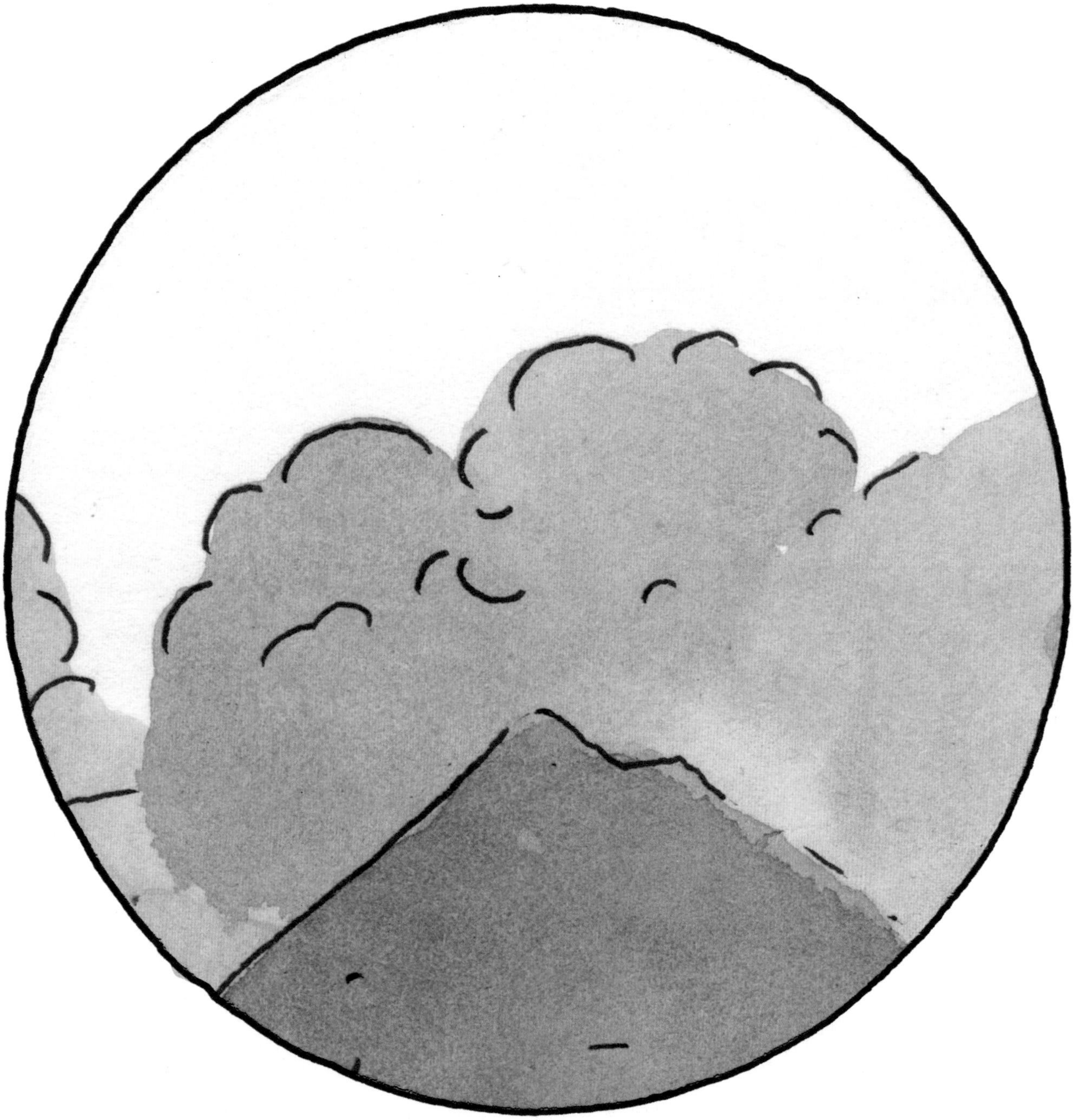

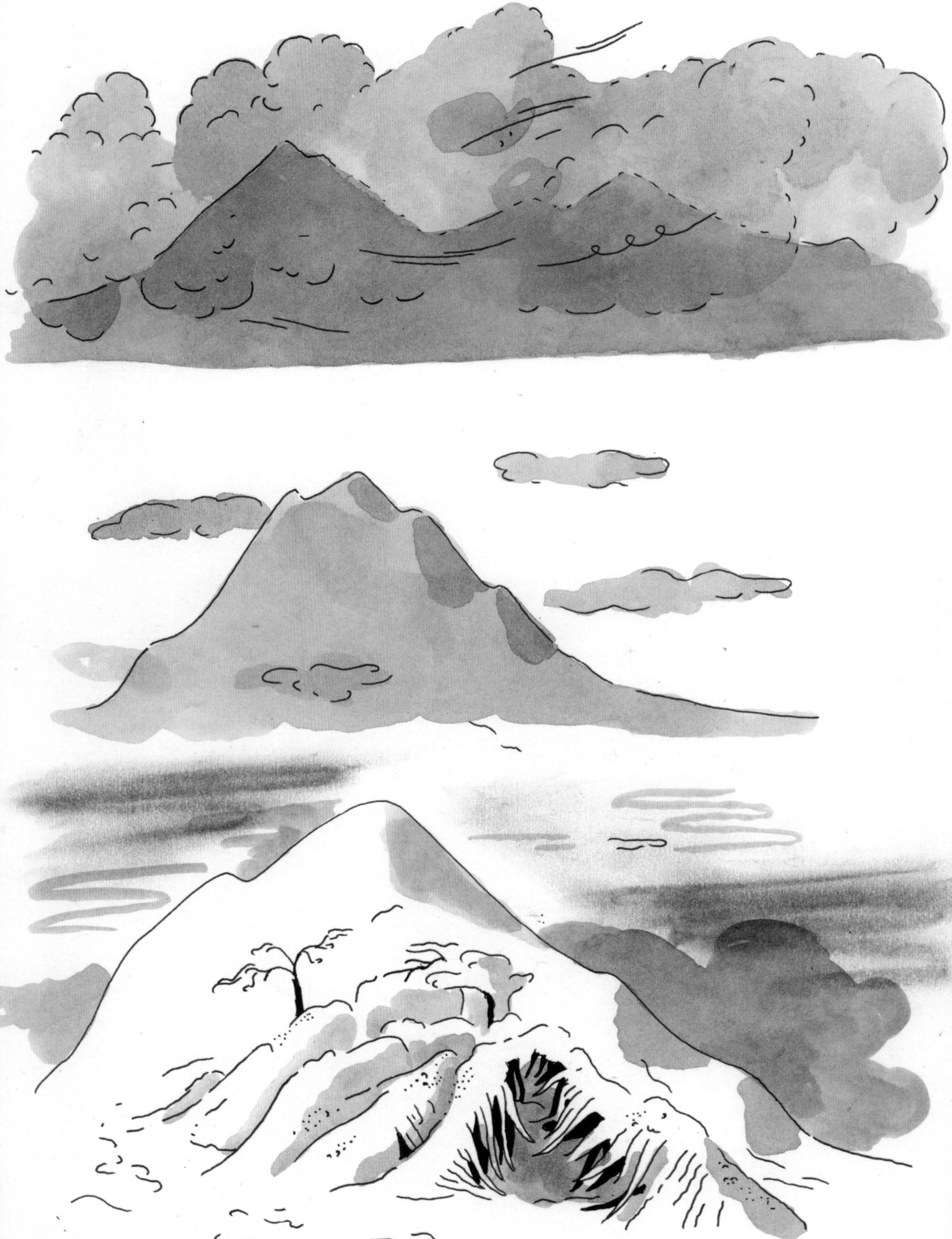

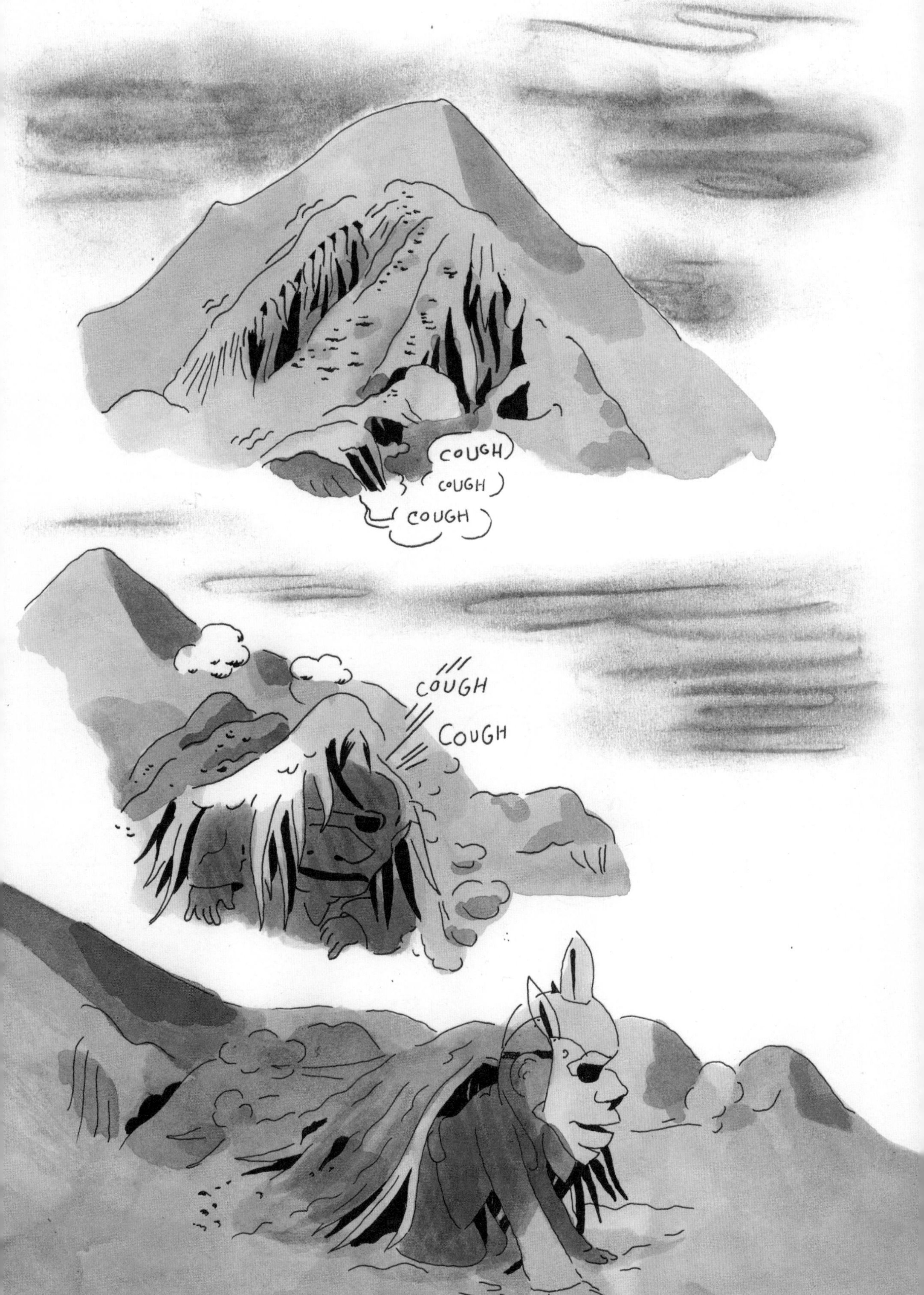
COUGH
COUGH
COUGH
COUGH
COUGH

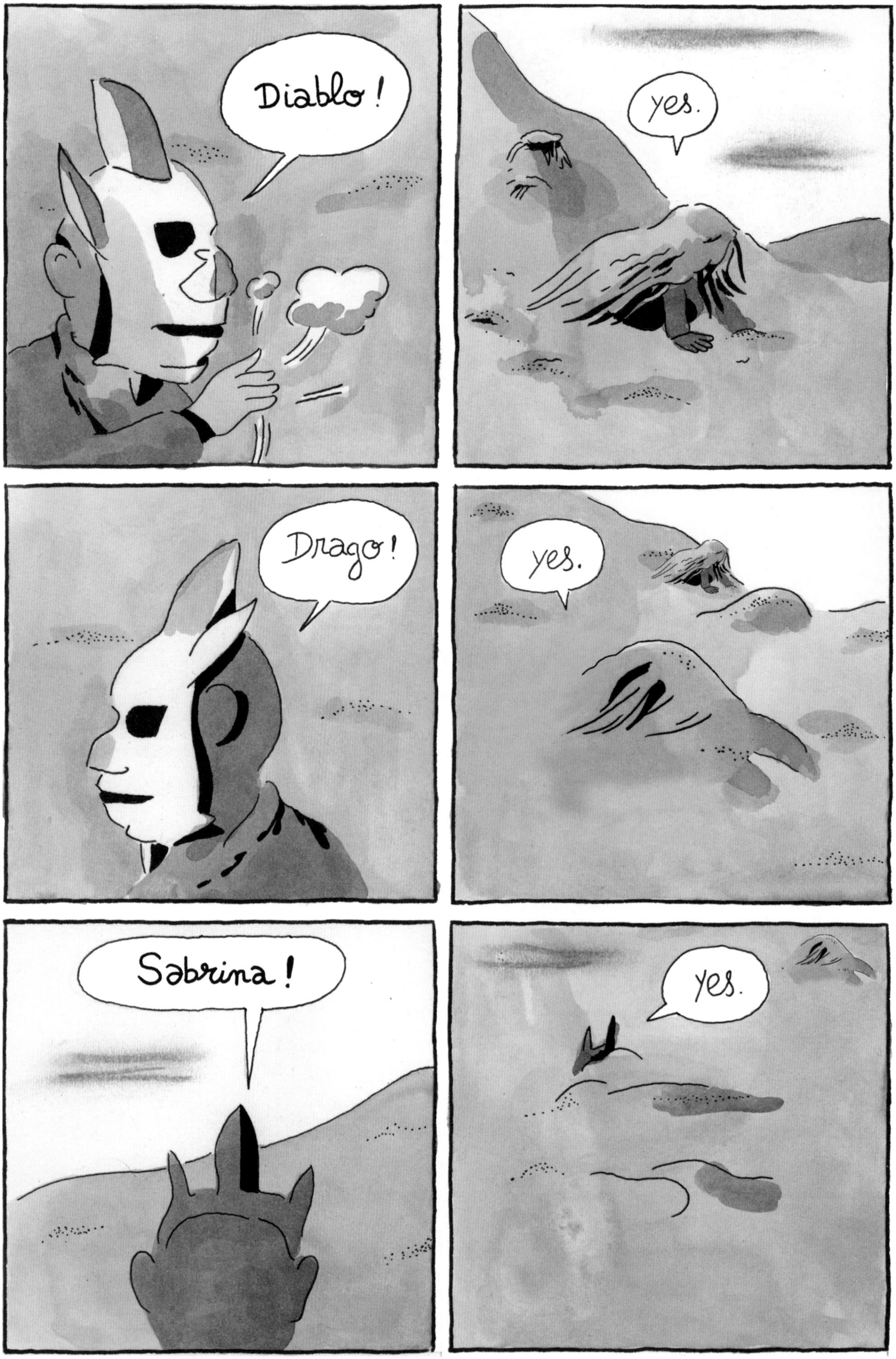
Diablo!
yes.
Drago!
yes.
Sabrina!
yes.

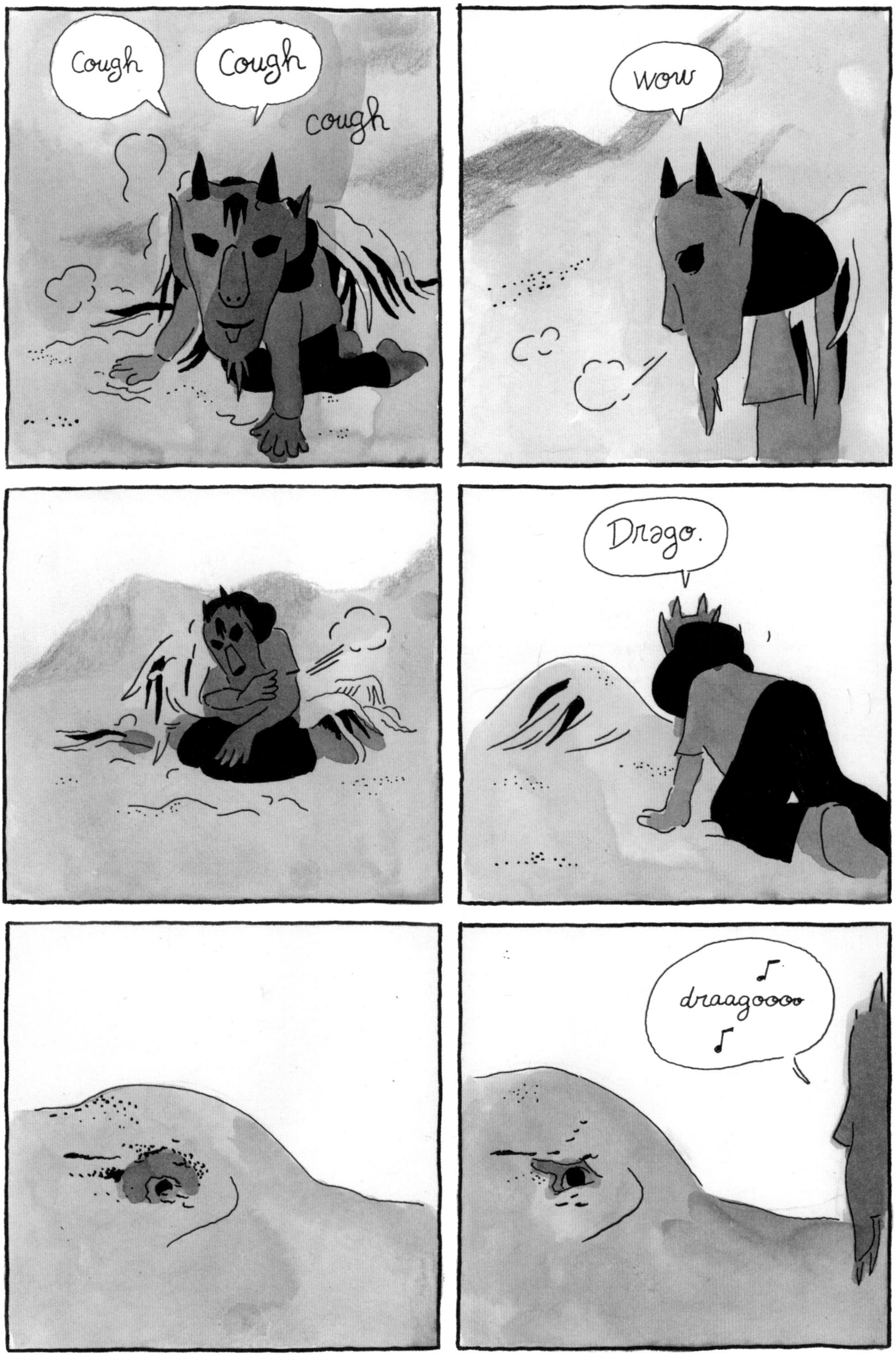
Cough
Cough
cough
wow
Drago.
draagoooo

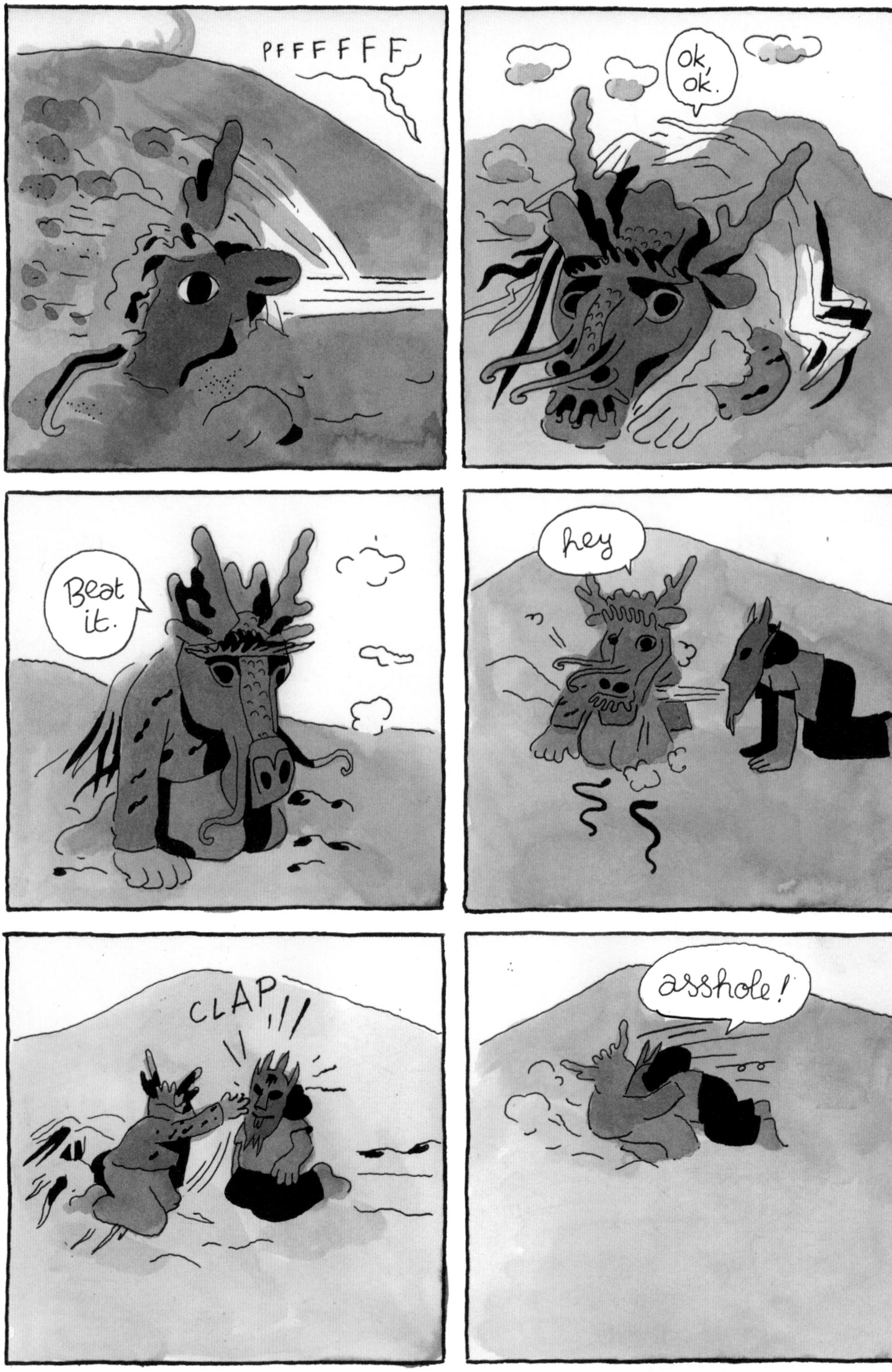
PFFFFFFF
Ok, ok.
Beat it.
hey
CLAP
asshole!

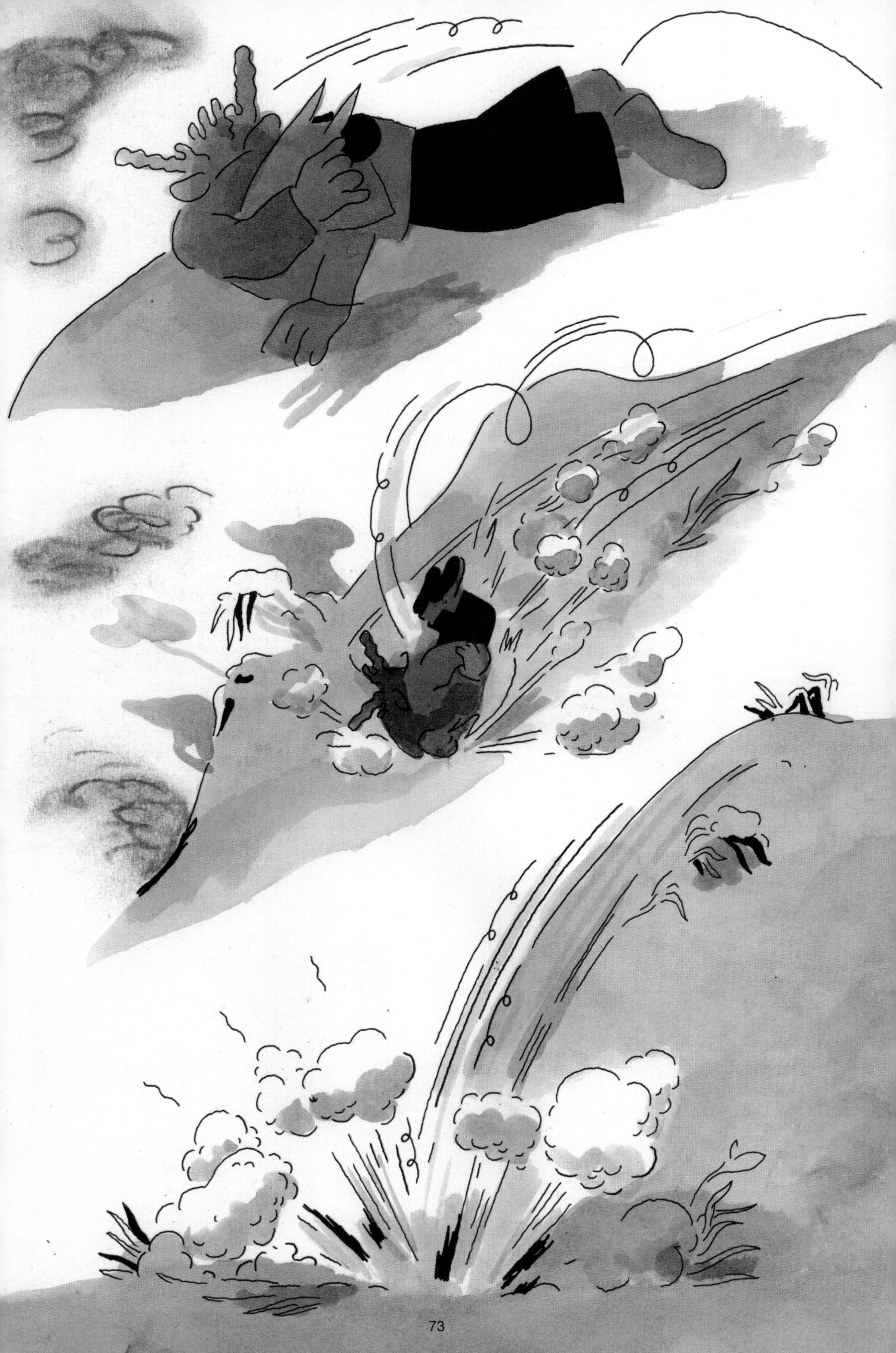

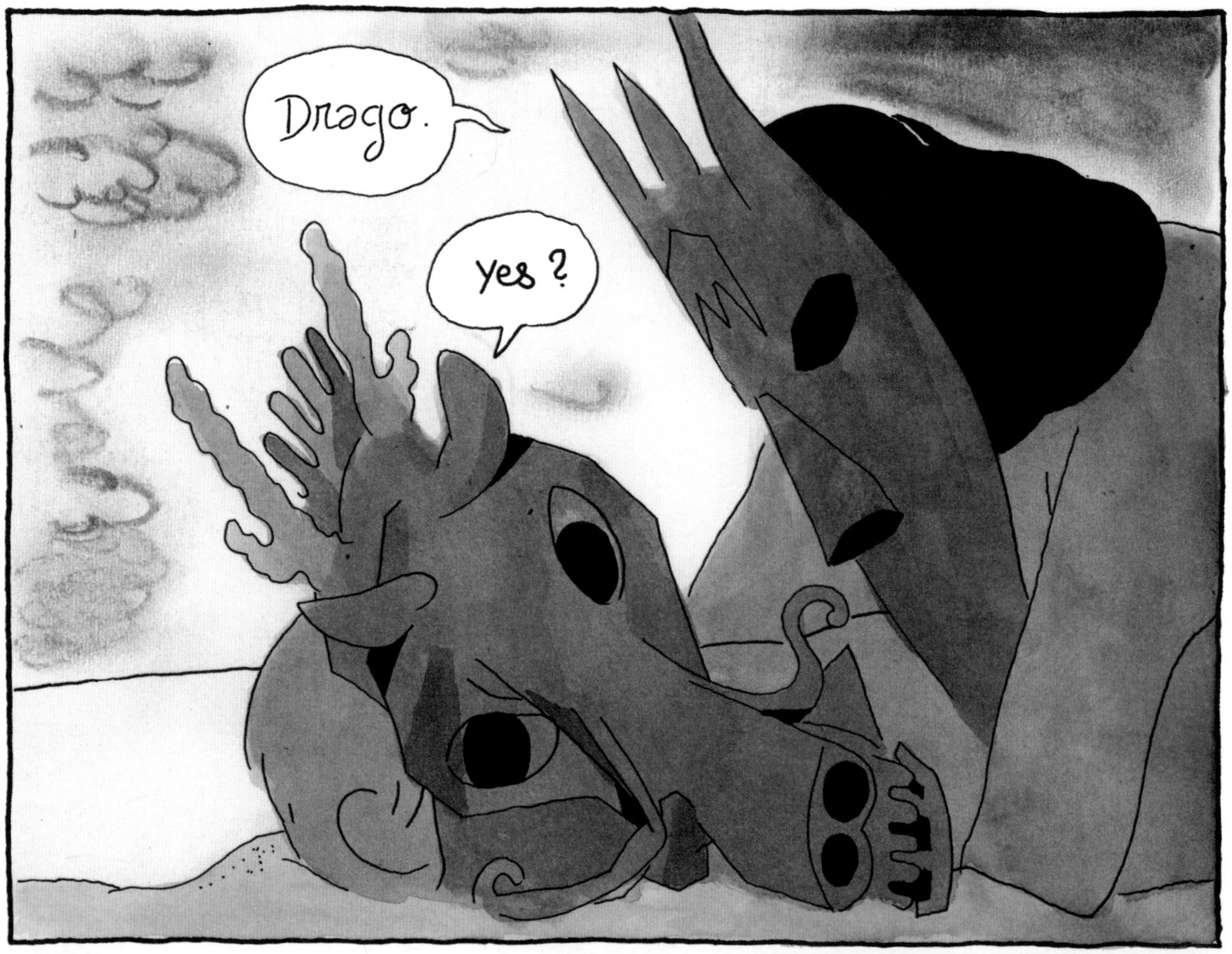
Drago.
yes ?

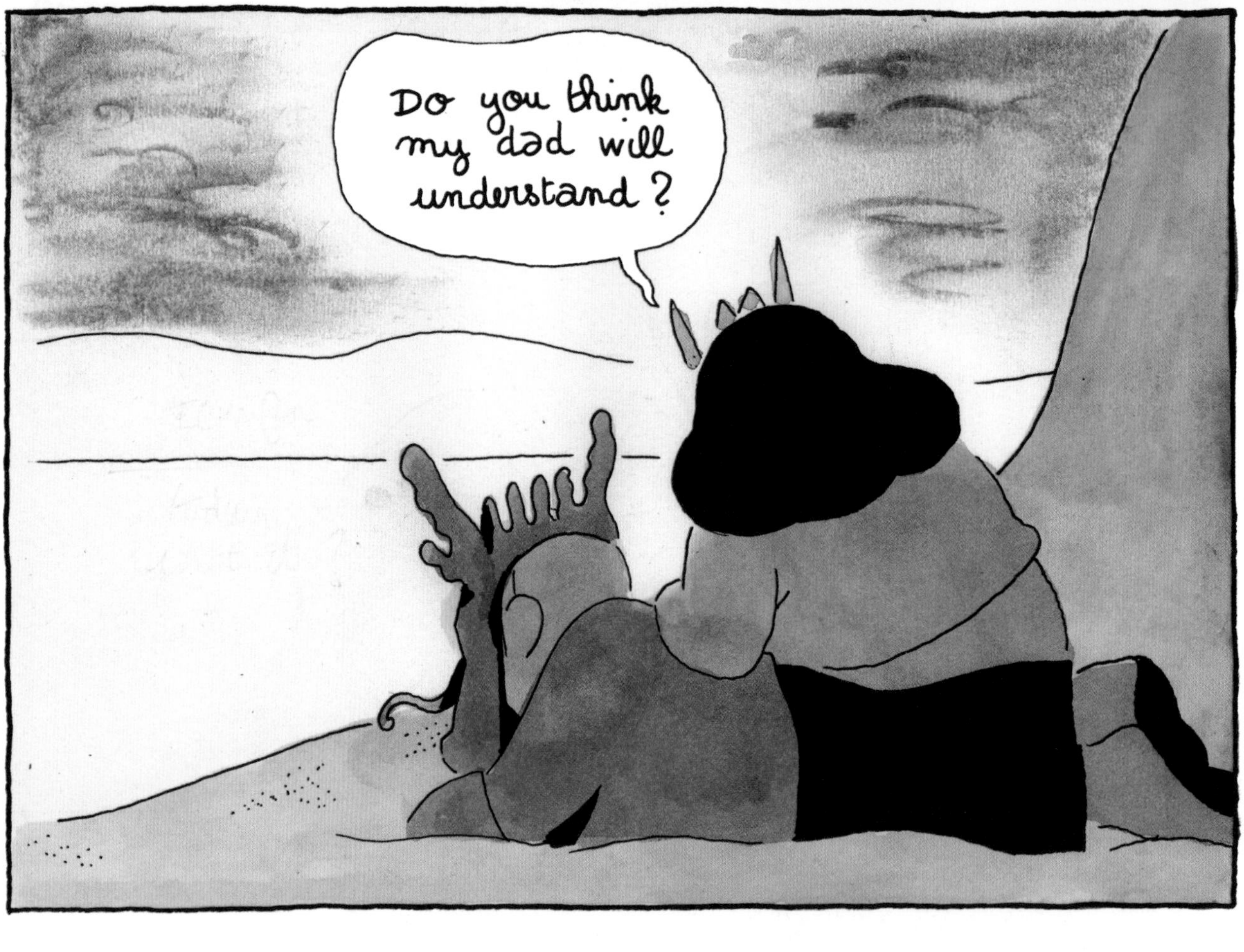
Do you think my dad will understand ?

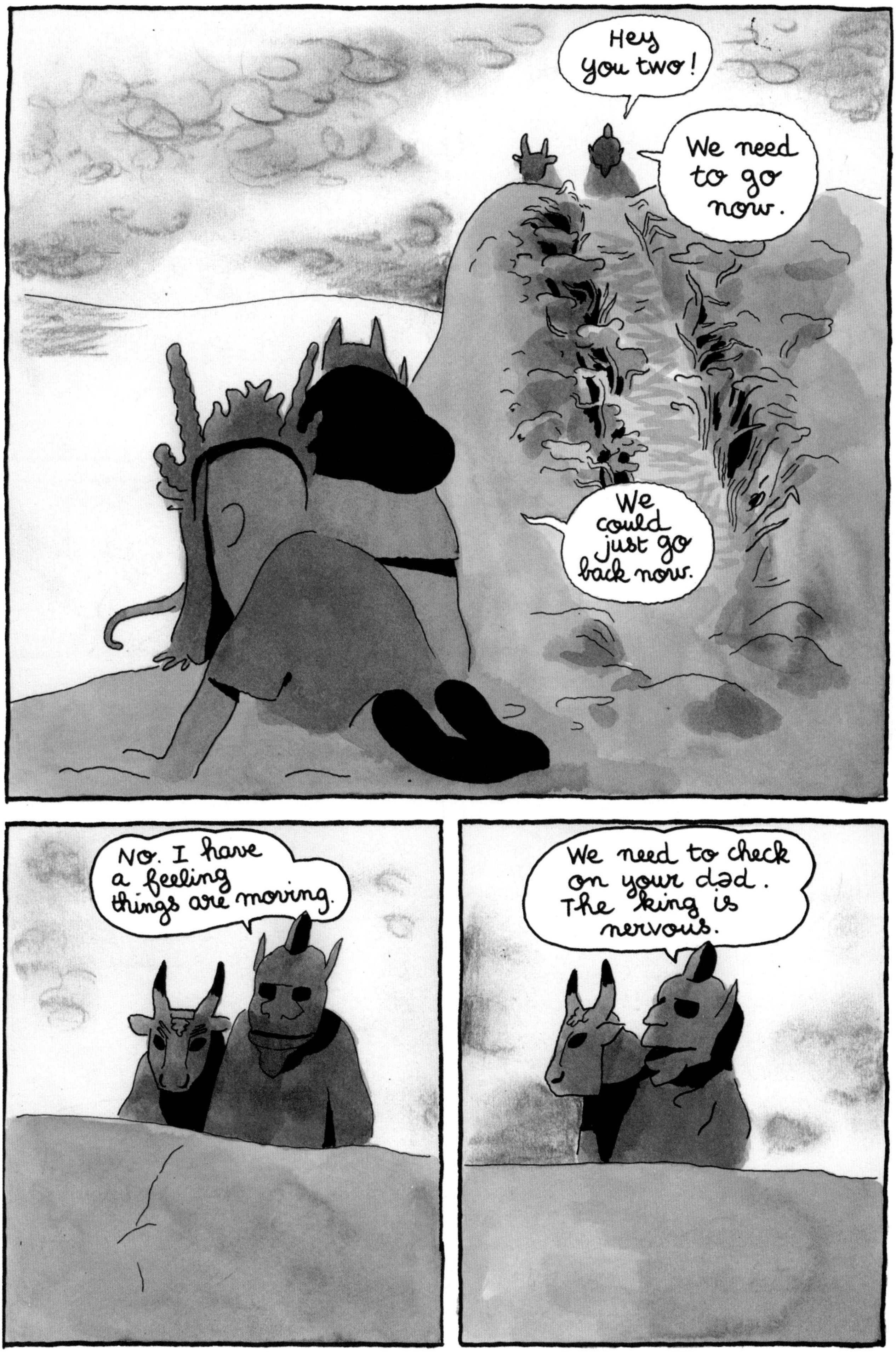
Hey you two!
We need to go now.
We could just go back now.
No. I have a feeling things are moving.
We need to check on your dad. The king is nervous.

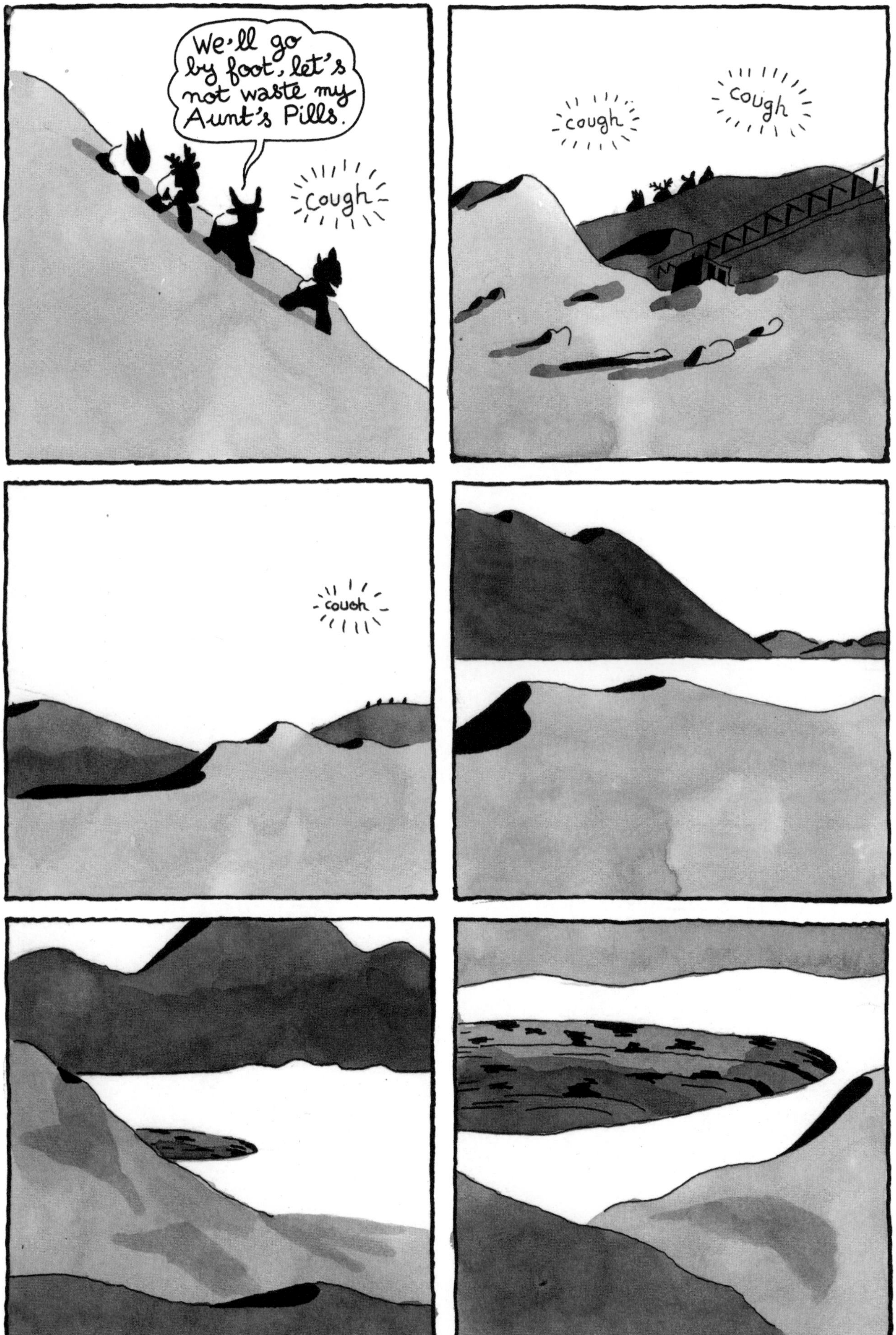
We'll go by foot, let's not waste my Aunt's Pills.
Cough
cough
Cough
cough

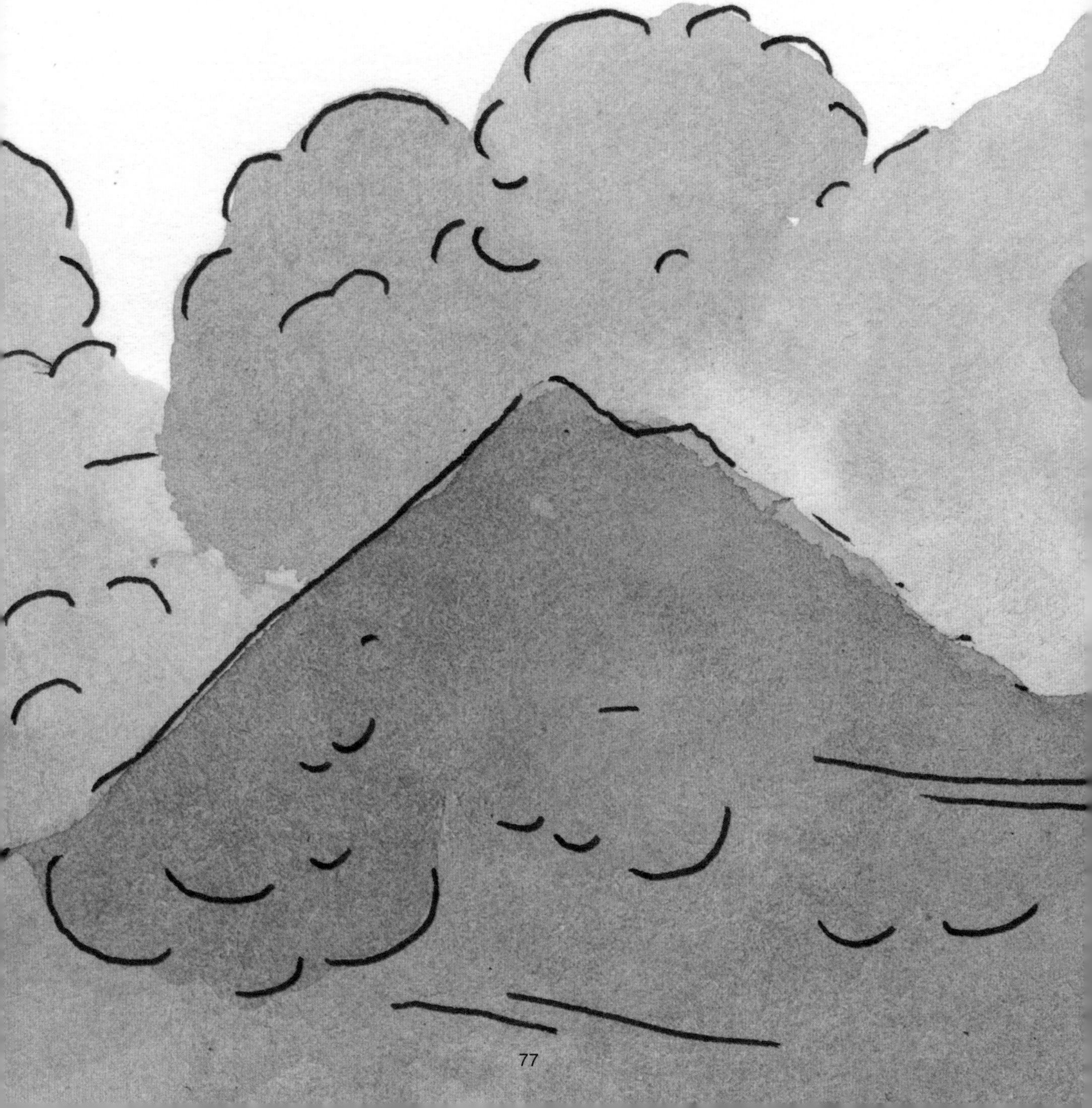

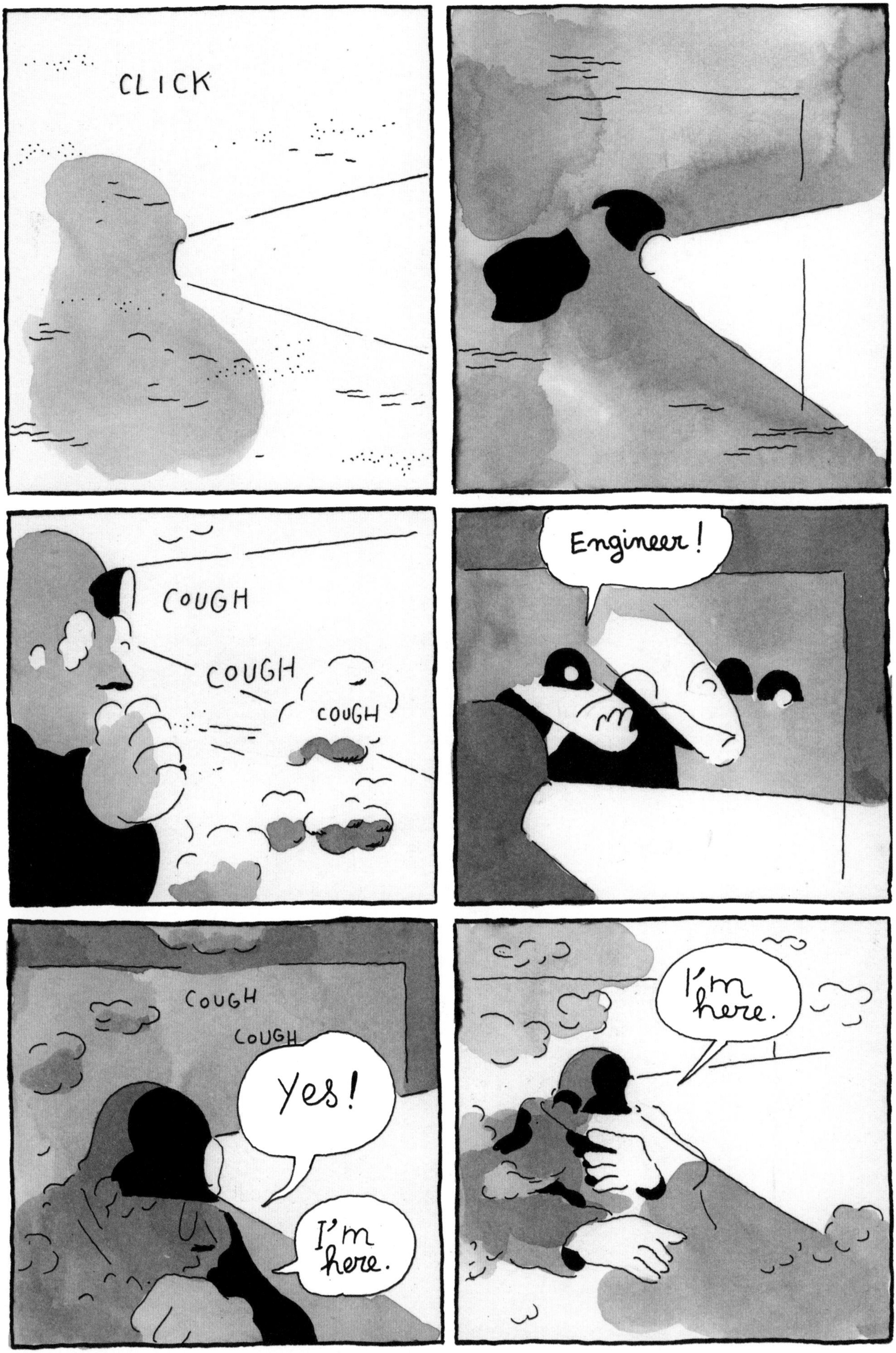
CLICK
COUGH
COUGH
COUGH
Engineer!
COUGH
COUGH
Yes!
I'm here.
I'm here.

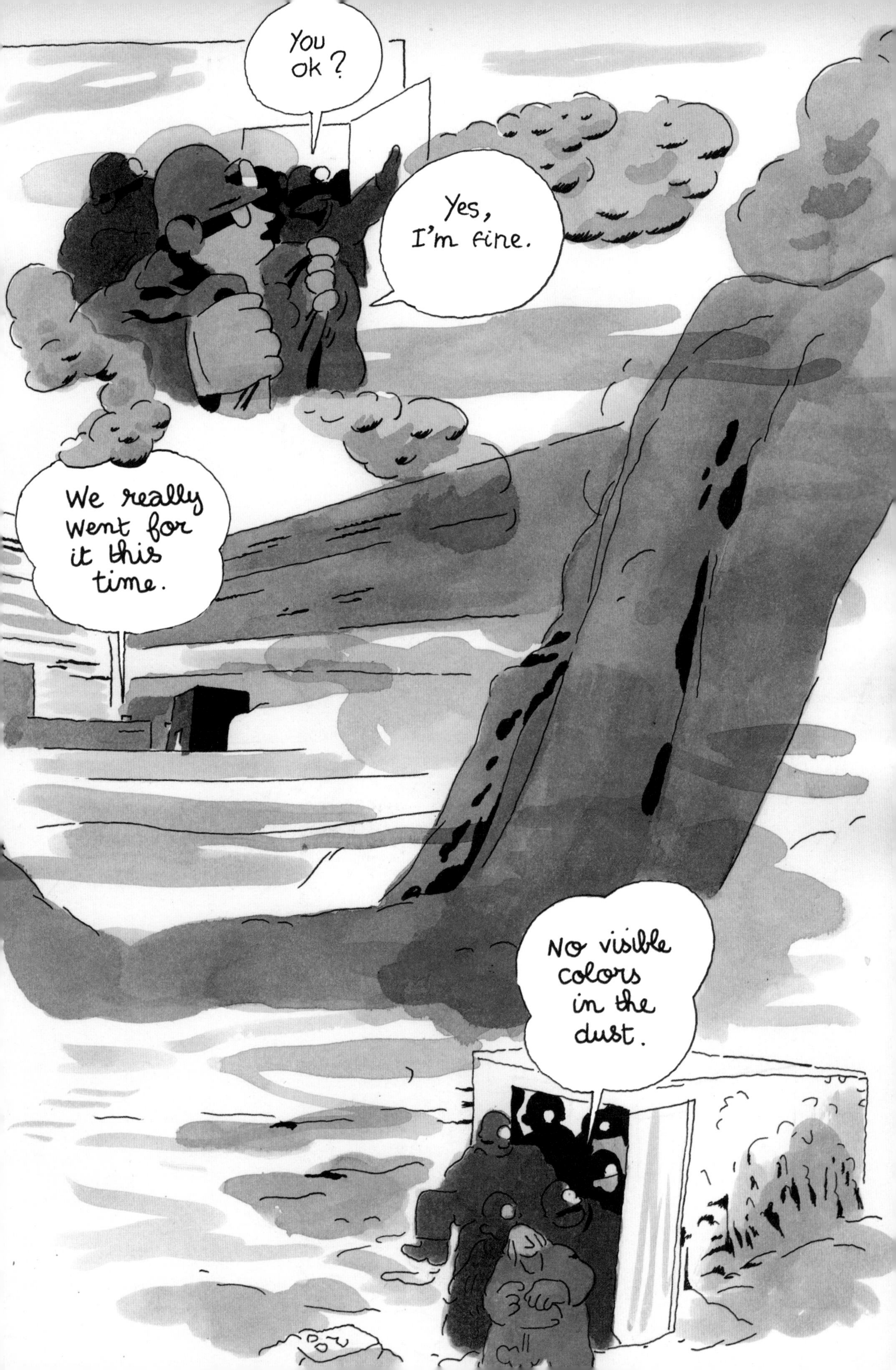
You ok?
Yes, I'm fine.
We really went for it this time.
No visible colors in the dust.

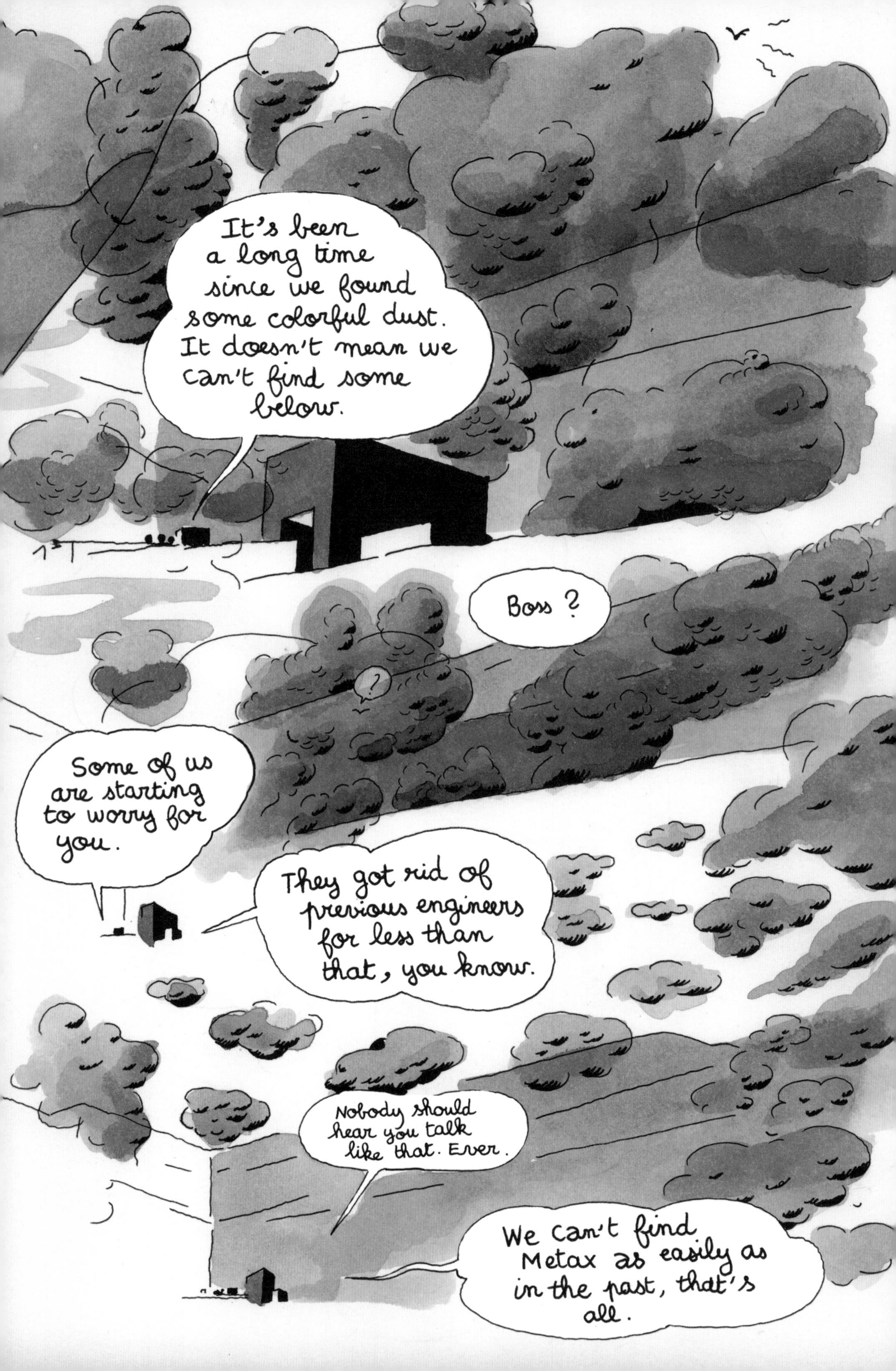
It's been a long time since we found some colorful dust. It doesn't mean we can't find some below.
Boss ?
?
Some of us are starting to worry for you.
They got rid of previous engineers for less than that, you know.
Nobody should hear you talk like that. Ever.
We can't find Metax as easily as in the past, that's all.

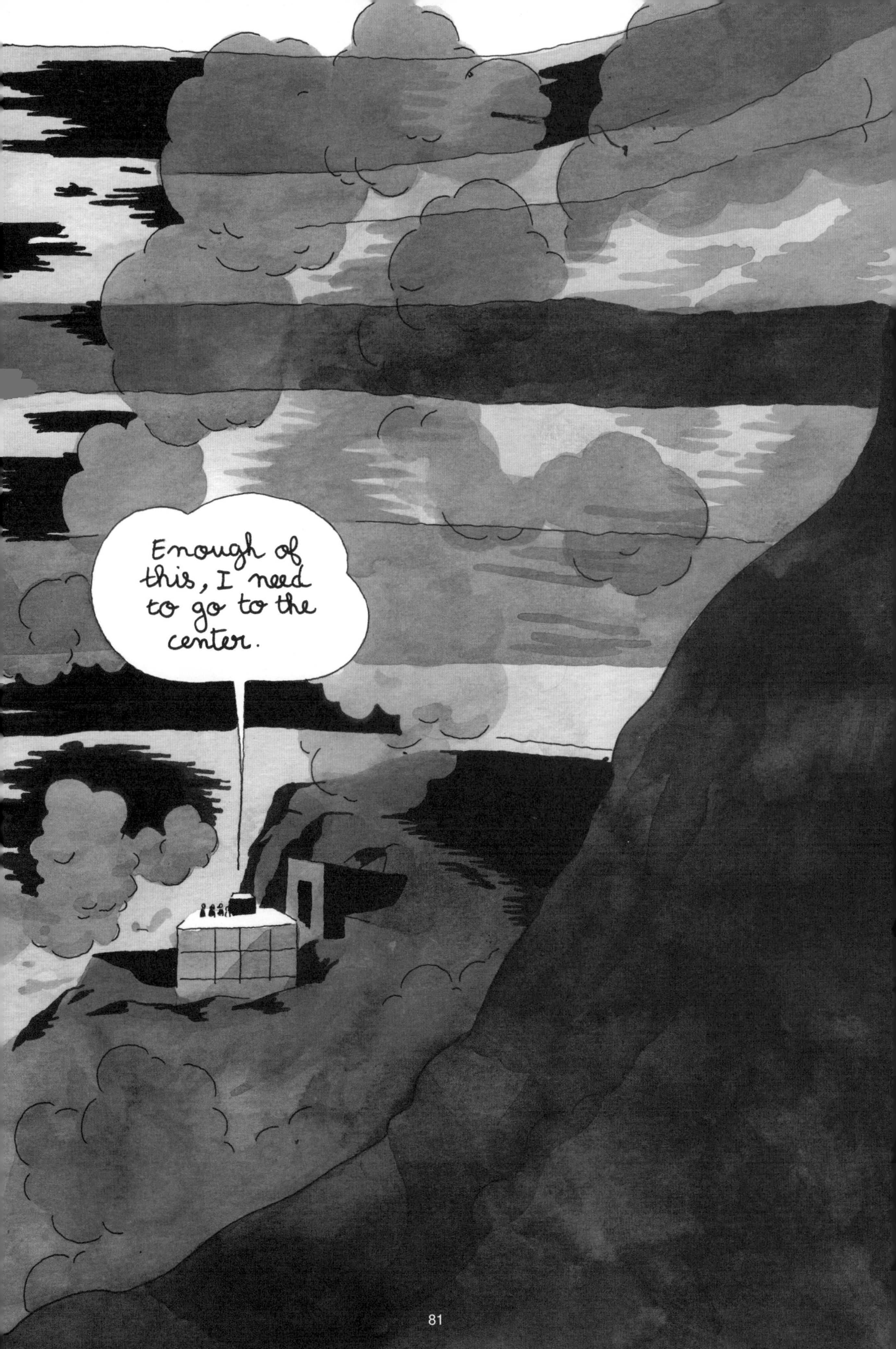
Enough of this, I need to go to the center.

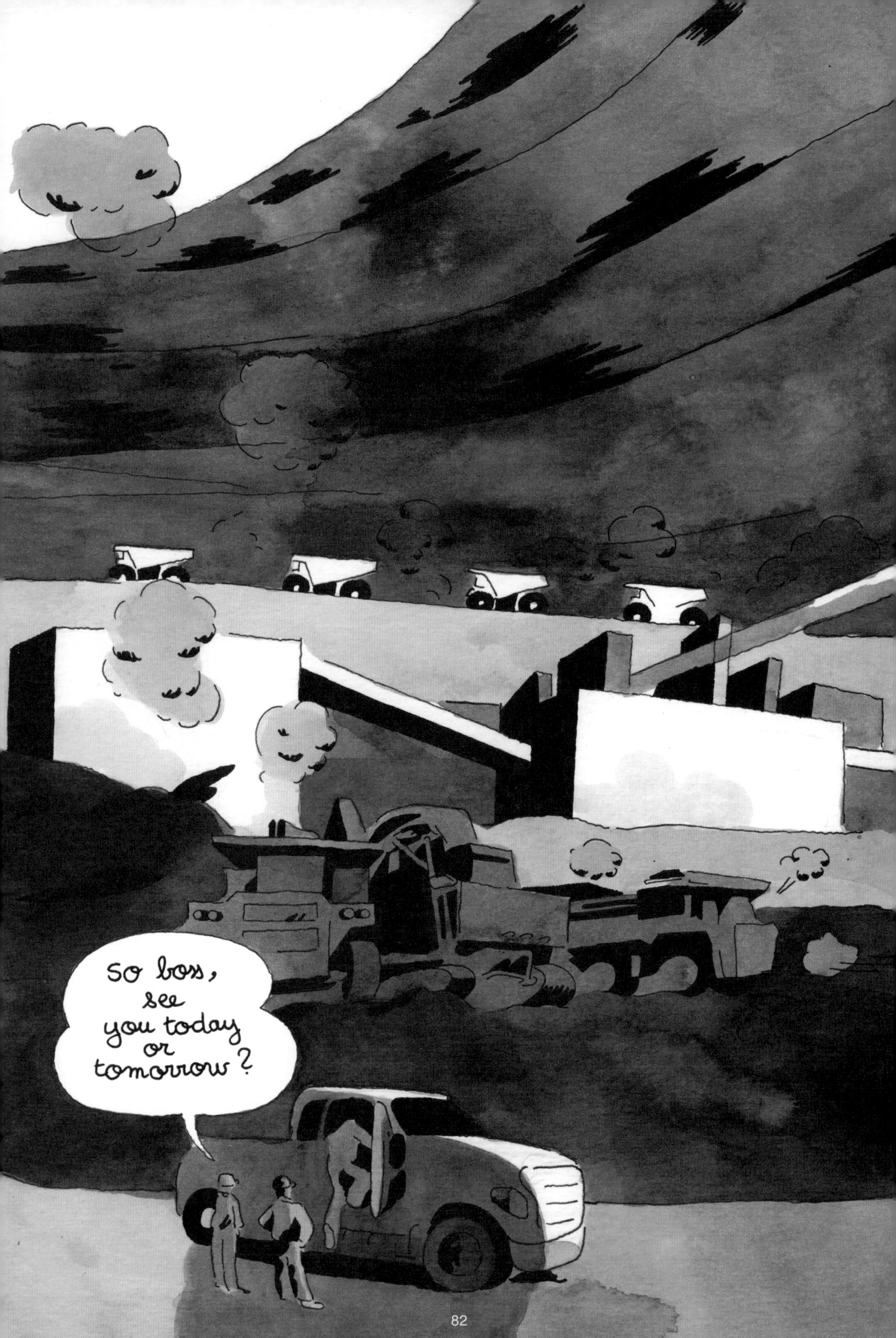
so boss, see you today or tomorrow?

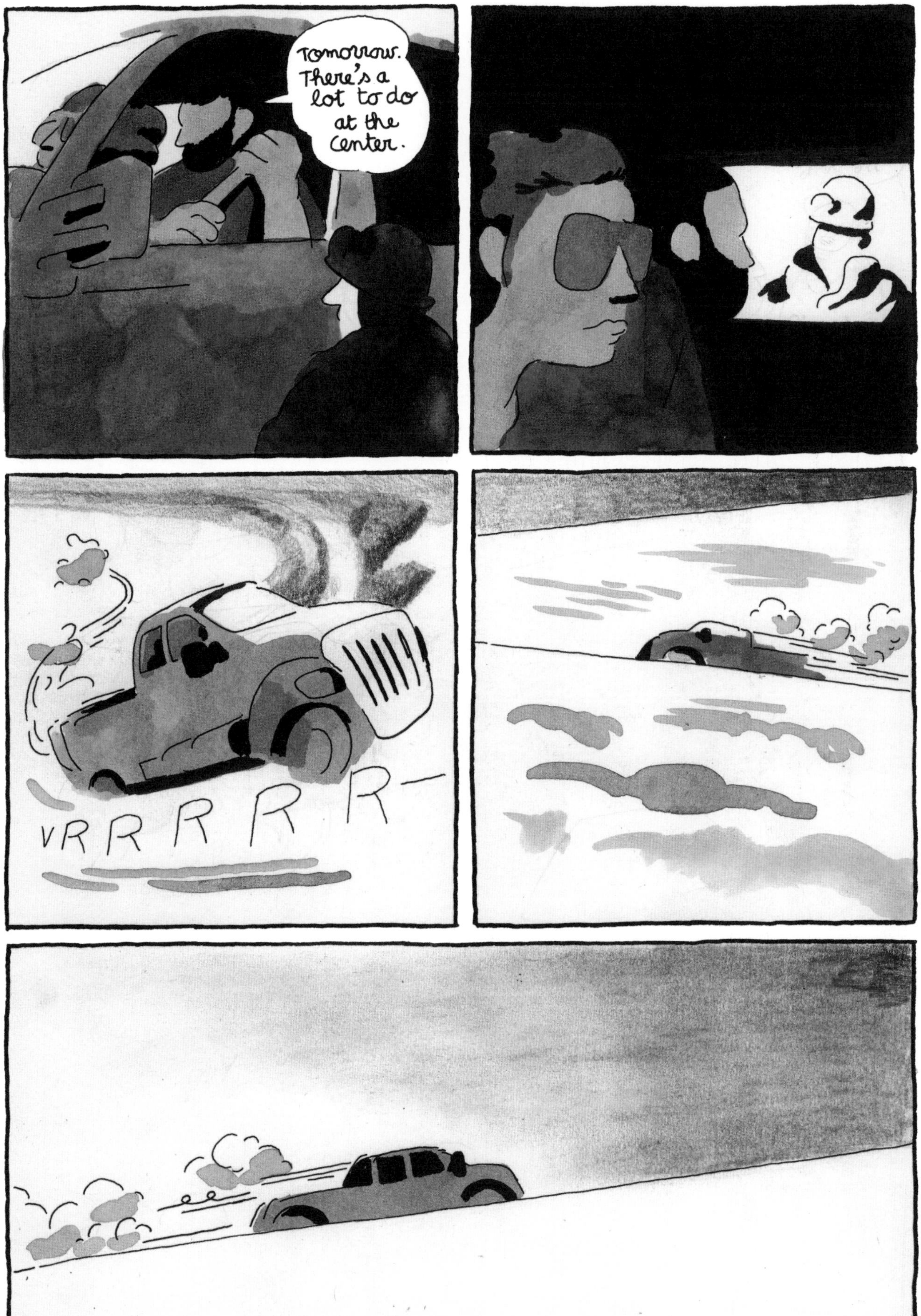
Tomorrow. There's a lot to do at the Center.
VRRRRR—

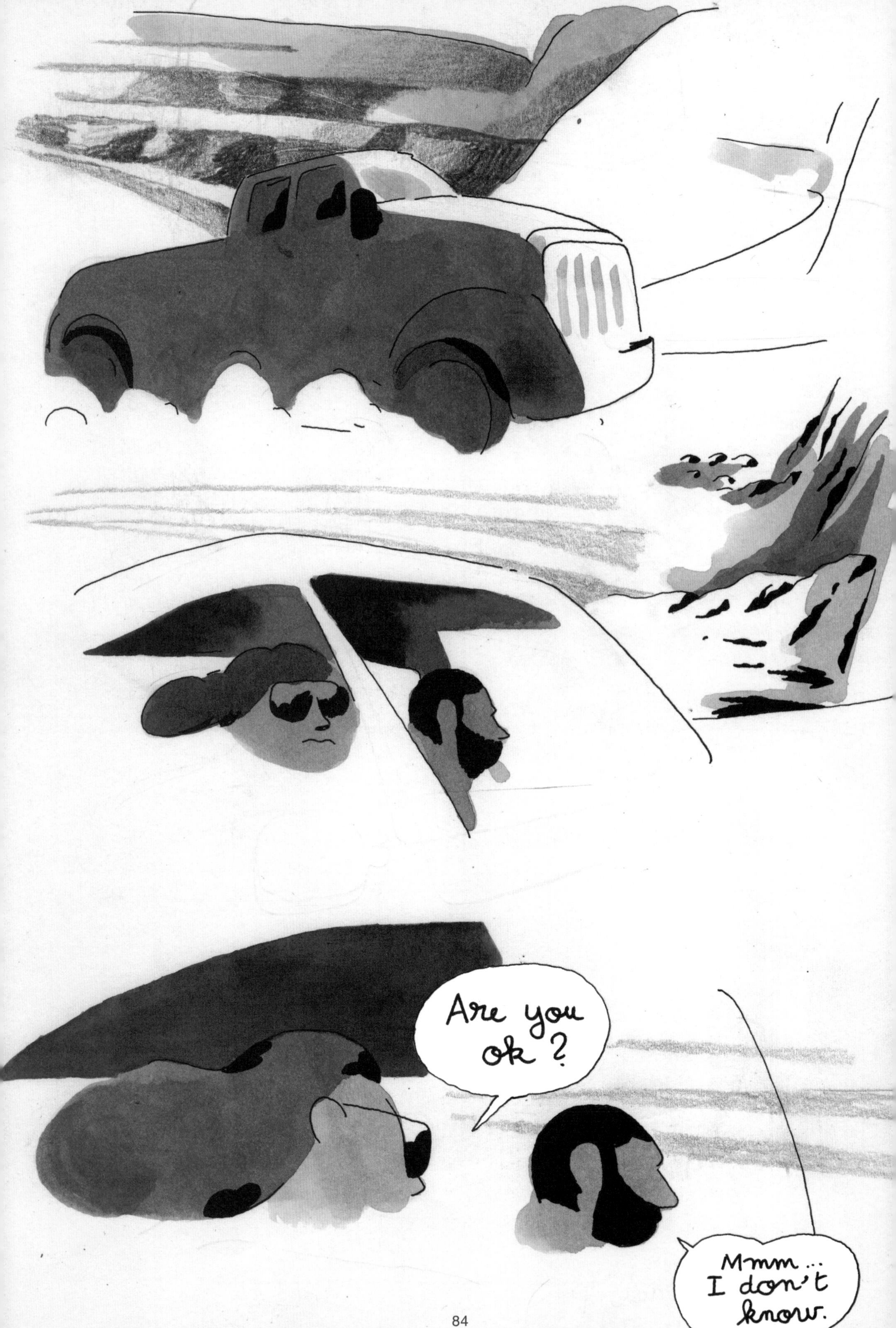
Are you ok?
Mmm... I don't know.

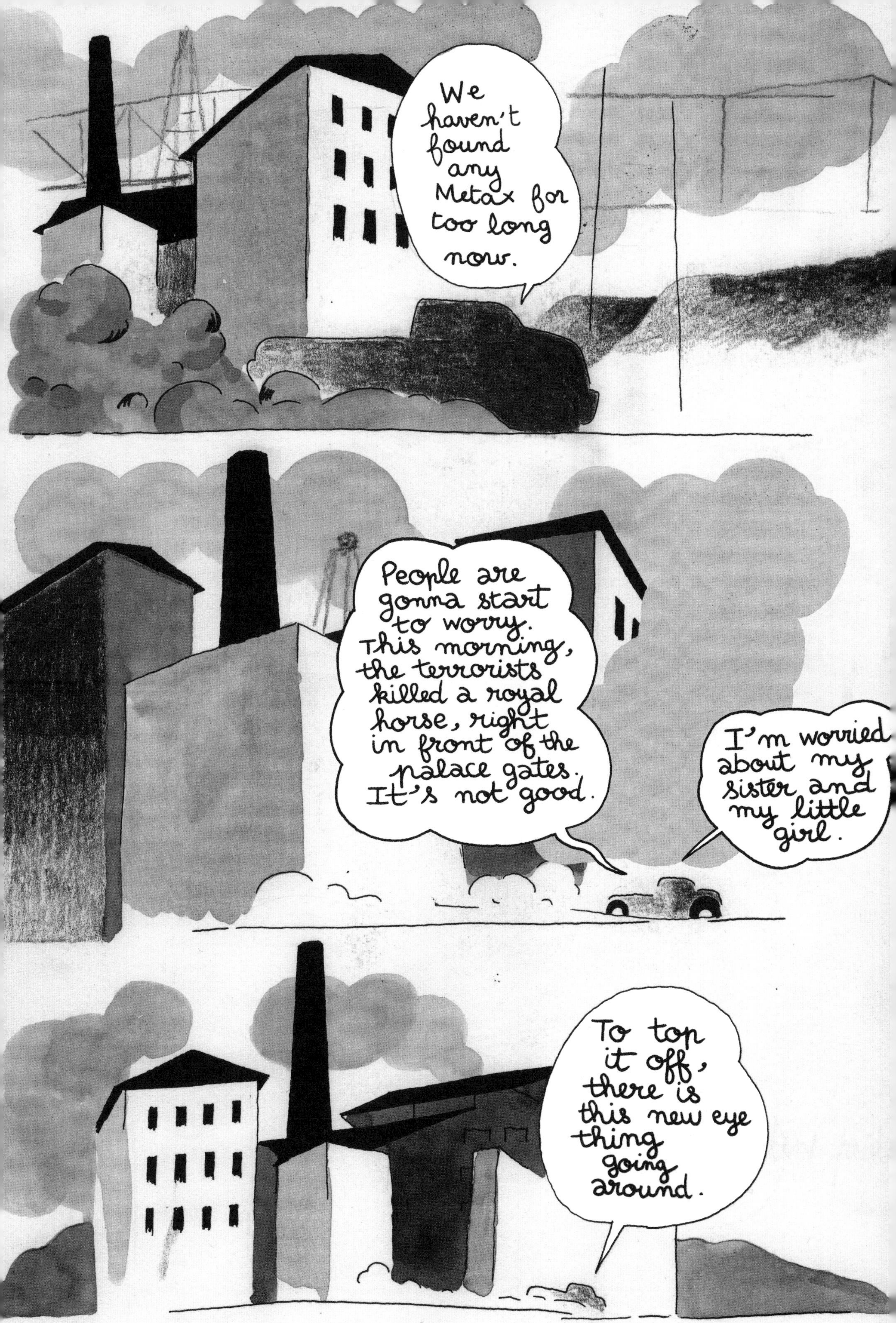
We haven't found any Metax for too long now.
People are gonna start to worry. This morning, the terrorists killed a royal horse, right in front of the palace gates. It's not good.
I'm worried about my sister and my little girl.
To top it off, there is this new eye thing going around.

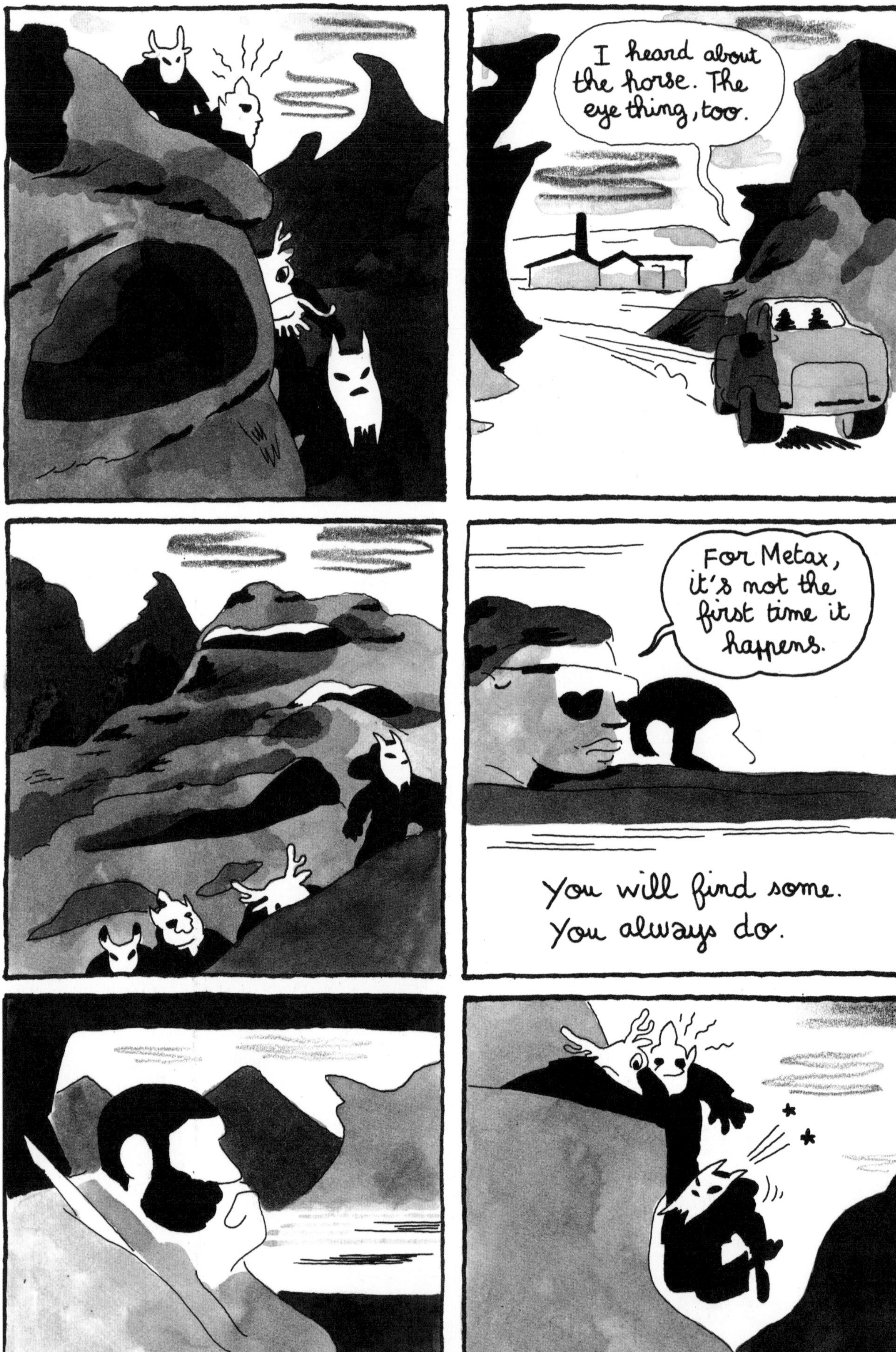
I heard about the horse. The eye thing, too.
For Metax, it's not the first time it happens.
You will find some. You always do.

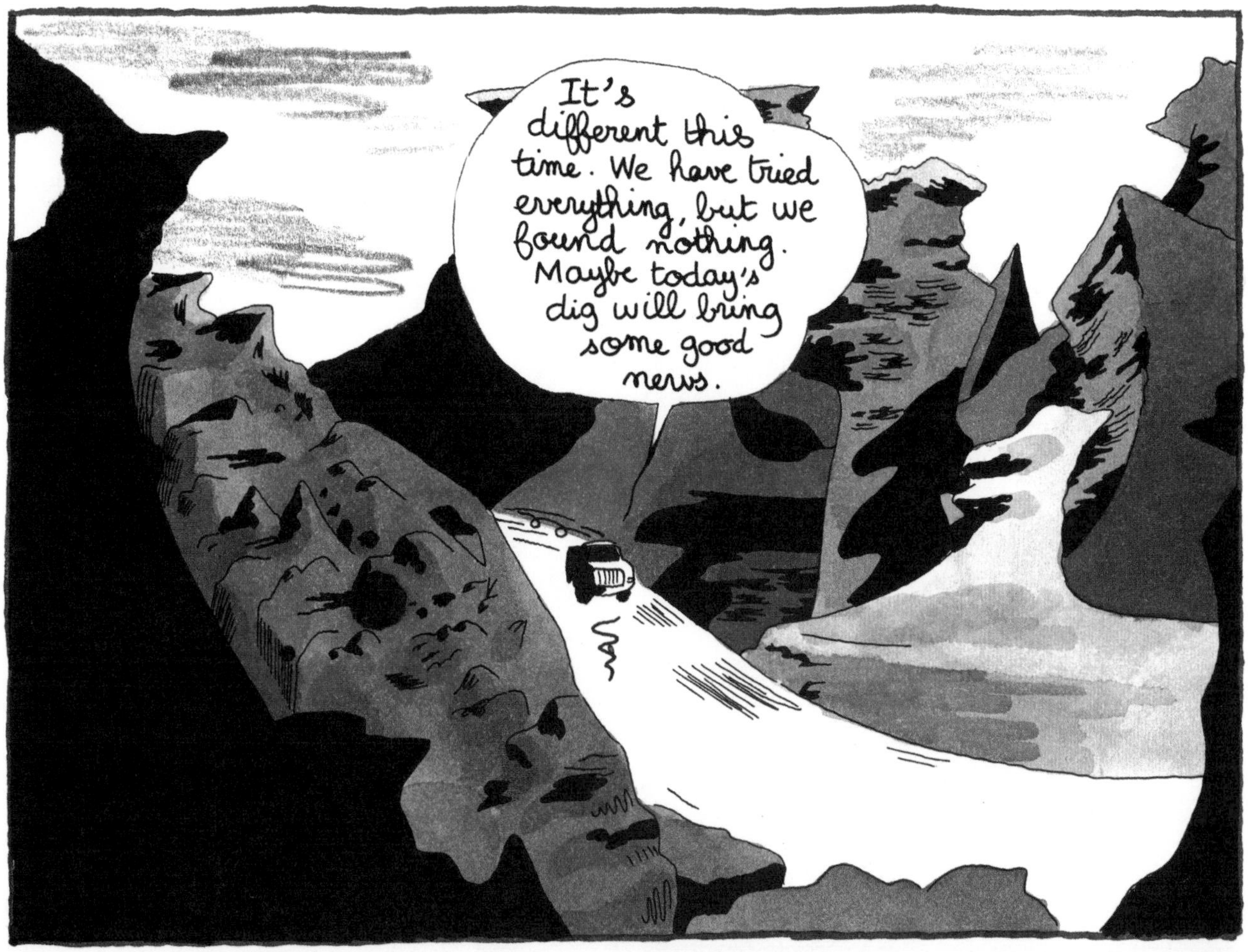
It's different this time. We have tried everything, but we found nothing. Maybe today's dig will bring some good news.

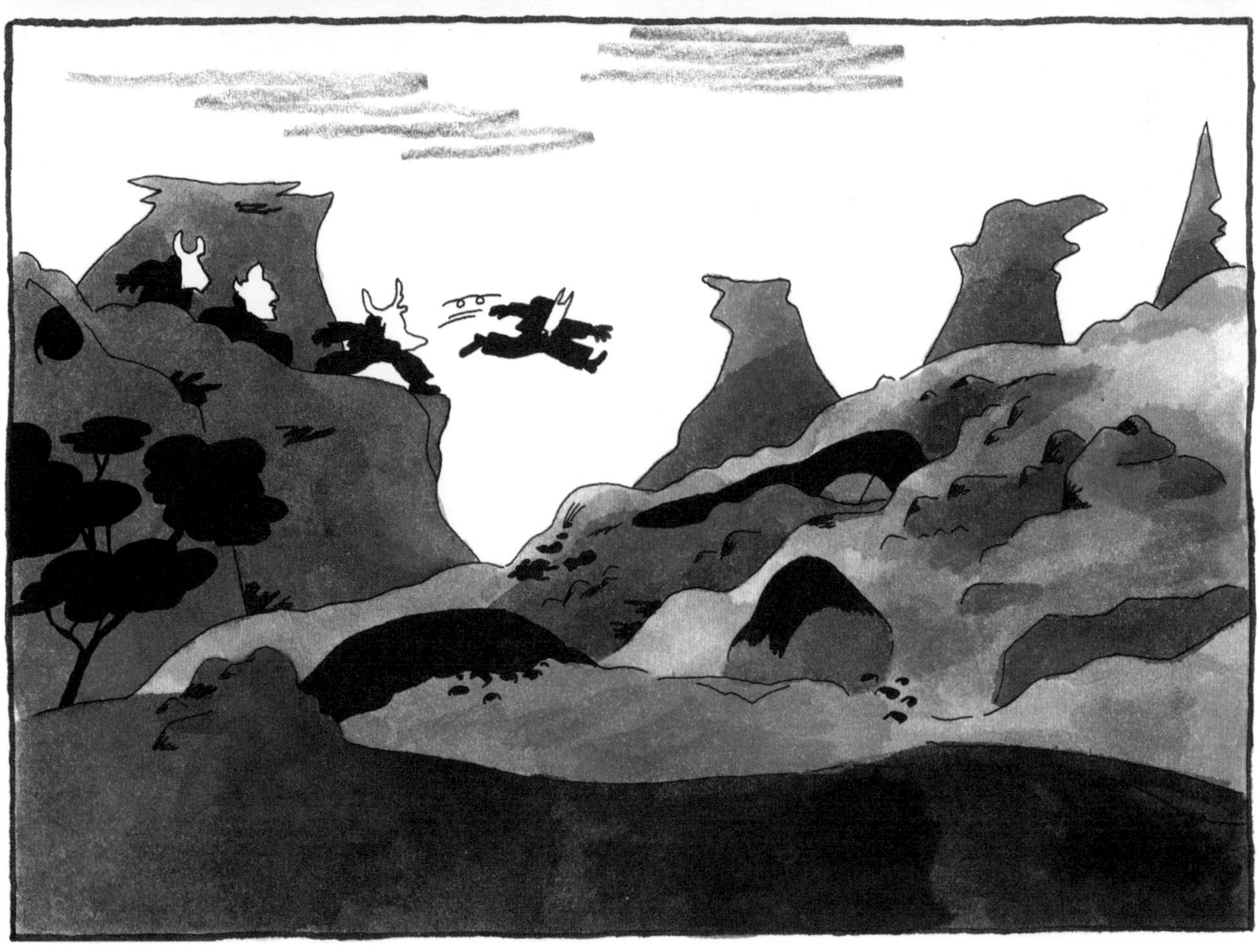

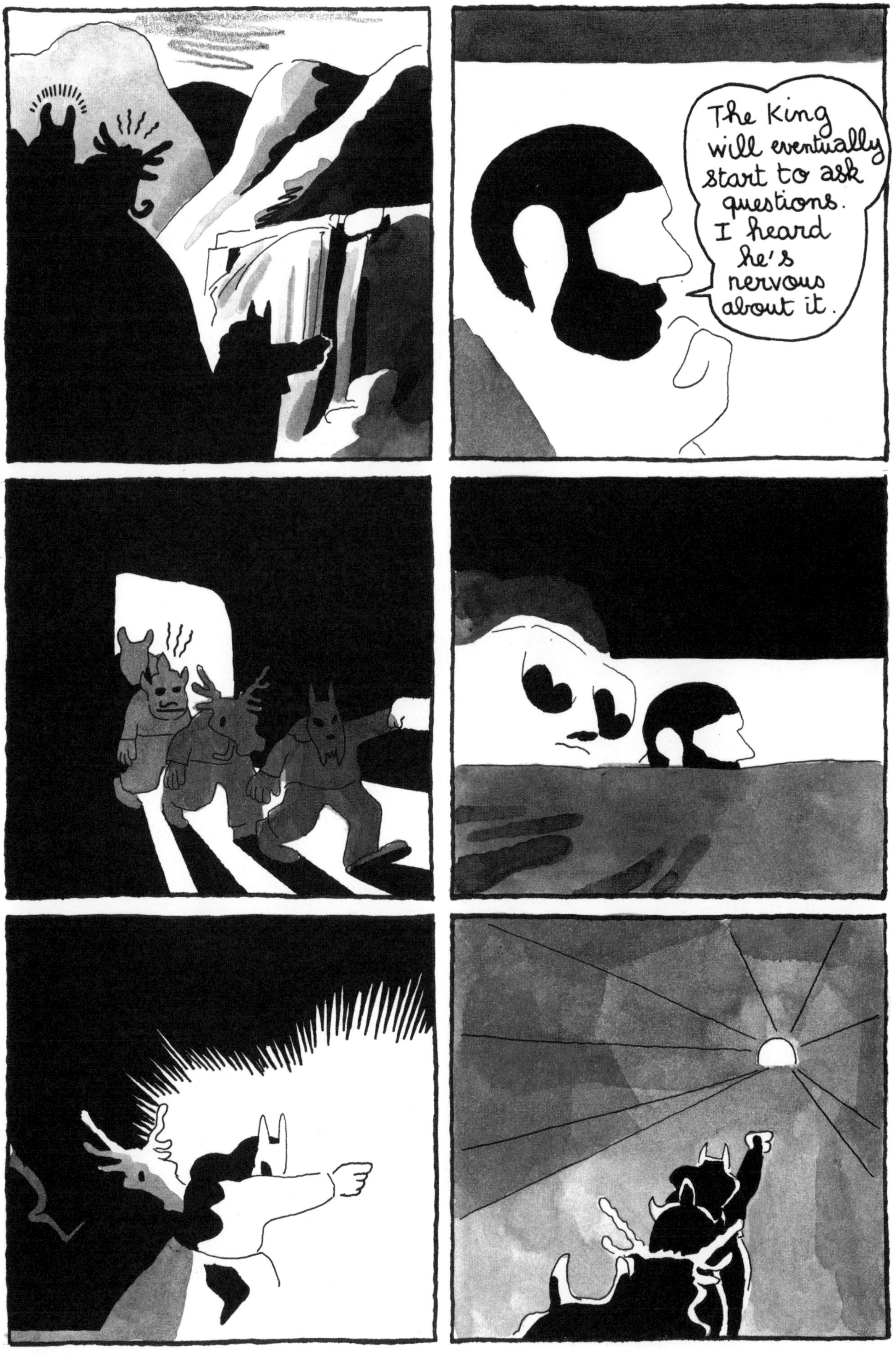
The King will eventually start to ask questions. I heard he's nervous about it.

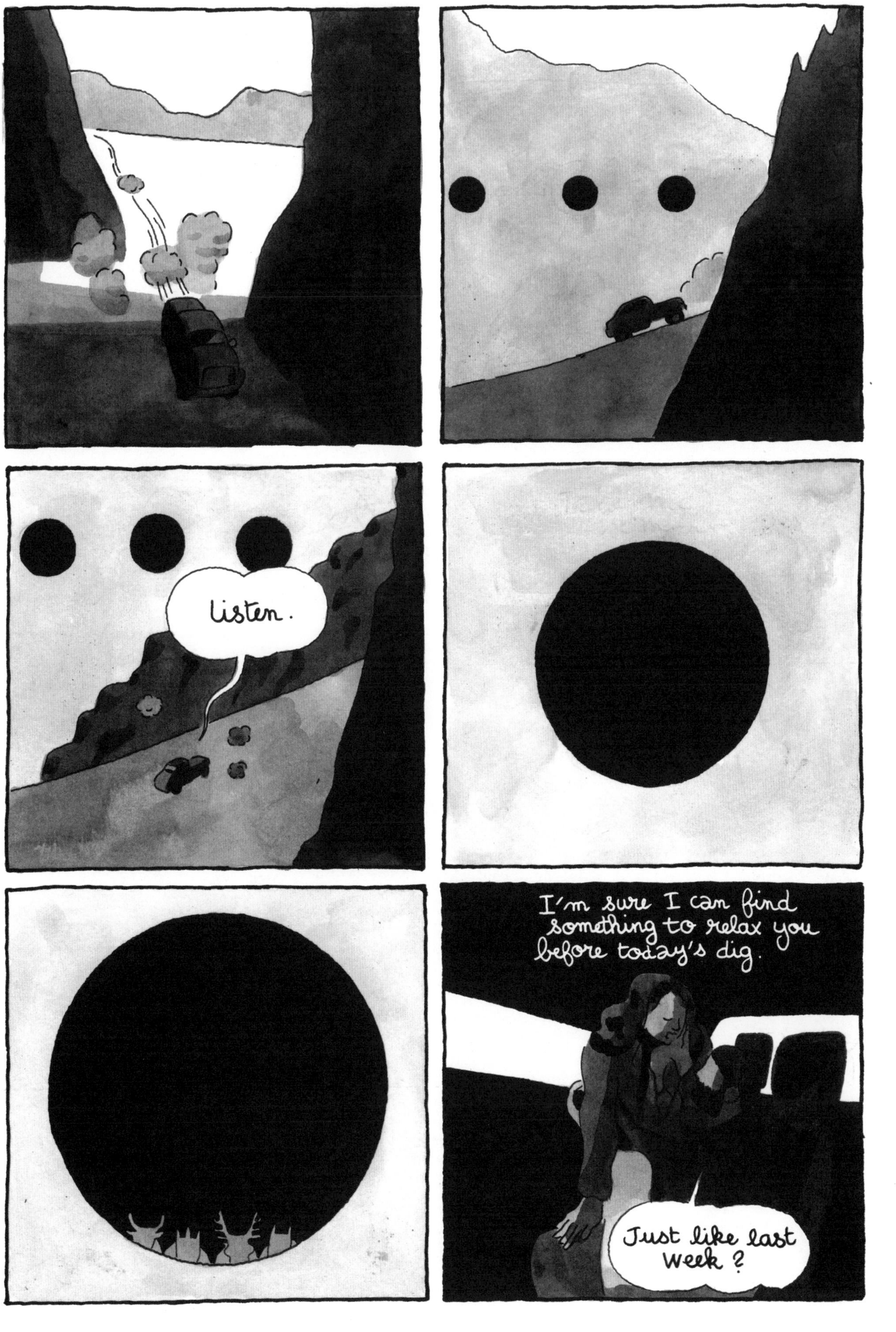
listen.
I'm sure I can find something to relax you before today's dig.
Just like last week?

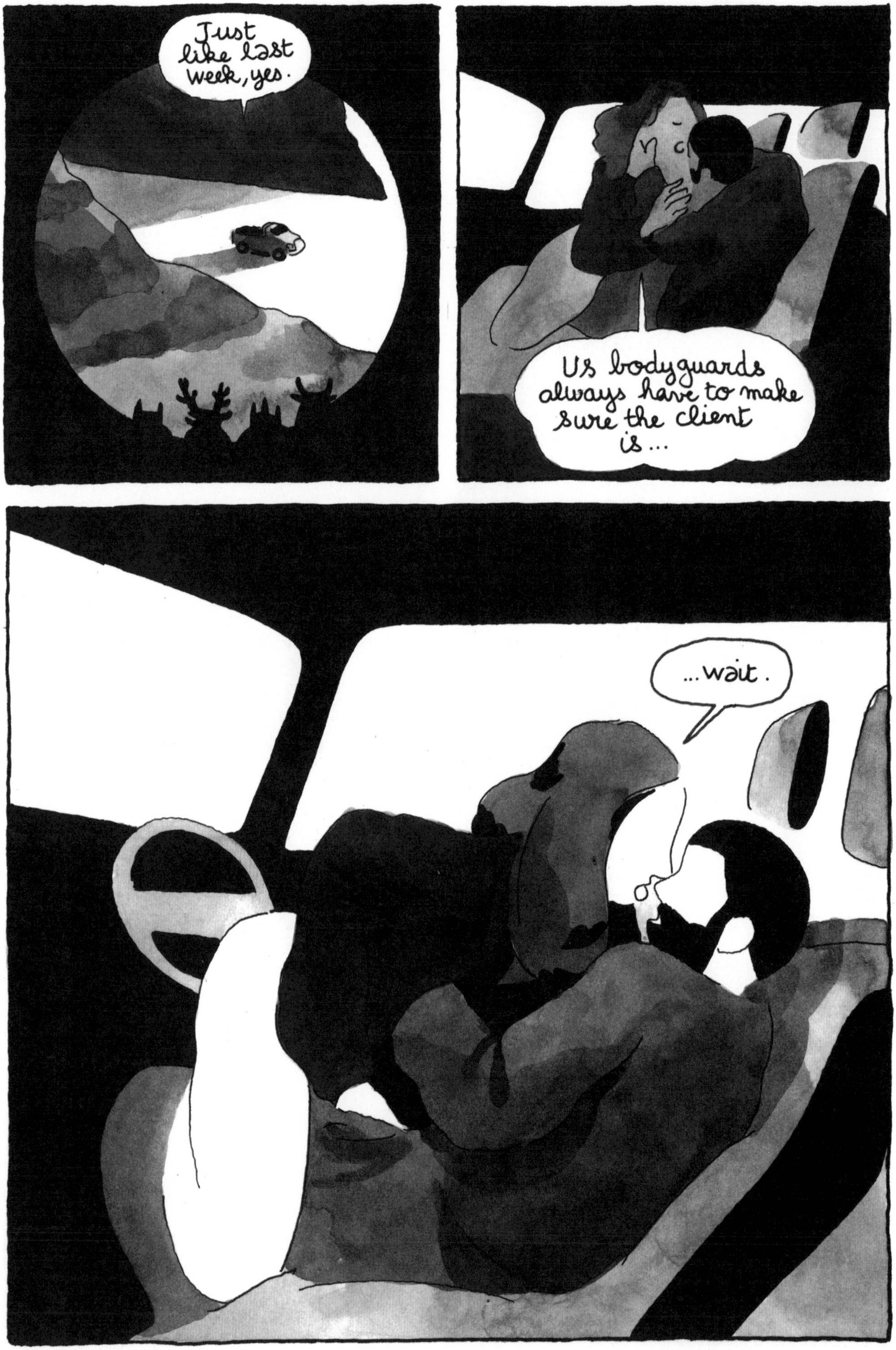
Just like last week, yes.
Us bodyguards always have to make sure the client is...
...wait.

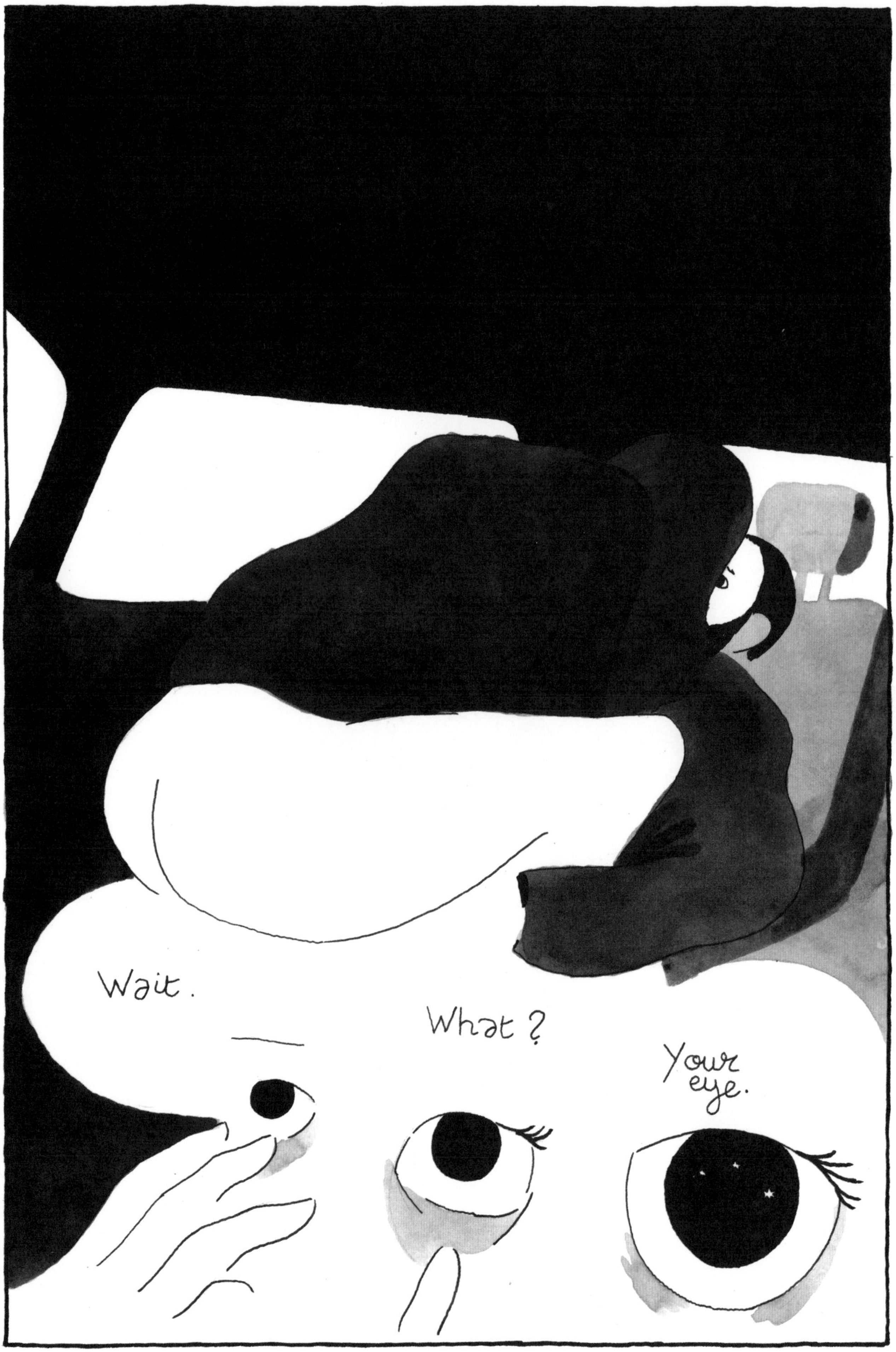
Wait.
What?
Your eye.

How long have
you had the stars
in your eye?

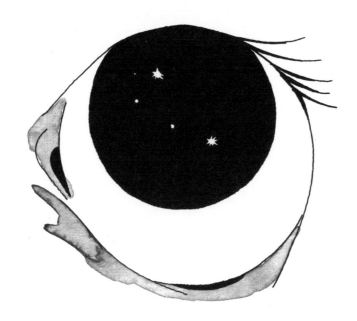

A few days...

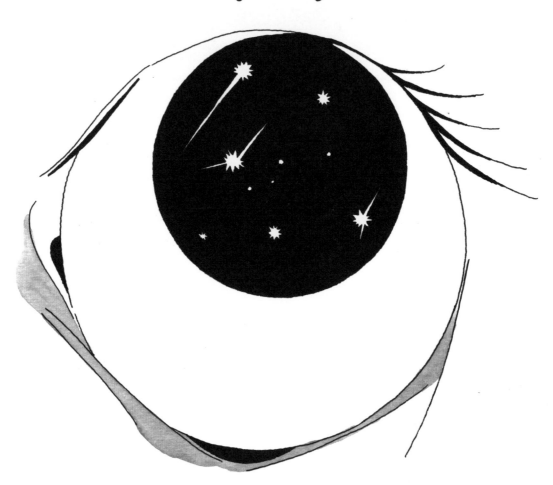

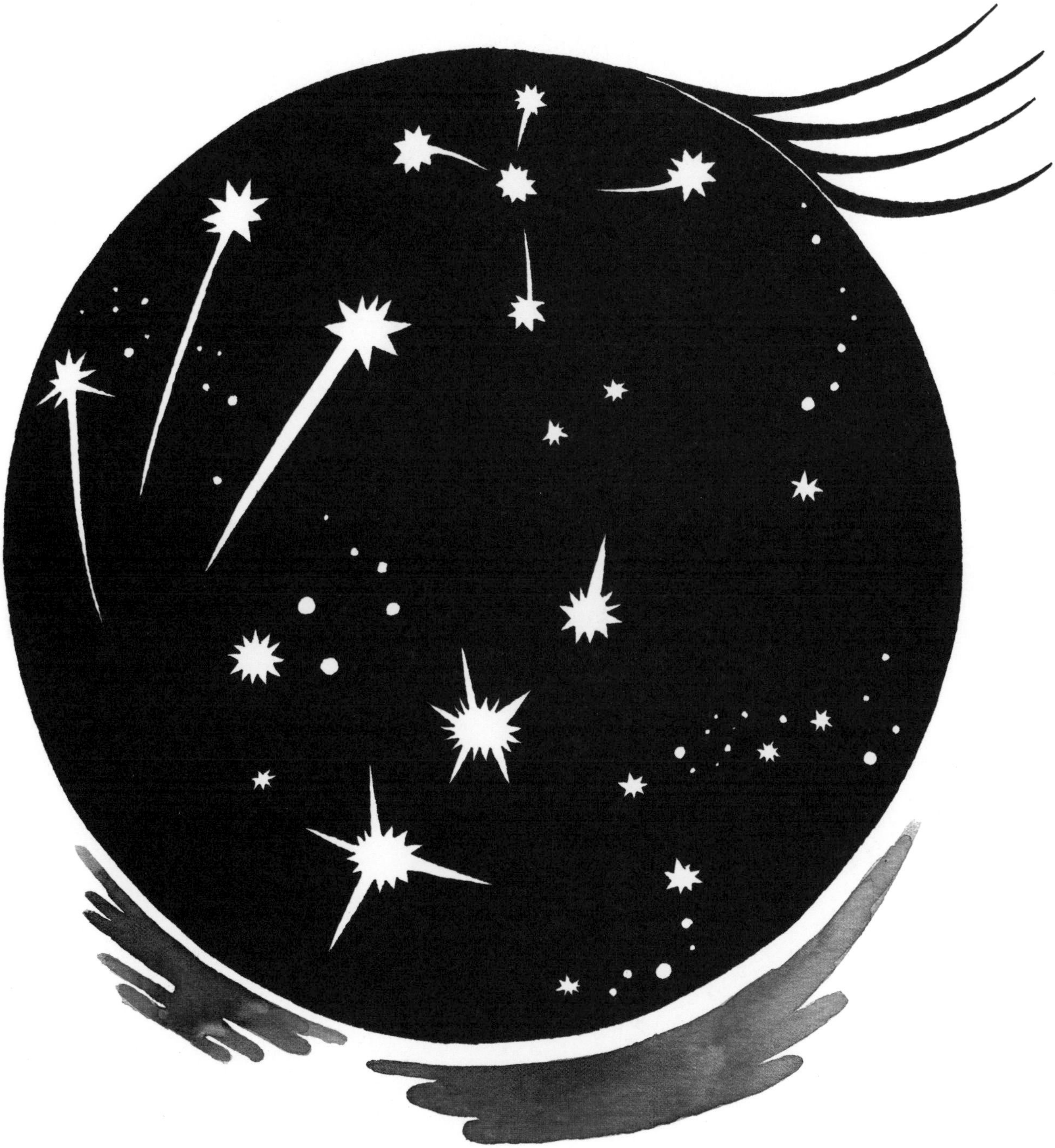

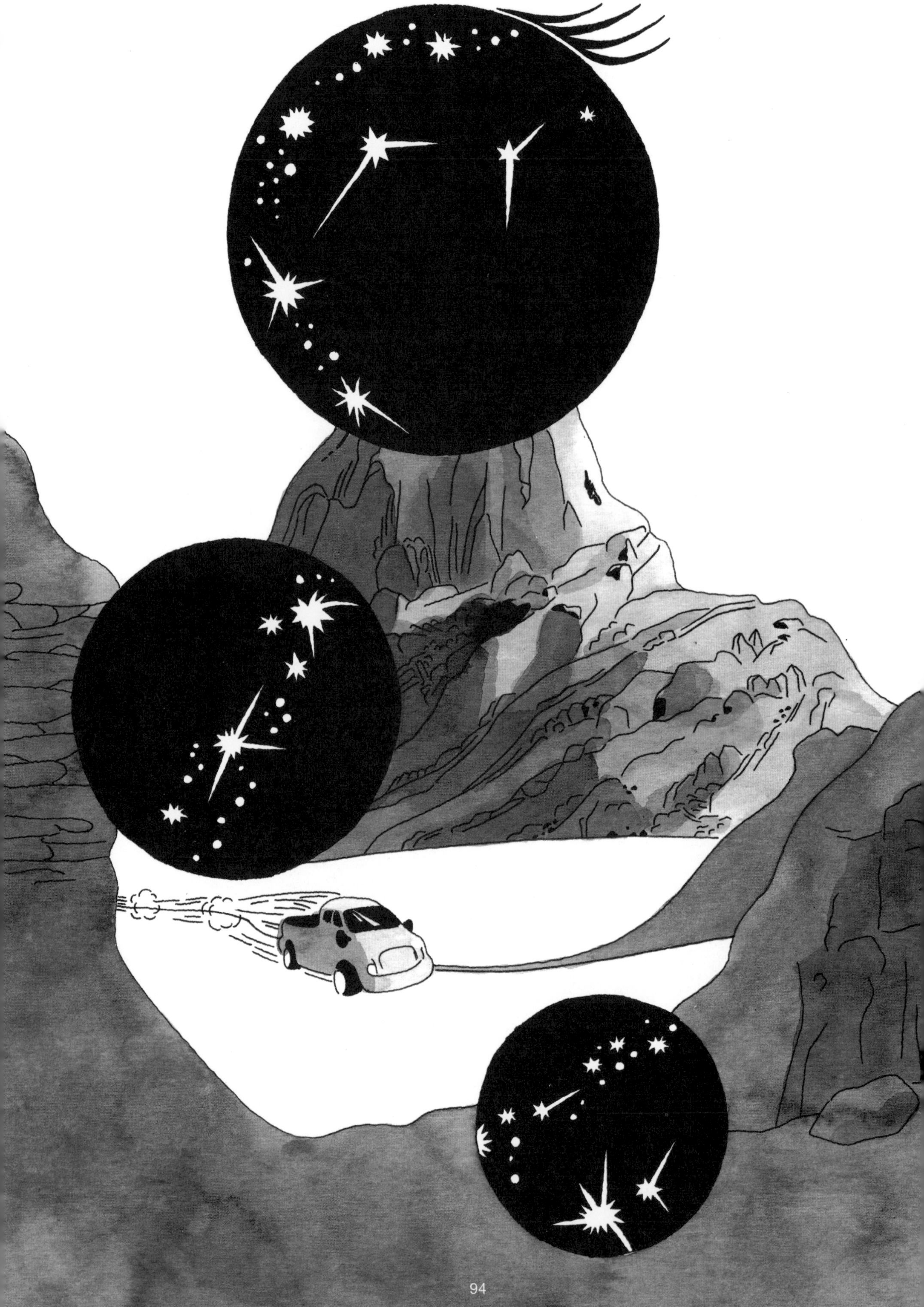

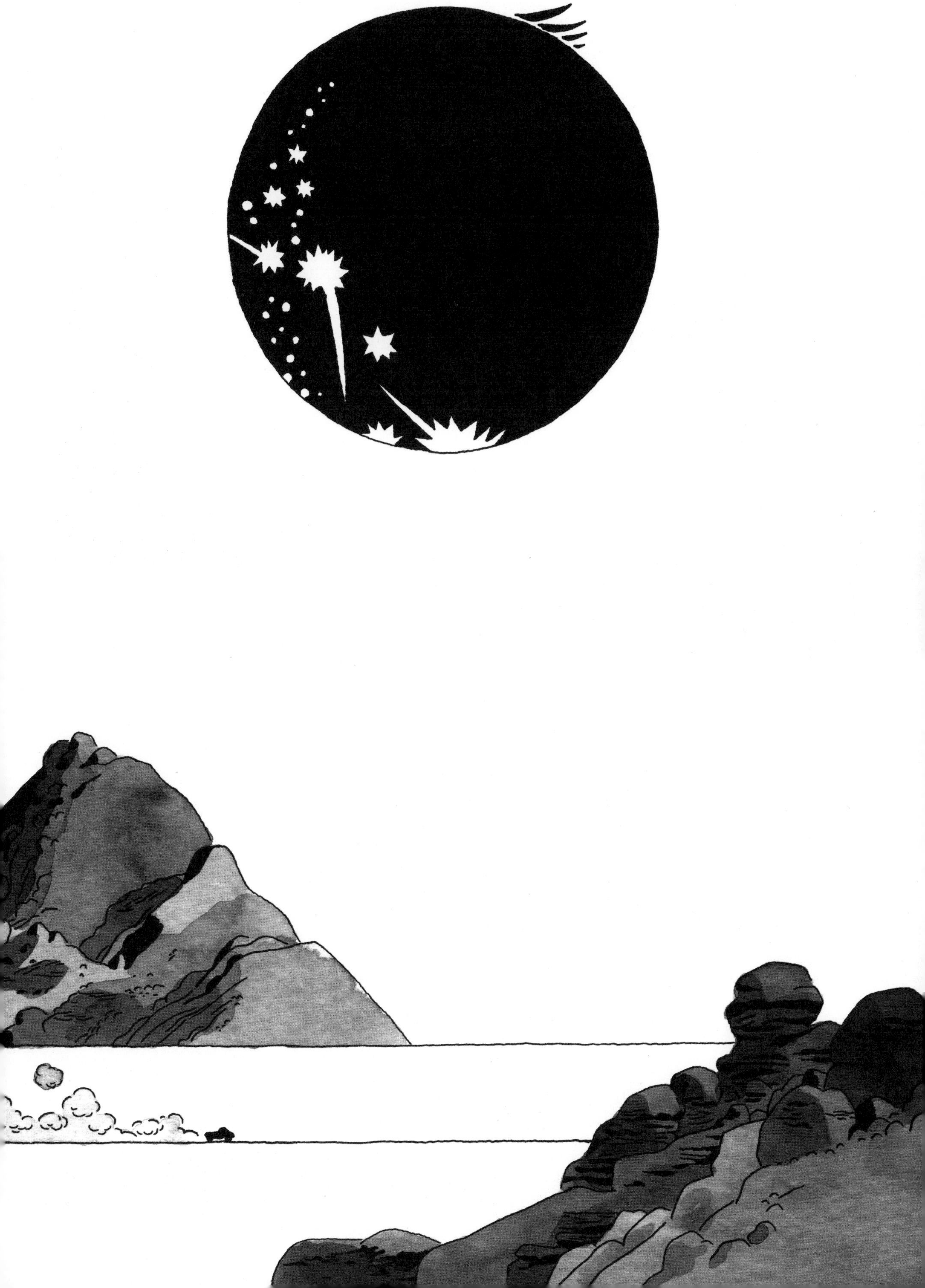

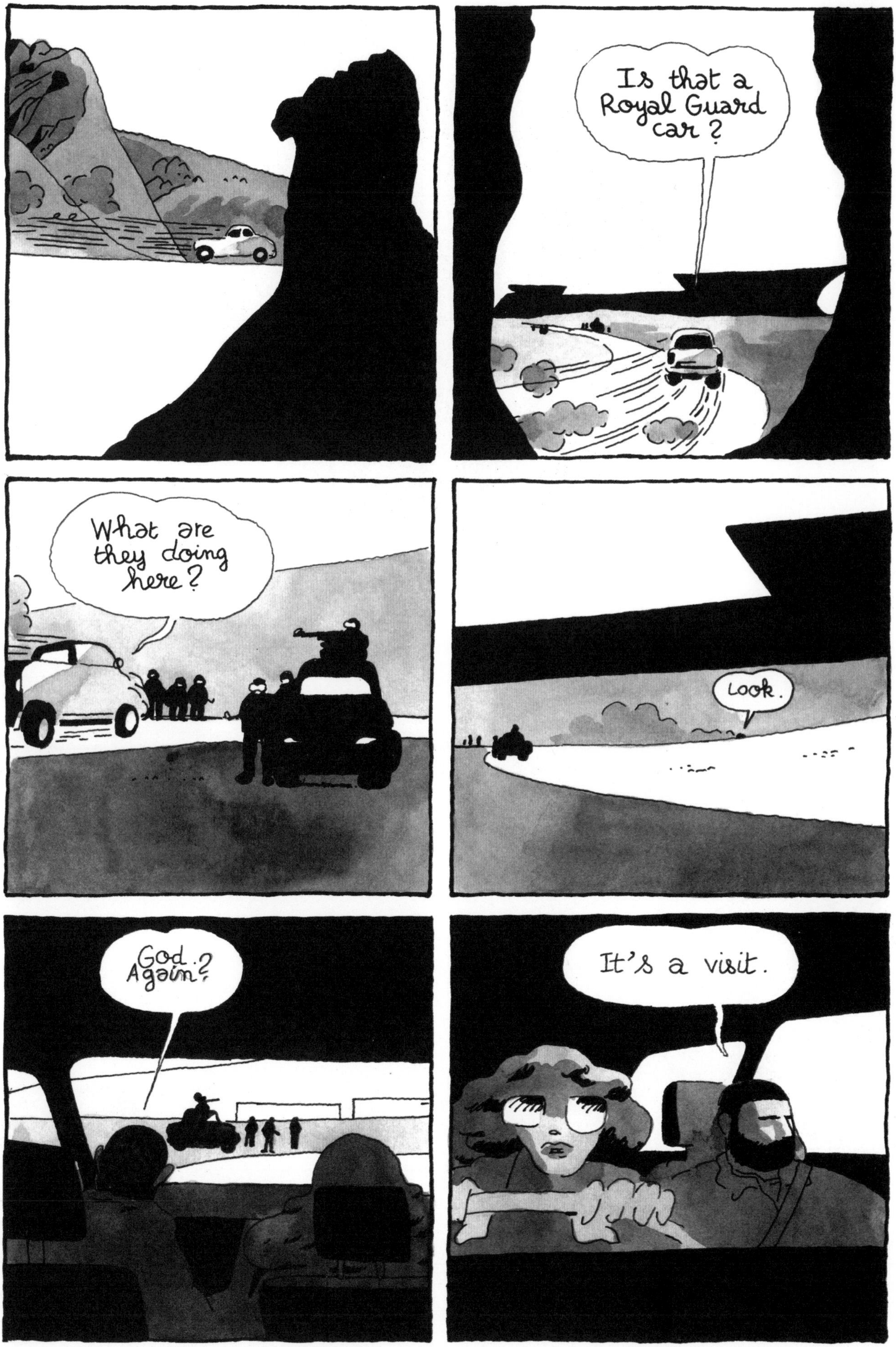
Is that a Royal Guard car?
What are they doing here?
Look.
God. Again?
It's a visit.

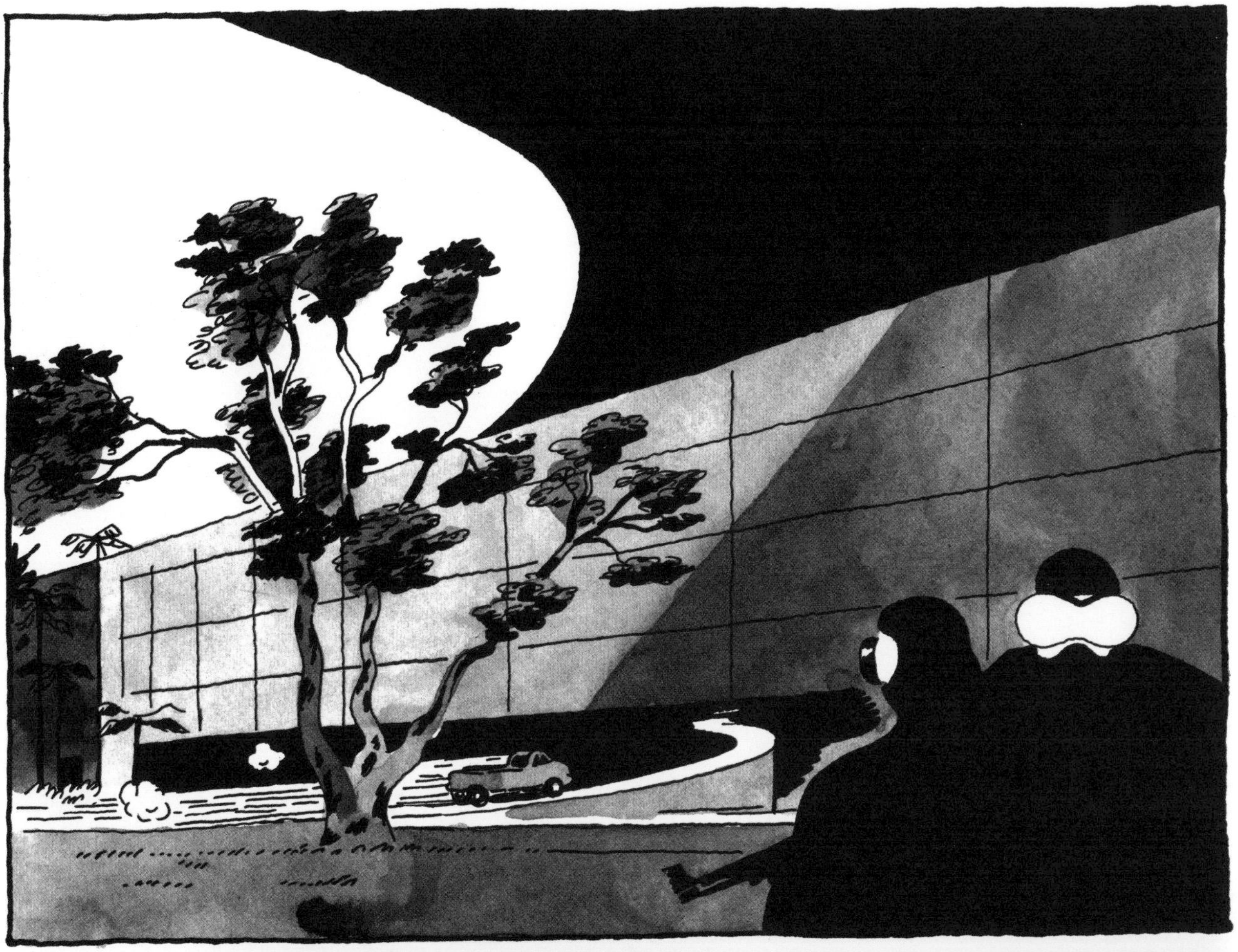

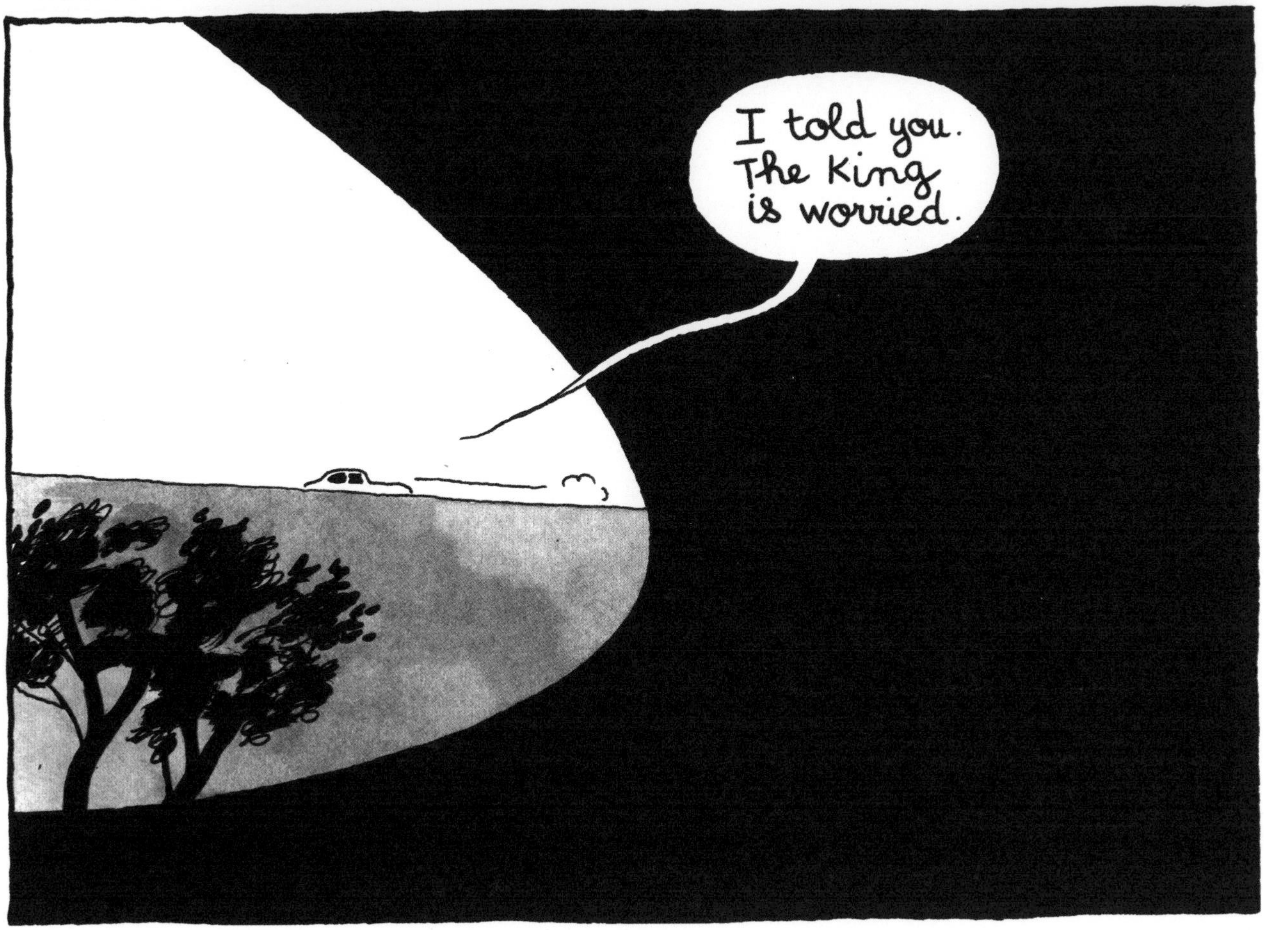
I told you. The King is worried.

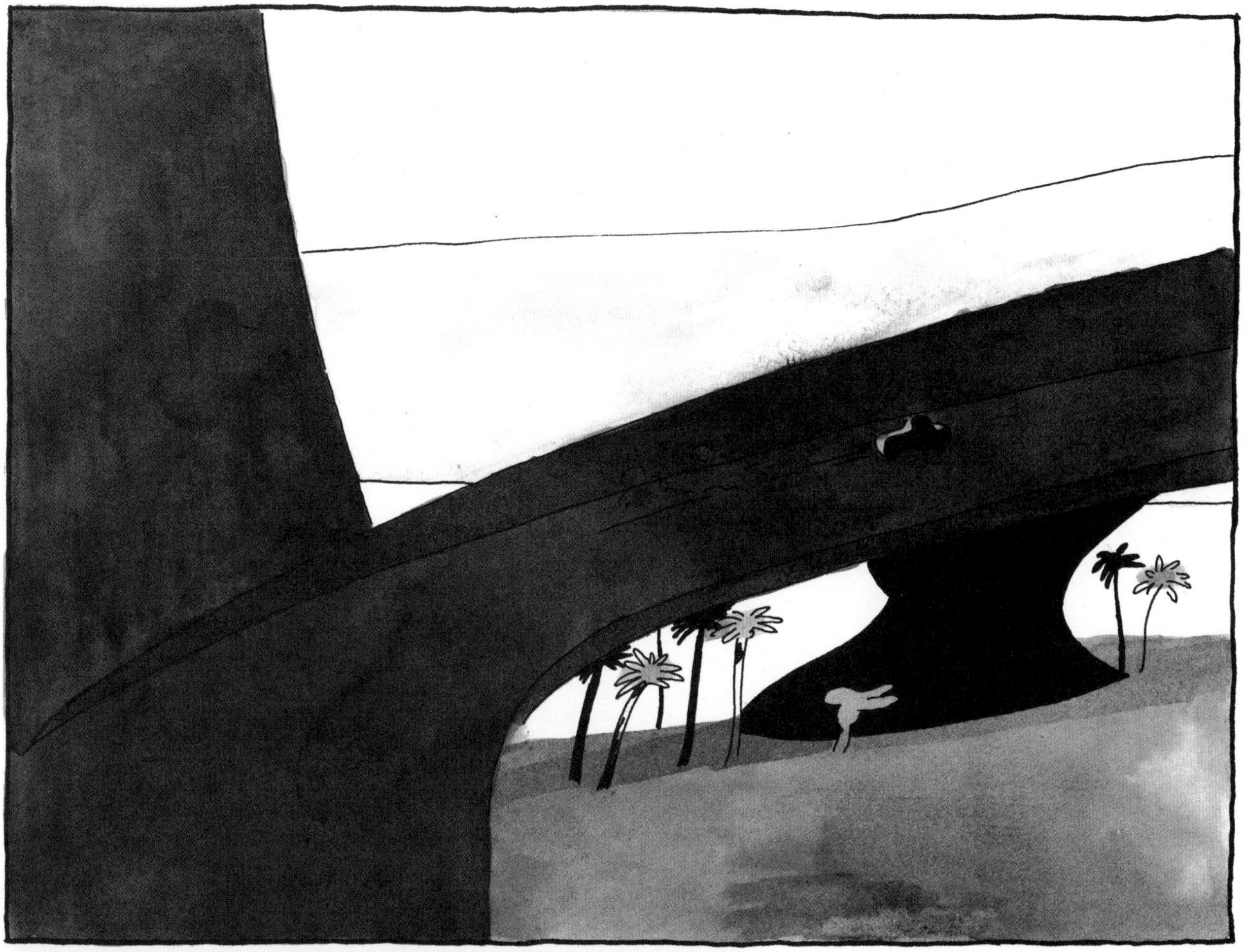

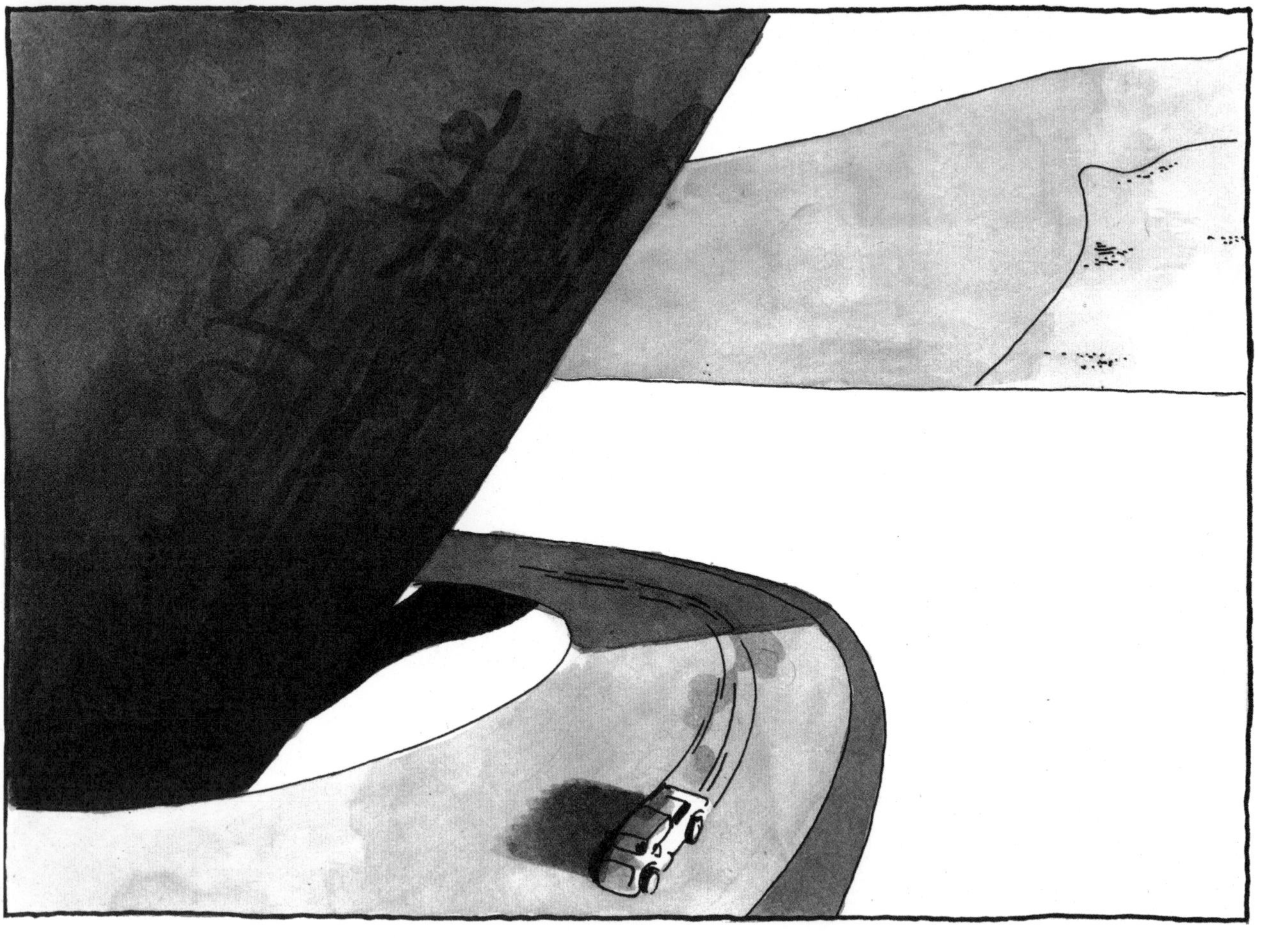

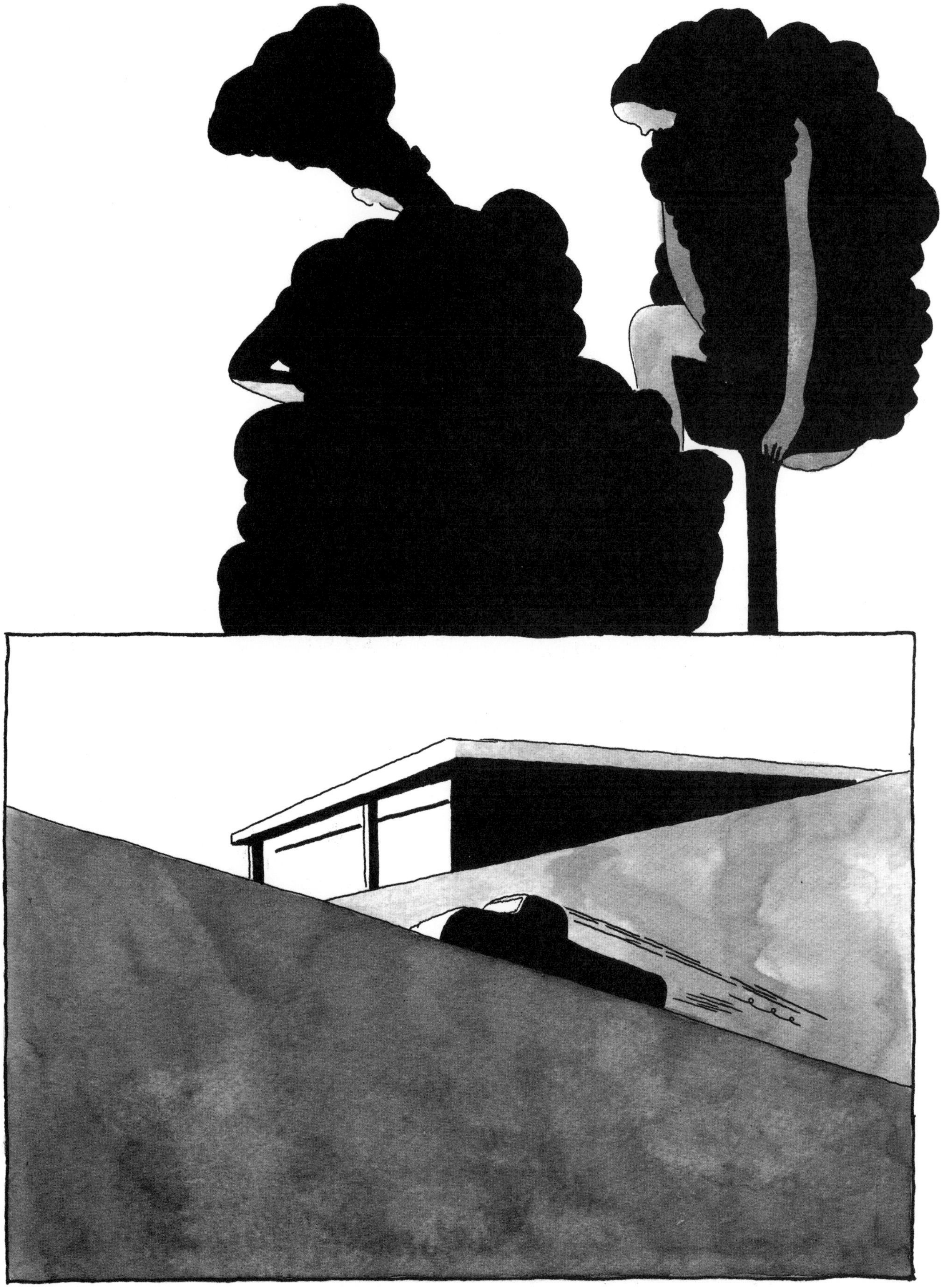

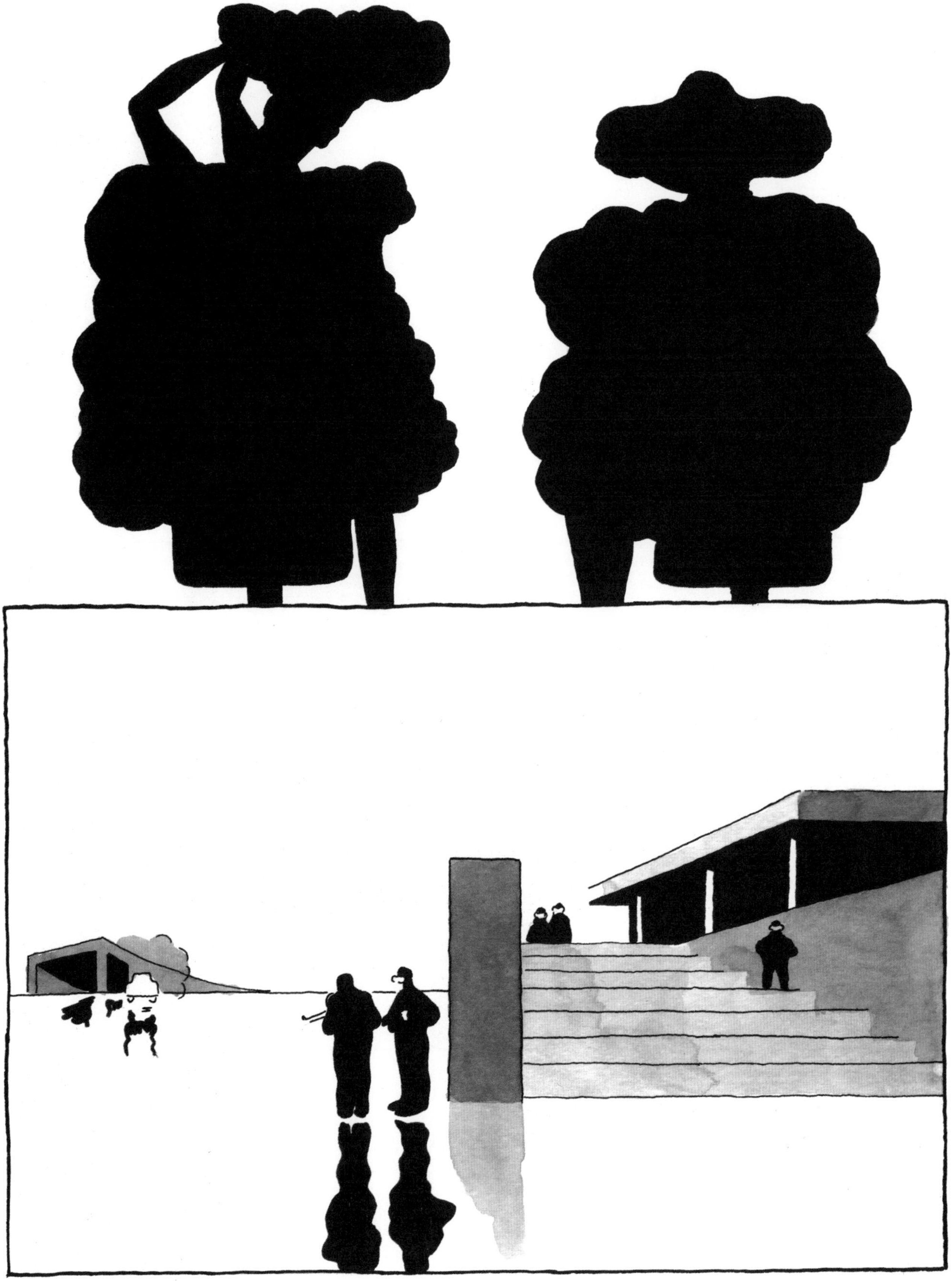

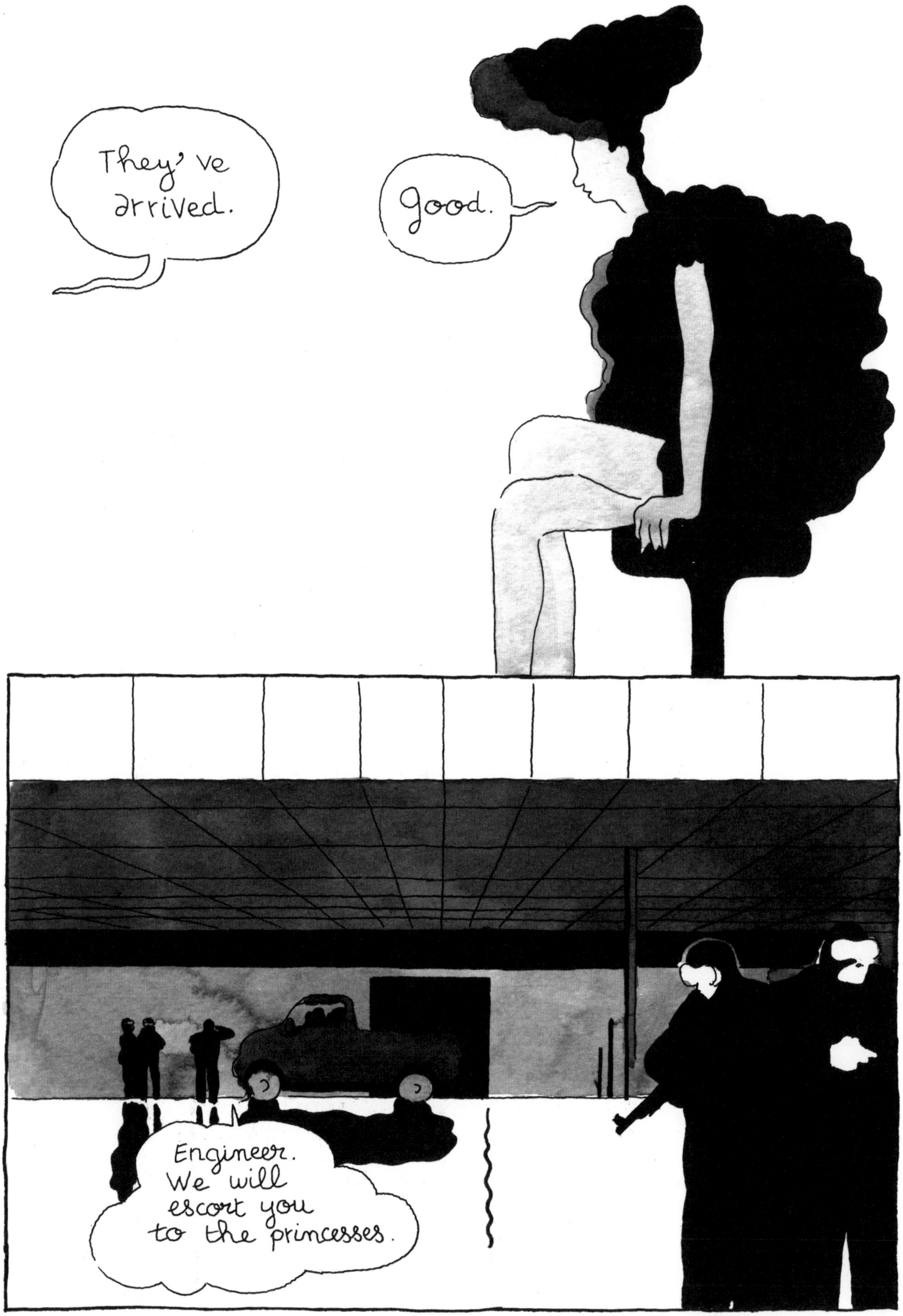
They've arrived.
Good.
Engineer. We will escort you to the princesses.

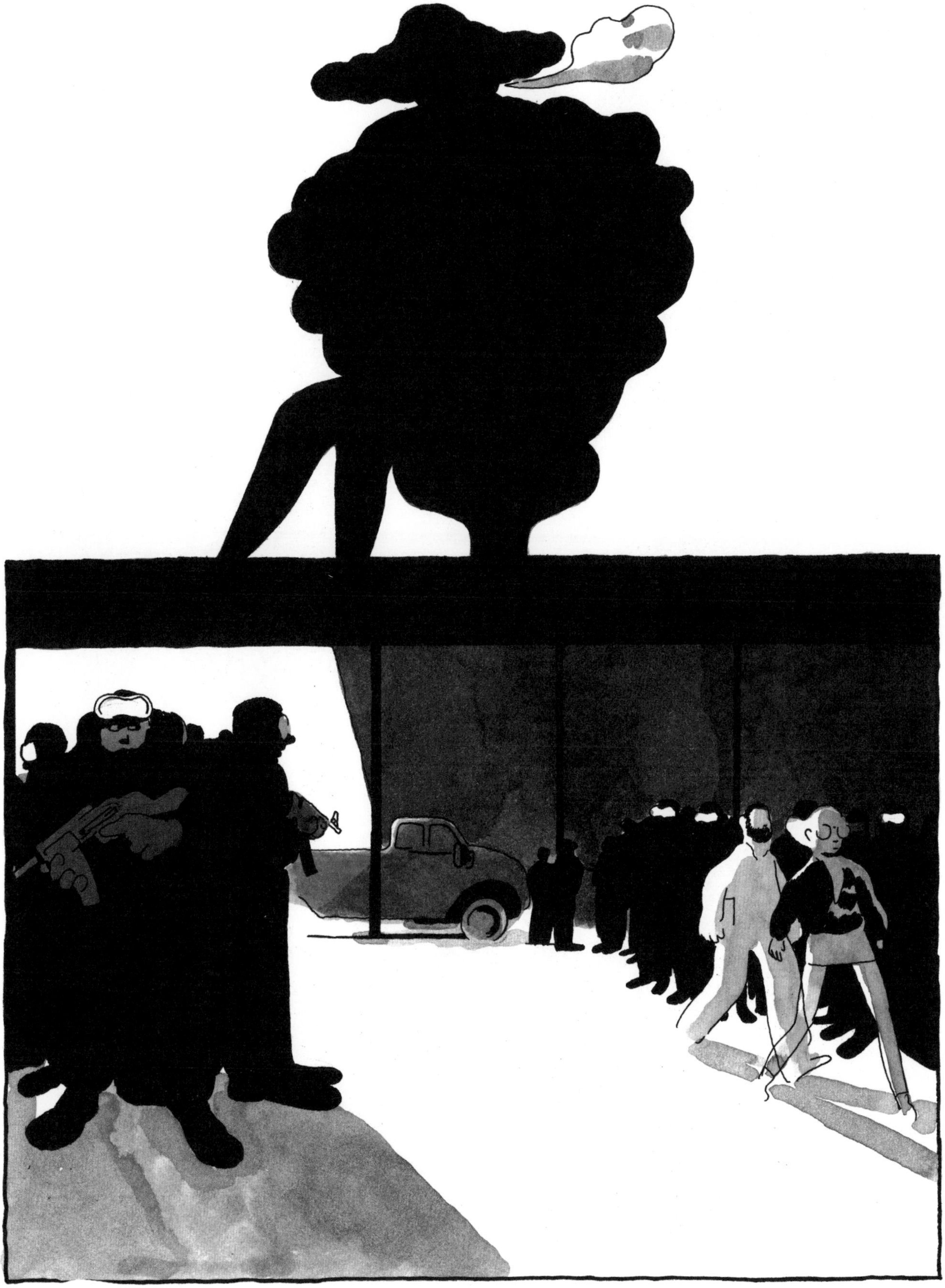

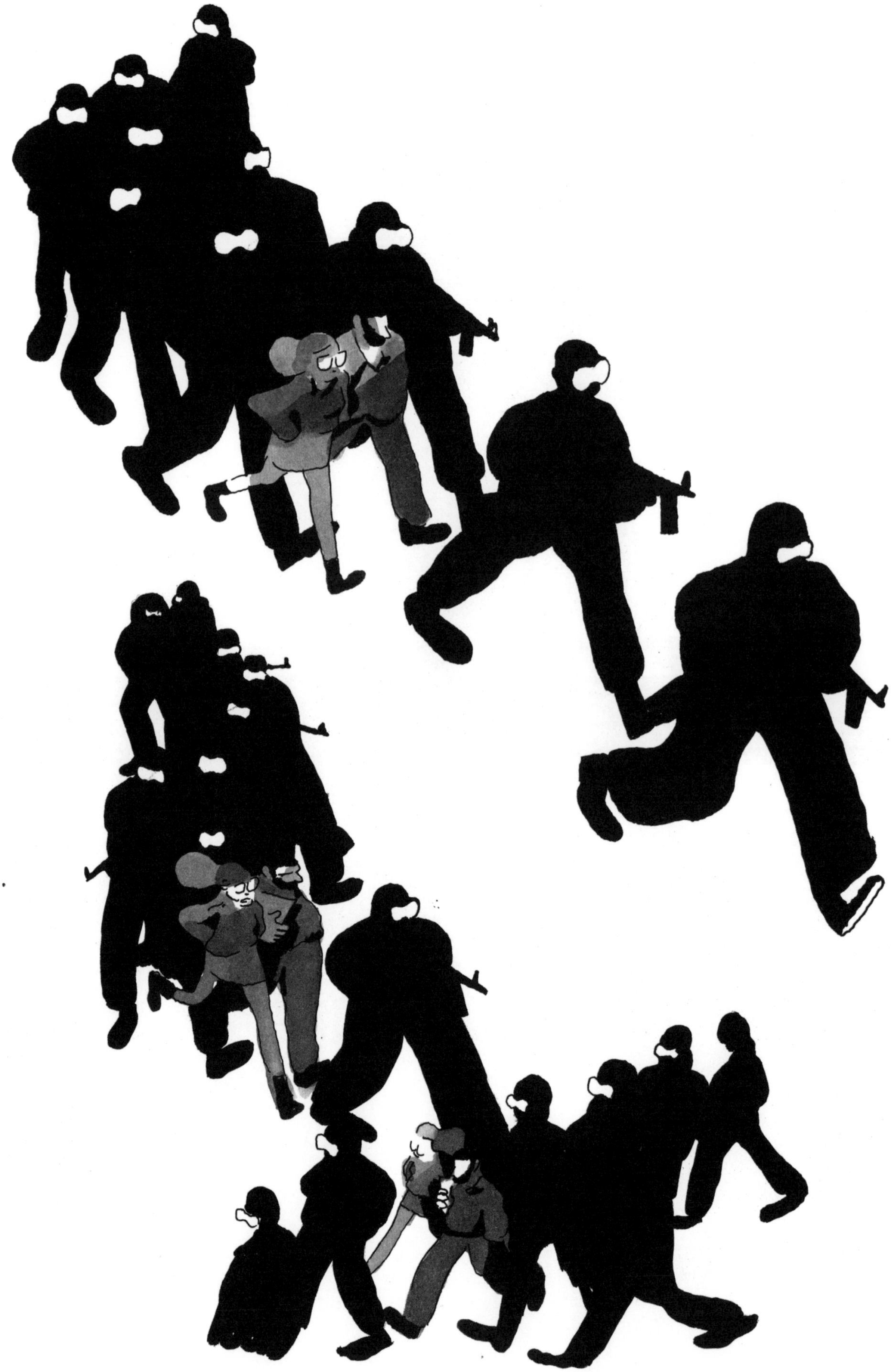

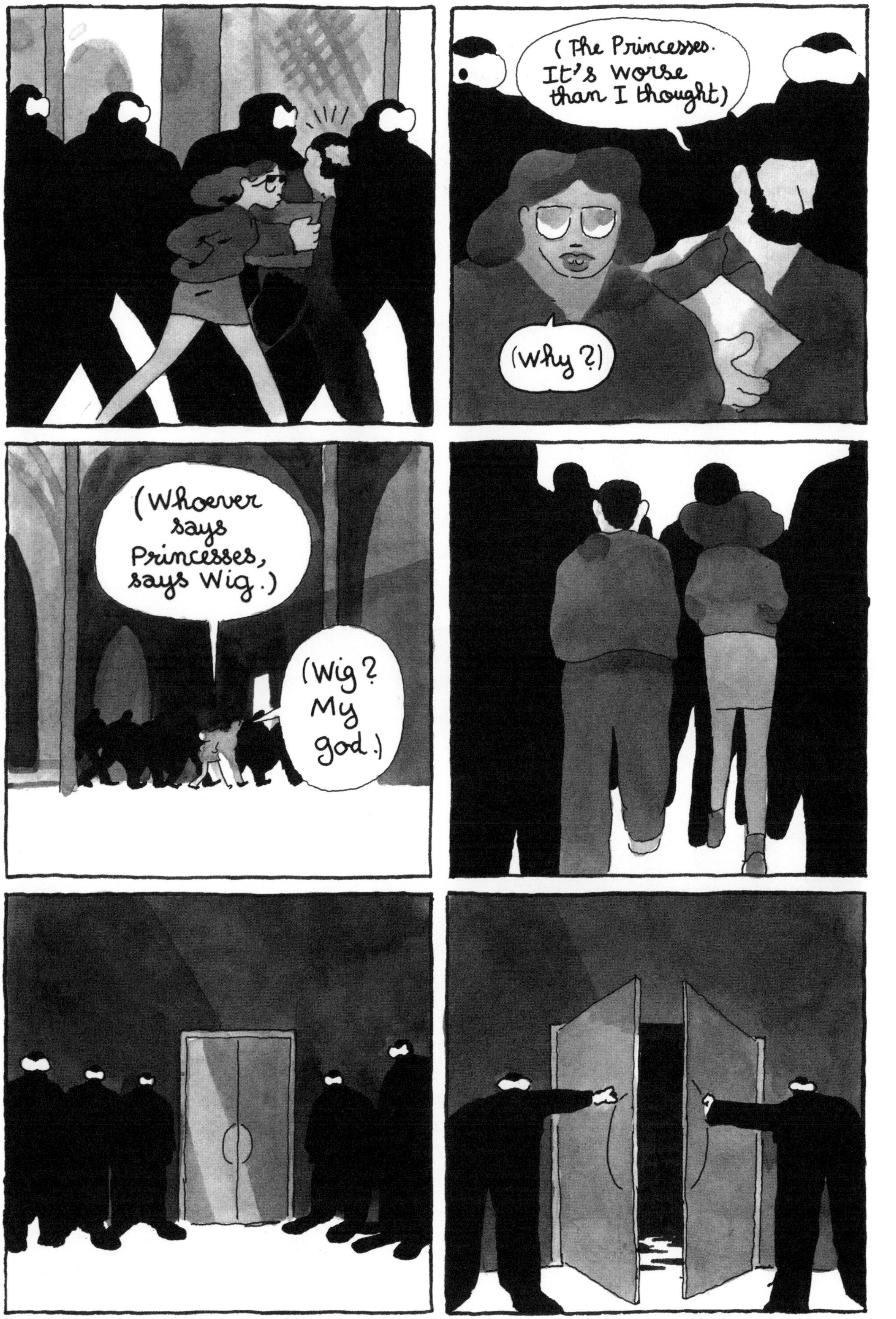
(The Princesses. It's worse than I thought)
(Why?)
(Whoever says Princesses, says Wig.)
(Wig? My god.)

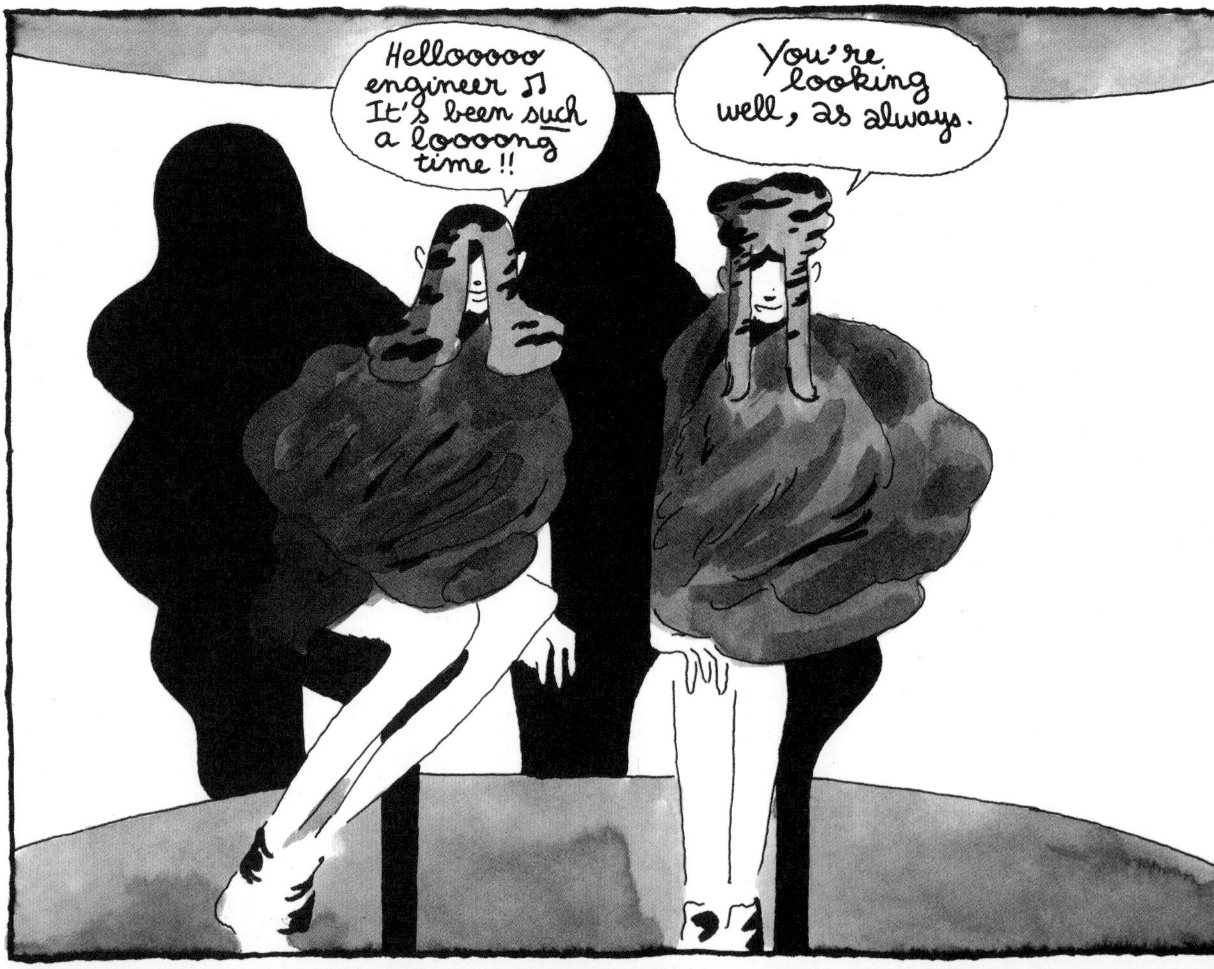
Hellooooo engineer ♫ It's been such a loooong time!!
You're looking well, as always.

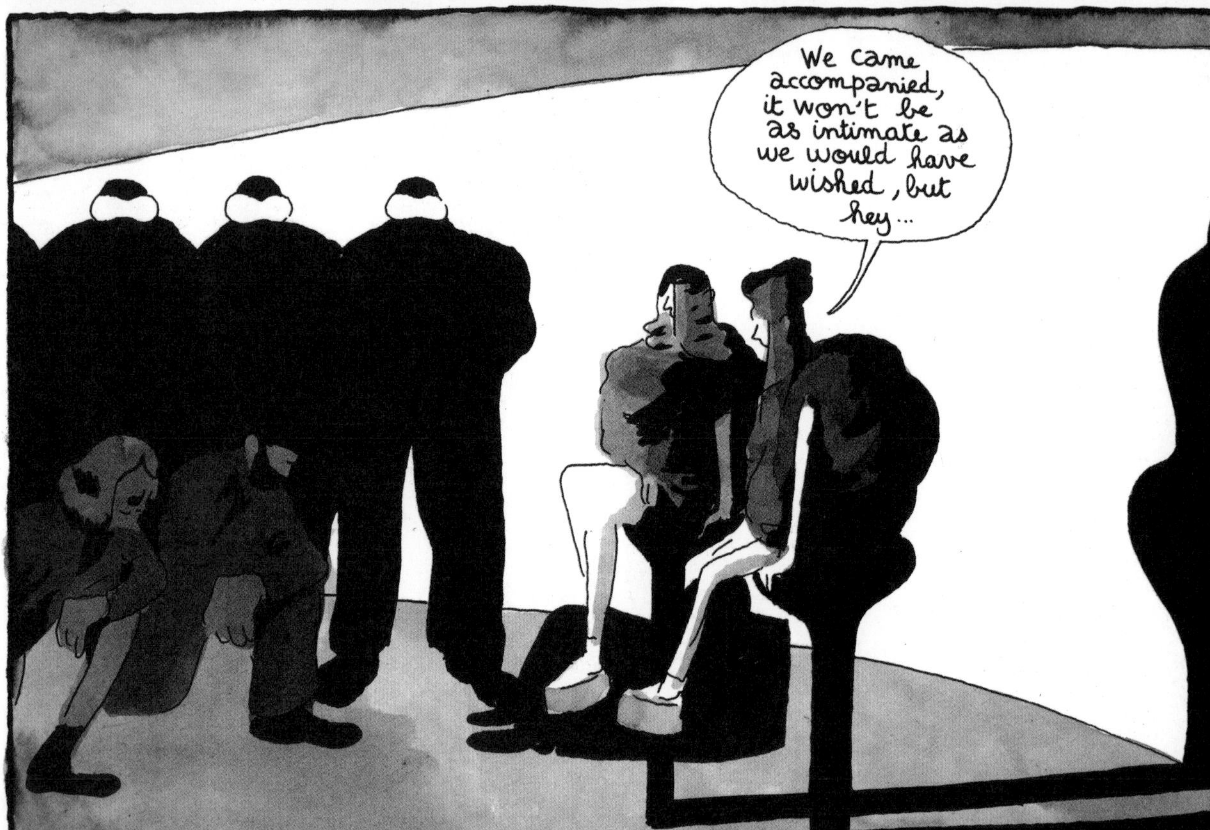
We came accompanied, it won't be as intimate as we would have wished, but hey...

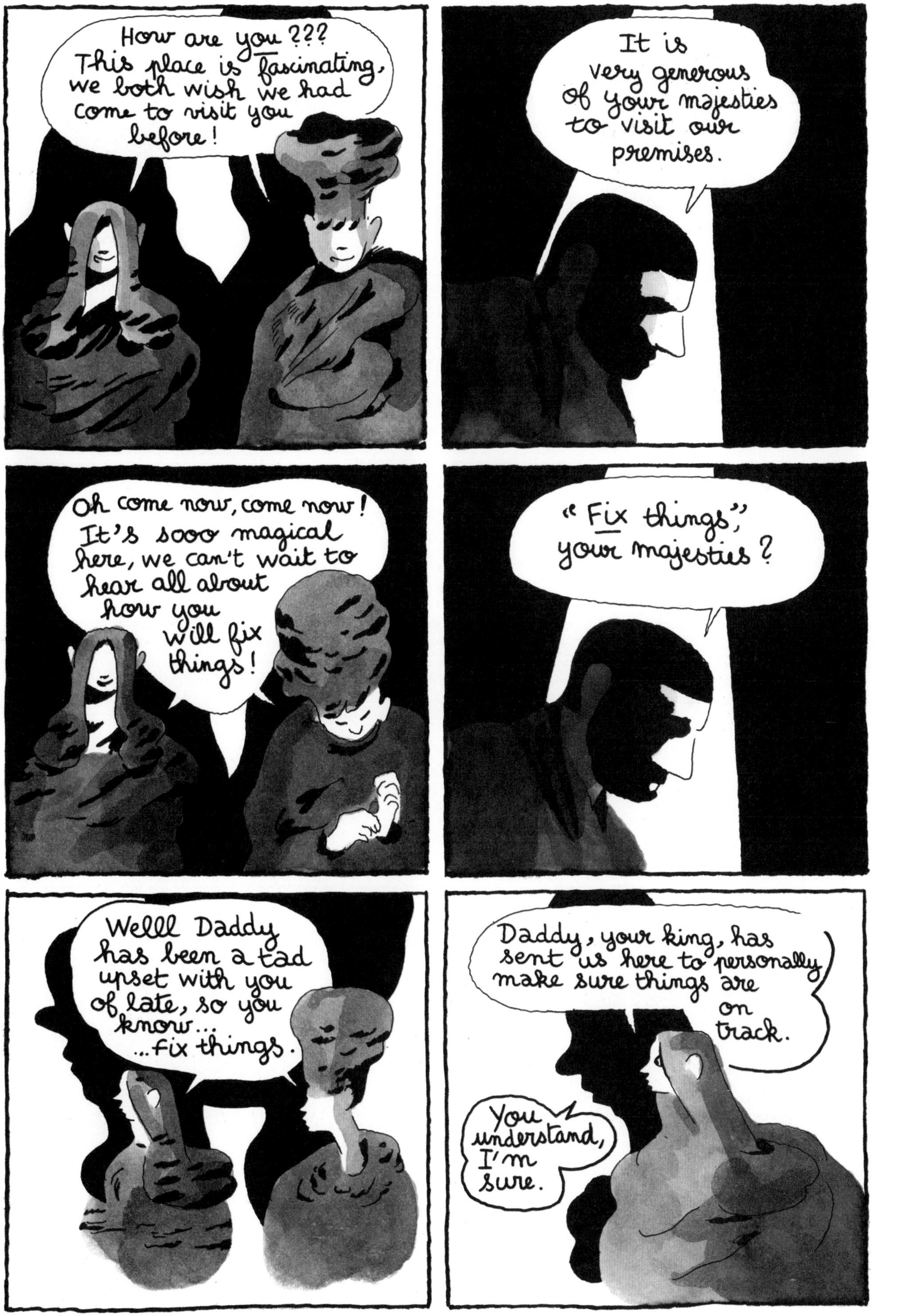
How are you??? This place is fascinating, we both wish we had come to visit you before!
It is very generous of your majesties to visit our premises.
Oh come now, come now! It's sooo magical here, we can't wait to hear all about how you will fix things!
"Fix things," your majesties?
Welll Daddy has been a tad upset with you of late, so you know... ...fix things.
Daddy, your king, has sent us here to personally make sure things are on track.
You understand, I'm sure.

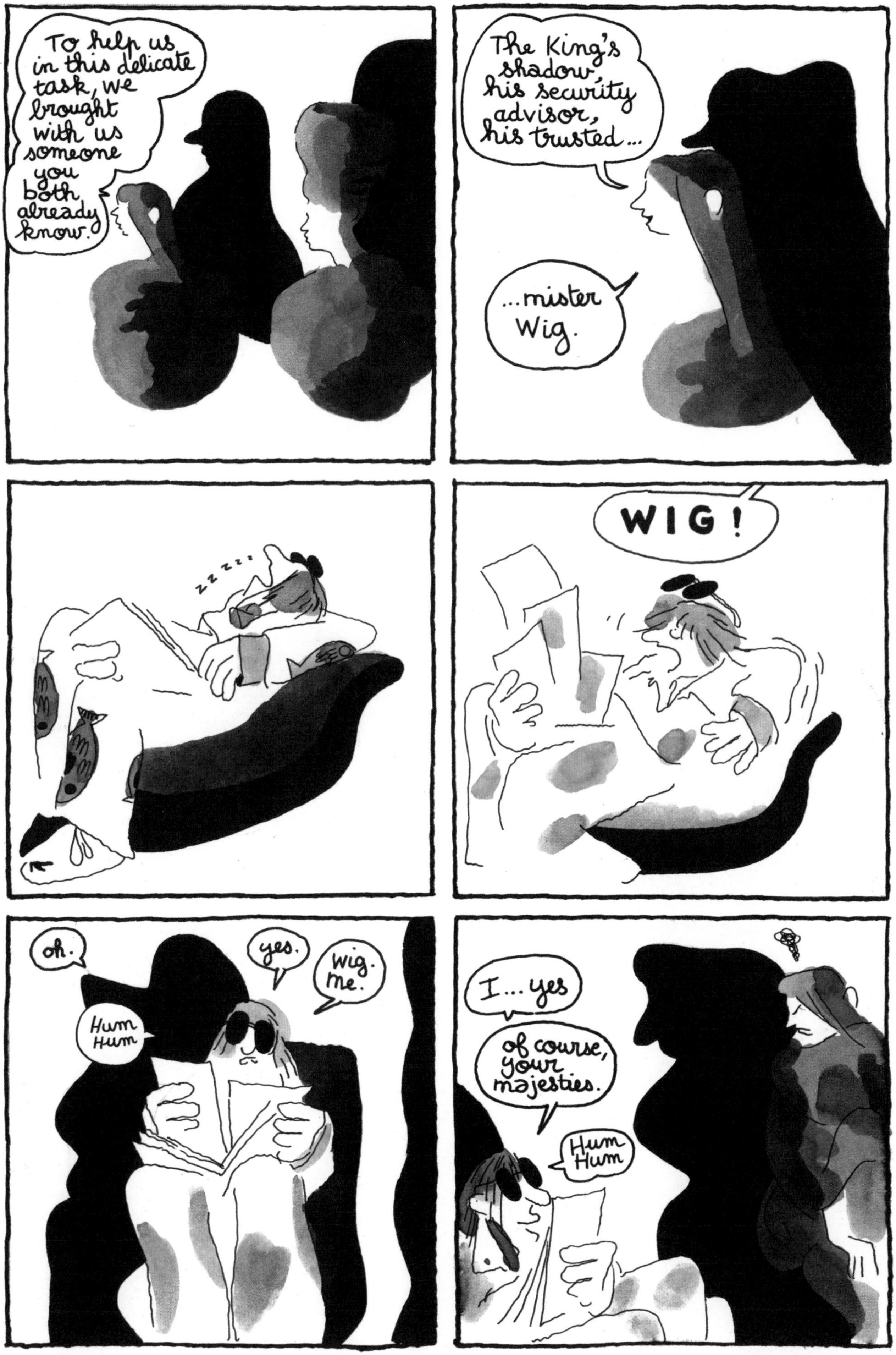
To help us in this delicate task, we brought with us someone you both already know.
The King's shadow, his security advisor, his trusted...
...mister Wig.
ZZZZZ
WIG!
oh.
yes.
Hum Hum
Wig. me.
I... yes
of course, your majesties.
Hum Hum

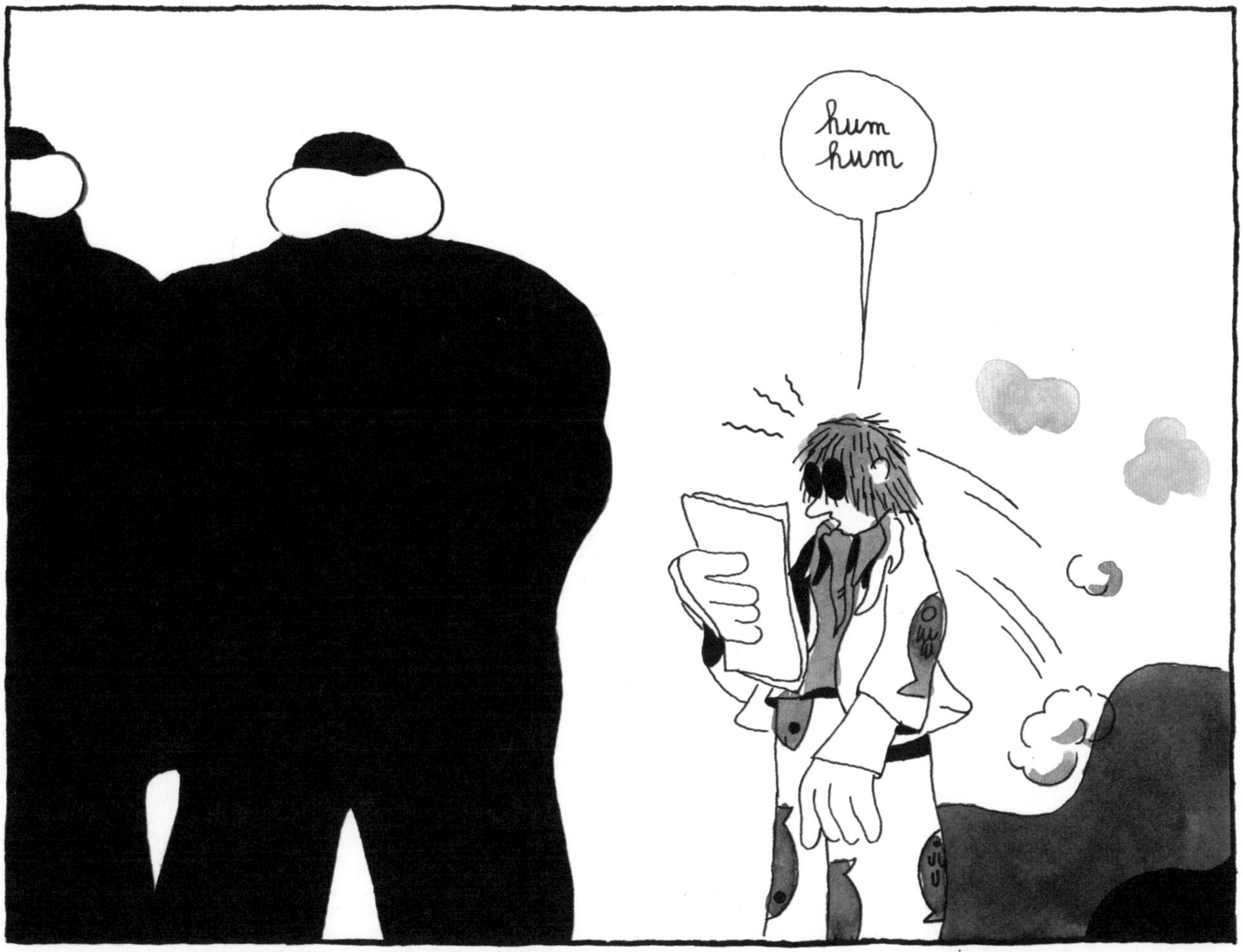
hum
hum

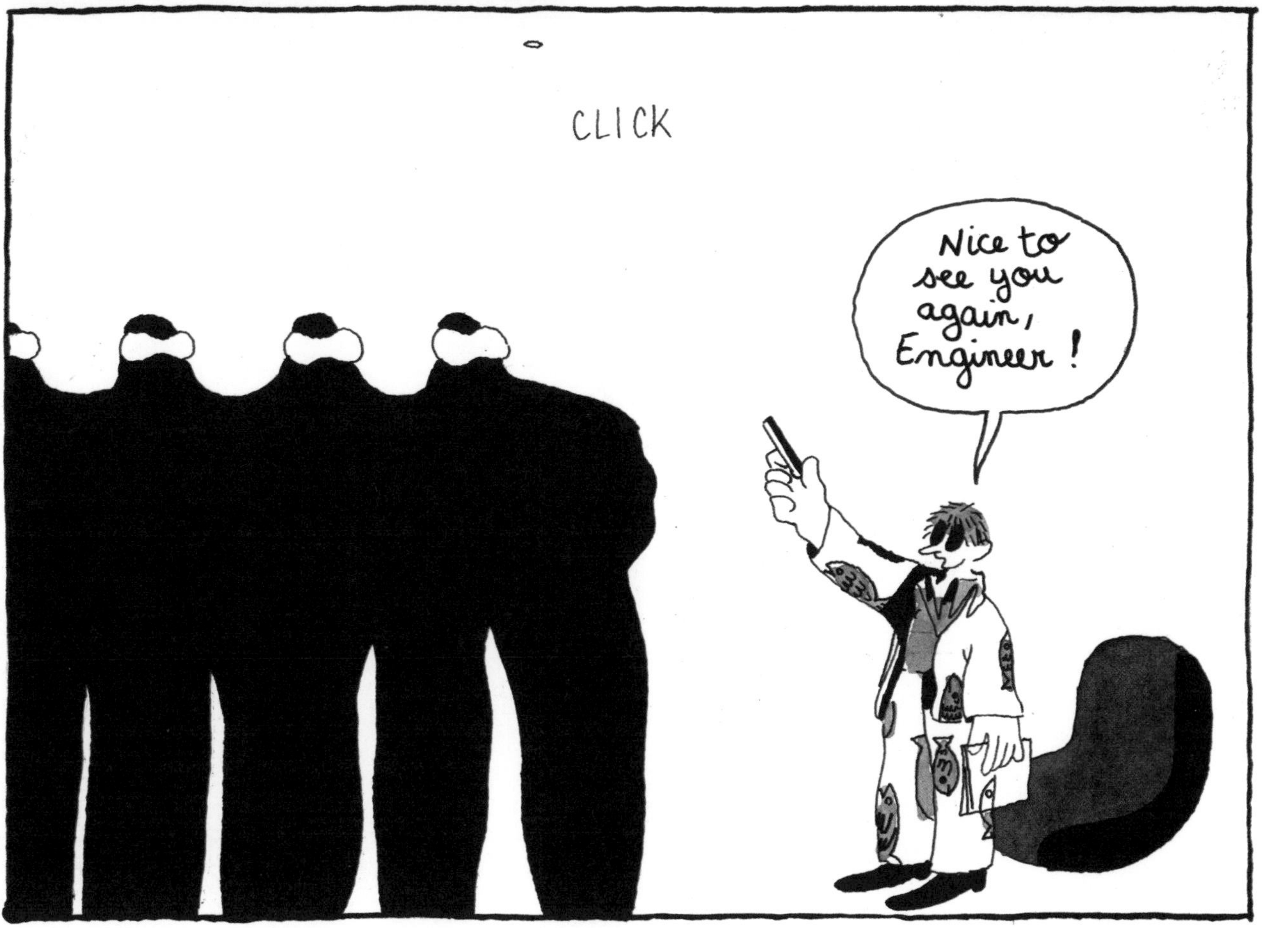
CLICK
Nice to see you again, Engineer!

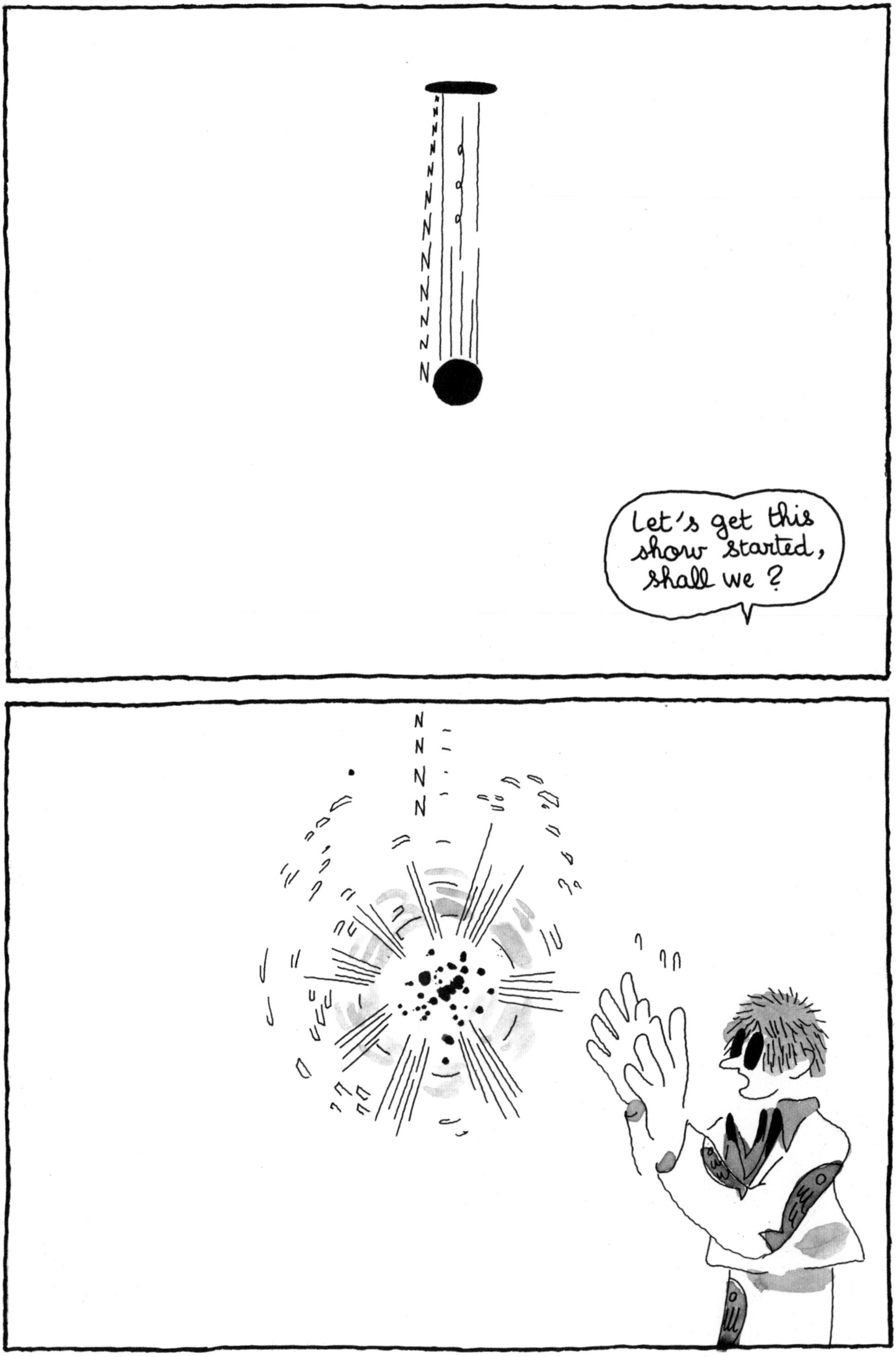
Let's get this show started, shall we ?

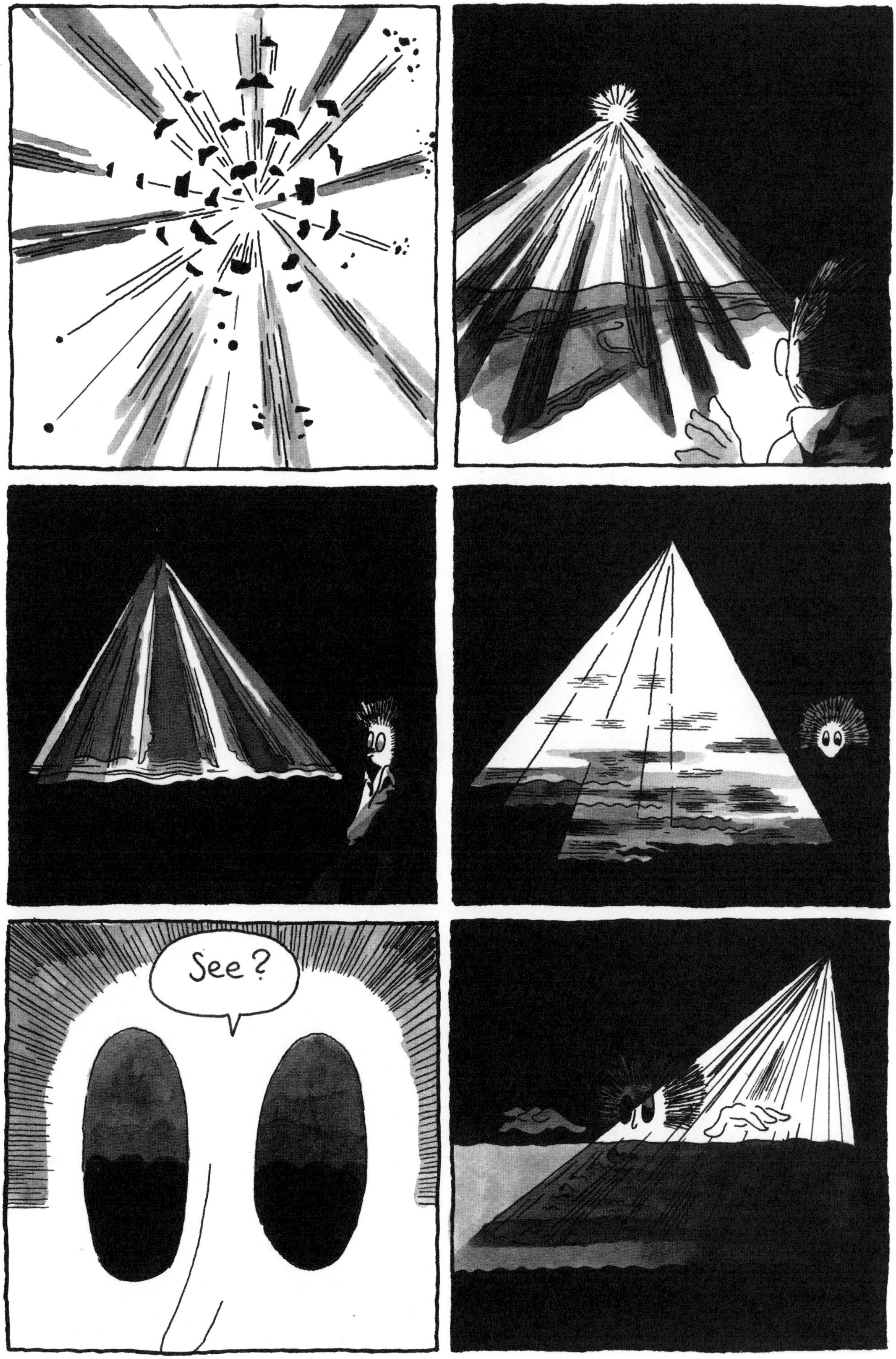
See?

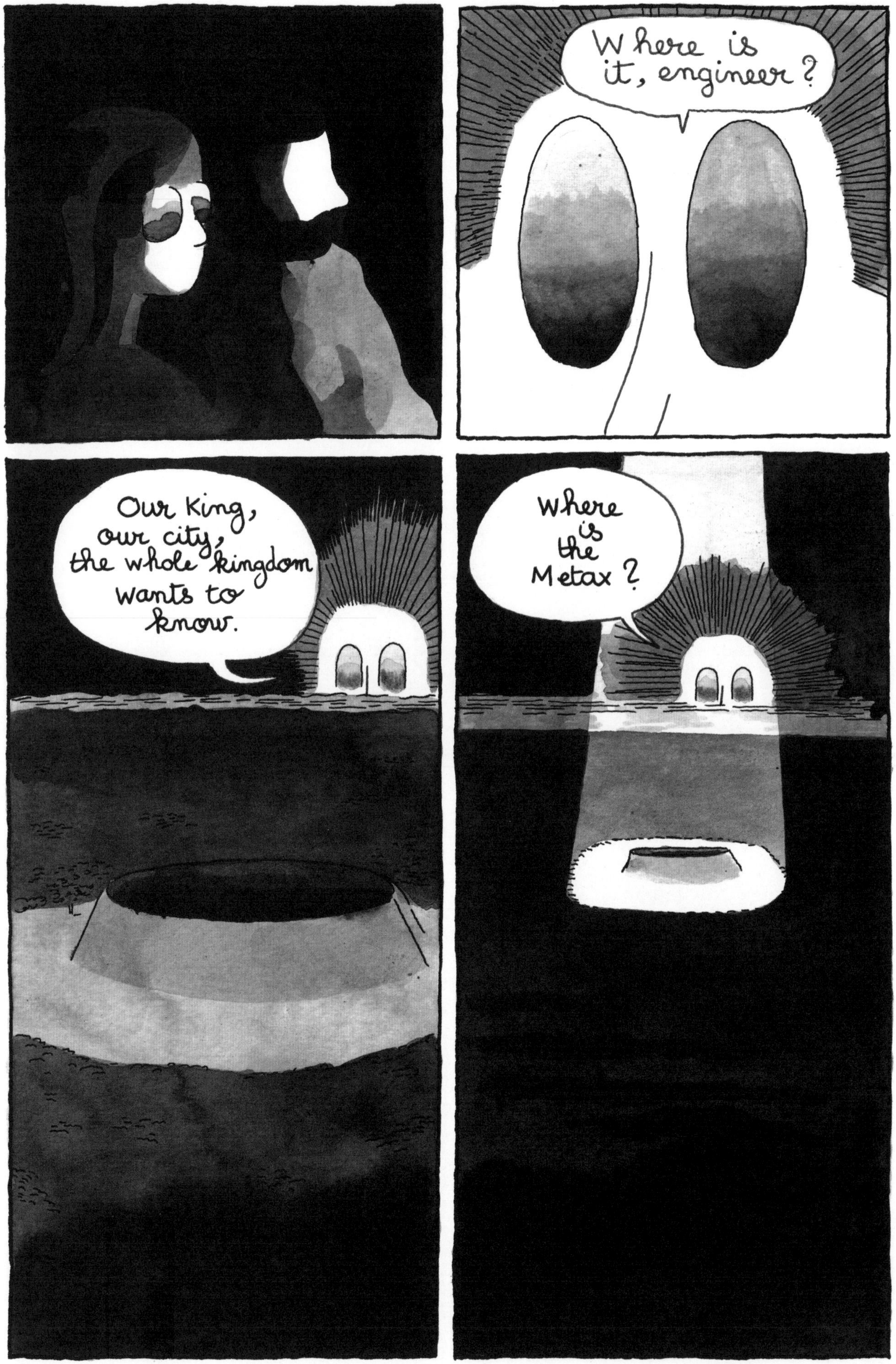
Where is it, engineer?
Our King, our city, the whole kingdom wants to know.
Where is the Metax?

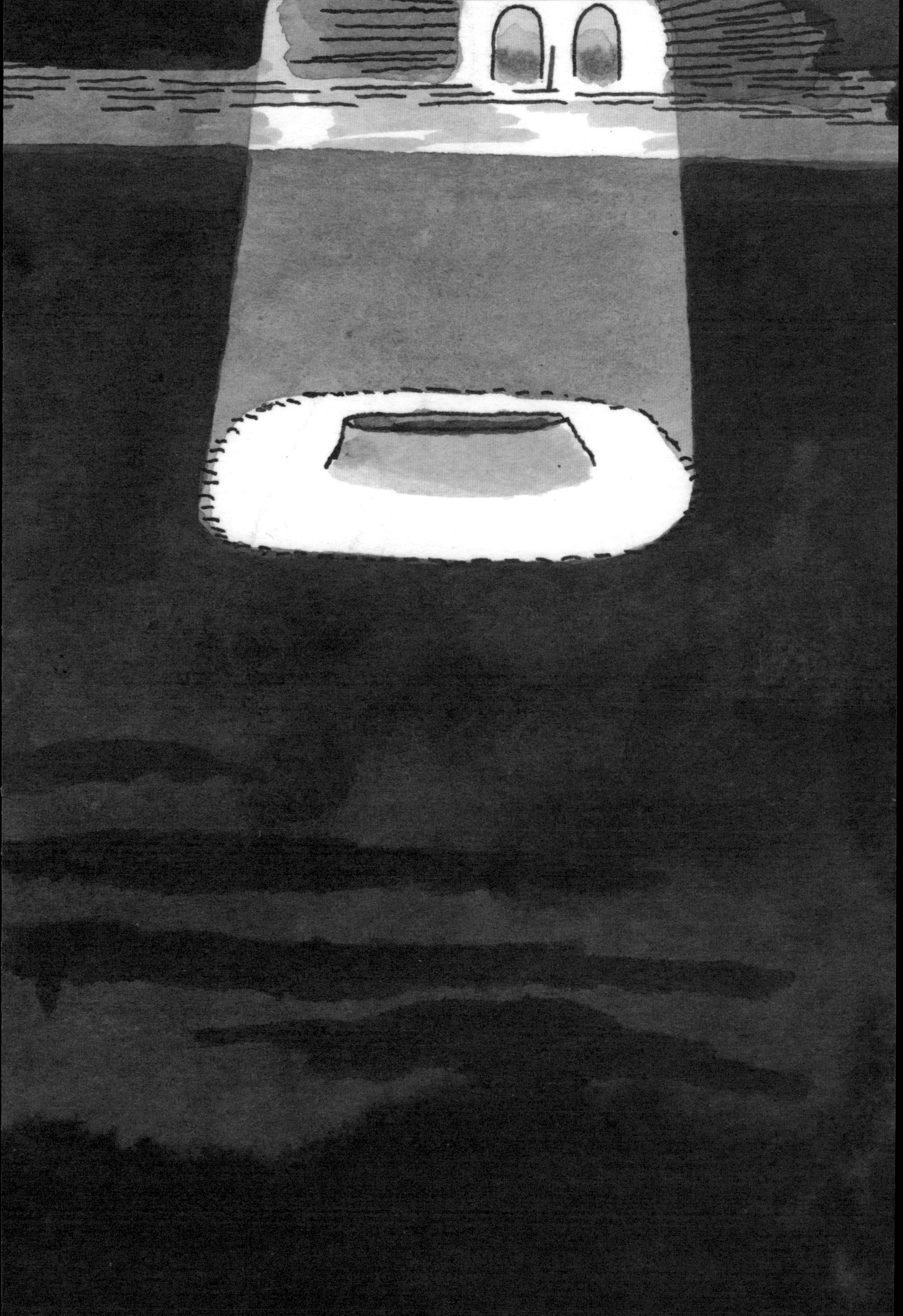

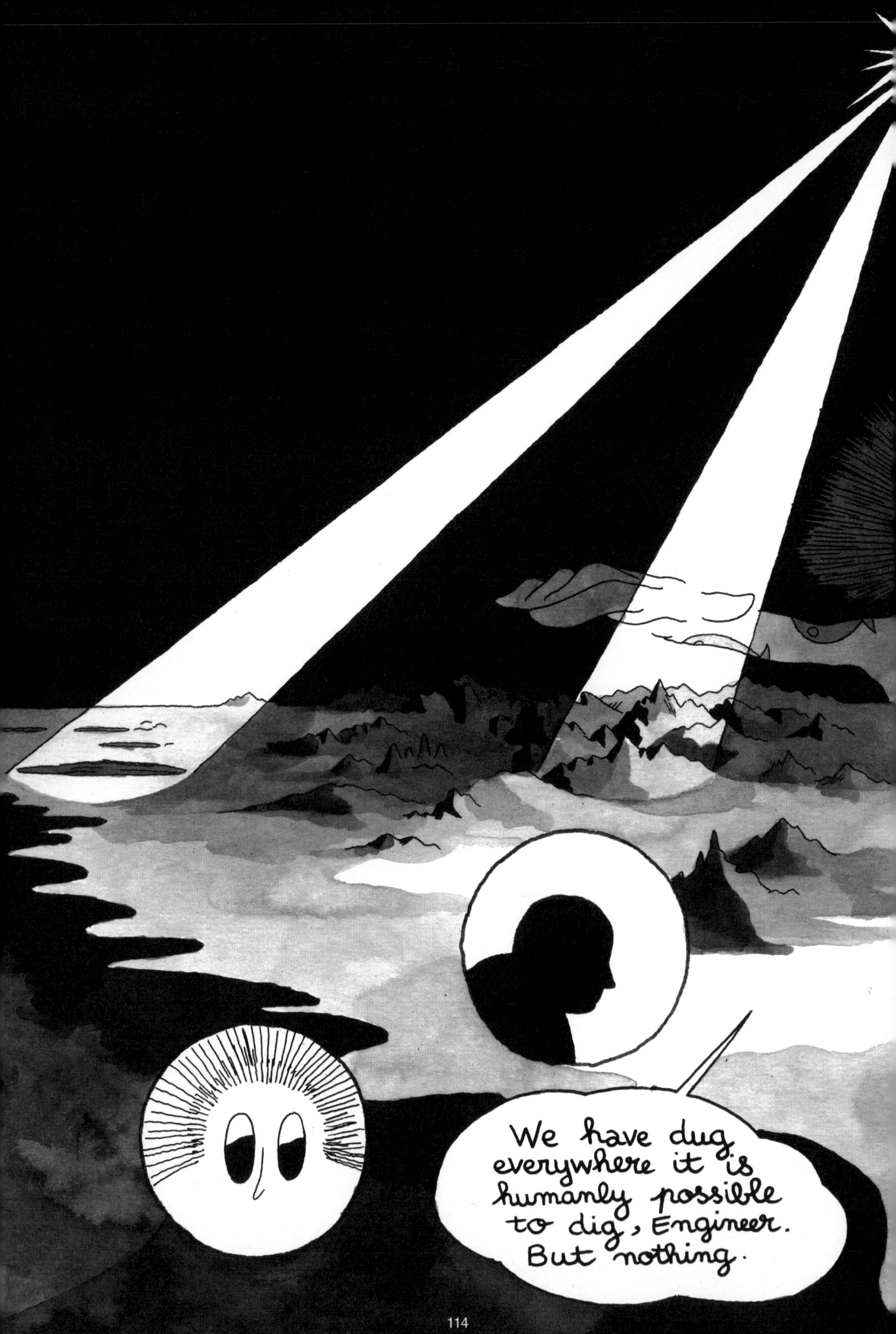
We have dug everywhere it is humanly possible to dig, Engineer. But nothing.

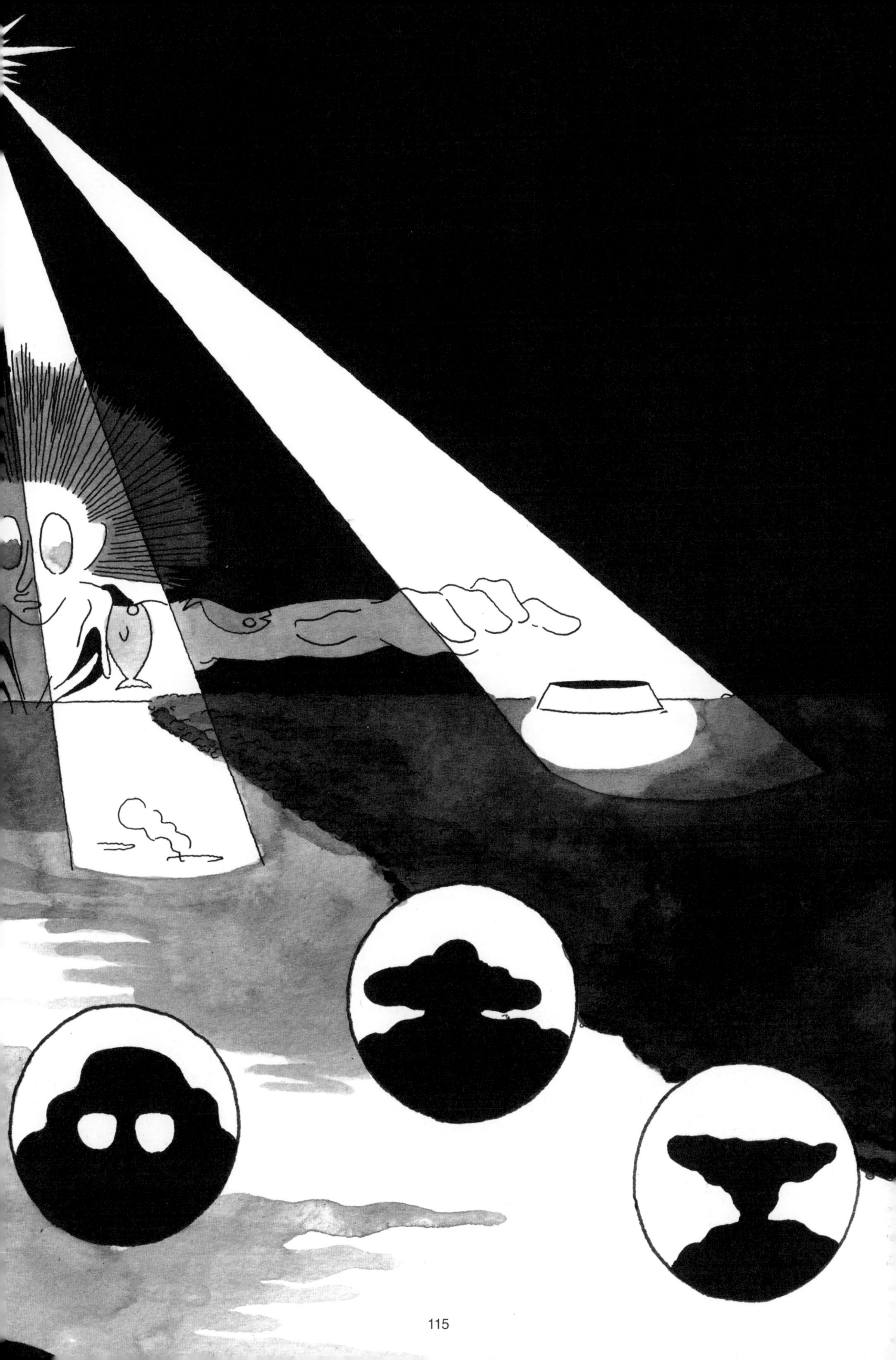

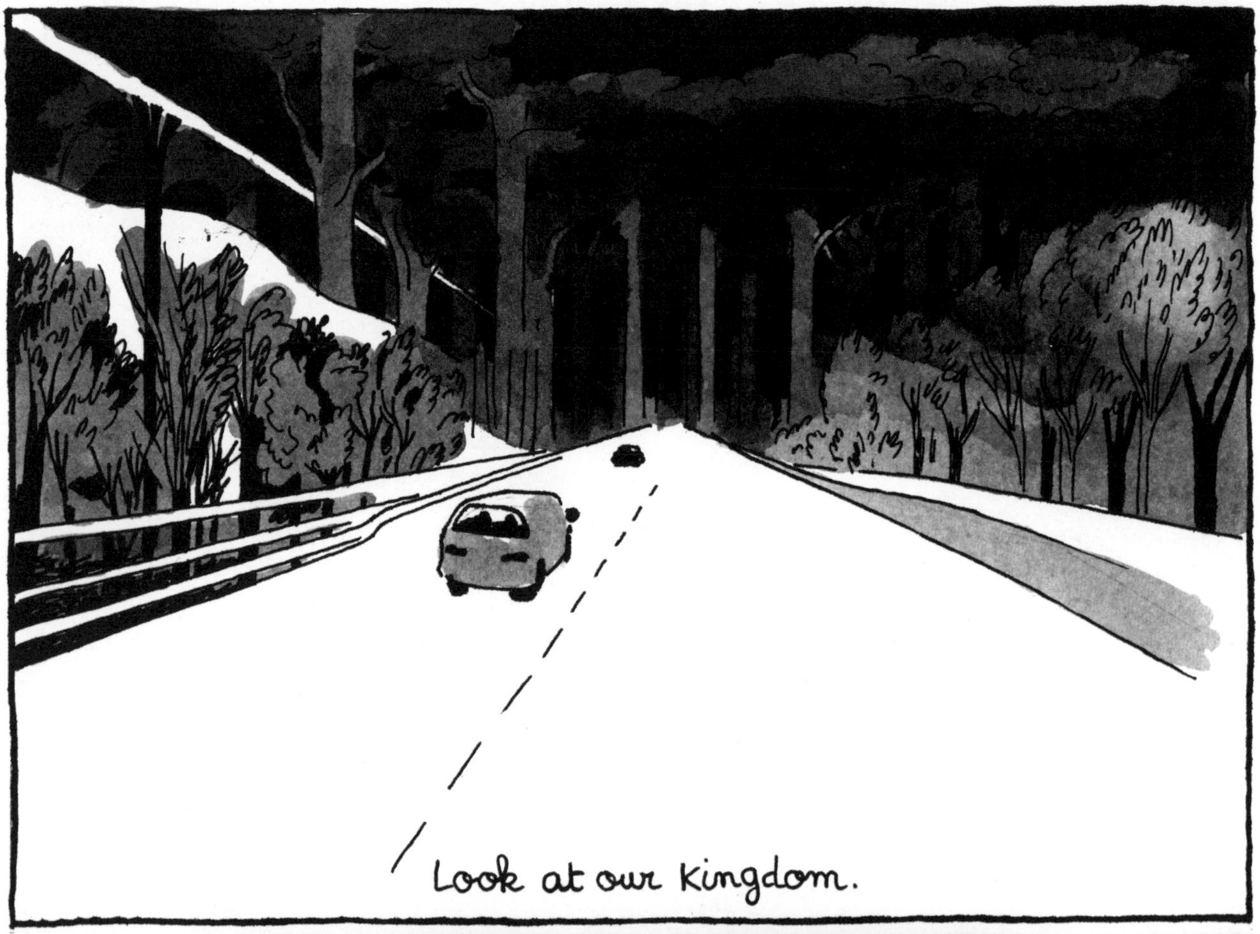
Look at our Kingdom.

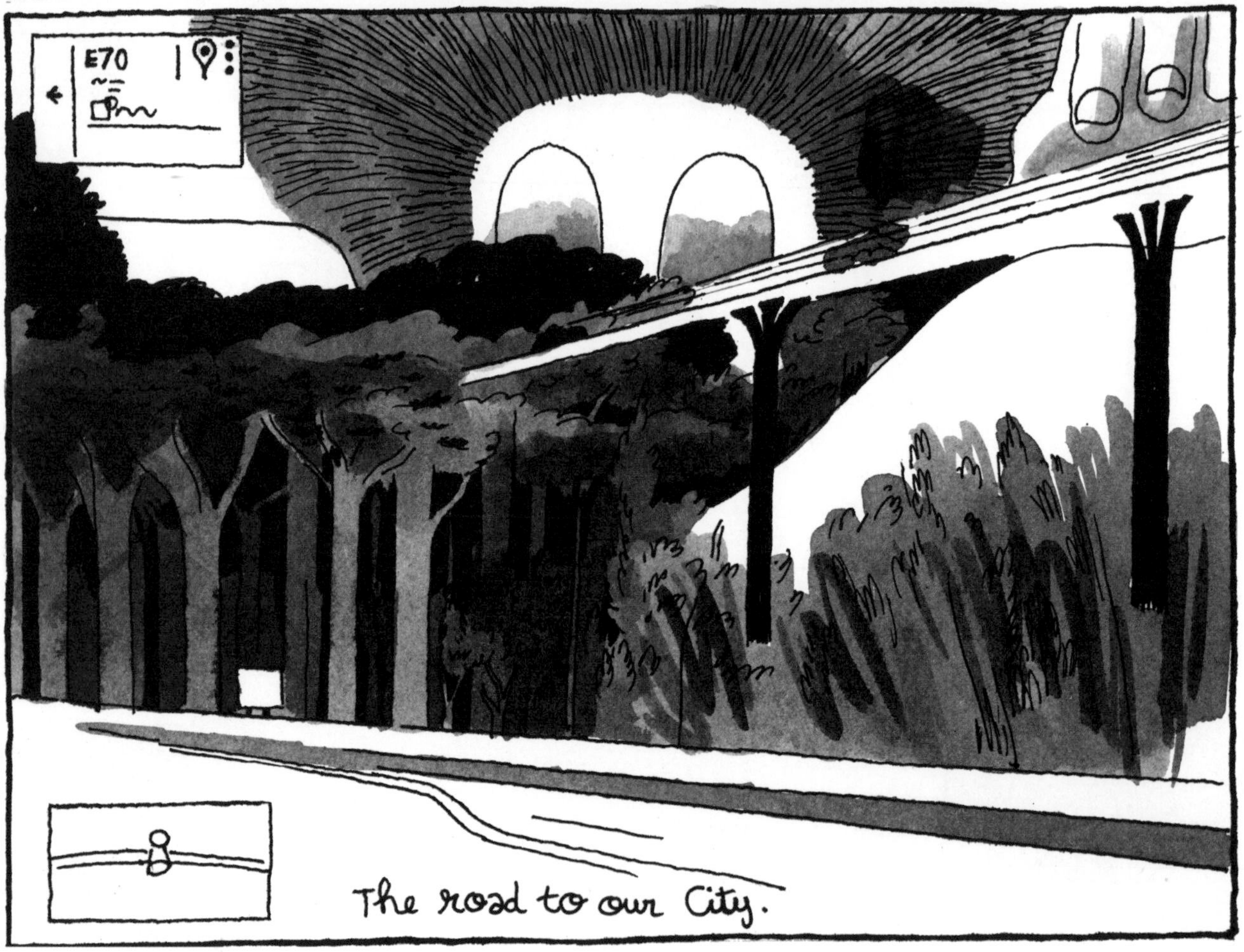
E70
The road to our City.

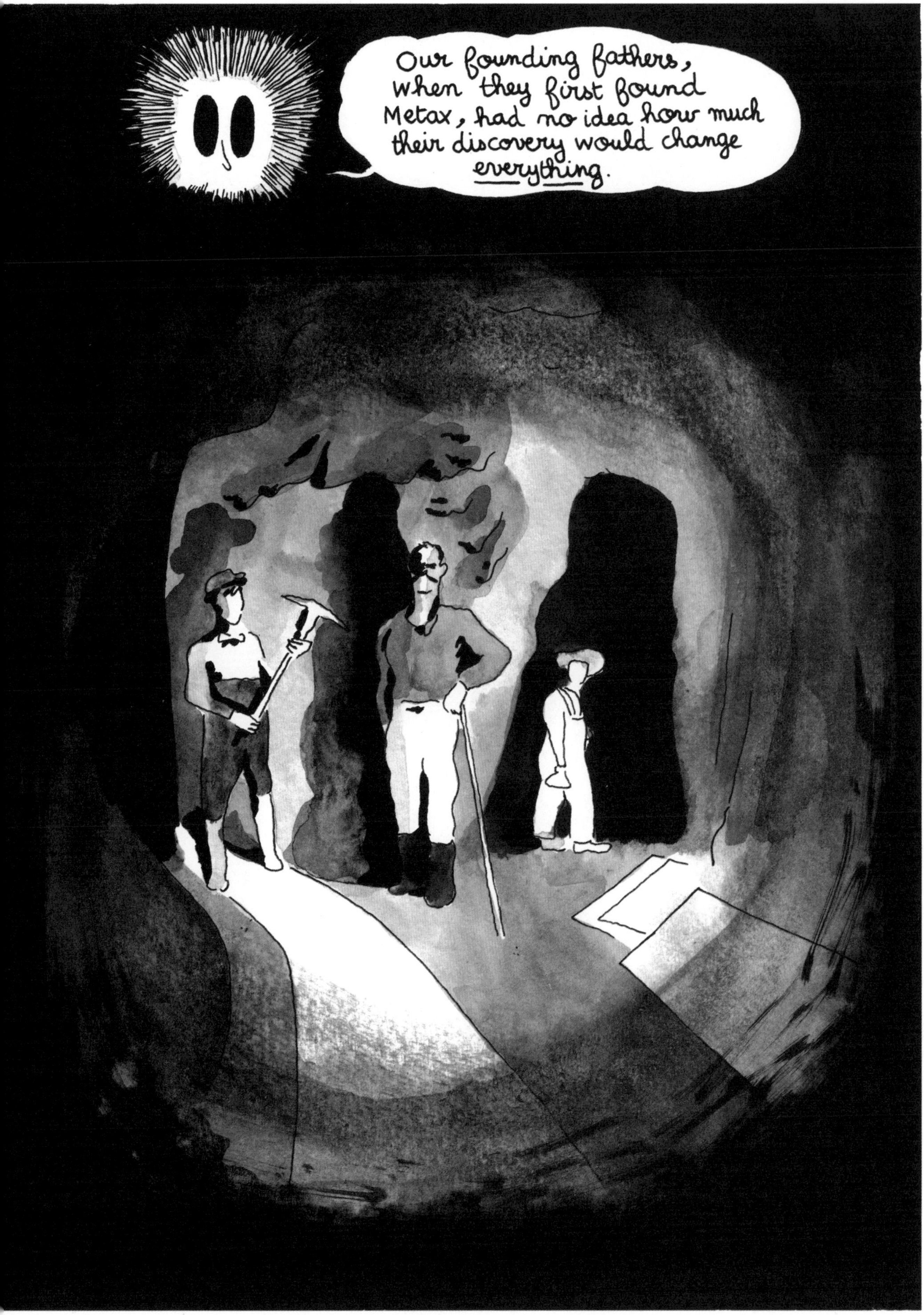
Our founding fathers, when they first found Metax, had no idea how much their discovery would change everything.

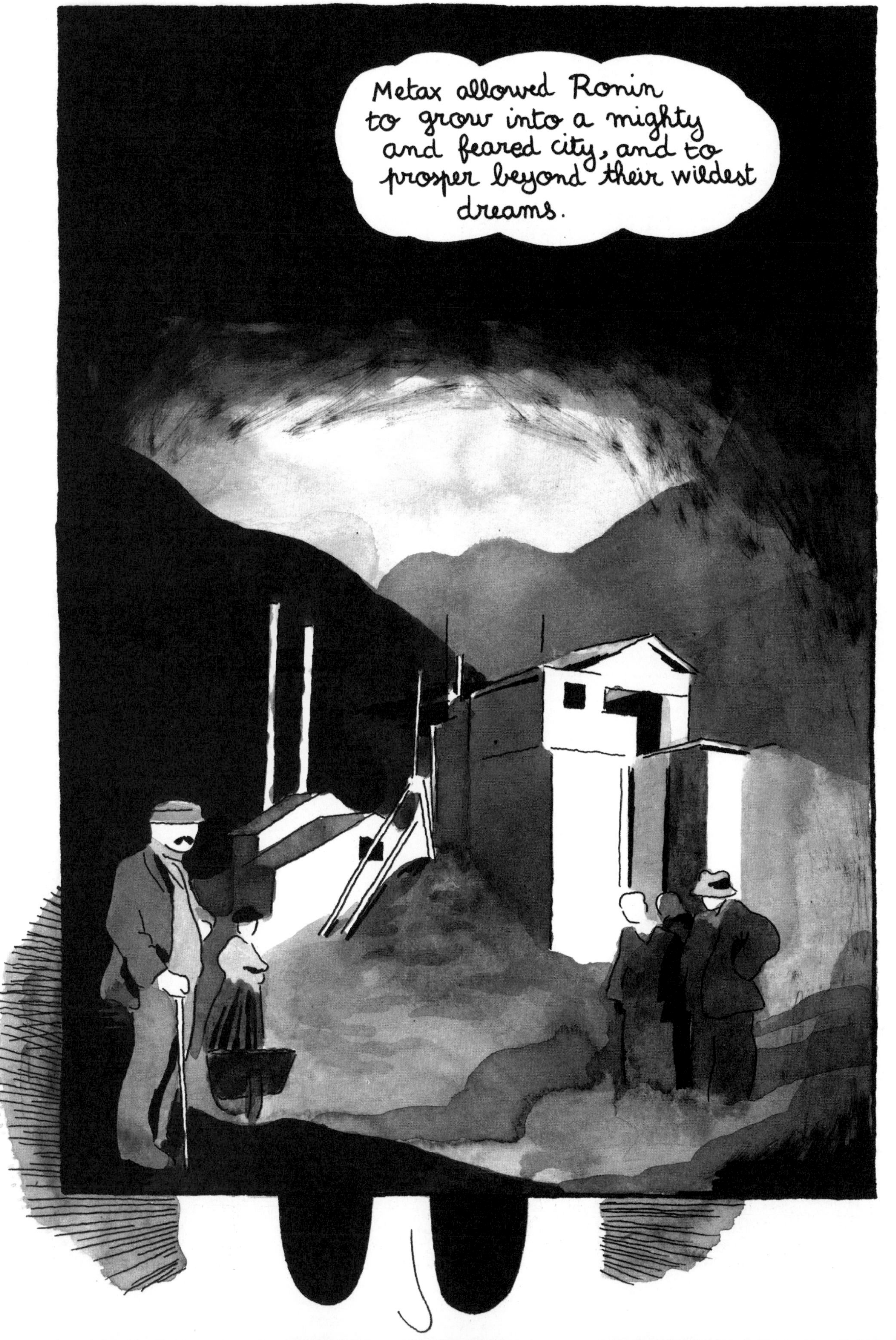
Metax allowed Ronin to grow into a mighty and feared city, and to prosper beyond their wildest dreams.

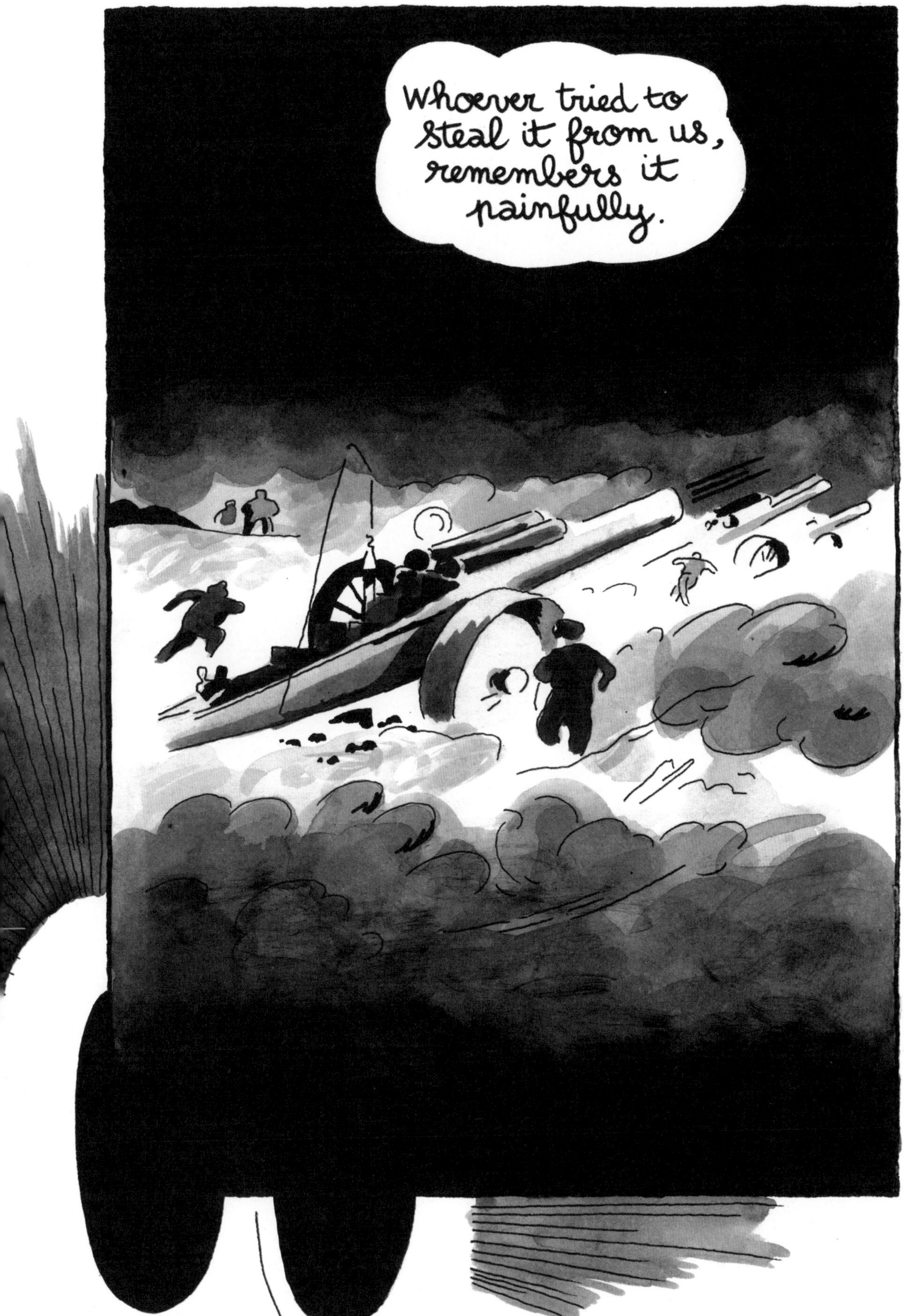
Whoever tried to steal it from us, remembers it painfully.

We built a wall to protect our city. You engineers helped our kingdom to thrive, by finding Metax with more and more ingenuity.

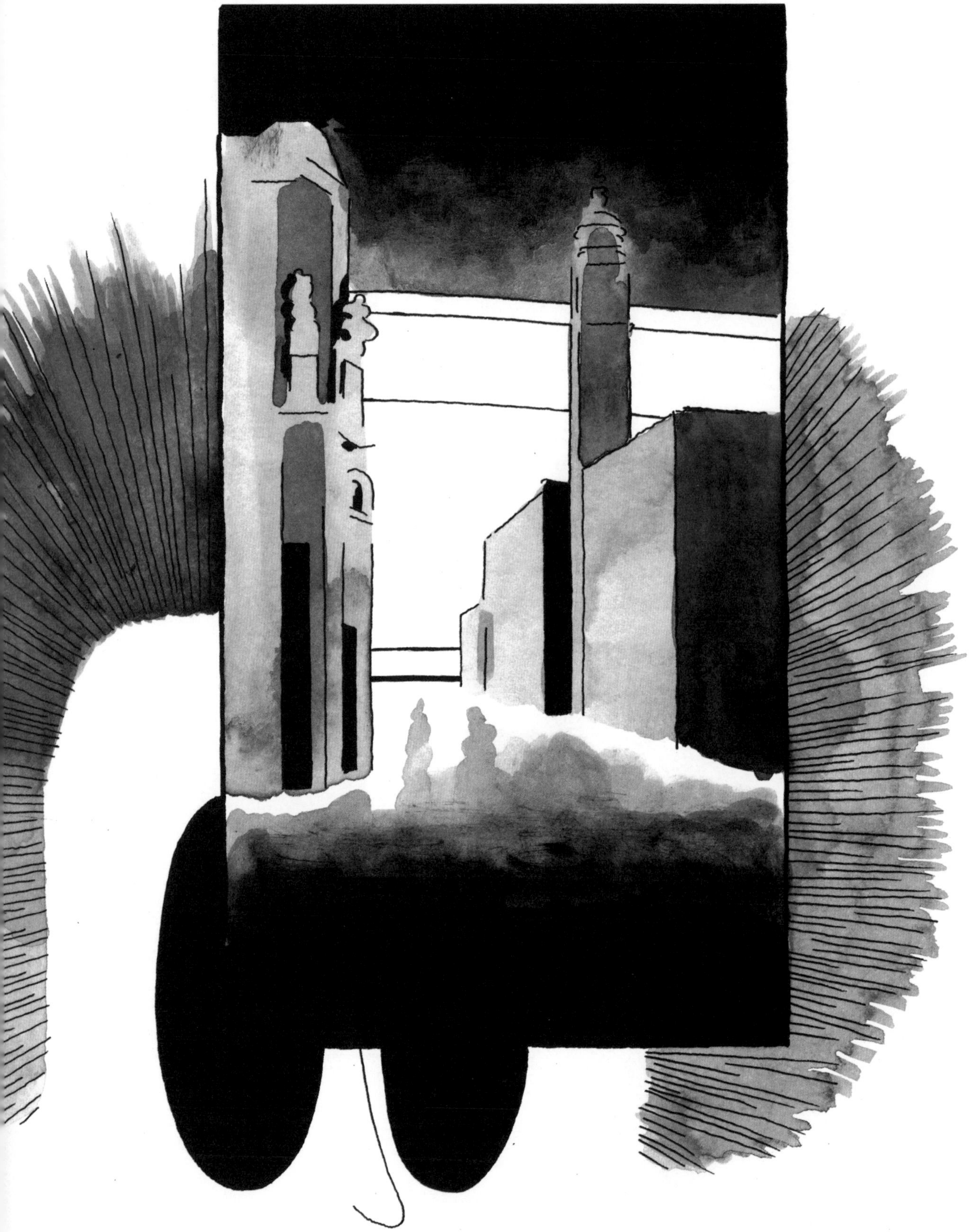

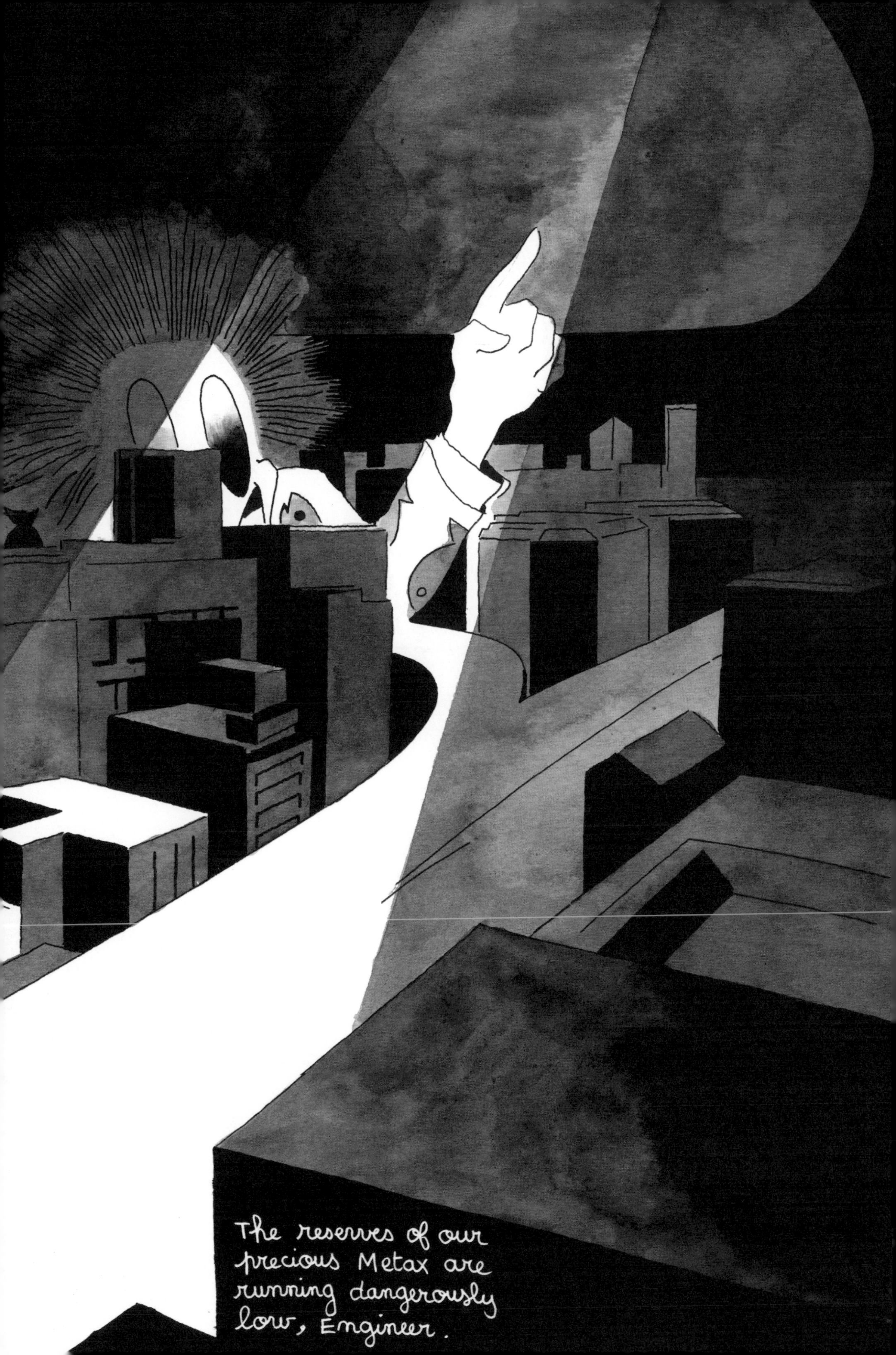
The reserves of our
precious Metax are
running dangerously
low, Engineer.

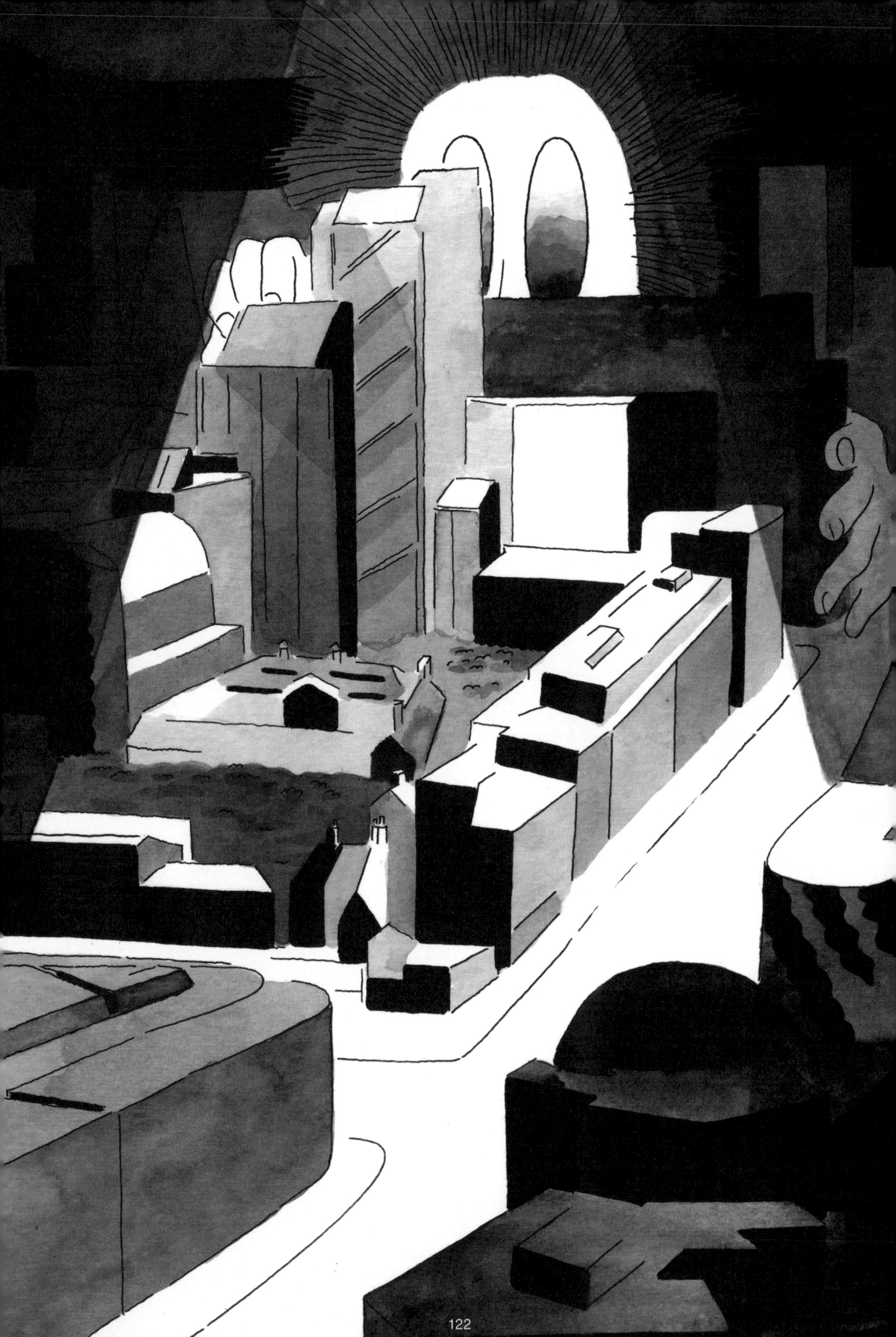

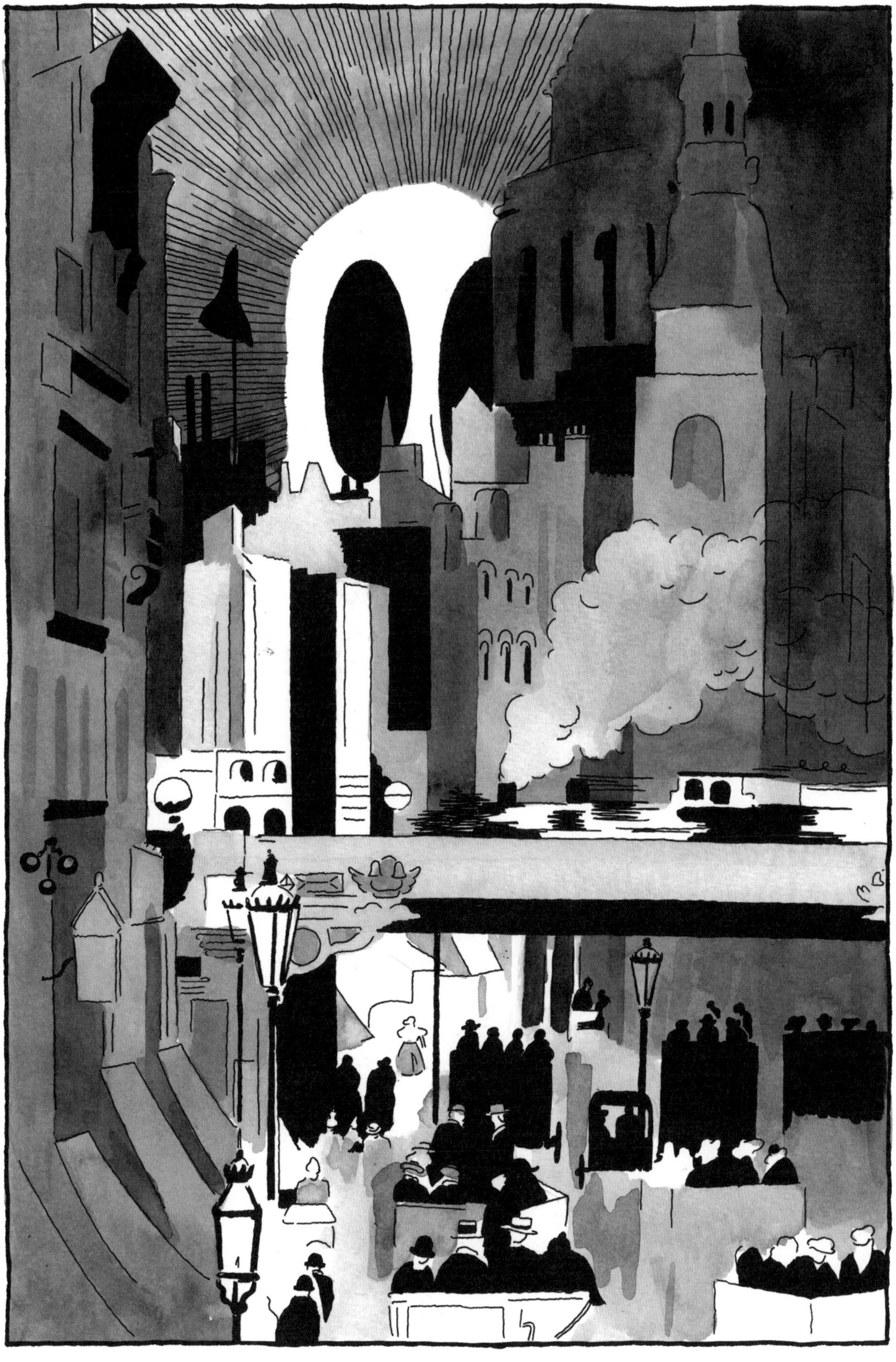

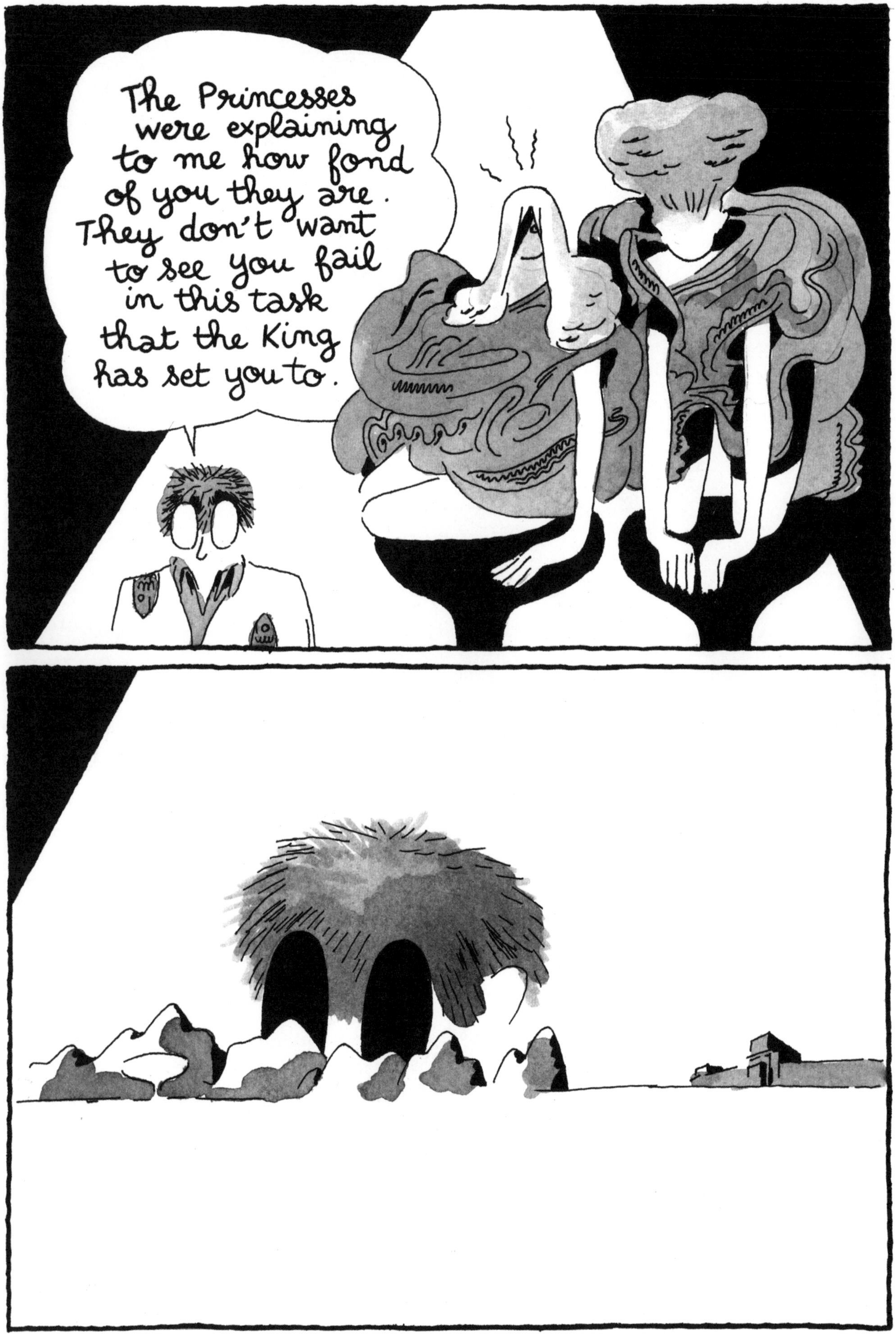
The Princesses were explaining to me how fond of you they are. They don't want to see you fail in this task that the King has set you to.

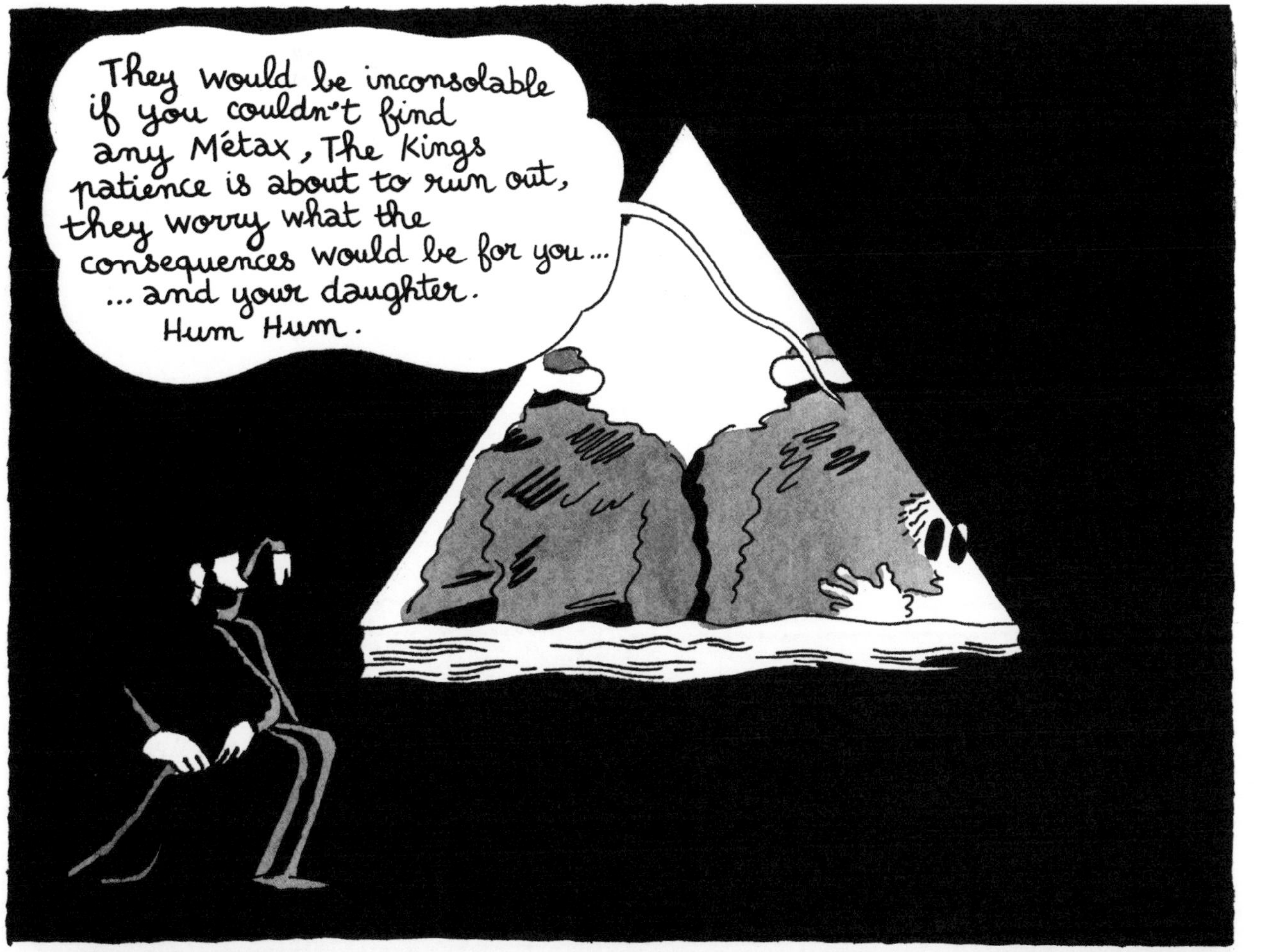
They would be inconsolable if you couldn't find any Métax, The Kings patience is about to run out, they worry what the consequences would be for you... ...and your daughter. Hum Hum.

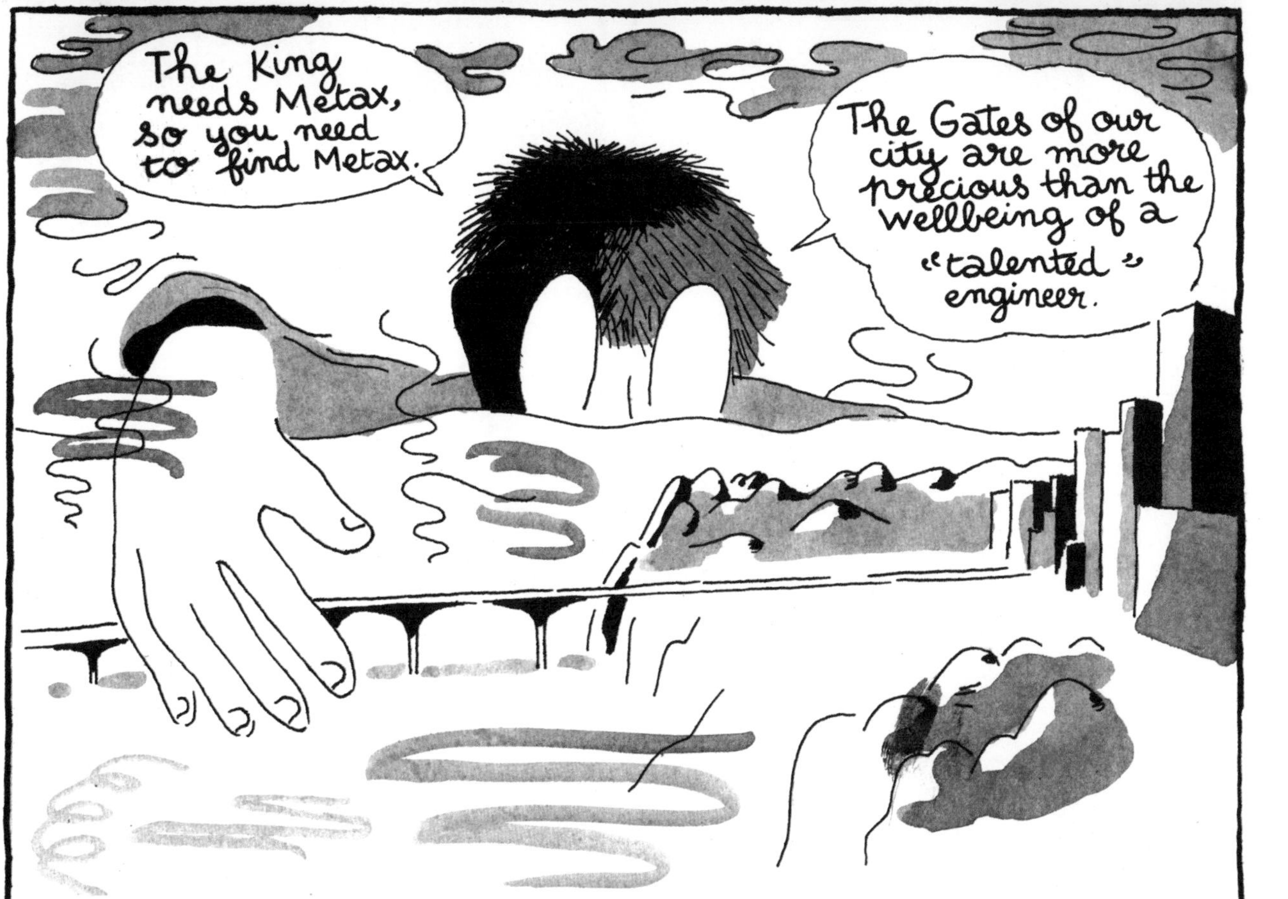
The King needs Metax, so you need to find Metax.
The Gates of our city are more precious than the wellbeing of a "talented" engineer.

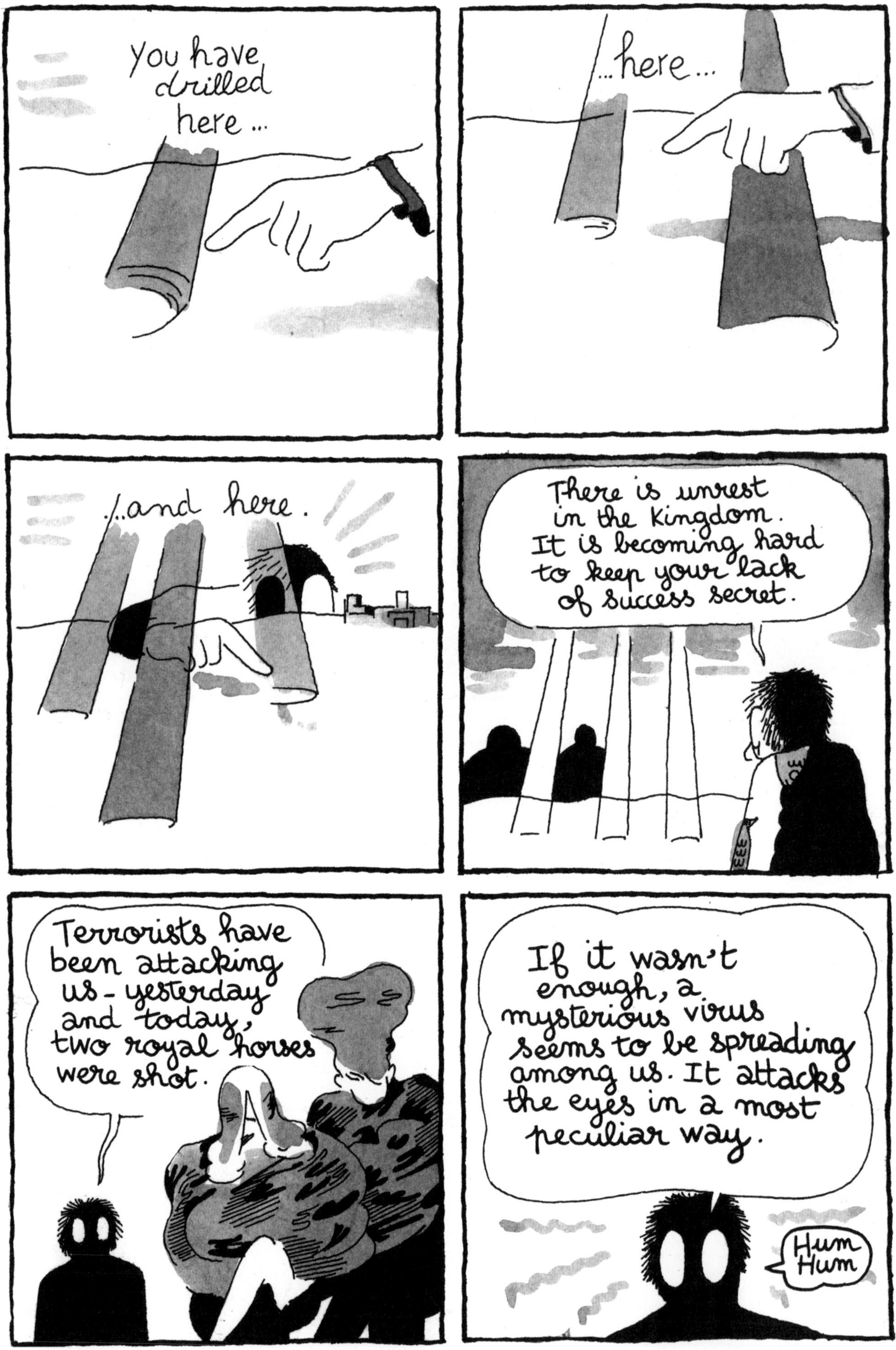
you have drilled here ...
... here ...
... and here.
There is unrest in the Kingdom. It is becoming hard to keep your lack of success secret.
Terrorists have been attacking us - yesterday and today, two royal horses were shot.
If it wasn't enough, a mysterious virus seems to be spreading among us. It attacks the eyes in a most peculiar way.
Hum Hum

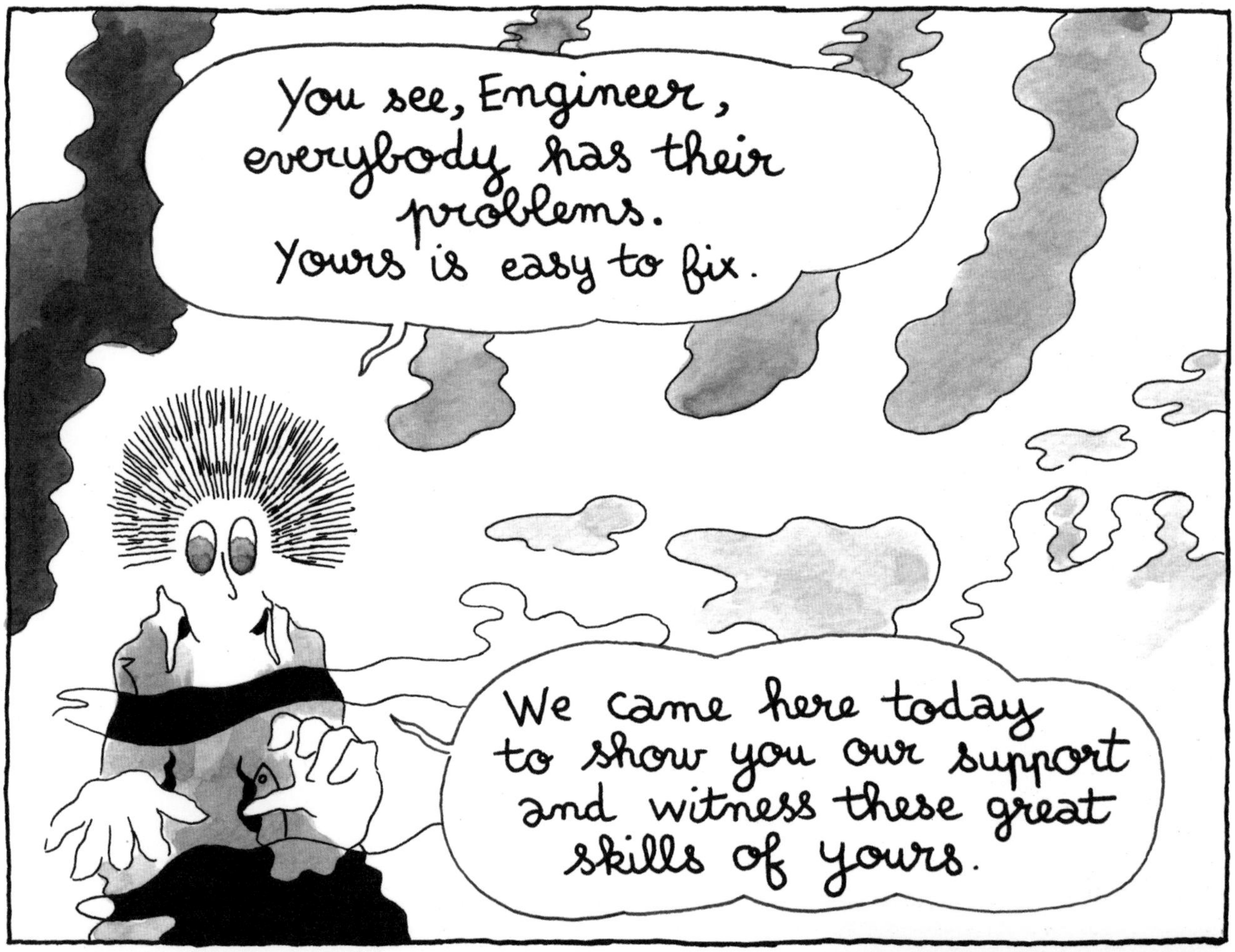
You see, Engineer, everybody has their problems. Yours is easy to fix.
We came here today to show you our support and witness these great skills of yours.

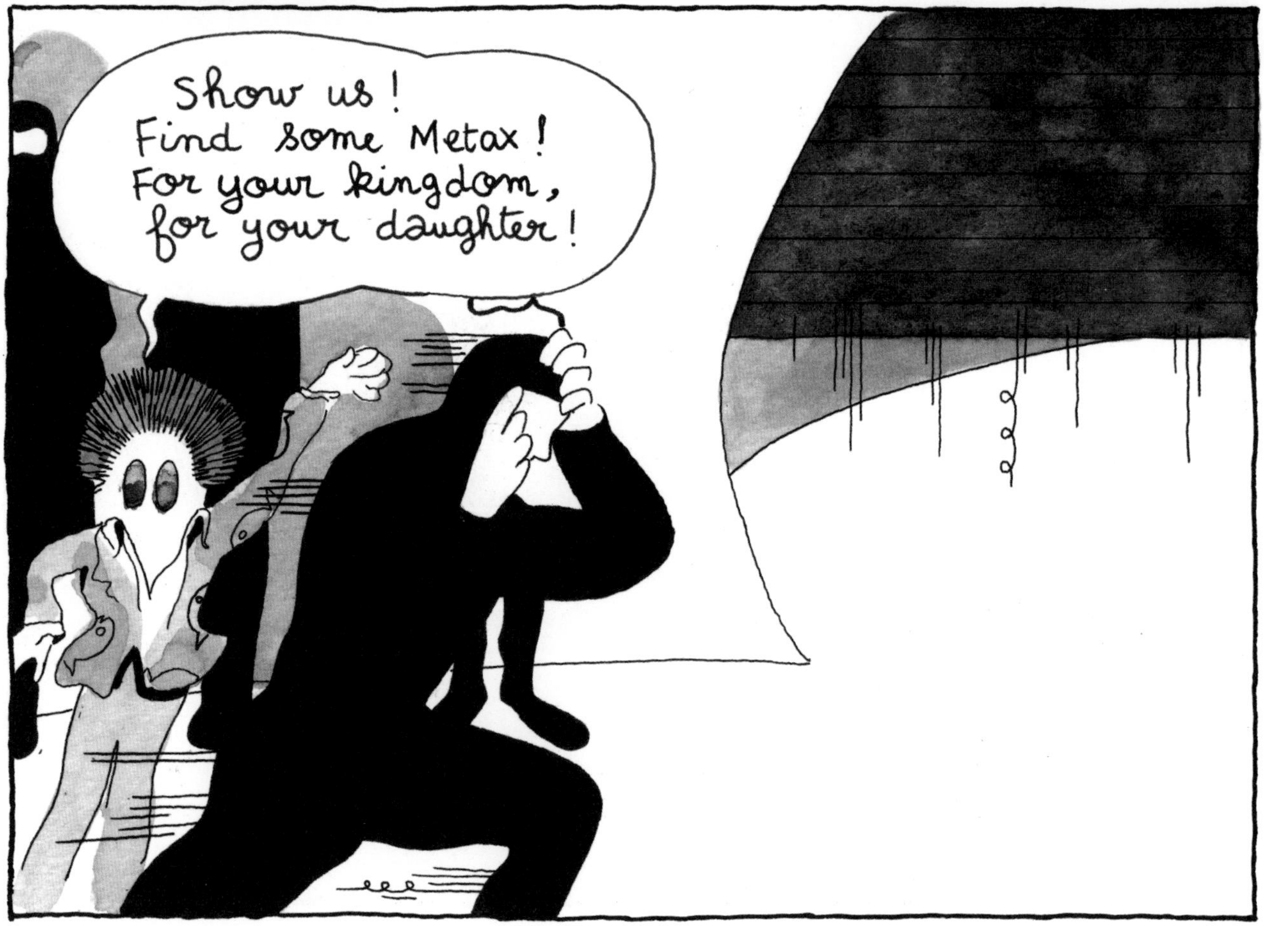
Show us! Find some Metax! For your kingdom, for your daughter!

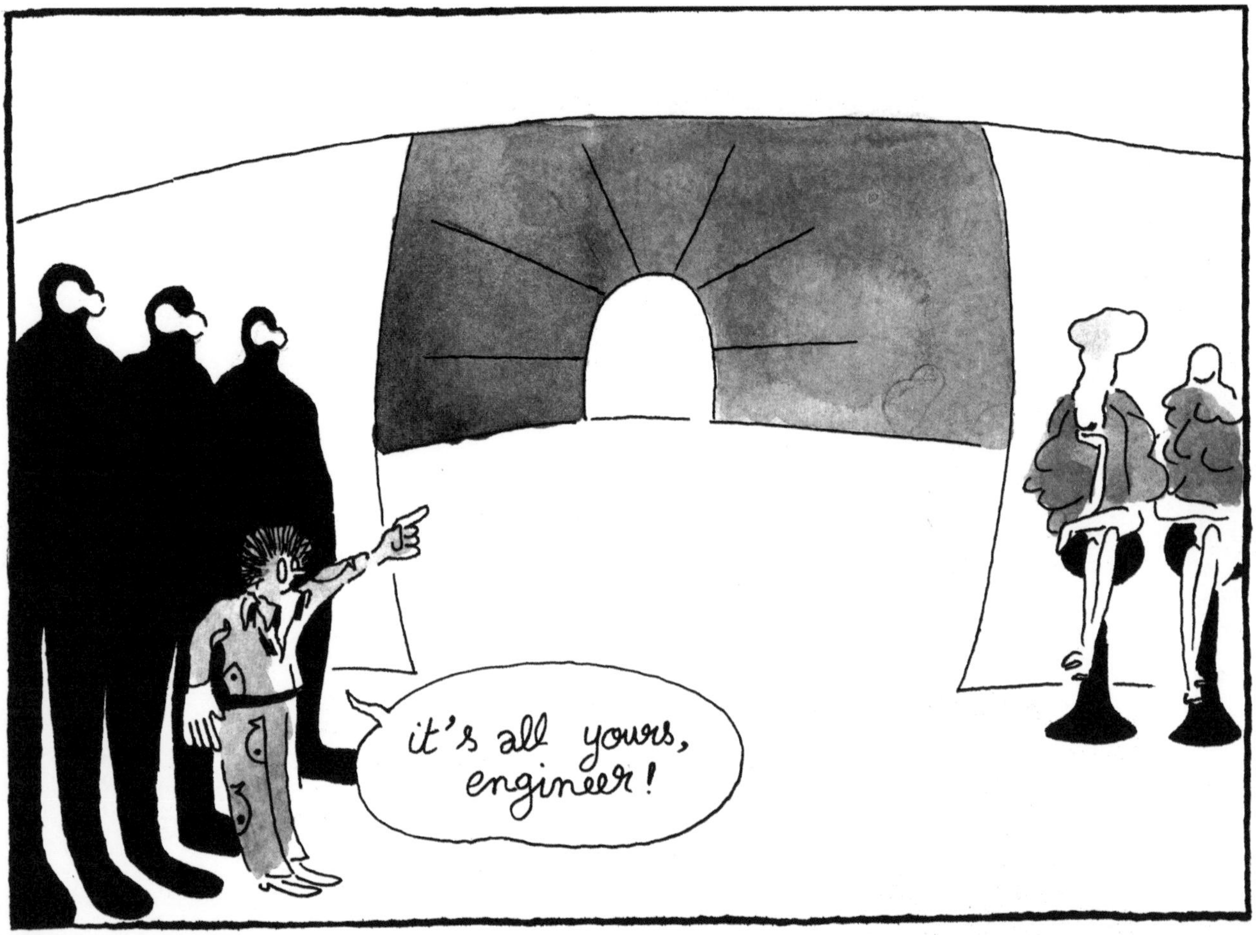
it's all yours, engineer!

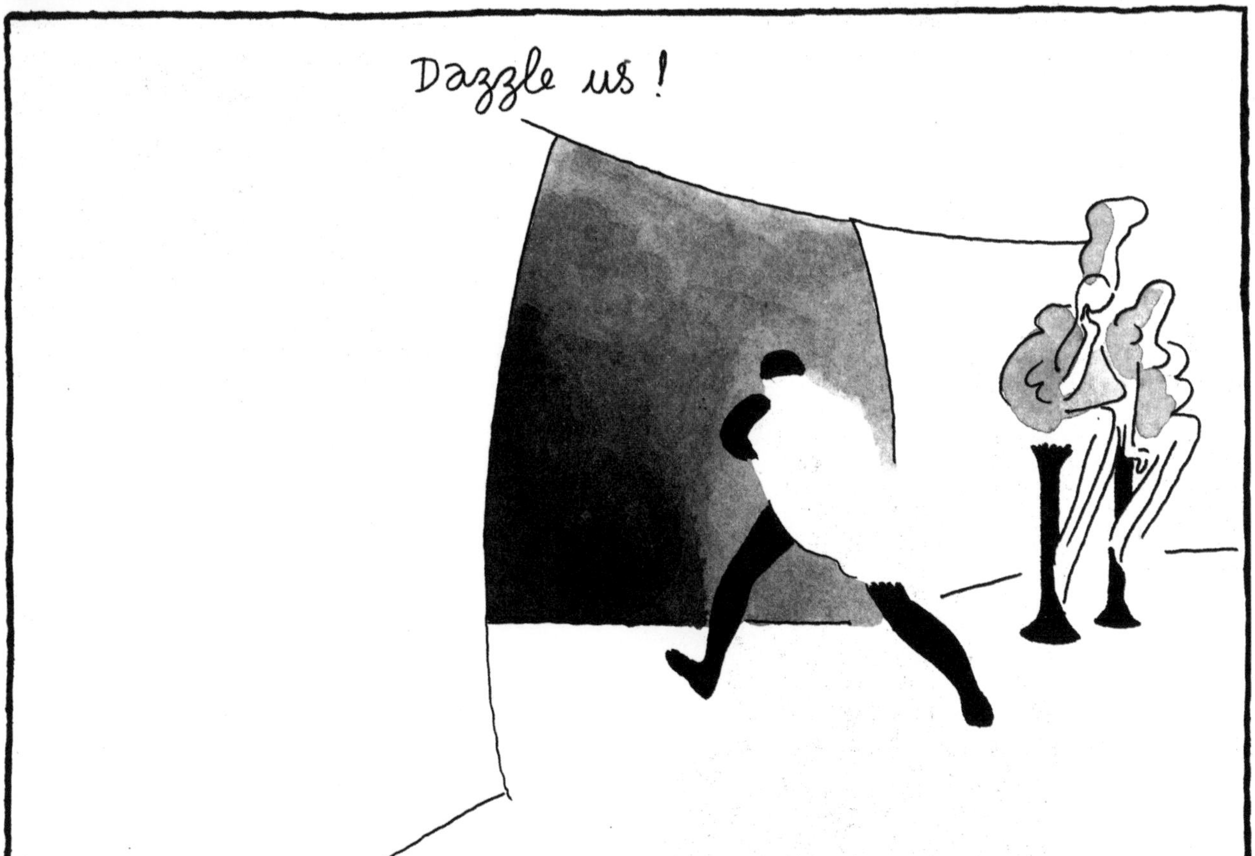
Dazzle us!

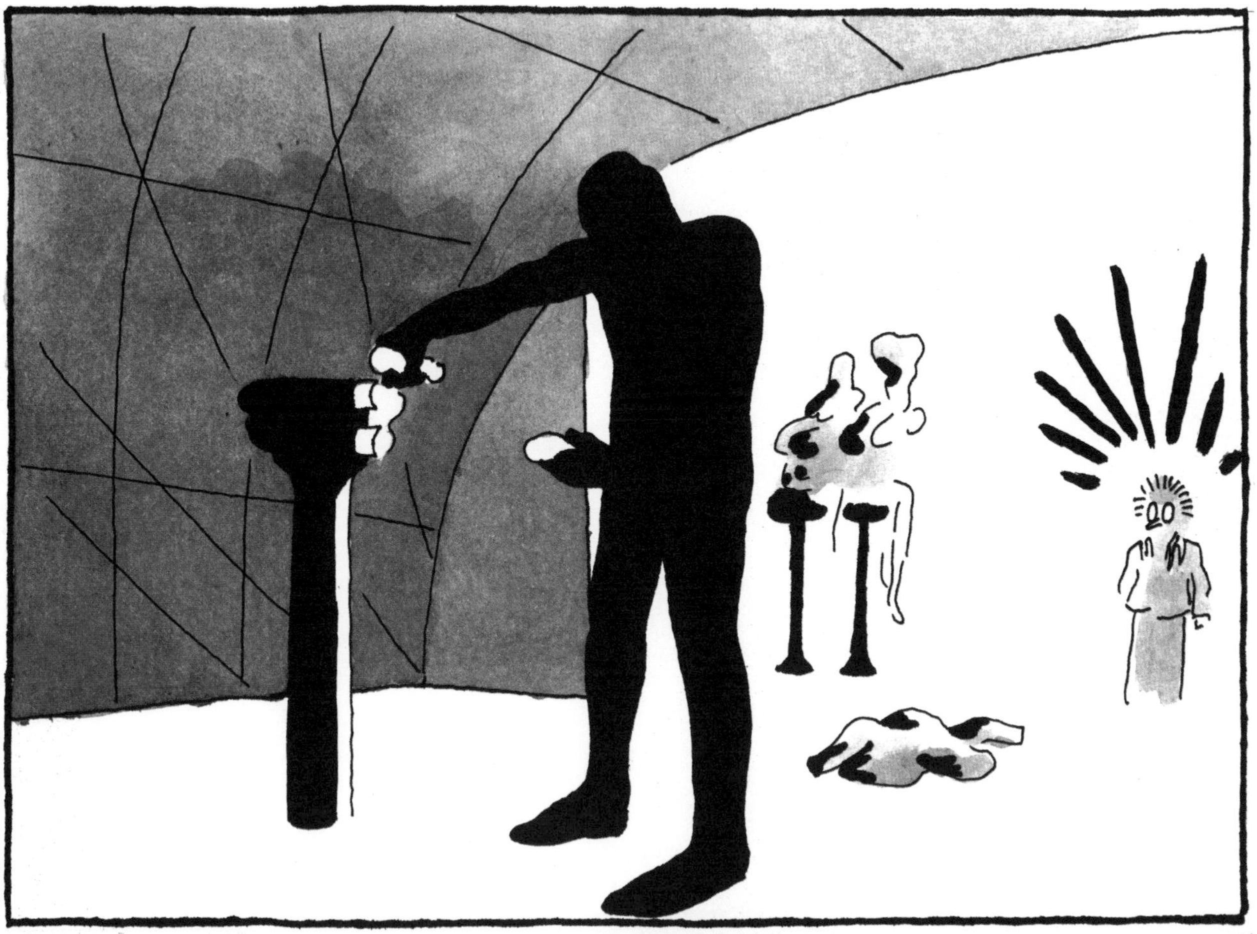

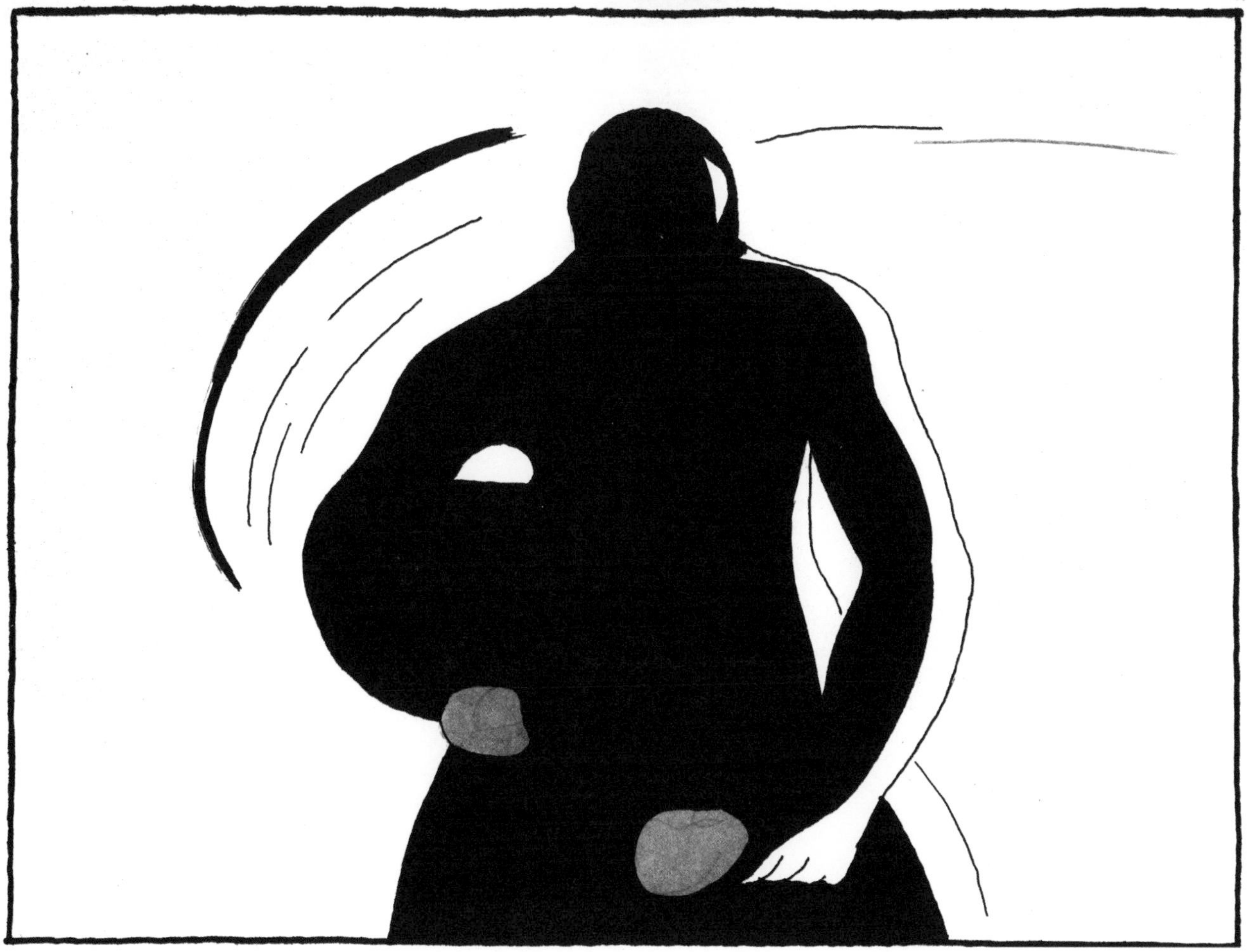

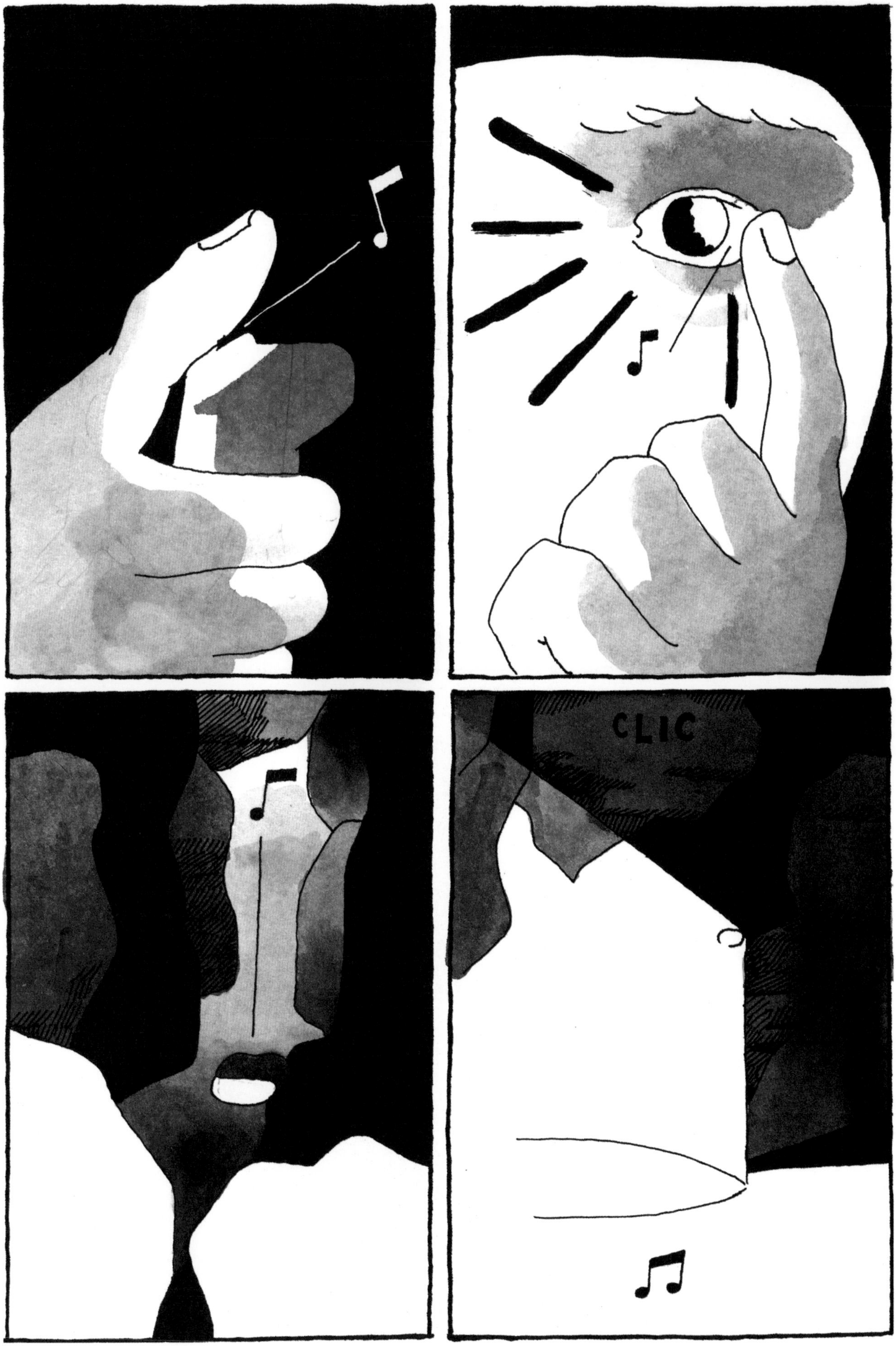
CLIC

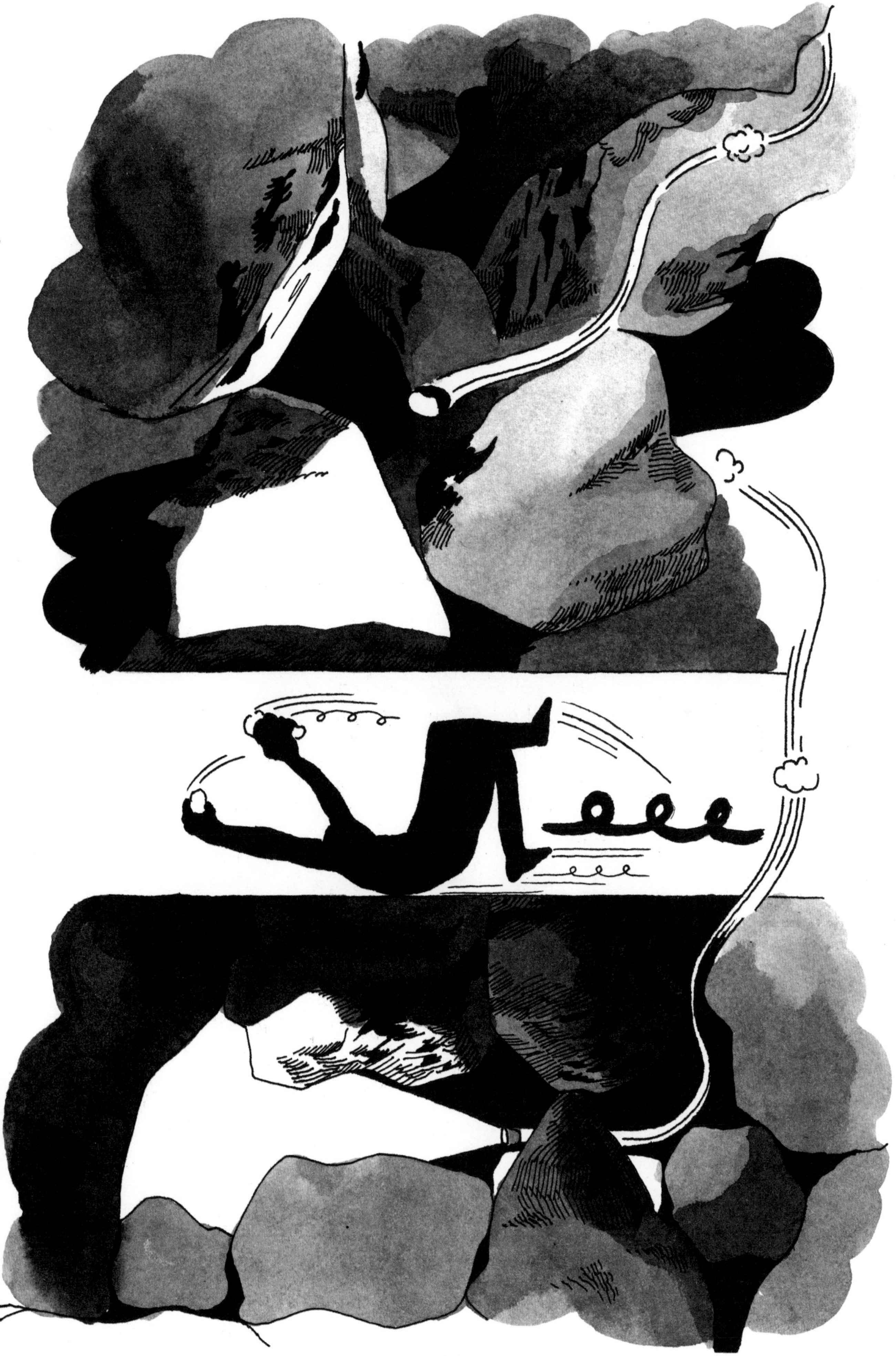

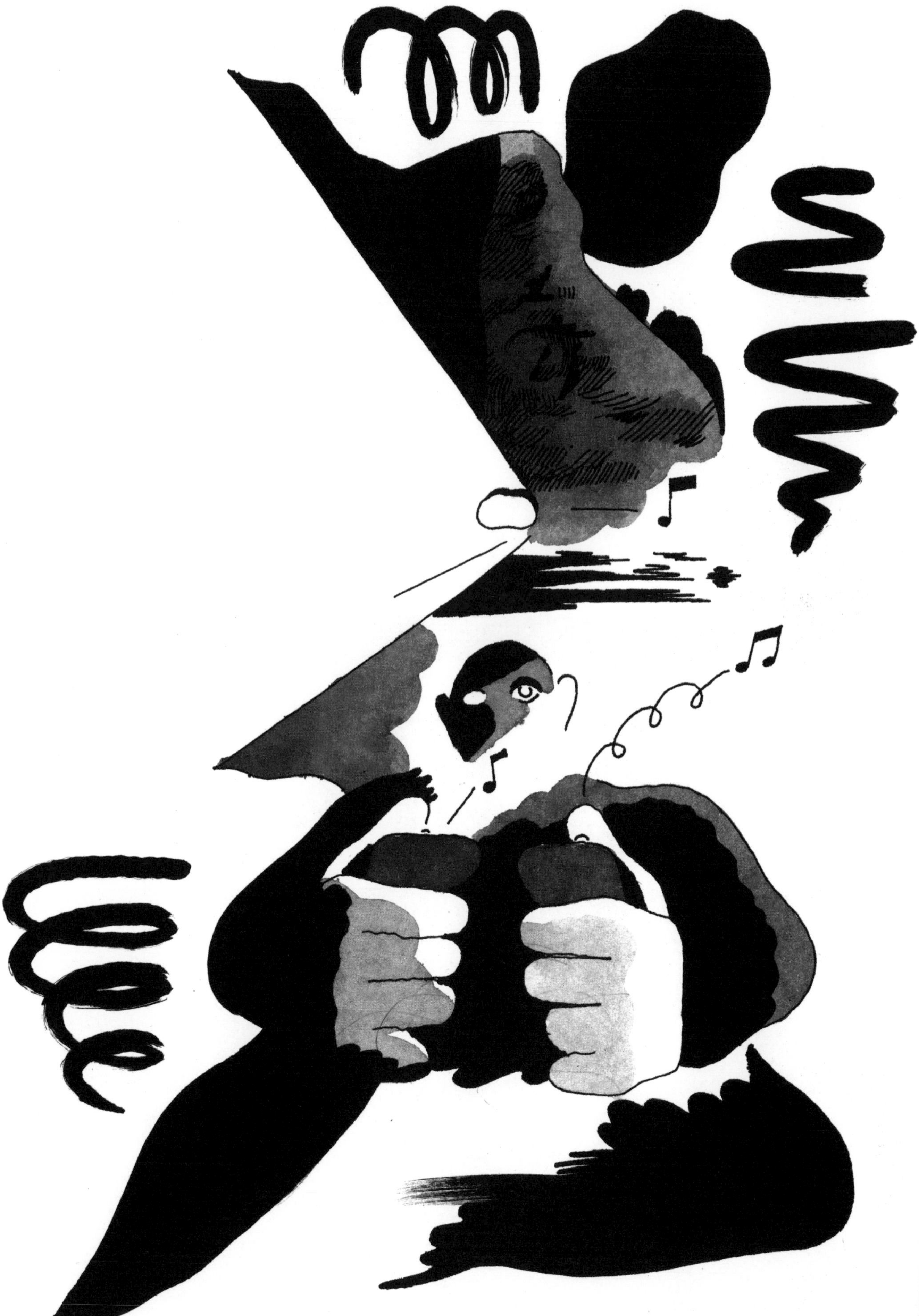

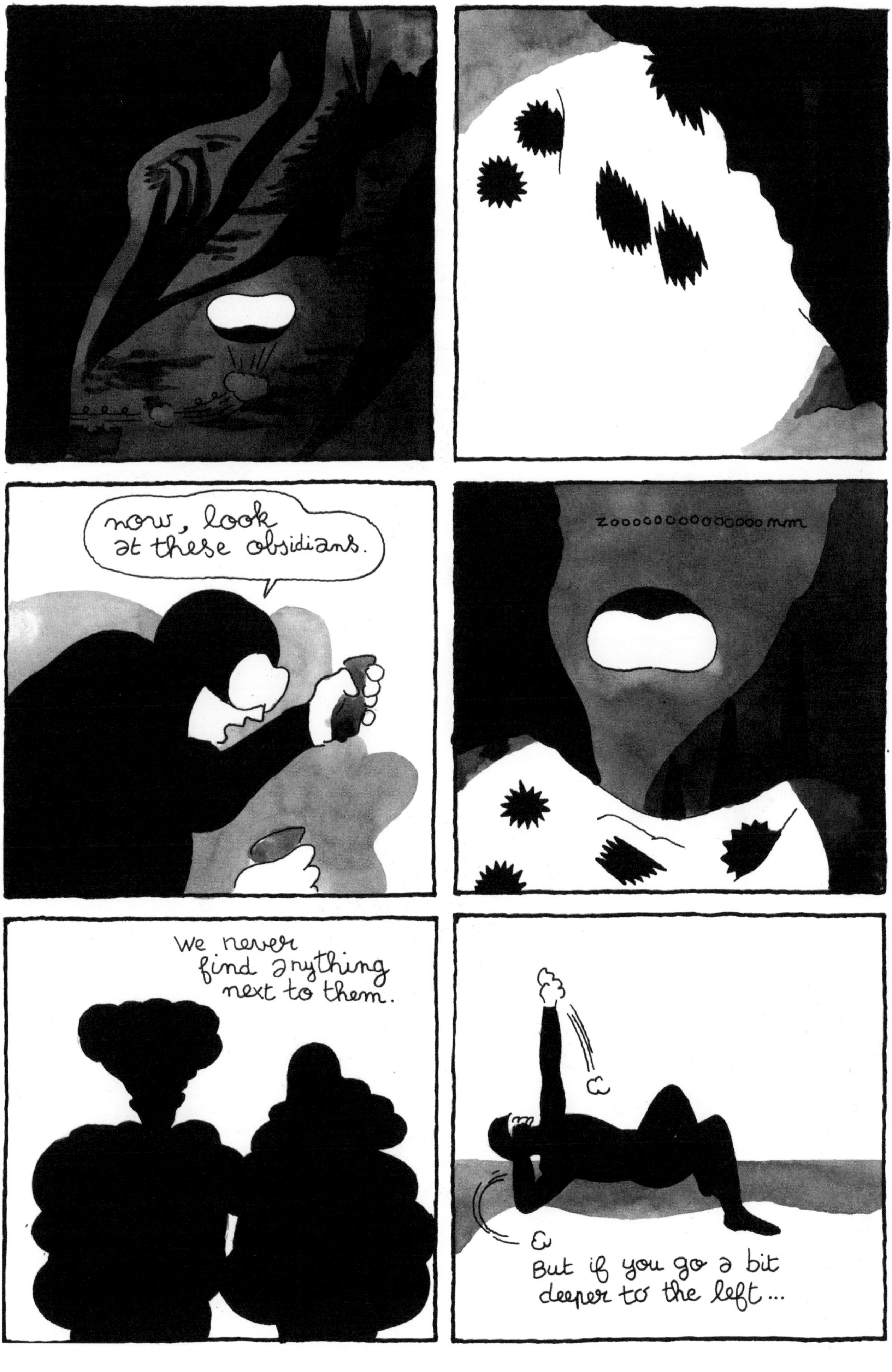
now, look at these obsidians.
Zoooooooooooooomm
We never find anything next to them.
But if you go a bit deeper to the left...

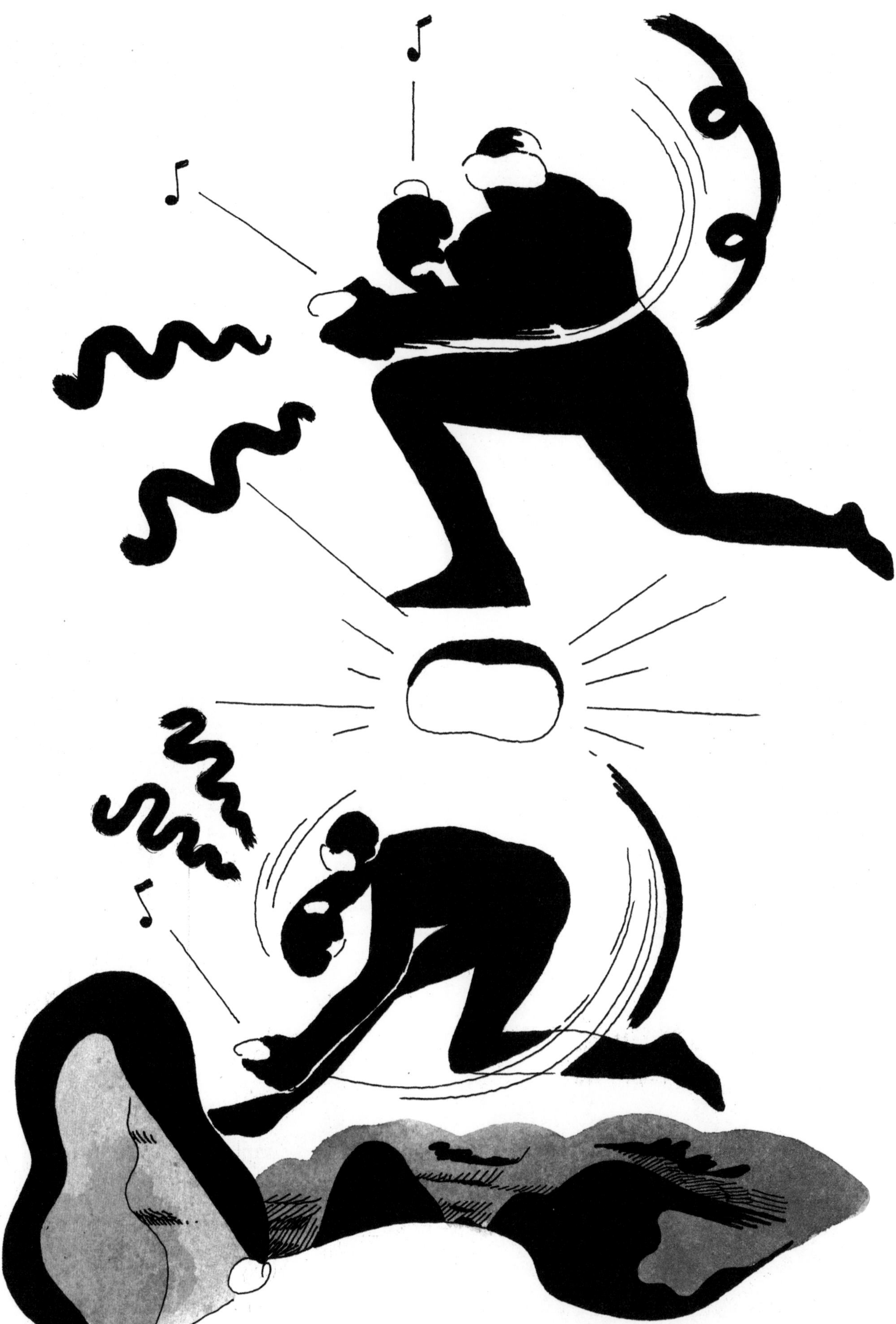

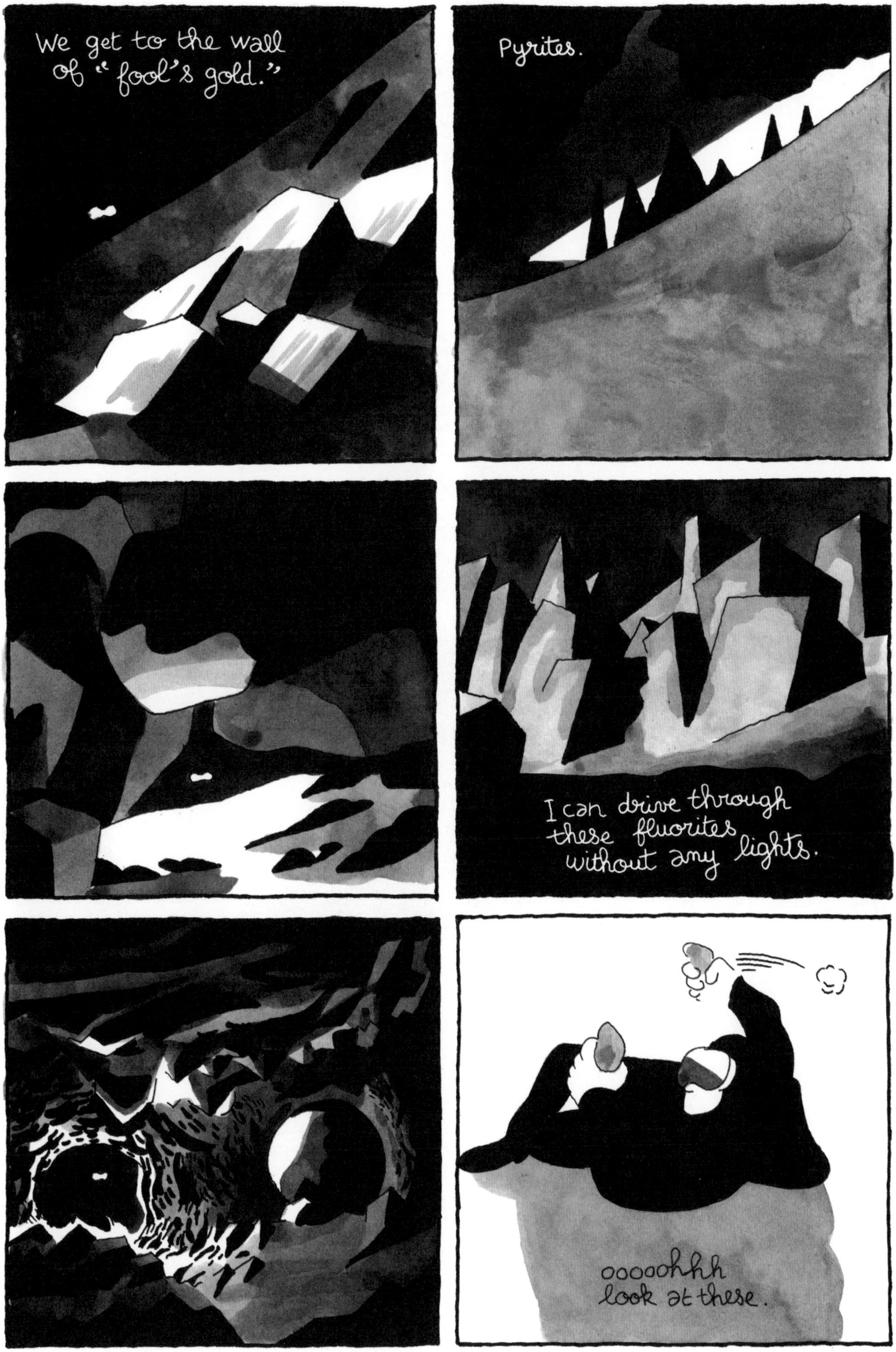
We get to the wall of "fool's gold."
Pyrites.
I can drive through these fluorites without any lights.
oooooohhh look at these.

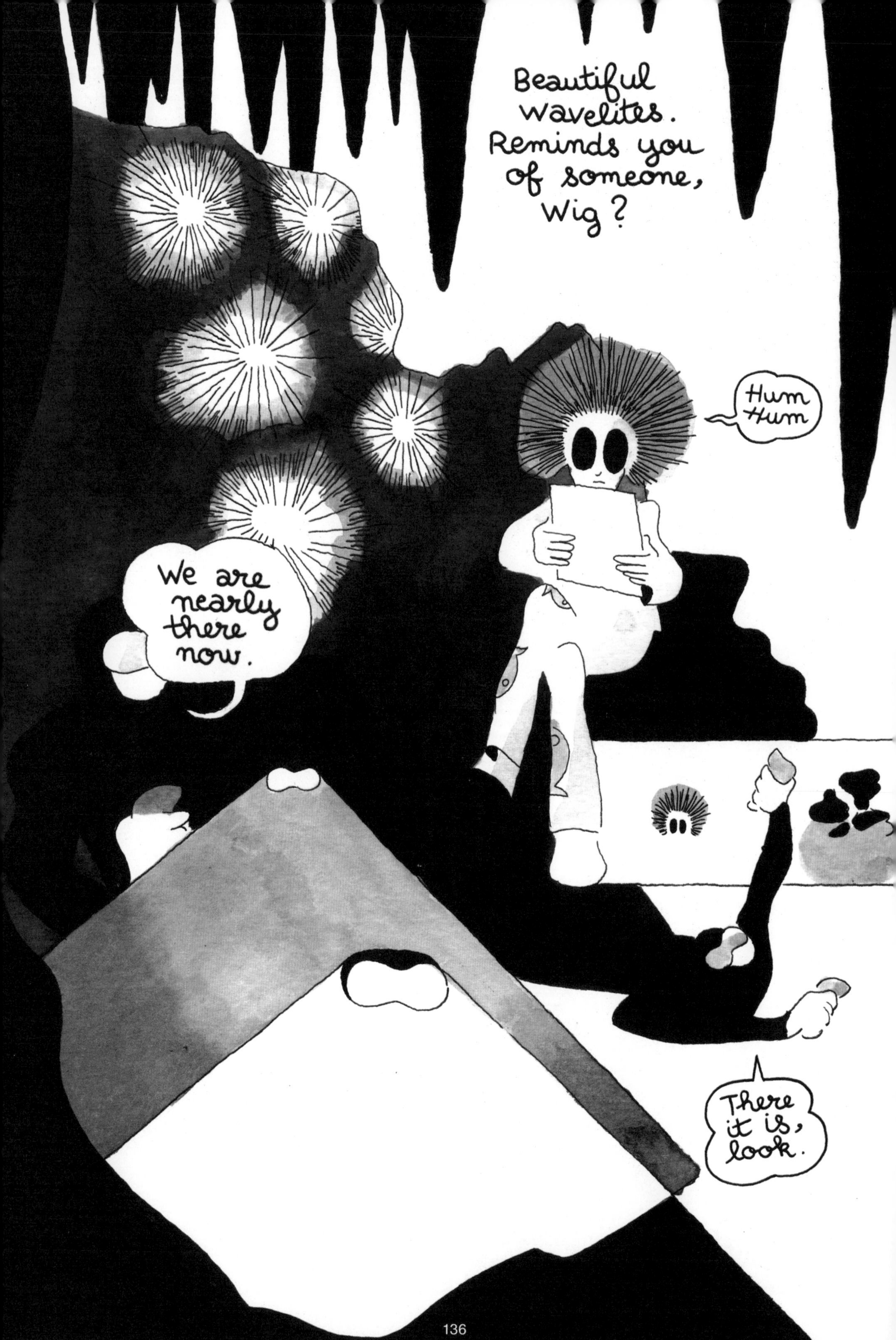
Beautiful wavelites. Reminds you of someone, Wig?
Hum Hum
We are nearly there now.
There it is, look.

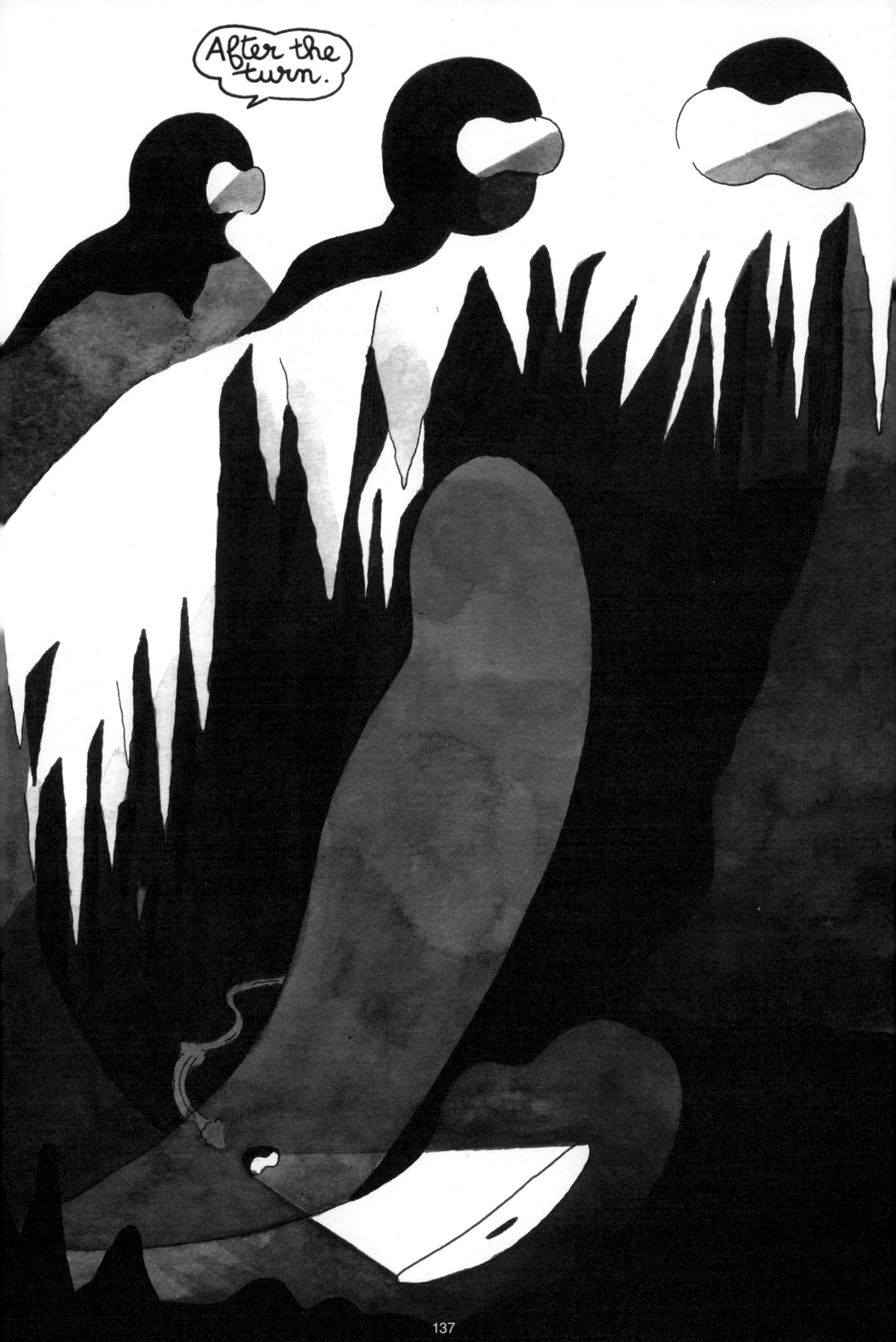
After the turn.

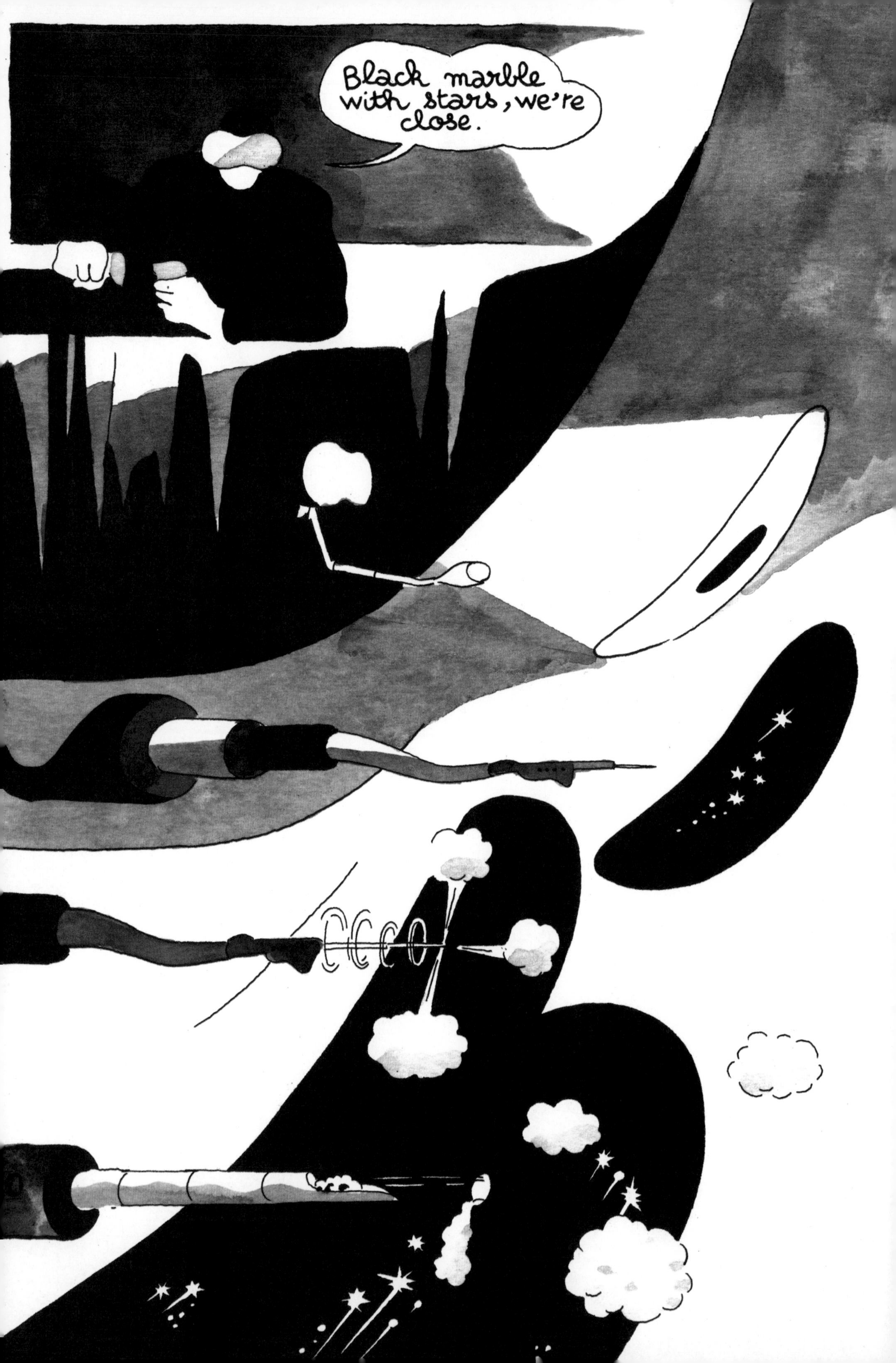
Black marble with stars, we're close.

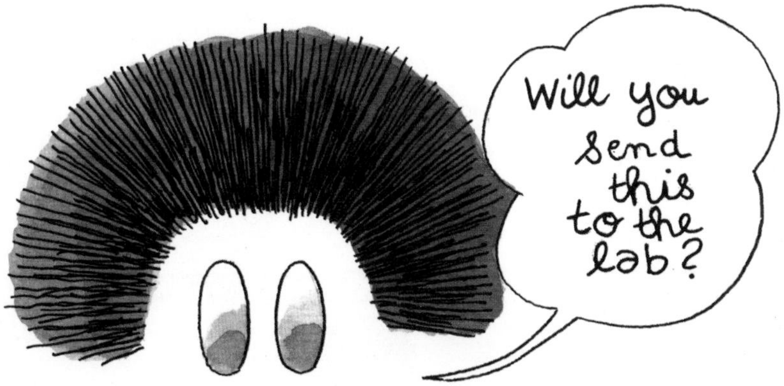
Will you send this to the lab?

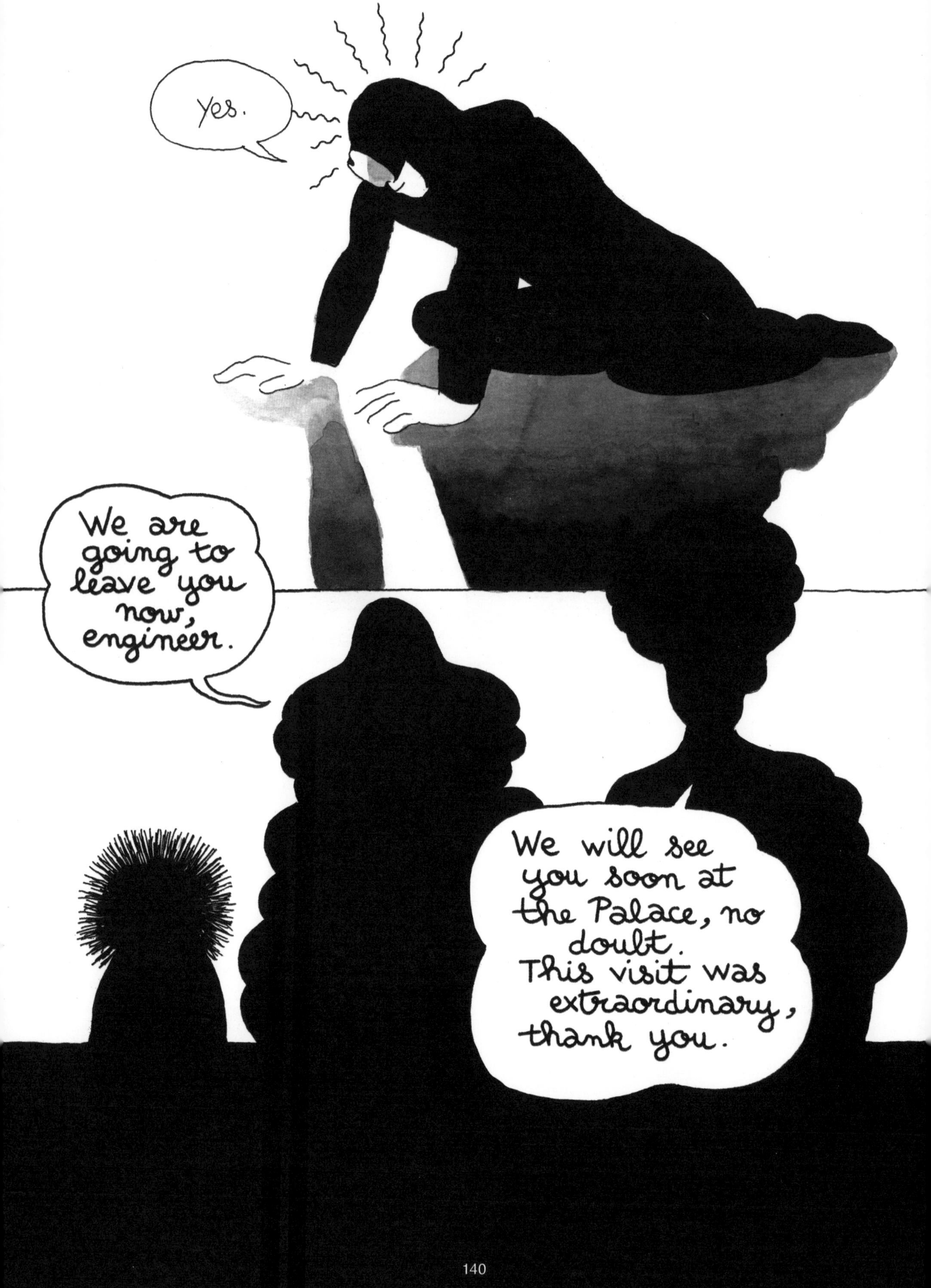
Yes.
We are going to leave you now, engineer.
We will see you soon at the Palace, no doubt. This visit was extraordinary, thank you.

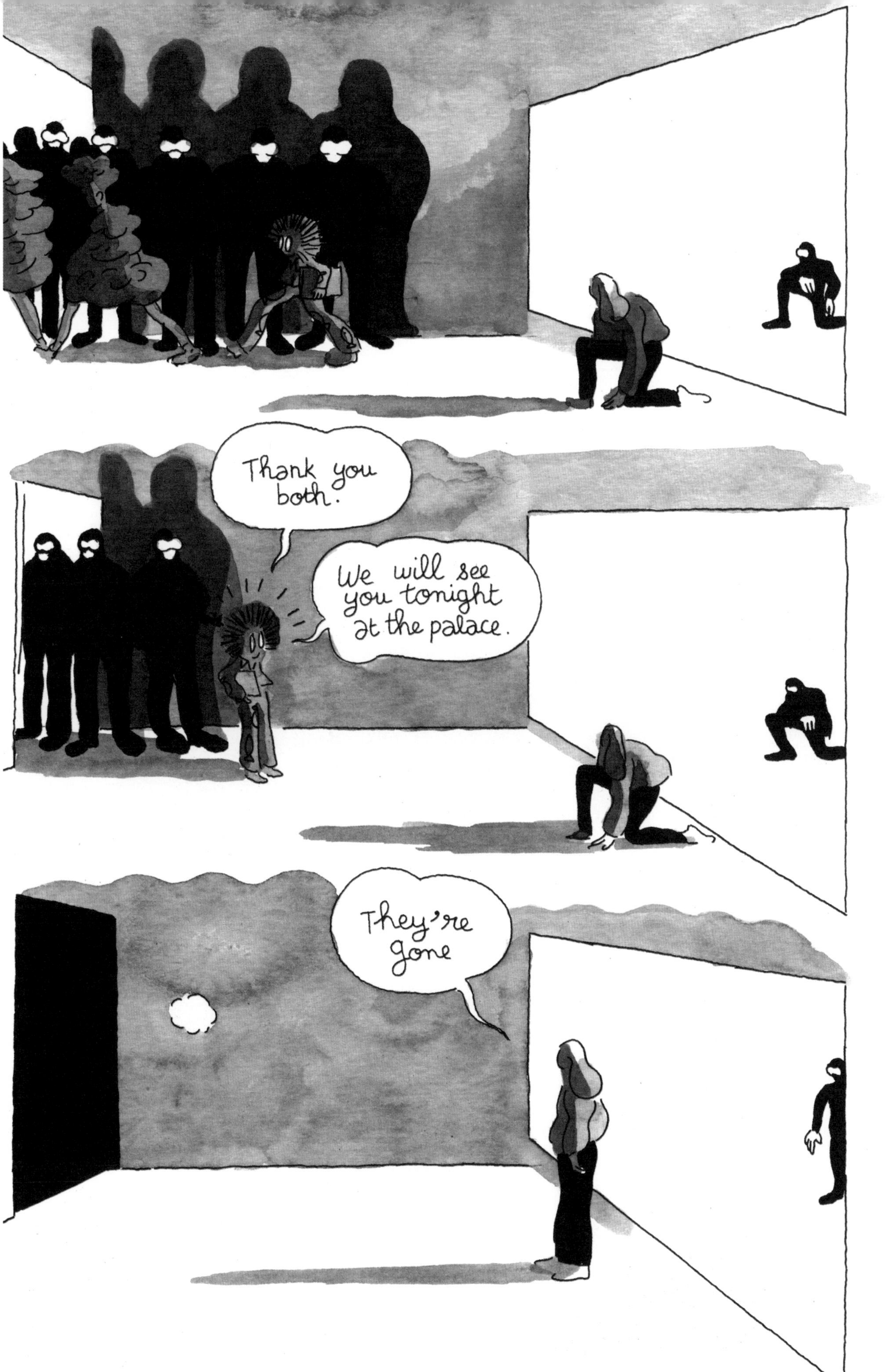
Thank you both.
We will see you tonight at the palace.
They're gone

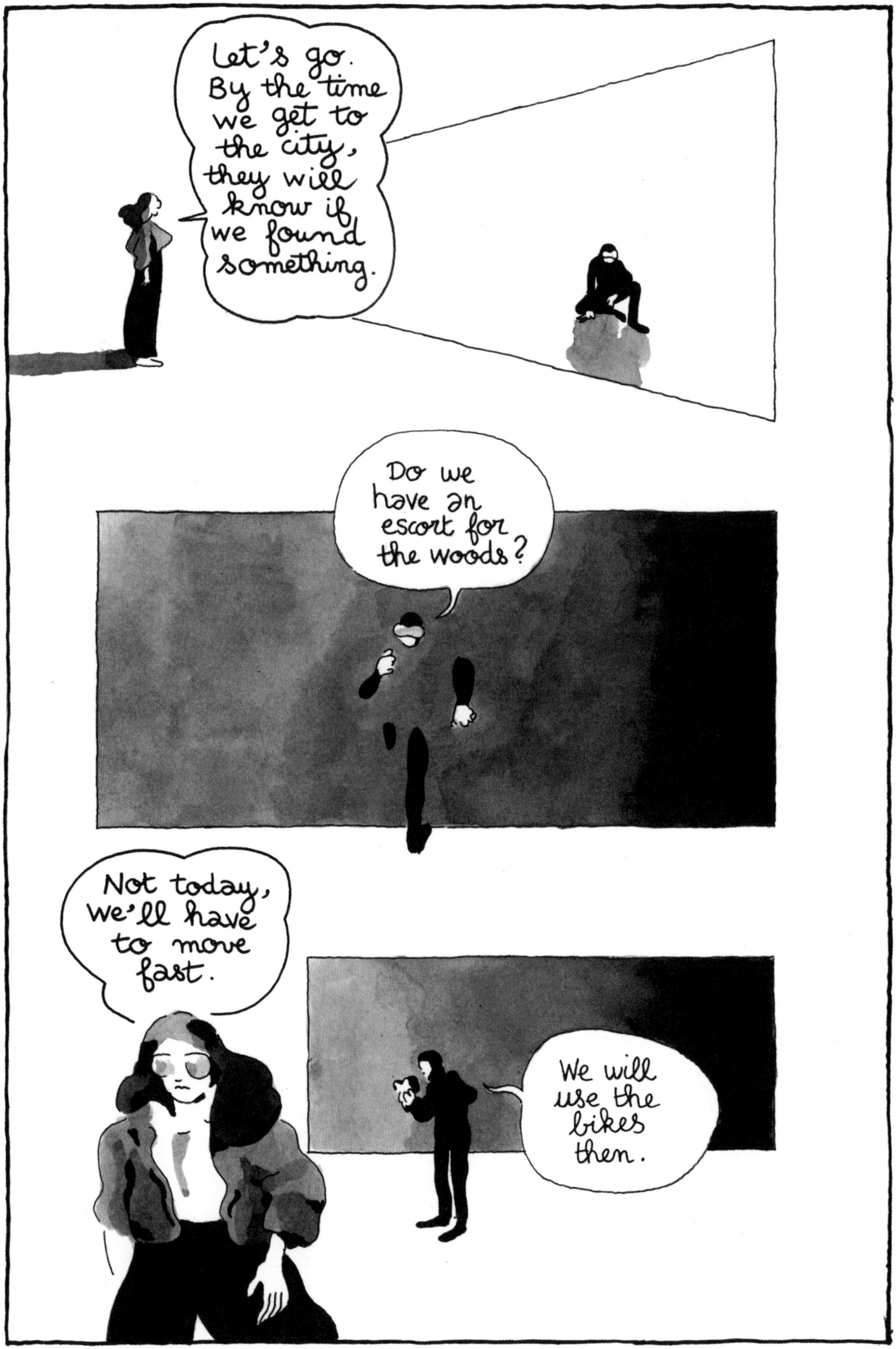
Let's go. By the time we get to the city, they will know if we found something.
Do we have an escort for the woods?
Not today, we'll have to move fast.
We will use the bikes then.

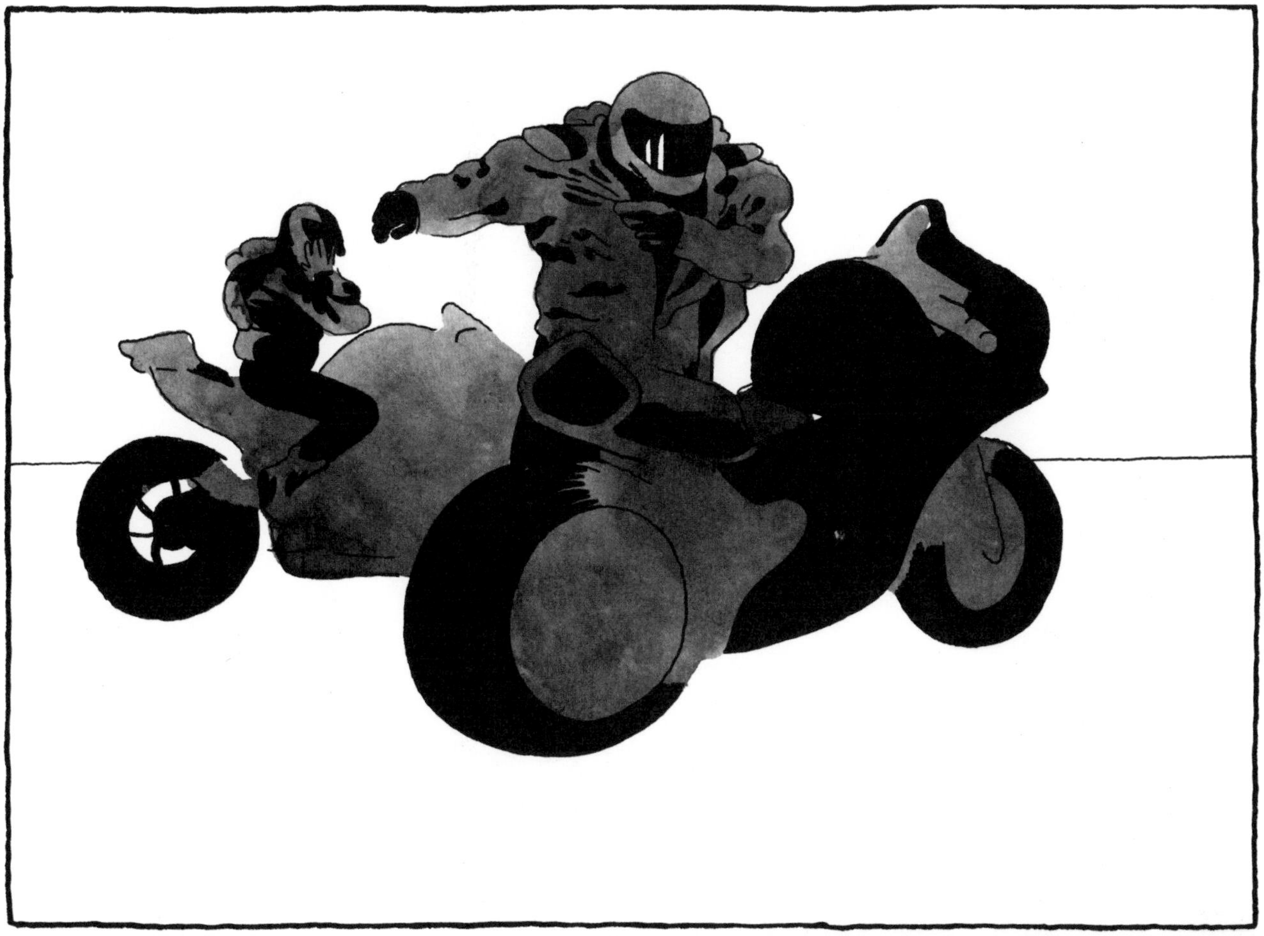

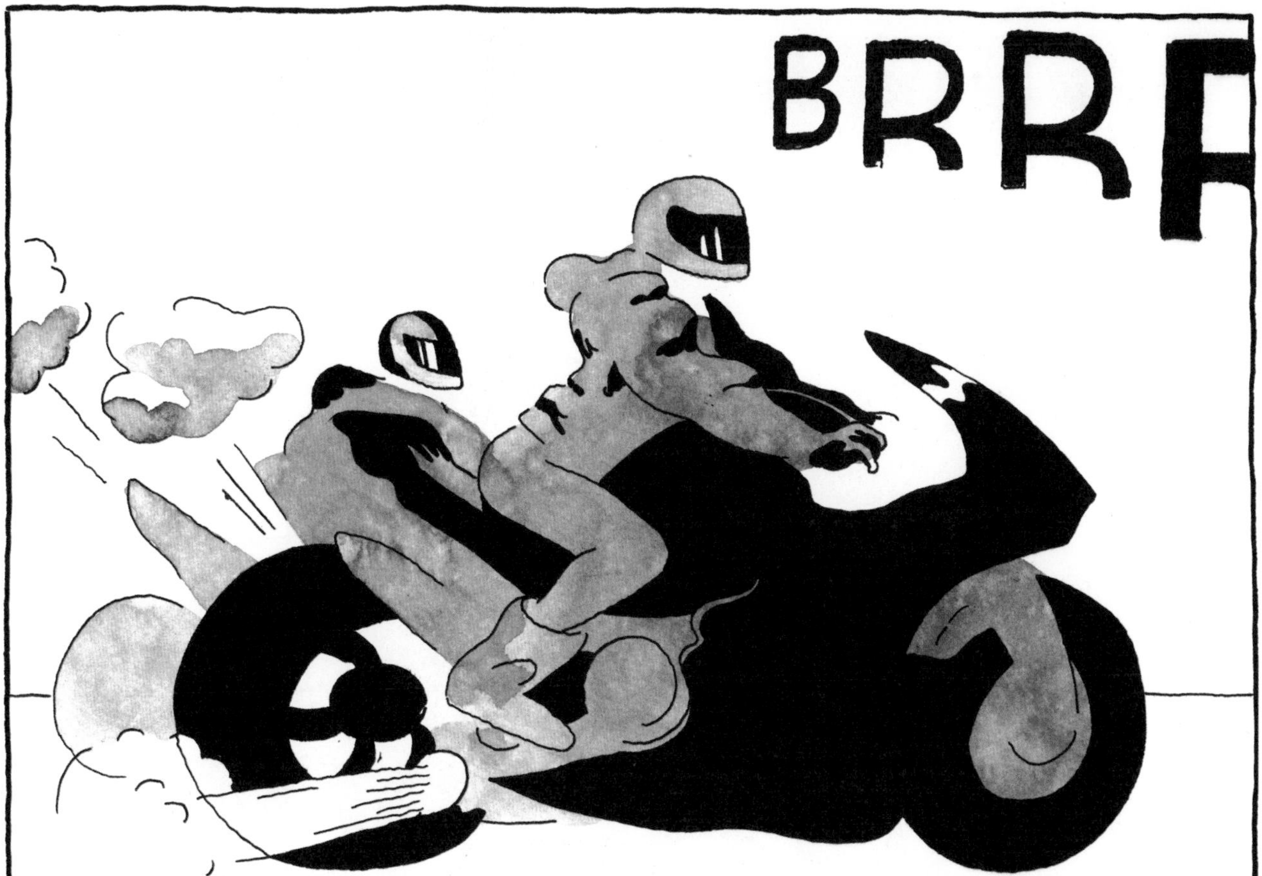
BRRR

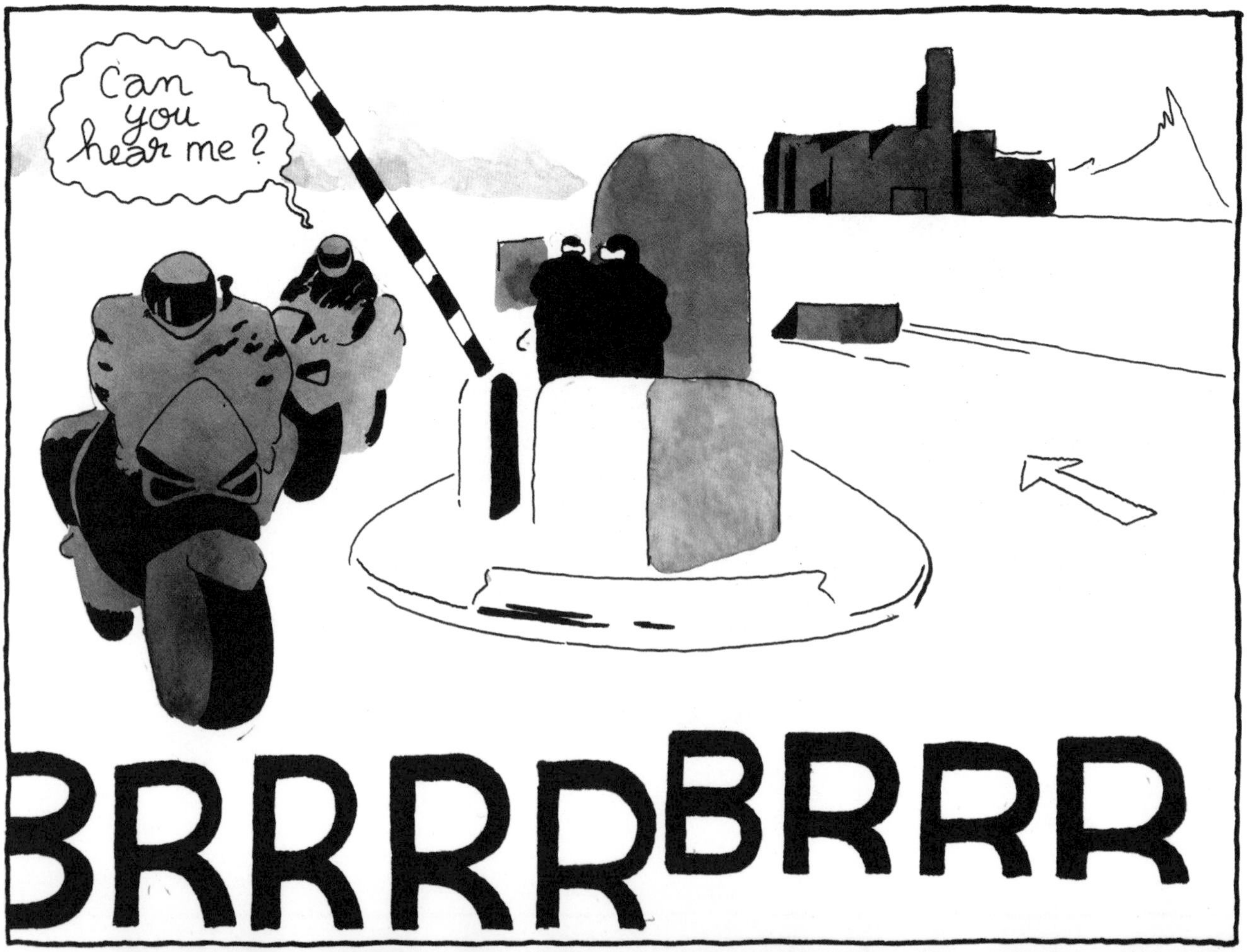
Can you hear me?
BRRRRBRRRR

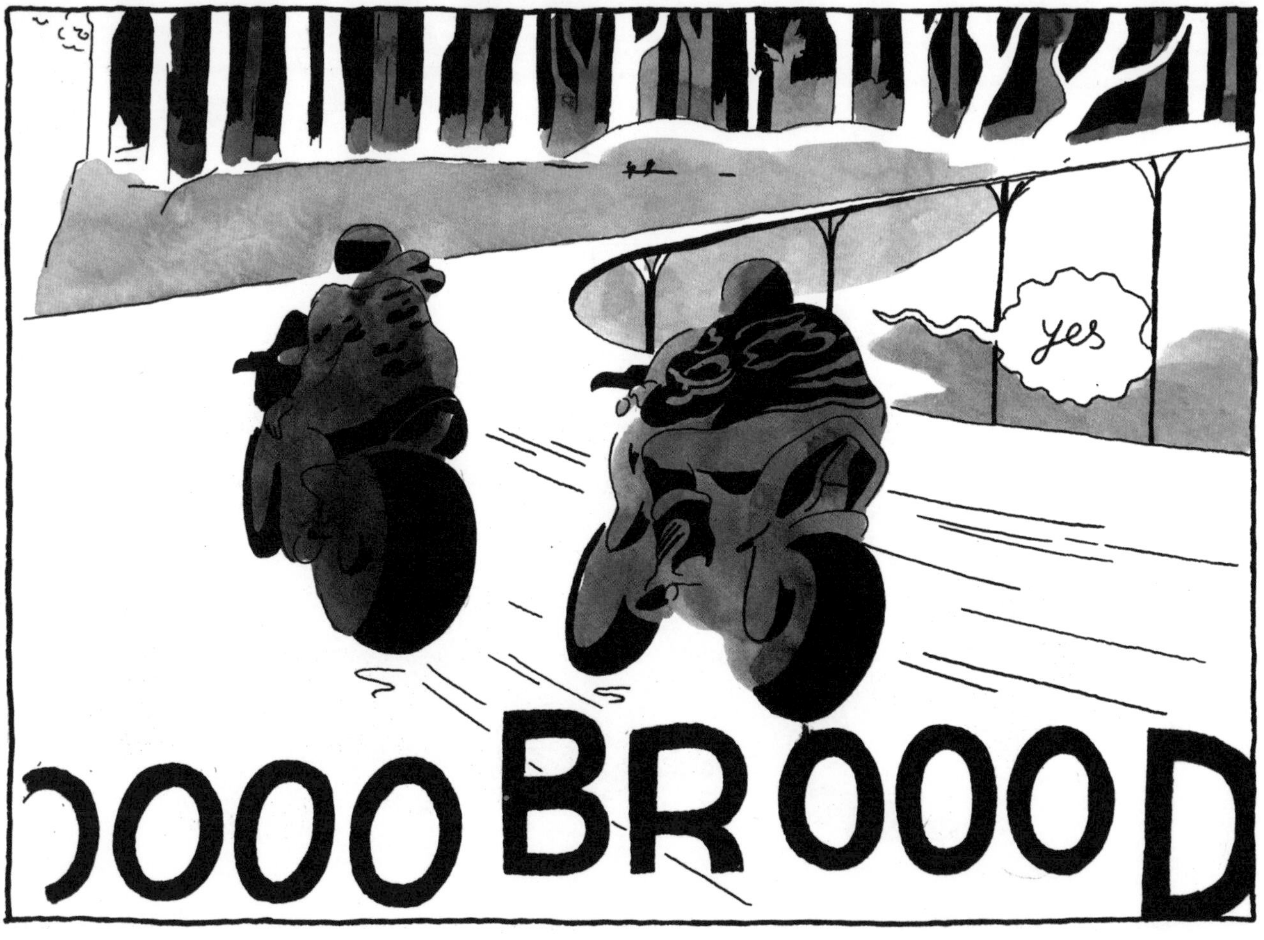
yes
OOOOBROOOD

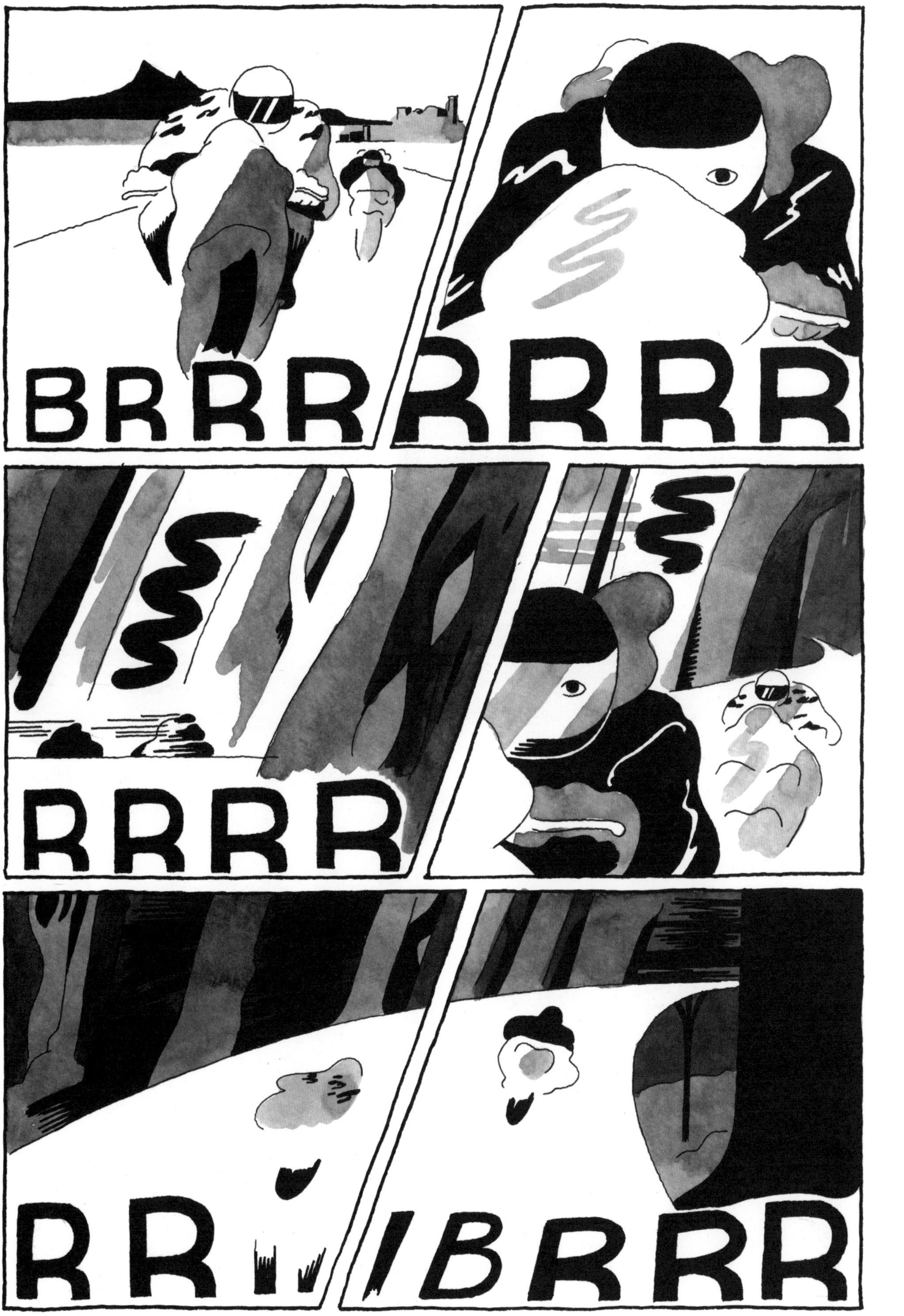
BRRR
RRRR
RRRR
RR
BRRR

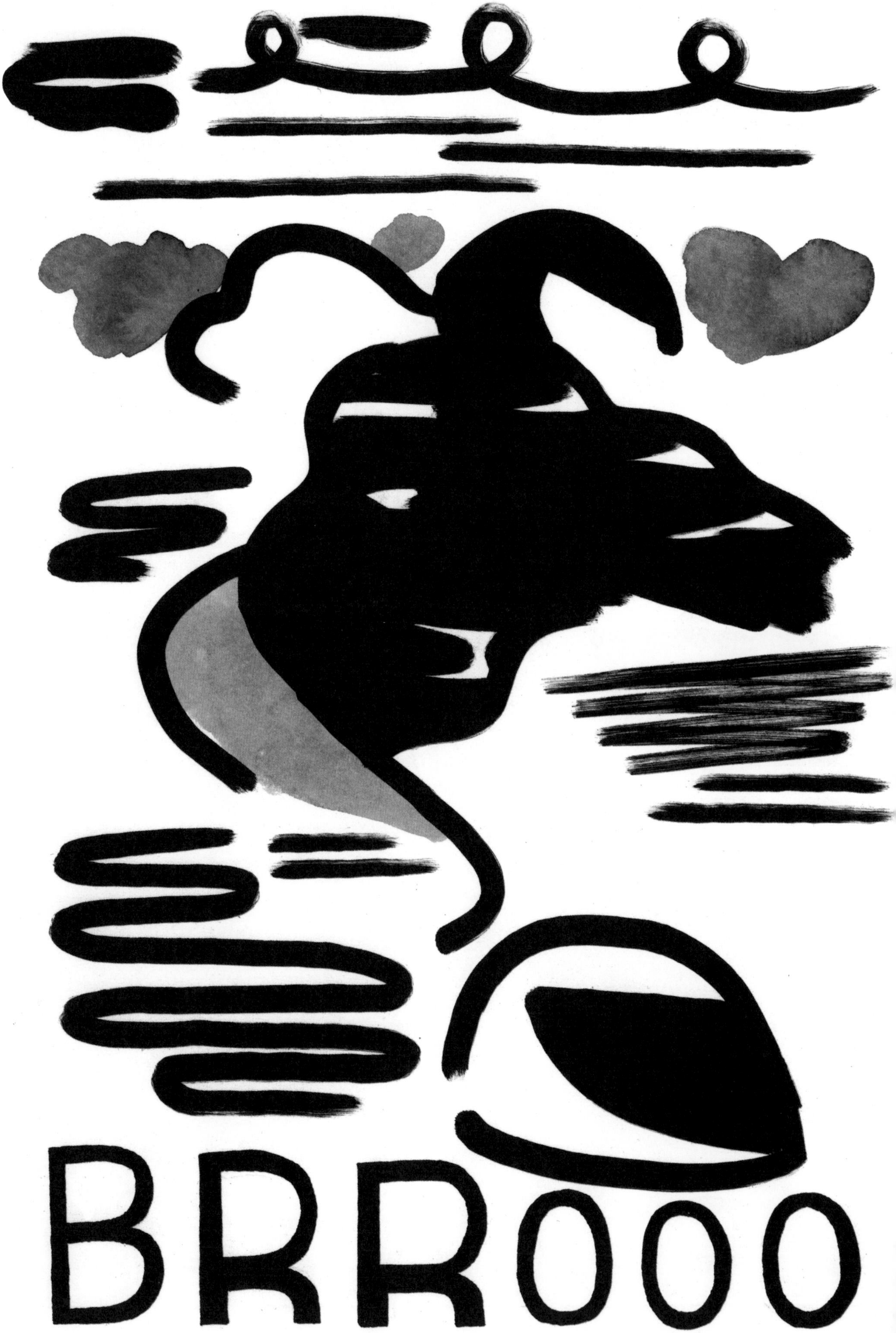
BRROOO

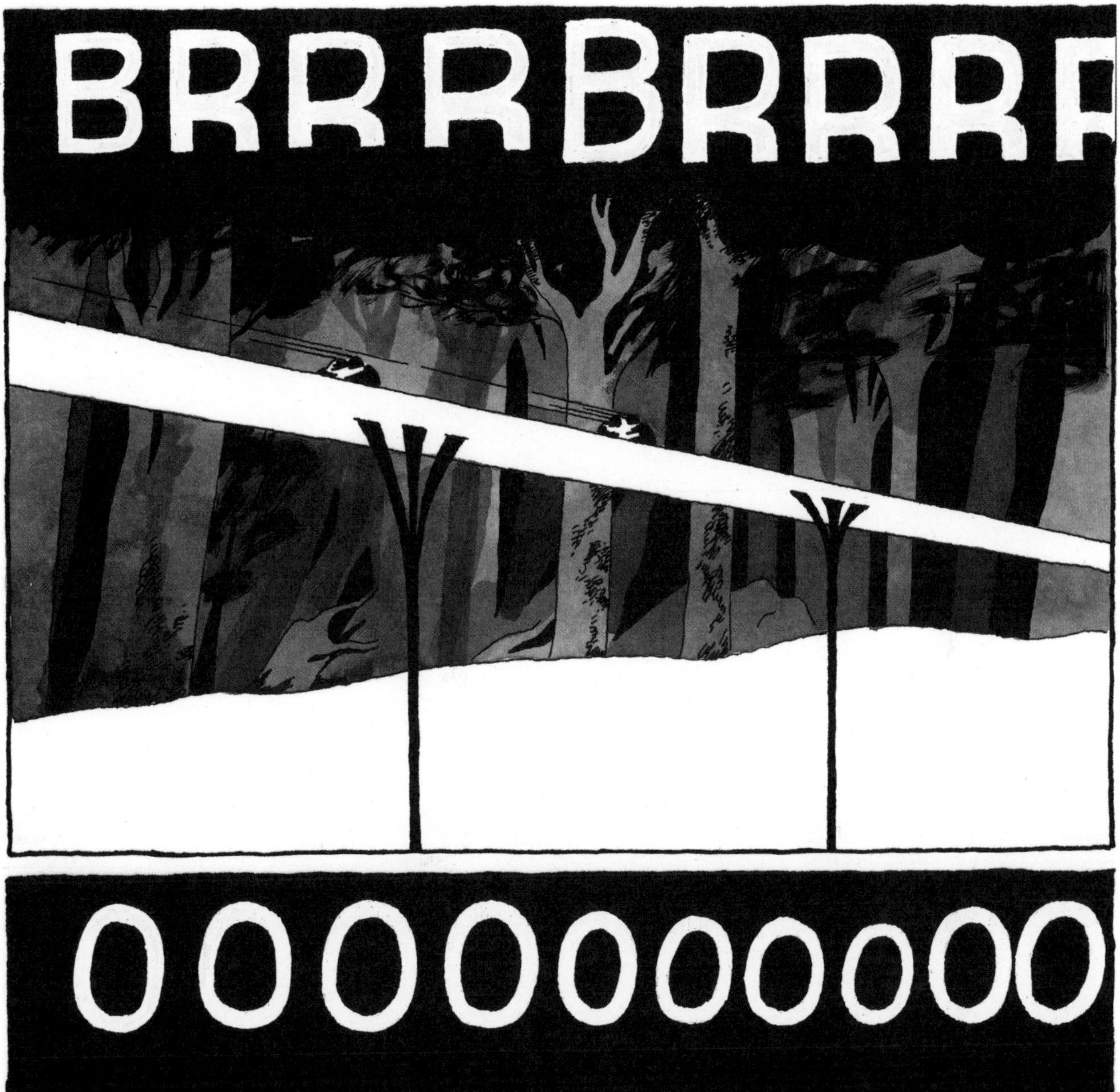
BRRRBRRRR

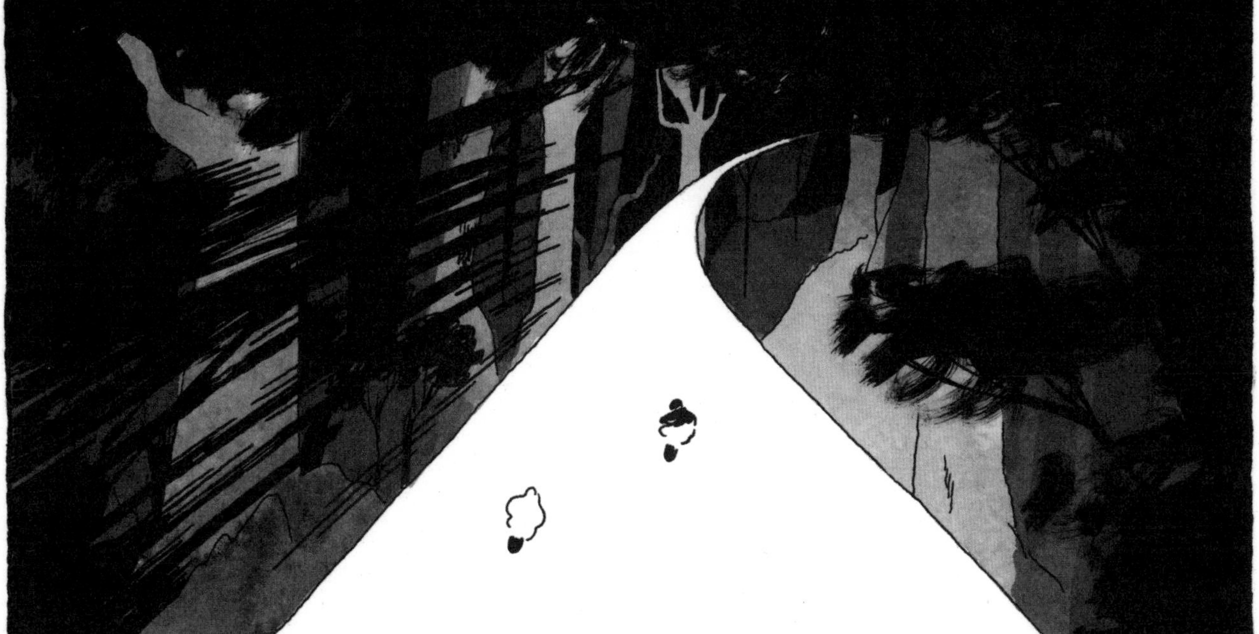
OOOOOOOOOO

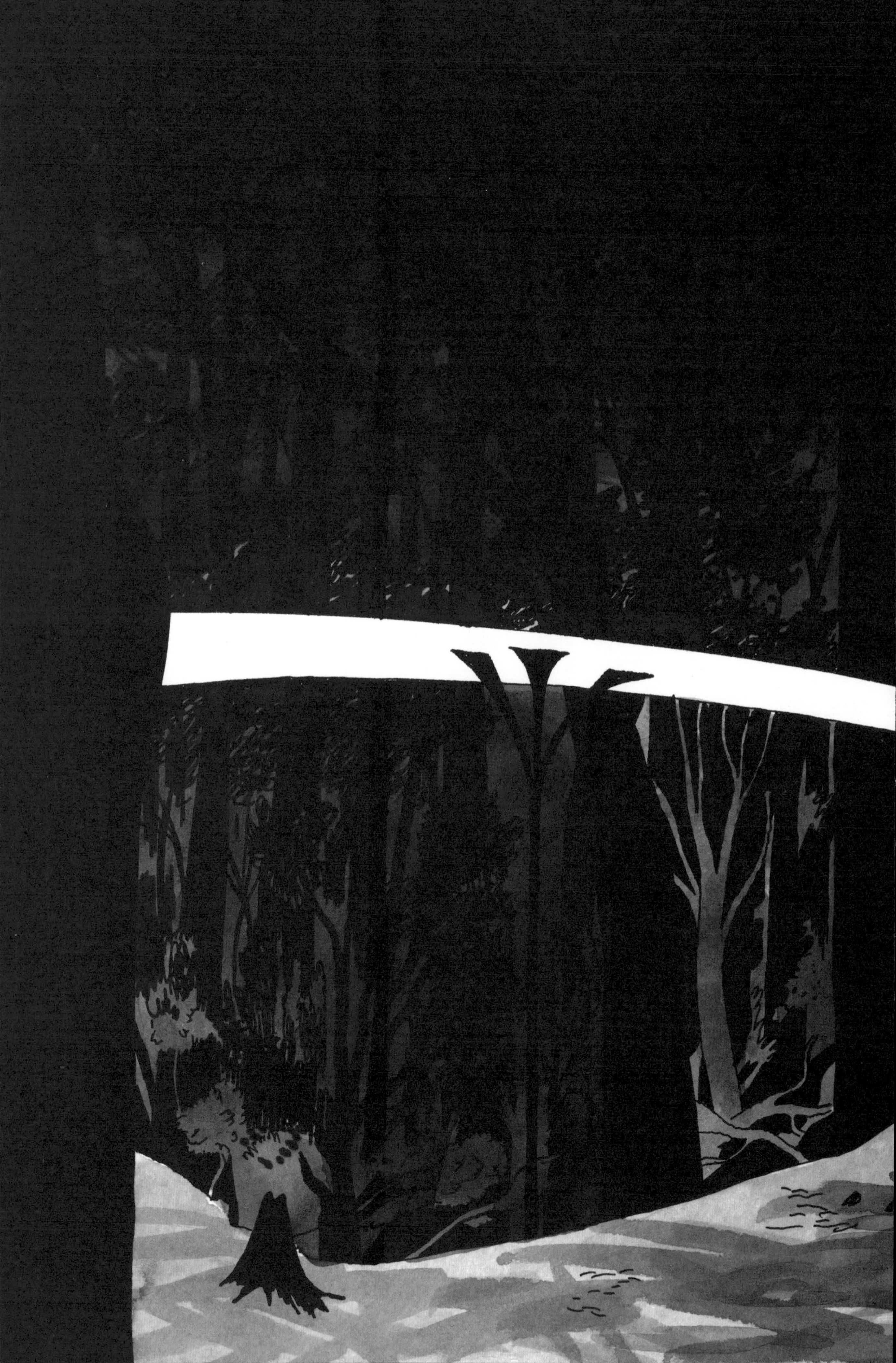

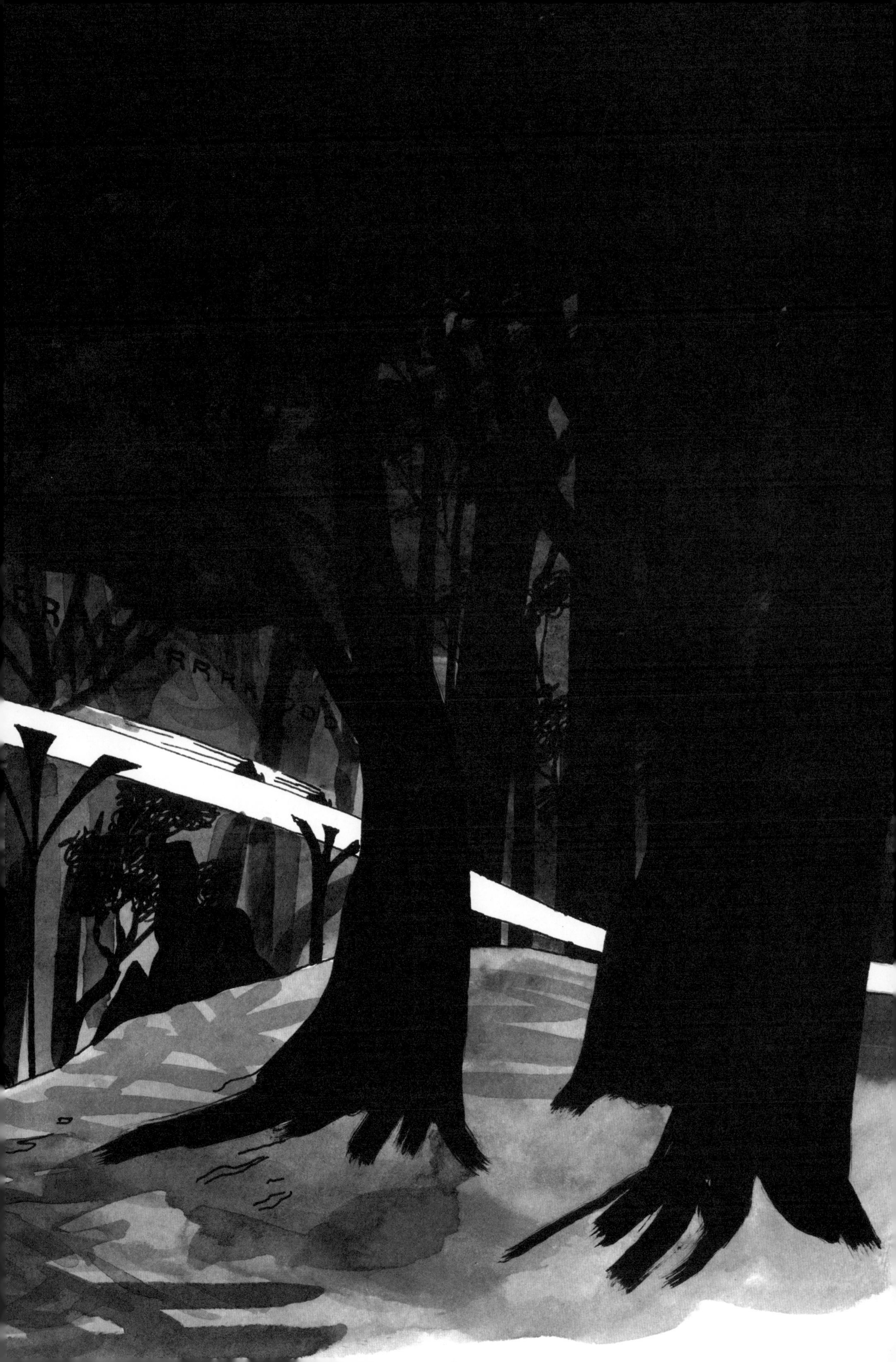

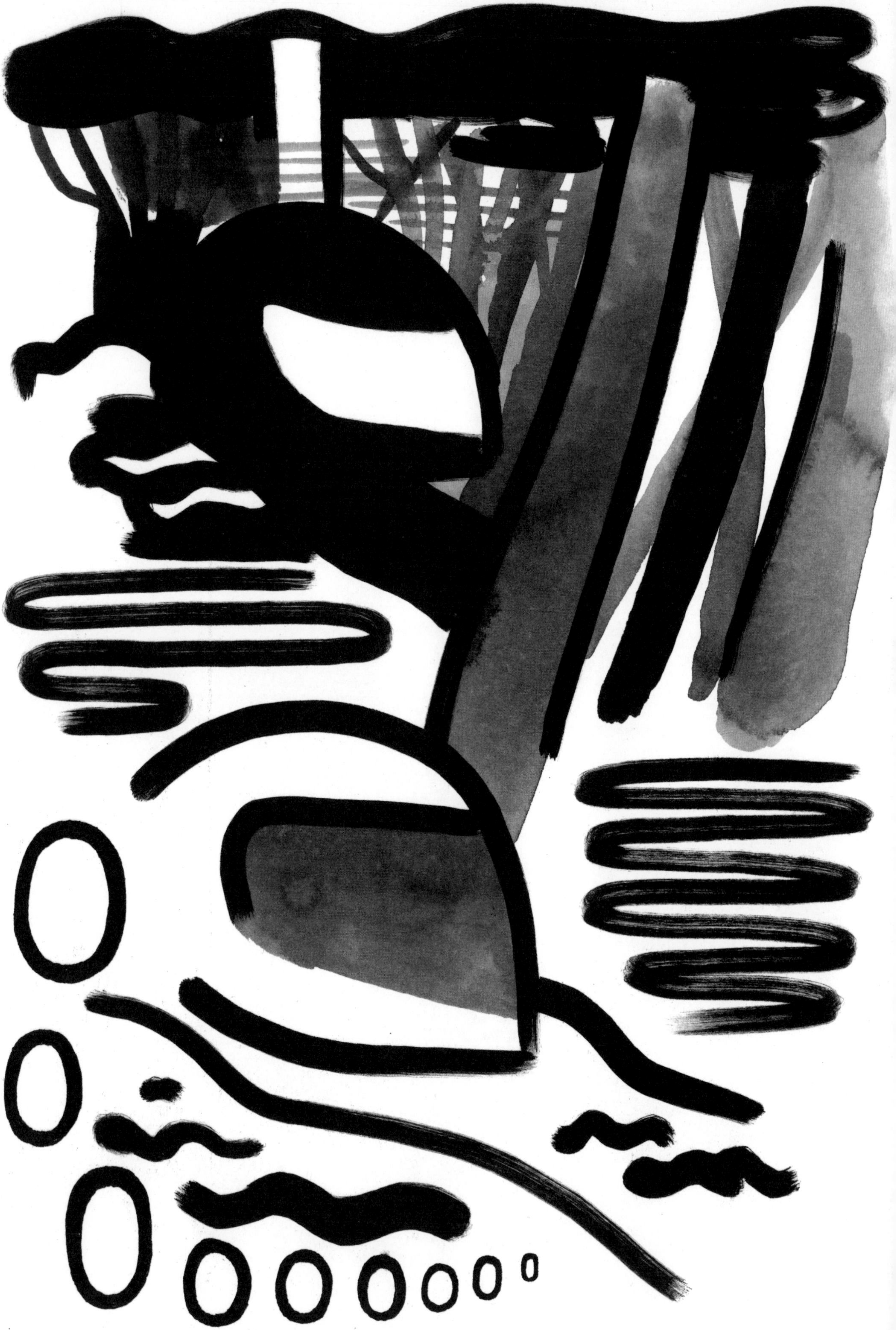

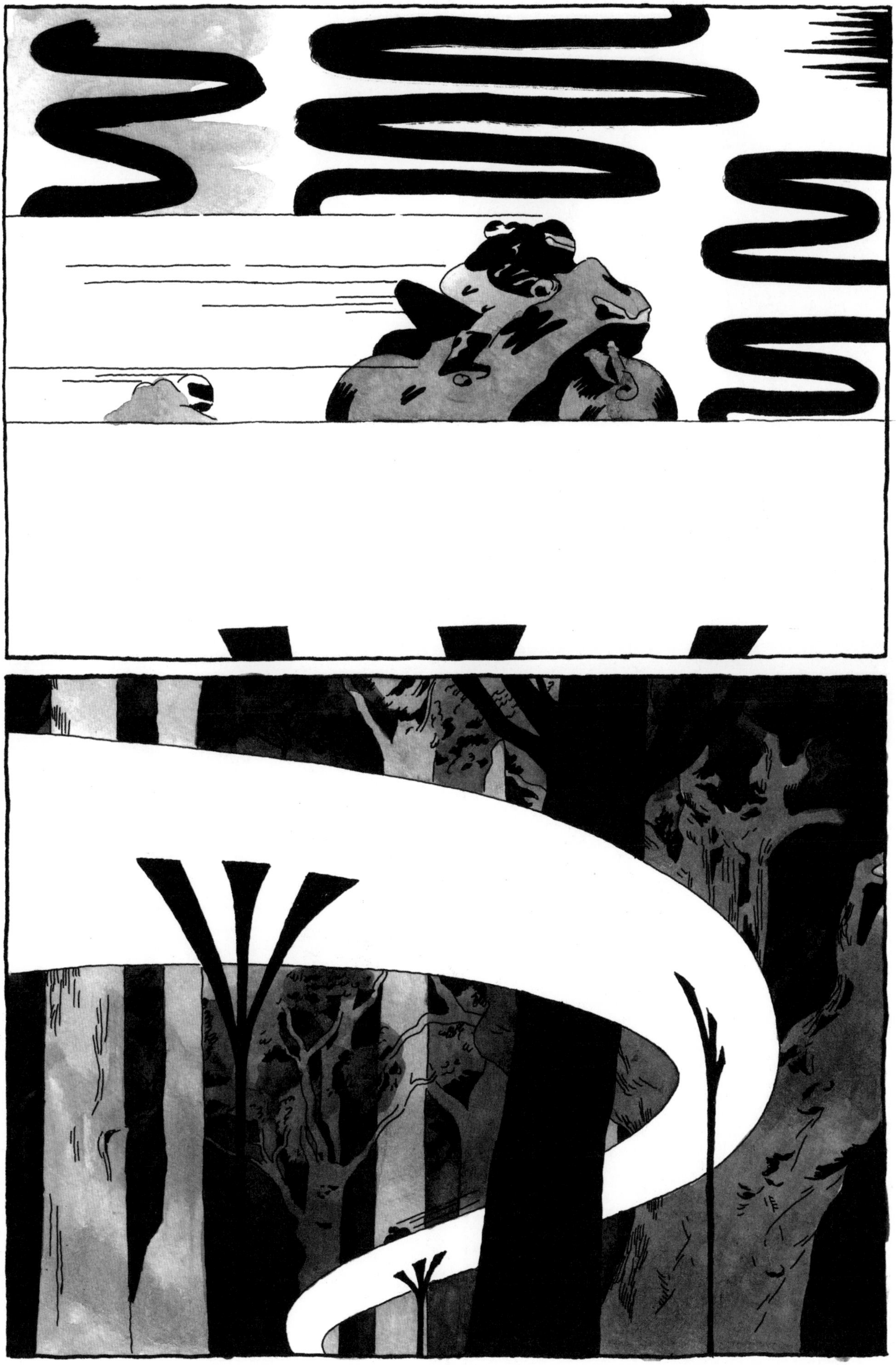

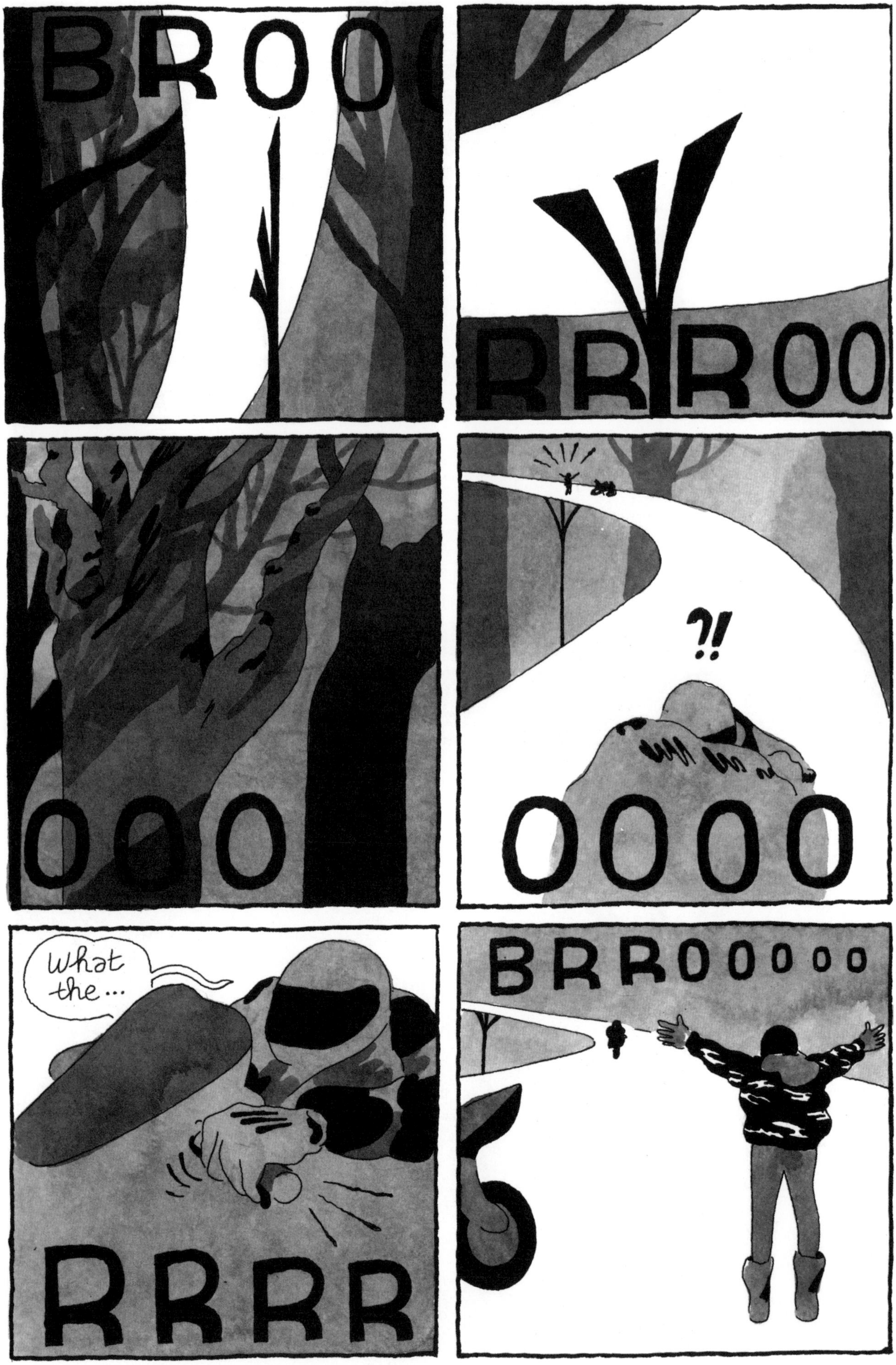

BROO
RRRROO
OOO
?!
OOOO
What the...
RRRR
BRROOOOO

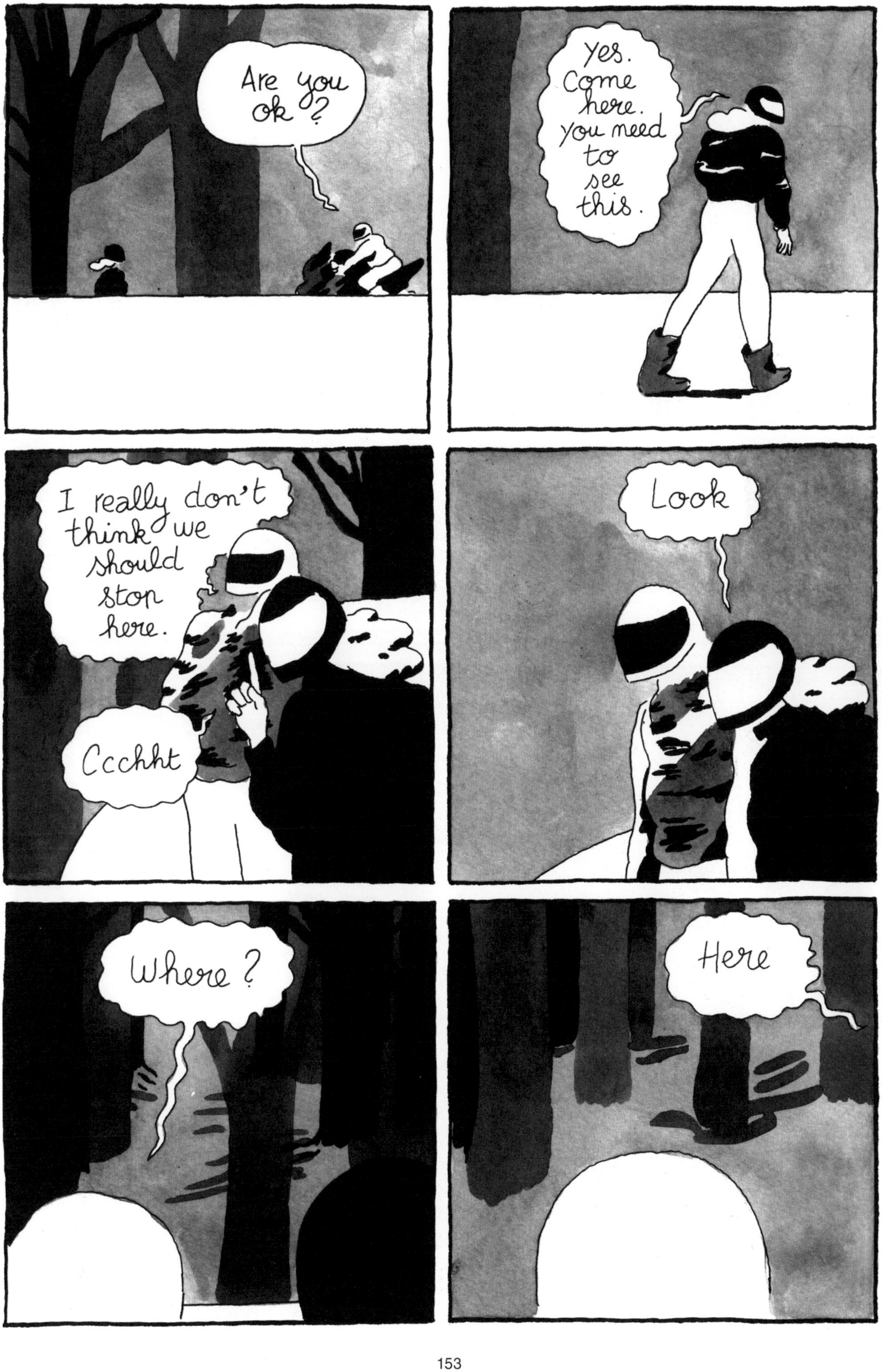
Are you ok?
Yes. Come here. You need to see this.
I really don't think we should stop here.
Ccchht
Look
Where?
Here

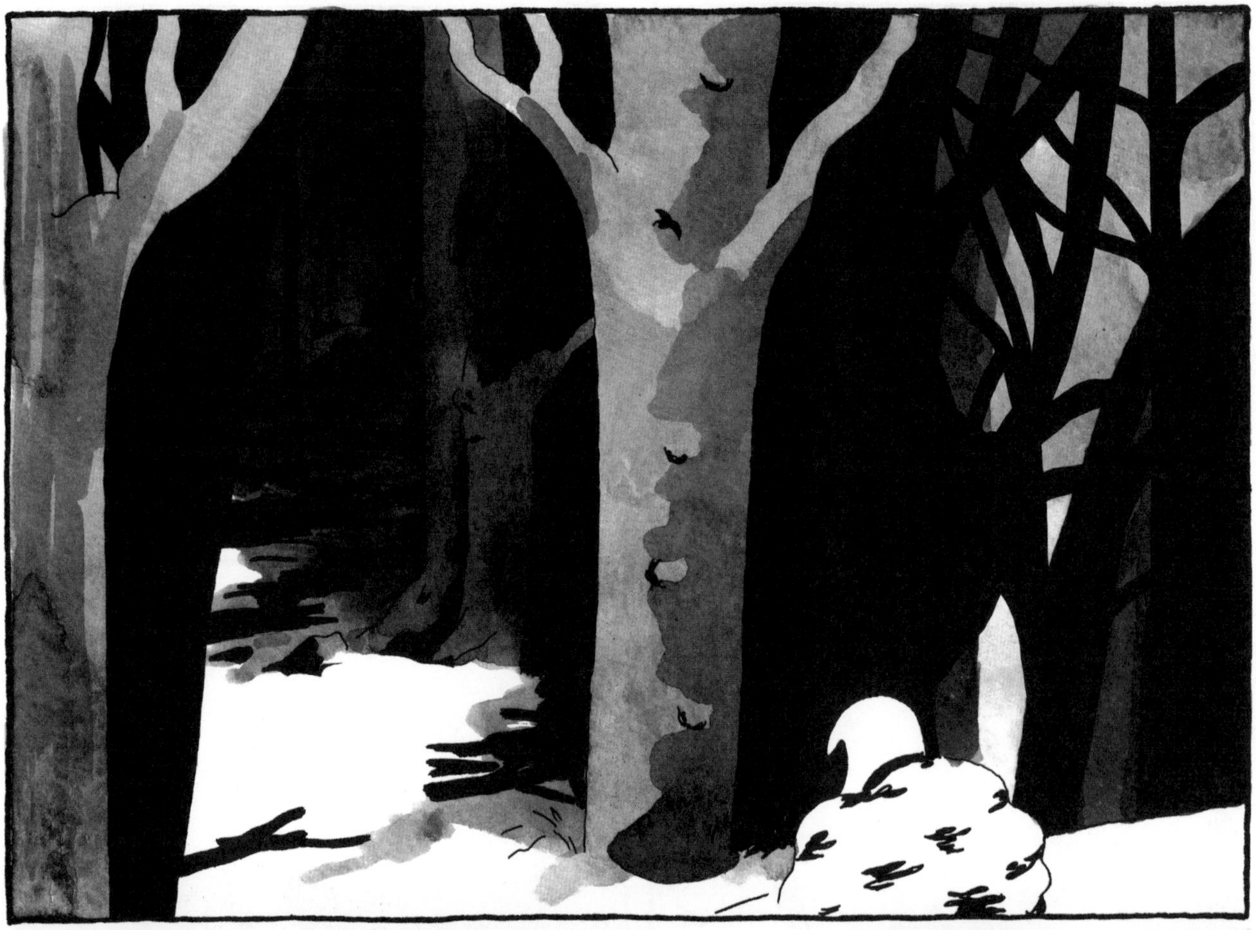

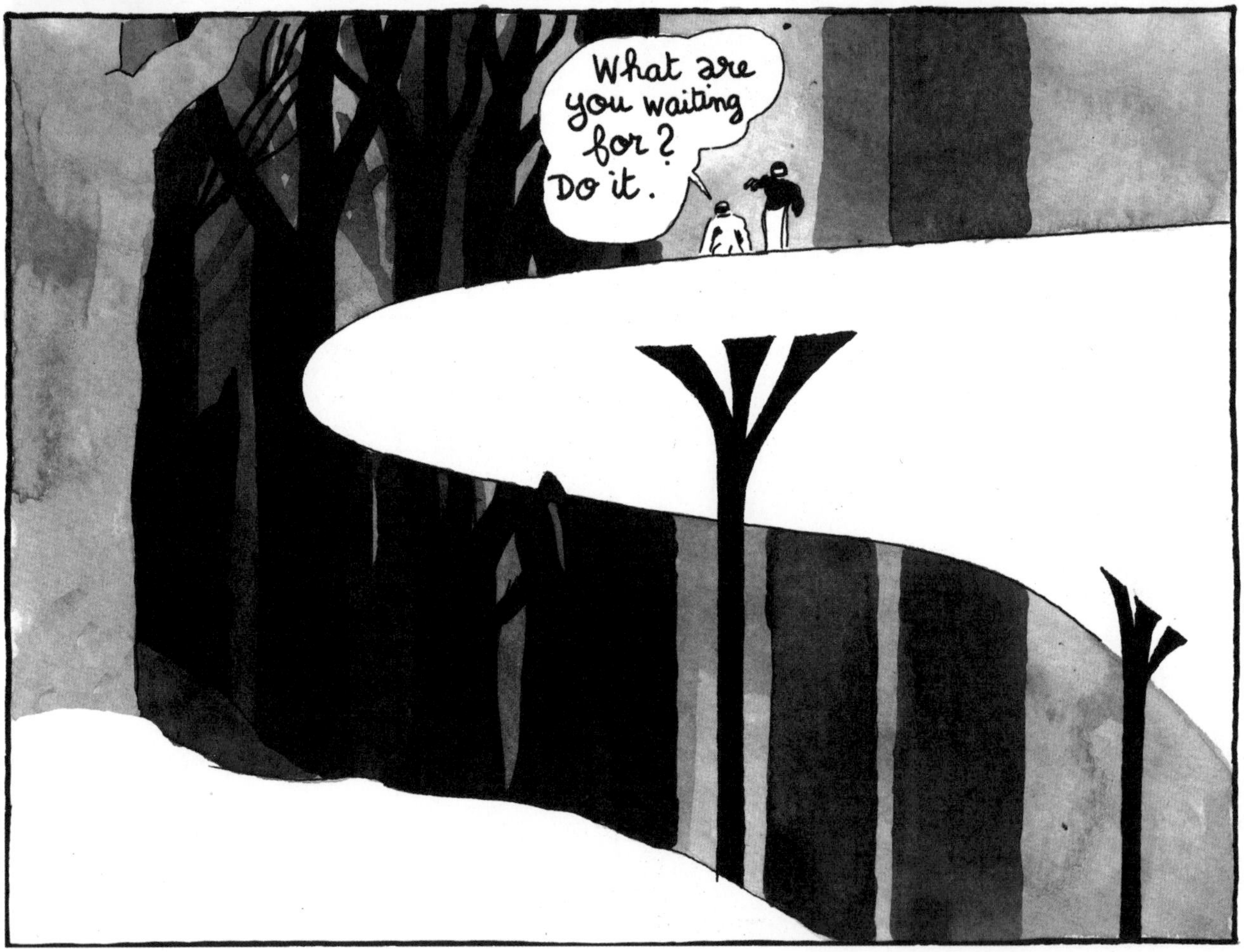
What are you waiting for? Do it.

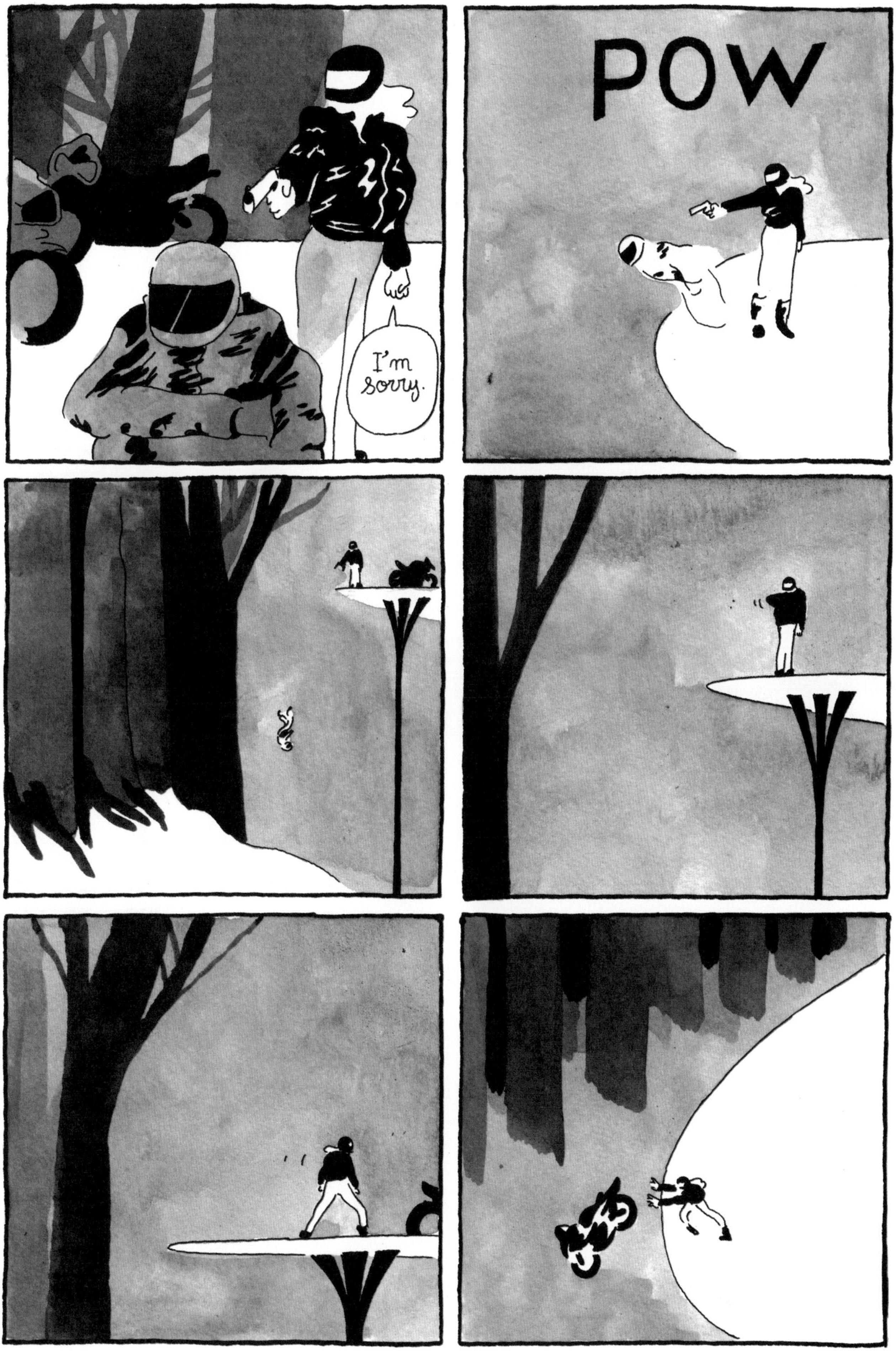
I'm sorry.
POW

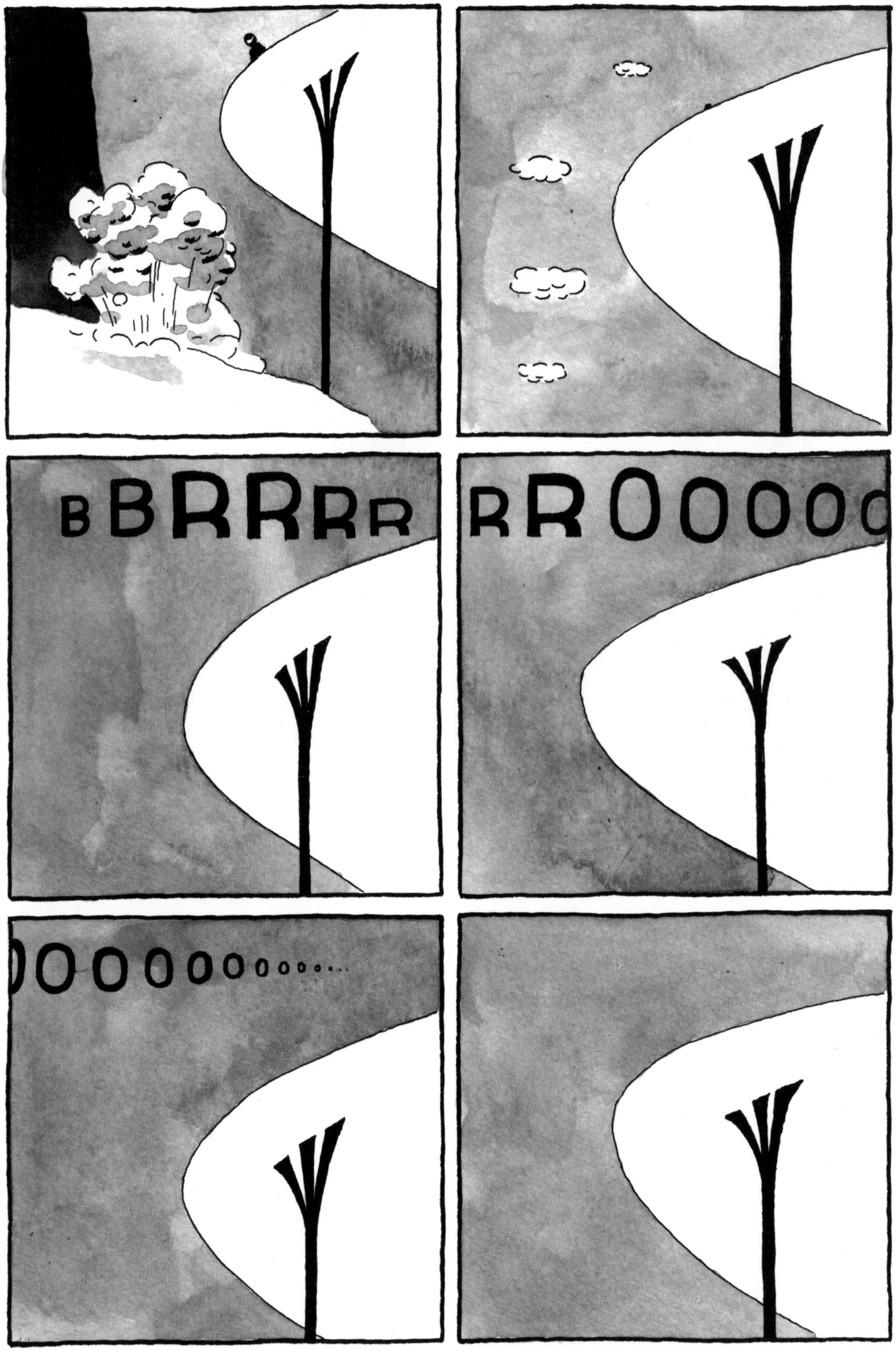
bBRRrr
rROOOOO
OOOOOOoooo...

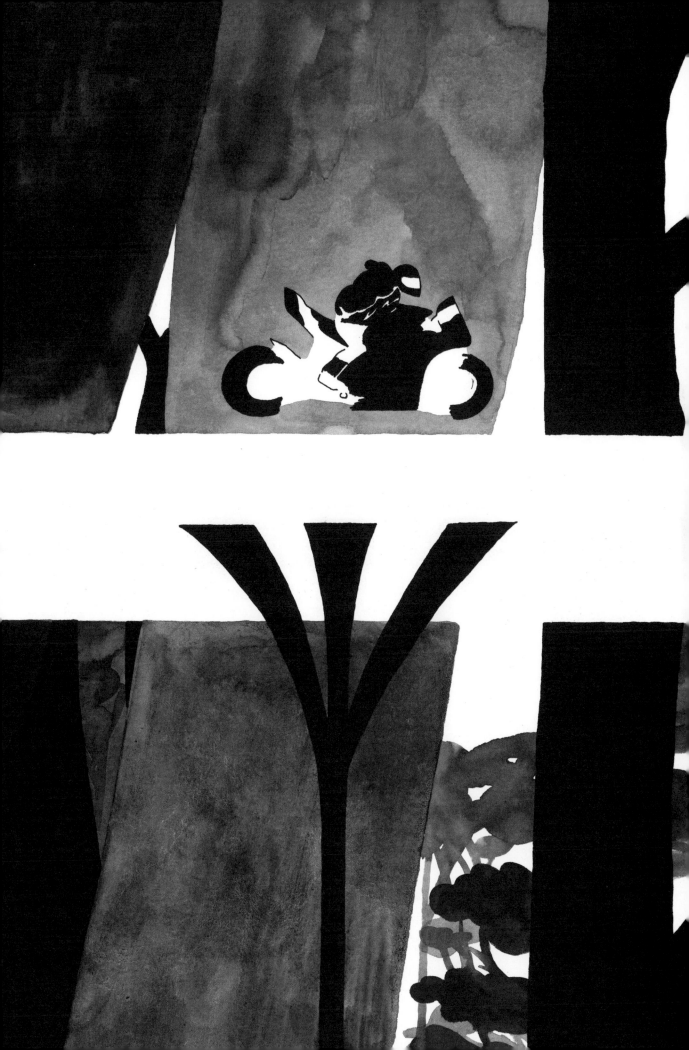

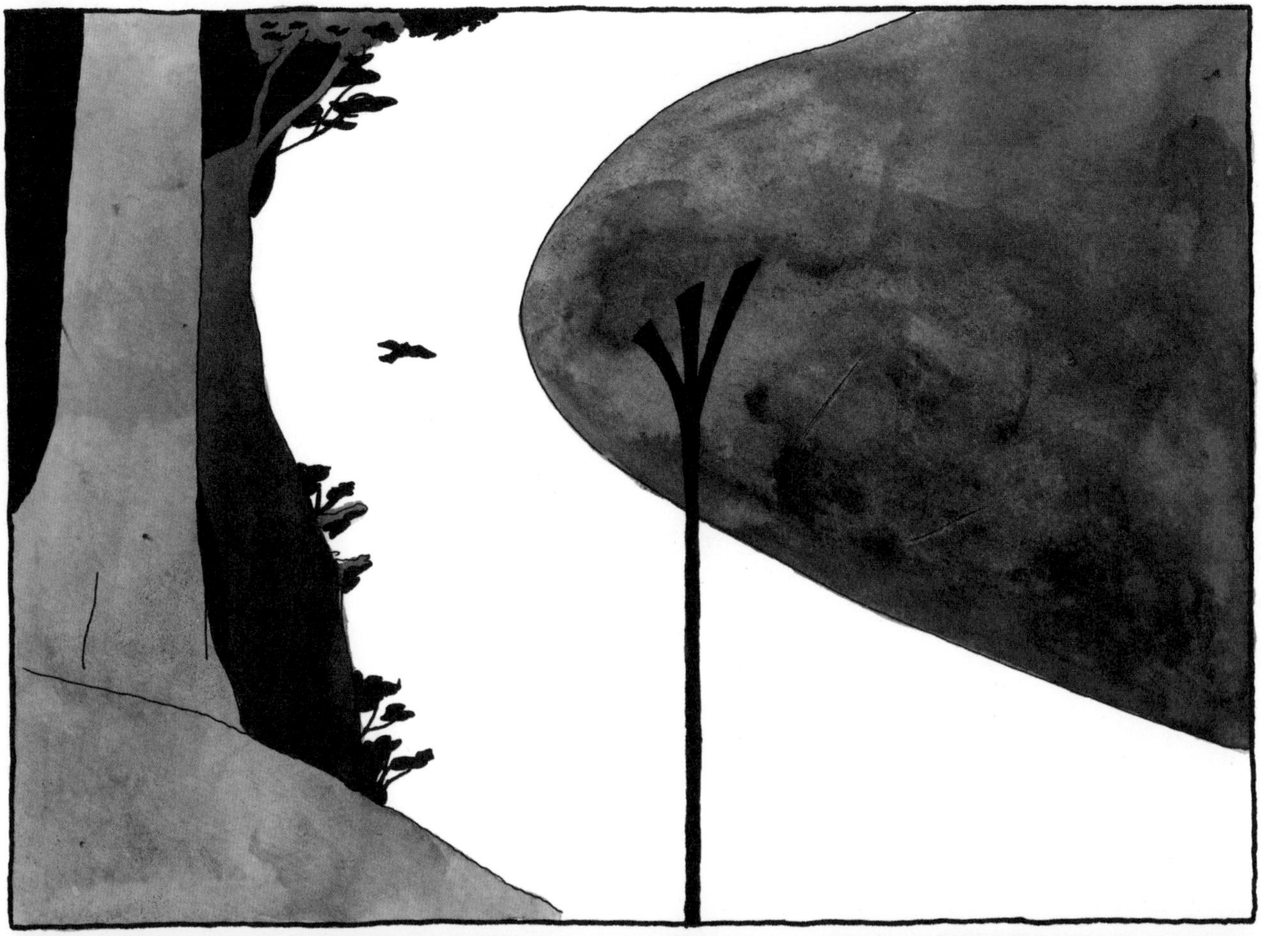

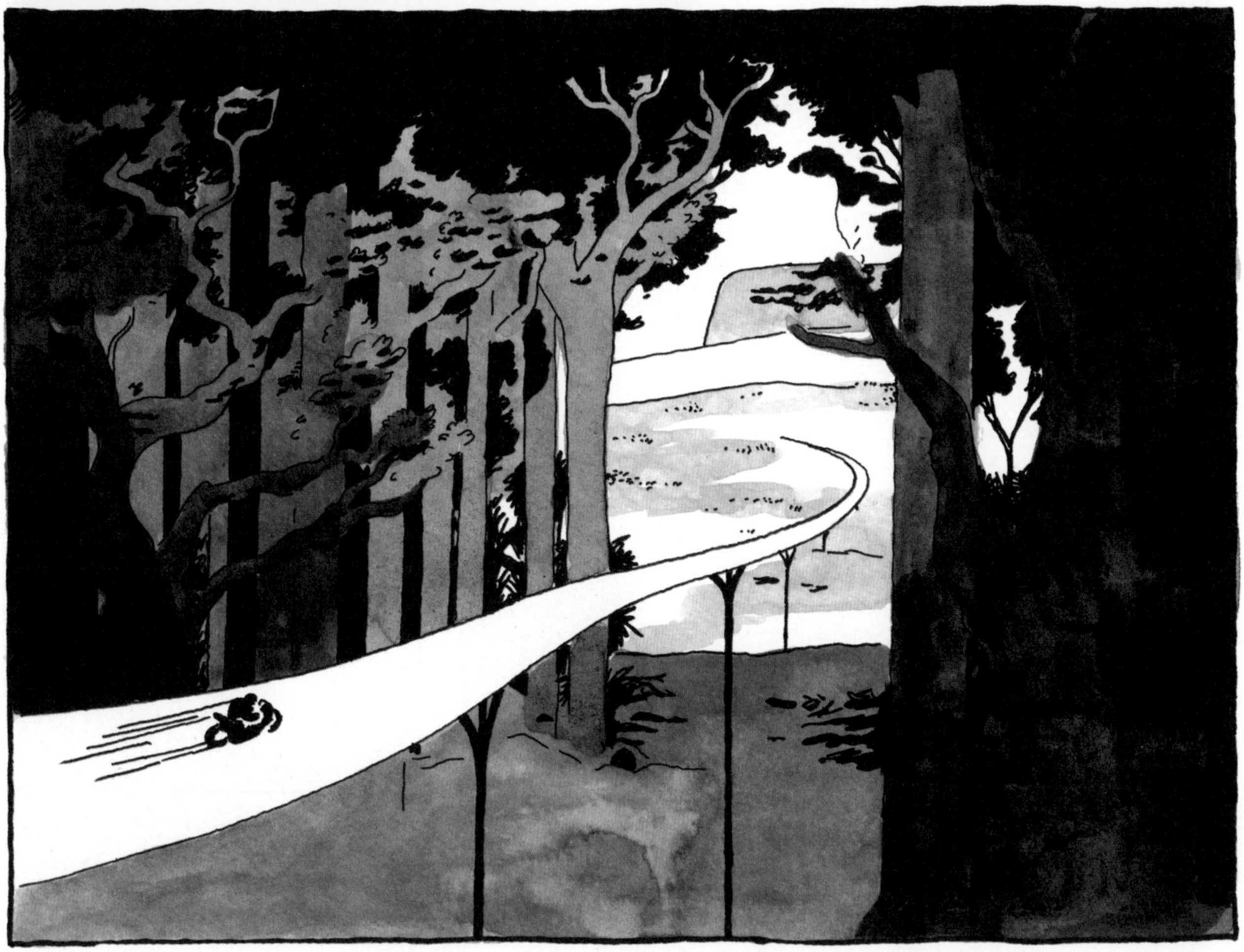

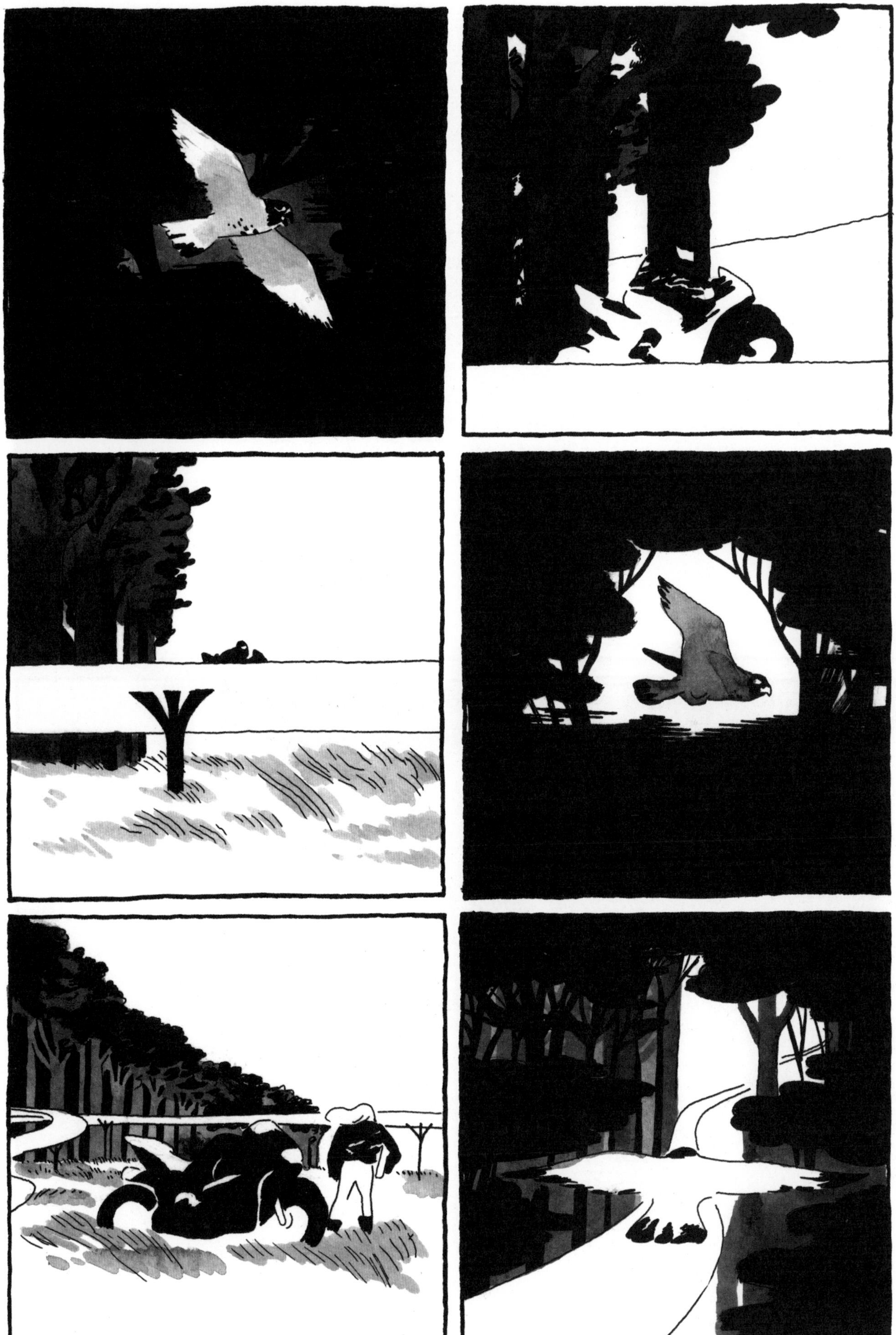

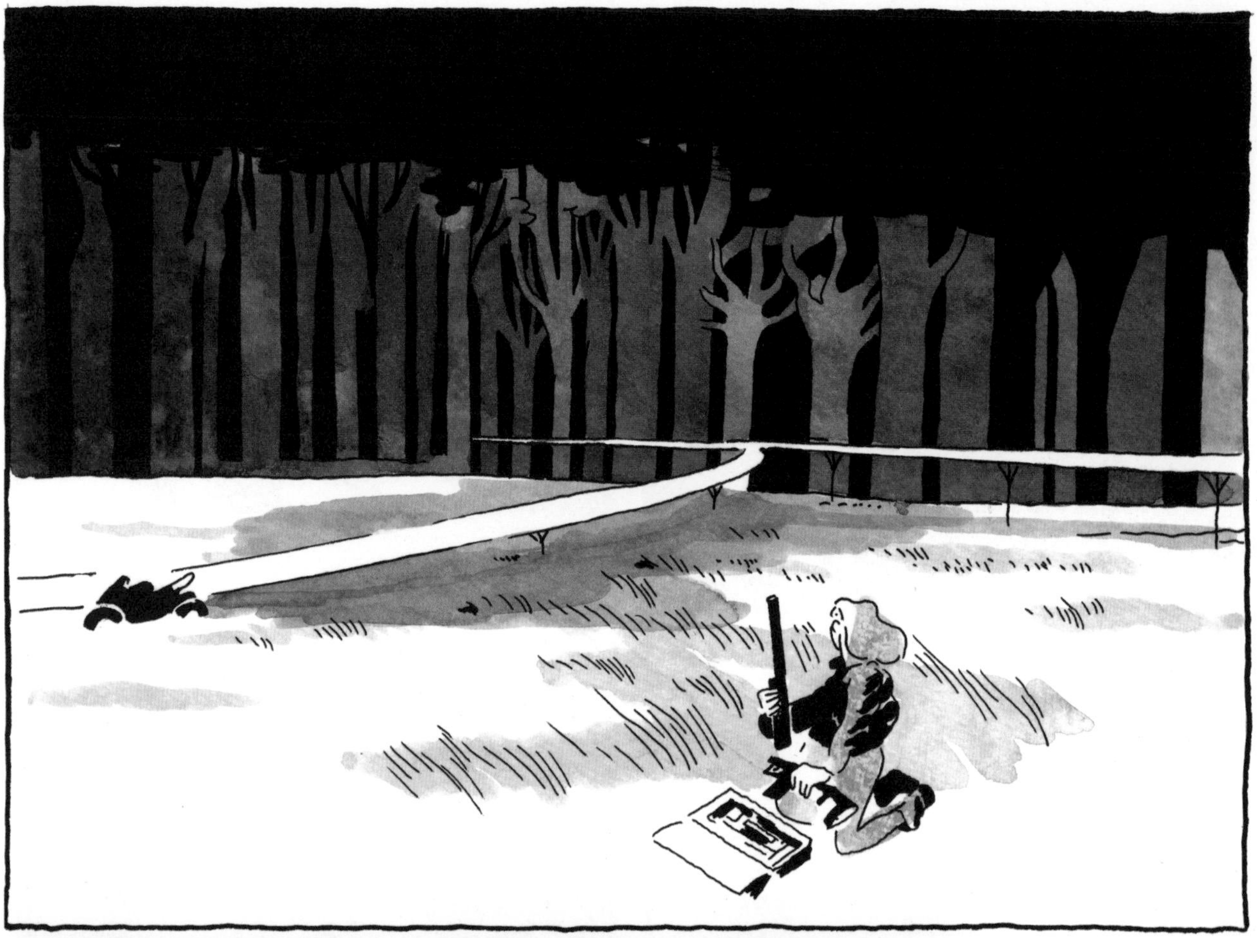

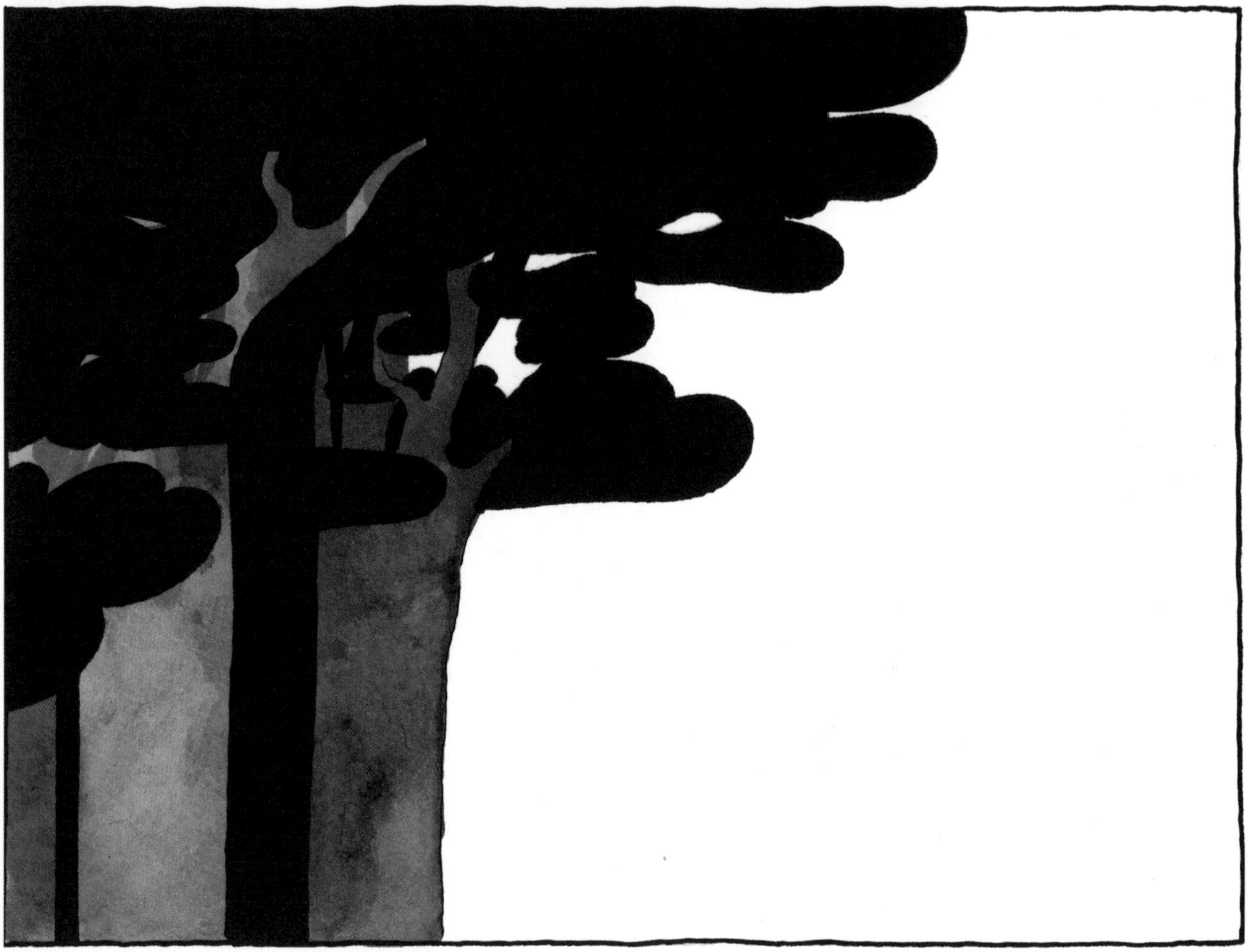

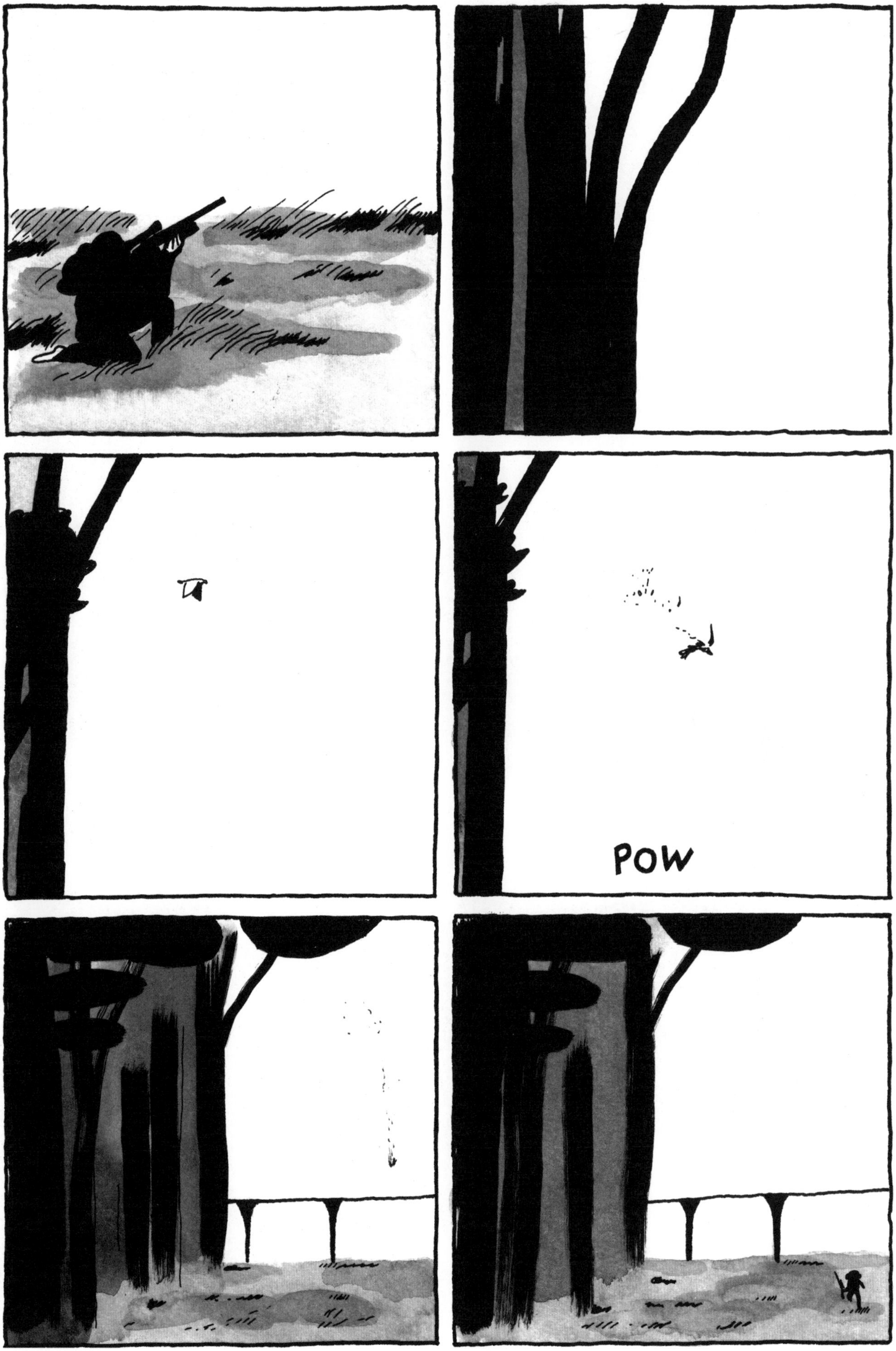
POW

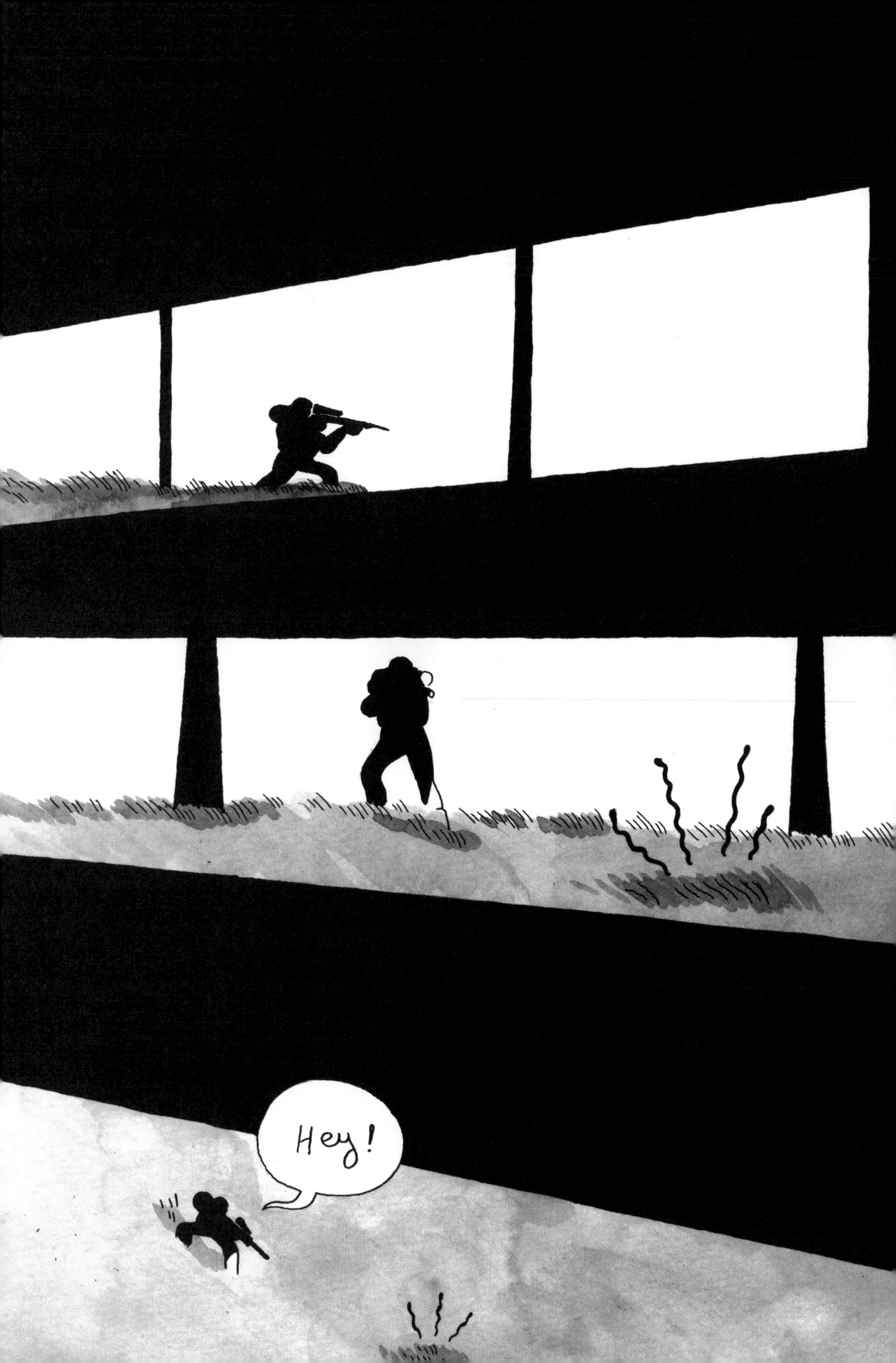
Hey!

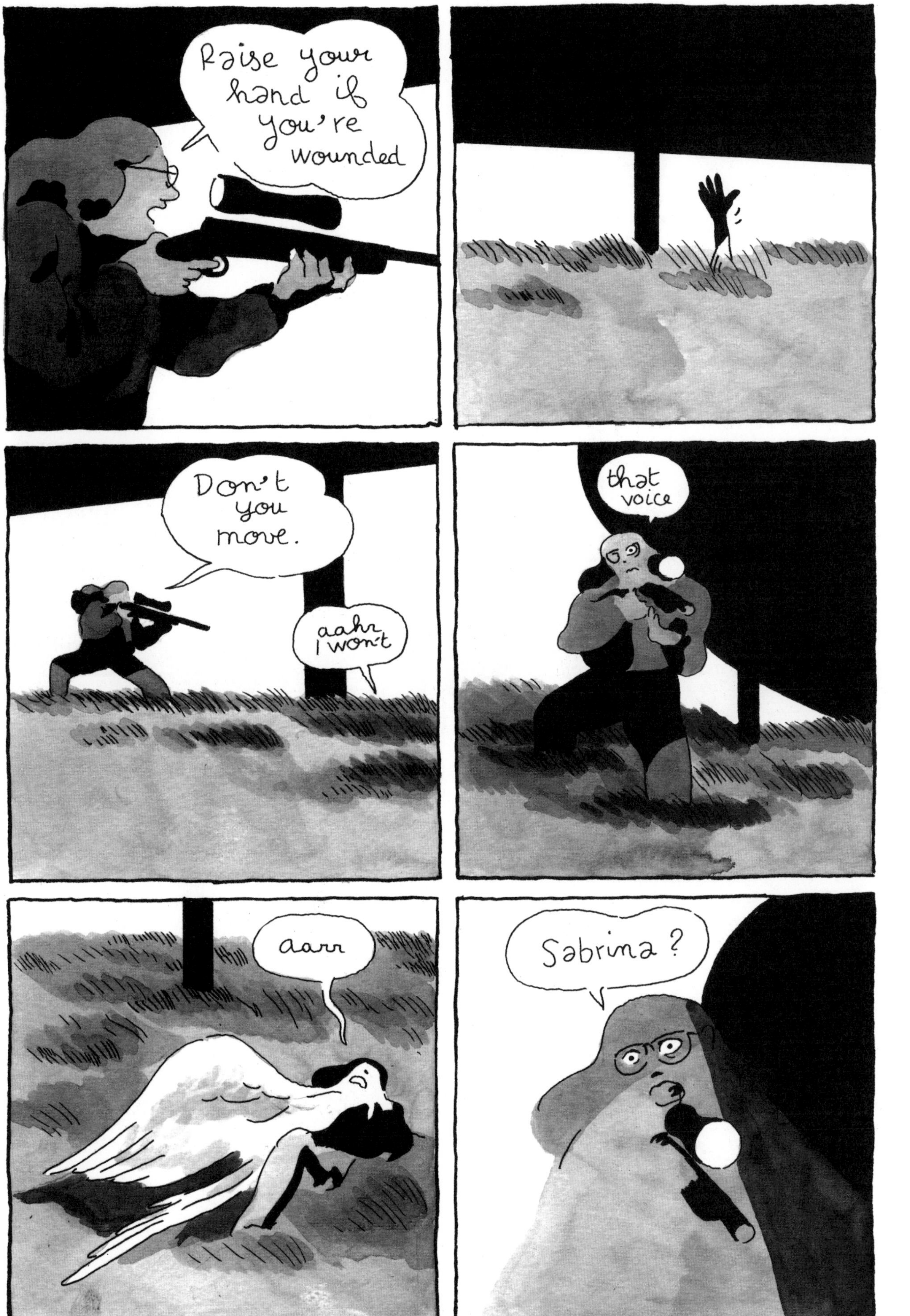
Raise your hand if you're wounded
Don't you move.
aahr I won't
that voice
aarr
Sabrina?

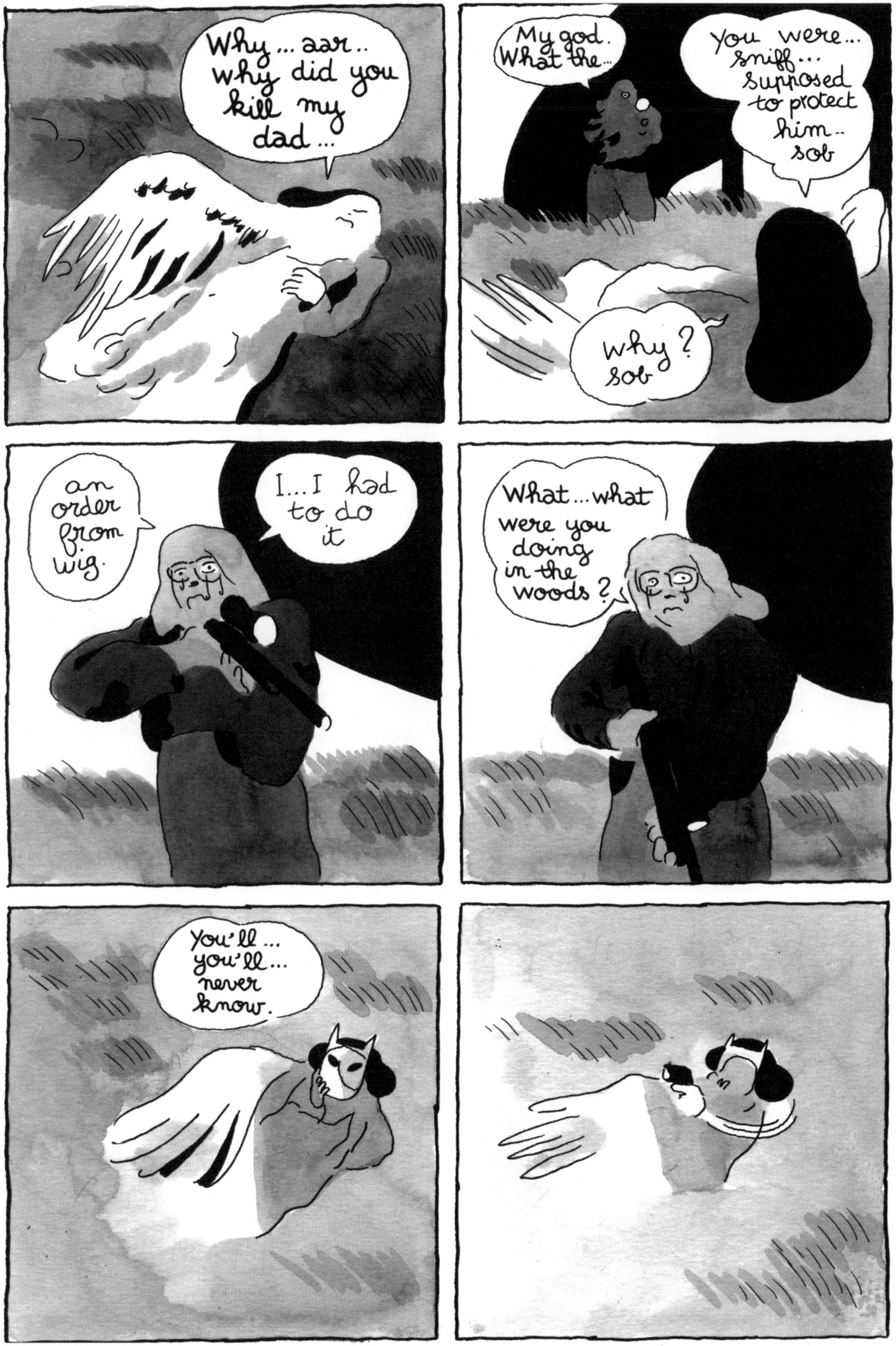
Why... aar.. why did you kill my dad...
My god. What the...
You were... sniff... supposed to protect him.. sob
Why? sob
an order from wig.
I... I had to do it
What... what were you doing in the woods?
You'll... you'll... never know.

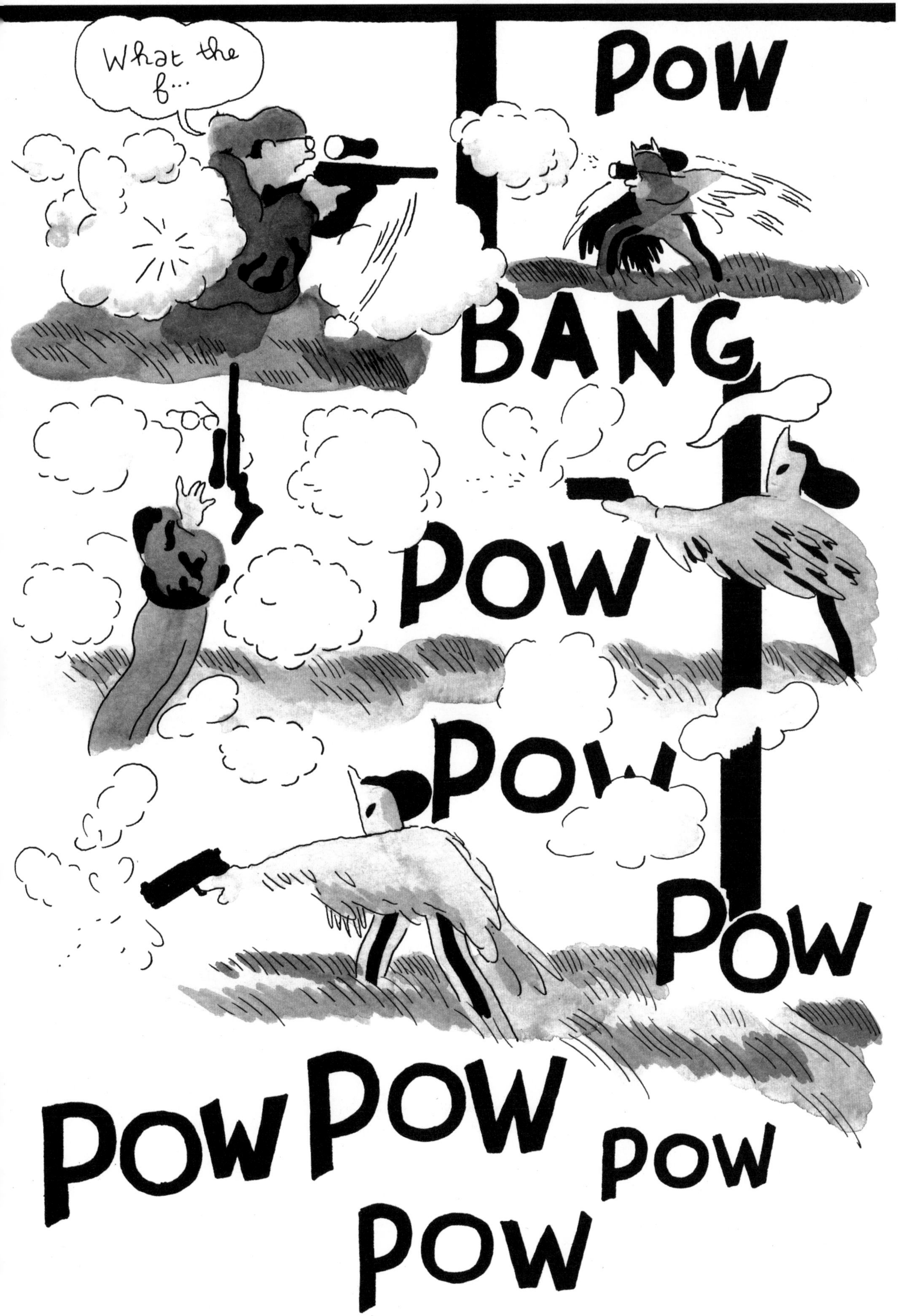
What the f...
POW
BANG
POW
POW
POW
POW POW pow
POW

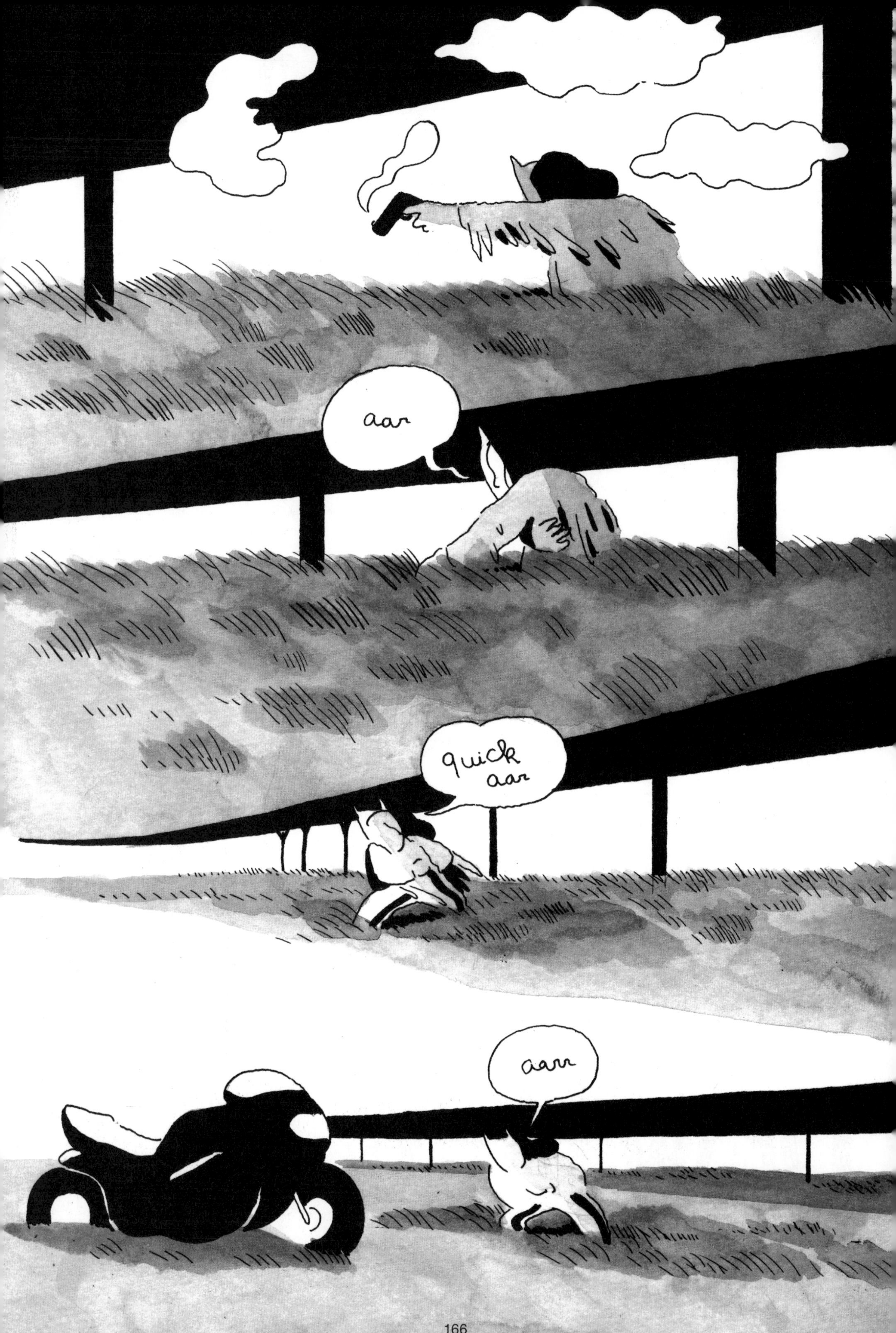
aar
quick
aar
aarr

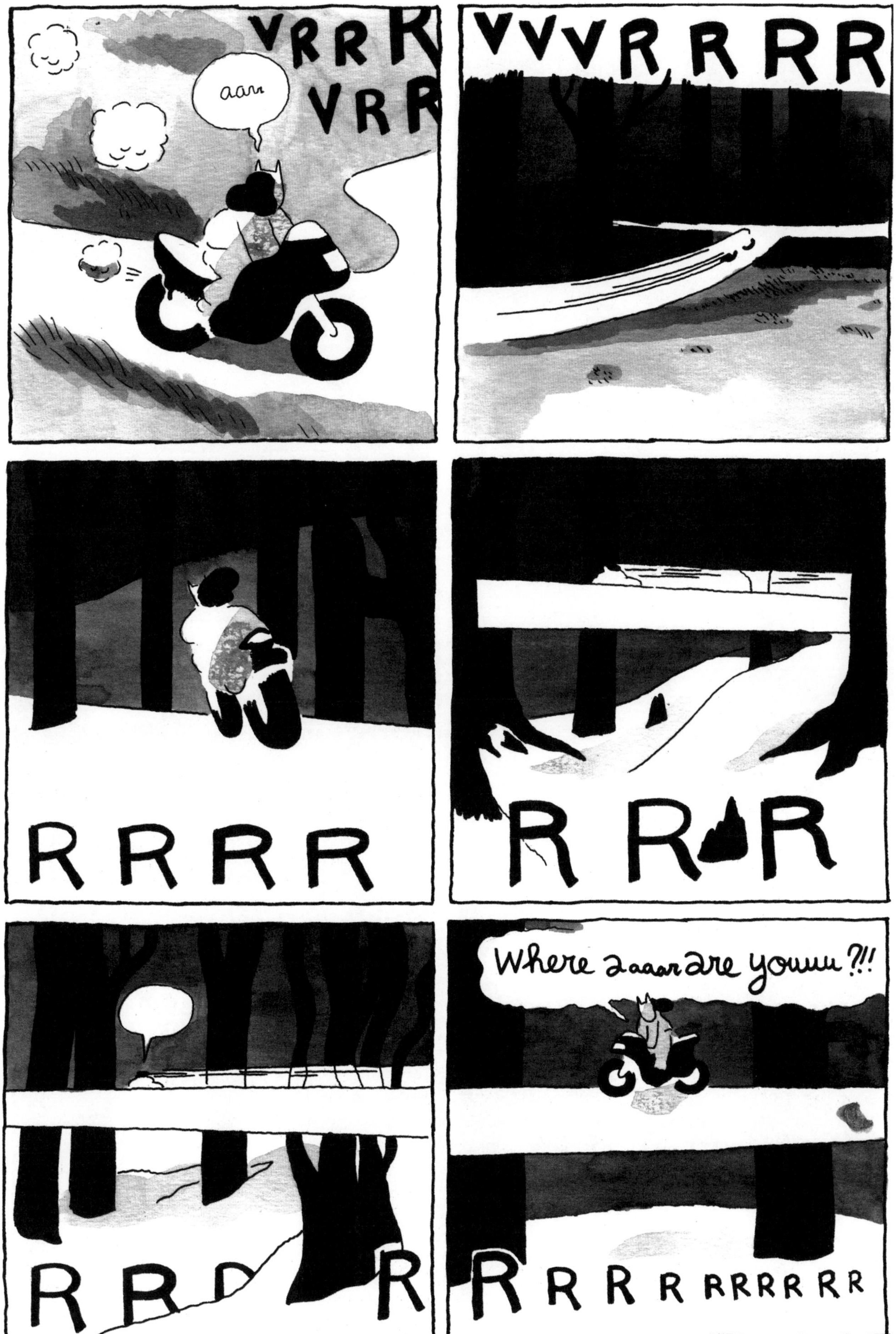
VRRR
VRR
aarr
VVVRRRR
RRRR
RRR
RRR R
Where aaaarare youuu?!!
RRRRRRRRRRR

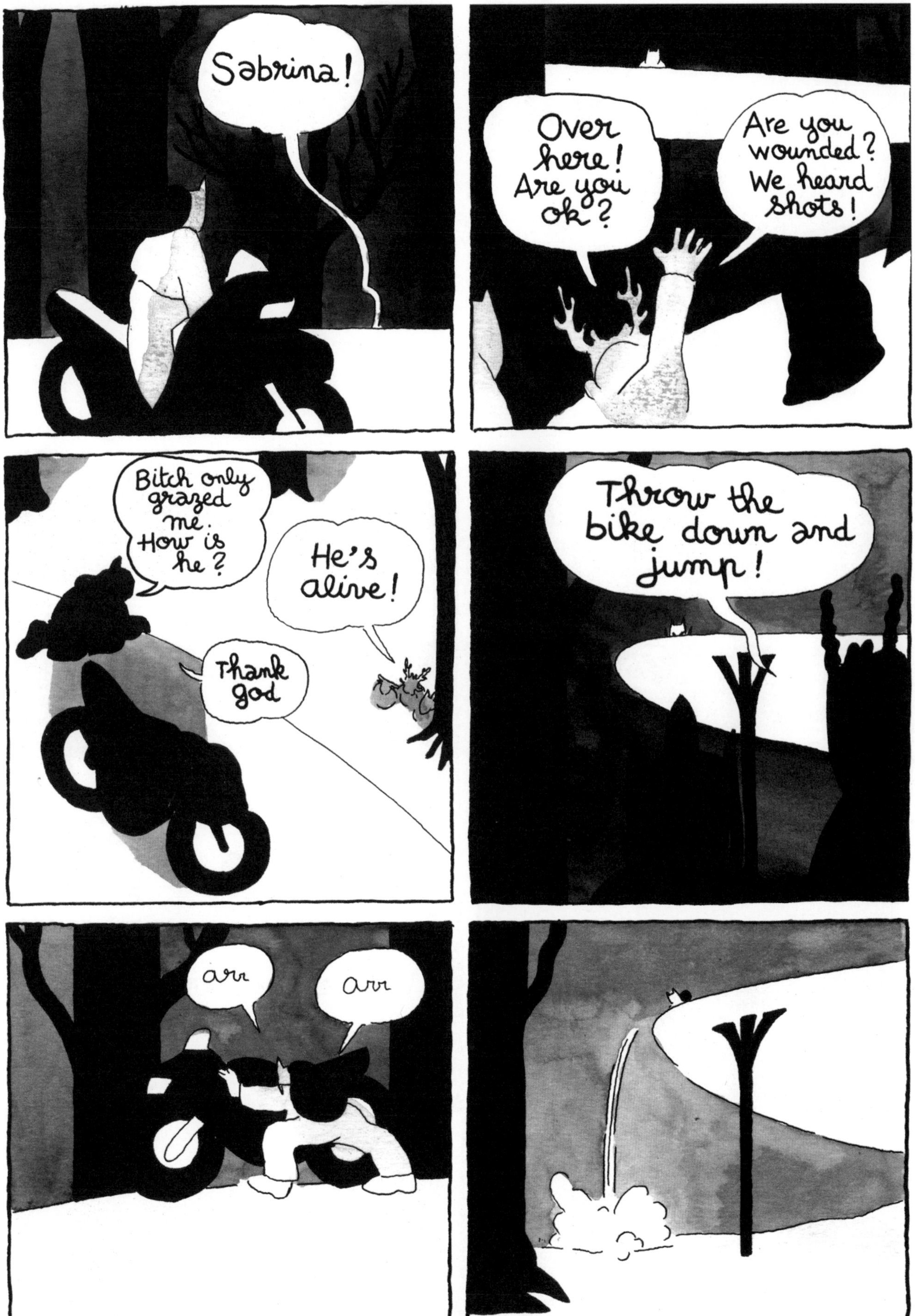

Sabrina!
Over here! Are you ok?
Are you wounded? We heard shots!
Bitch only grazed me. How is he?
He's alive!
Thank god
Throw the bike down and jump!
arr
arr

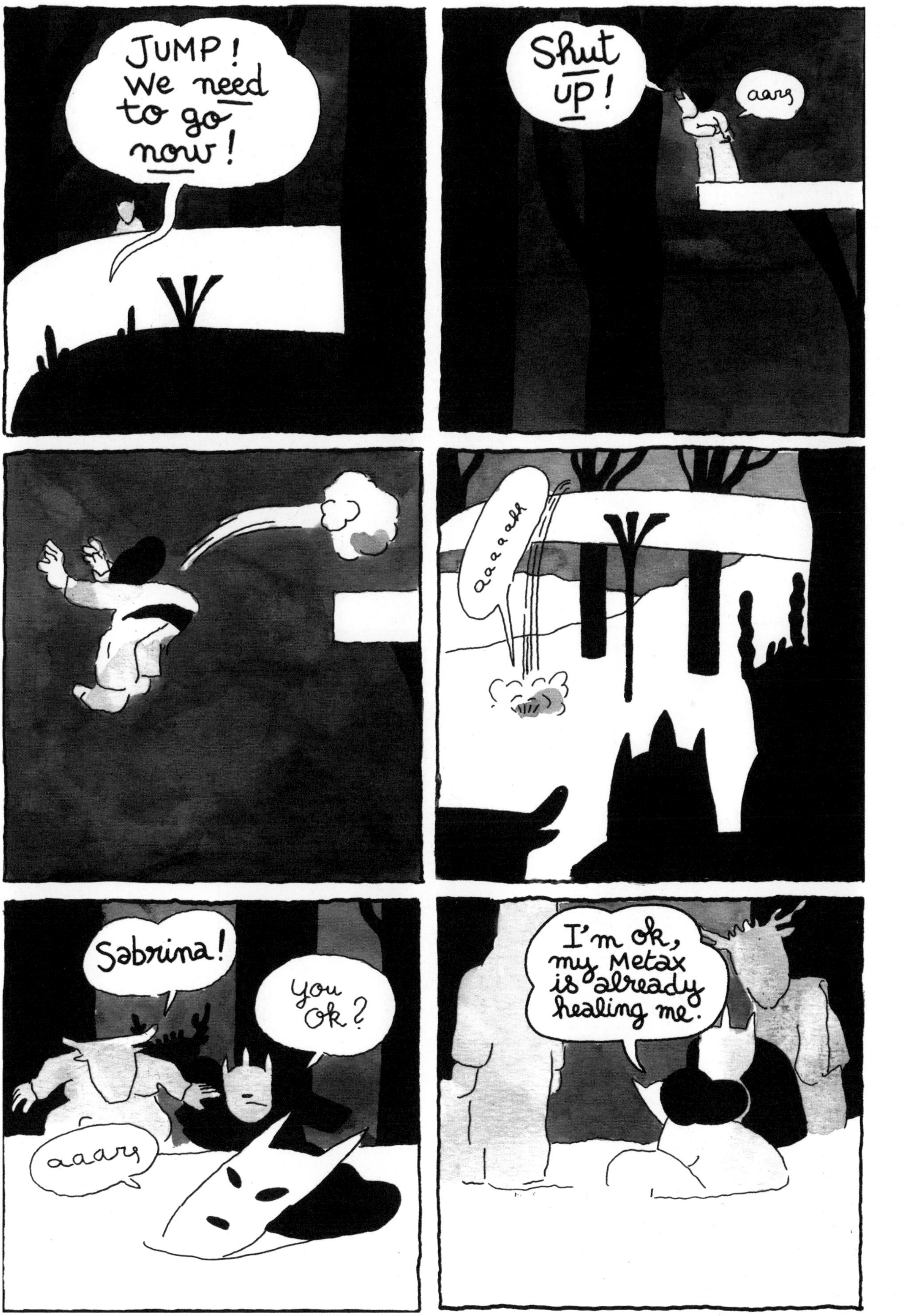
JUMP! We need to go now!
Shut up!
aarg
aaaaahh
Sabrina!
You Ok?
aaarg
I'm ok, my Metax is already healing me.

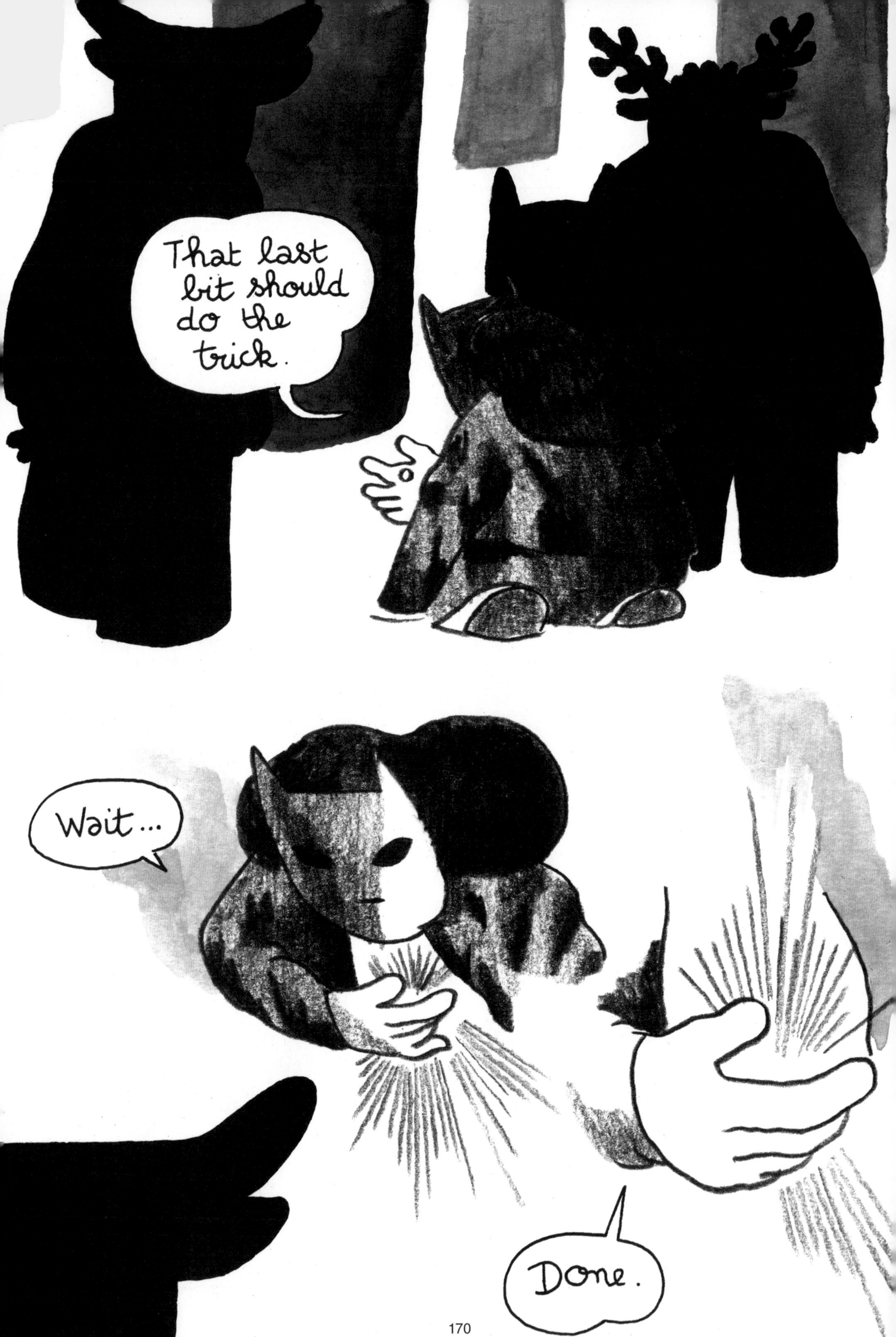
That last bit should do the trick.
Wait...
Done.

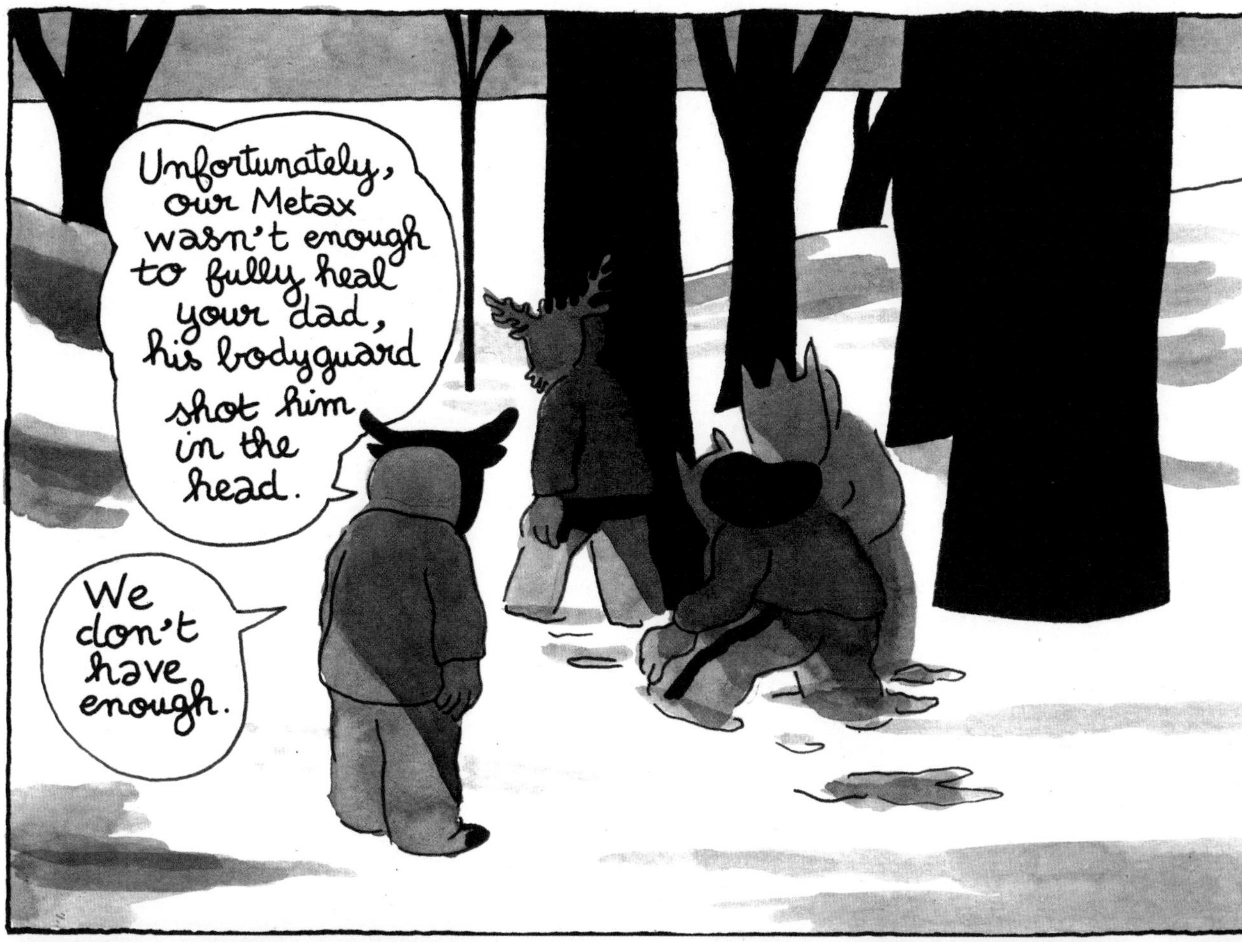
Unfortunately, our Metax wasn't enough to fully heal your dad, his bodyguard shot him in the head.
We don't have enough.

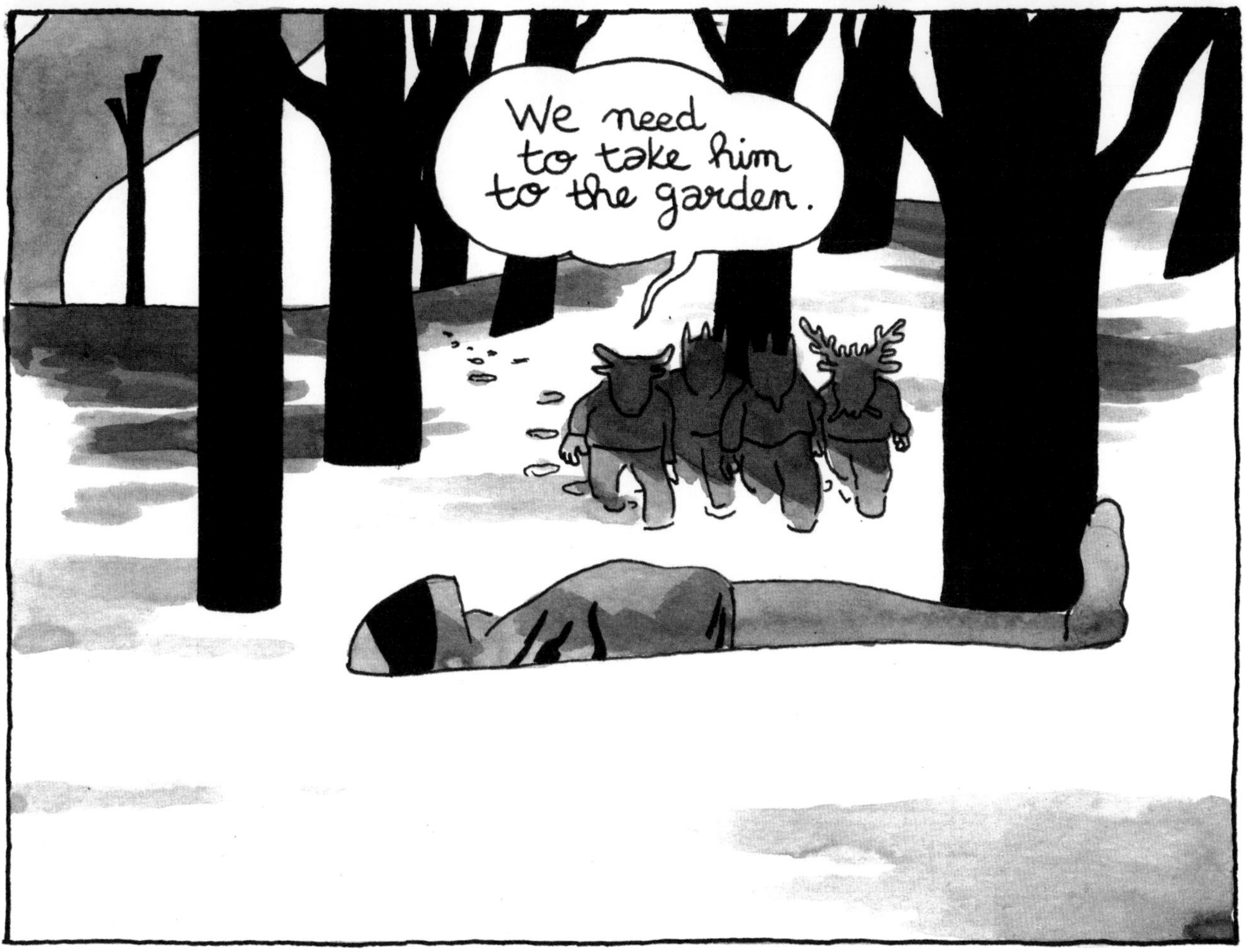
We need to take him to the garden.

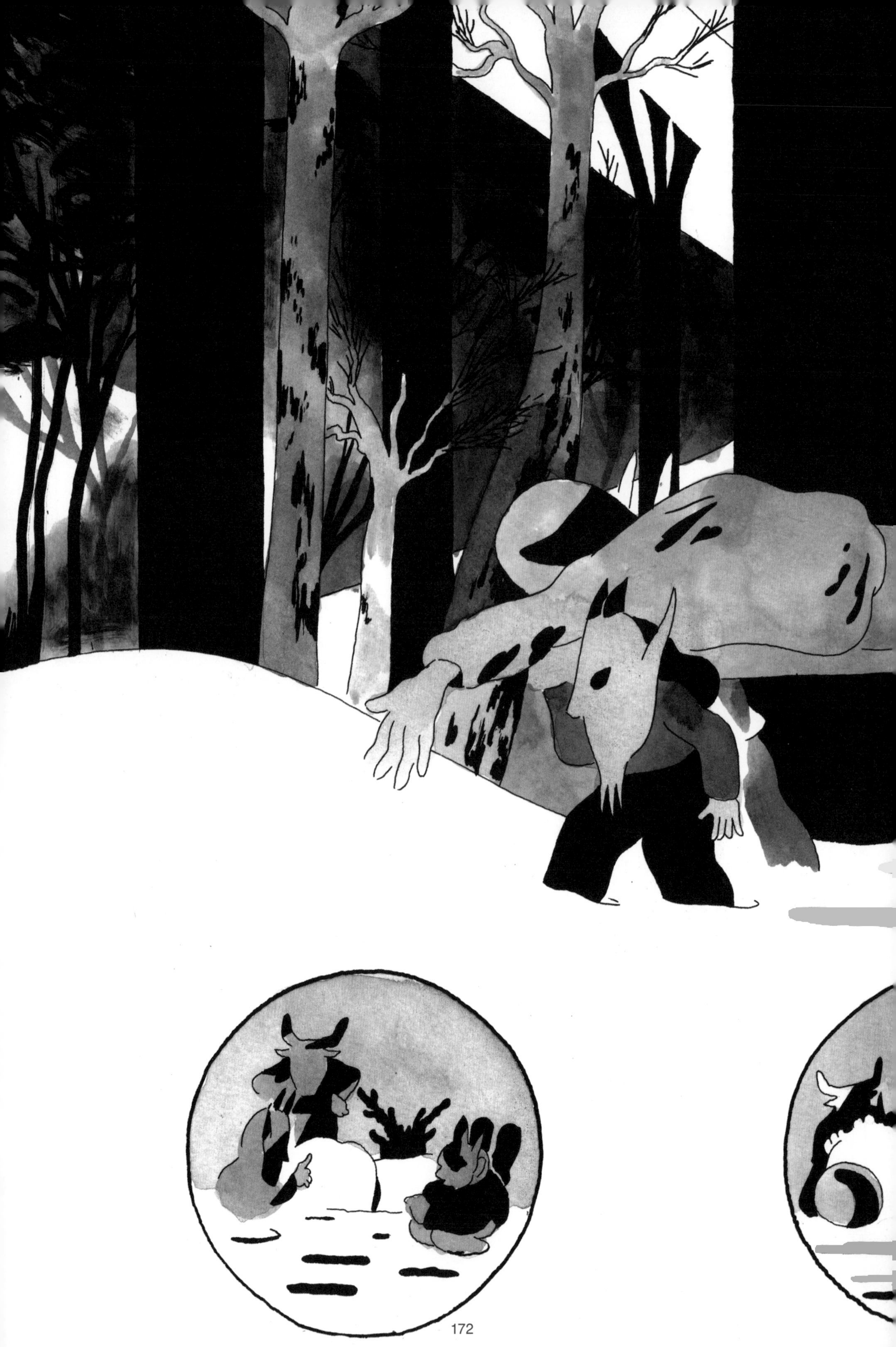

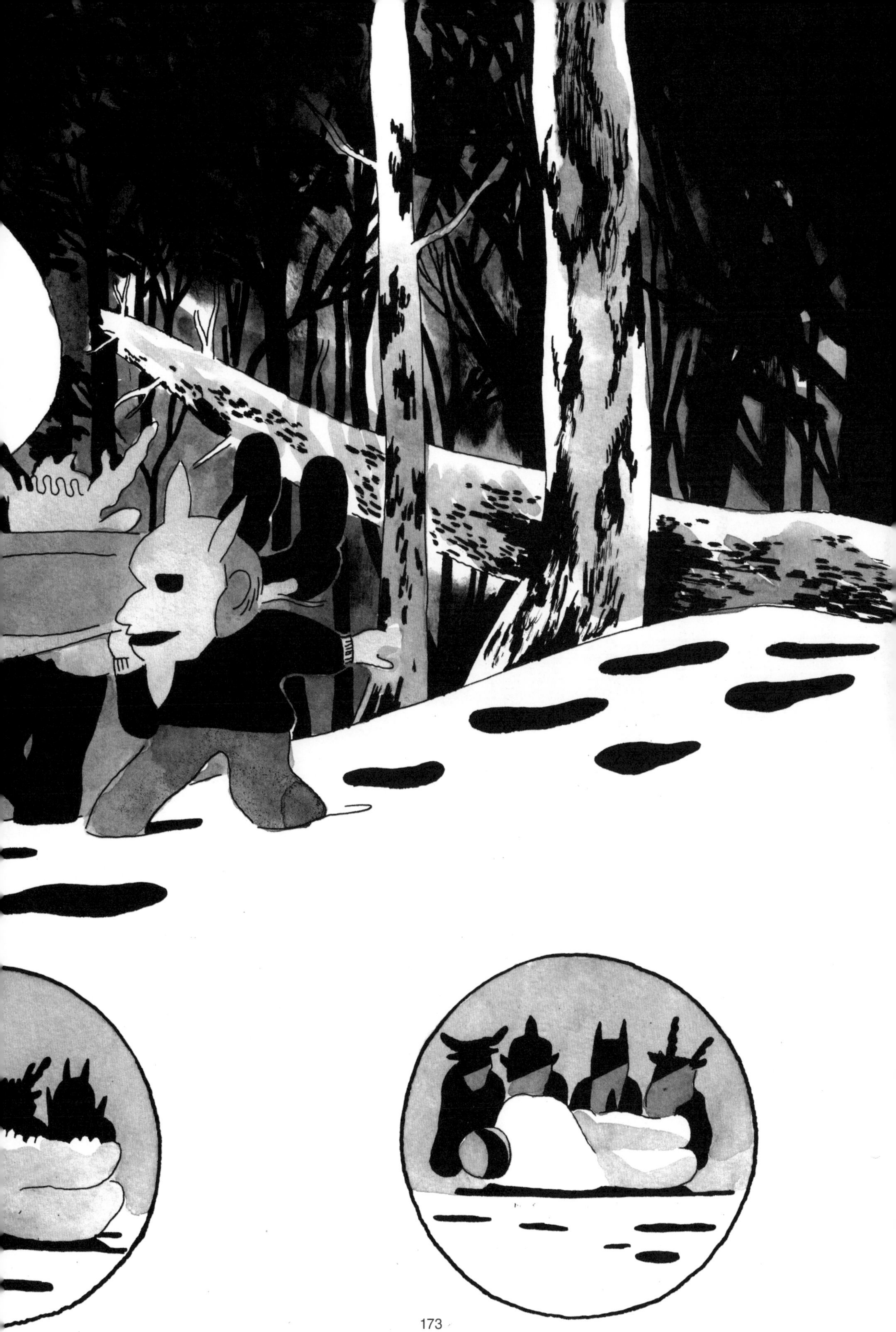

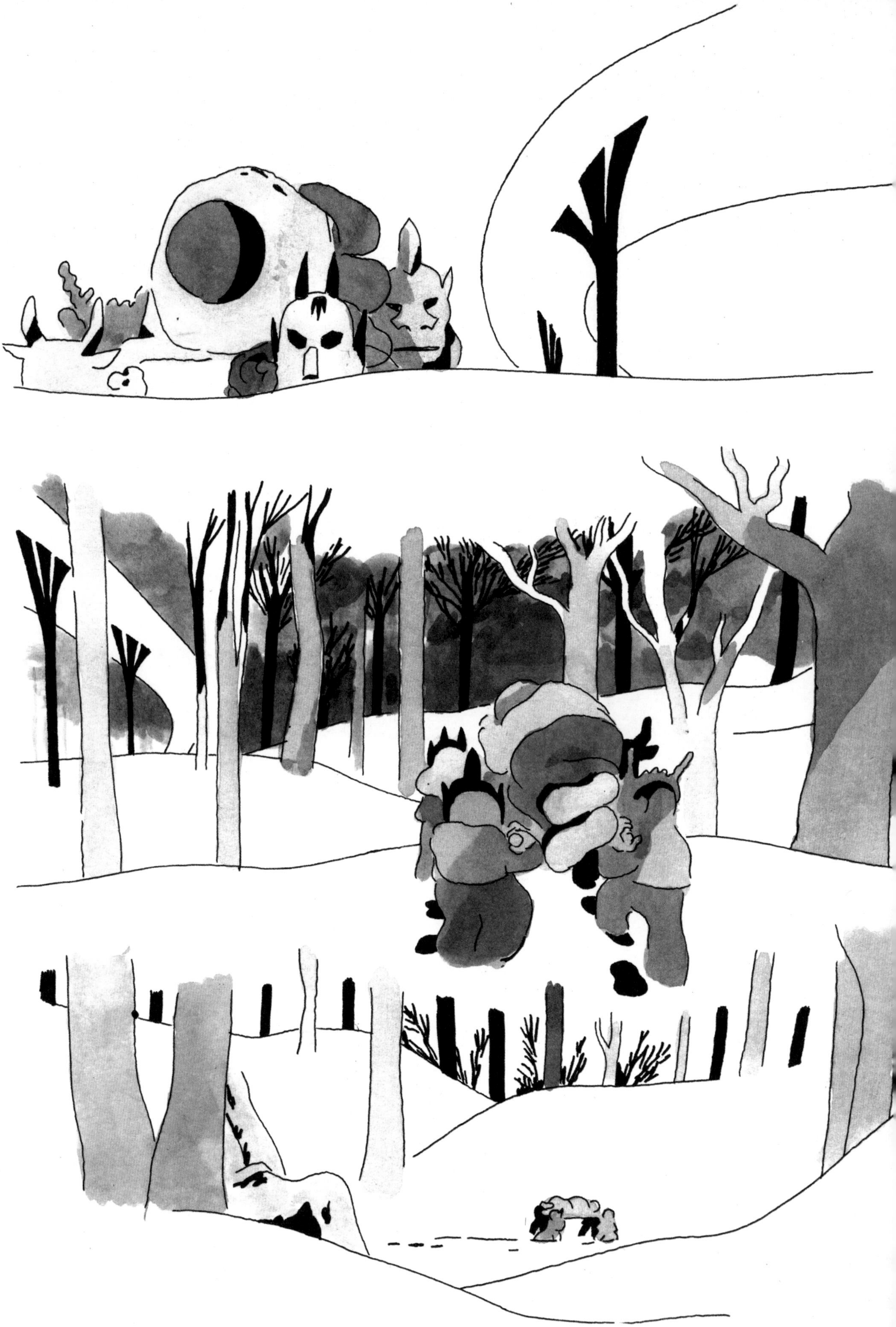

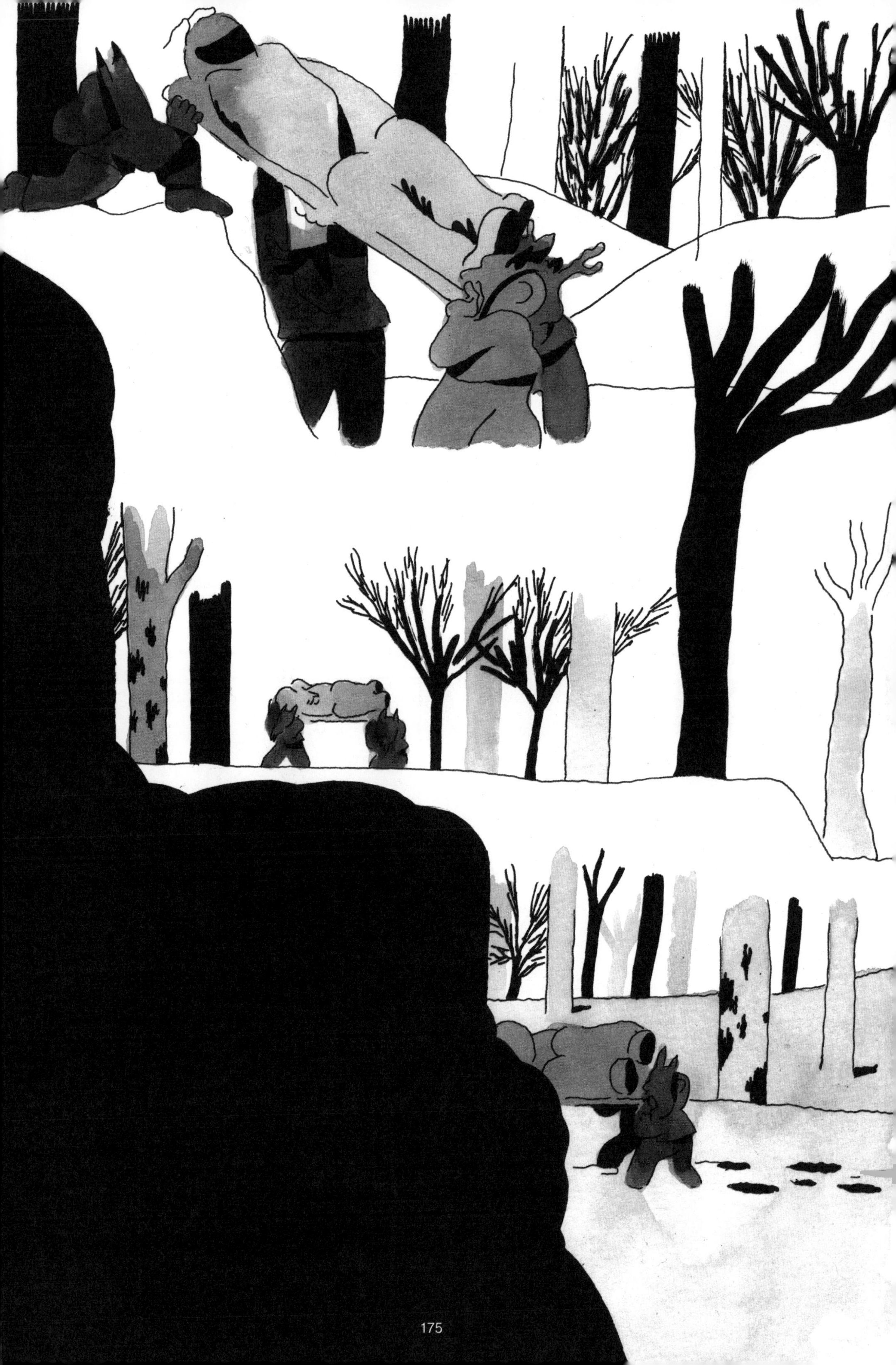

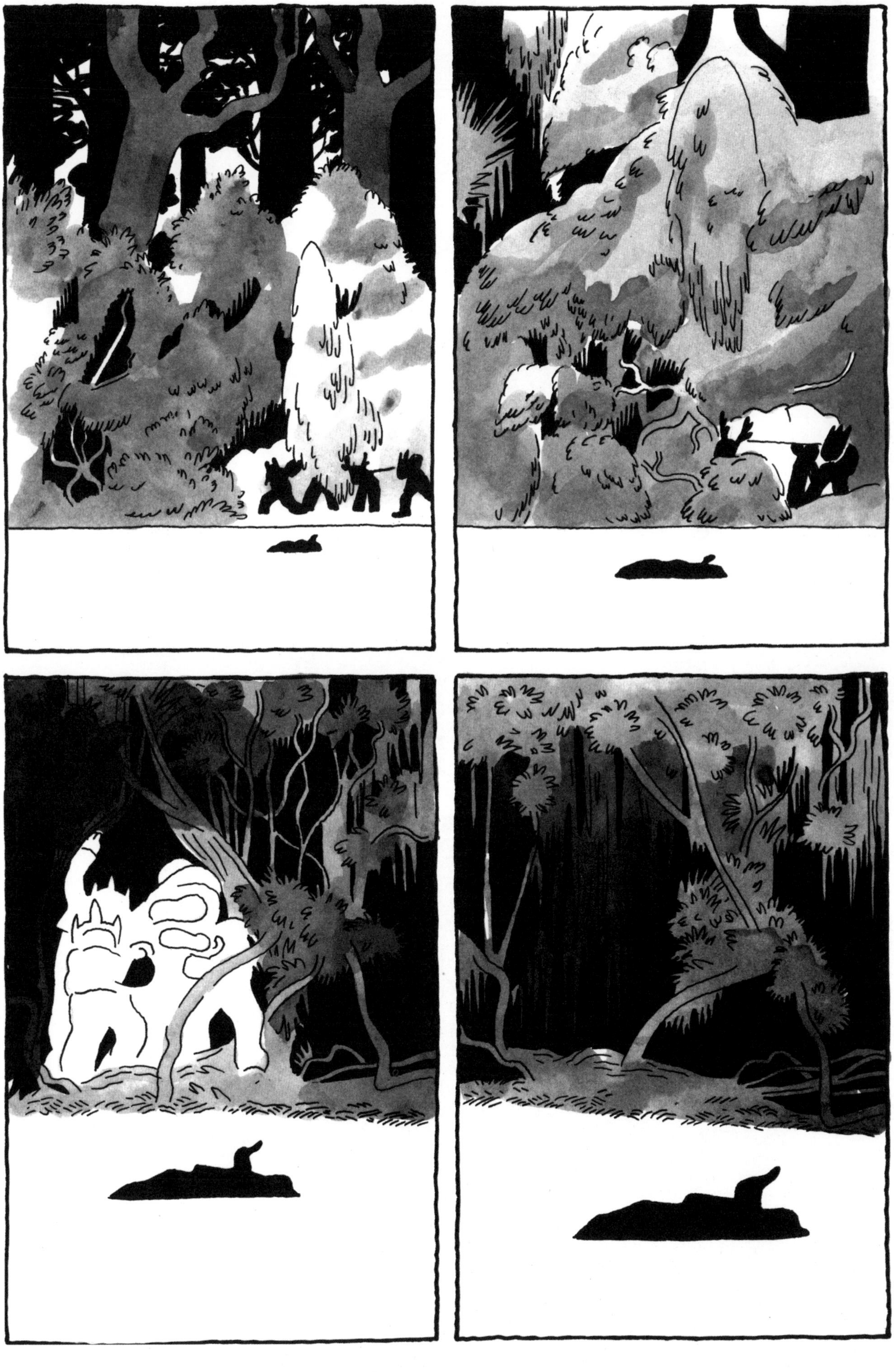

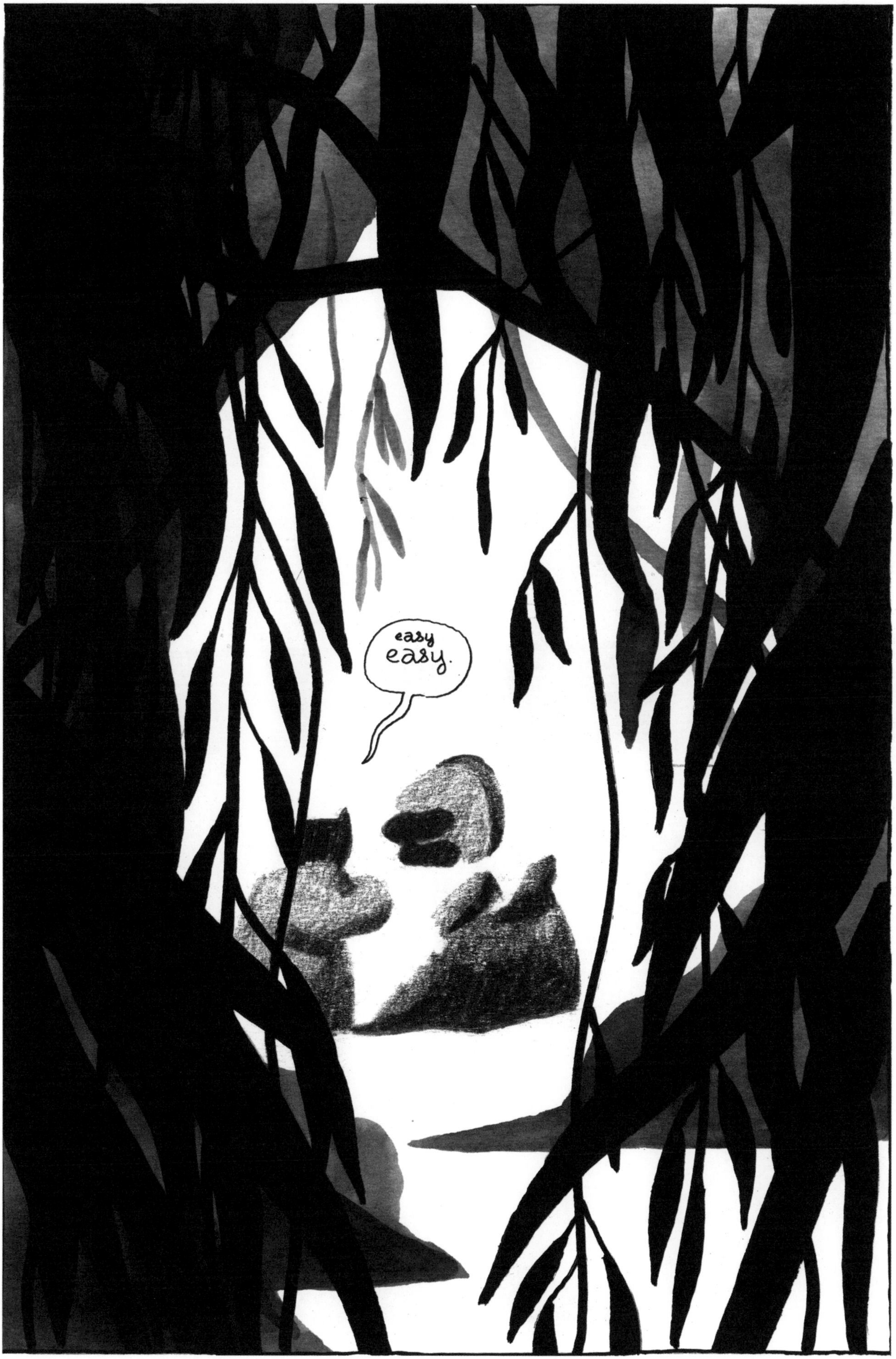
easy easy.

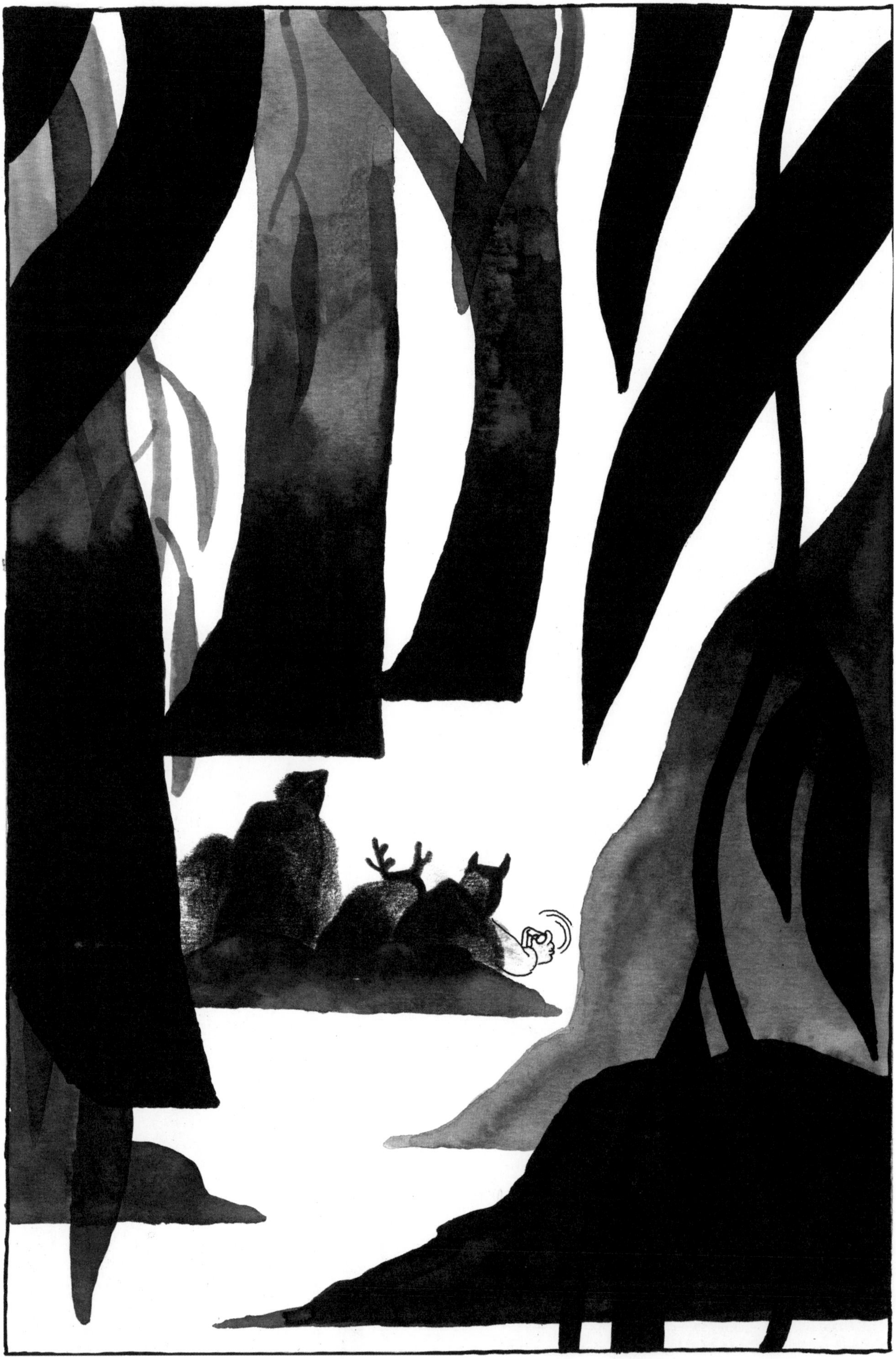

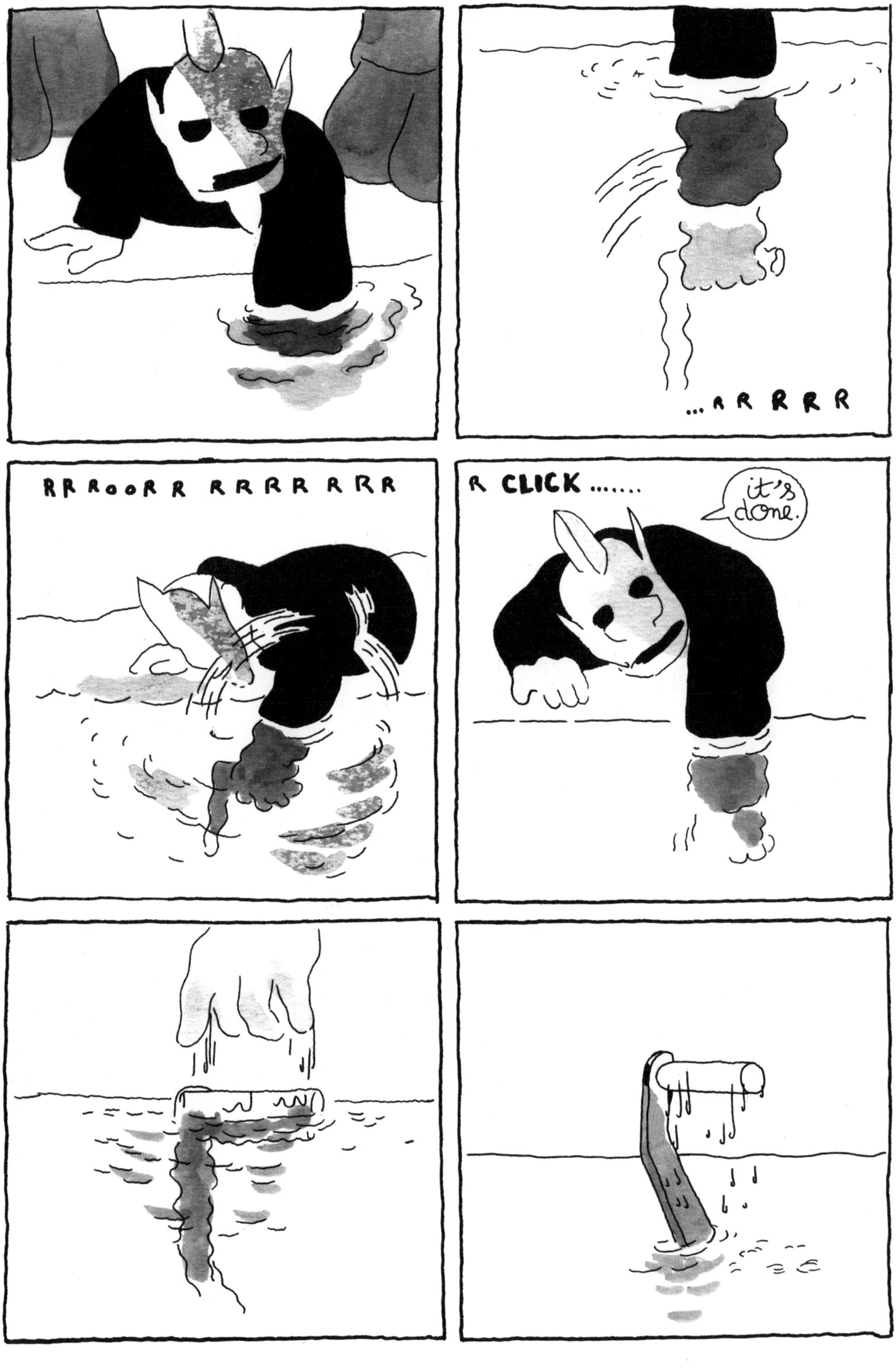
...R R R R R
RR ROOR R RRRR RRR
R CLICK.......
it's done.

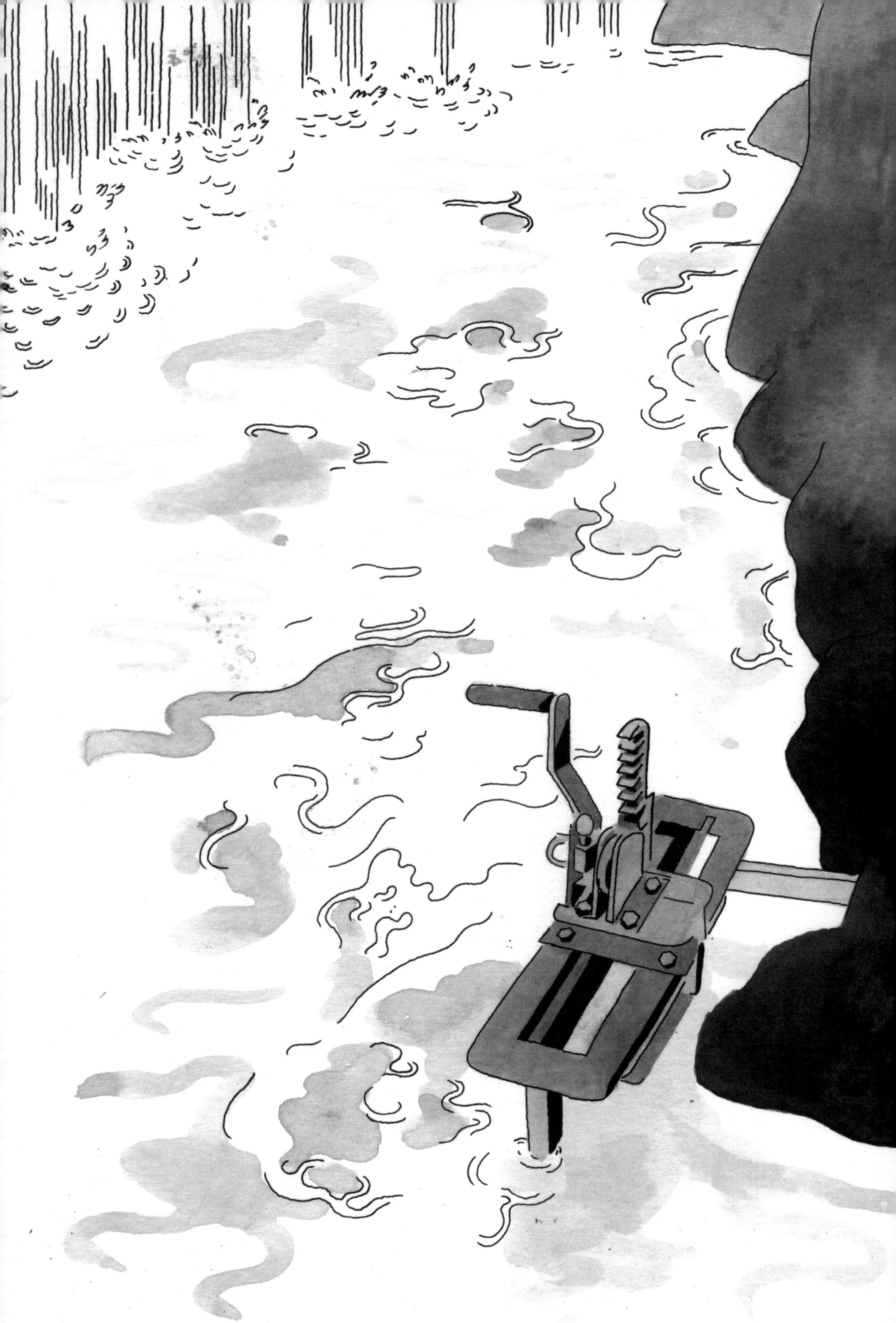

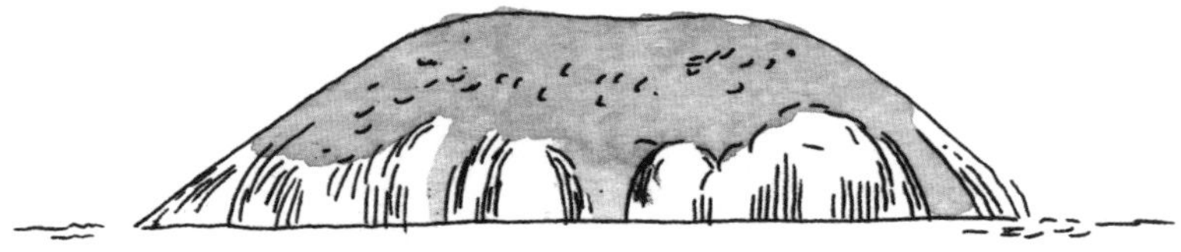

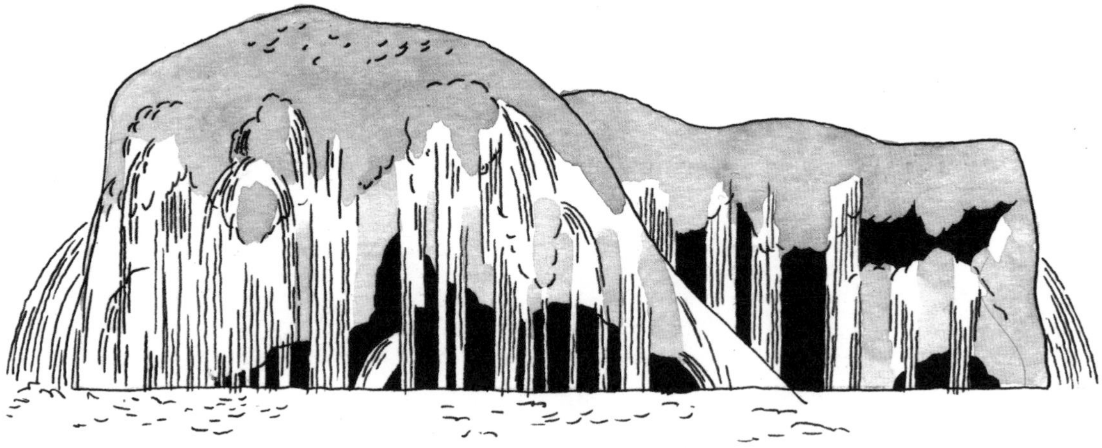

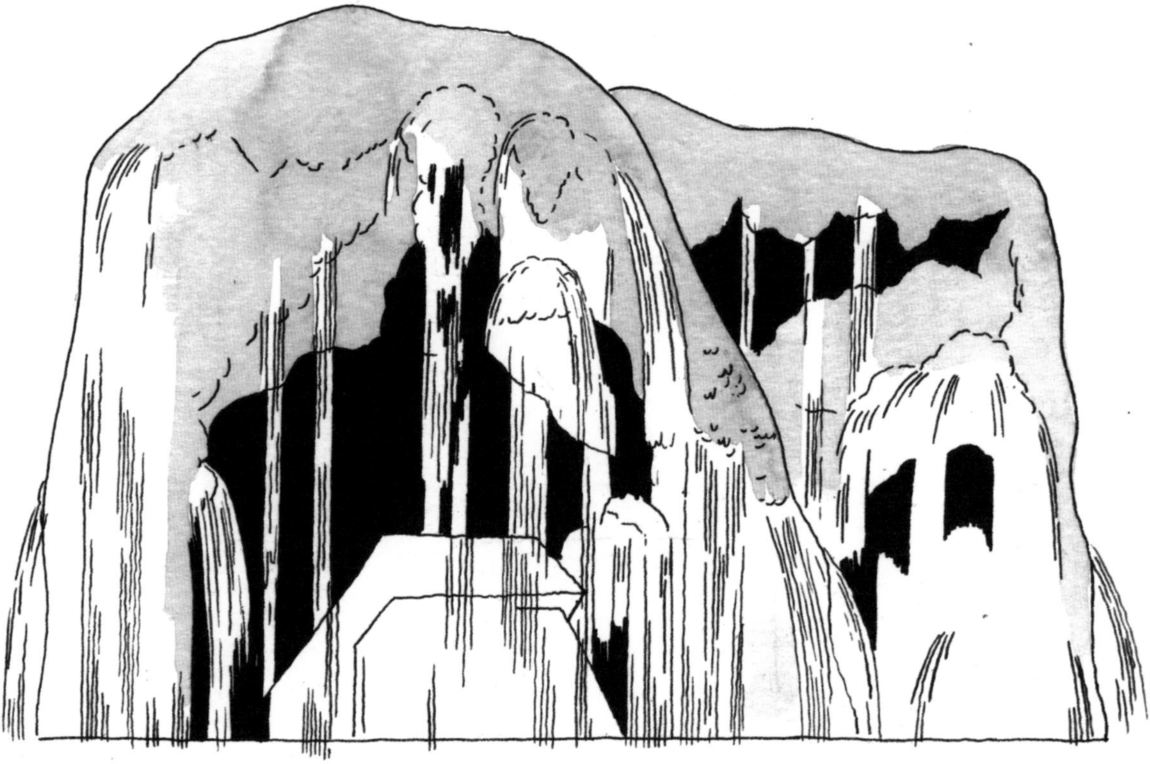

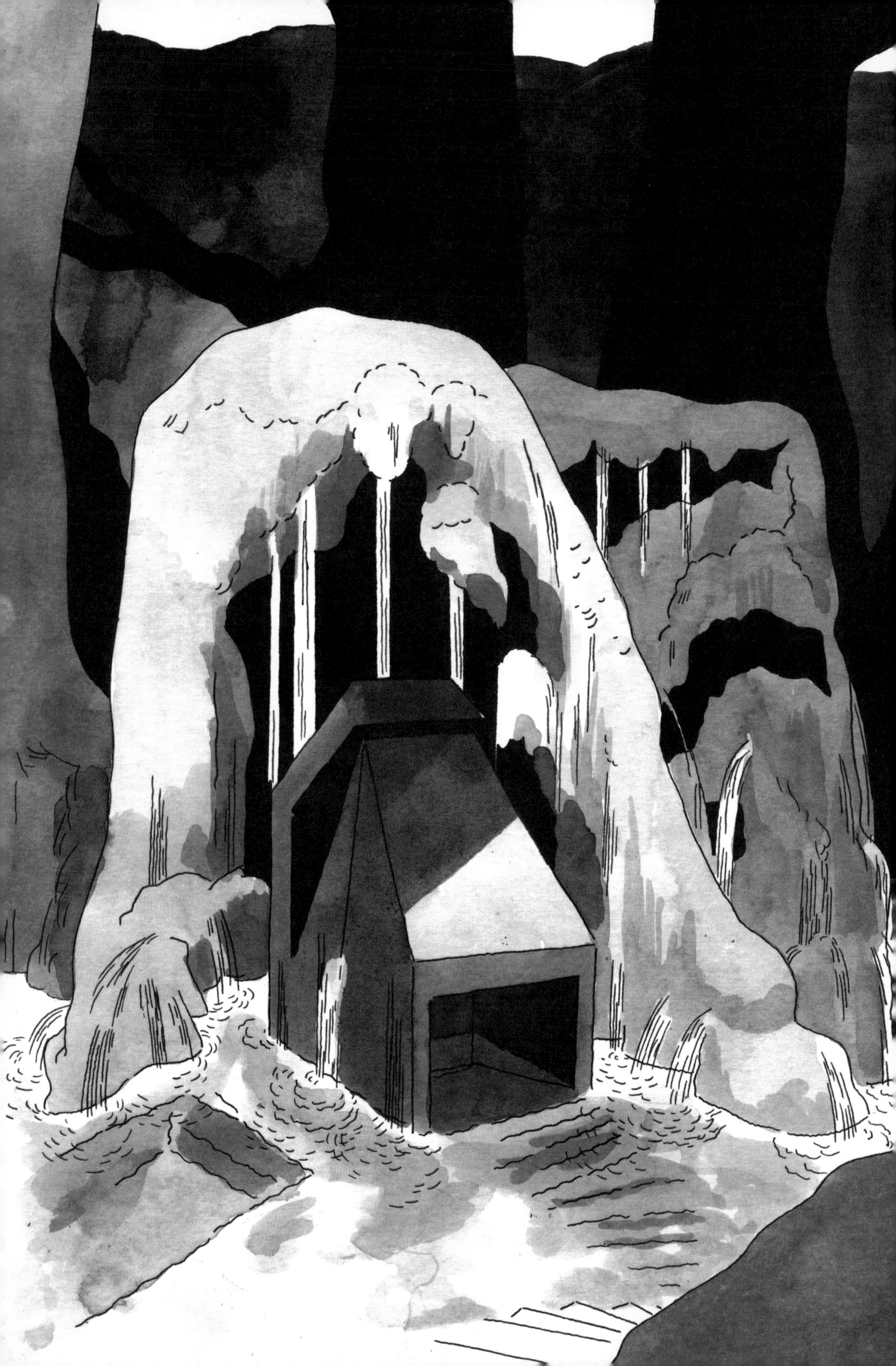

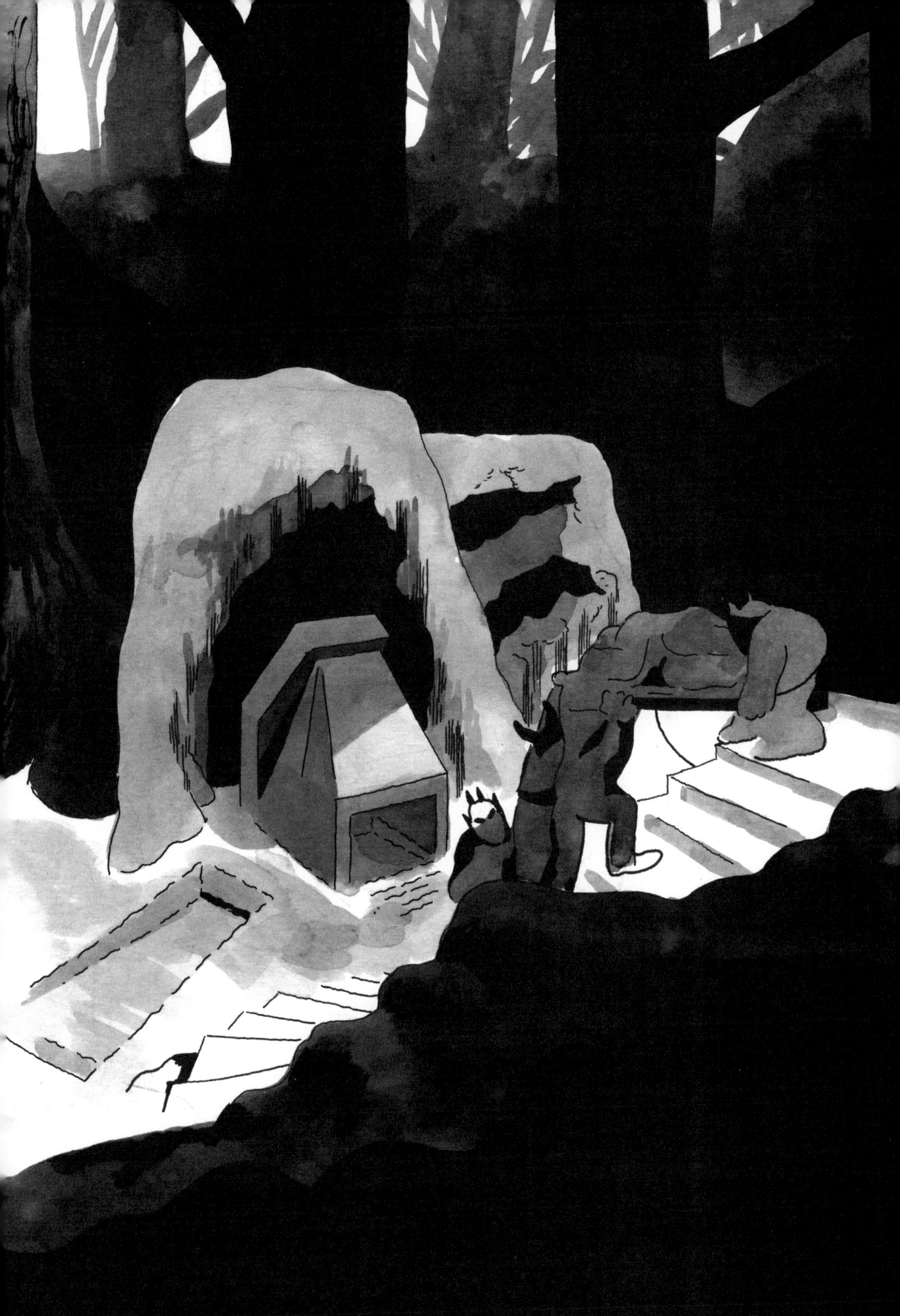

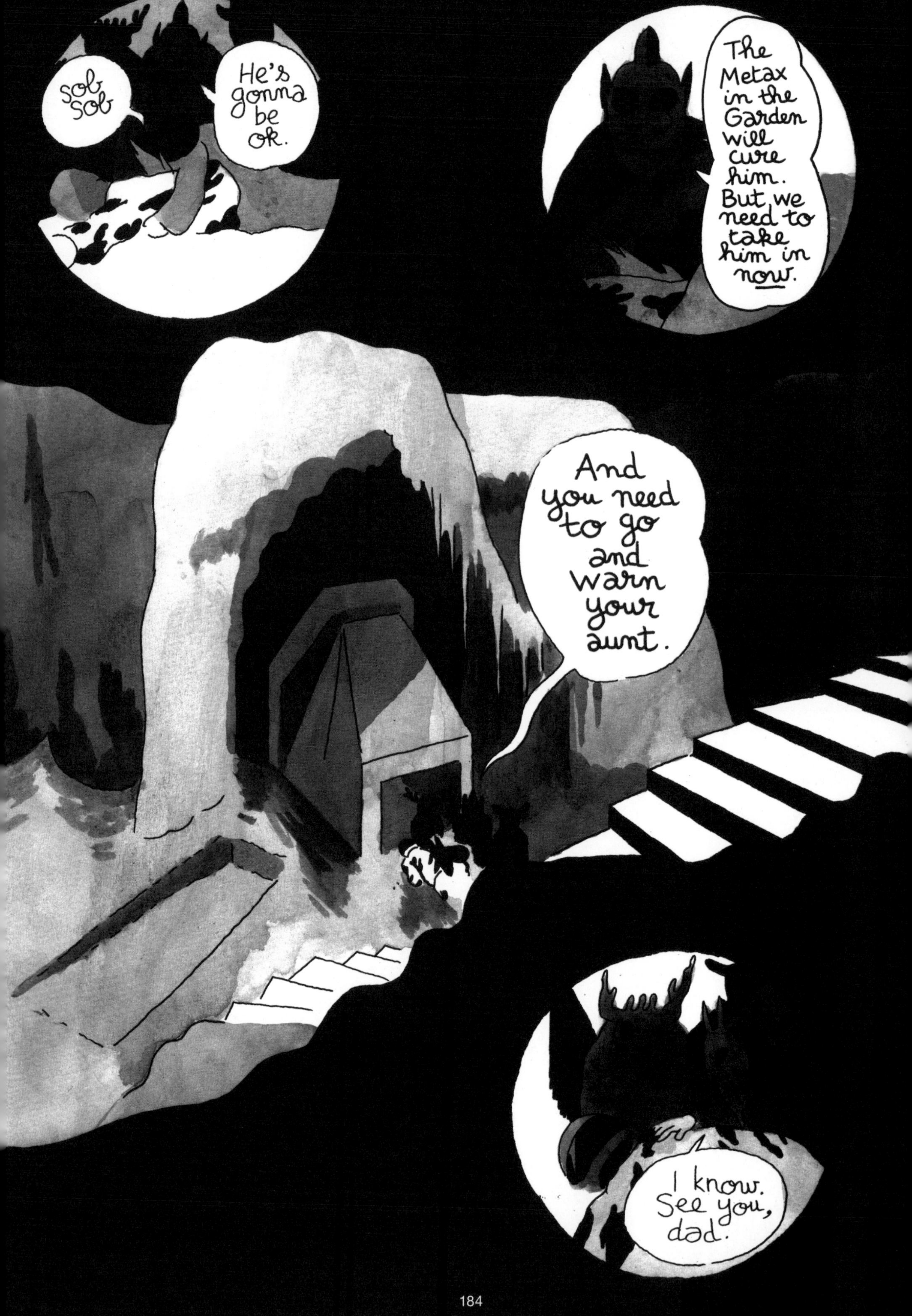
sob sob
He's gonna be ok.
The Metax in the Garden will cure him. But we need to take him in now.
And you need to go and warn your aunt.
I know. See you, dad.

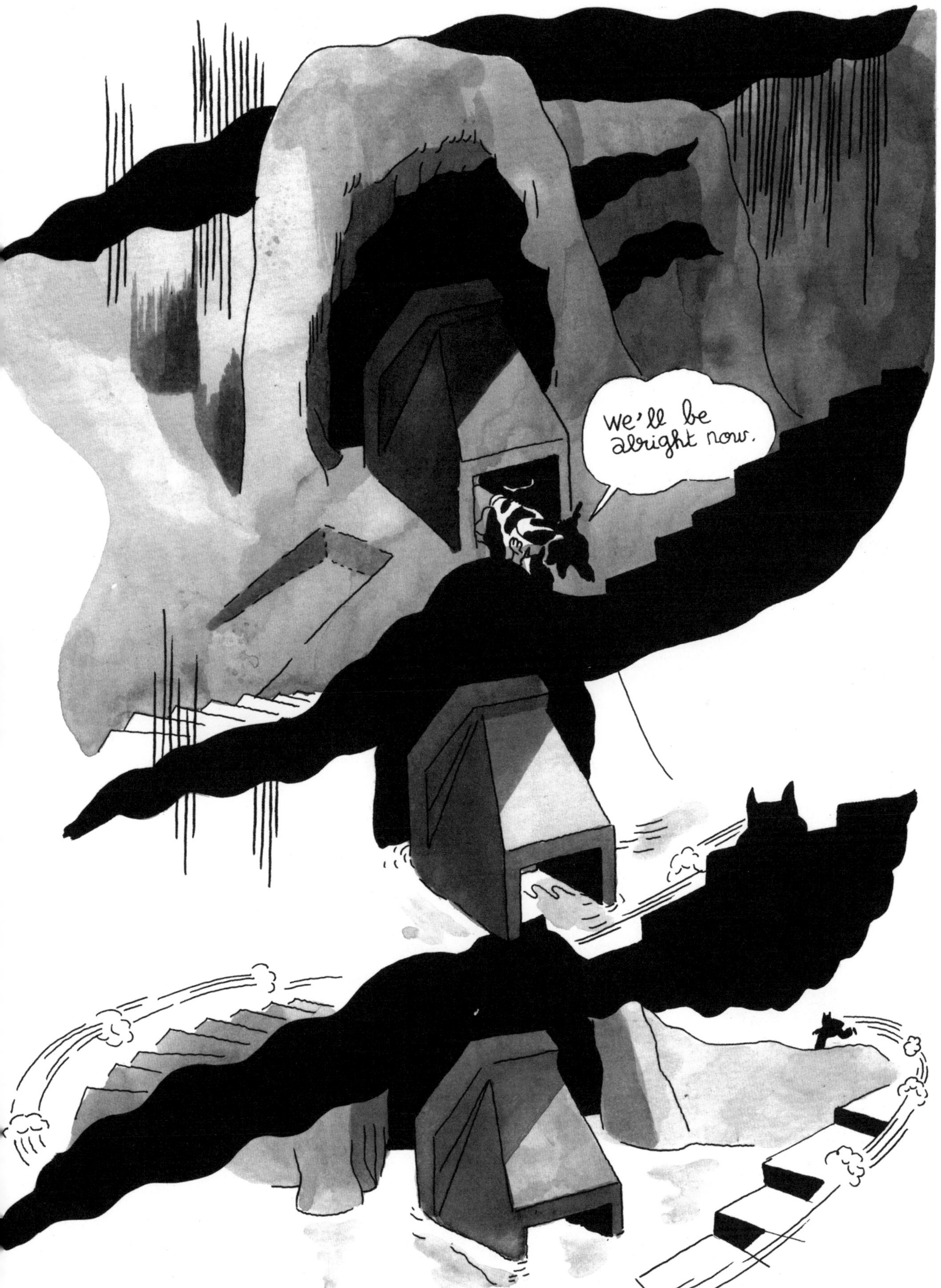
We'll be alright now.

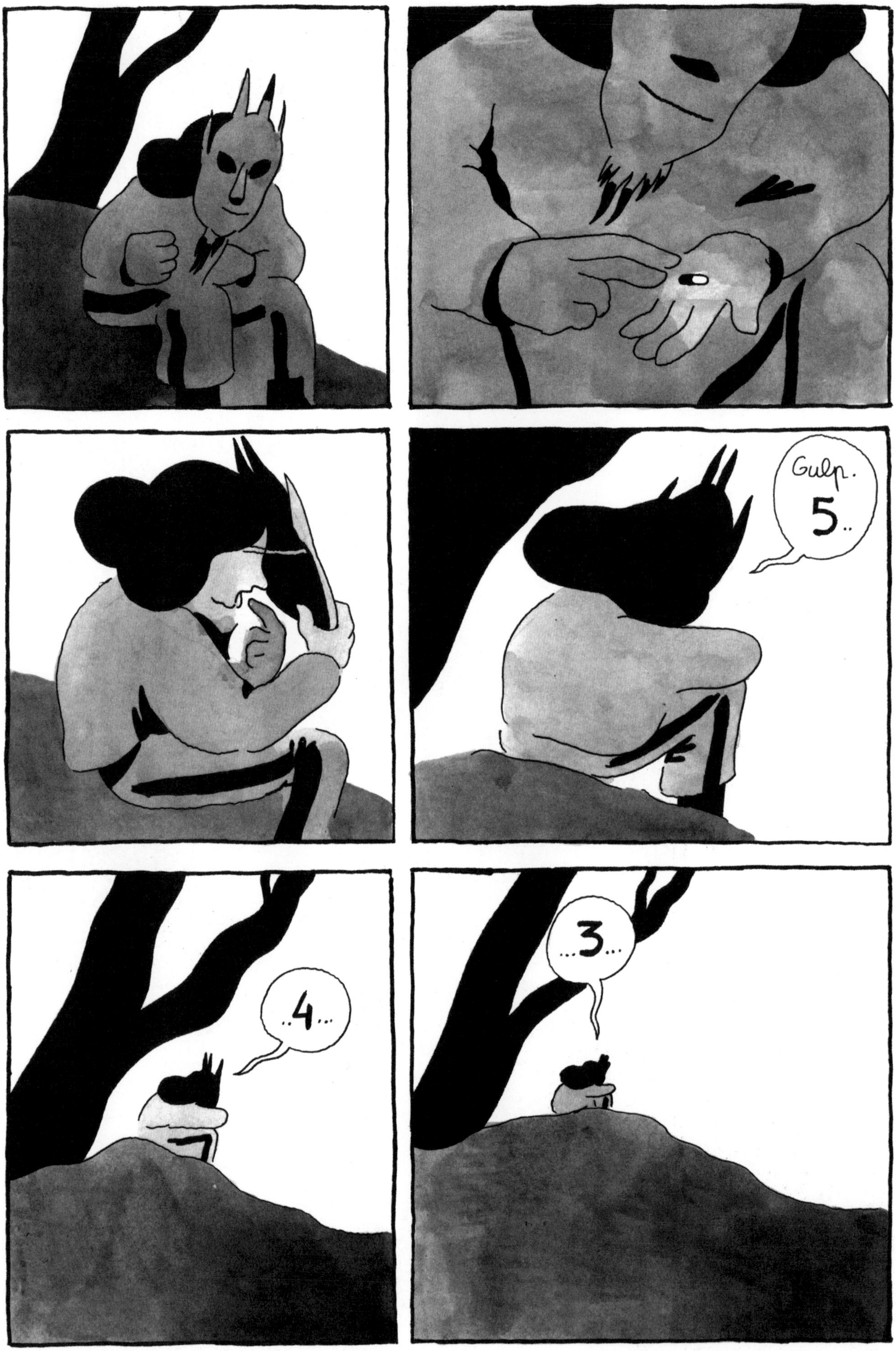
Gulp.
5..
..4...
...3...

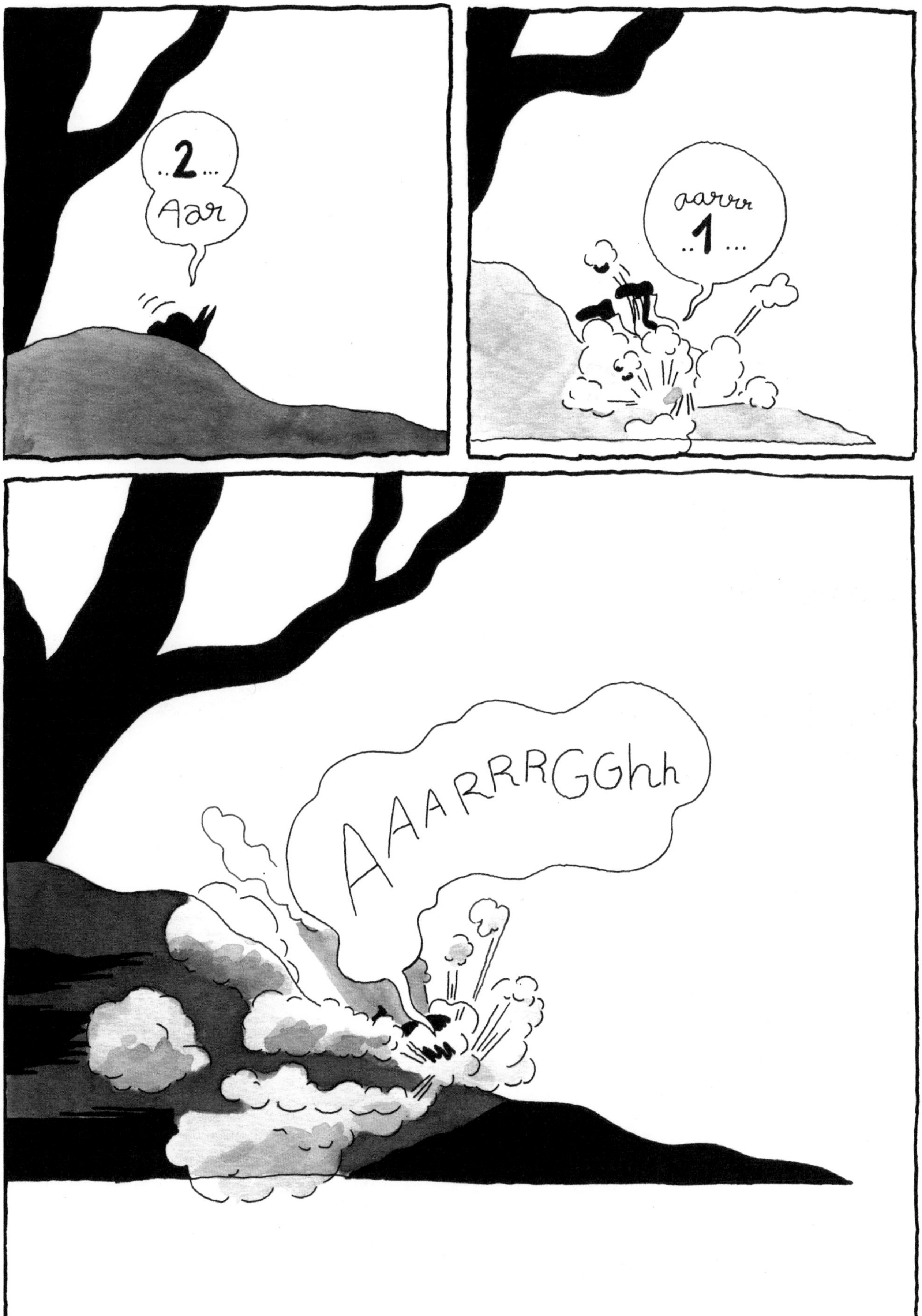
..2...
Aar
aarrr
..1...
AAARRRGhh

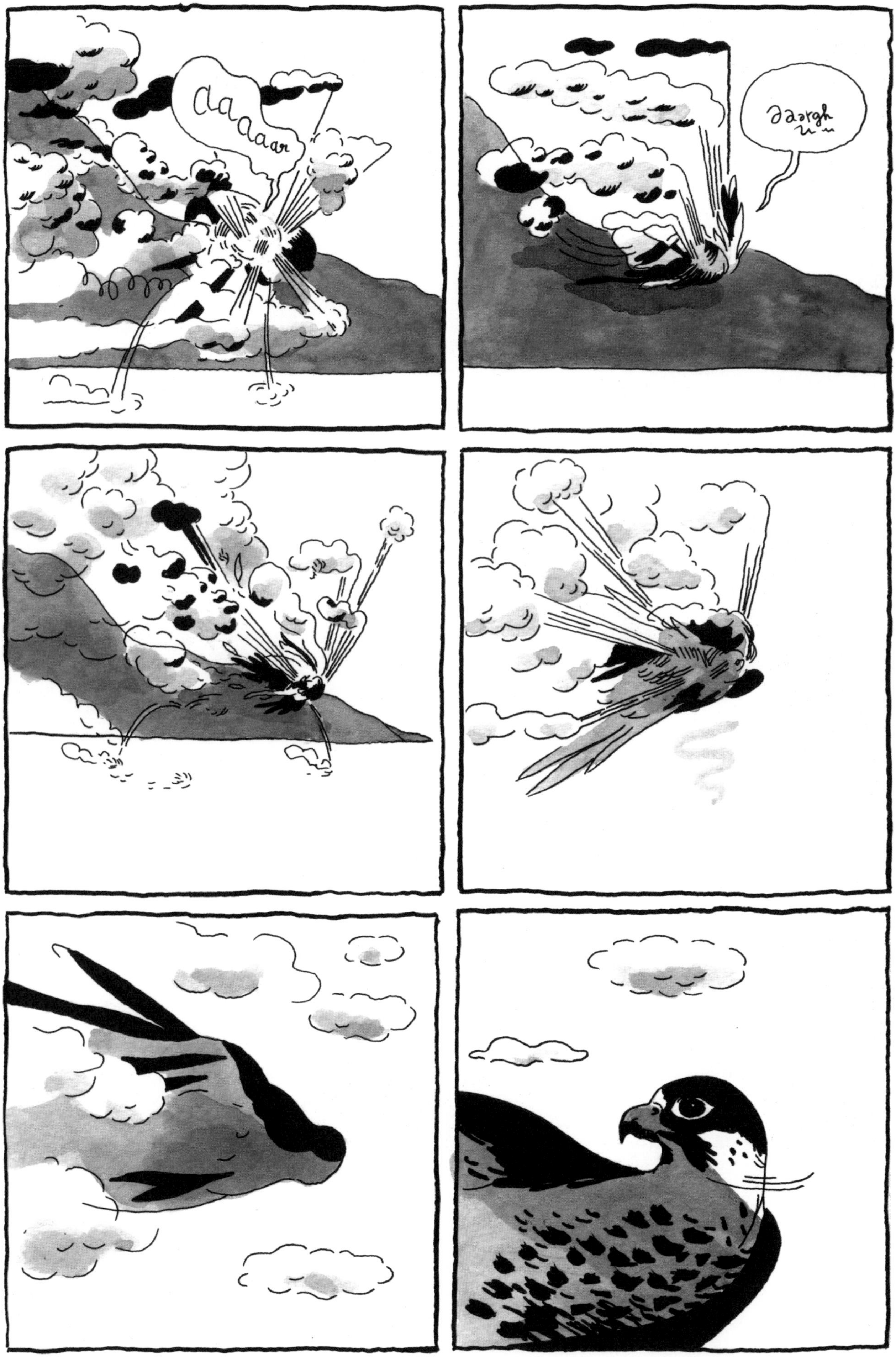
aaaaar
aaargh

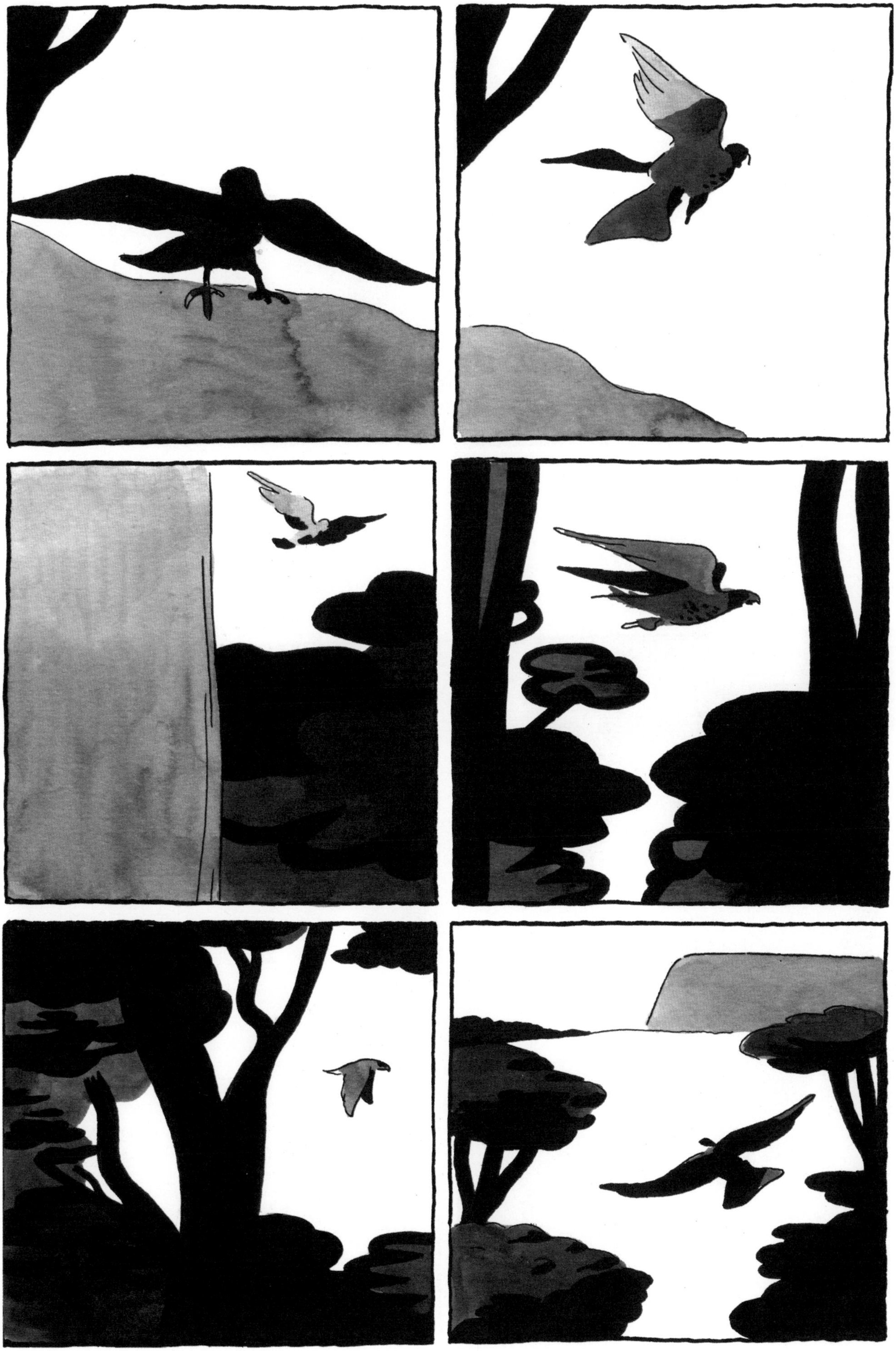

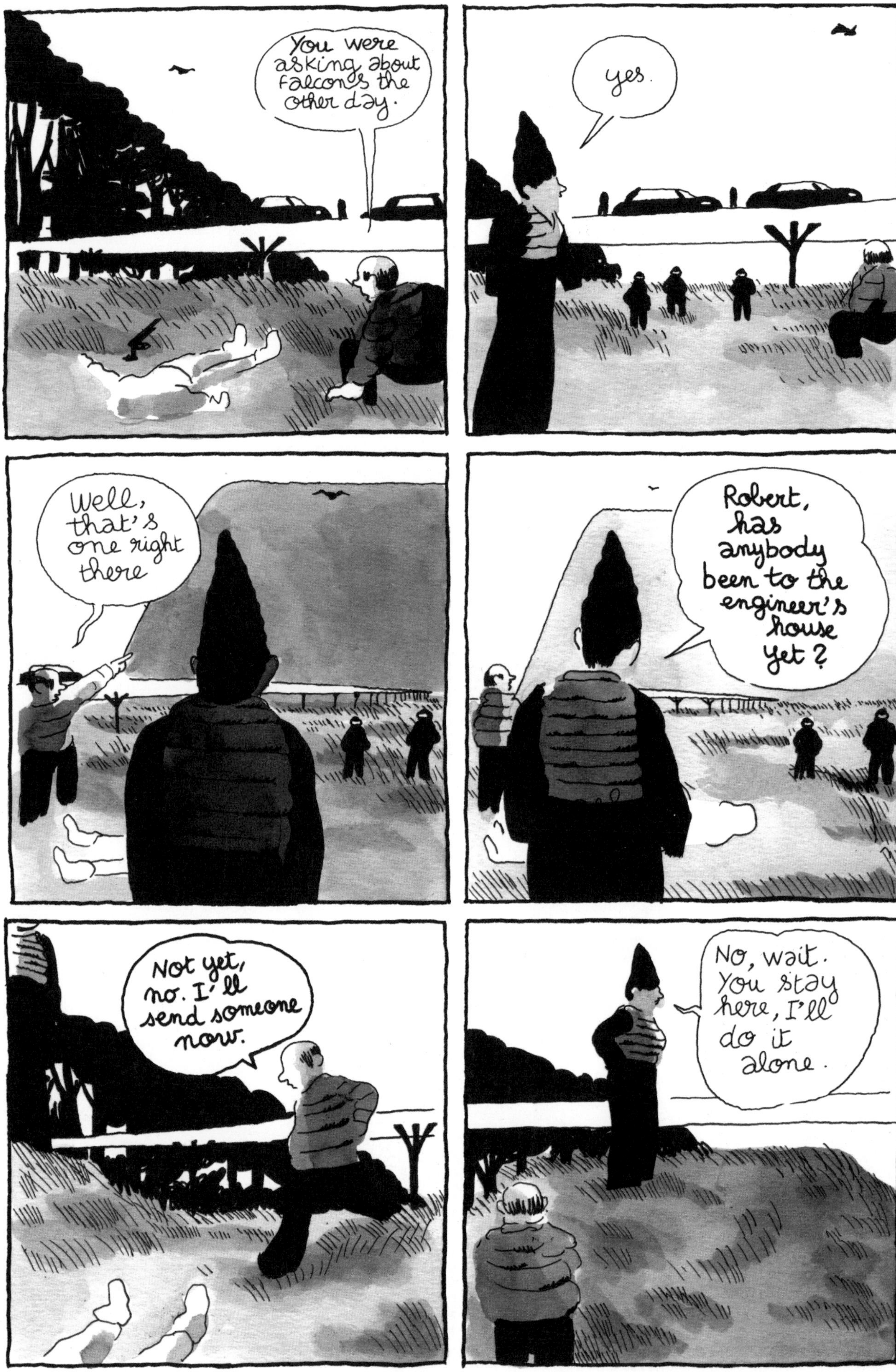
You were asking about falcons the other day.
yes.
Well, that's one right there
Robert, has anybody been to the engineer's house yet?
Not yet, no. I'll send someone now.
No, wait. You stay here, I'll do it alone.

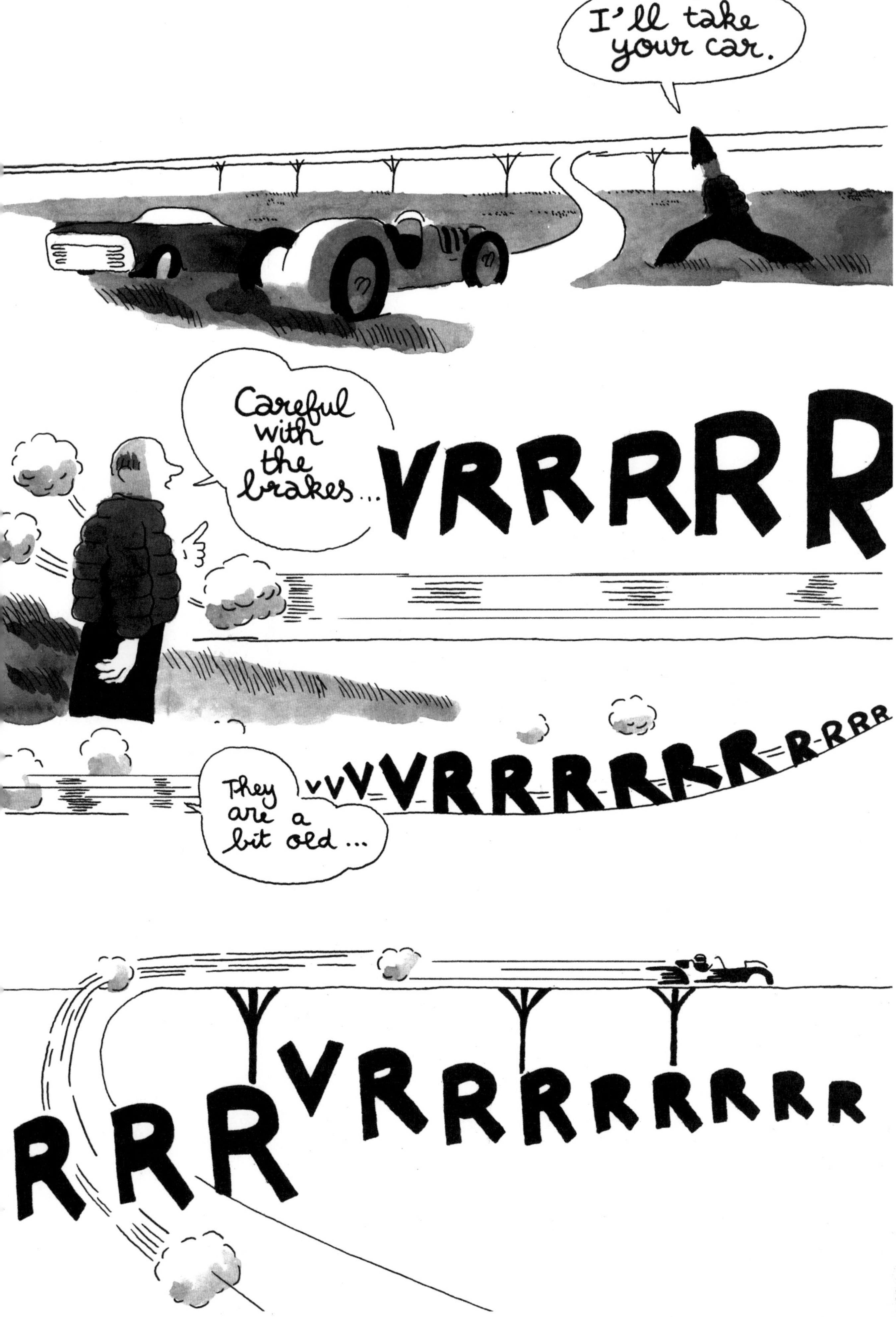

I'll take your car.
Careful with the brakes...
VRRRRRR
They are a bit old...
VVVVRRRRRRR-R-RRR
RRRVRRRRRRRRR

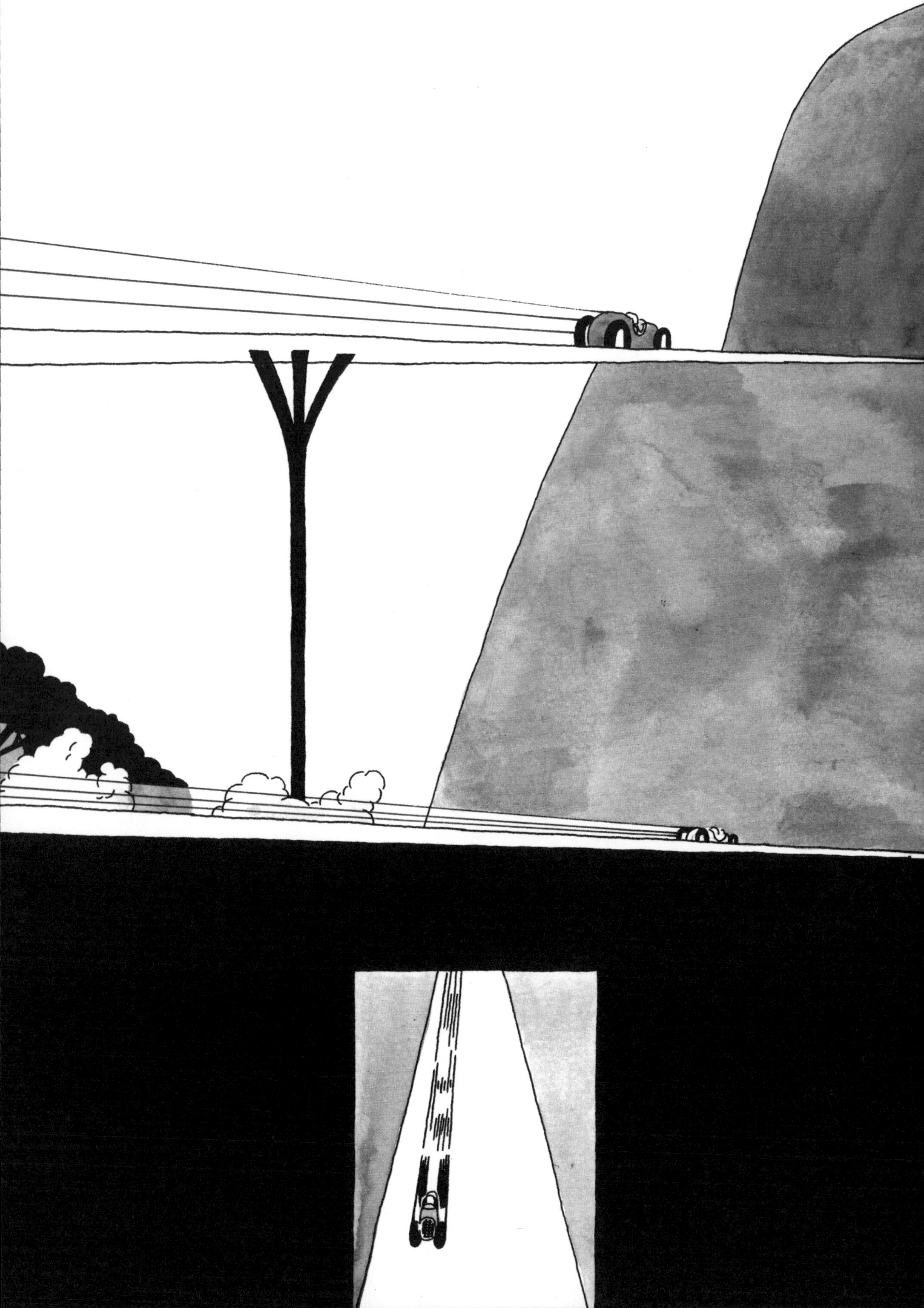

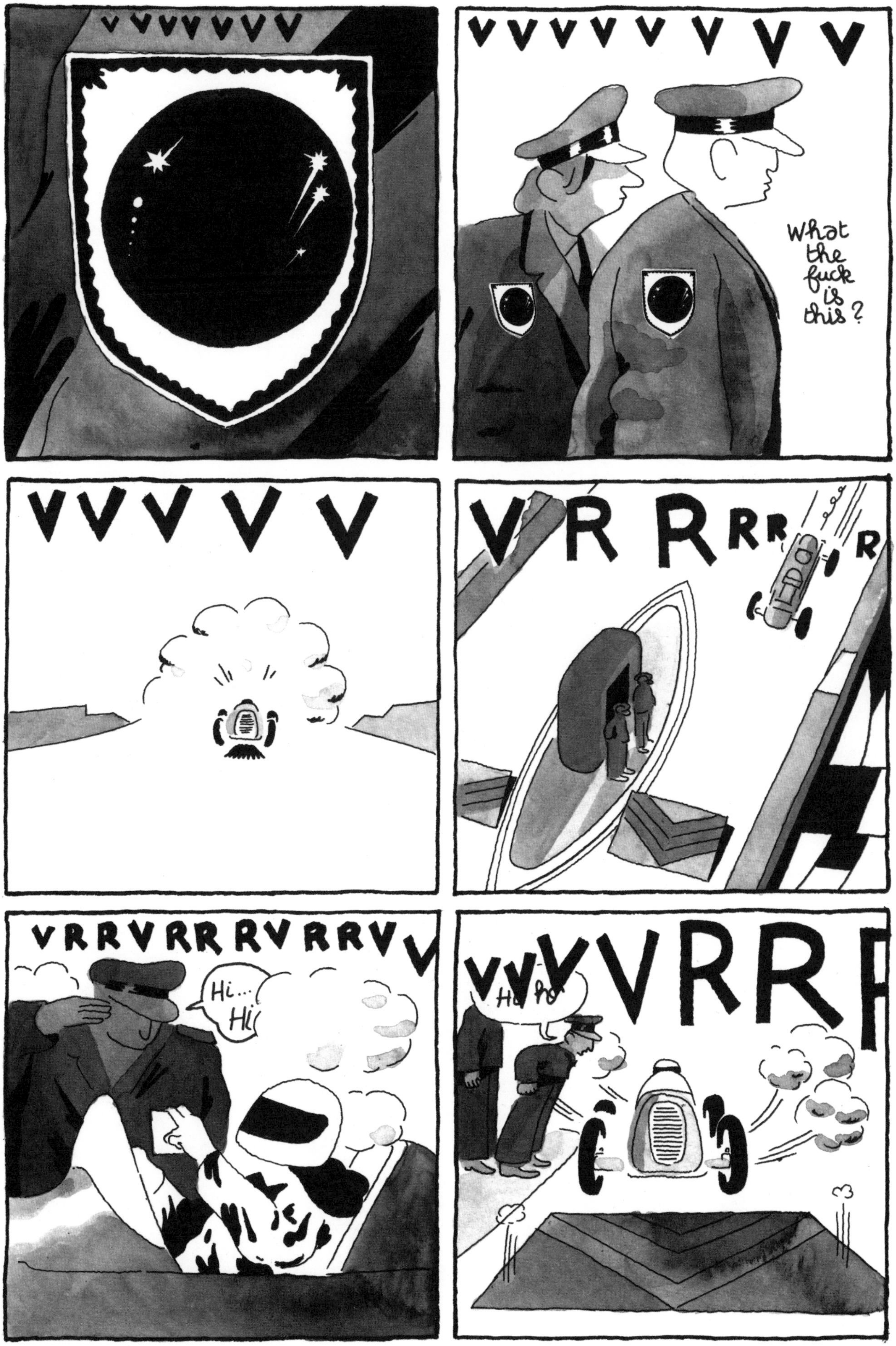
VVVVVVVV
VVVVVVVV
What the fuck is this?
VVVVV
VRRRRR
VRRVRRRVRRRVV
Hi... Hi
VVVVRR

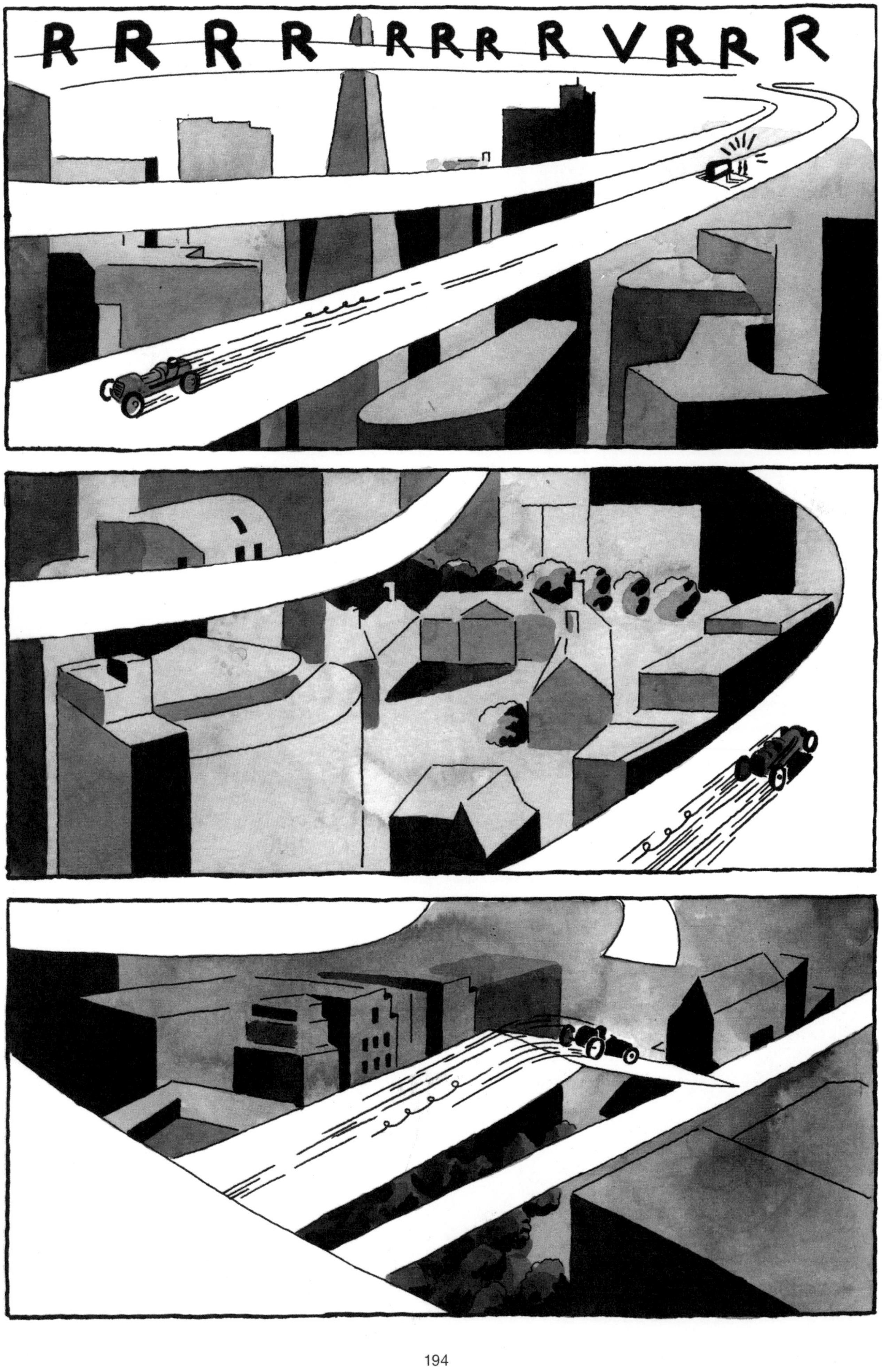
R R R R RRR R VRRR R

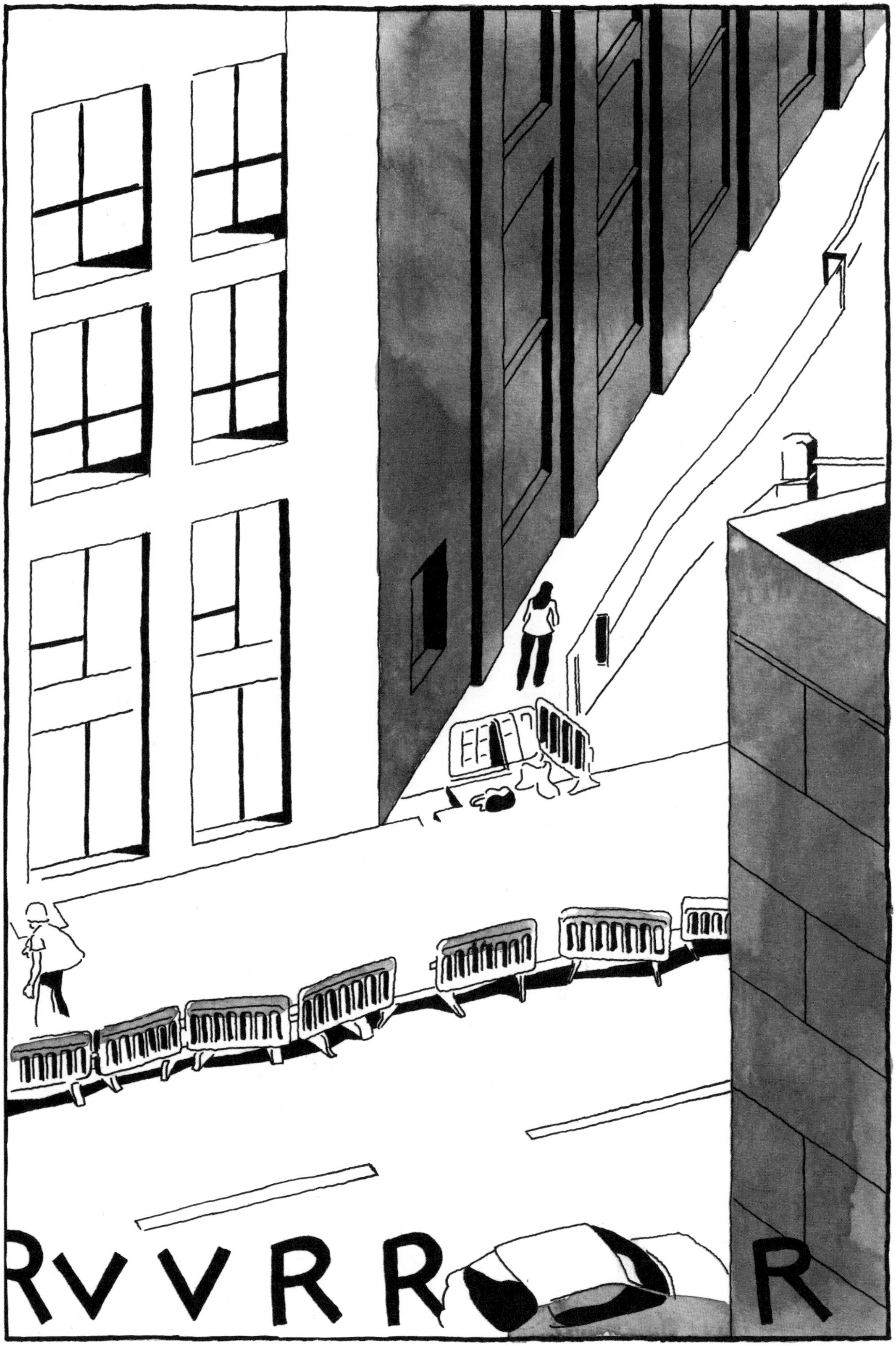
RVVRR R

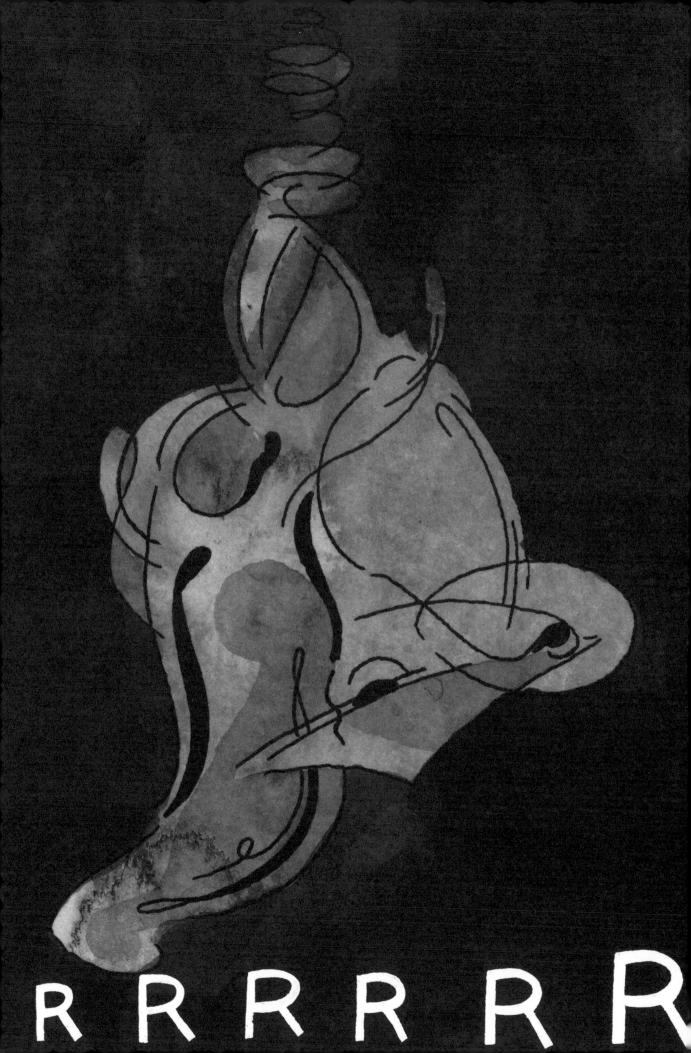

RRRRRR

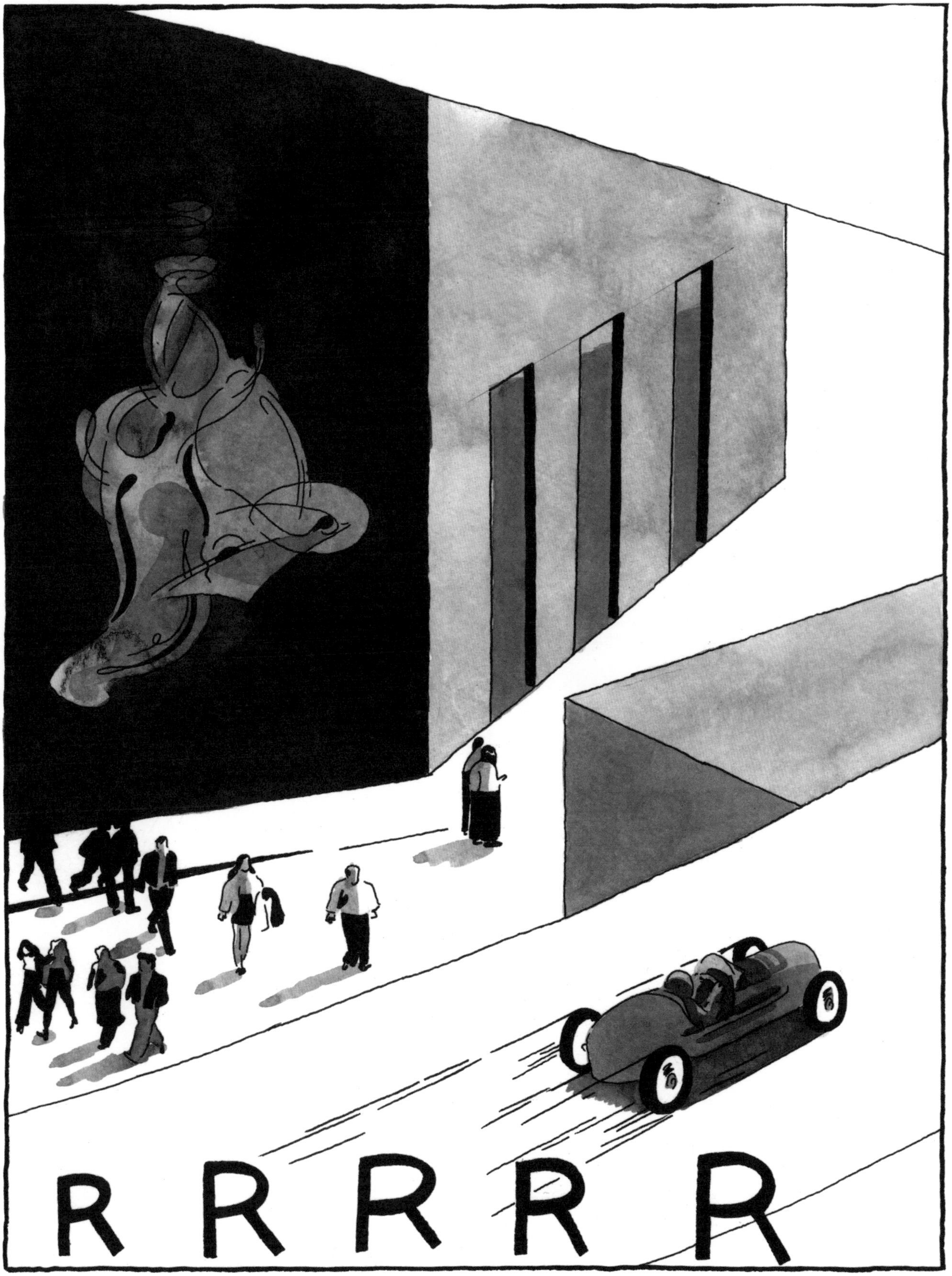
RRRRR

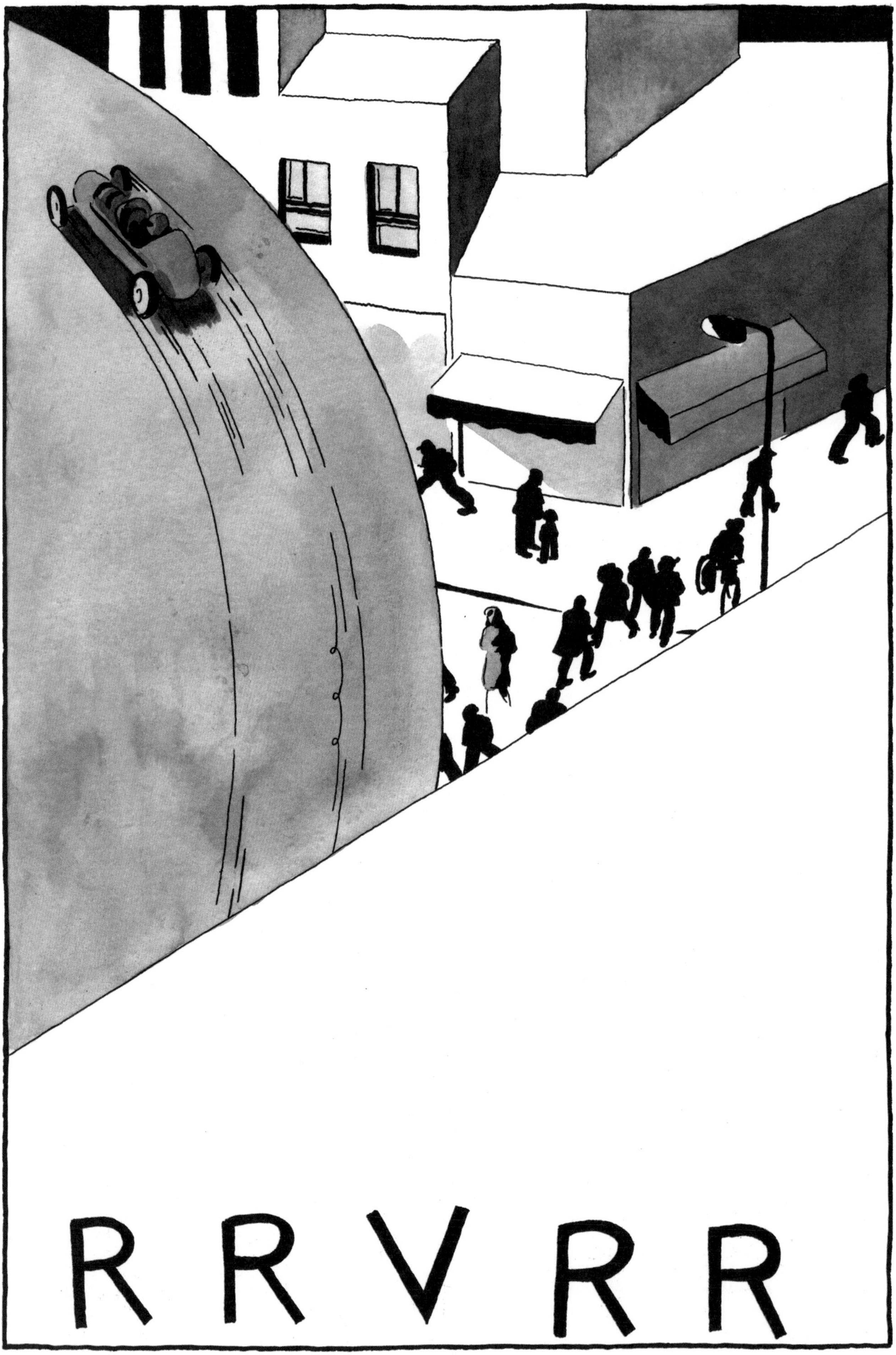
RRVRR

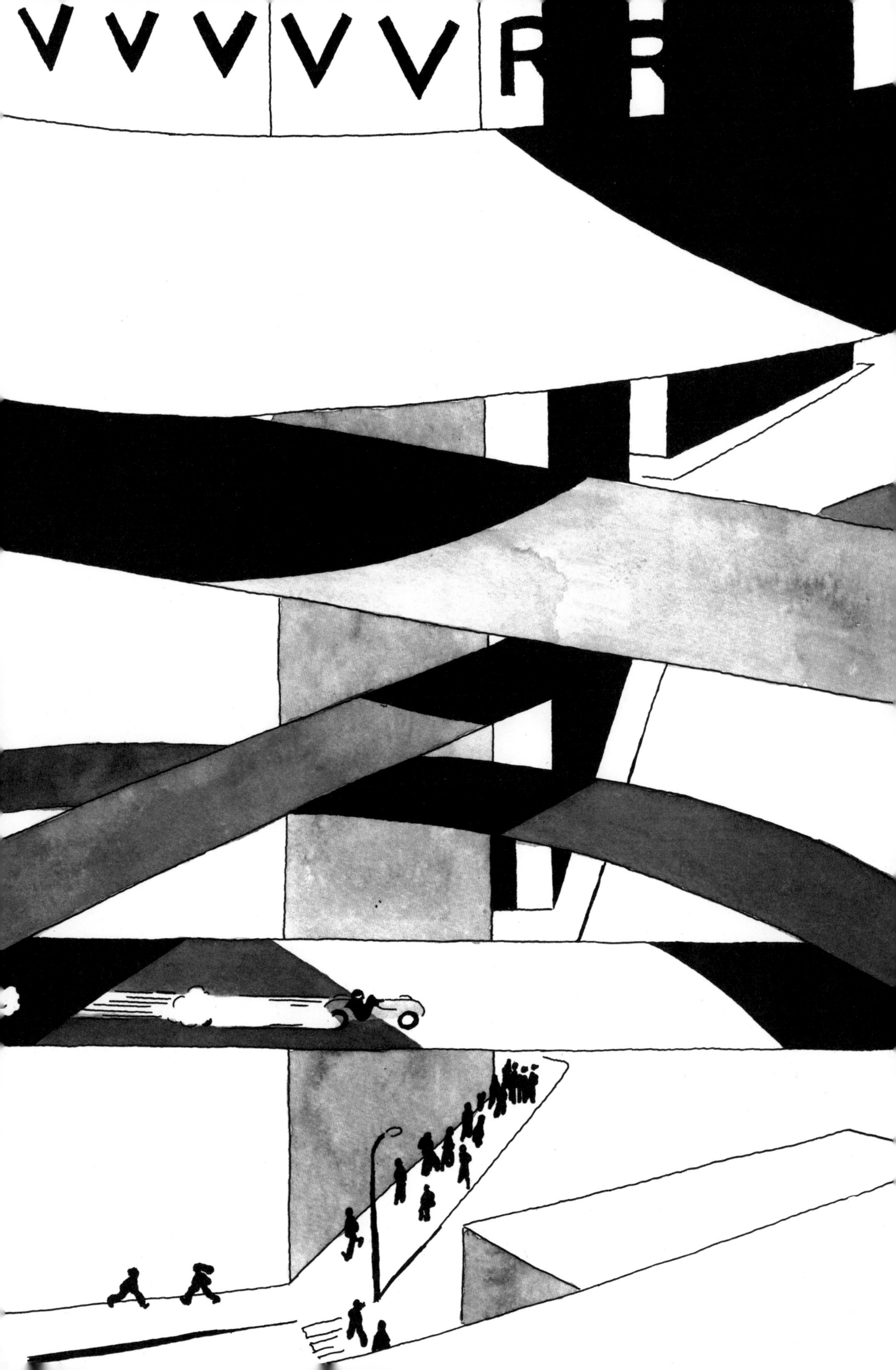
VVVVVRR

V V R
R R
V V V
RooRooR R R
R R
Road down!!
RRR R ROOOOR
Thanks!
V V R
RRRROOO

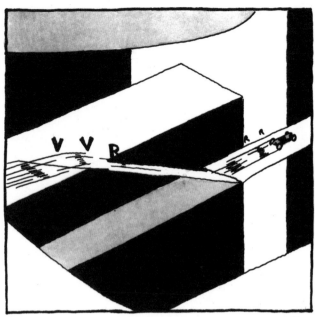

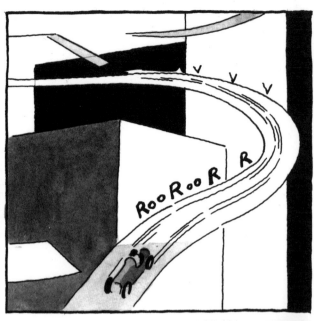

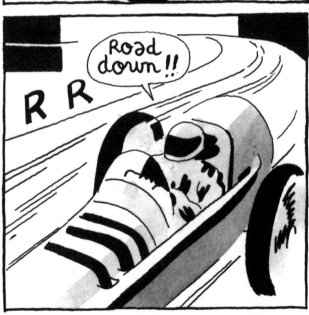

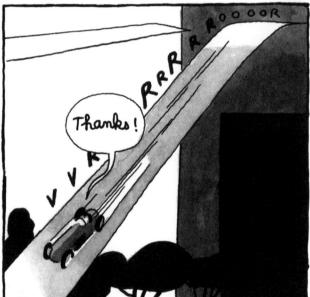

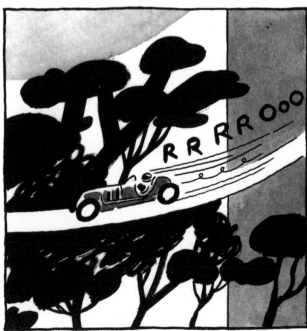

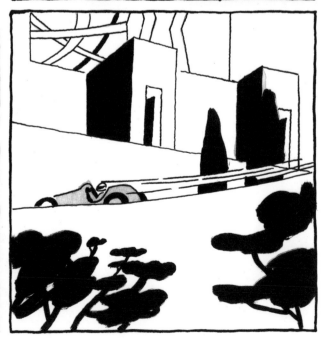

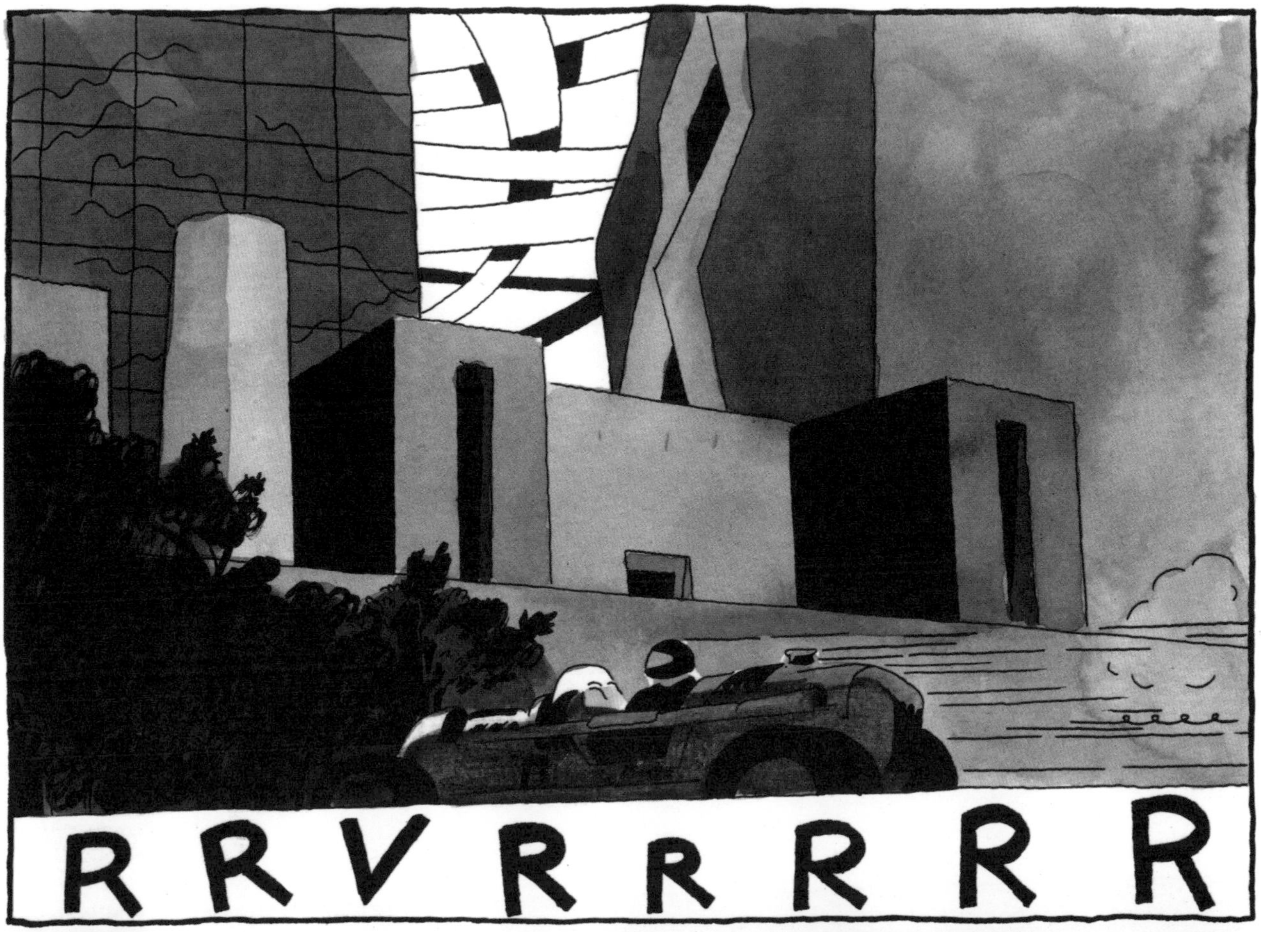
RRVRRRRRR

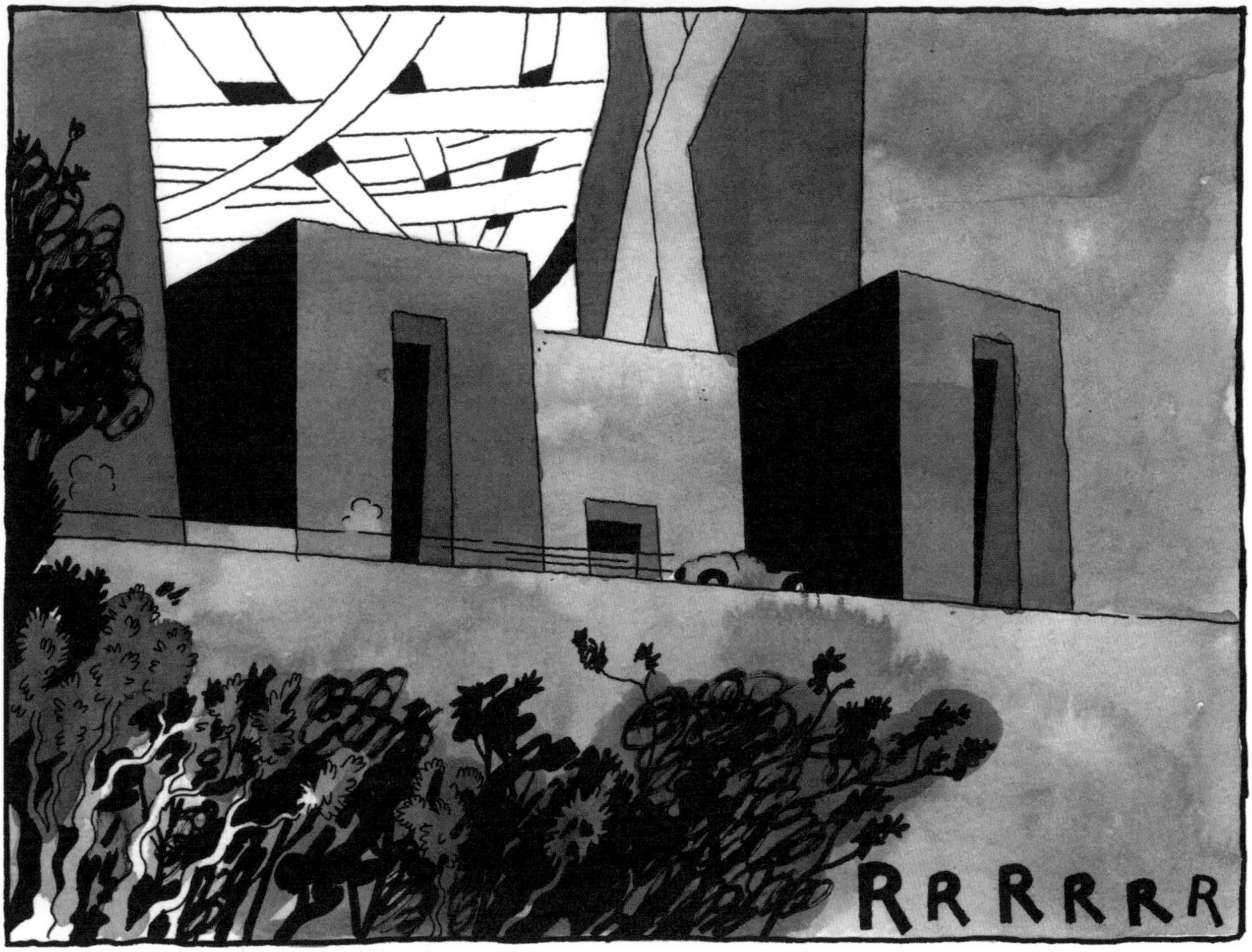
RRRRRR

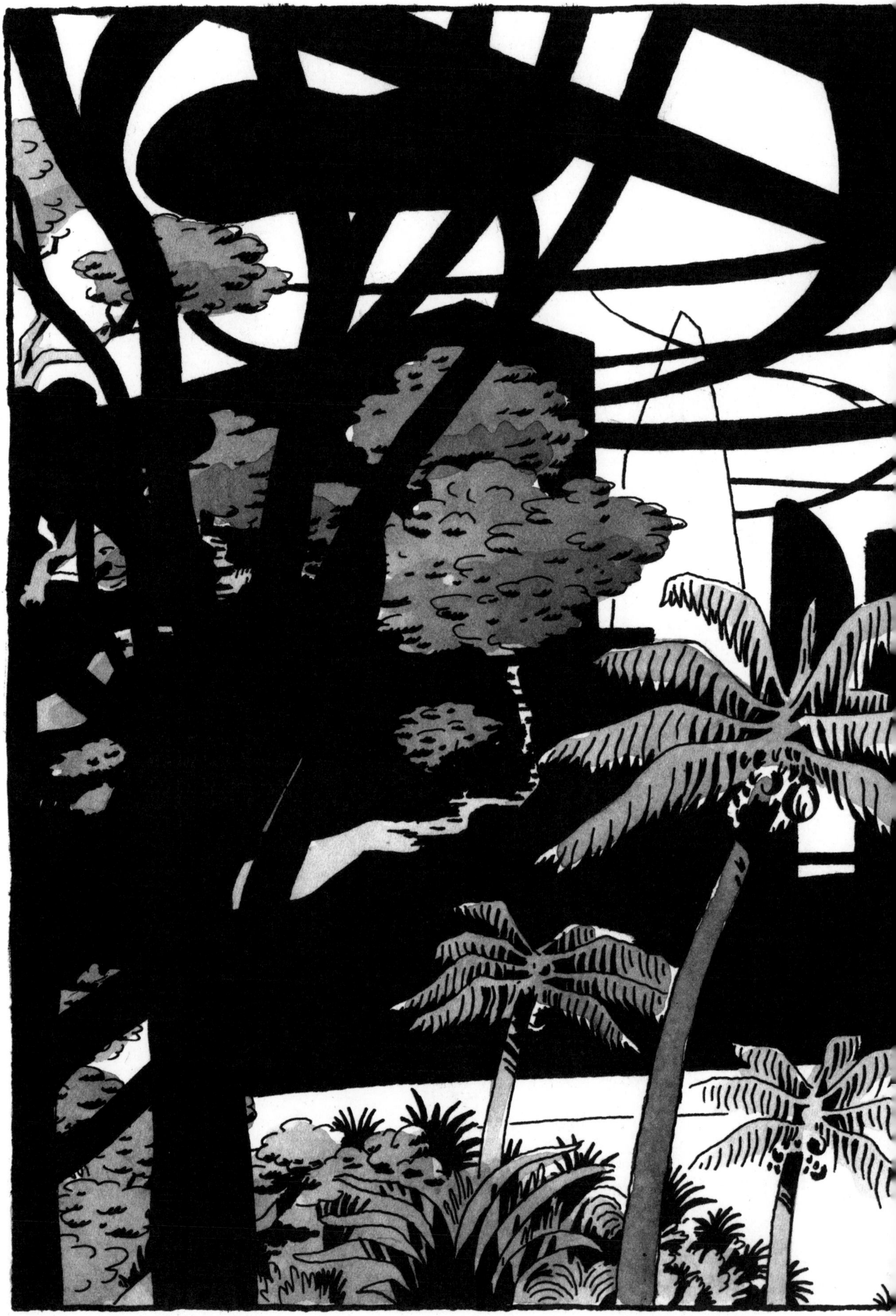

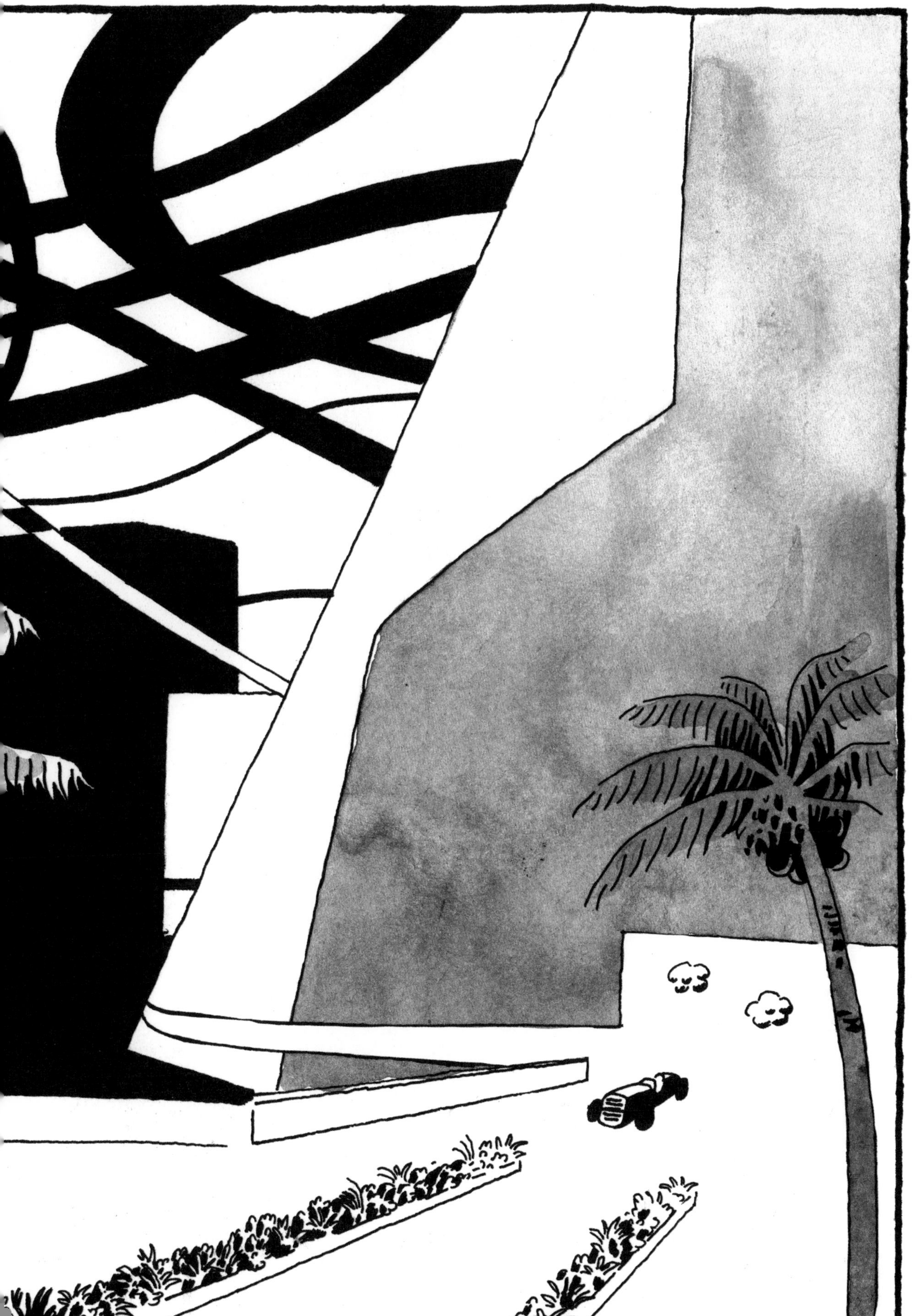

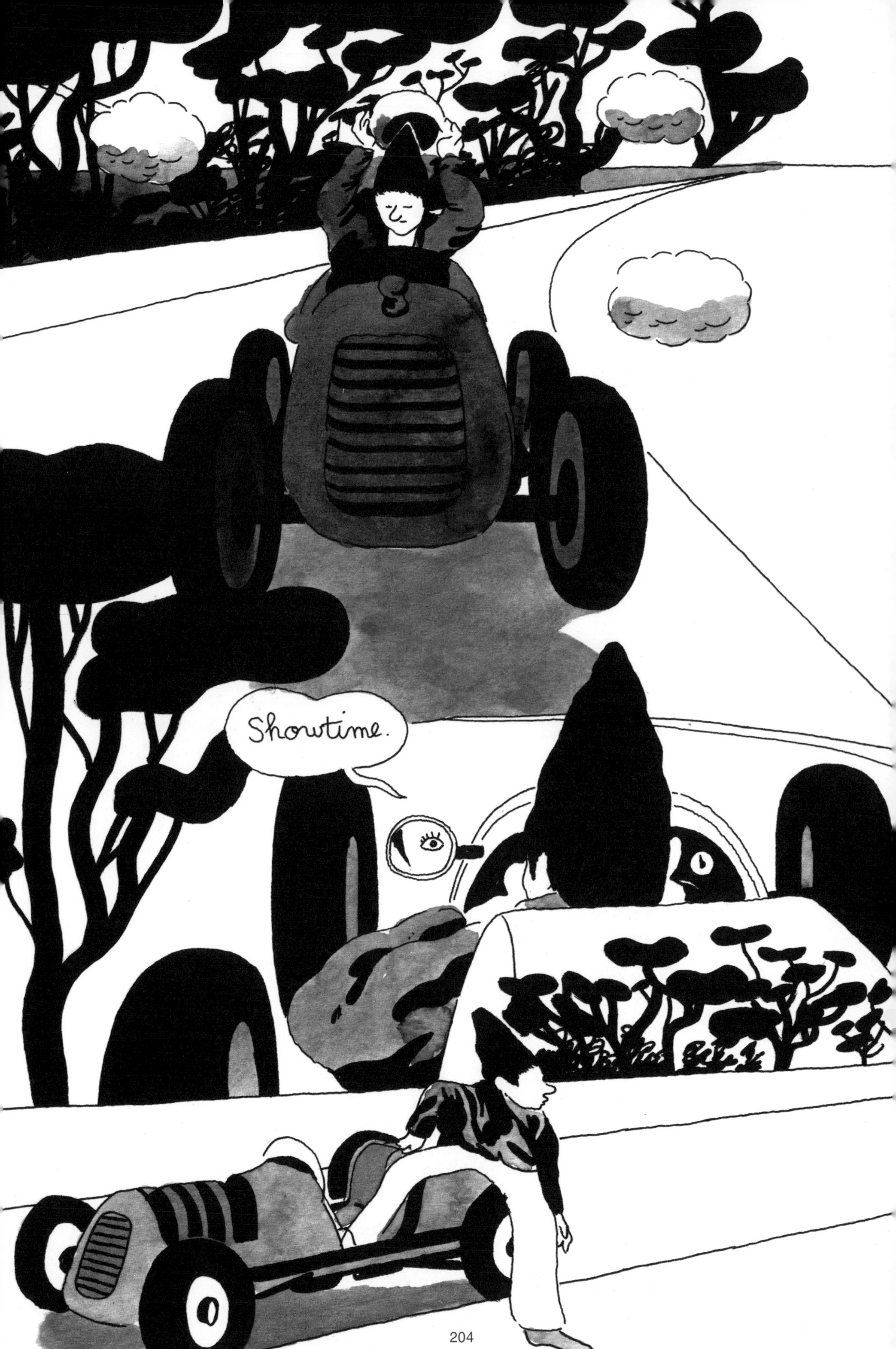
Showtime.

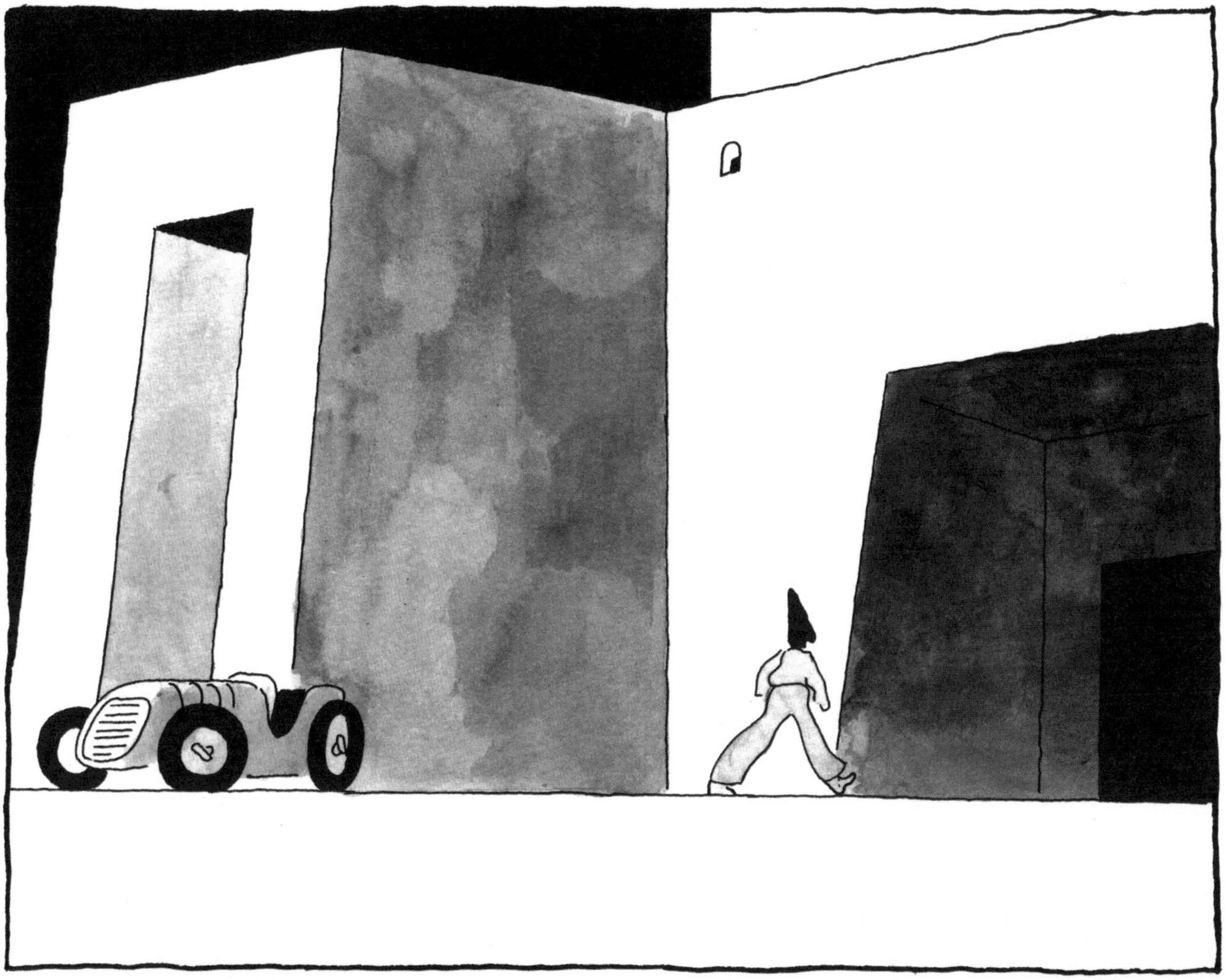

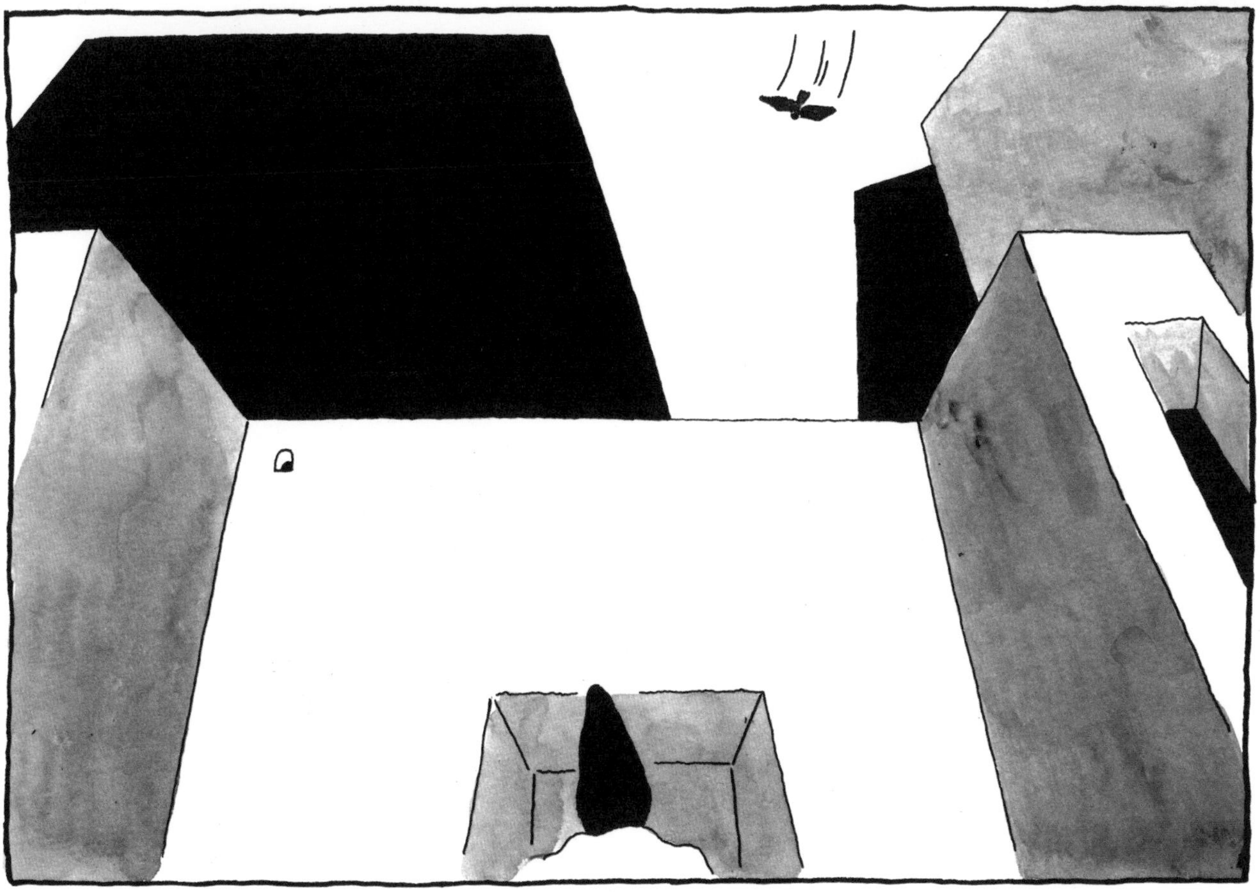

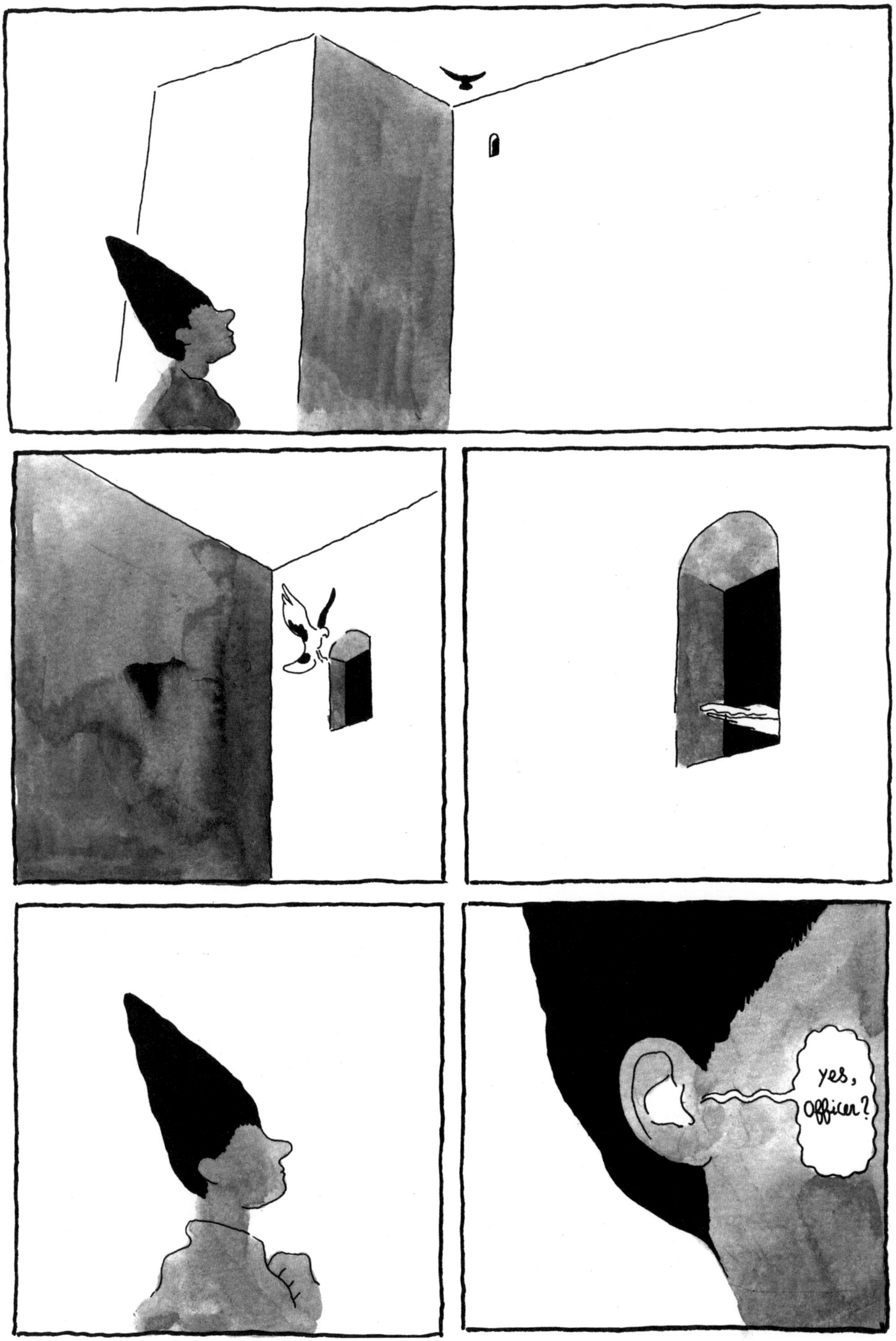
yes,
Officer?

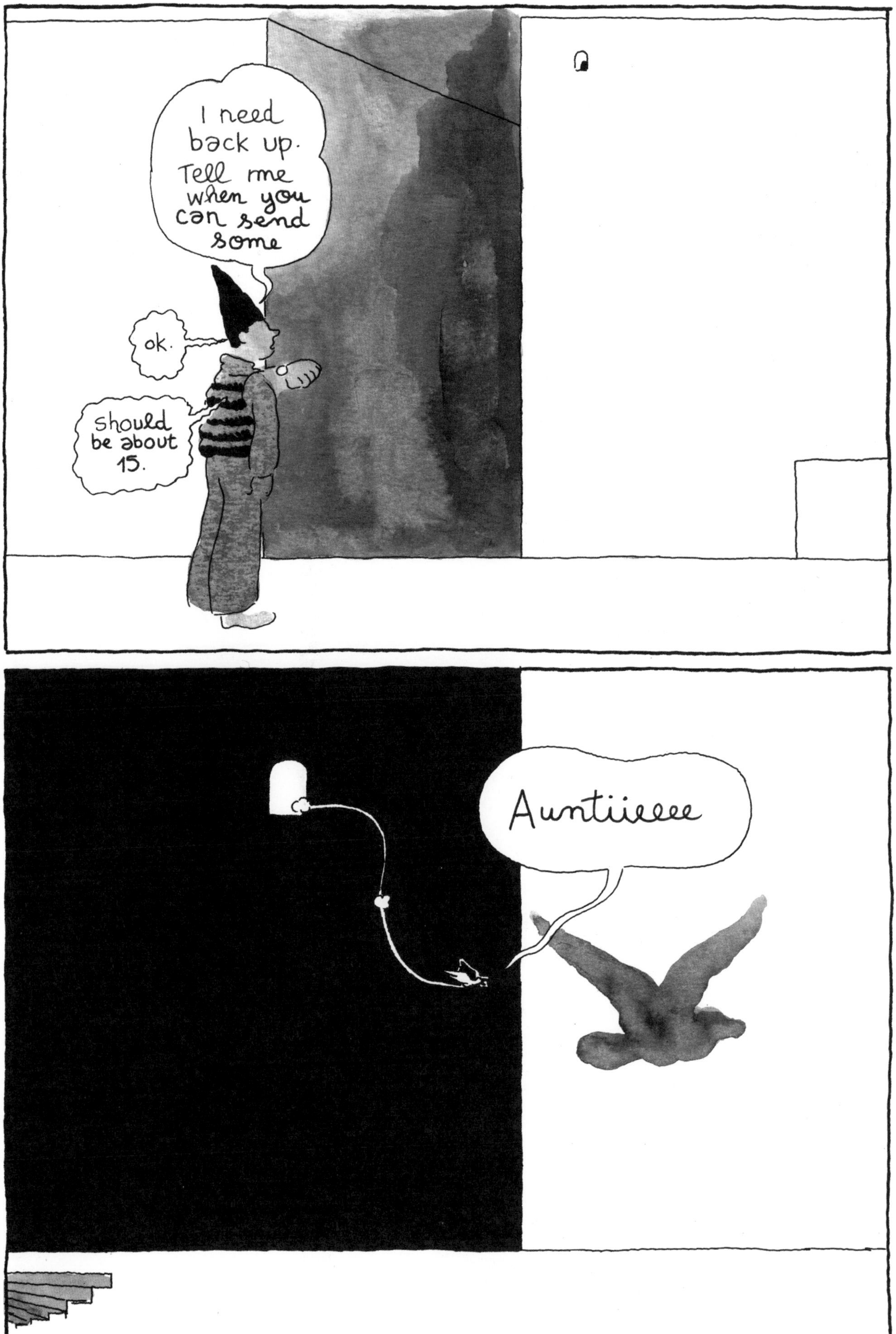
I need back up. Tell me when you can send some
ok.
should be about 15.
Auntiieeee

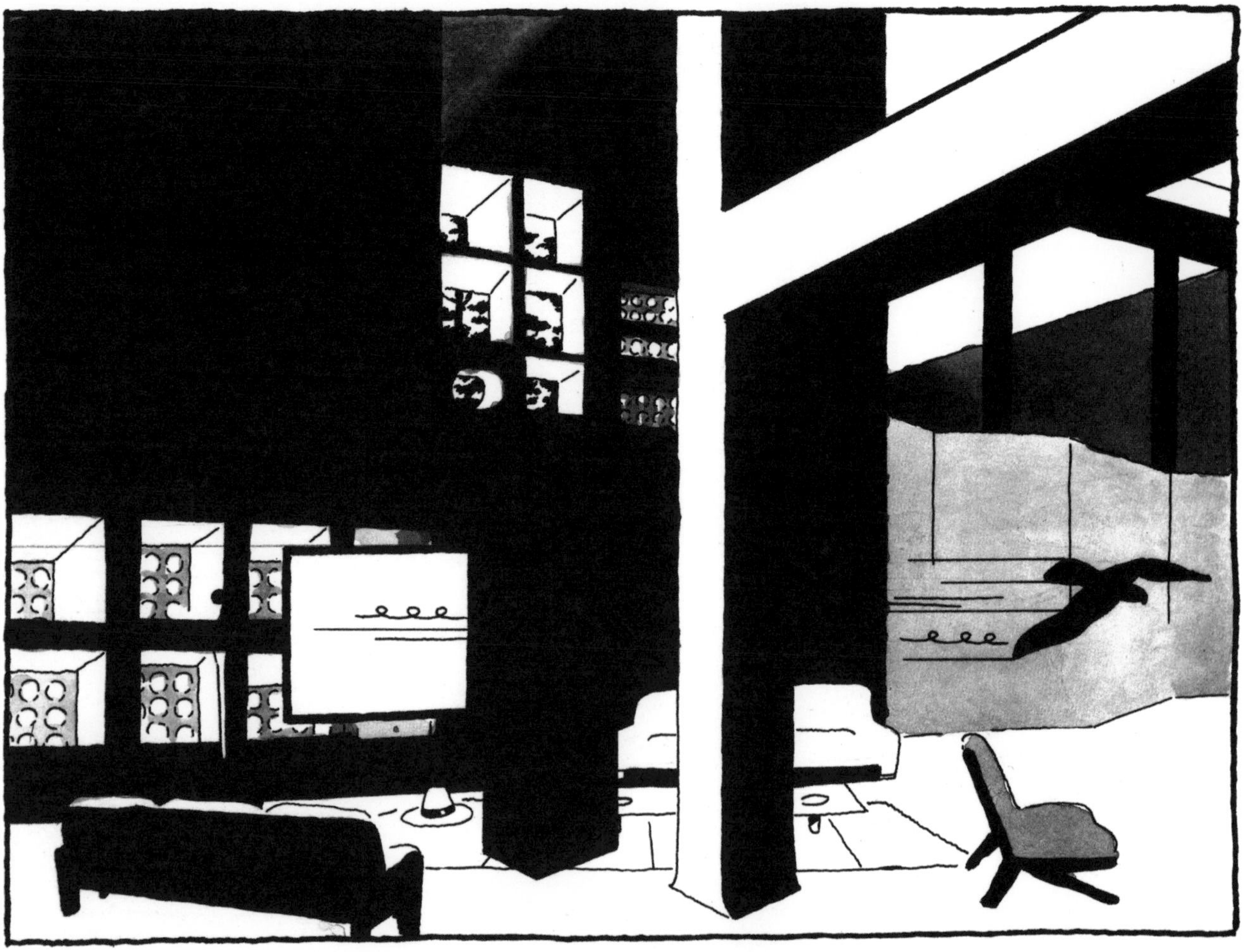

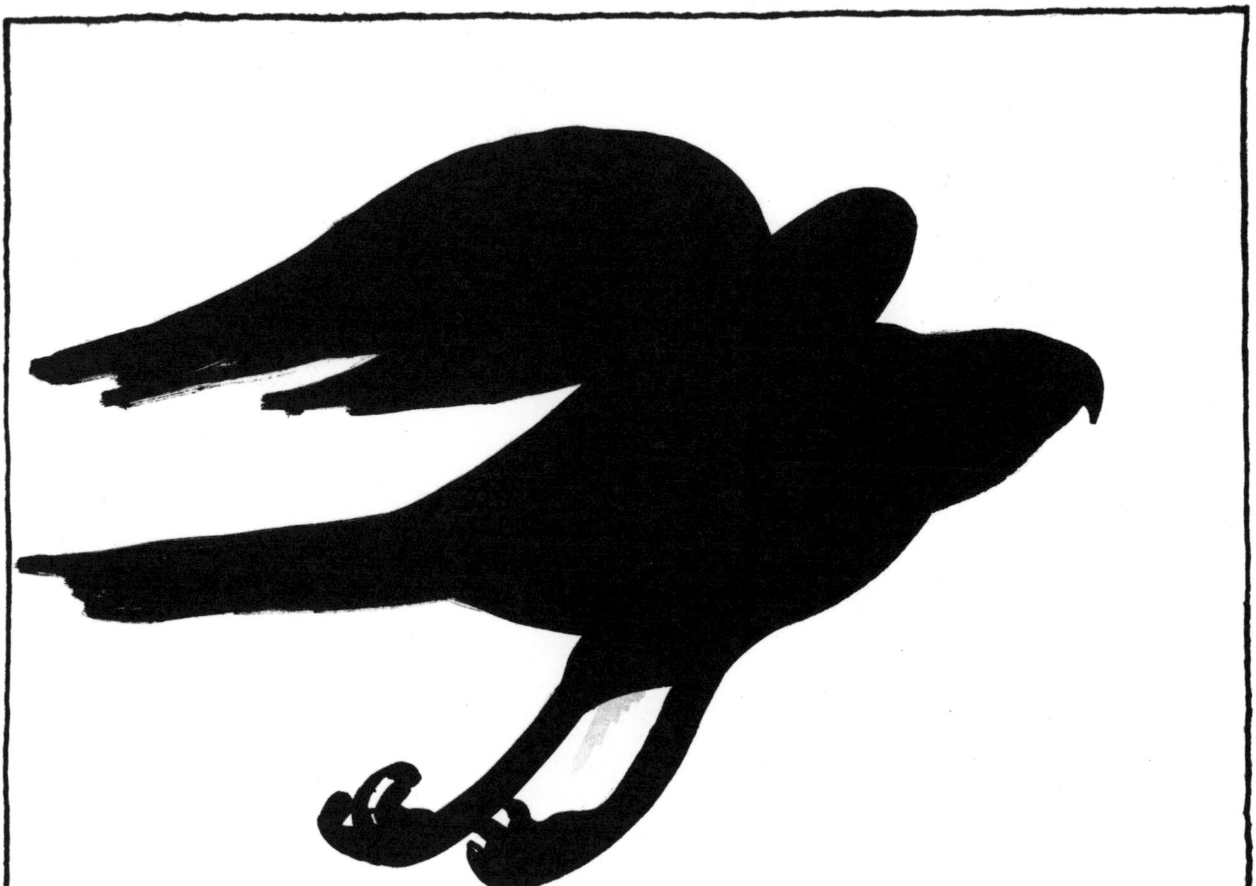

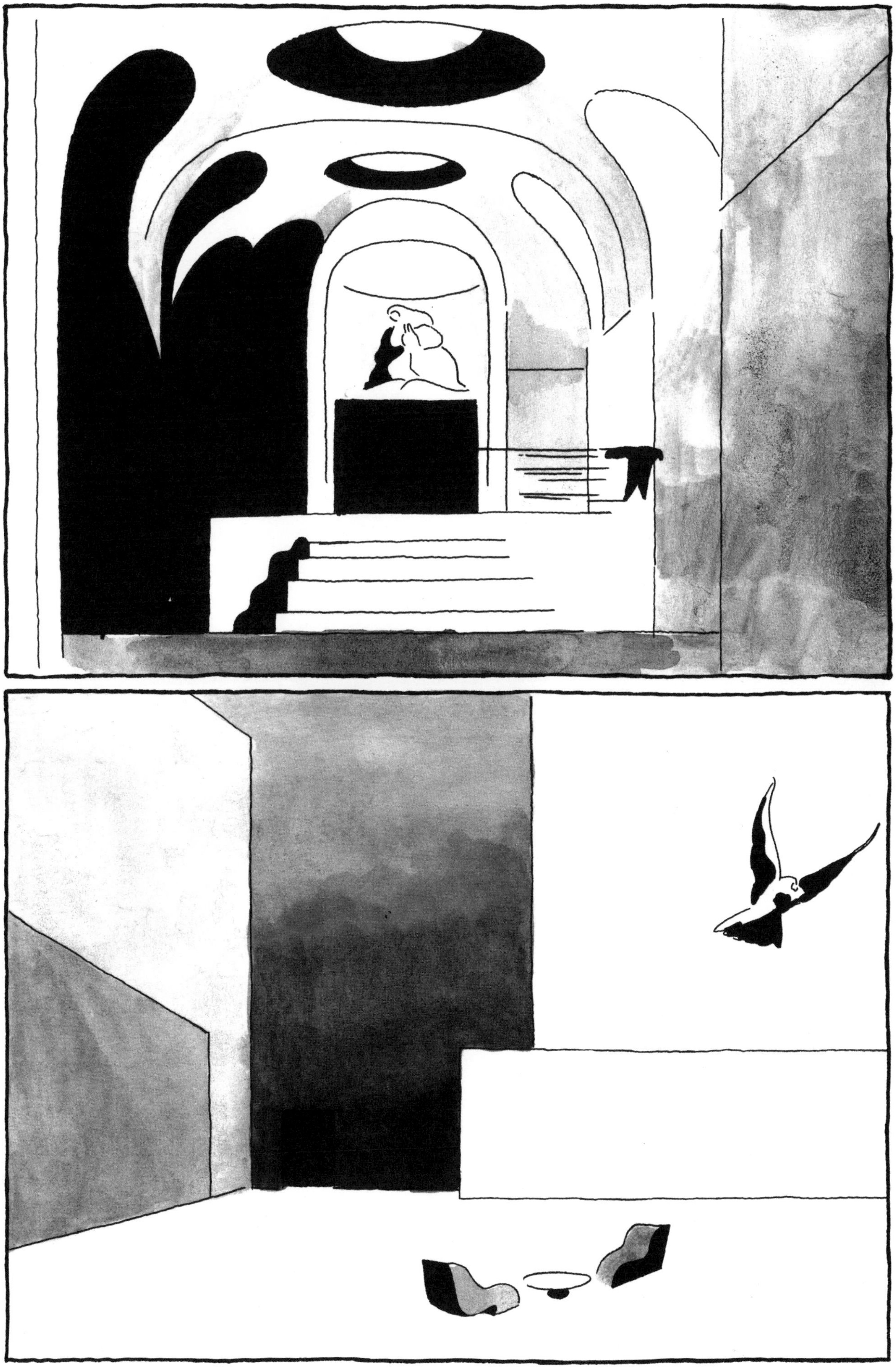

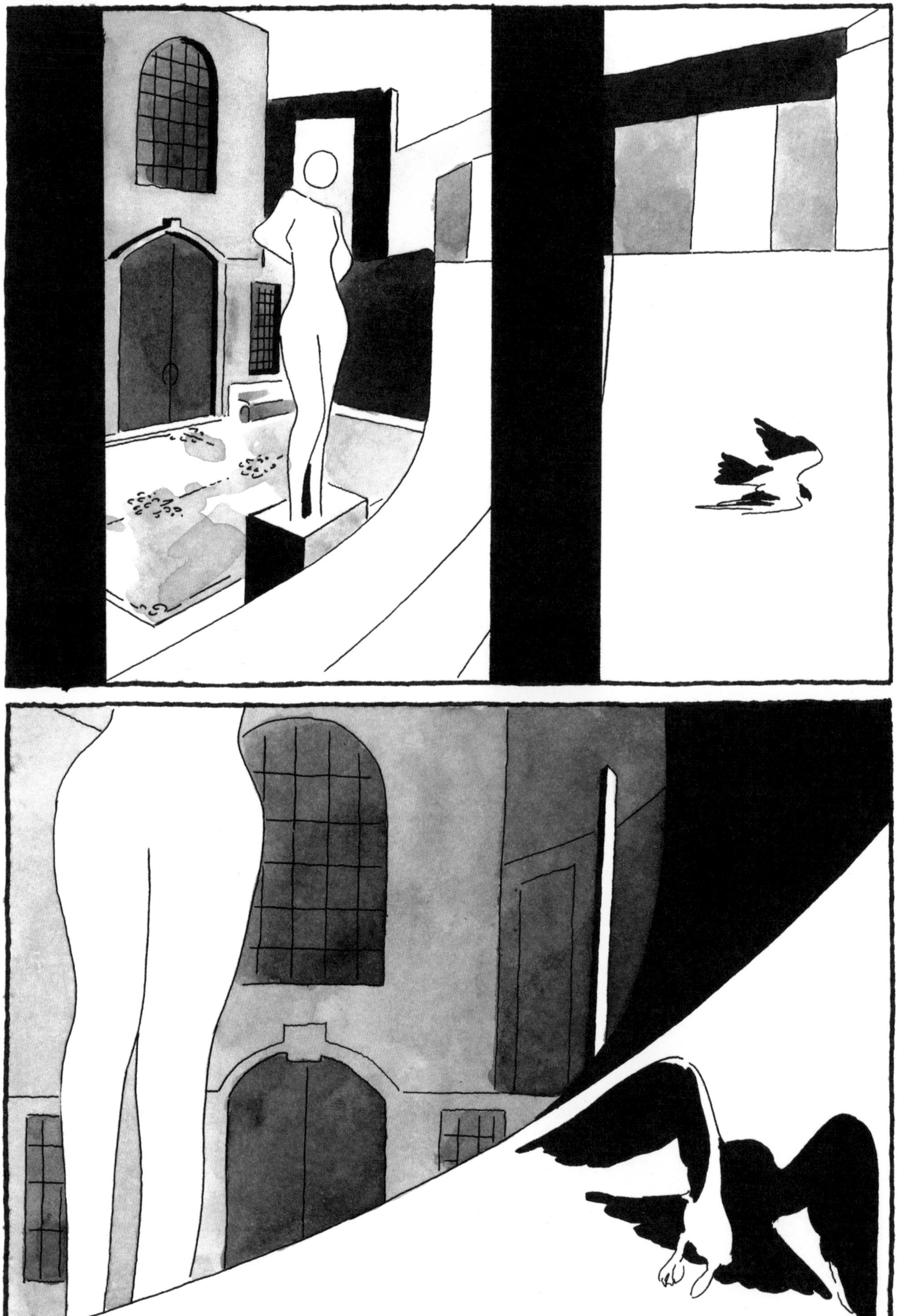

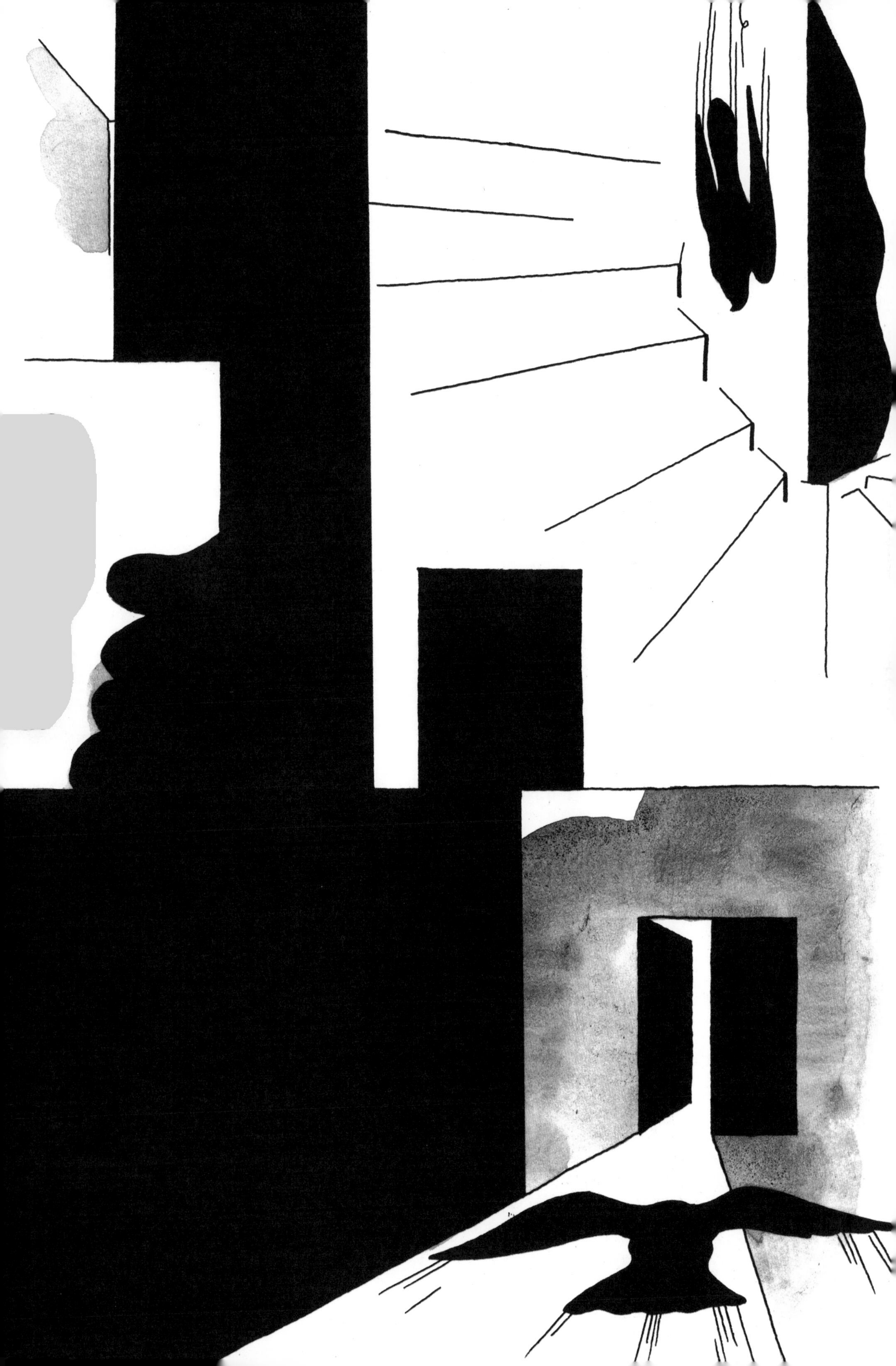

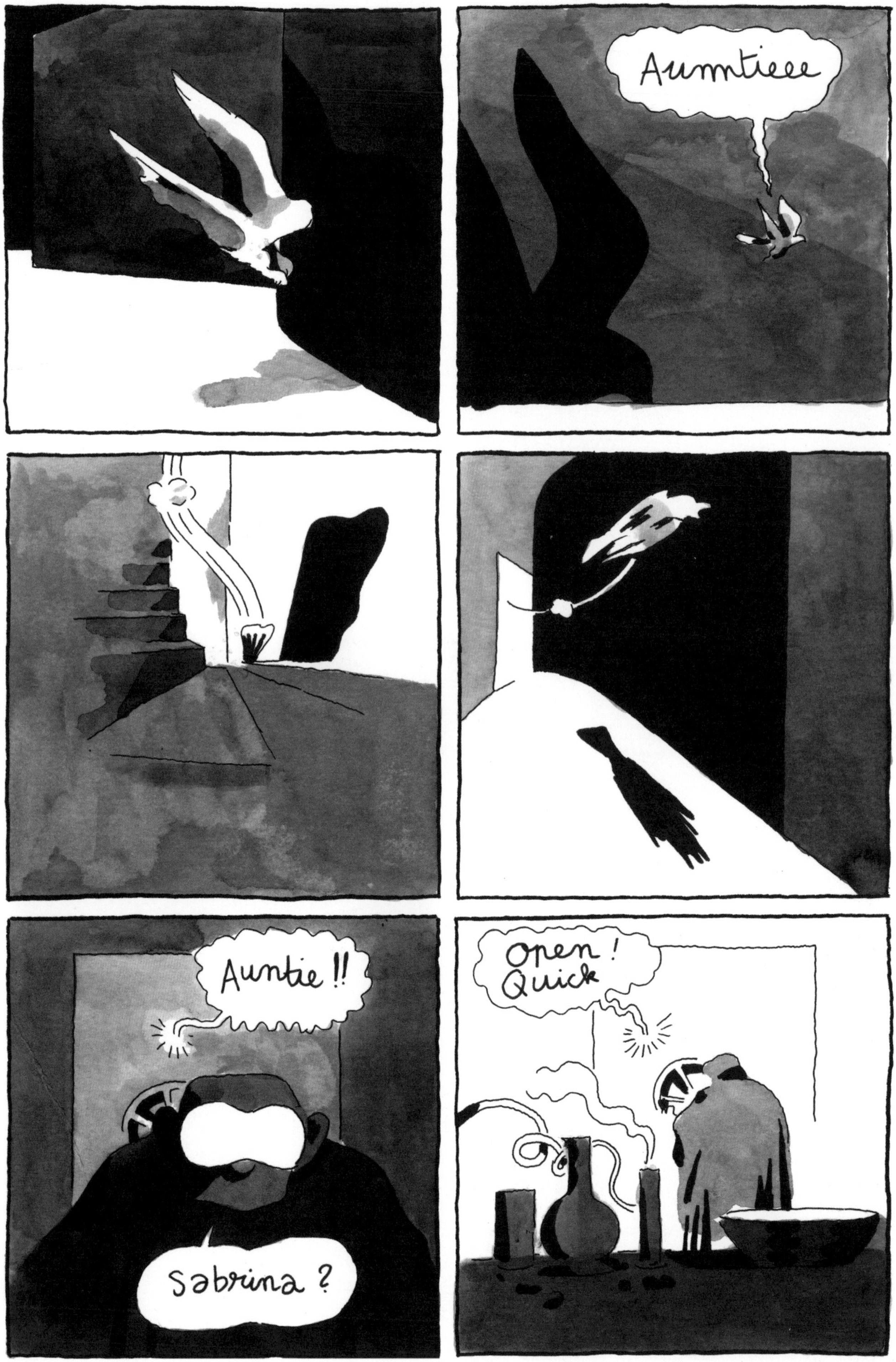
Aumtieee
Auntie !!
Sabrina ?
Open !
Quick

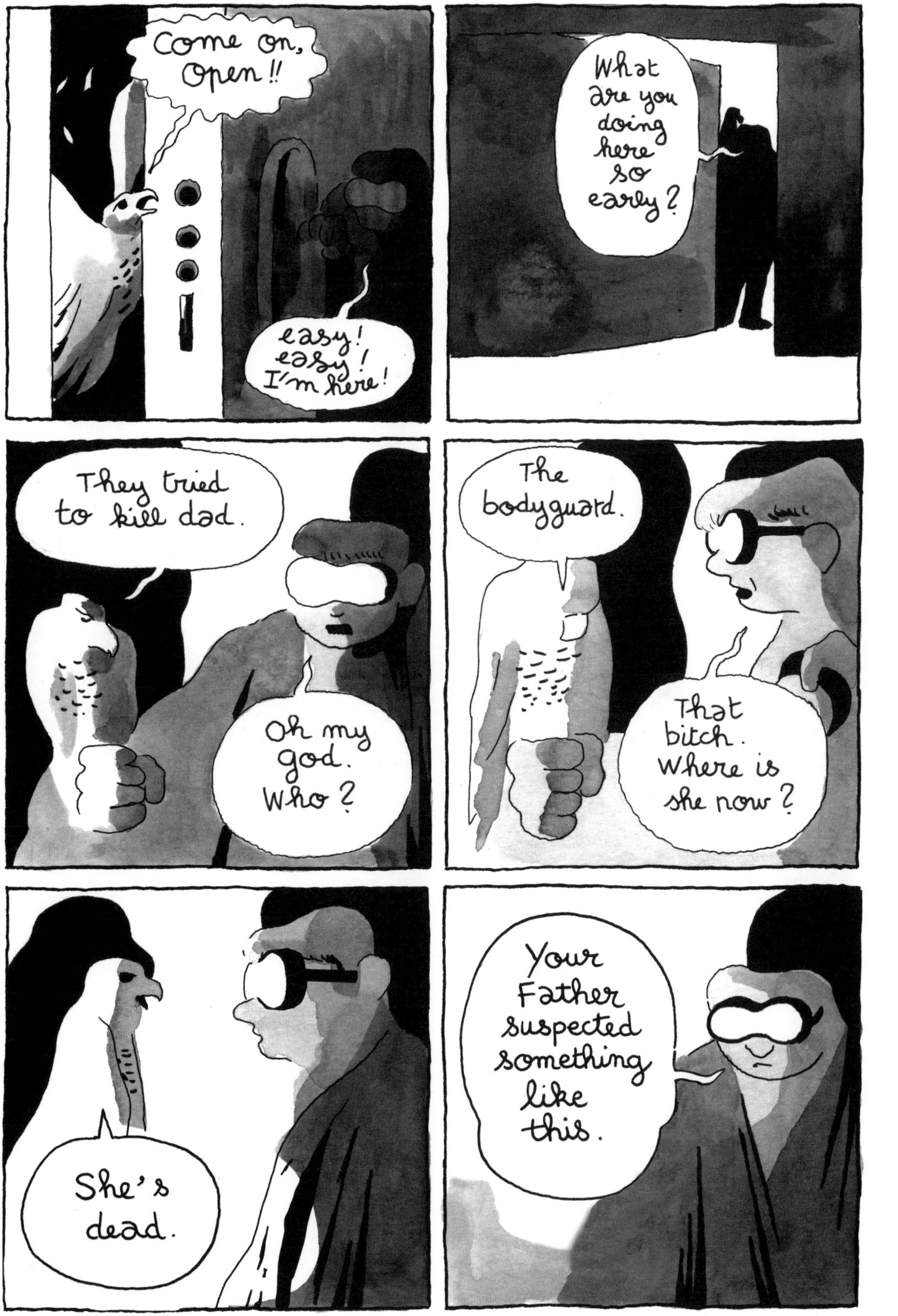
Come on, Open!!
easy! easy! I'm here!
What are you doing here so early?
They tried to kill dad.
Oh my god. Who?
The bodyguard.
That bitch. Where is she now?
She's dead.
Your Father suspected something like this.

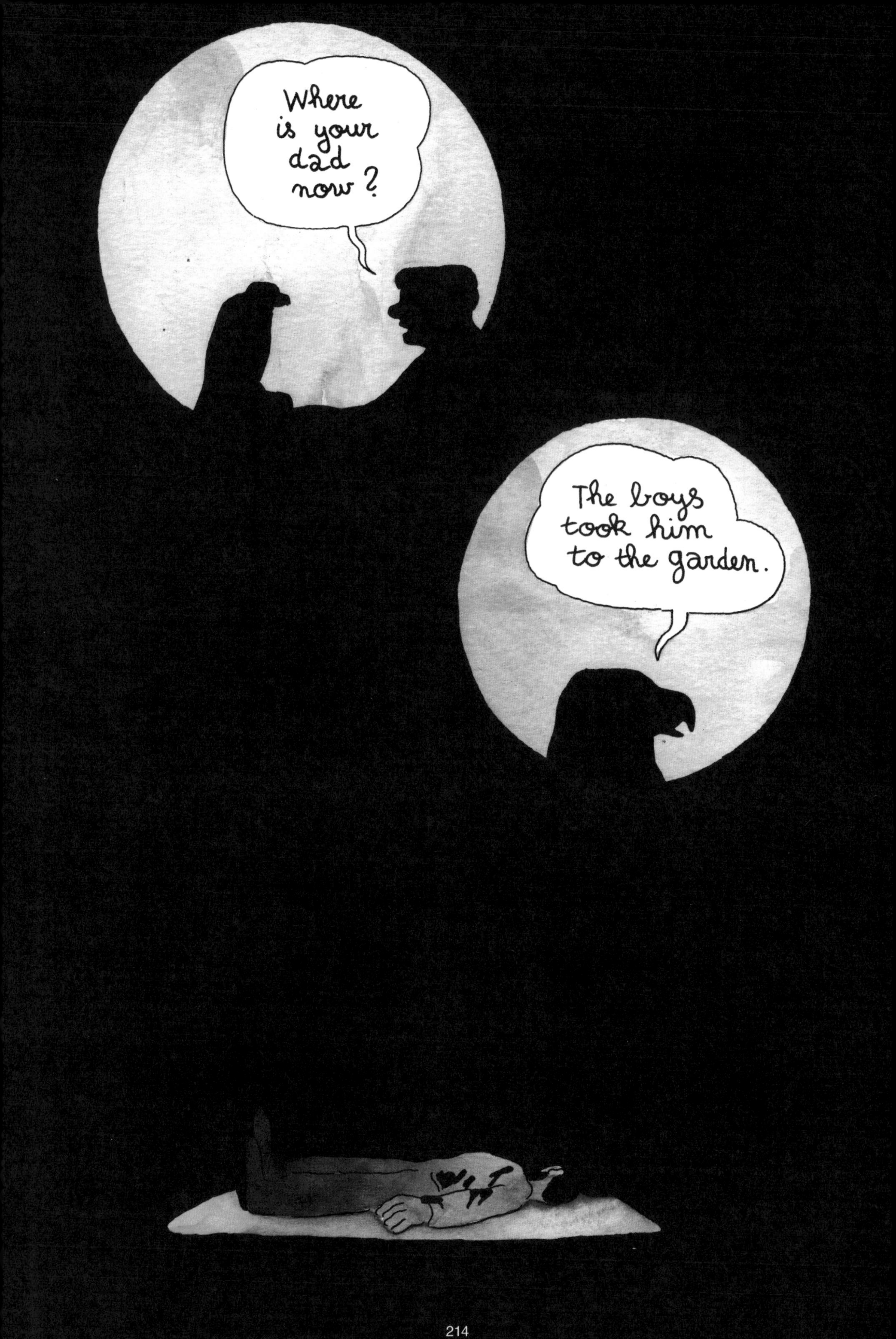
Where is your dad now?
The boys took him to the garden.

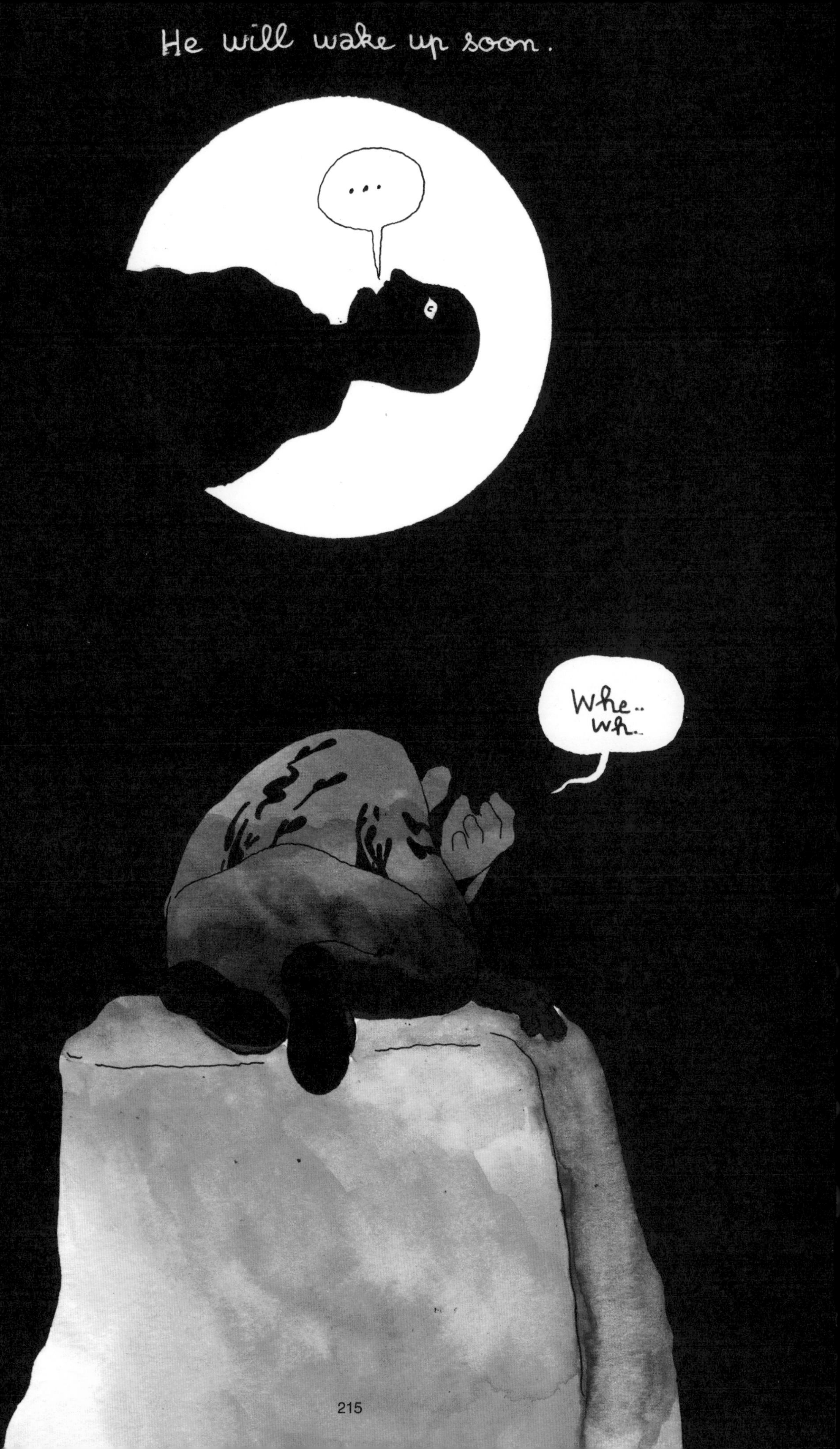
He will wake up soon.
...
Whe..
wh..

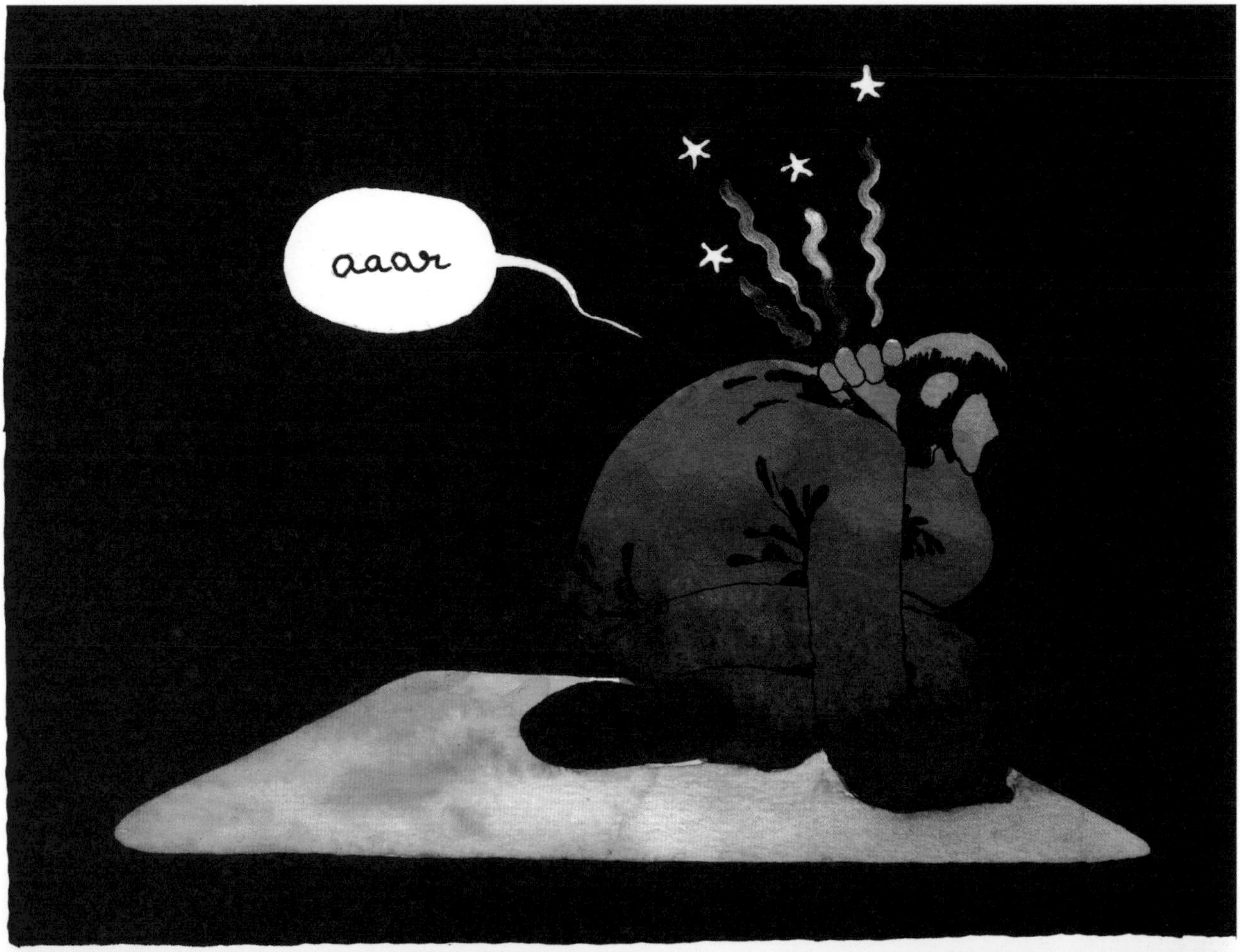
aaar

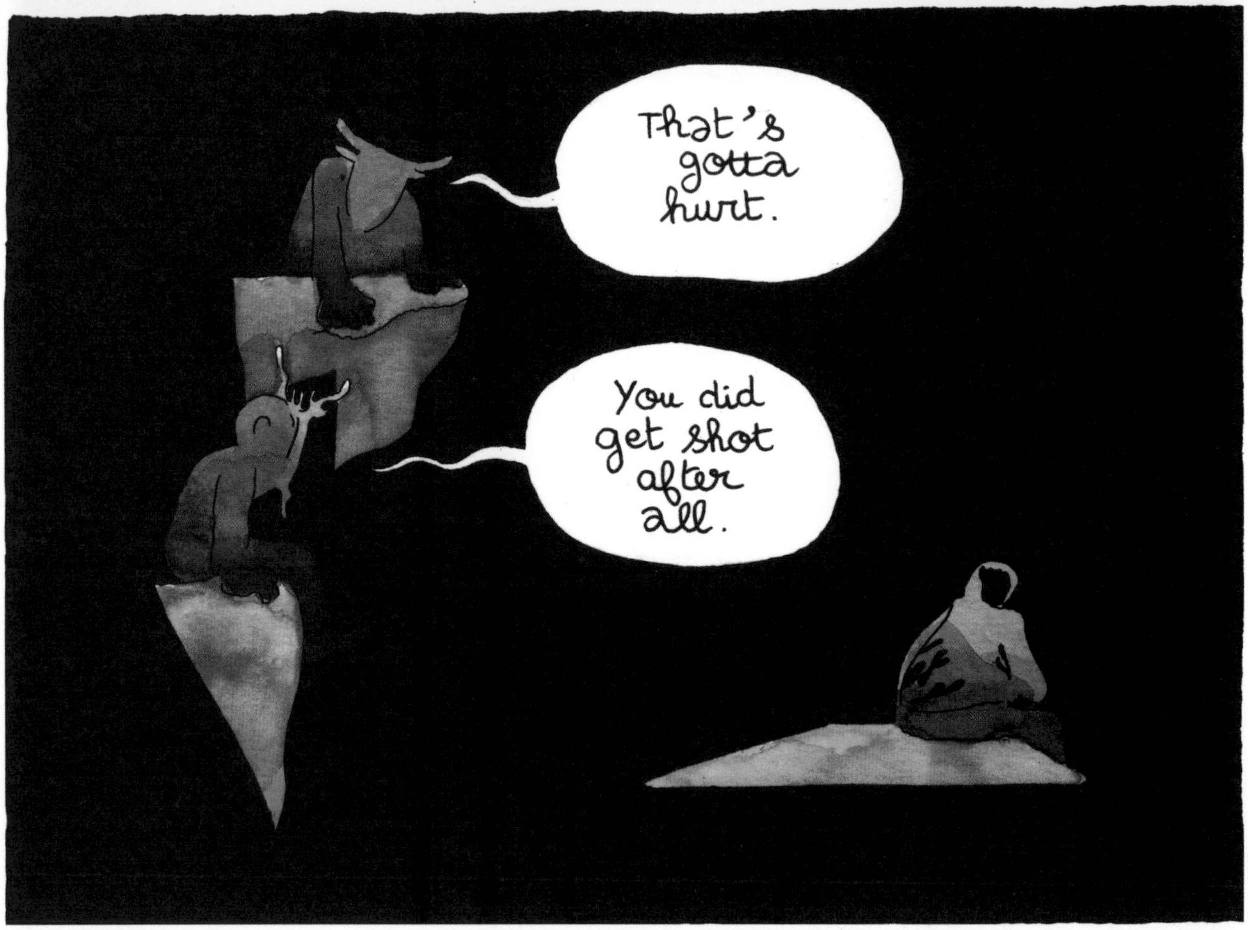
That's gotta hurt.
You did get shot after all.

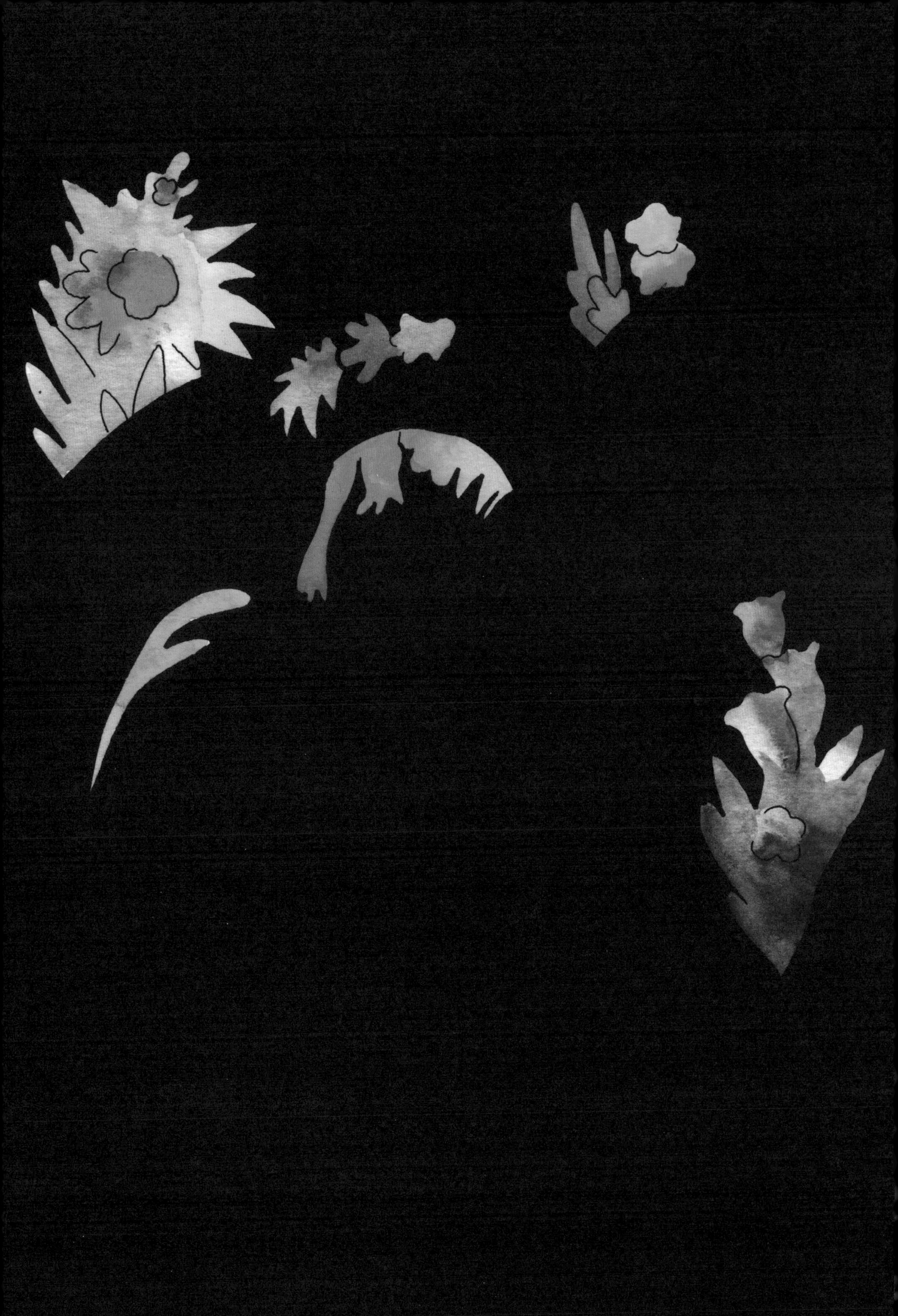

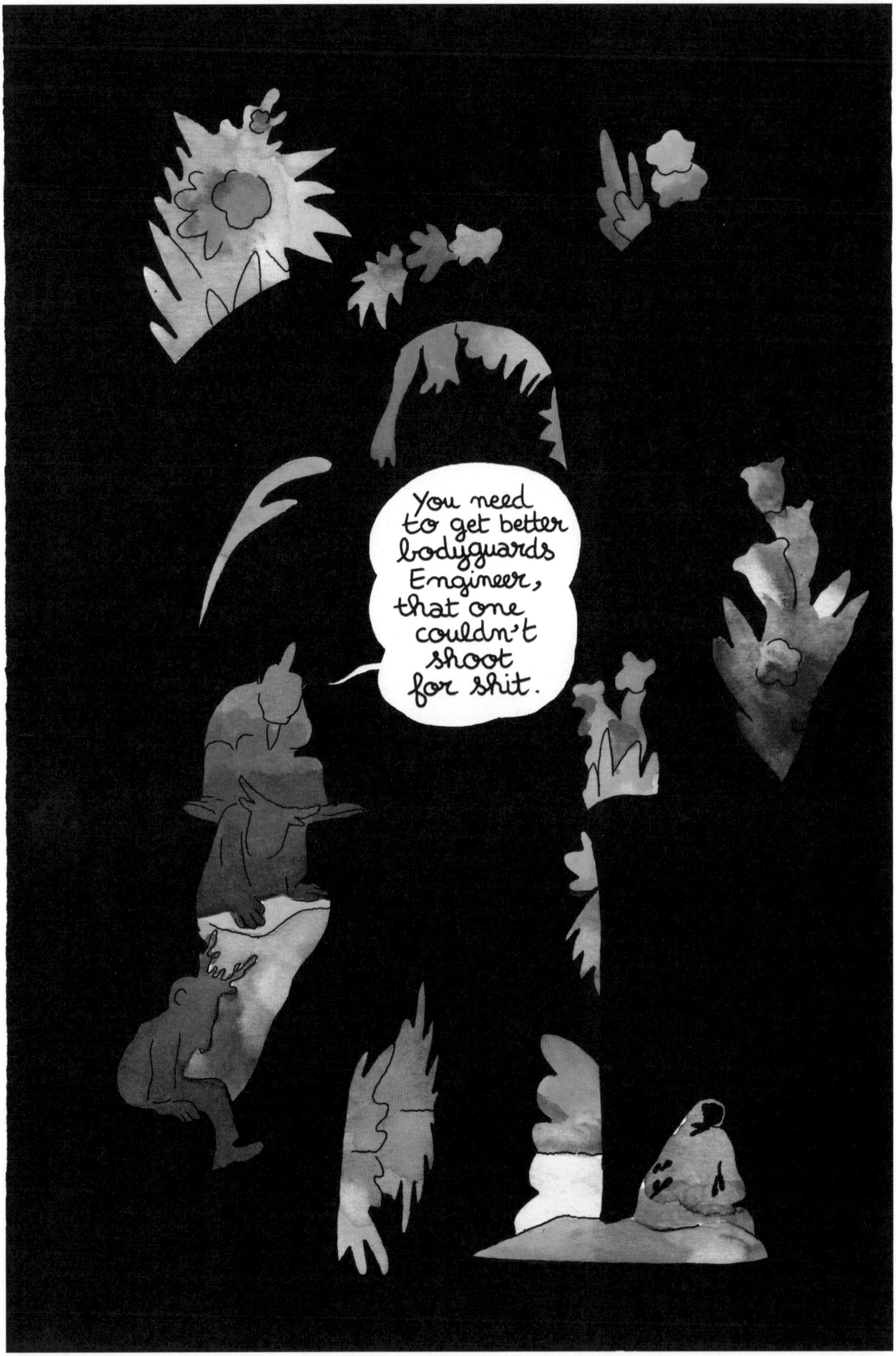
You need to get better bodyguards Engineer, that one couldn't shoot for shit.

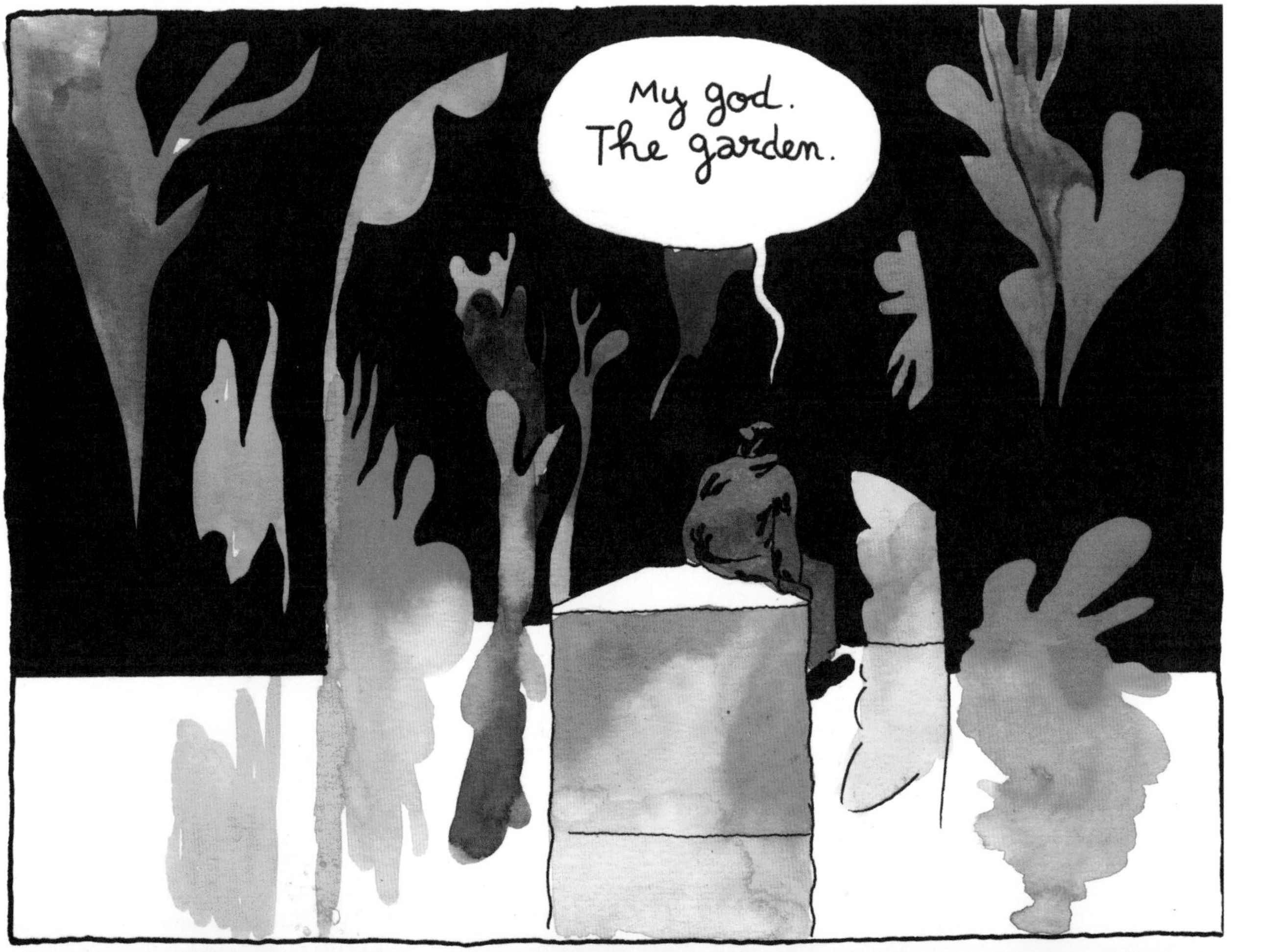
My god.
The garden.

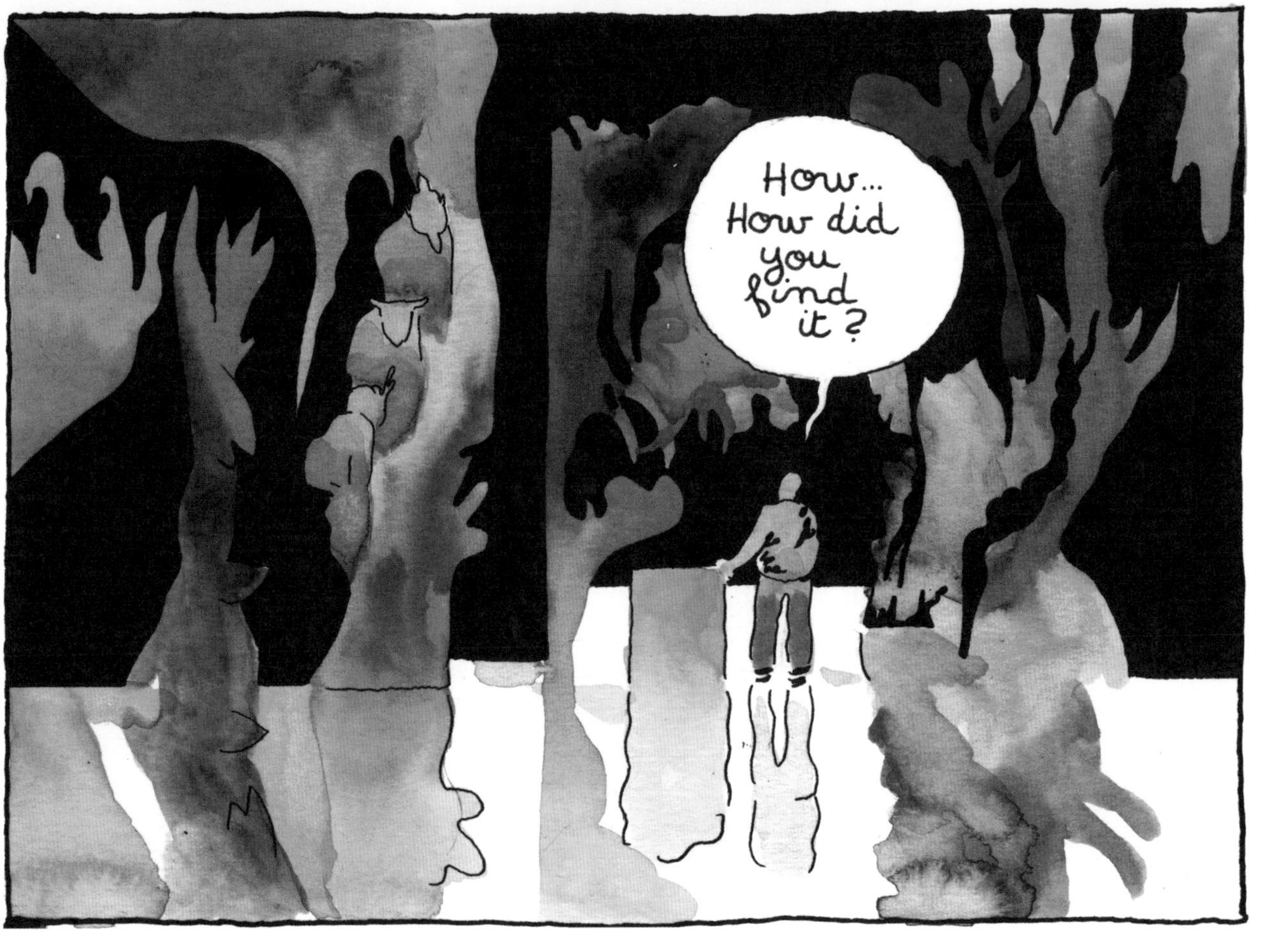
How...
How did you find it?

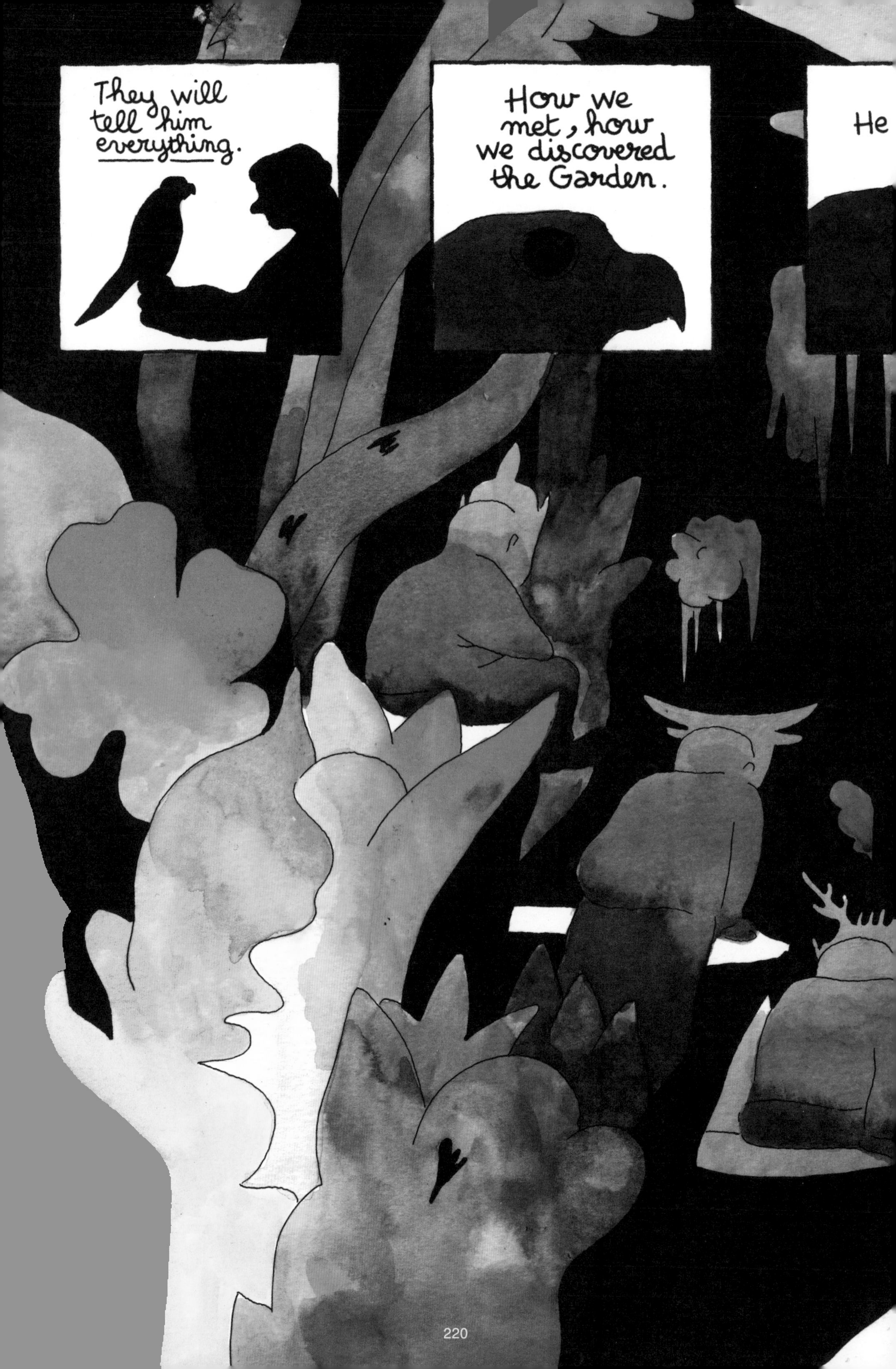

They will tell him everything.
How we met, how we discovered the Garden.
He

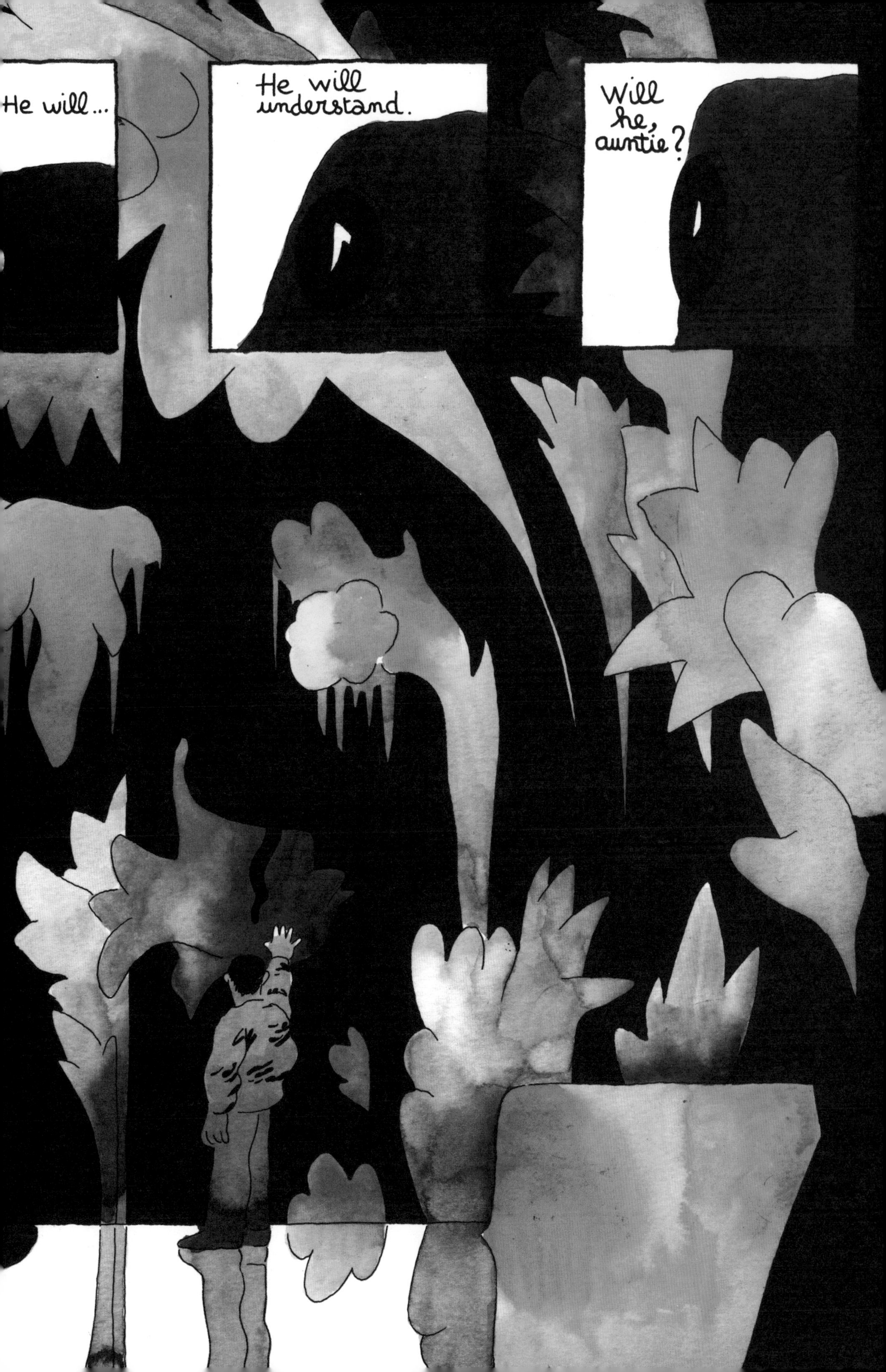
He will...
He will understand.
Will he, auntie?

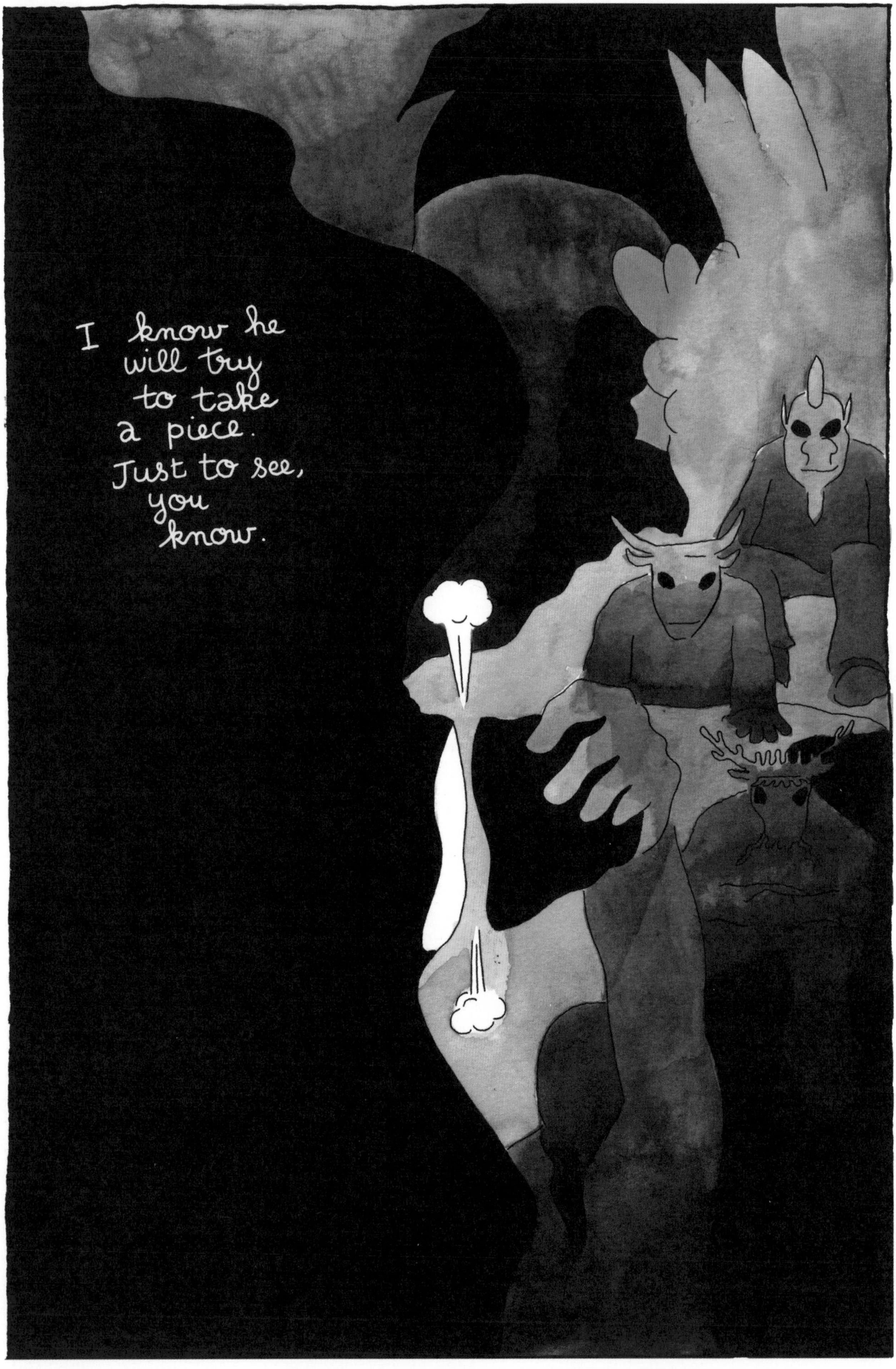
I know he
will try
to take
a piece.
Just to see,
you
know.

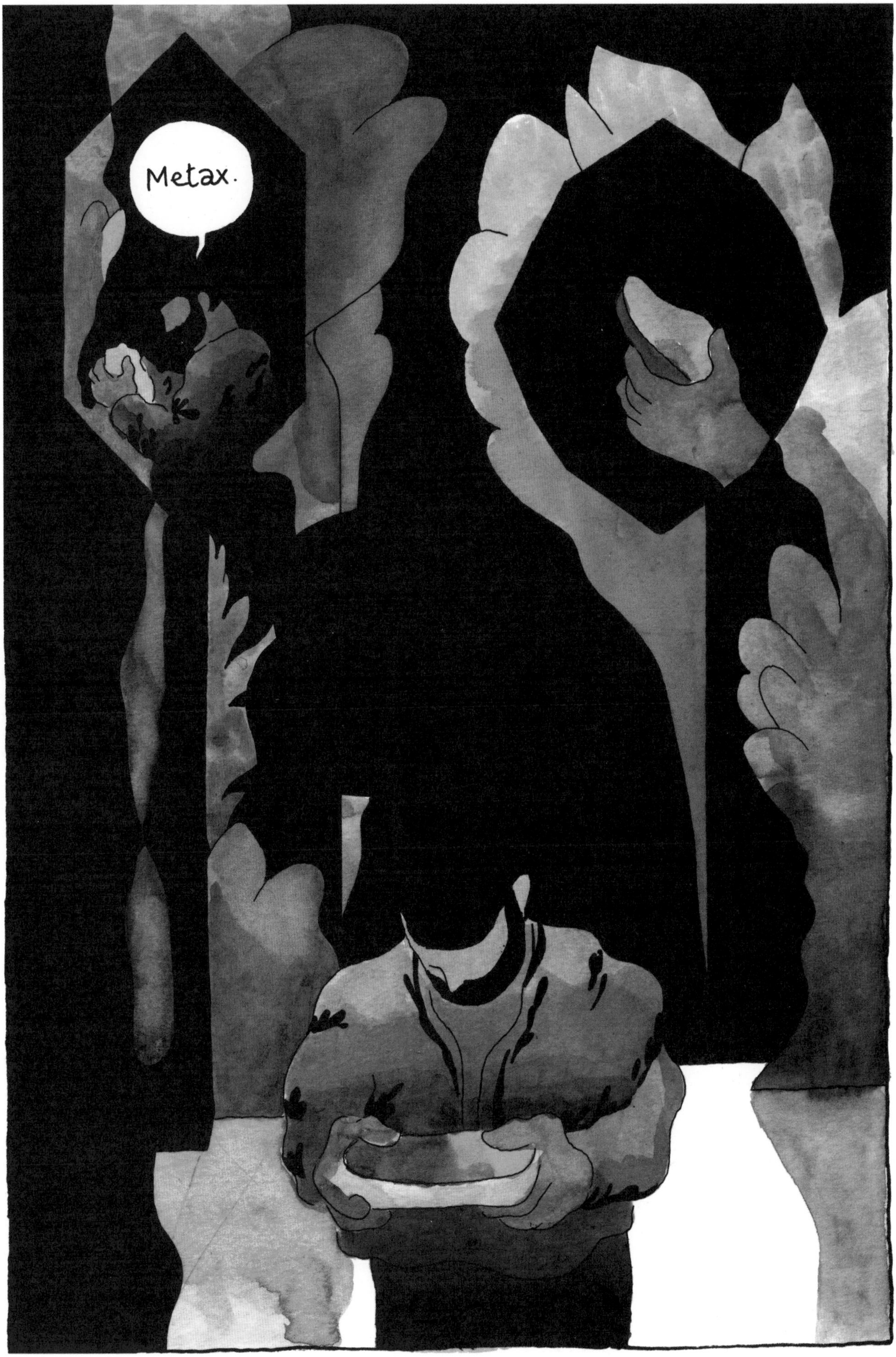
Metax.

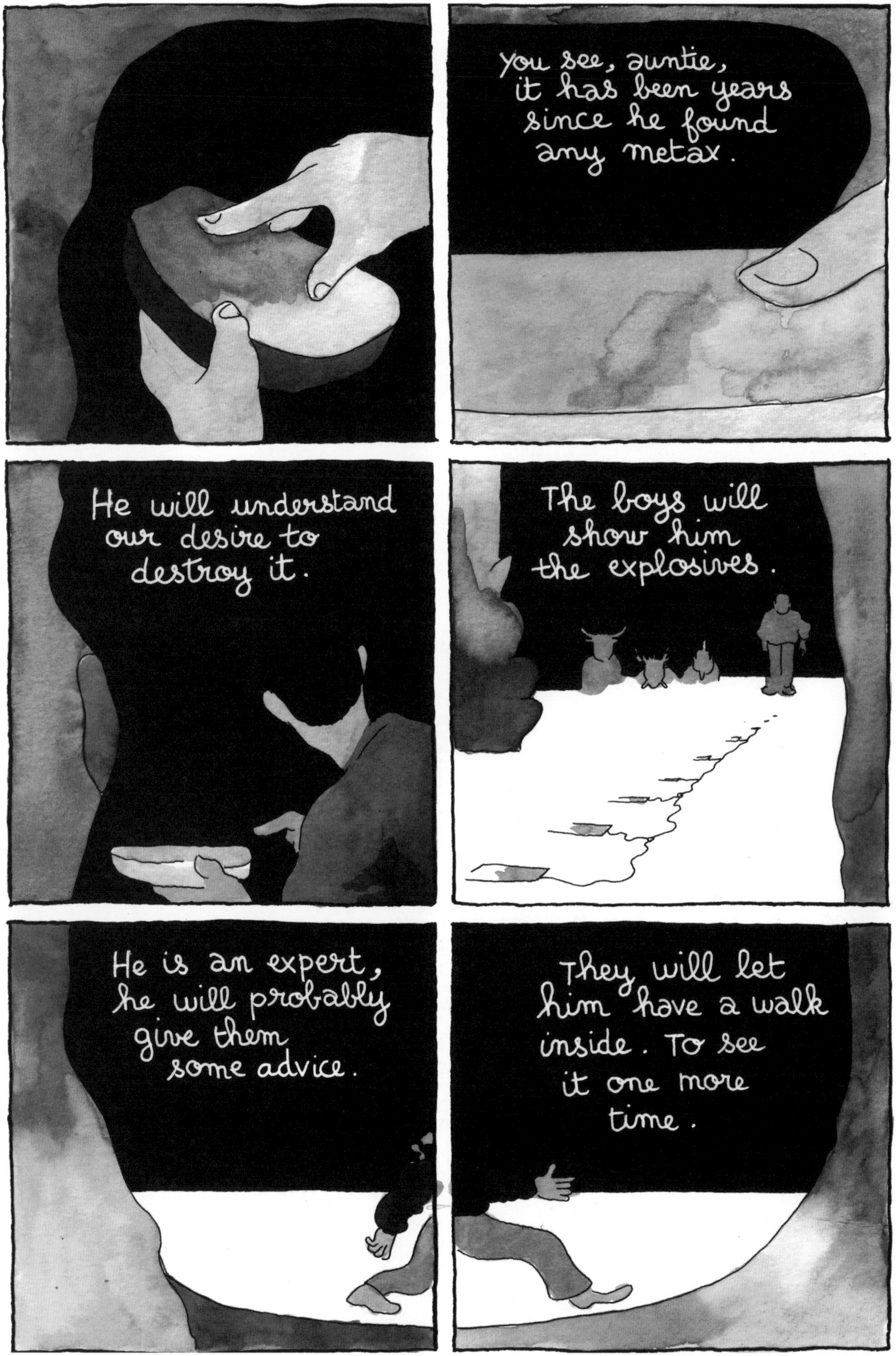
you see, auntie,
it has been years
since he found
any metax.
He will understand
our desire to
destroy it.
The boys will
show him
the explosives.
He is an expert,
he will probably
give them
some advice.
They will let
him have a walk
inside. To see
it one more
time.

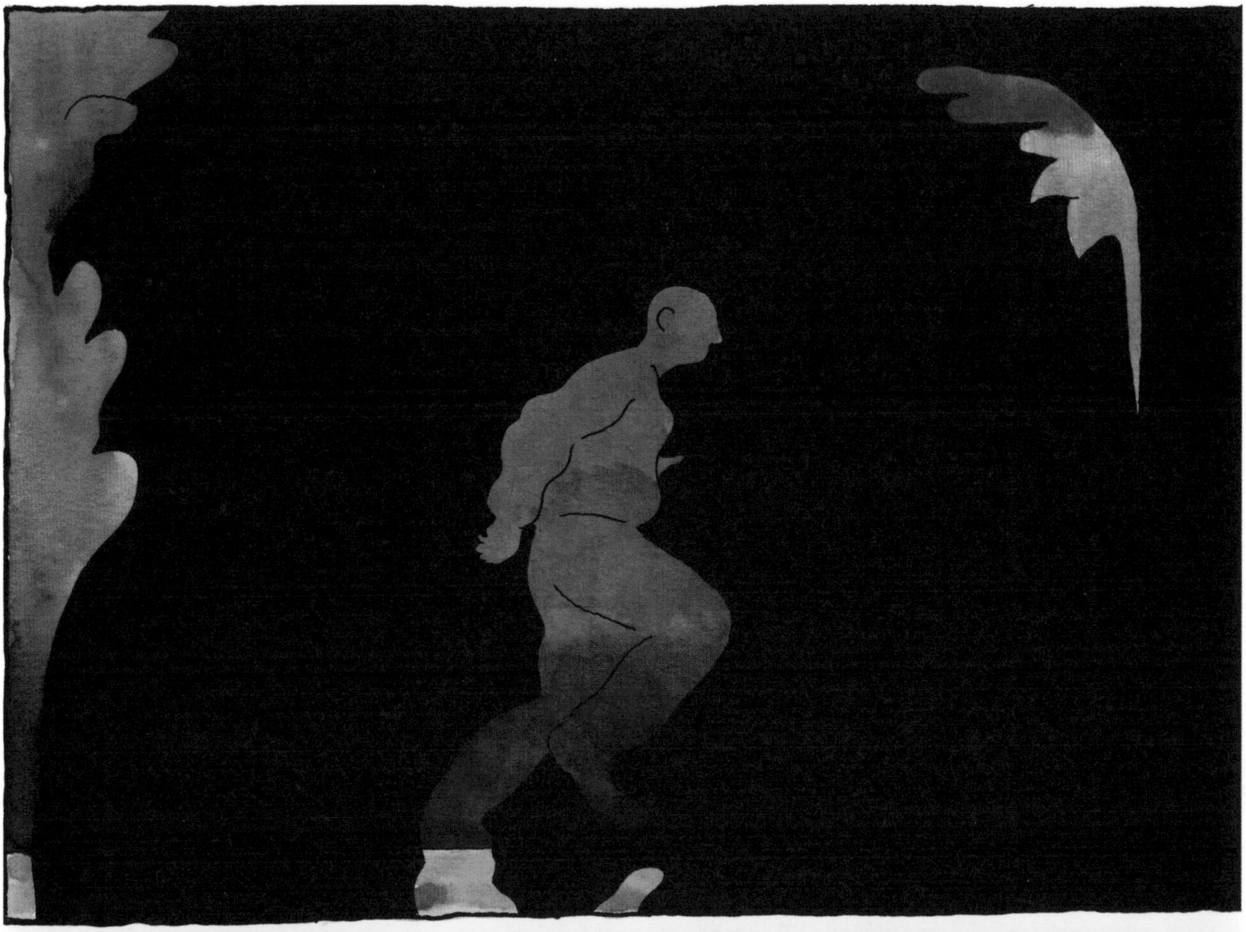

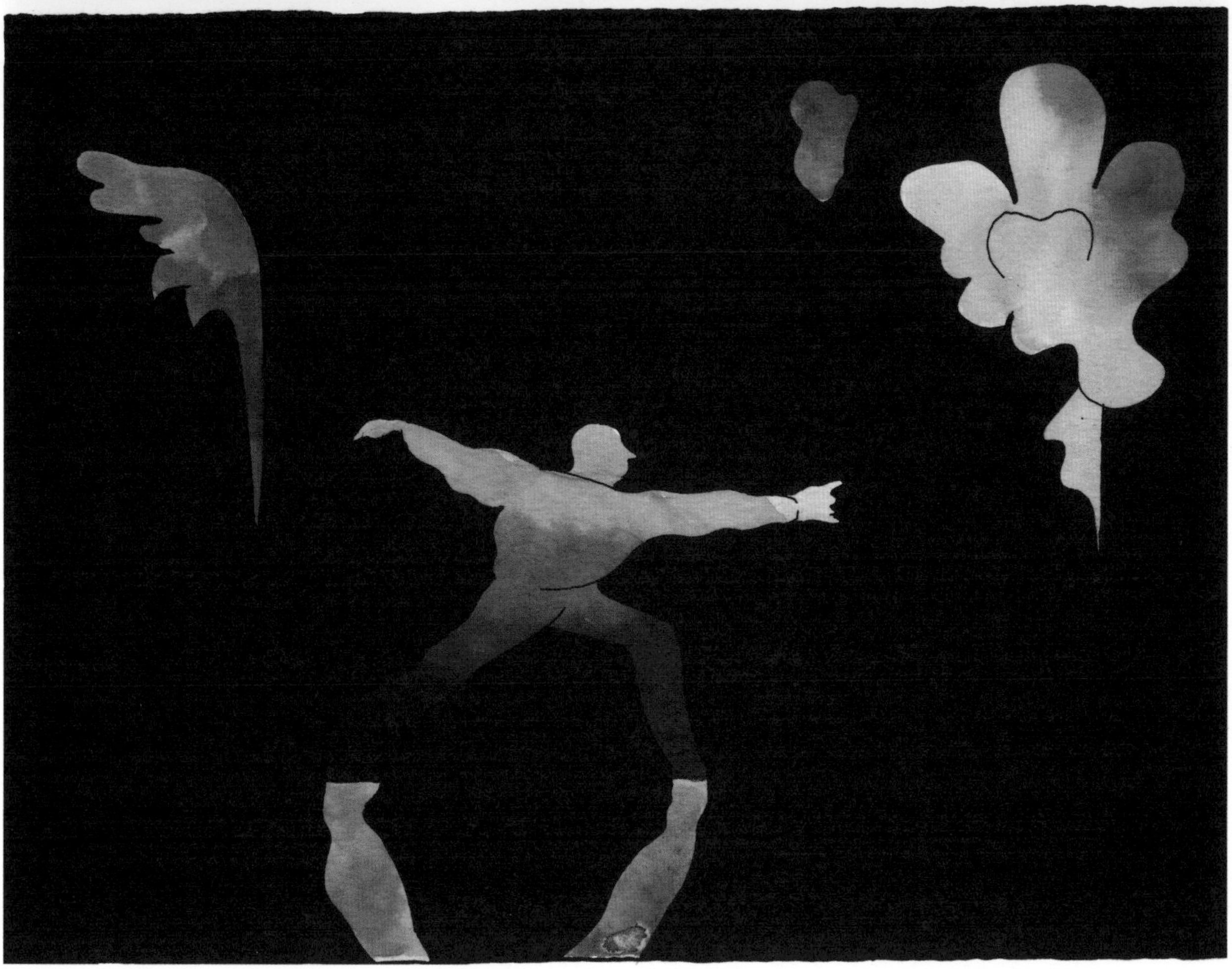

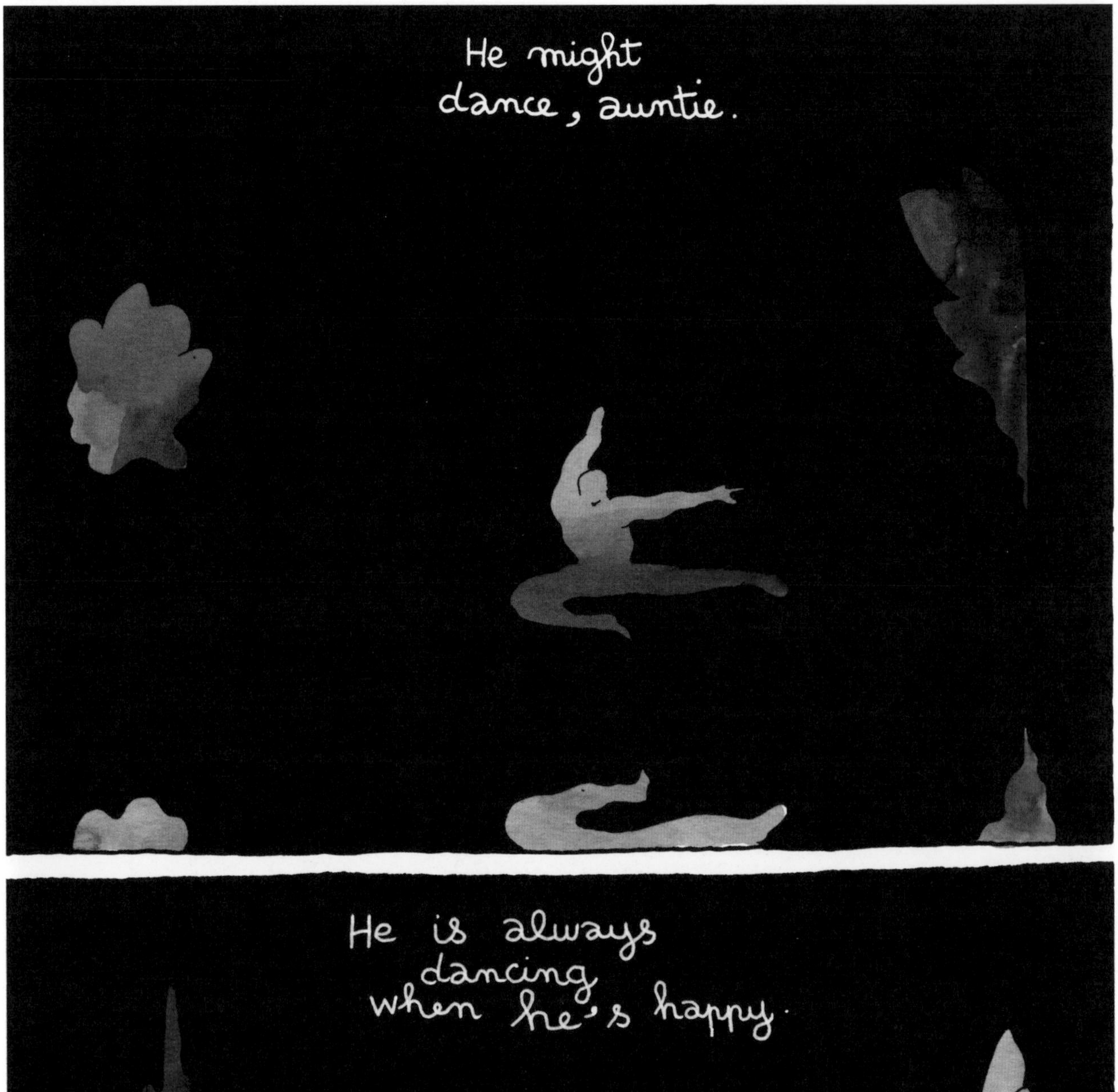
He might dance, auntie.

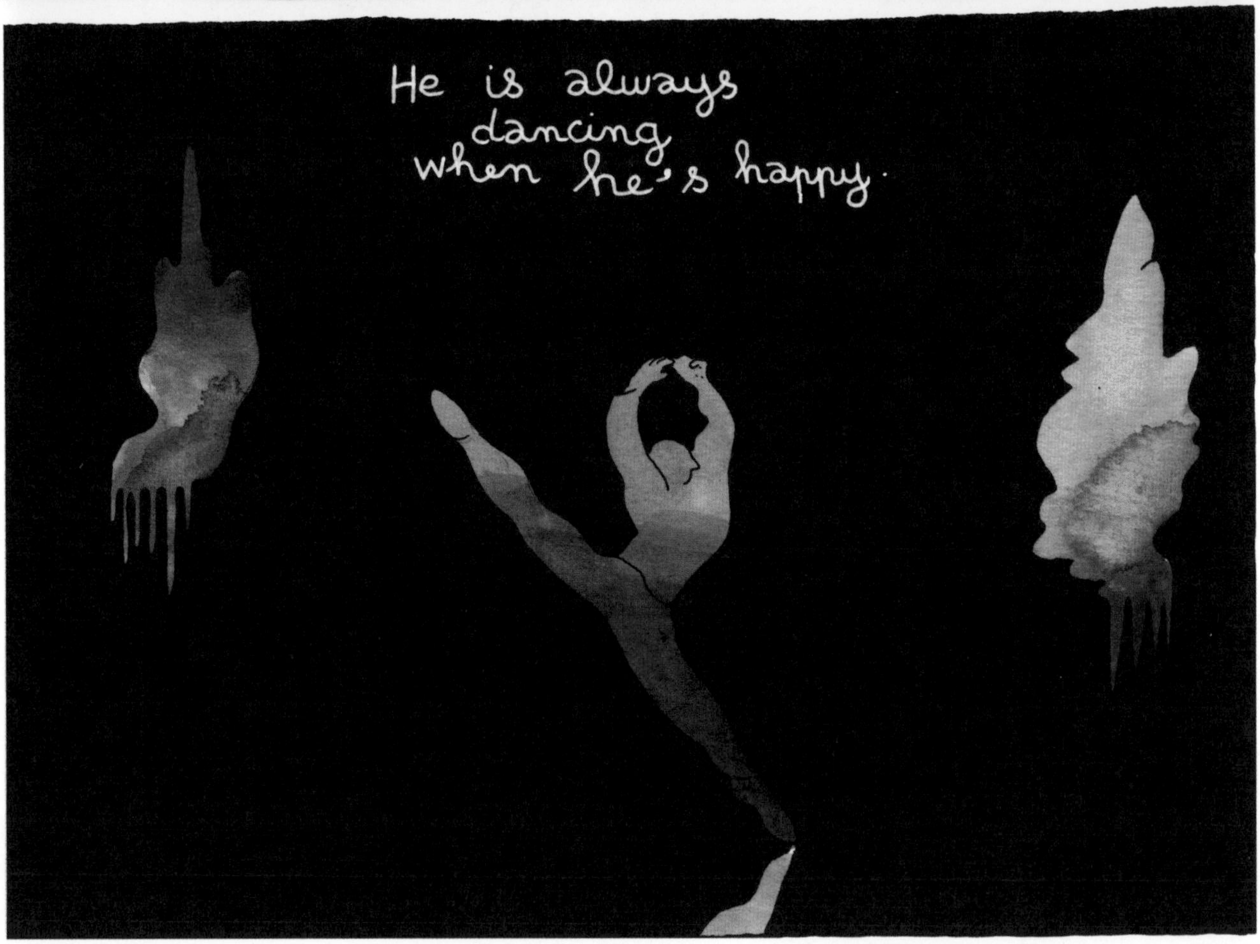
He is always dancing when he's happy.

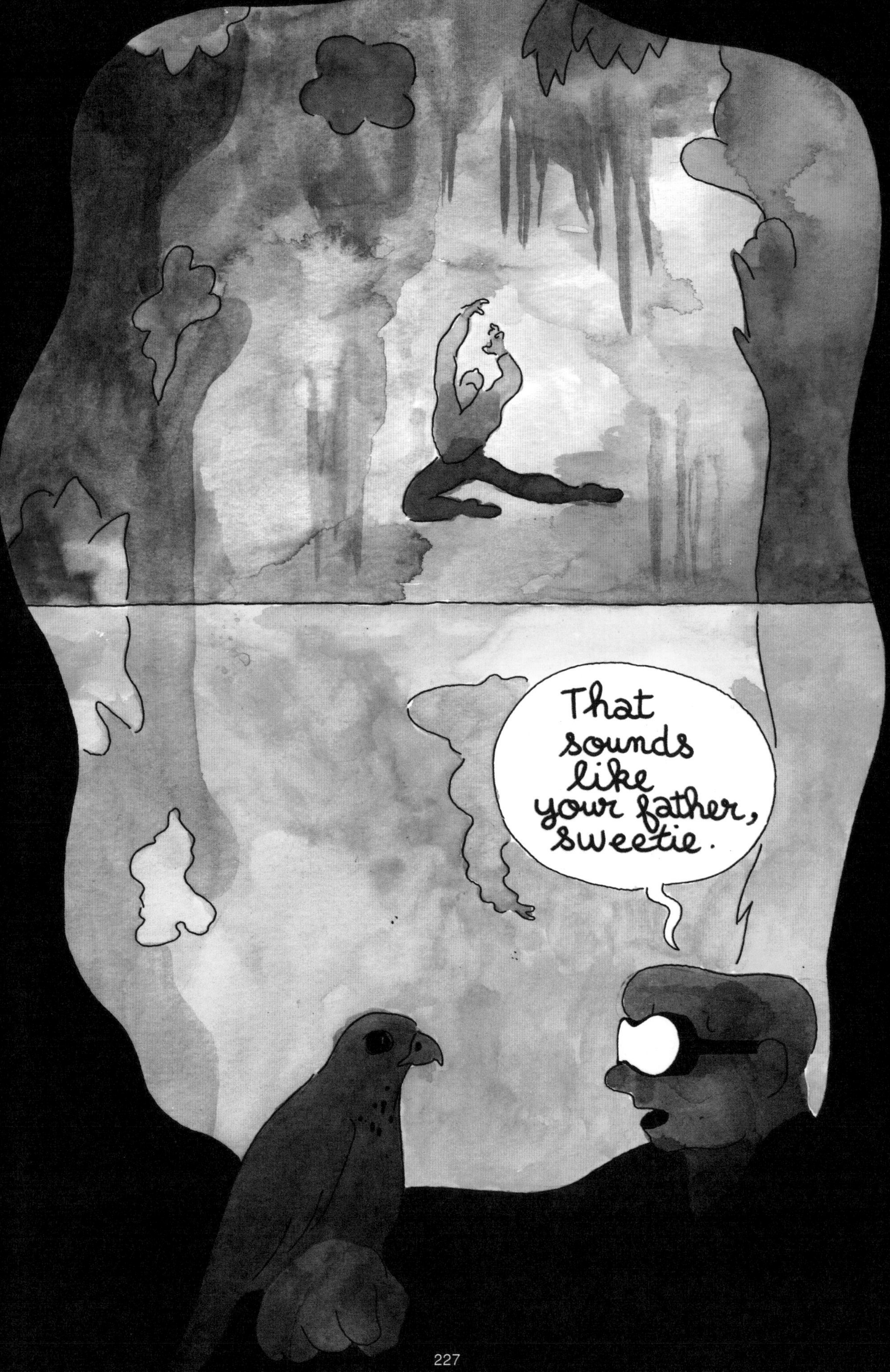
That sounds like your father, sweetie.

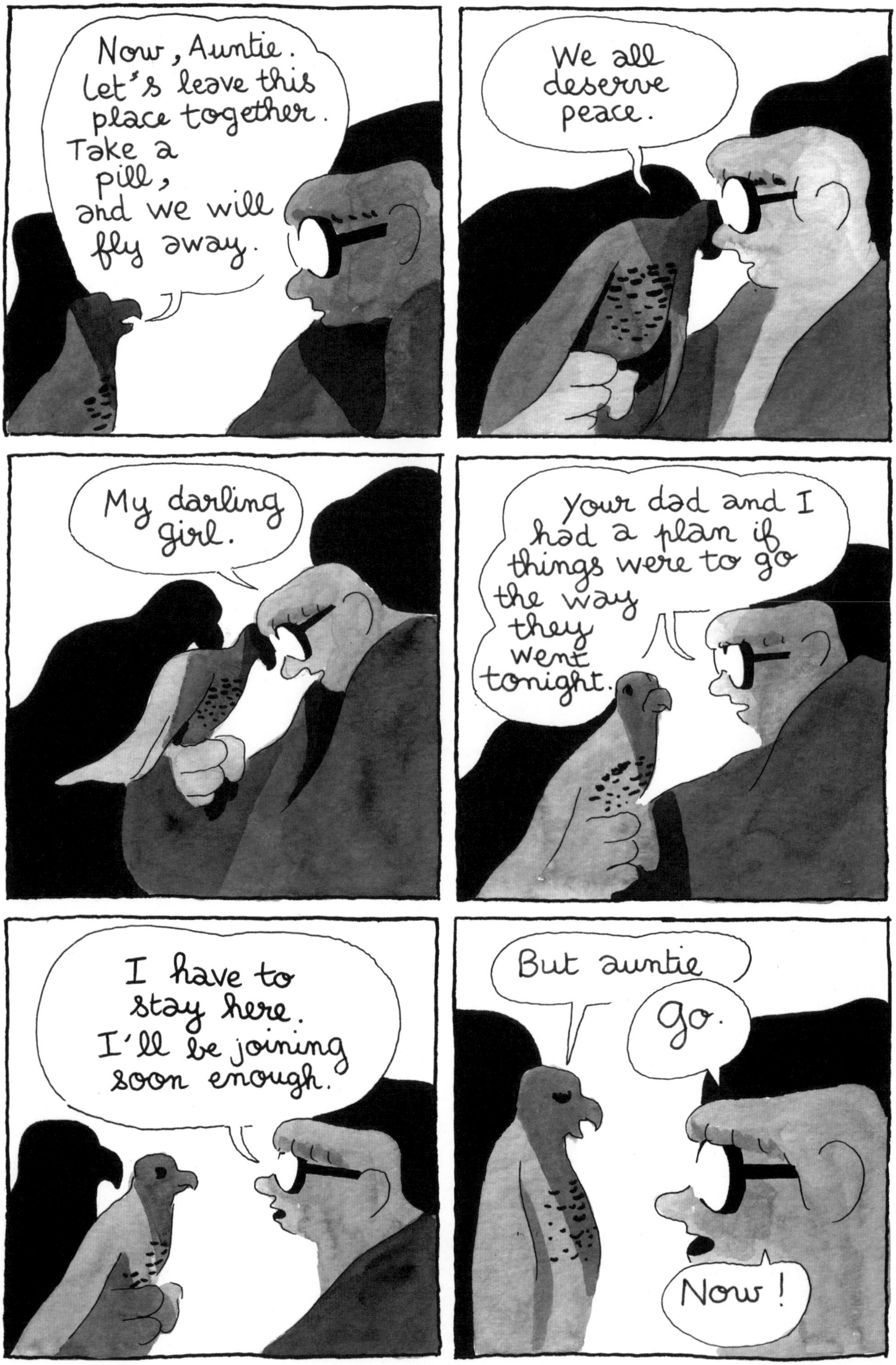
Now, Auntie. Let's leave this place together. Take a pill, and we will fly away.
We all deserve peace.
My darling girl.
Your dad and I had a plan if things were to go the way they went tonight.
I have to stay here. I'll be joining soon enough.
But auntie
Go.
Now!

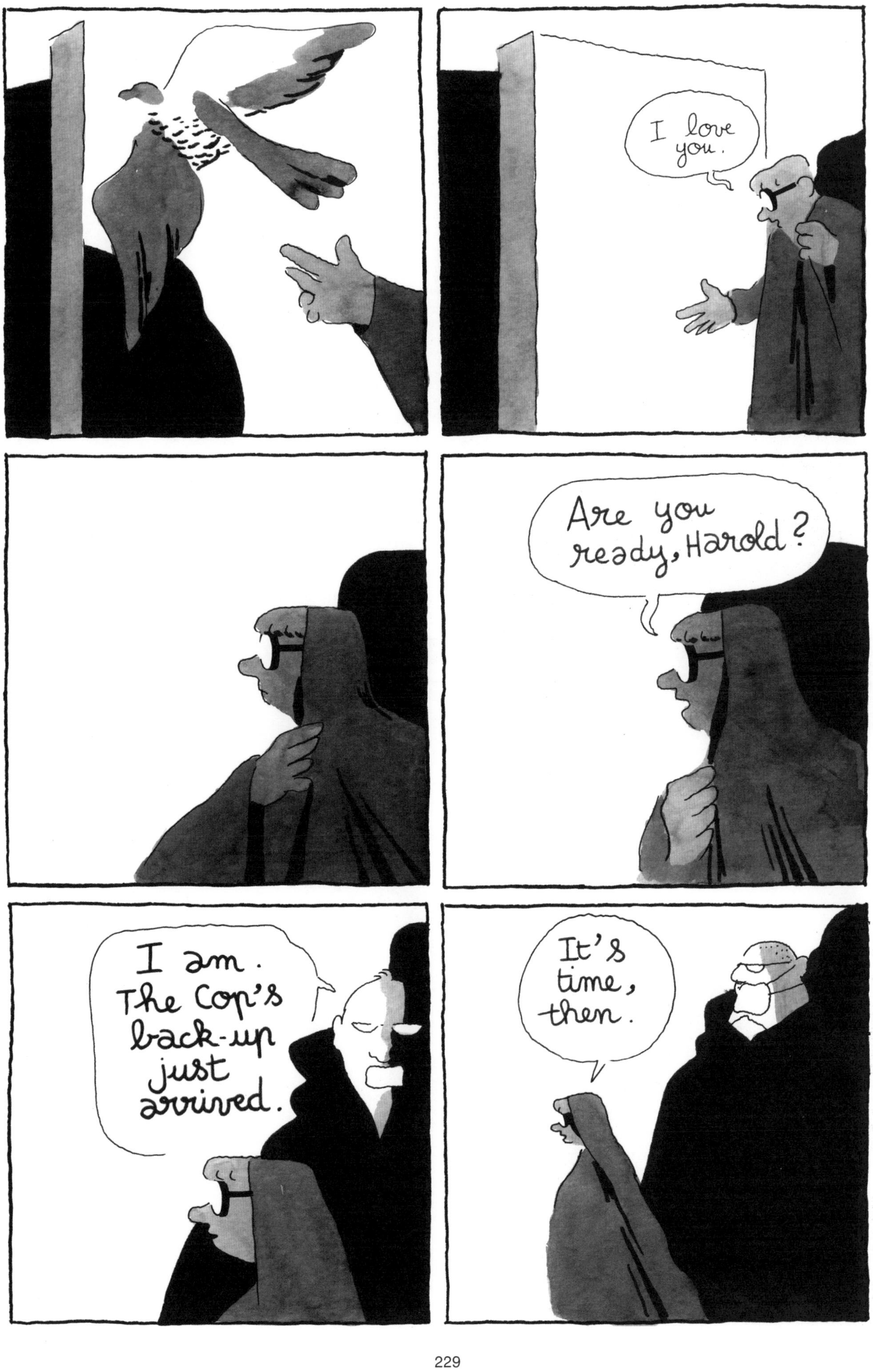
I love you.
Are you ready, Harold?
I am. The cop's back-up just arrived.
It's time, then.

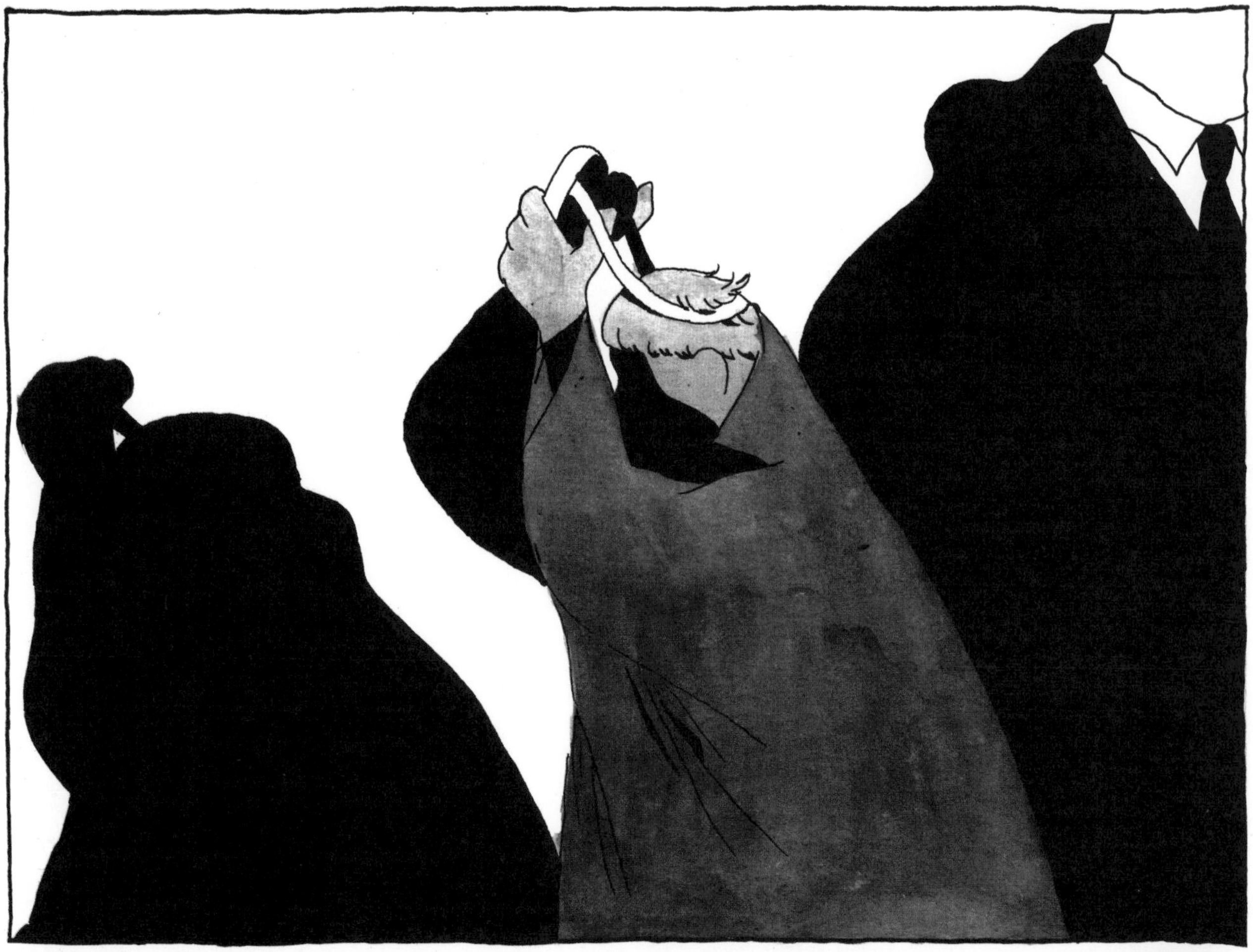

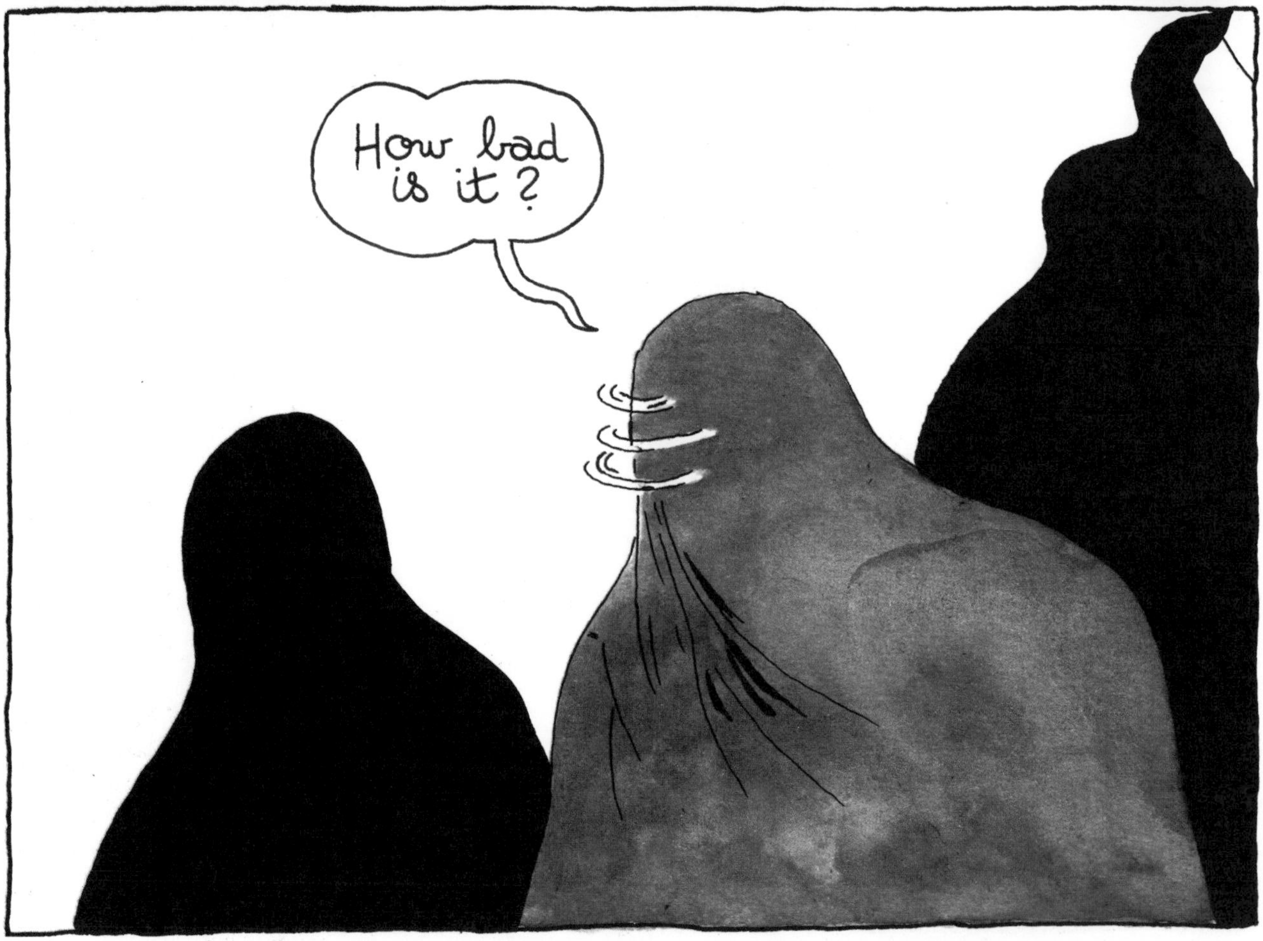
How bad is it?

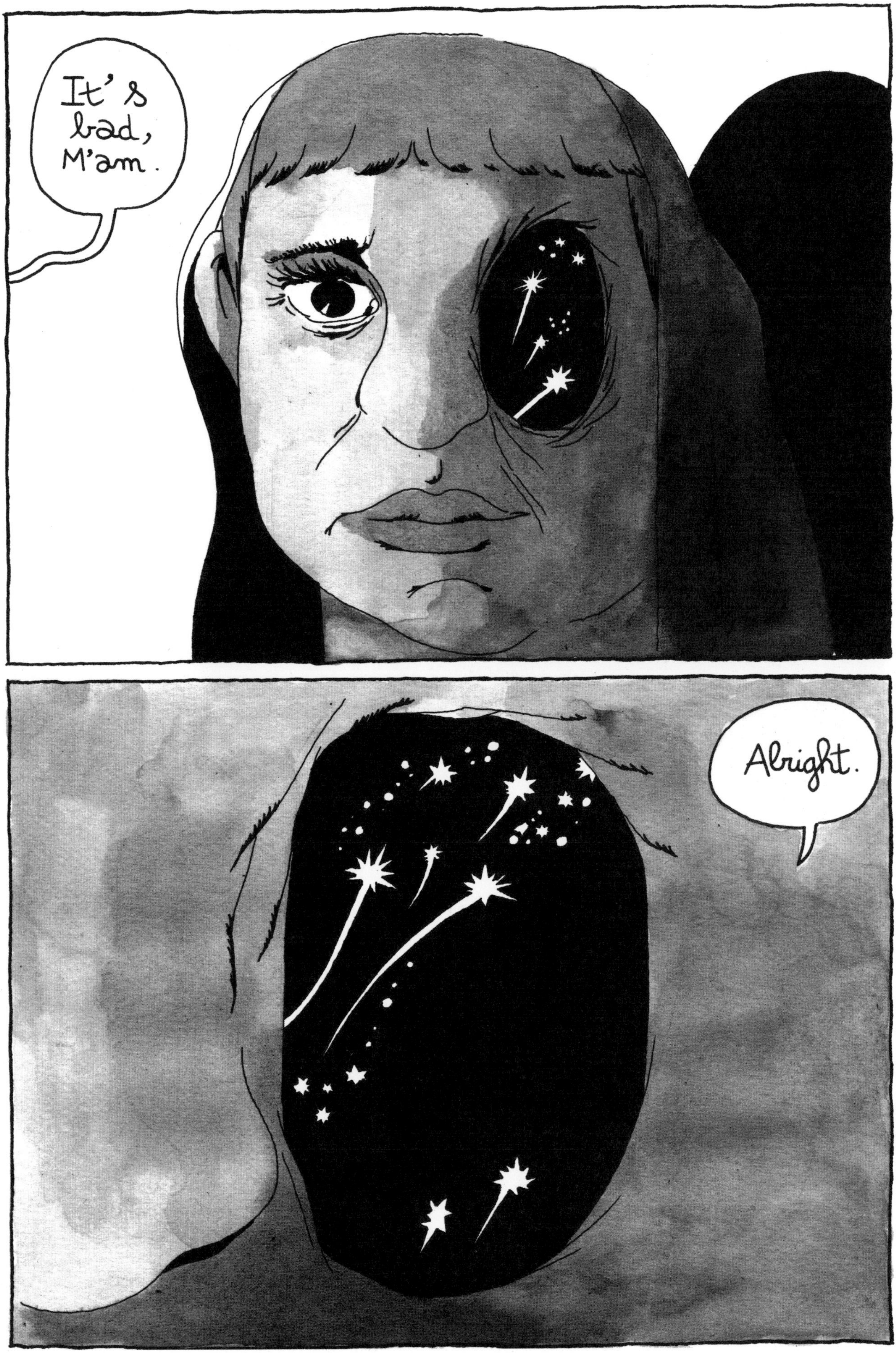
It's bad, M'am.
Alright.

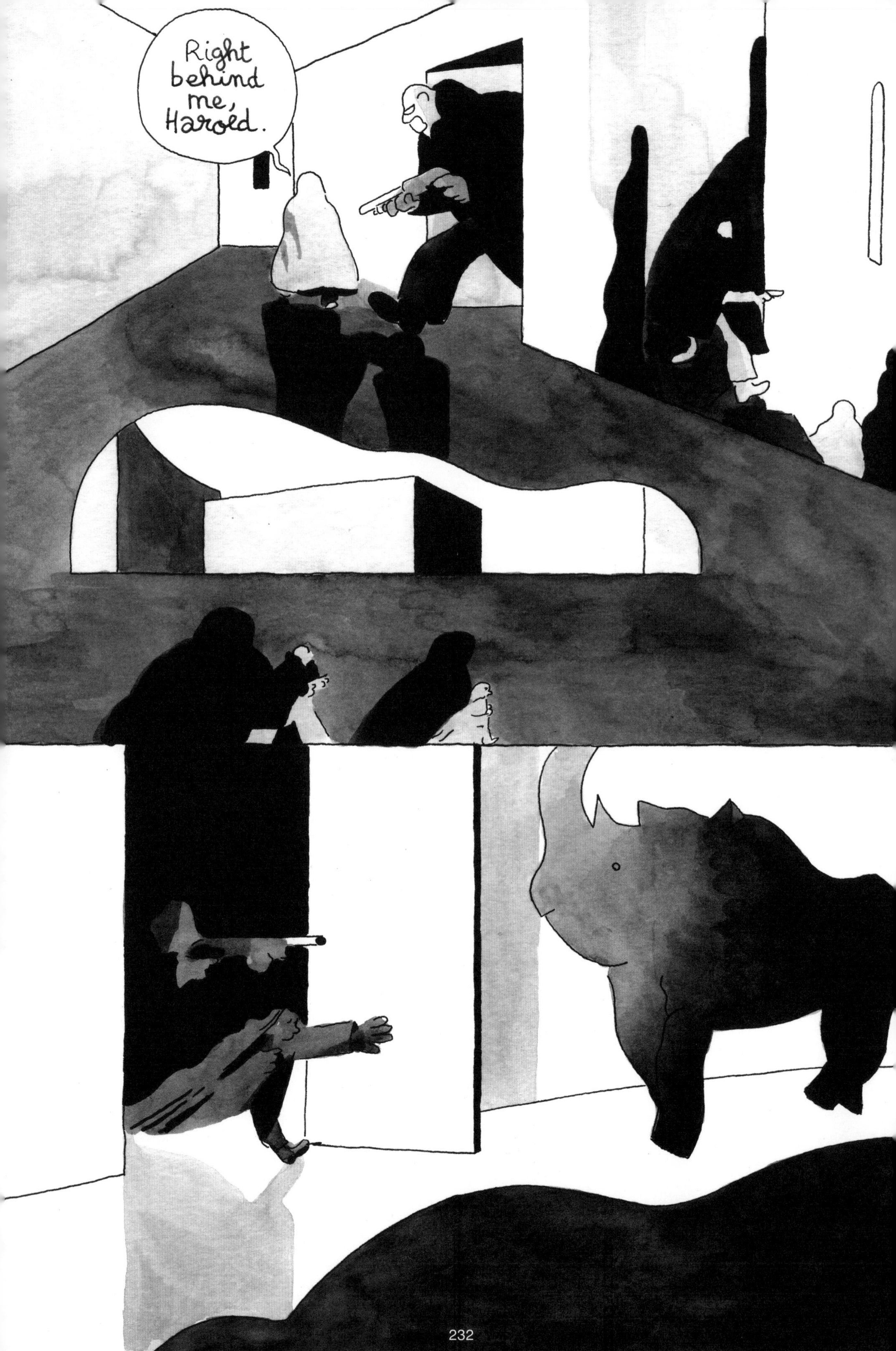
Right behind me, Harold.

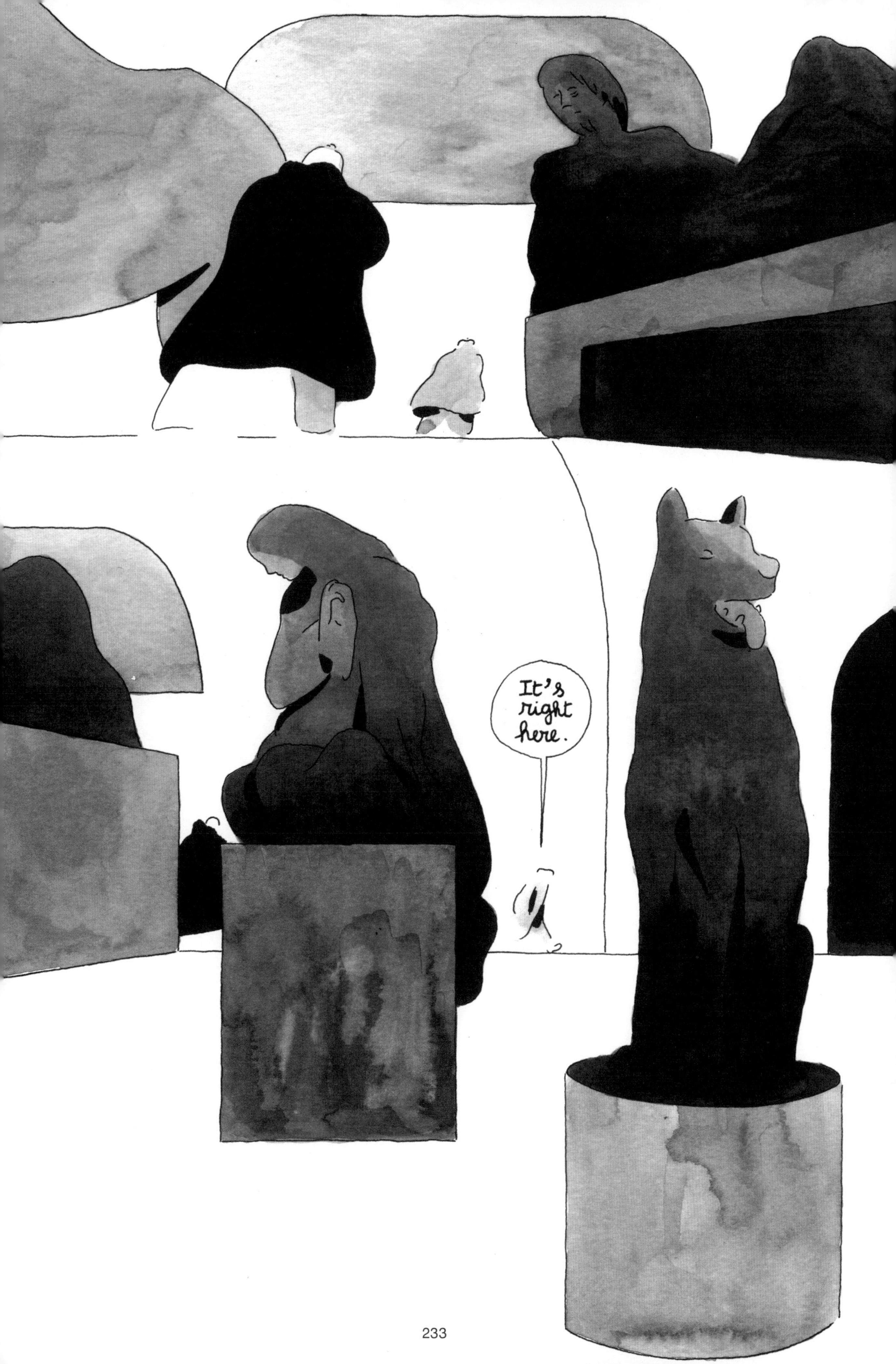
It's right here.

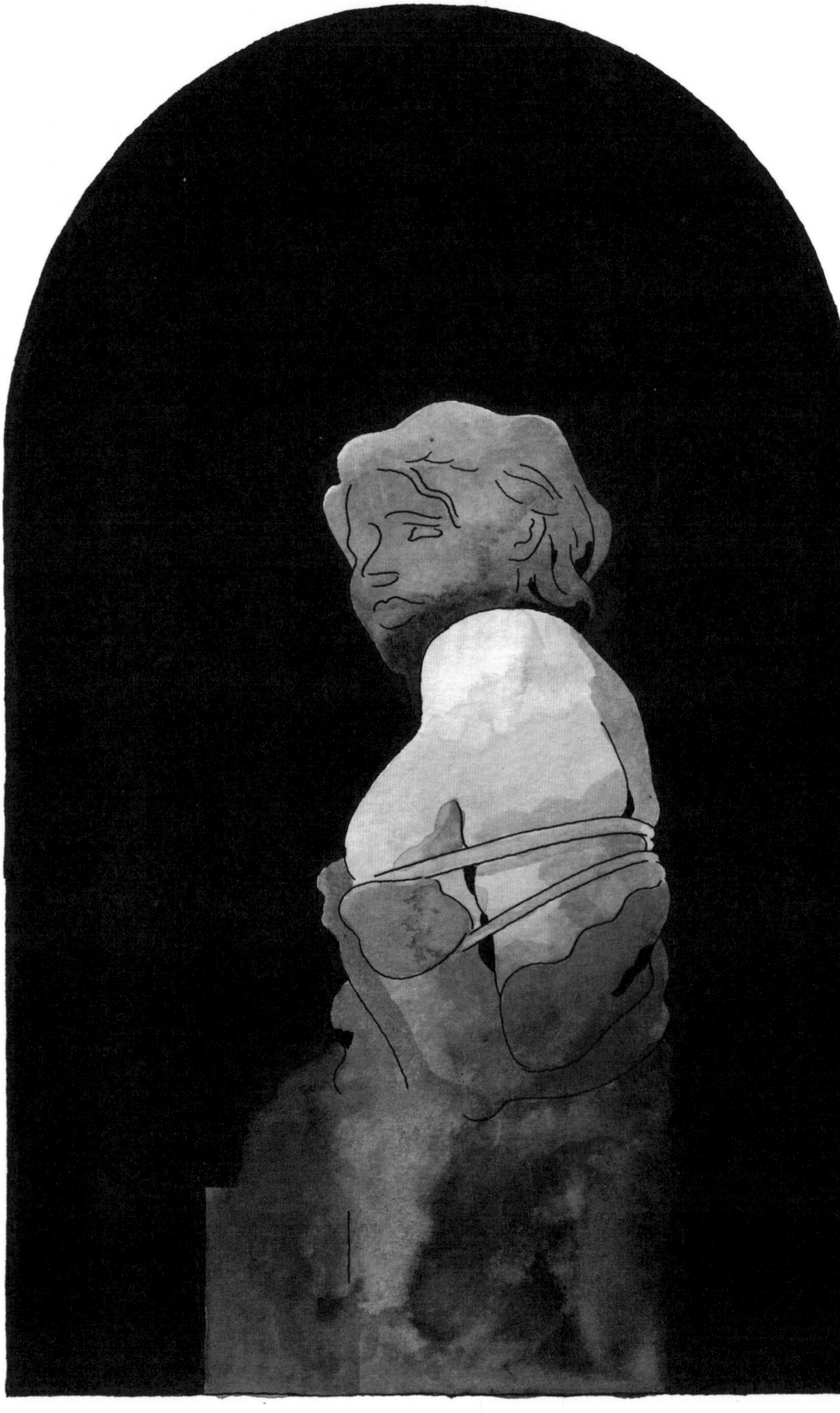

Hello, my old friend.

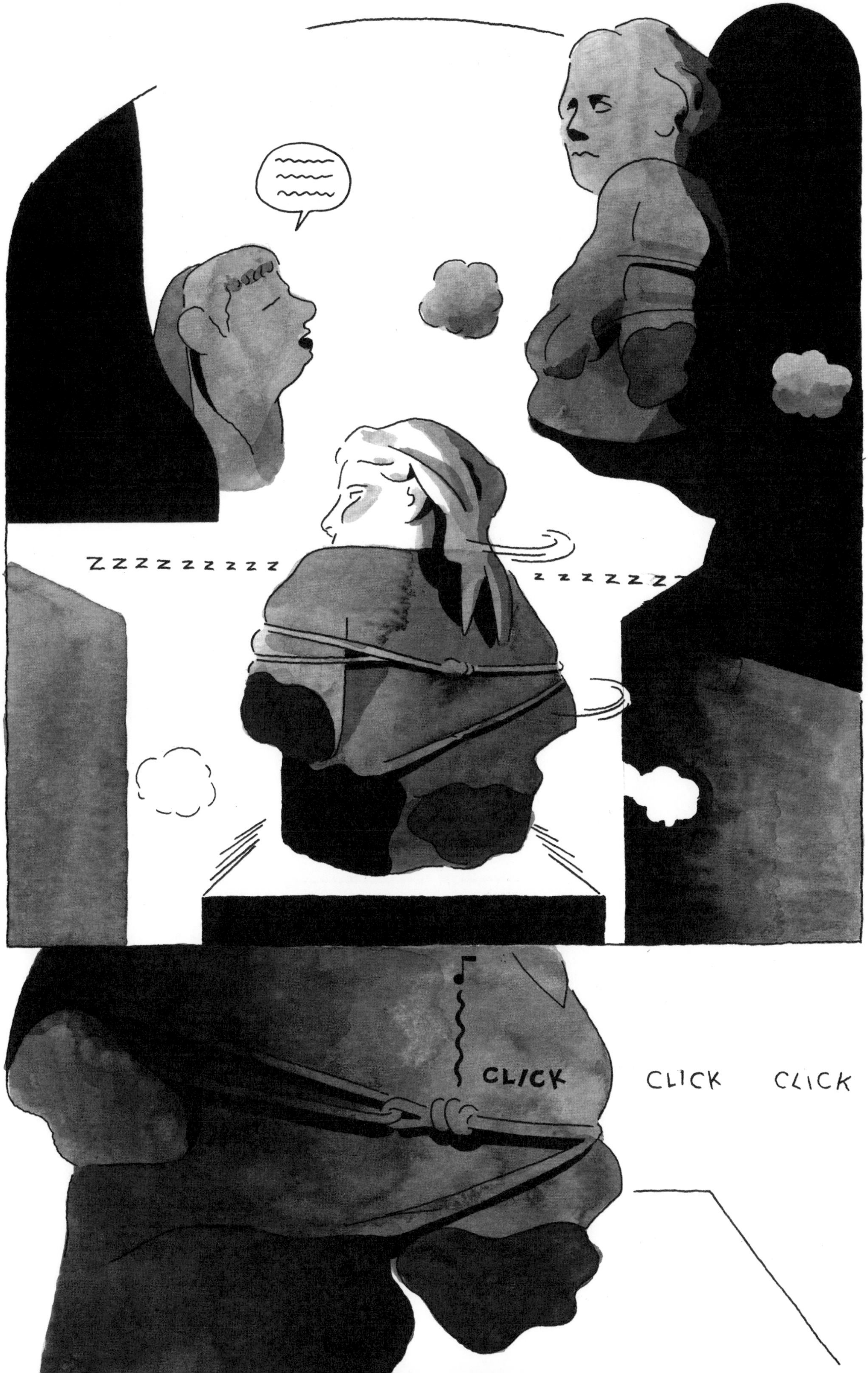

ZZZZZZZZZ
ZZZZZZZ
CLICK
CLICK
CLICK

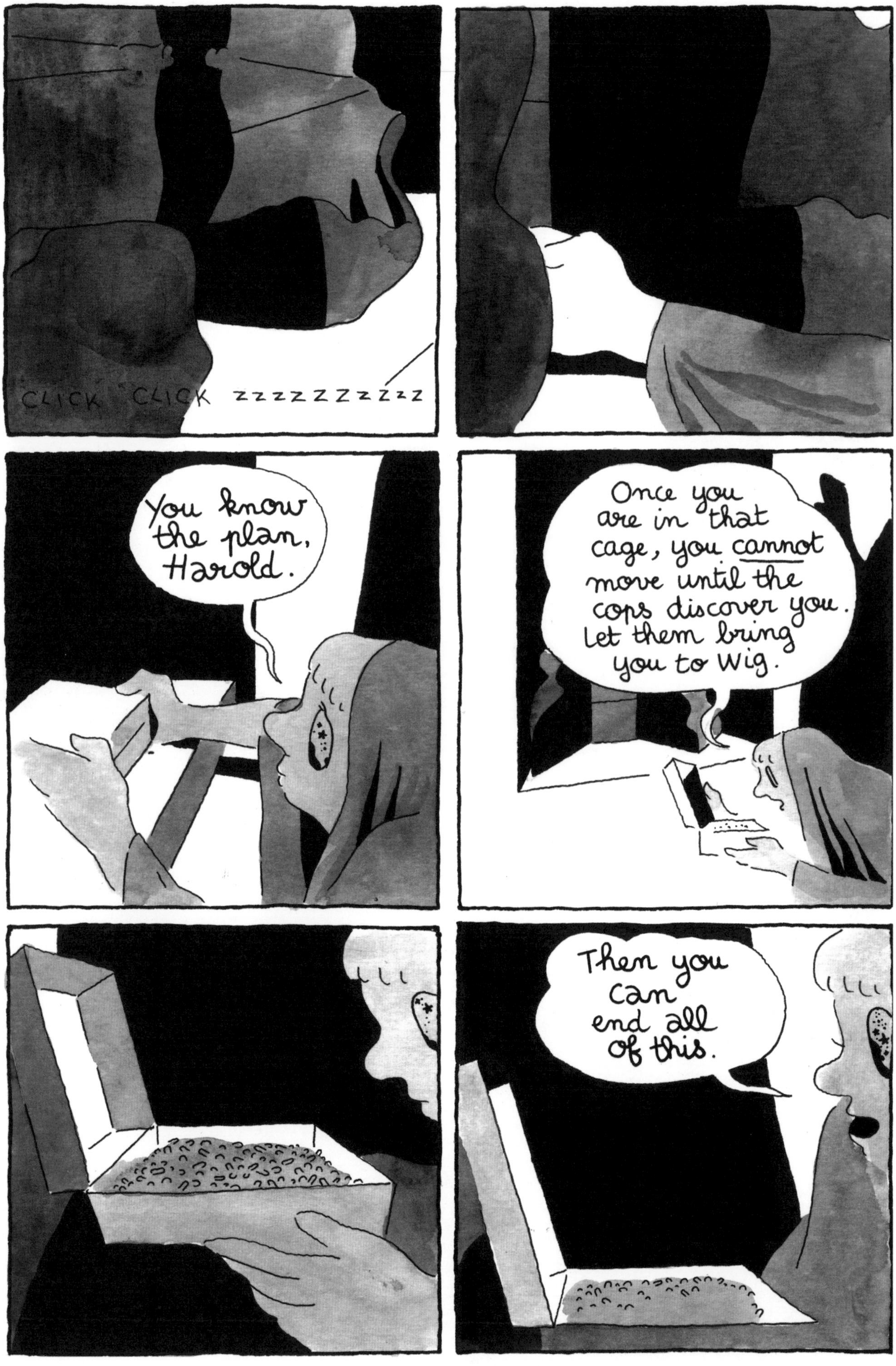
CLICK CLICK ZZZZZZZZZ
You know the plan, Harold.
Once you are in that cage, you cannot move until the cops discover you. Let them bring you to Wig.
Then you can end all of this.

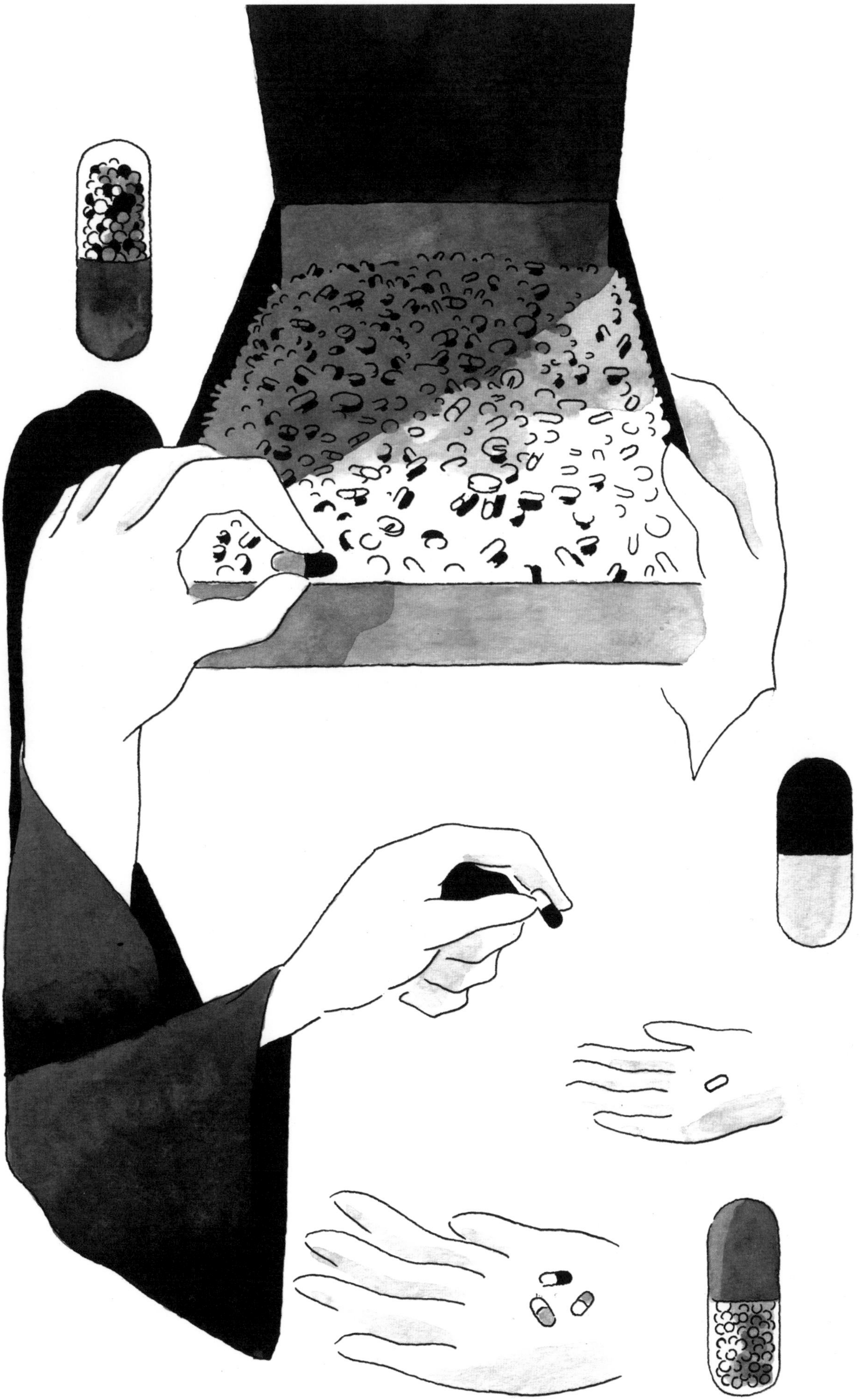

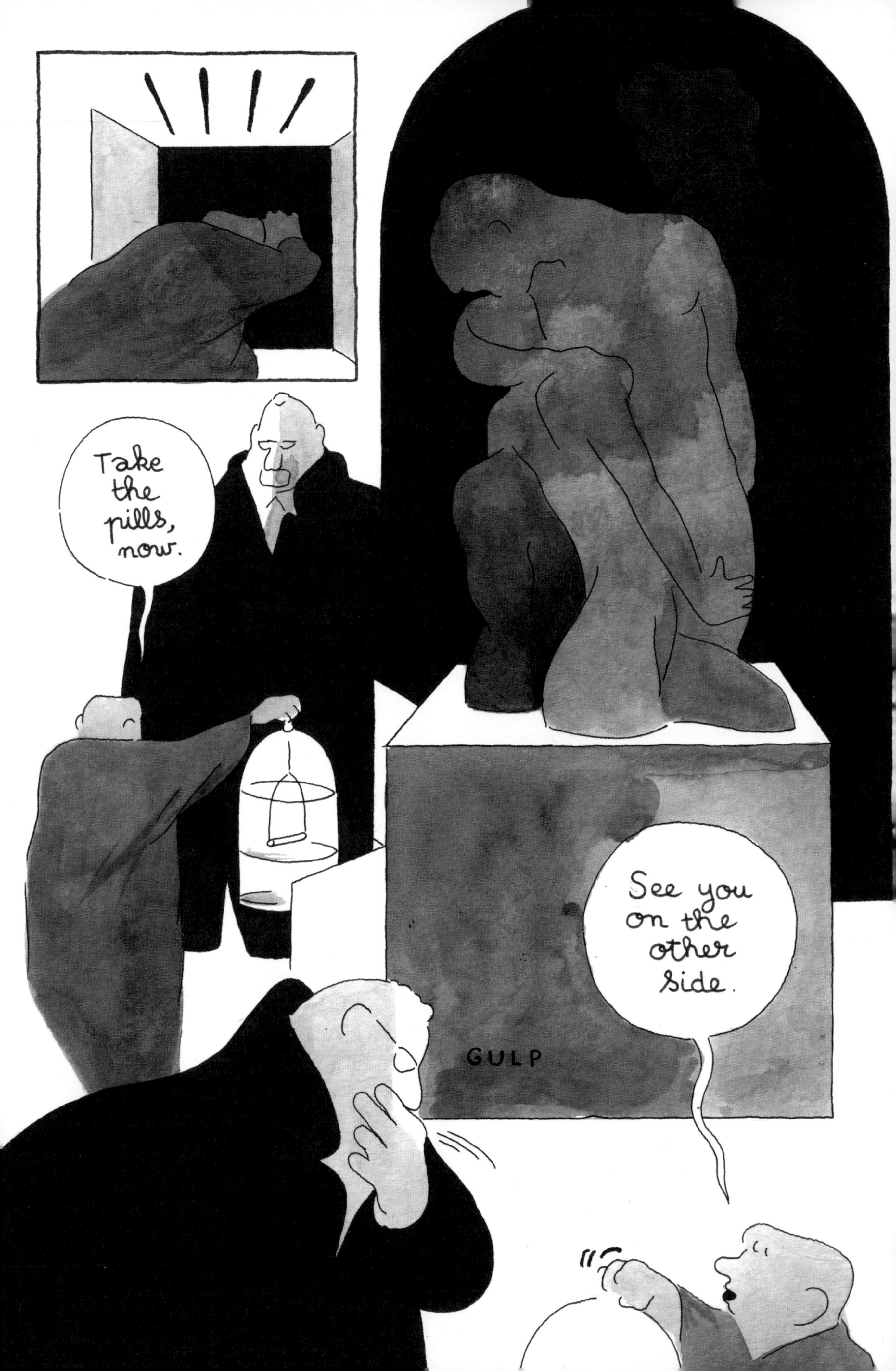
Take the pills, now.
See you on the other side.
GULP

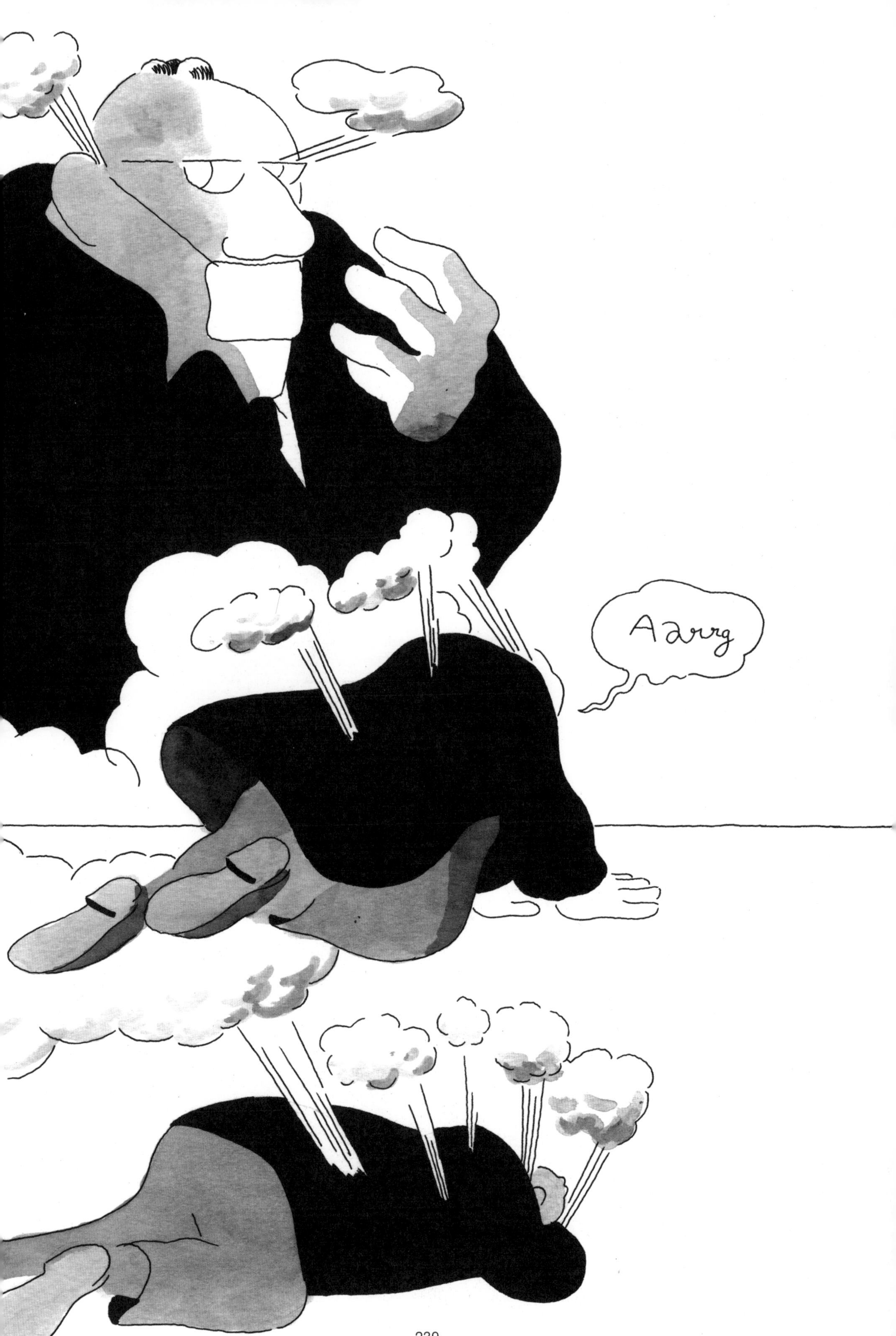
Aarrg

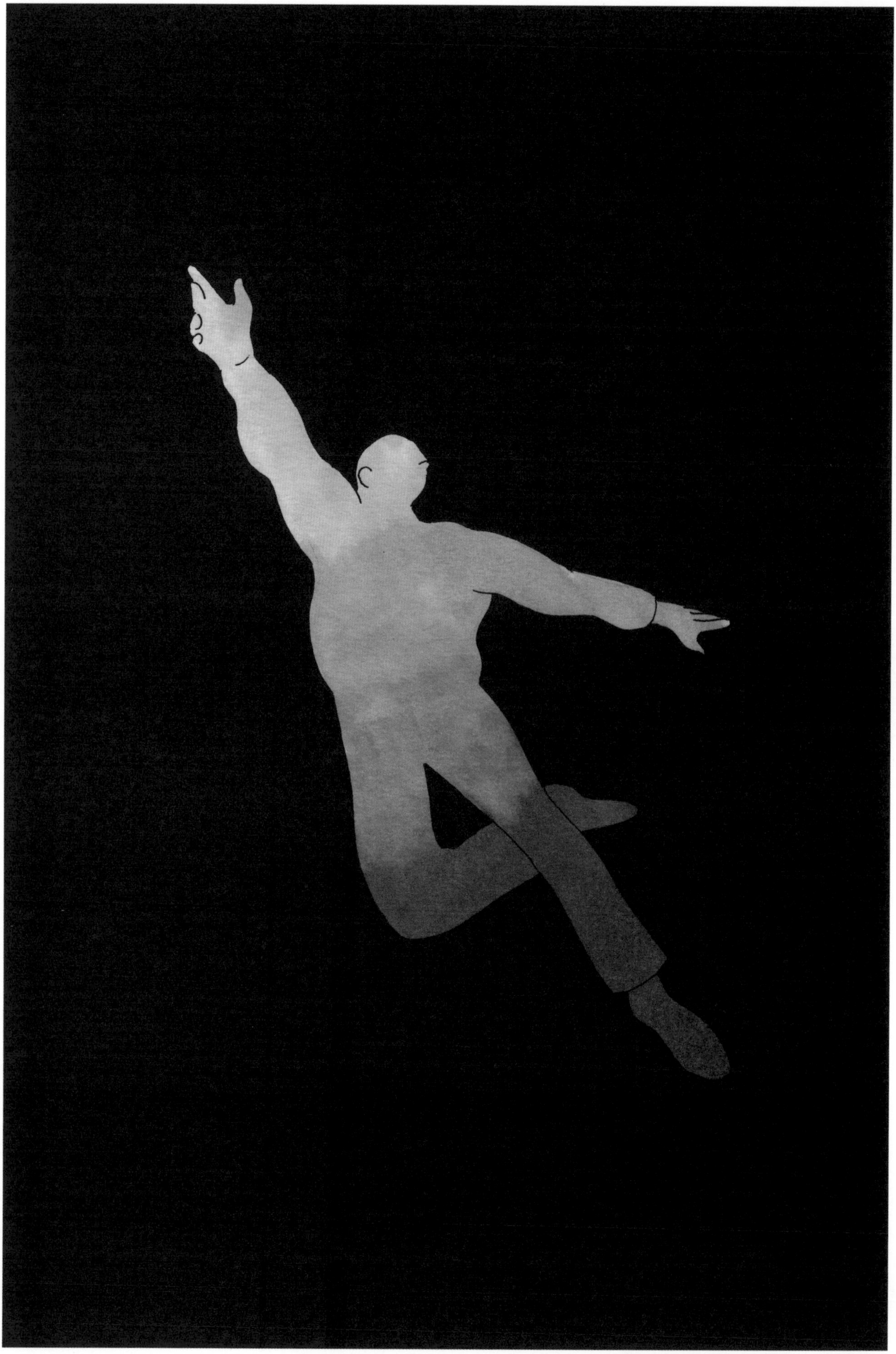

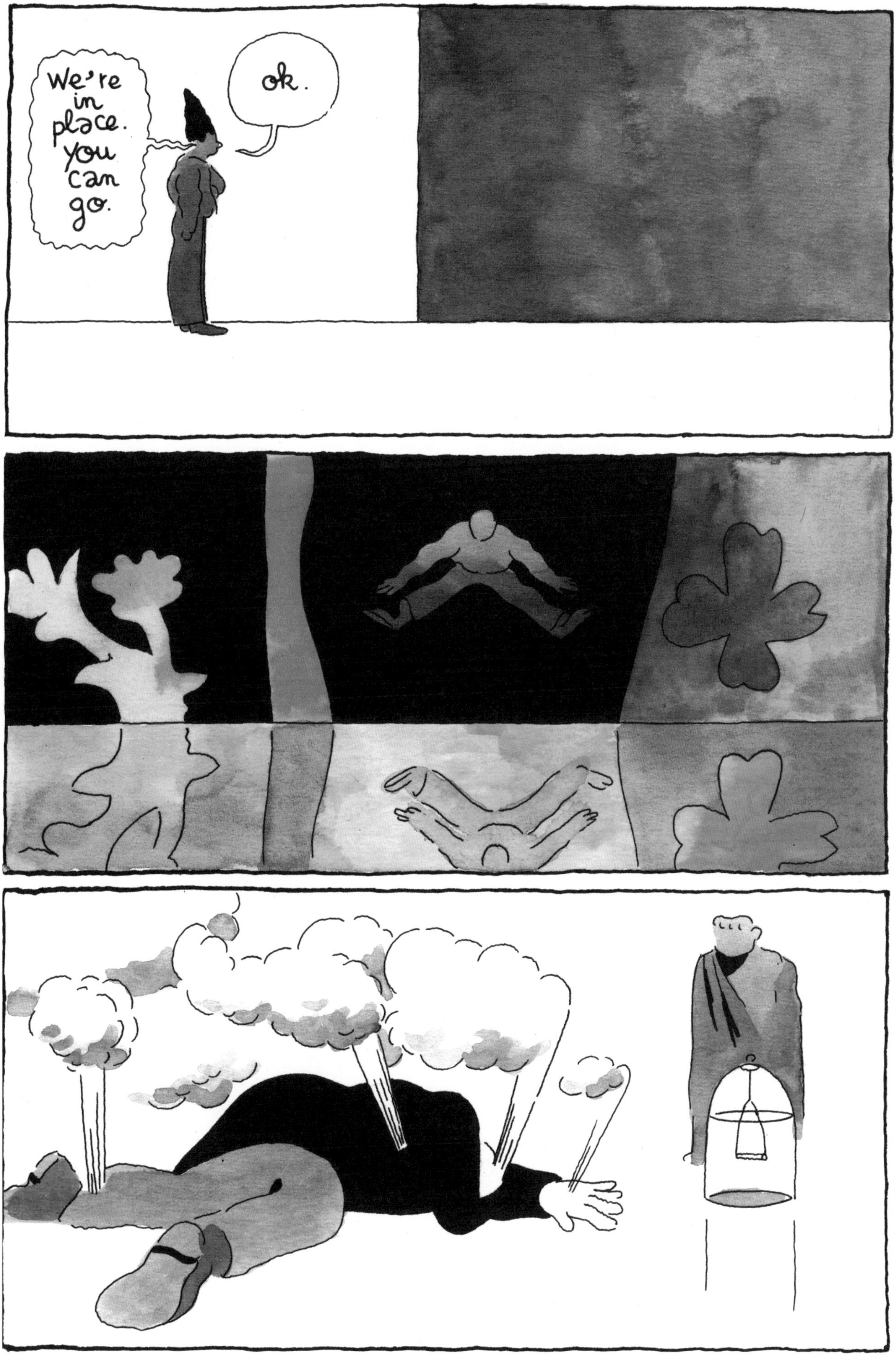
We're in place. you can go.
ok.

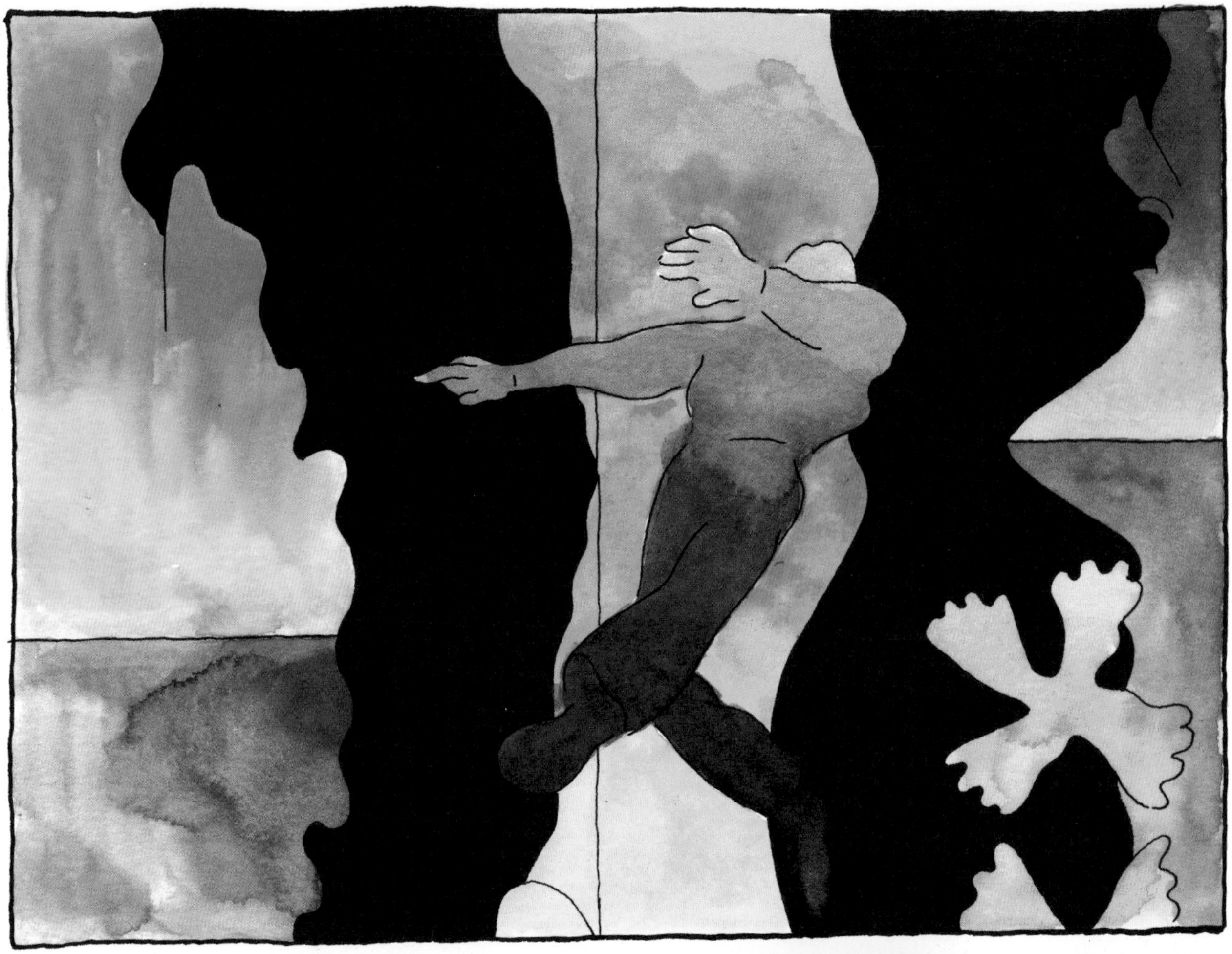

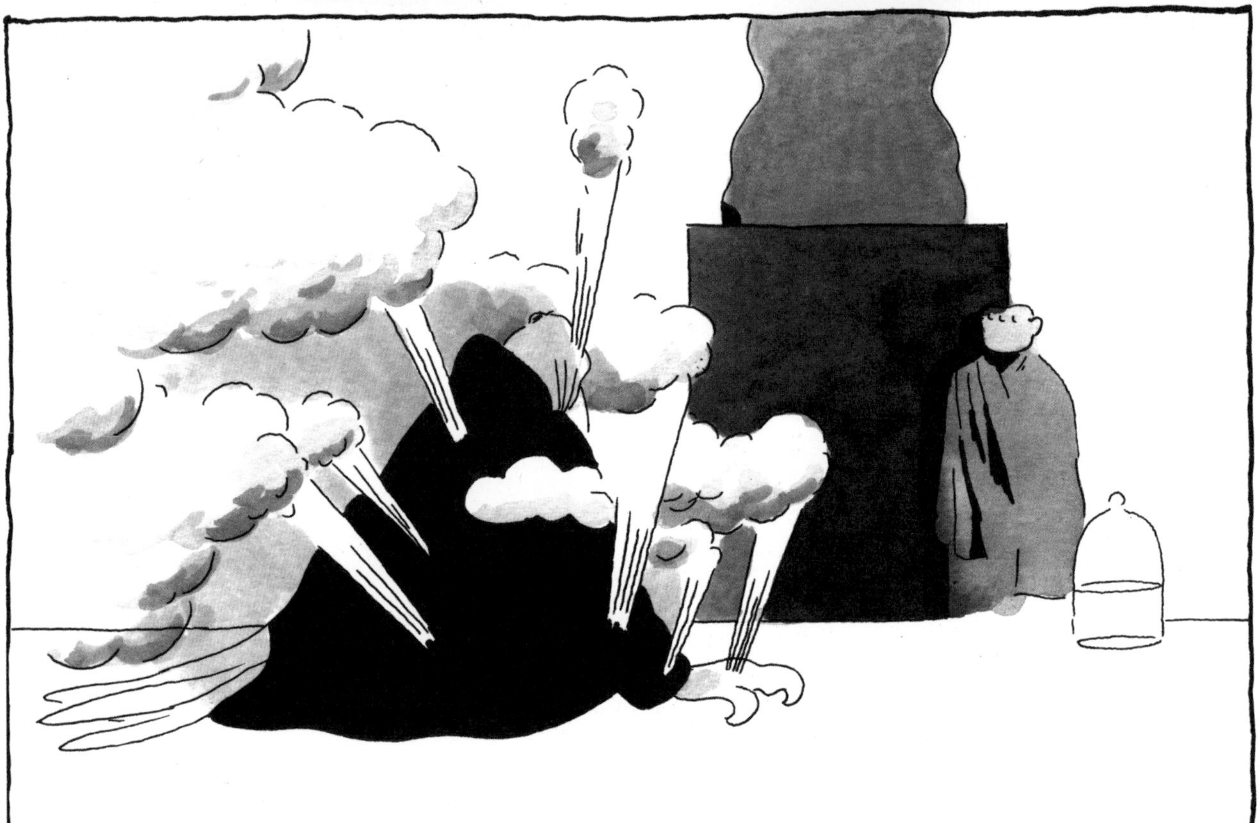

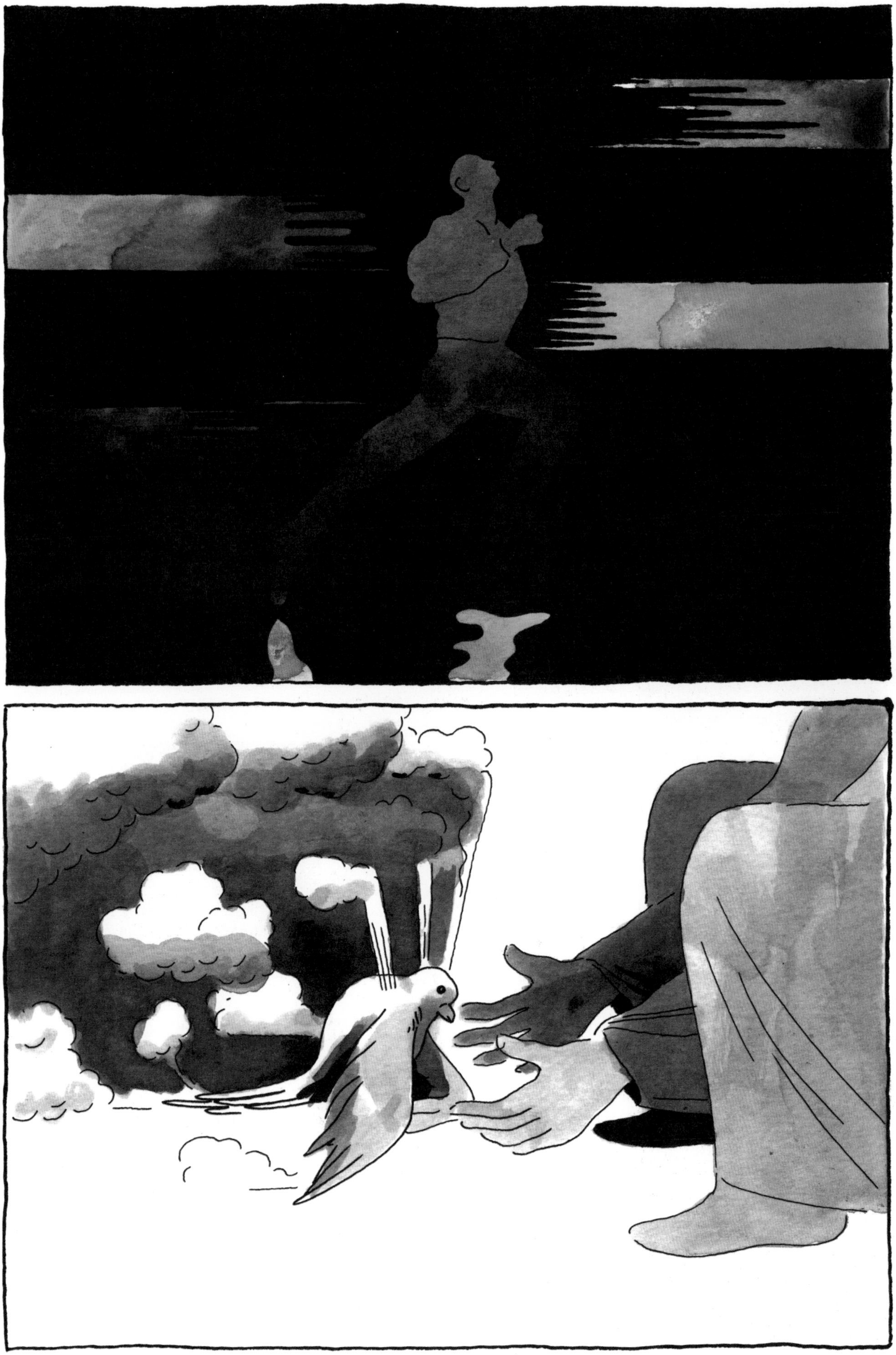

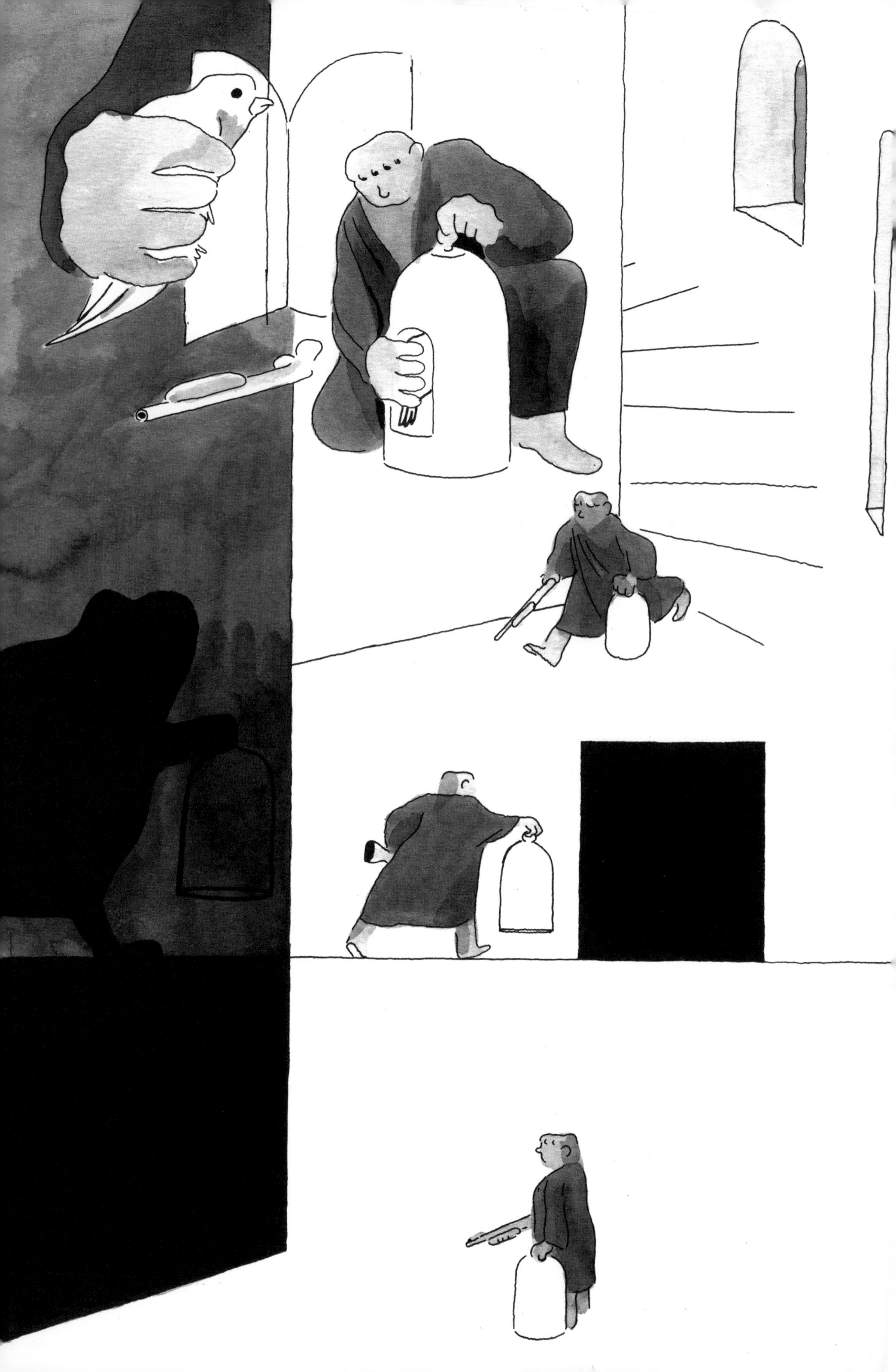

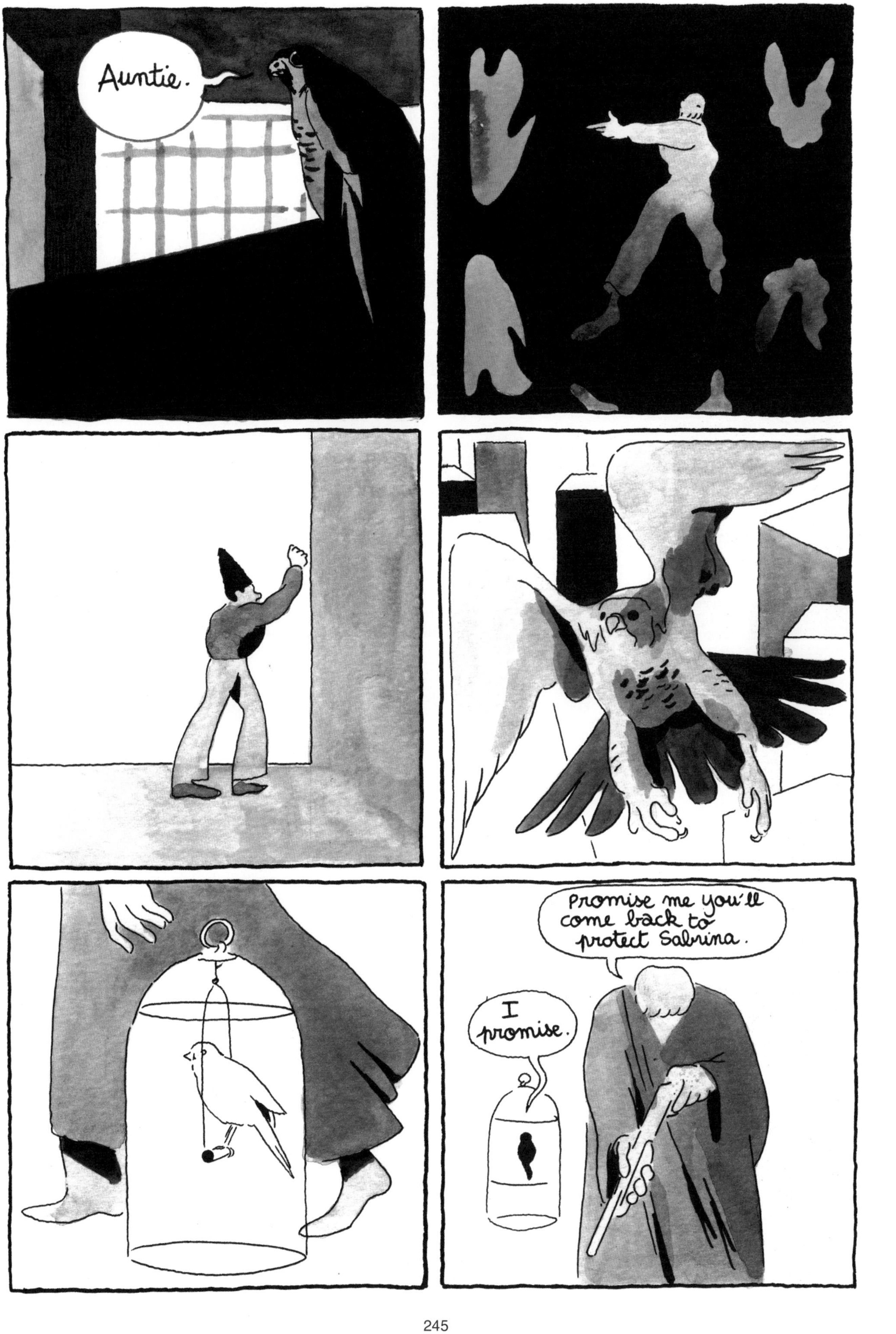
Auntie.
Promise me you'll come back to protect Sabrina.
I promise.

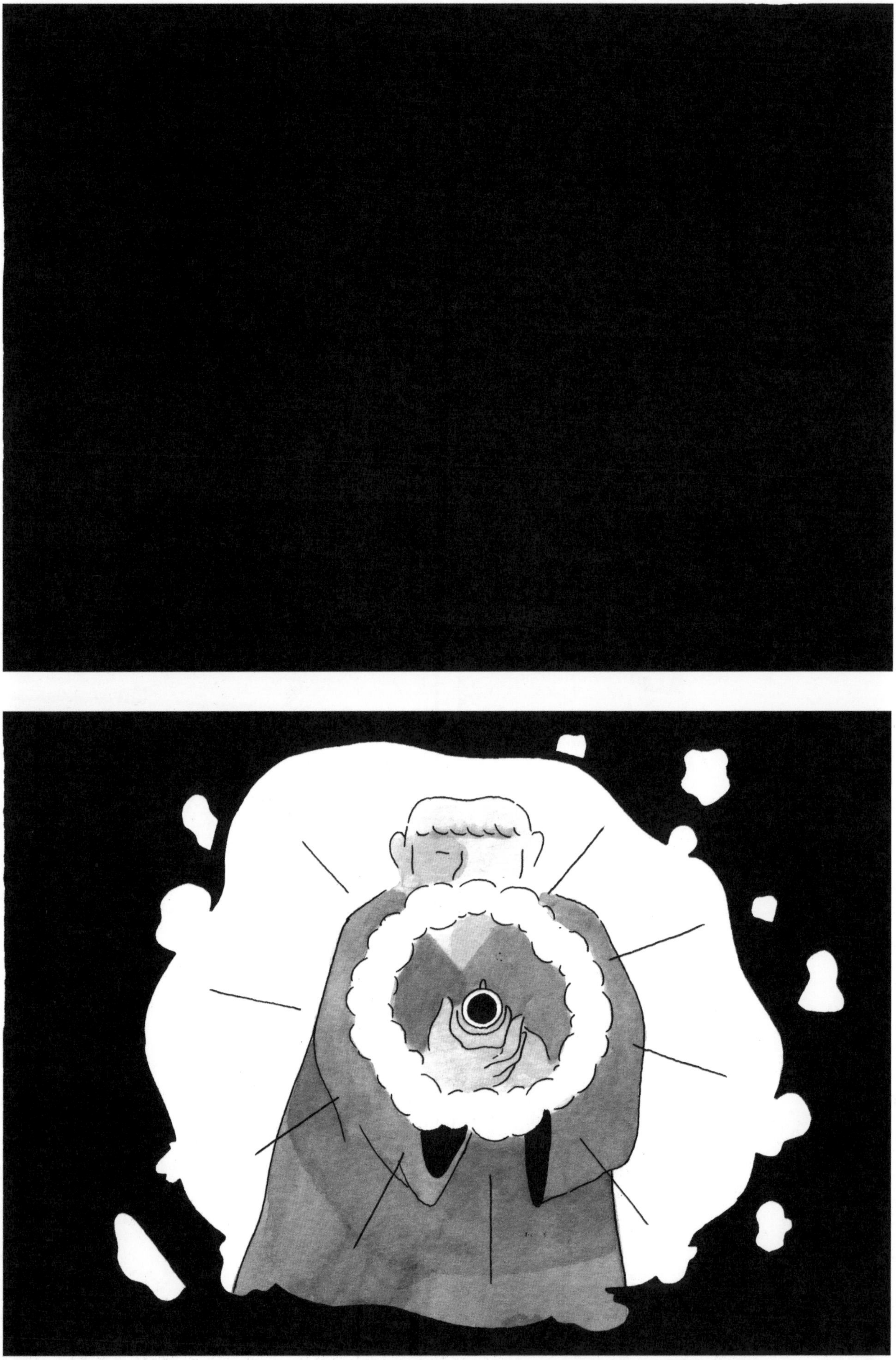

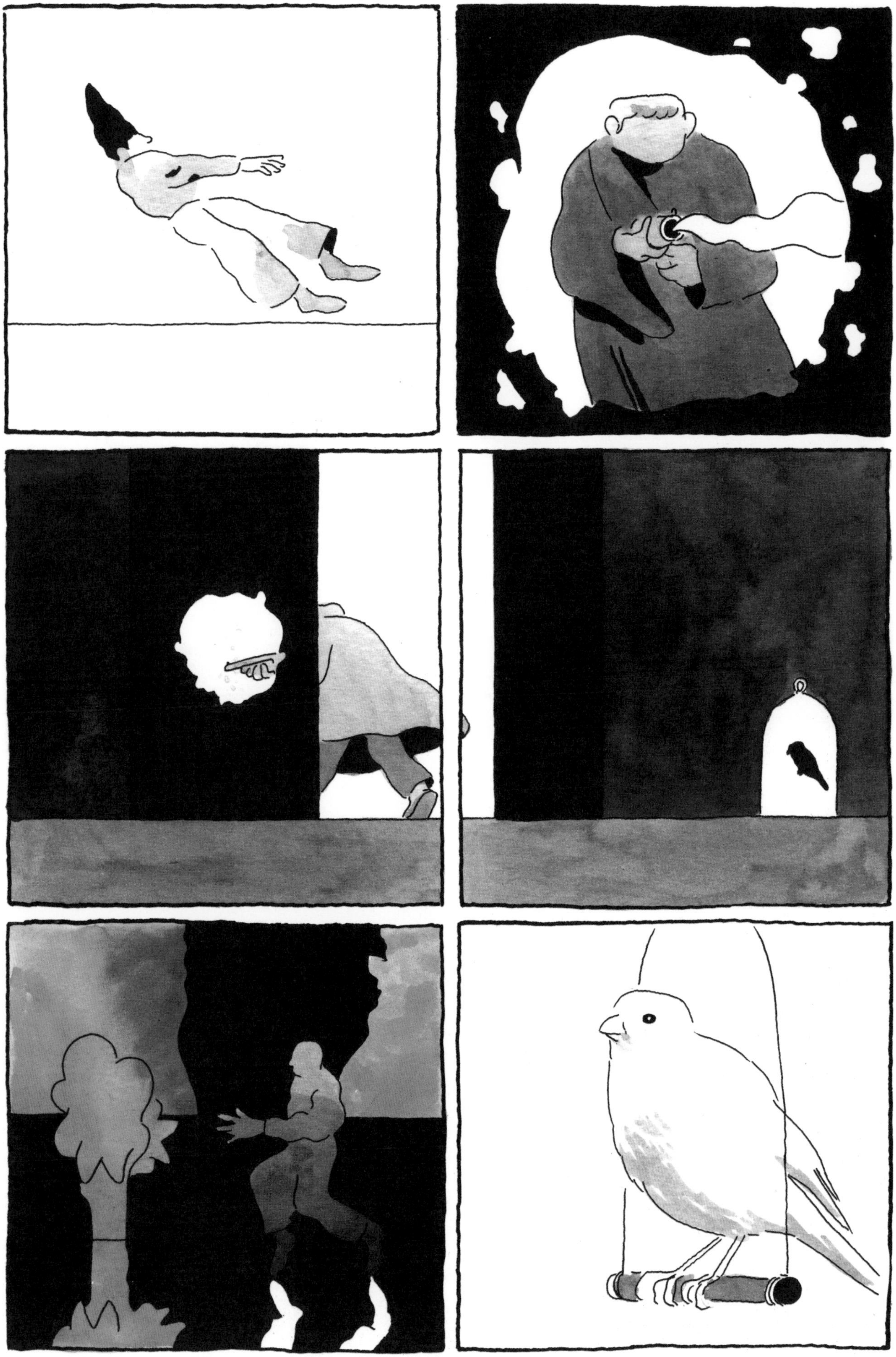

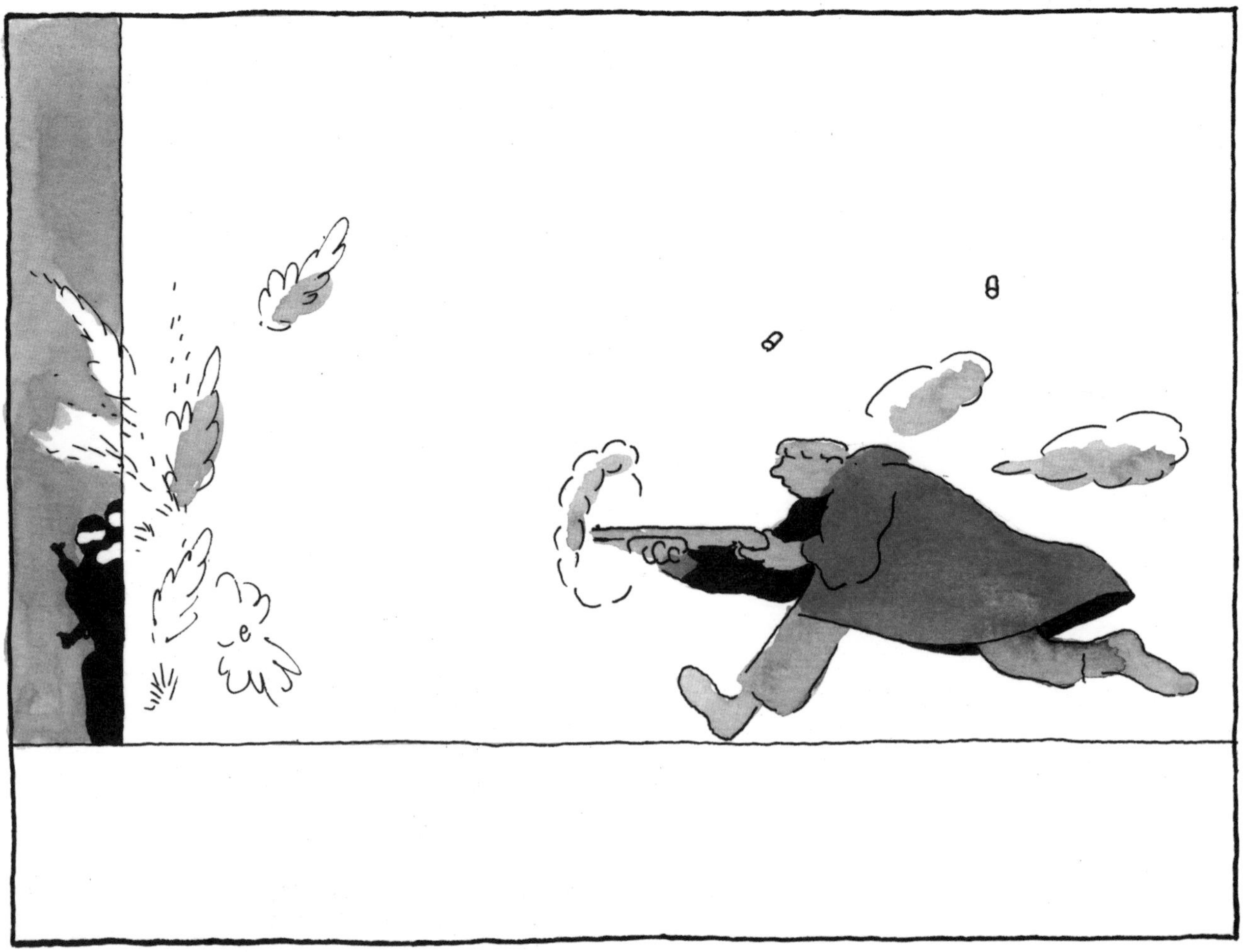

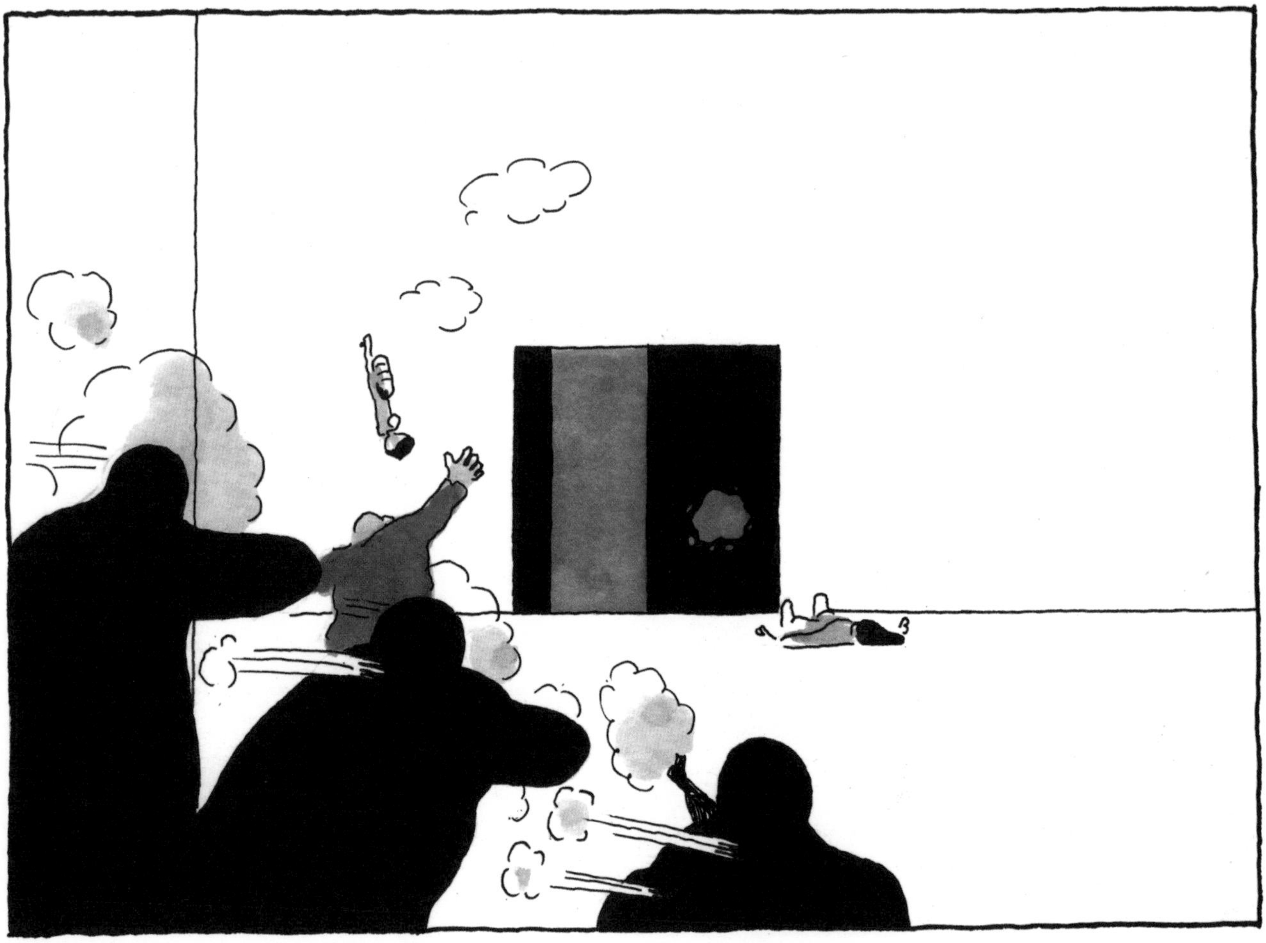

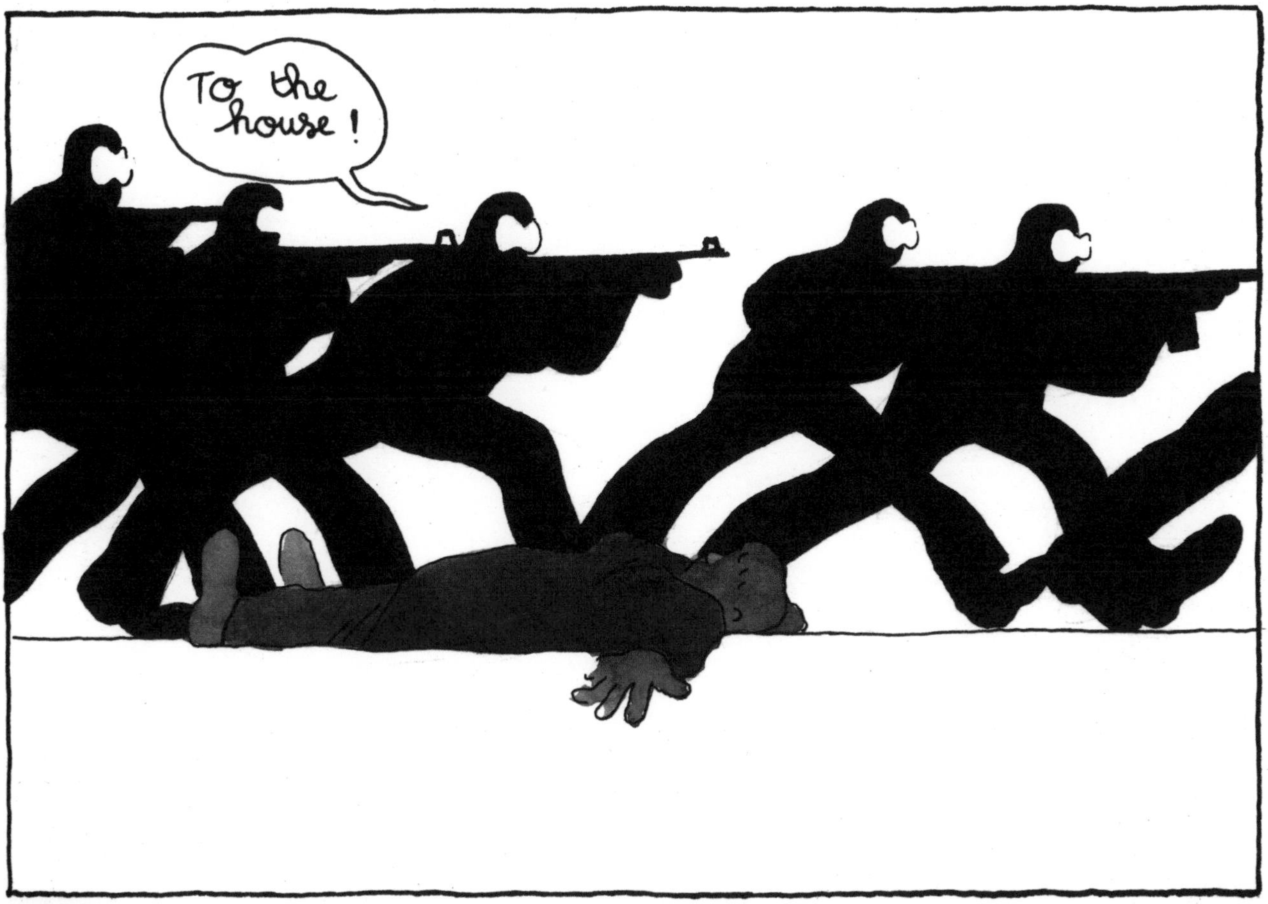
To the house!

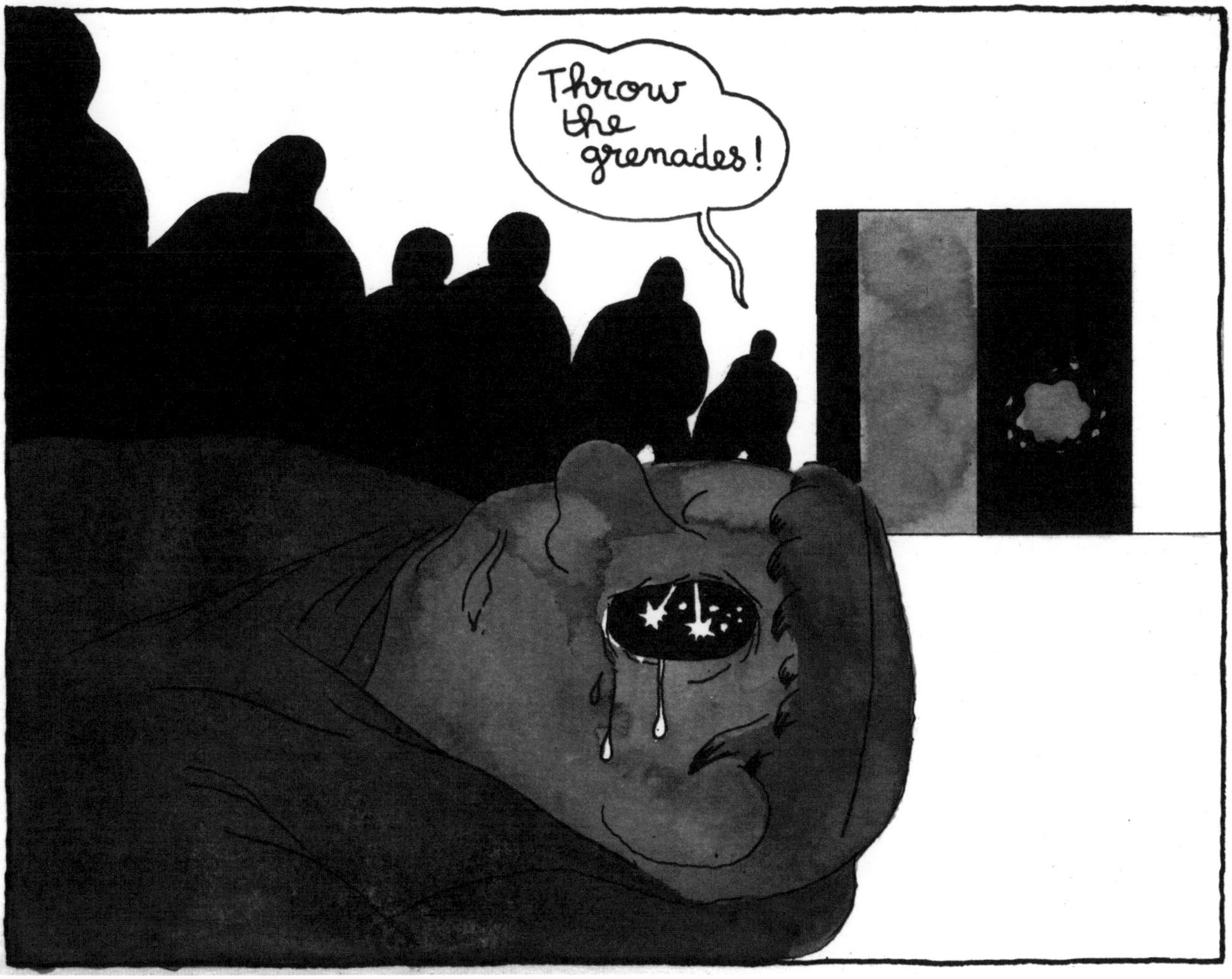
Throw the grenades!

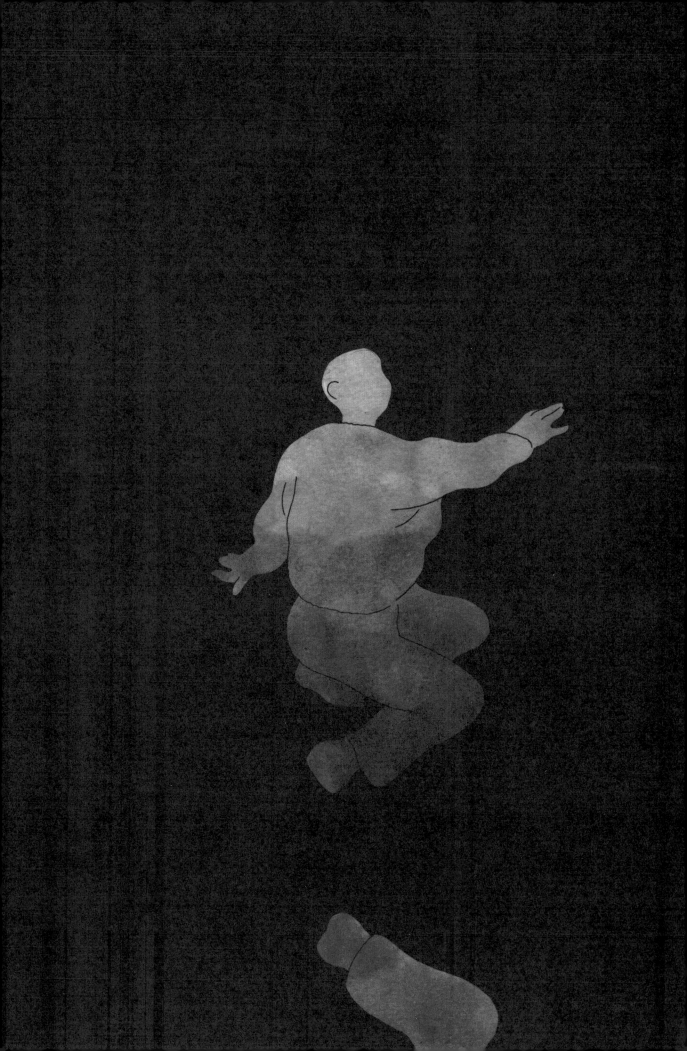

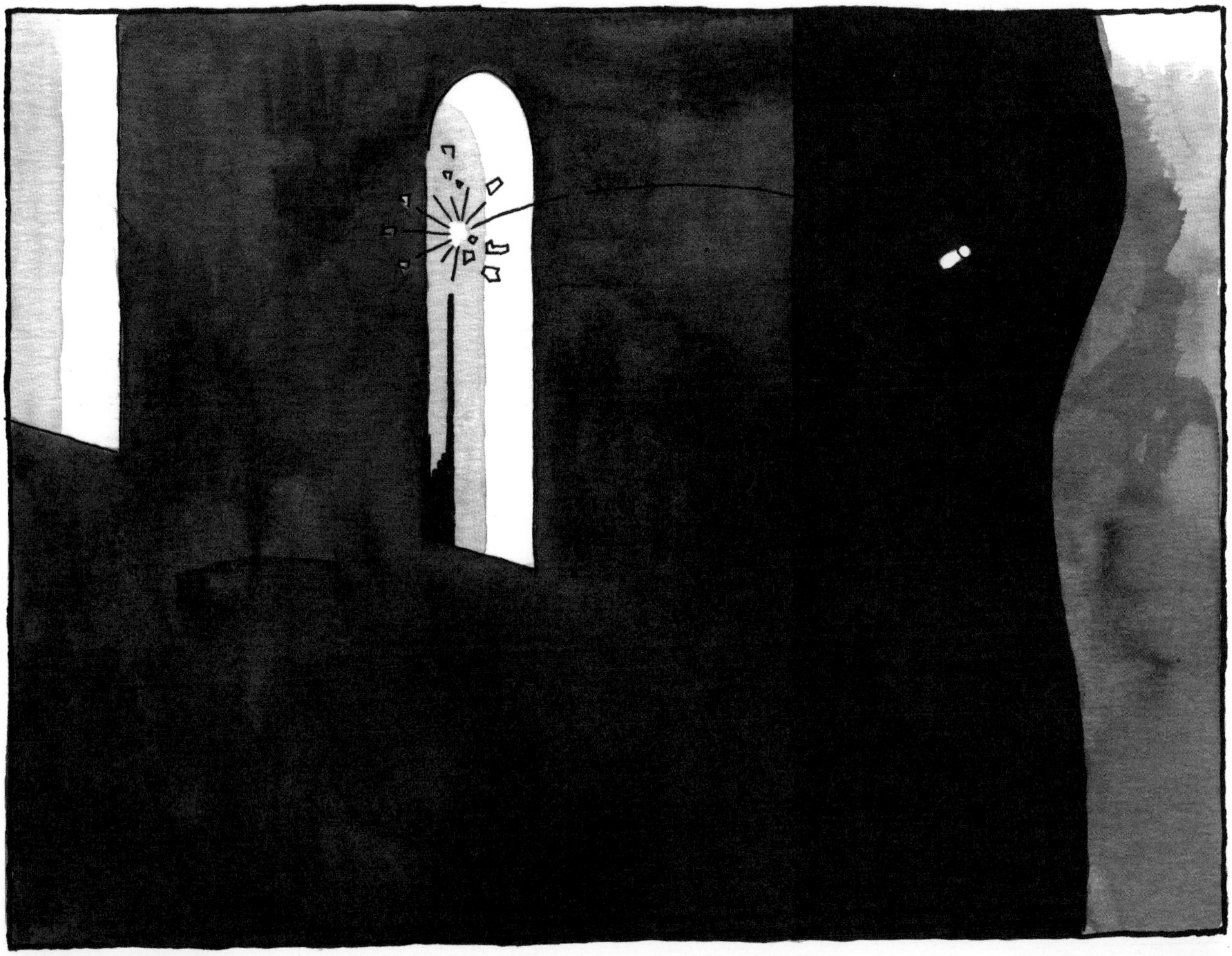

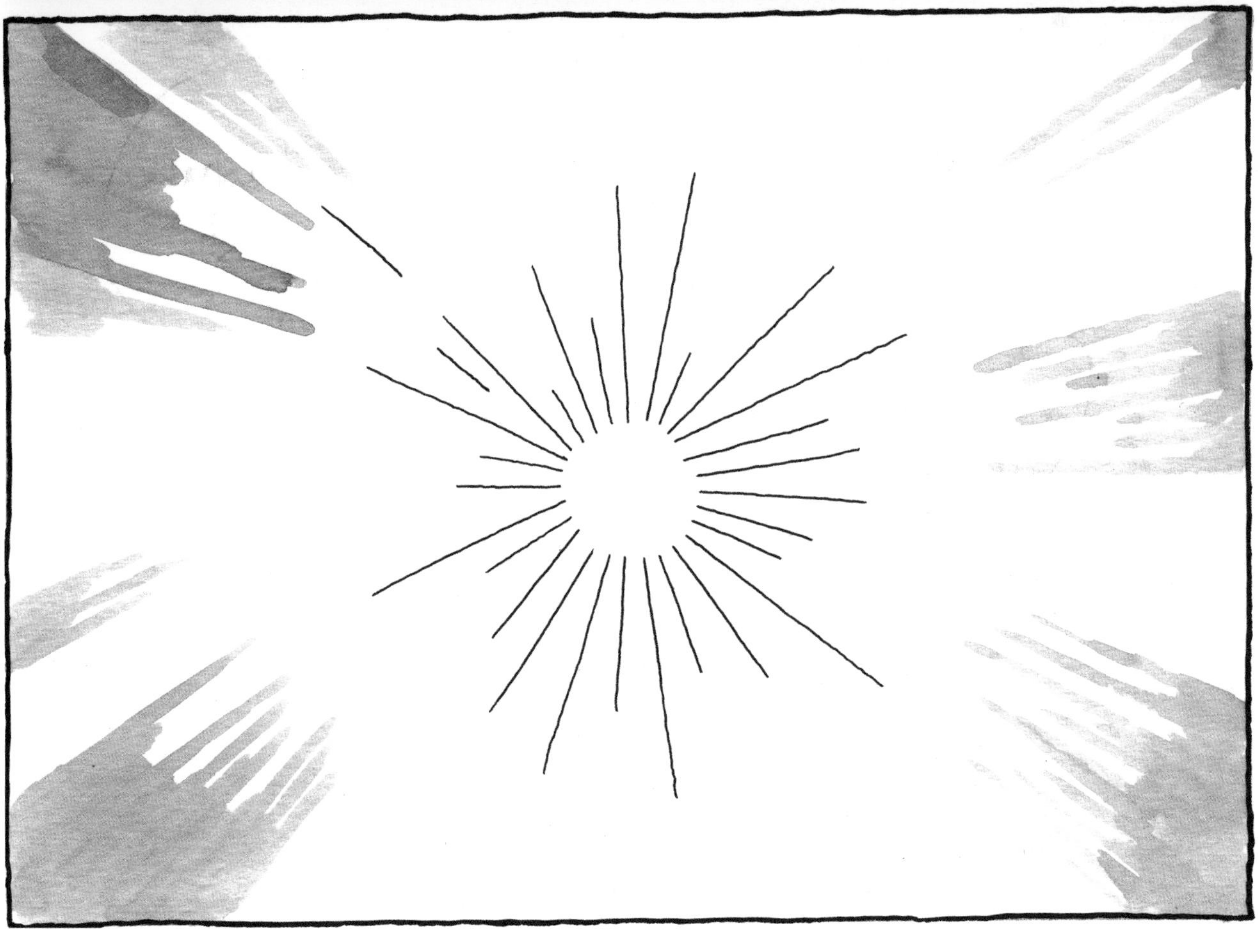

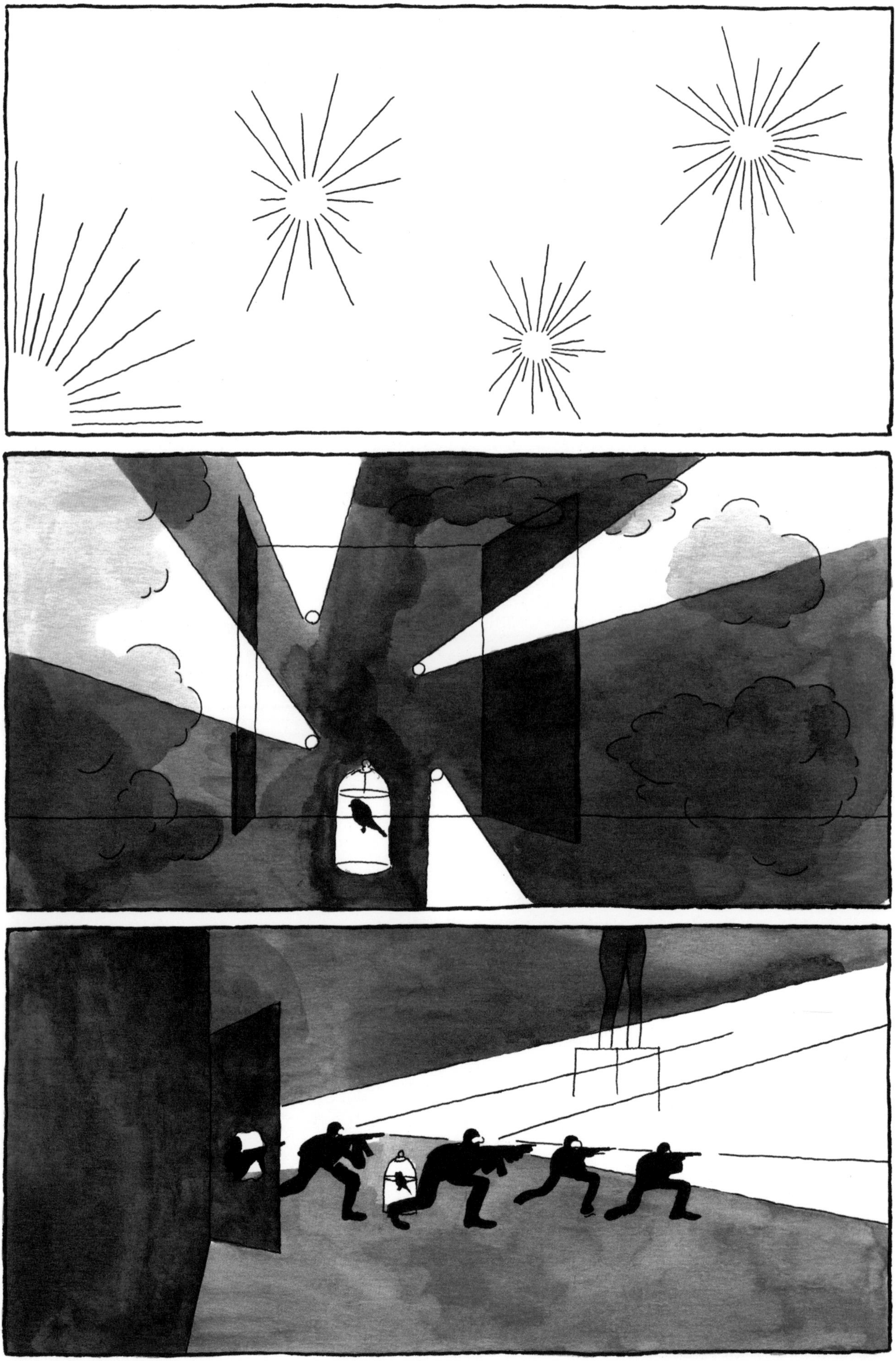

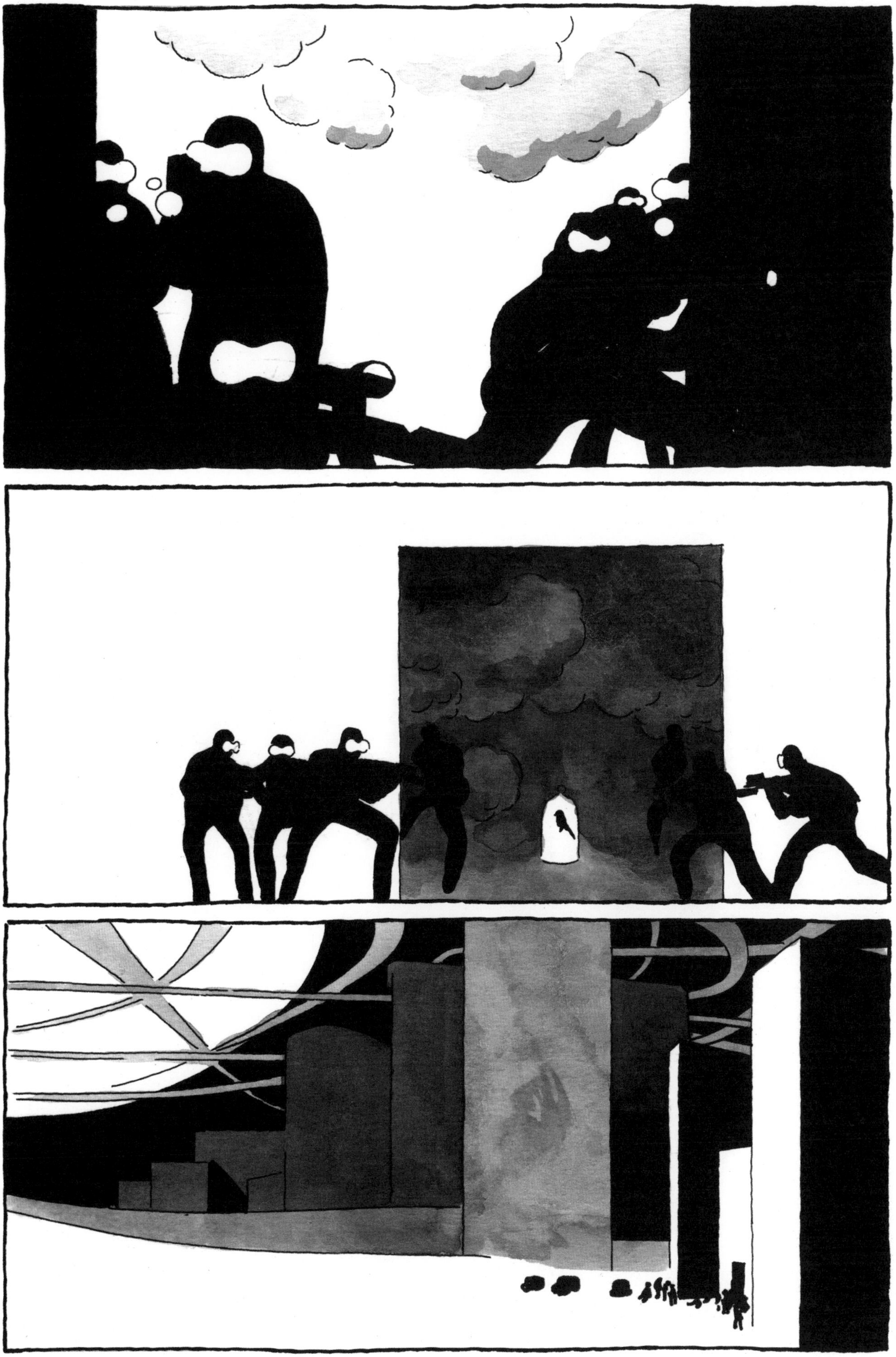

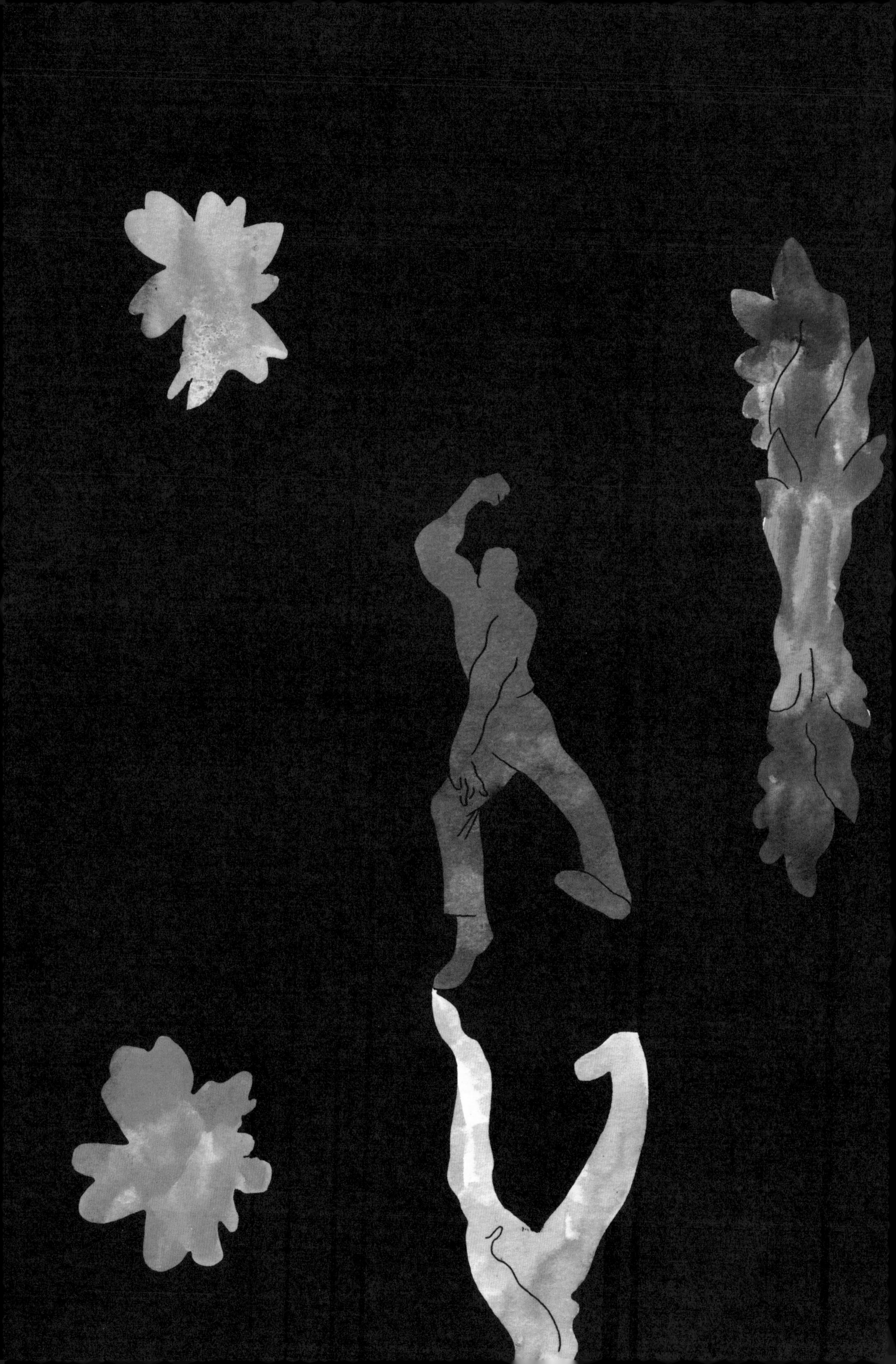

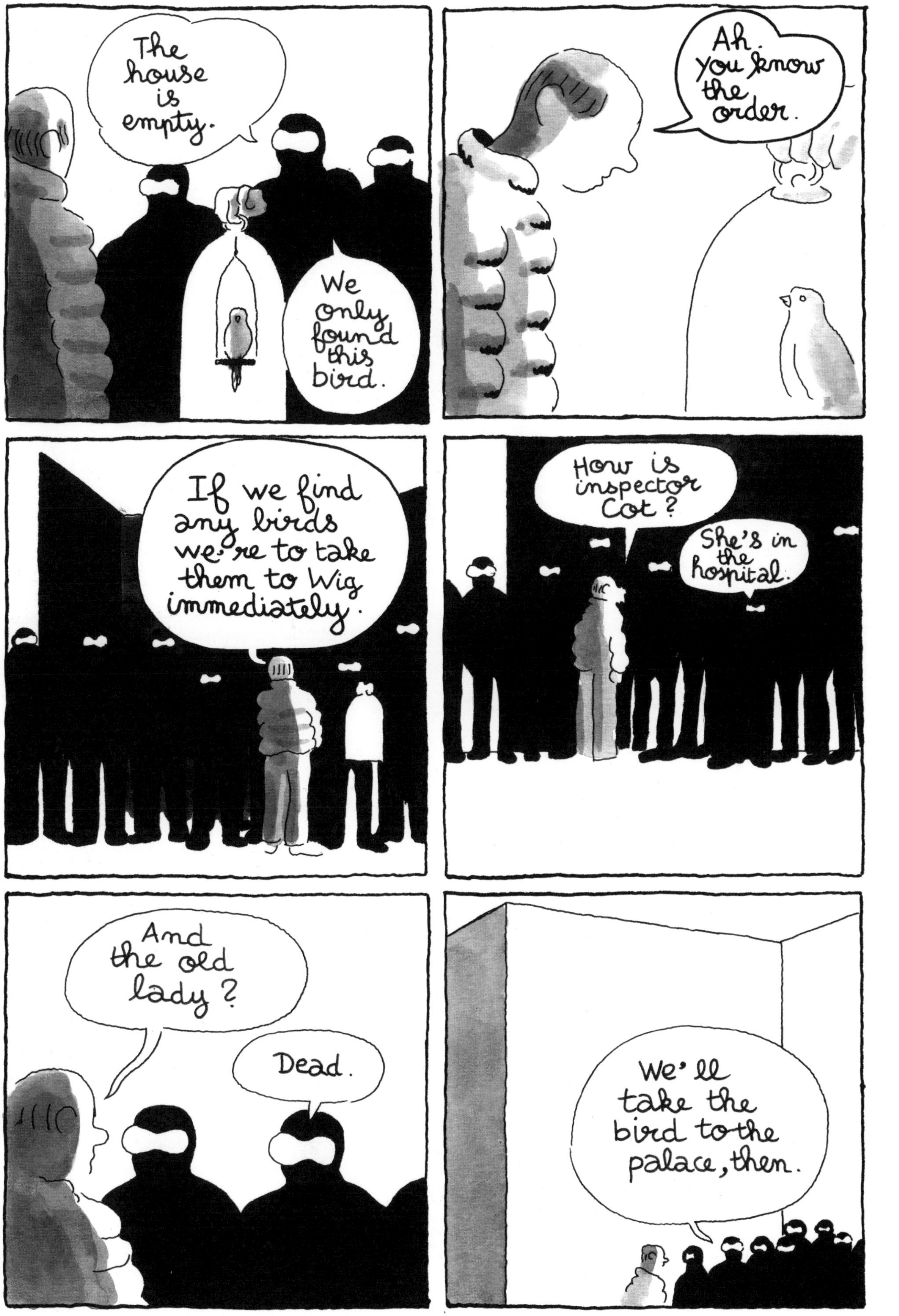

The house is empty.
We only found this bird.
Ah. you know the order.
If we find any birds we're to take them to Wig immediately.
How is inspector Cot?
She's in the hospital.
And the old lady?
Dead.
We'll take the bird to the palace, then.

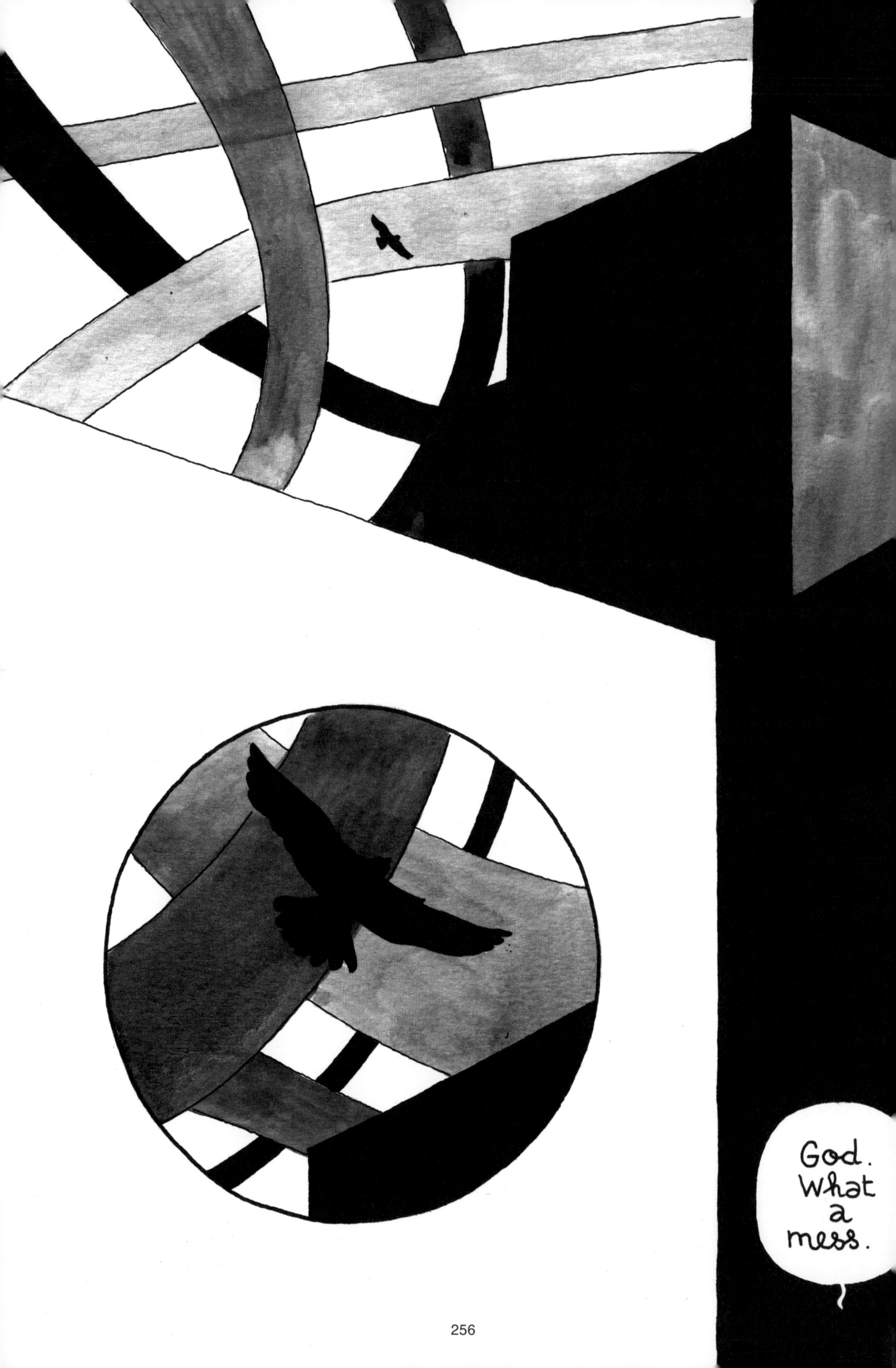
God. What a mess.

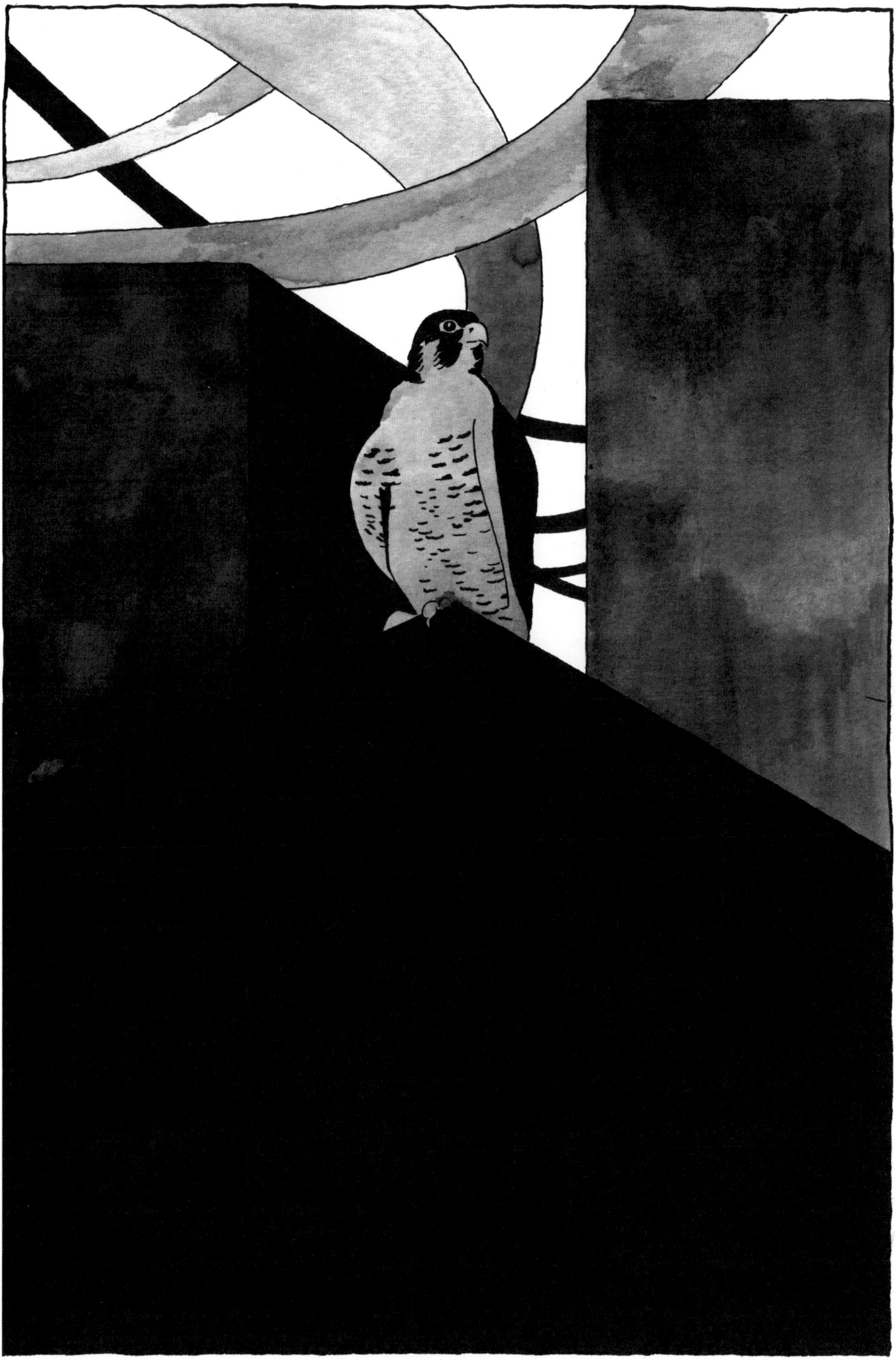

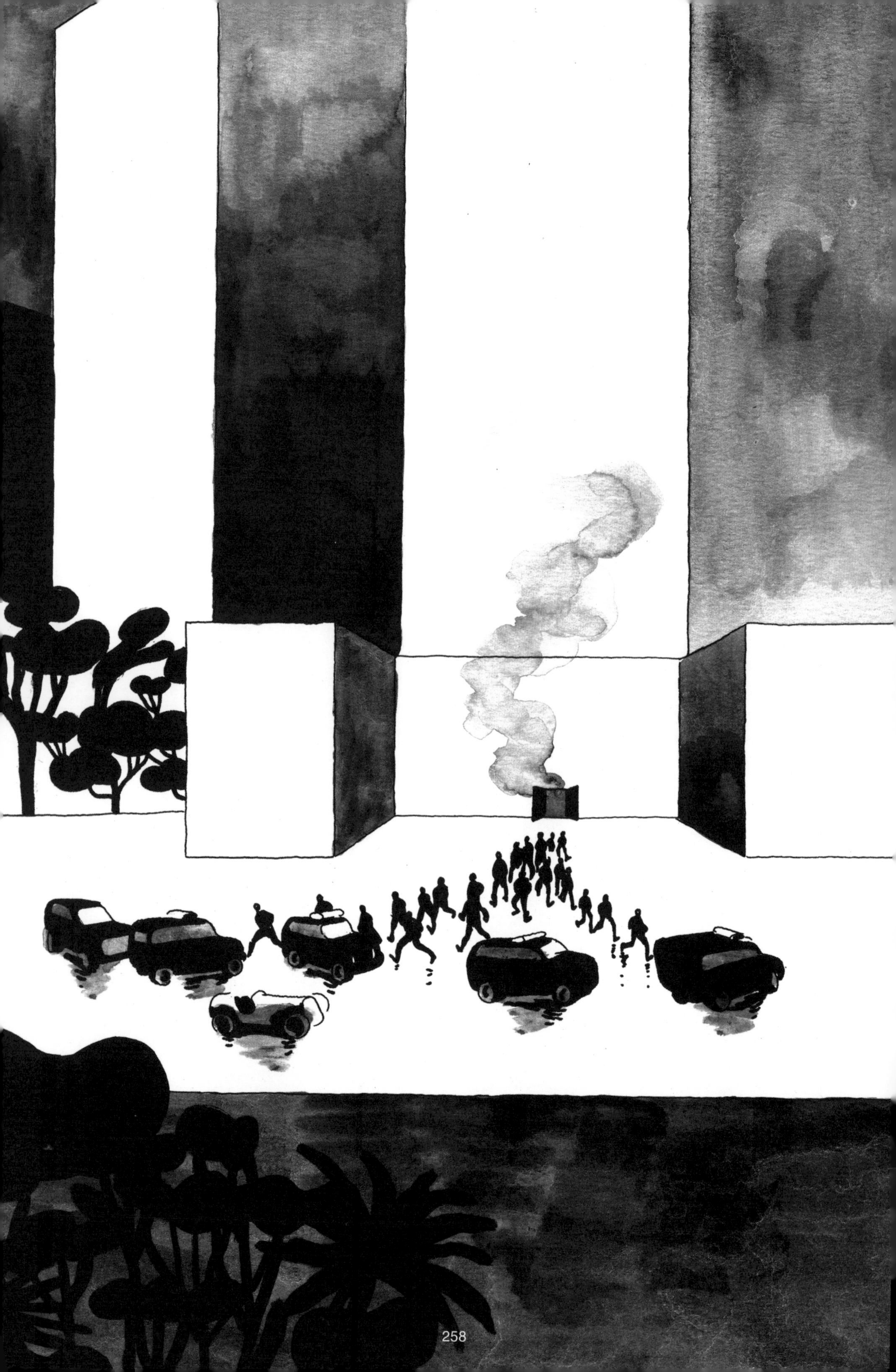

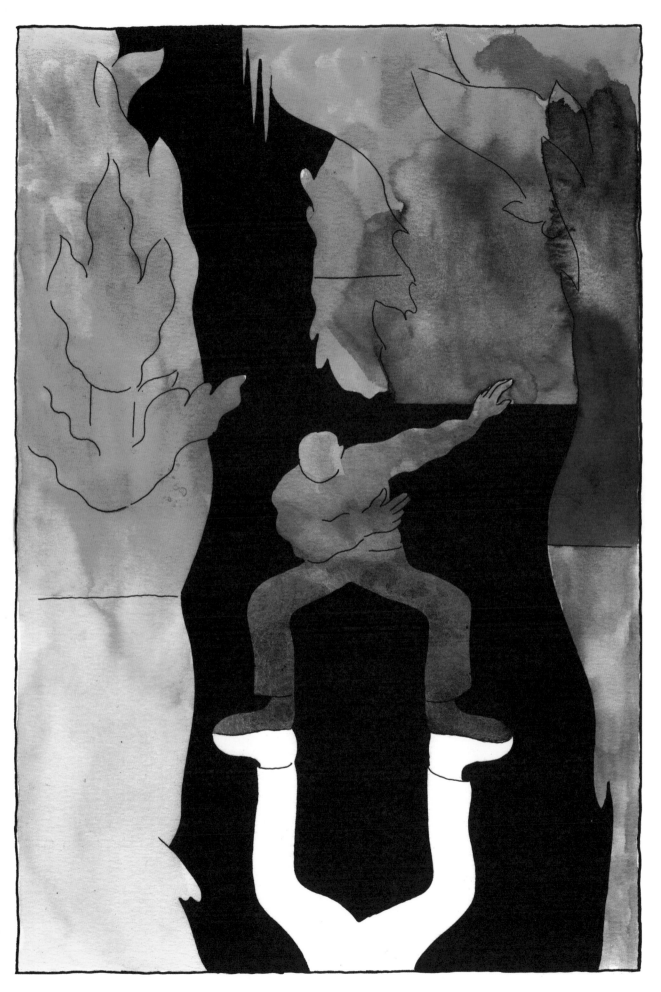

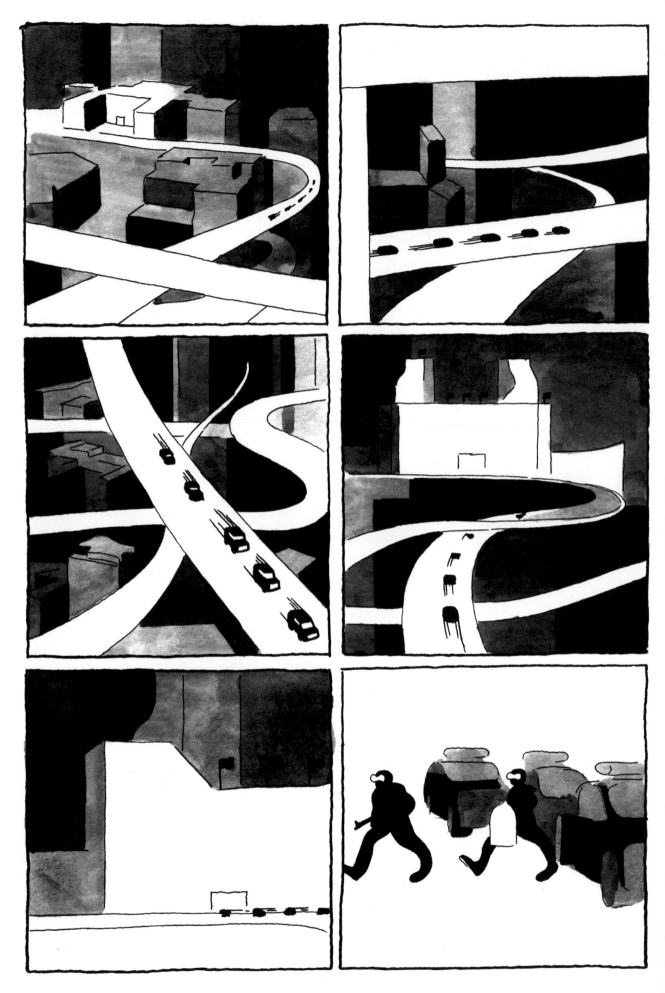

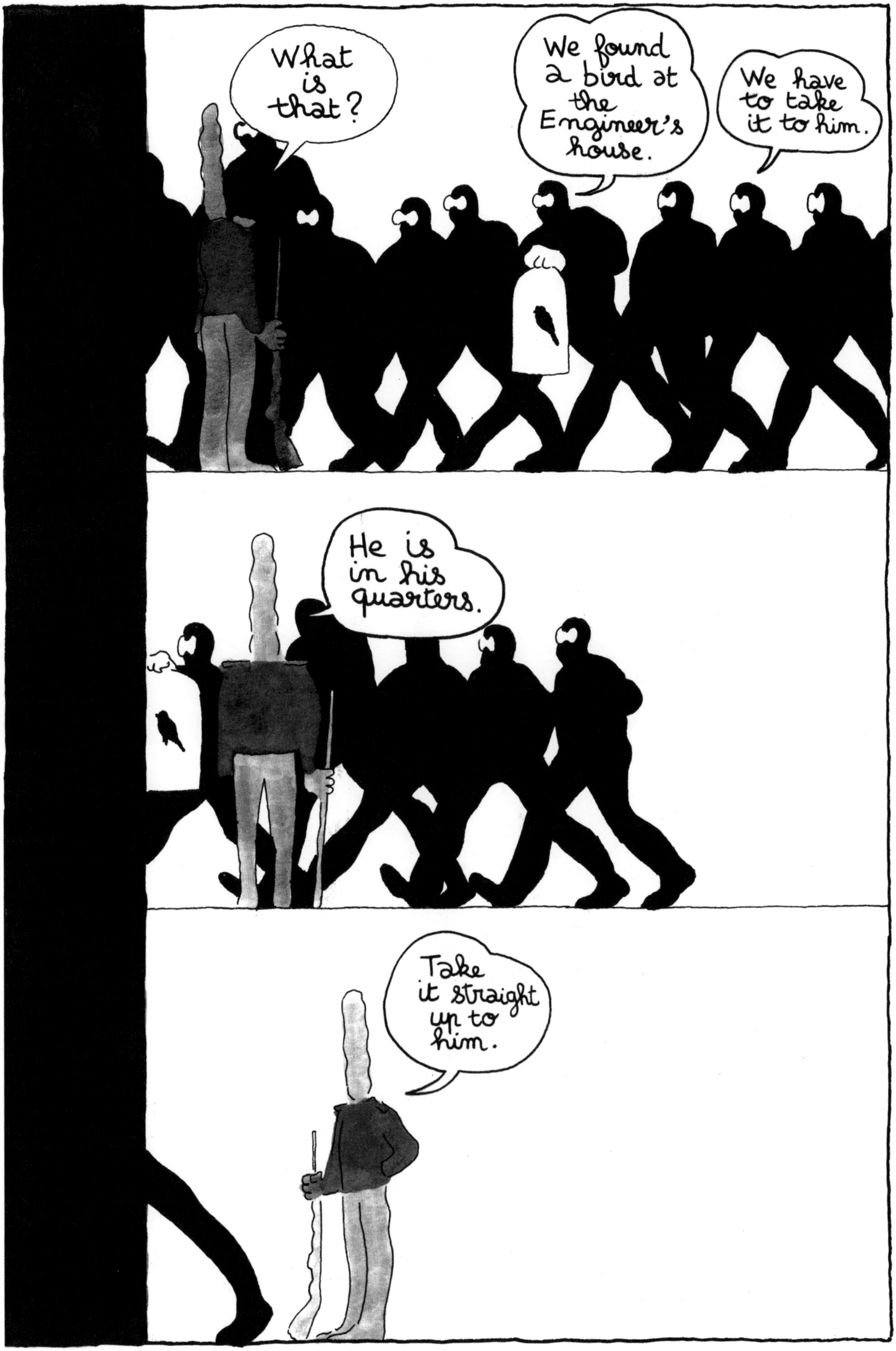
What is that?
We found a bird at the Engineer's house.
We have to take it to him.
He is in his quarters.
Take it straight up to him.

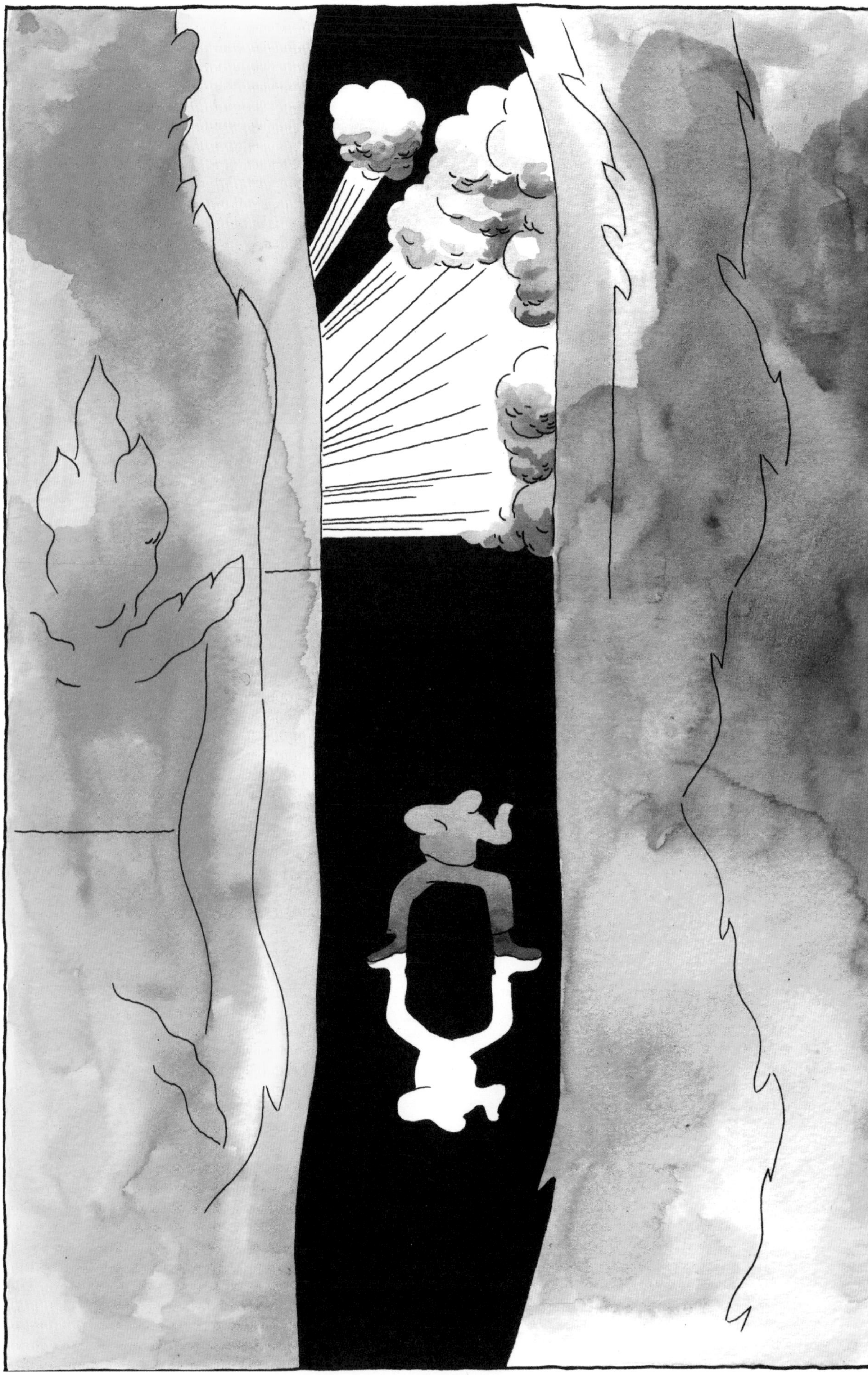

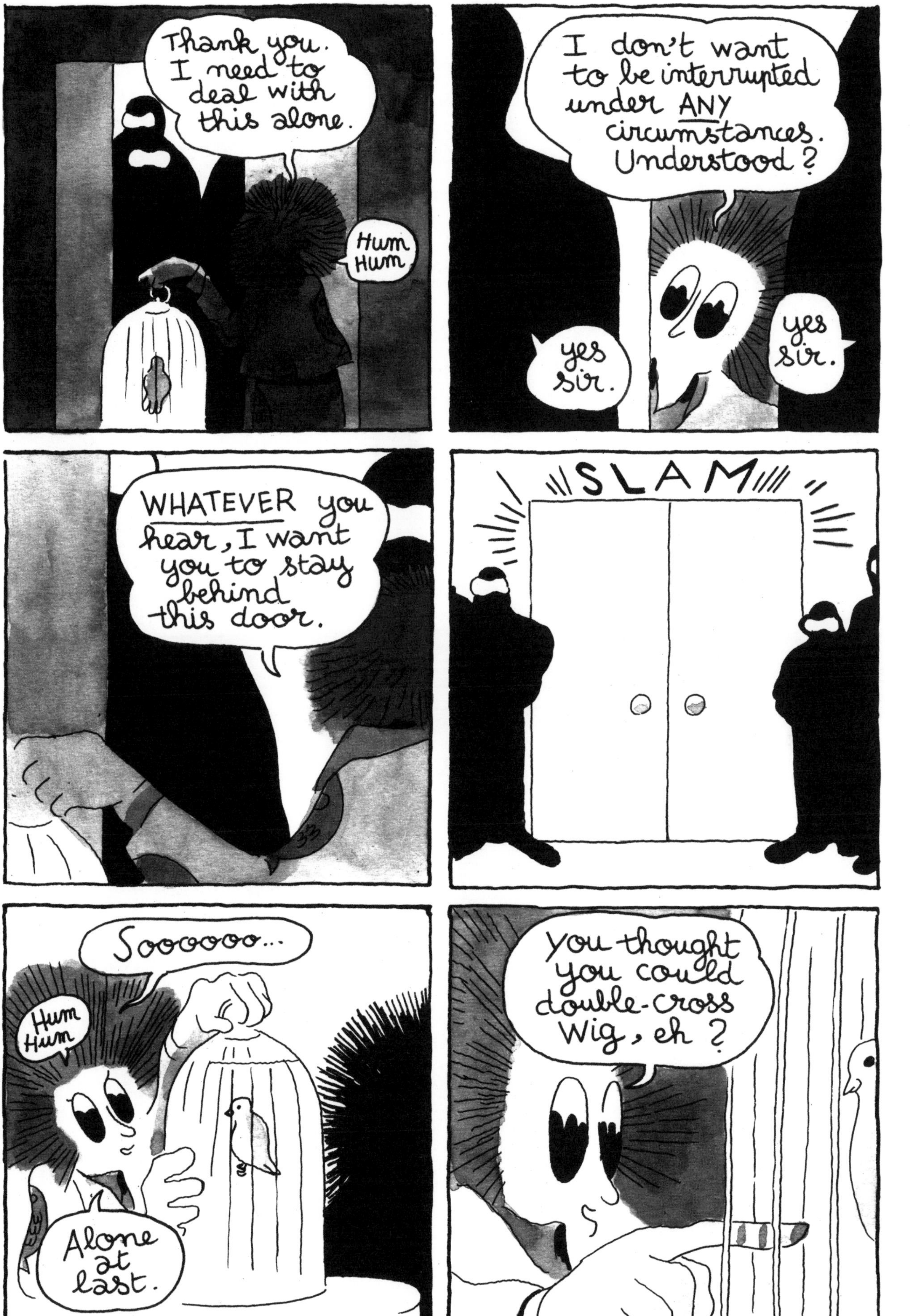
Thank you. I need to deal with this alone.
Hum Hum
I don't want to be interrupted under ANY circumstances. Understood?
yes sir.
yes sir.
WHATEVER you hear, I want you to stay behind this door.
SLAM
Soooooo...
Hum Hum
Alone at last.
You thought you could double-cross Wig, eh?

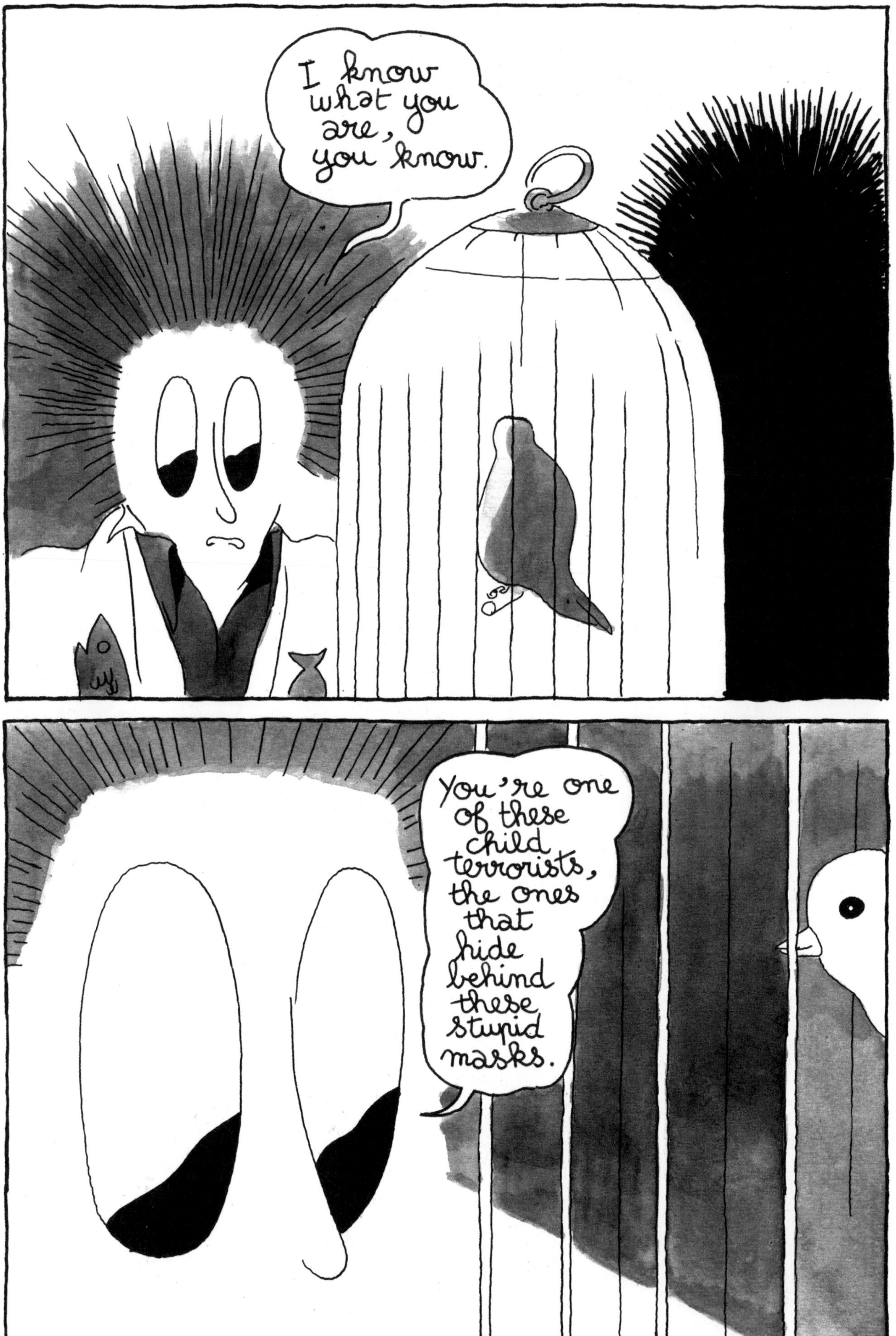
I know what you are, you know.
You're one of these child terrorists, the ones that hide behind these stupid masks.

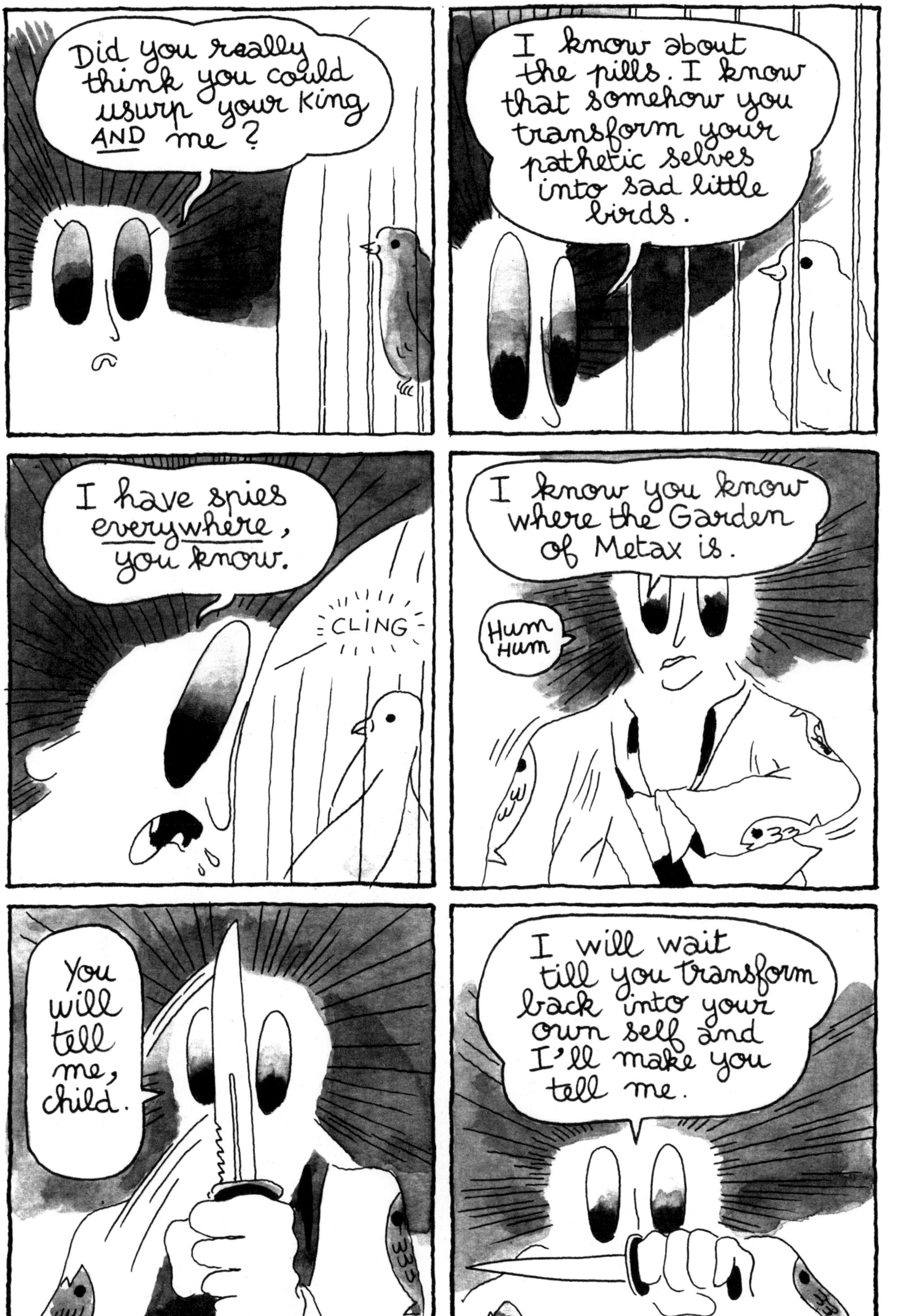
Did you really think you could usurp your King AND me?
I know about the pills. I know that somehow you transform your pathetic selves into sad little birds.
I have spies everywhere, you know.
CLING
I know you know where the Garden of Metax is.
Hum Hum
You will tell me, child.
I will wait till you transform back into your own self and I'll make you tell me.

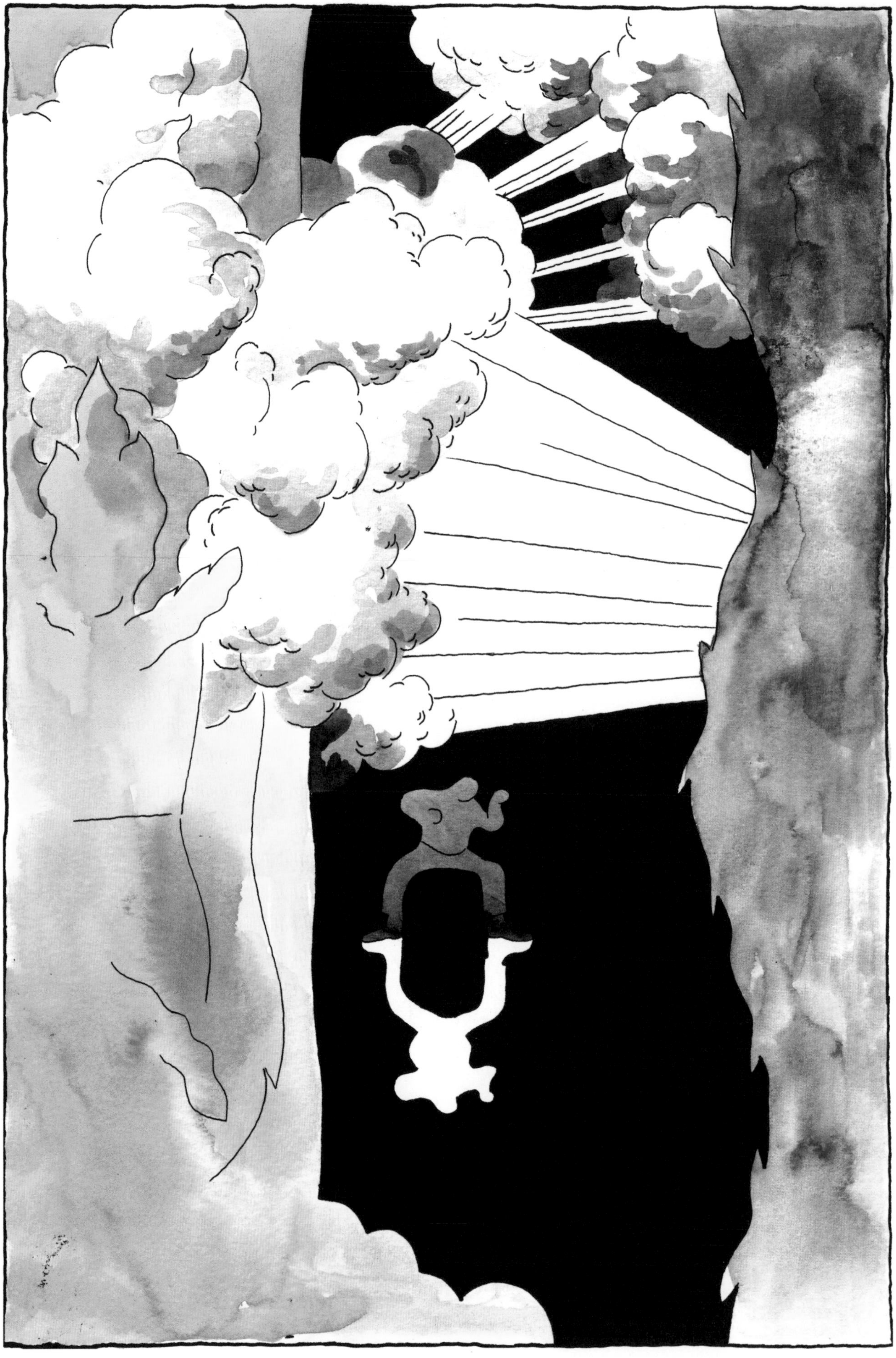

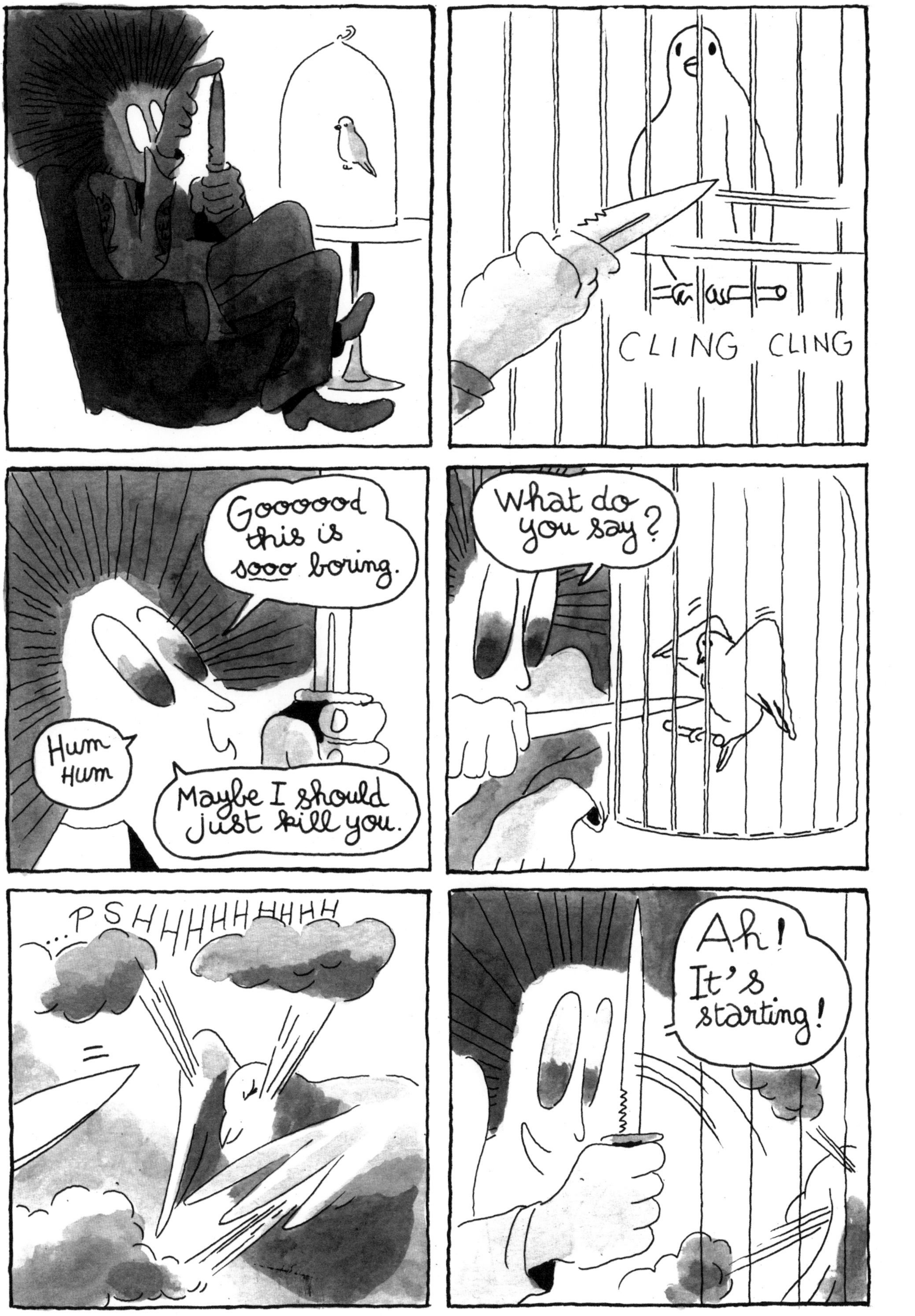
CLING CLING
Gooooood this is sooo boring.
Hum Hum
Maybe I should just kill you.
What do you say?
...PSHHHHHHHHH
Ah! It's starting!

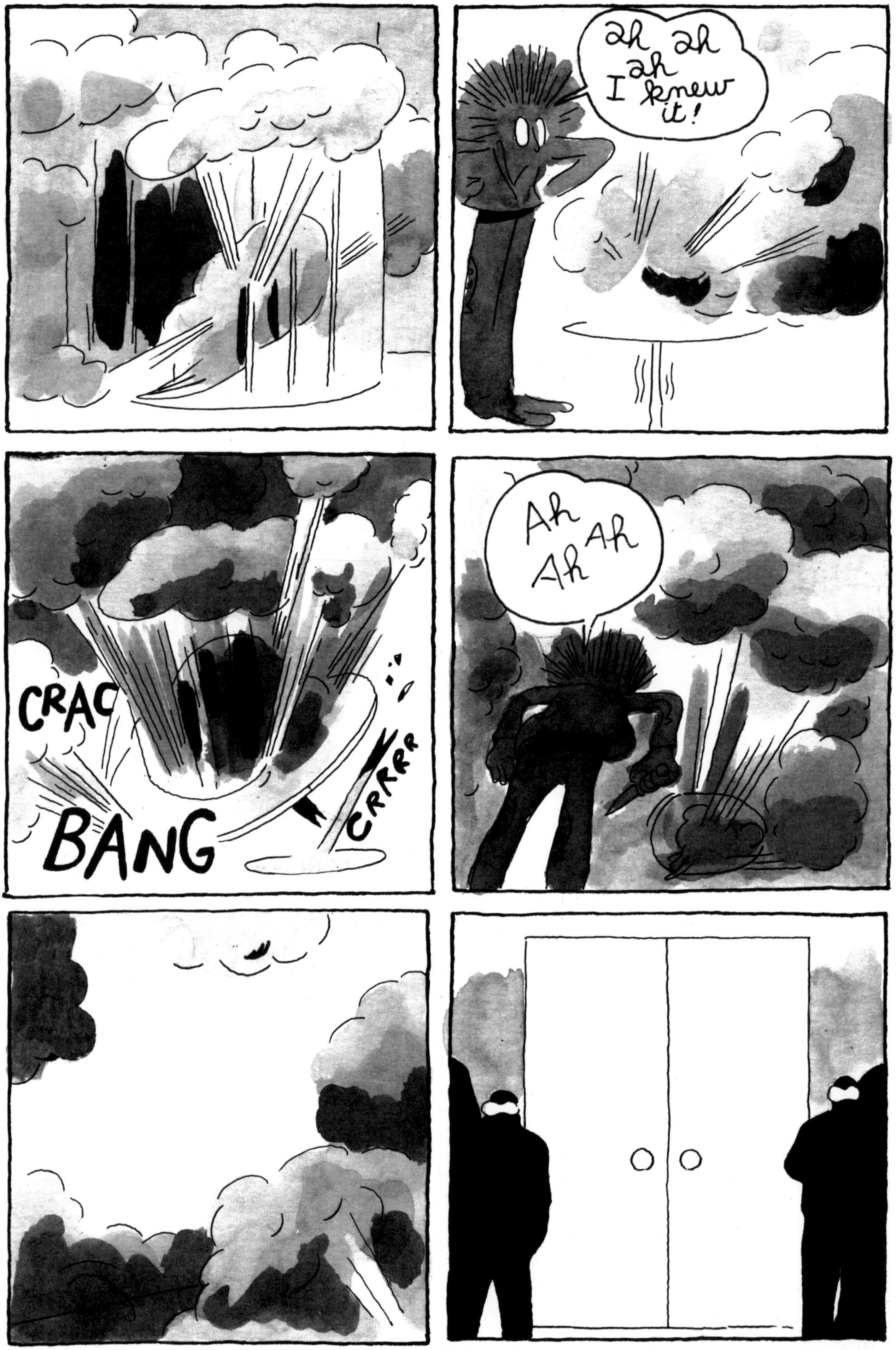
ah ah ah I knew it!
CRAC
BANG
CRRRR
Ah Ah Ah

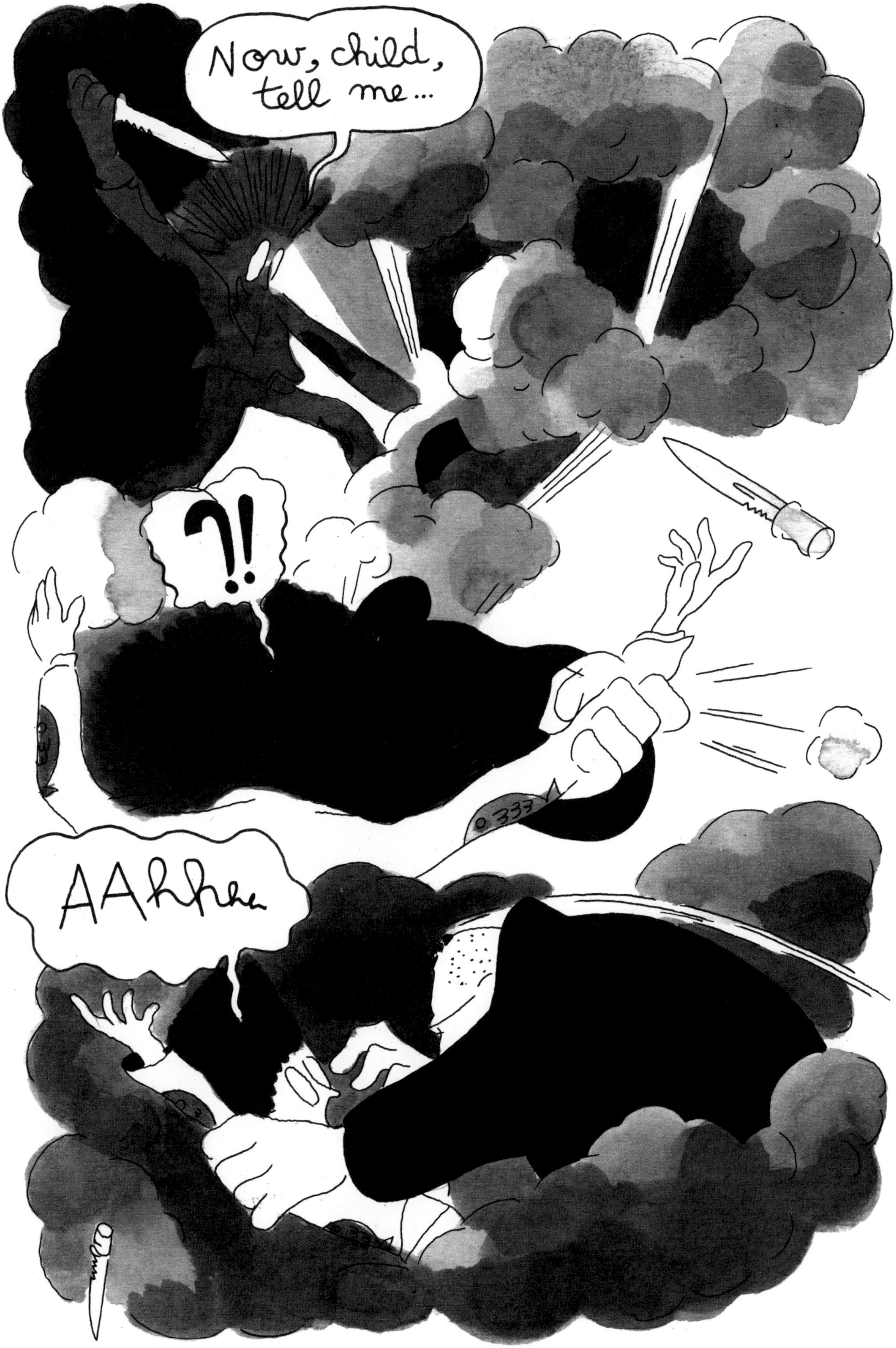
Now, child, tell me...
?!
AAhhh

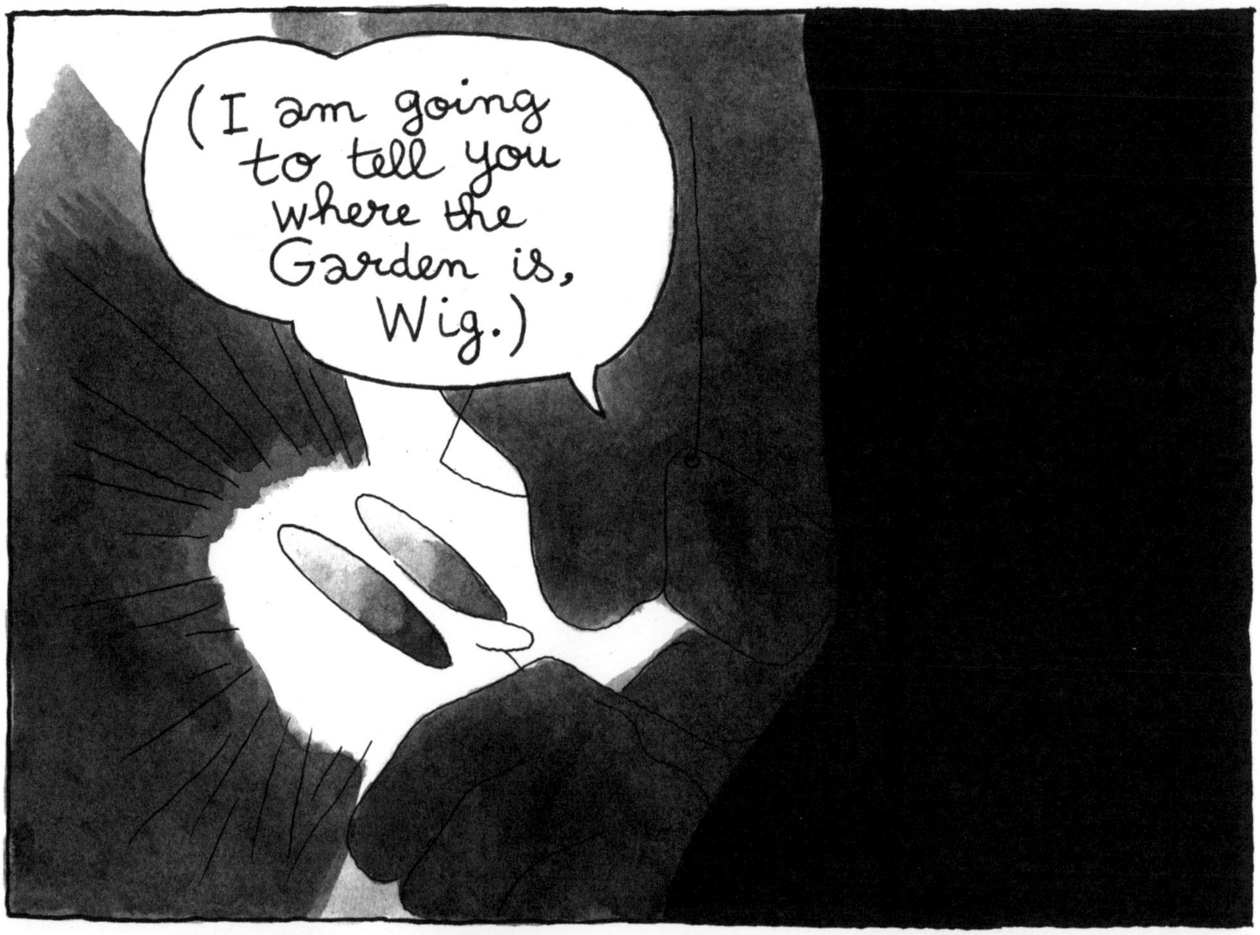
(I am going to tell you where the Garden is, Wig.)

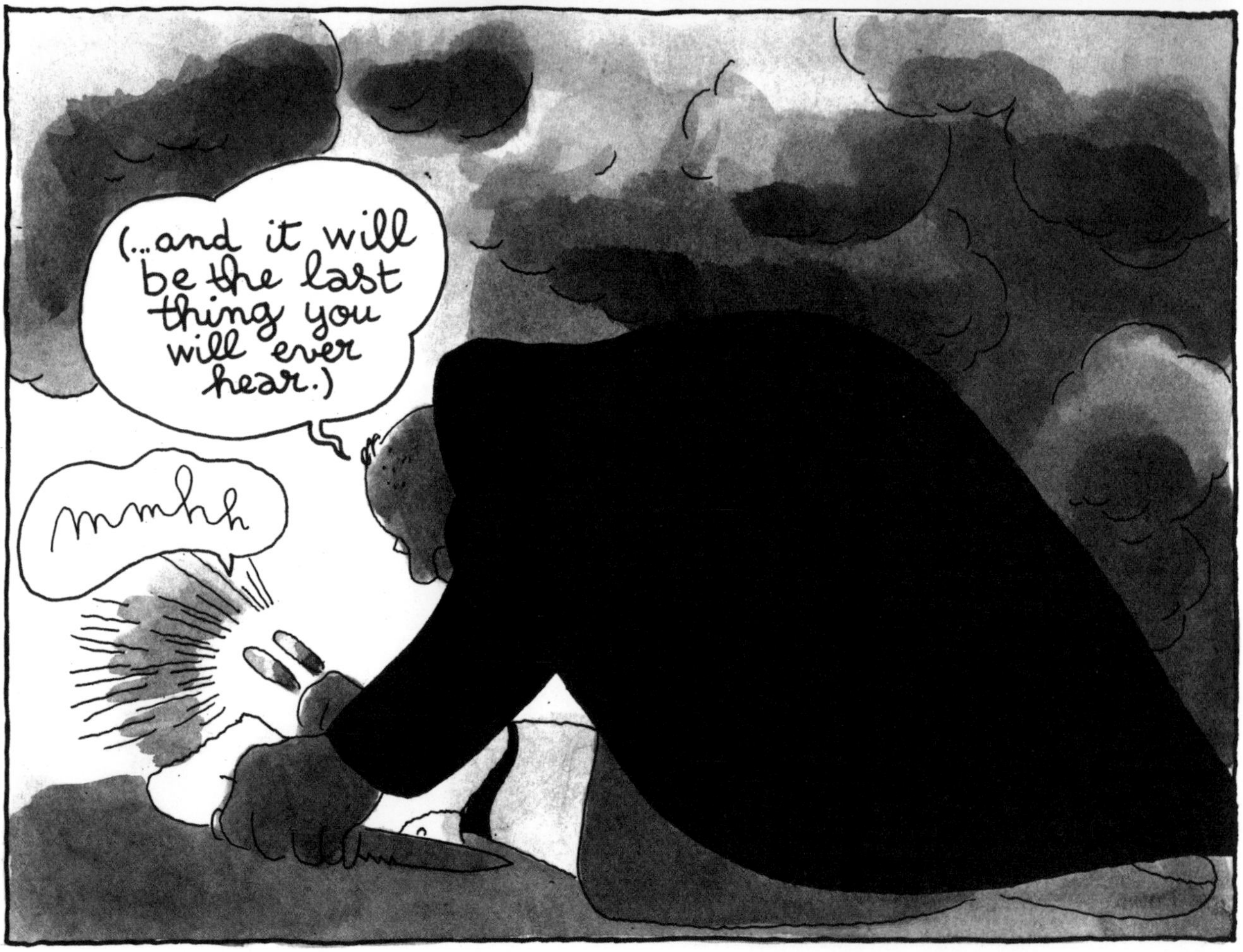
(...and it will be the last thing you will ever hear.)
mmhh

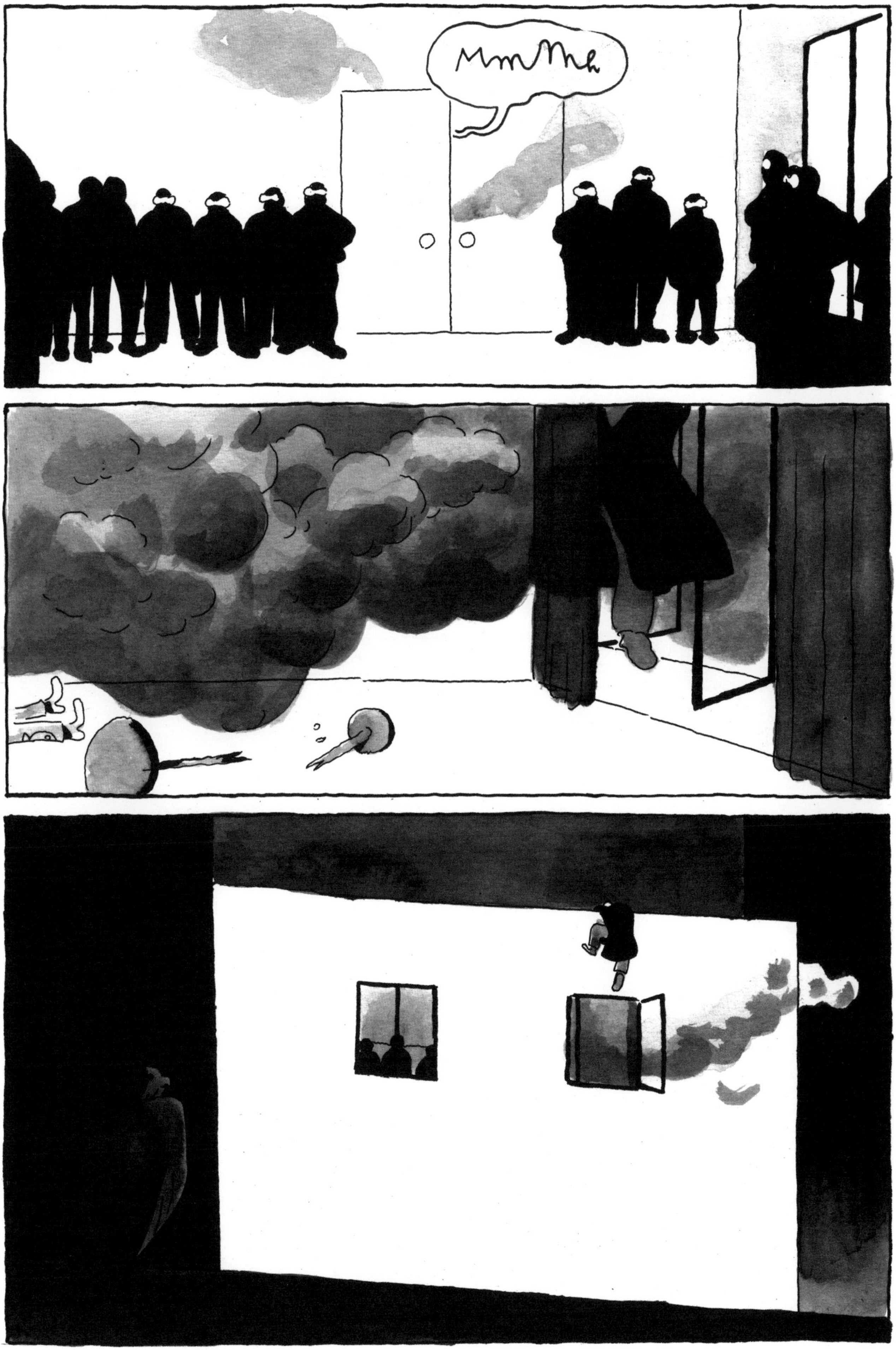

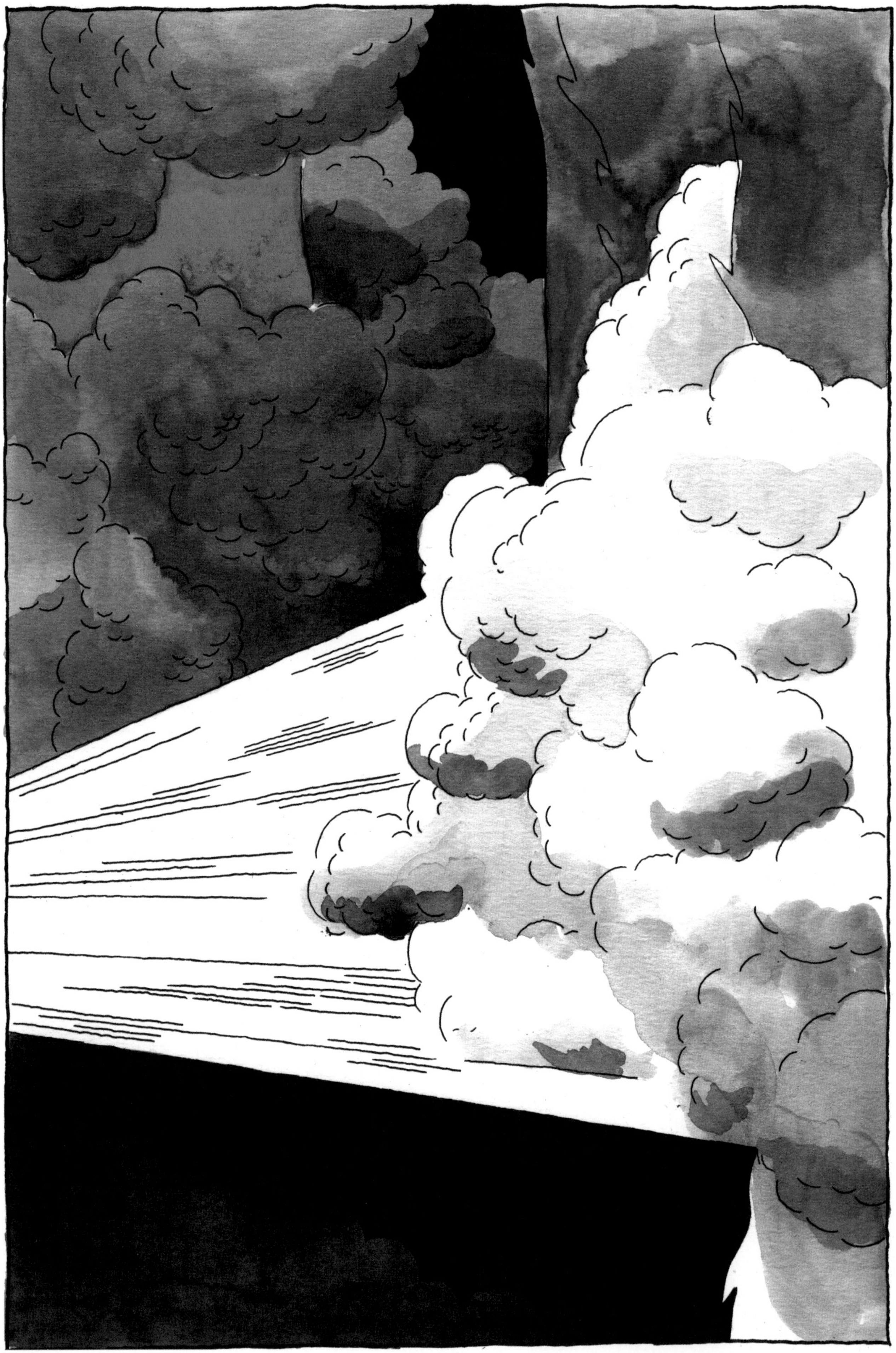

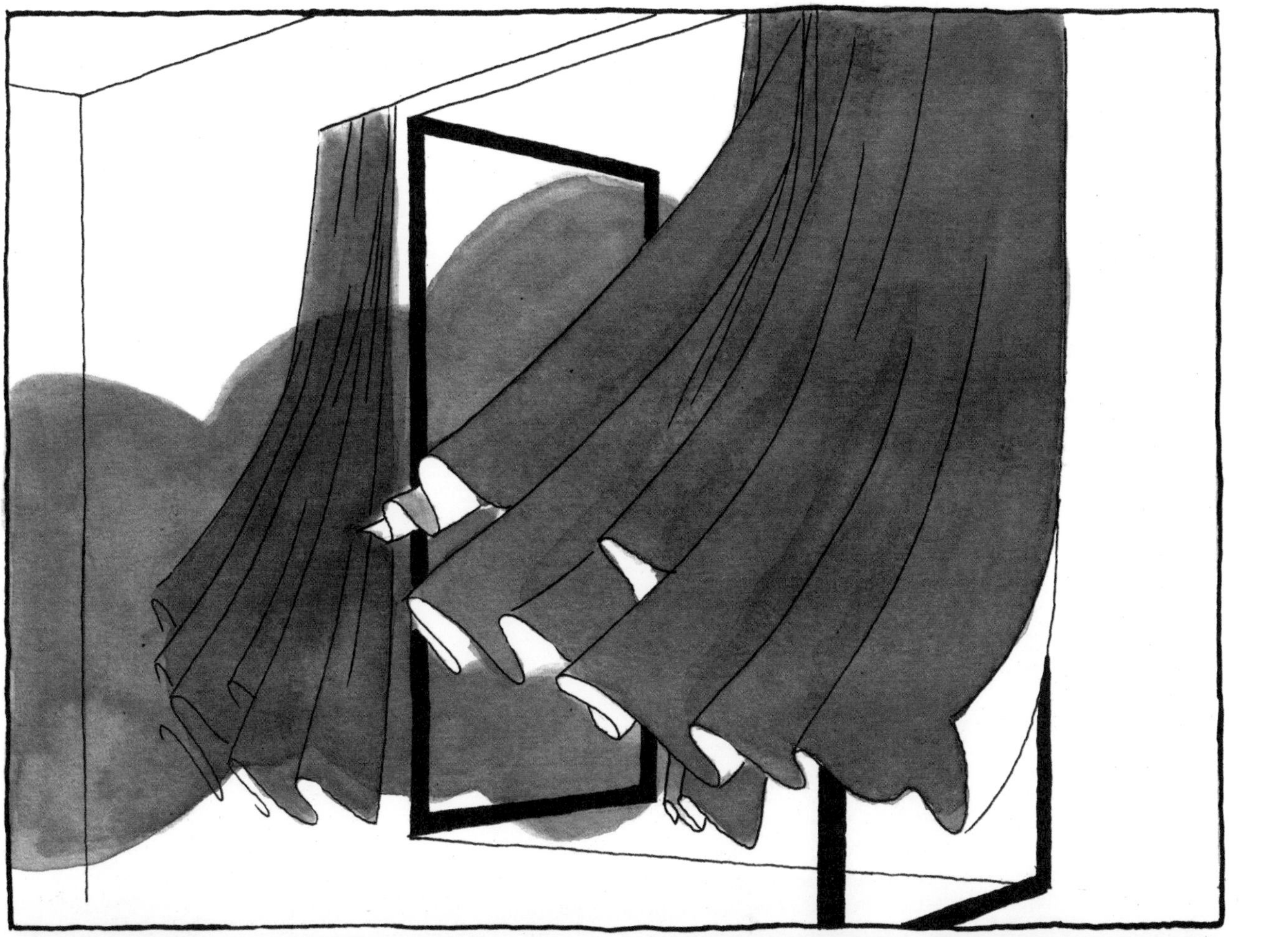

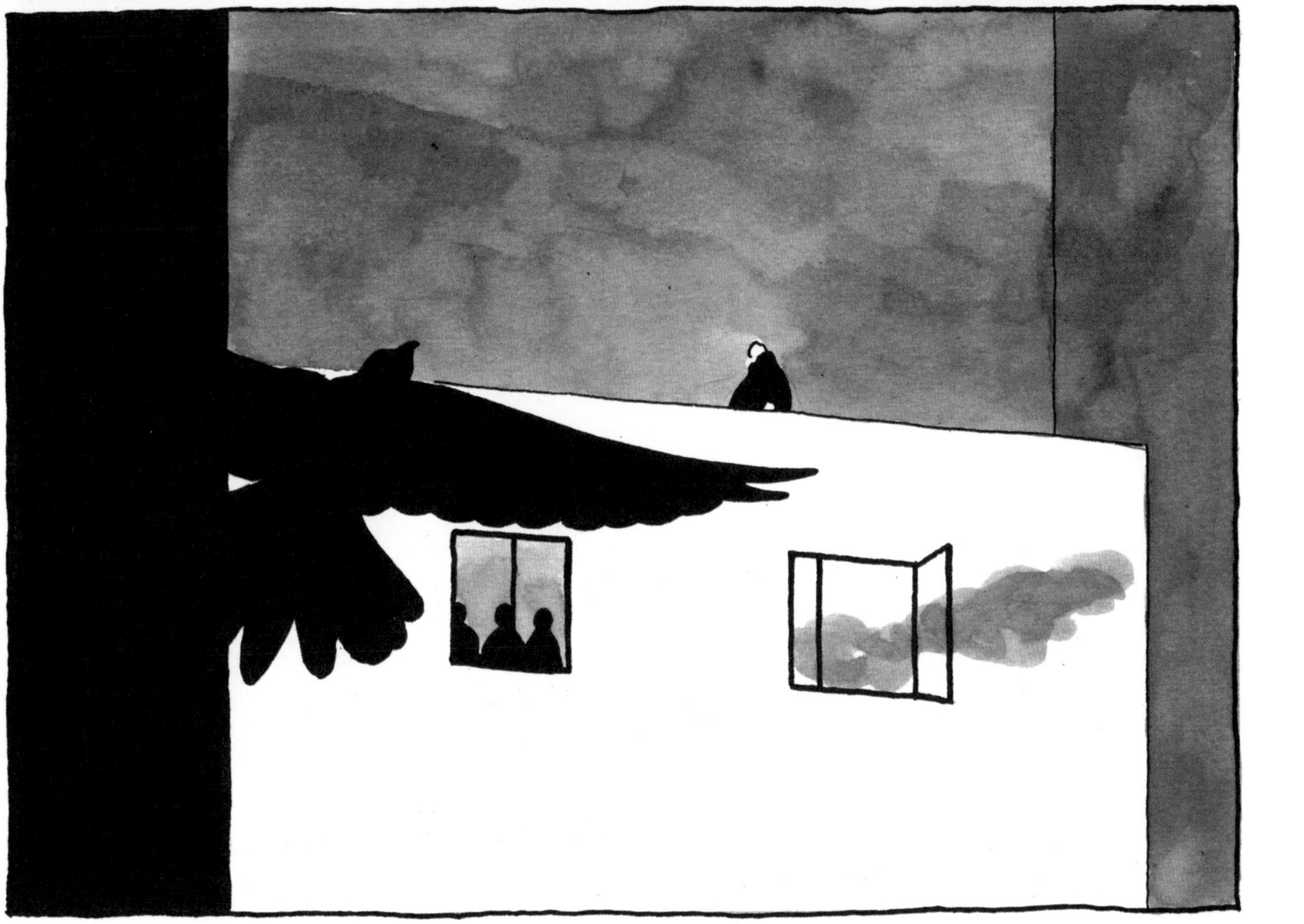

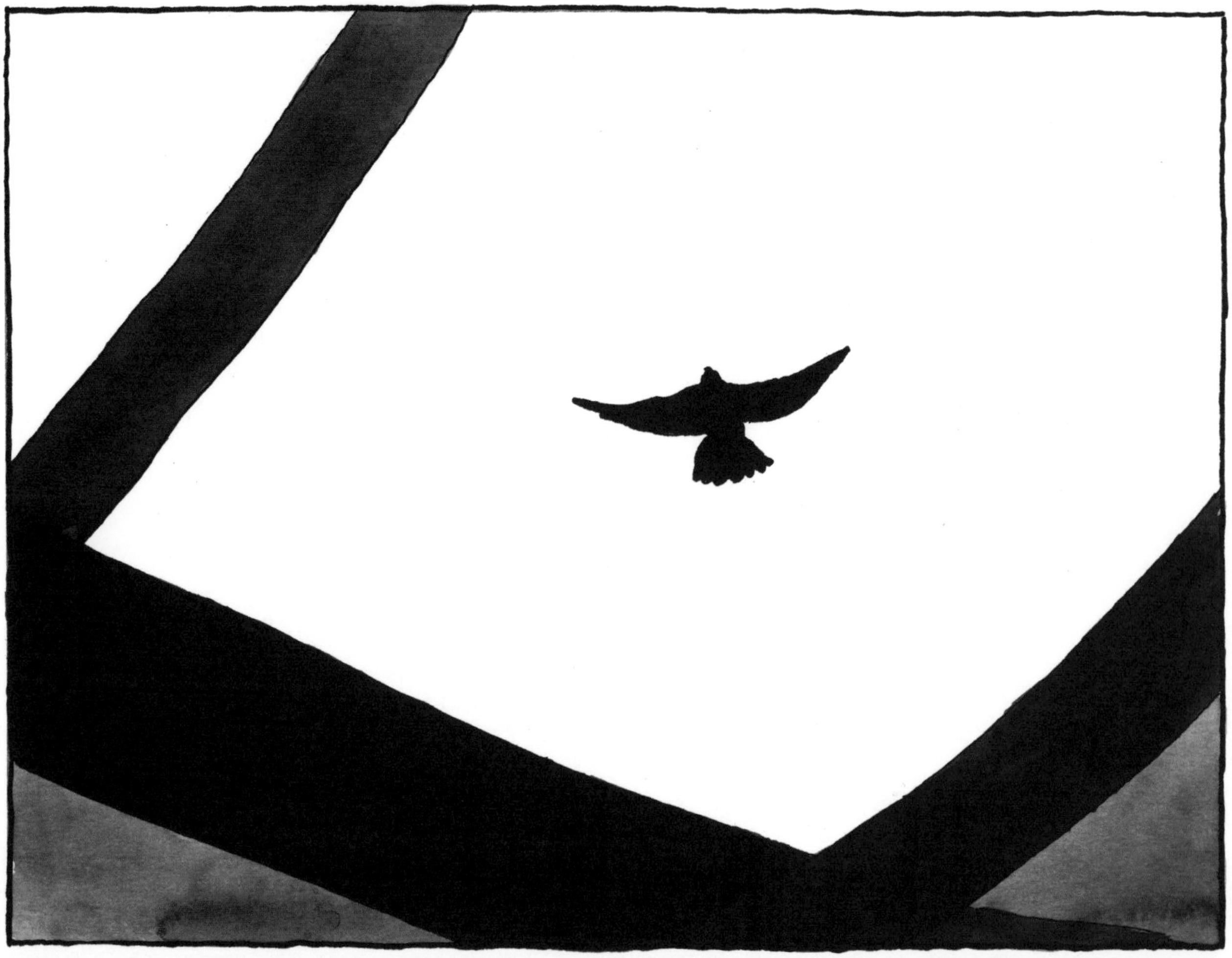

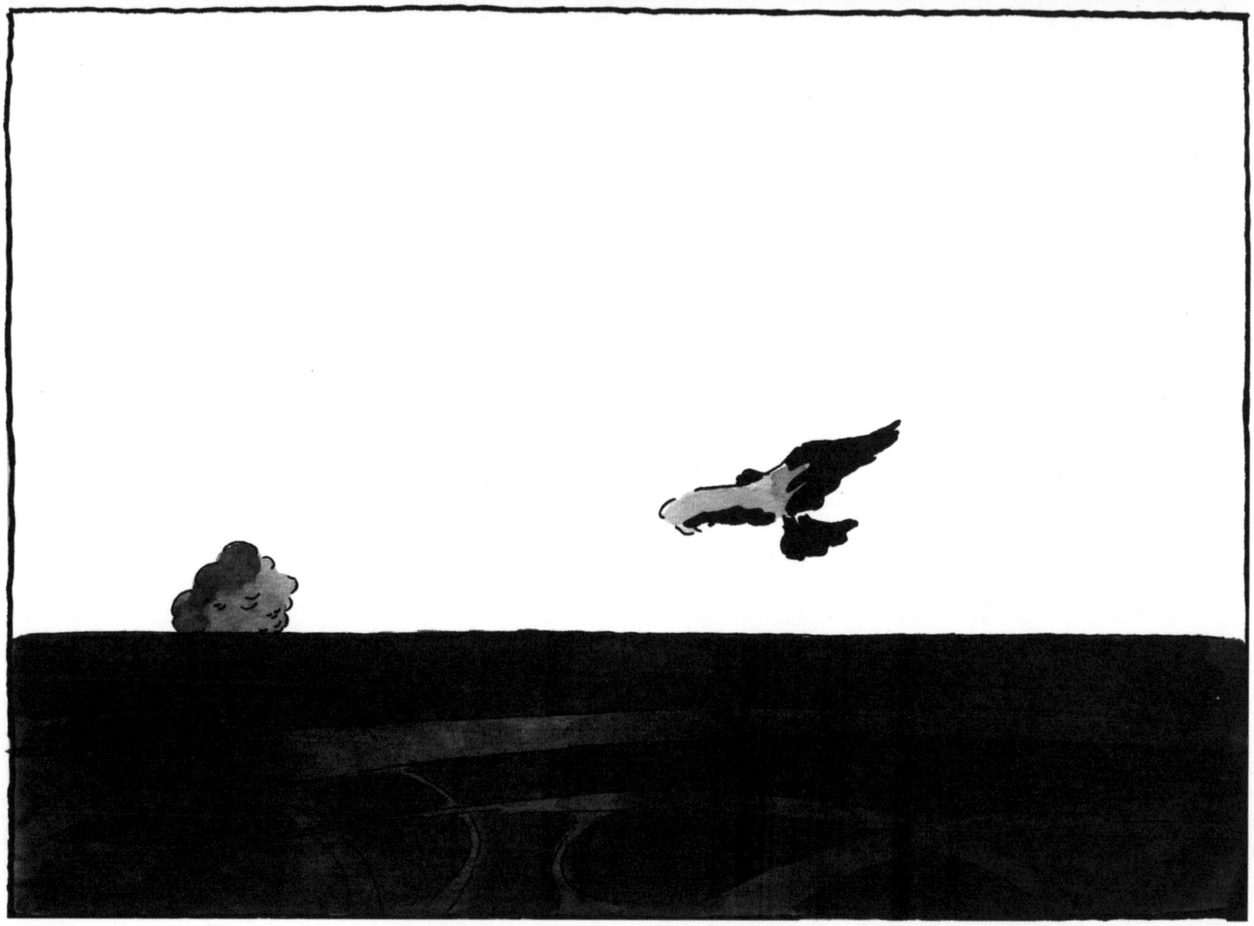

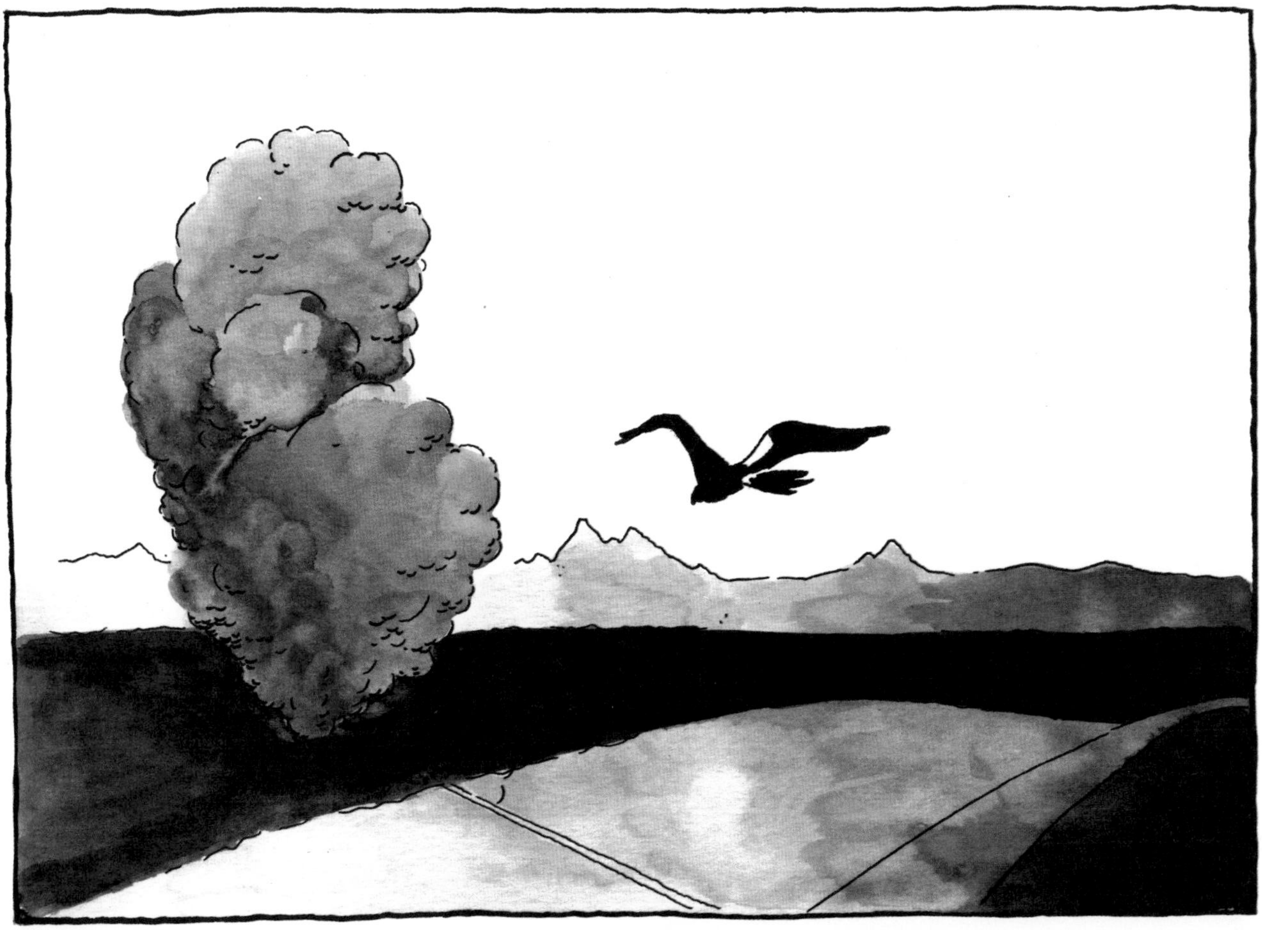

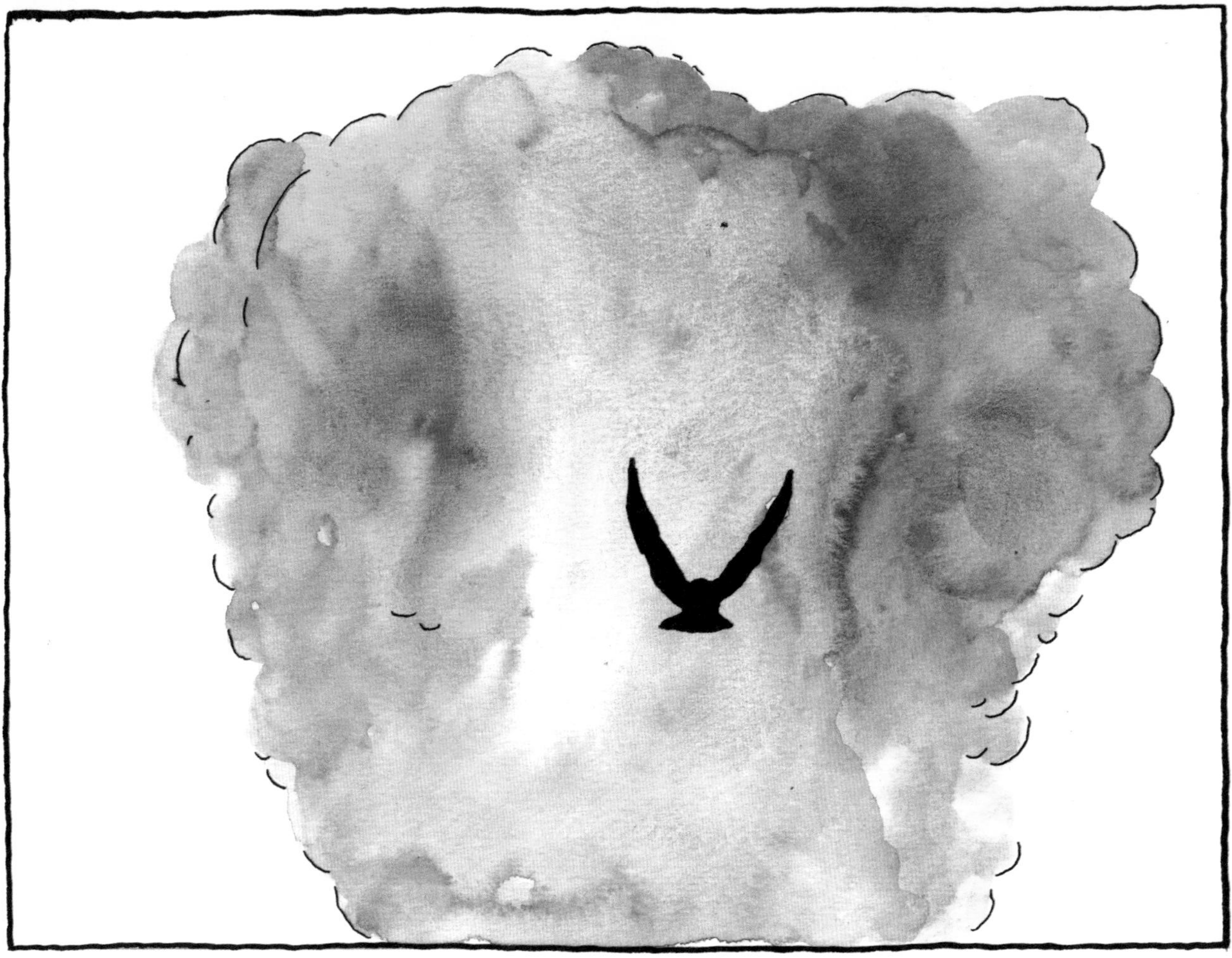

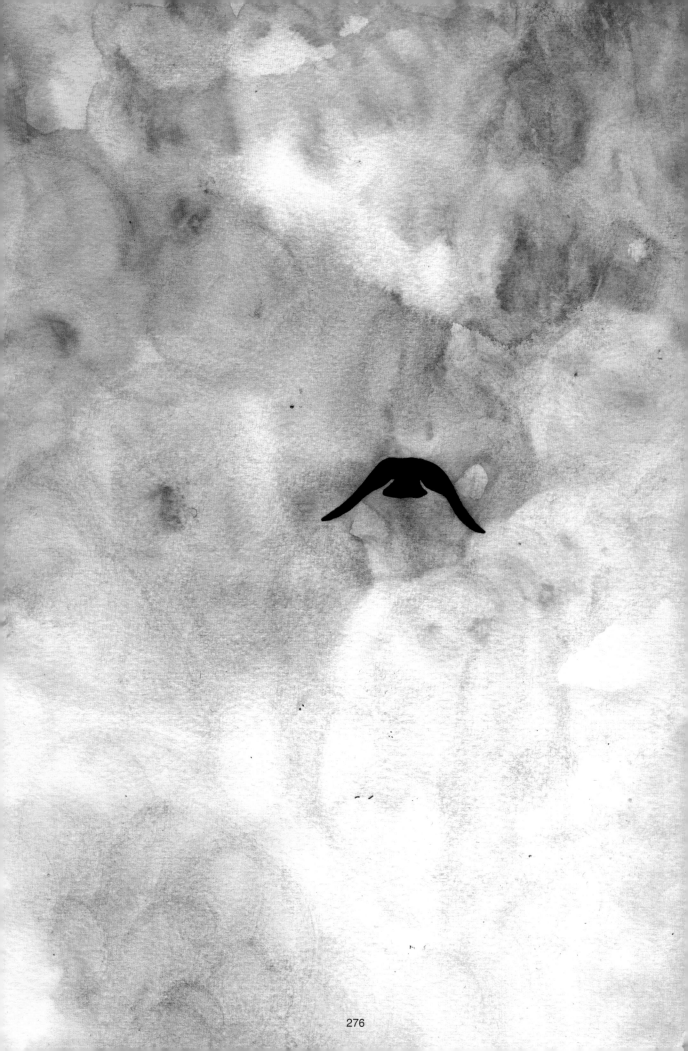

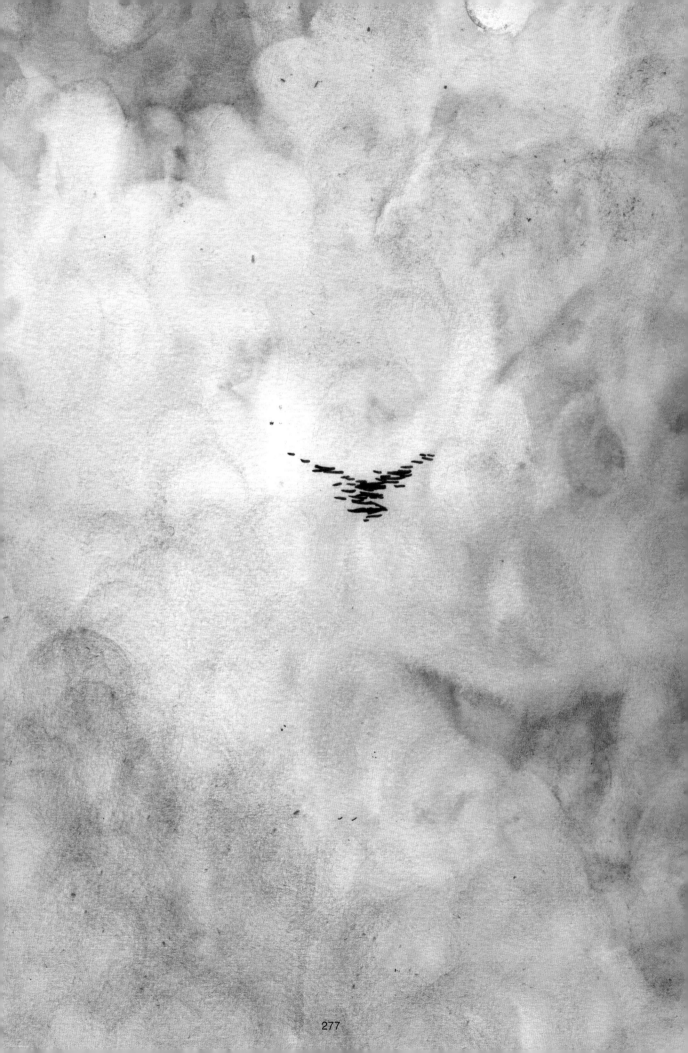

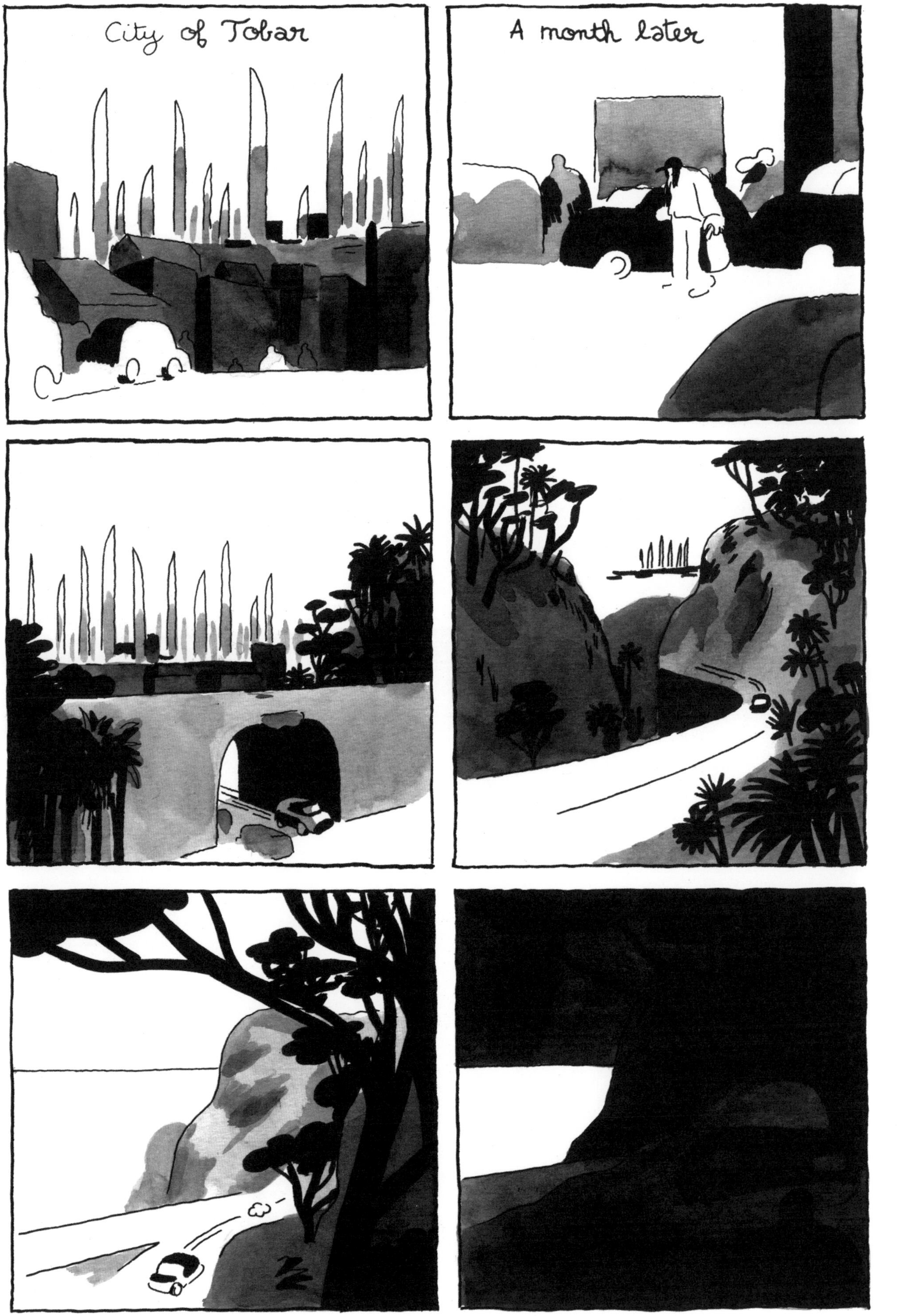
City of Tobar
A month later

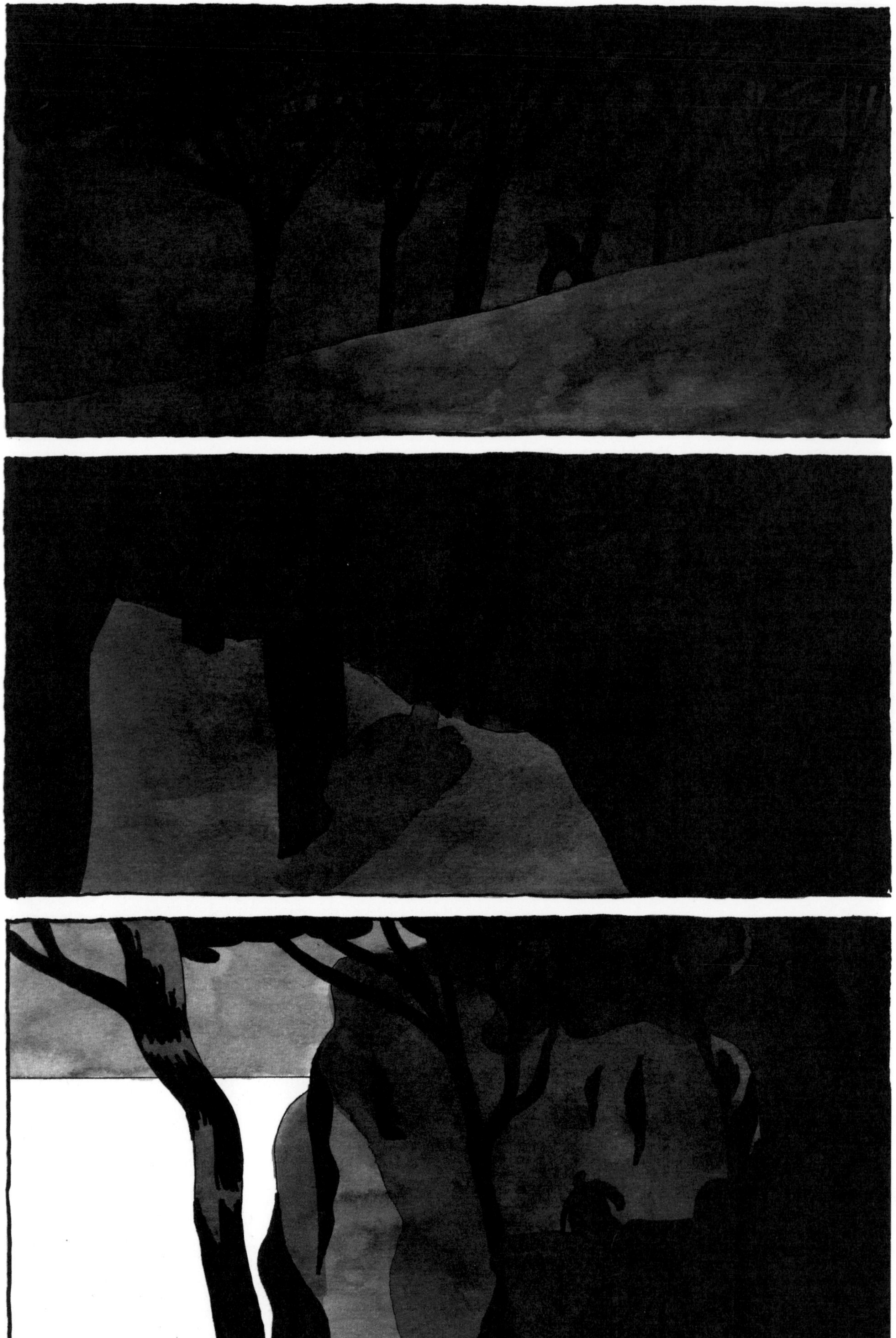

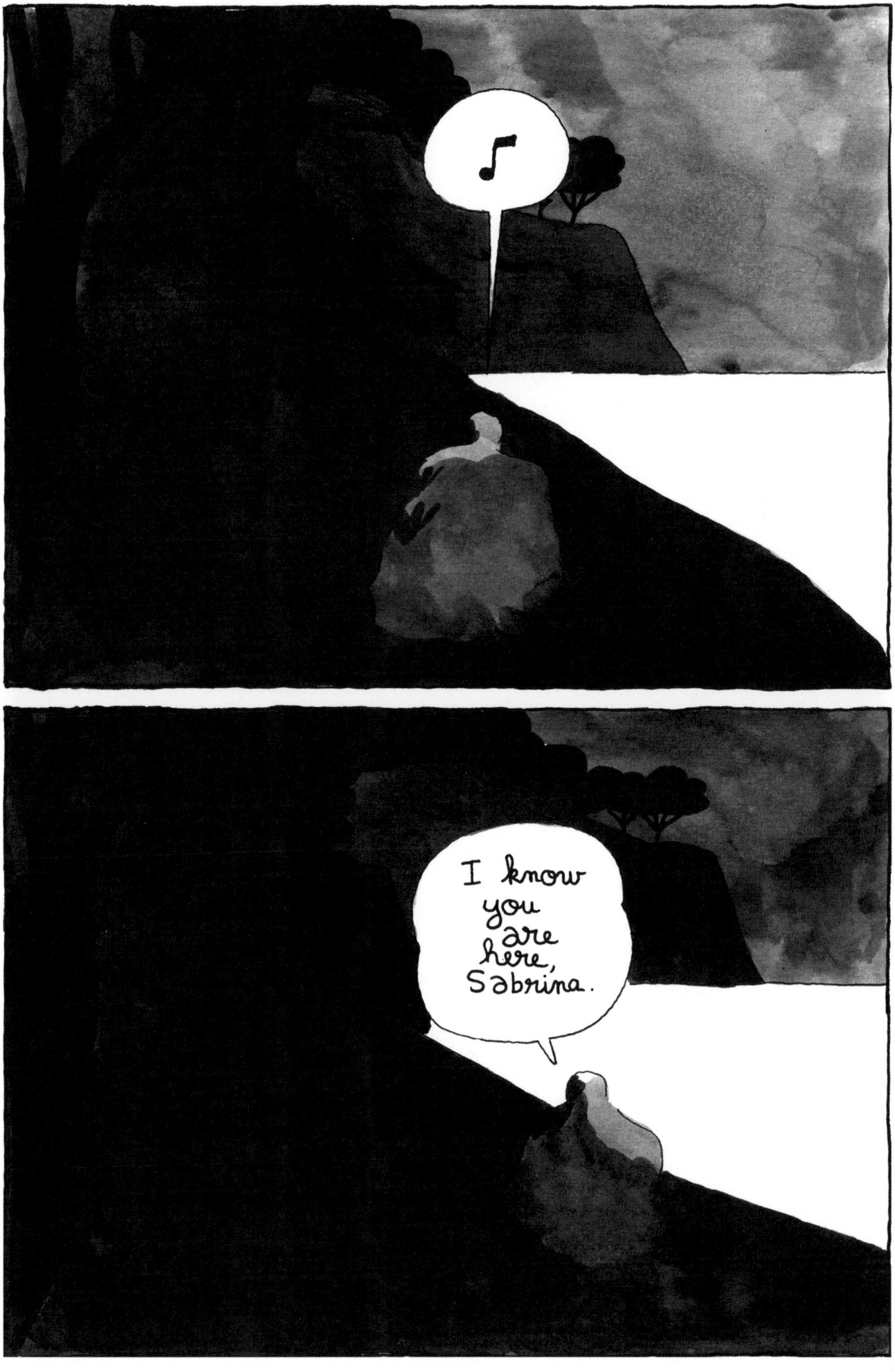
♪
I know you are here, Sabrina.

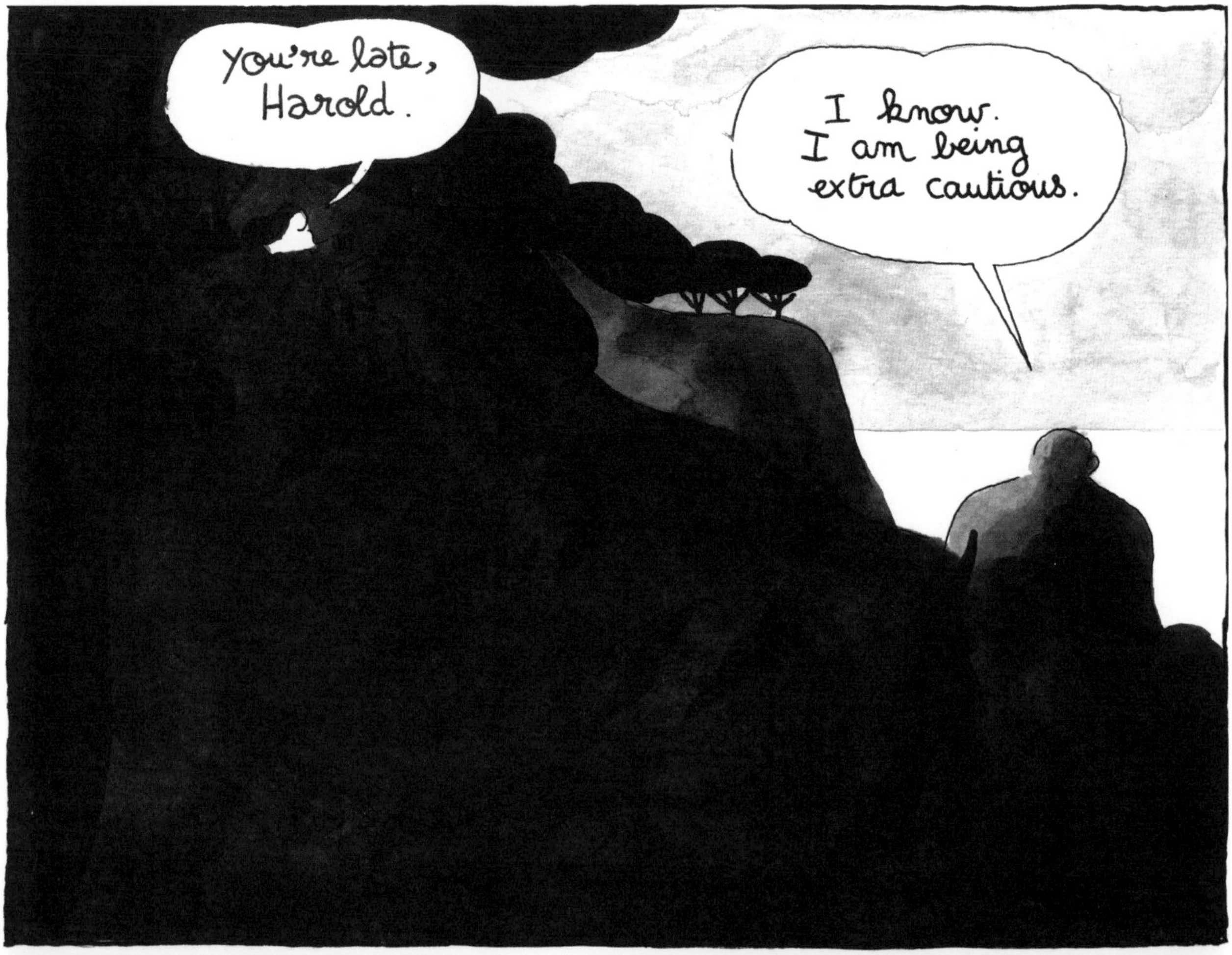
You're late, Harold.
I know. I am being extra cautious.

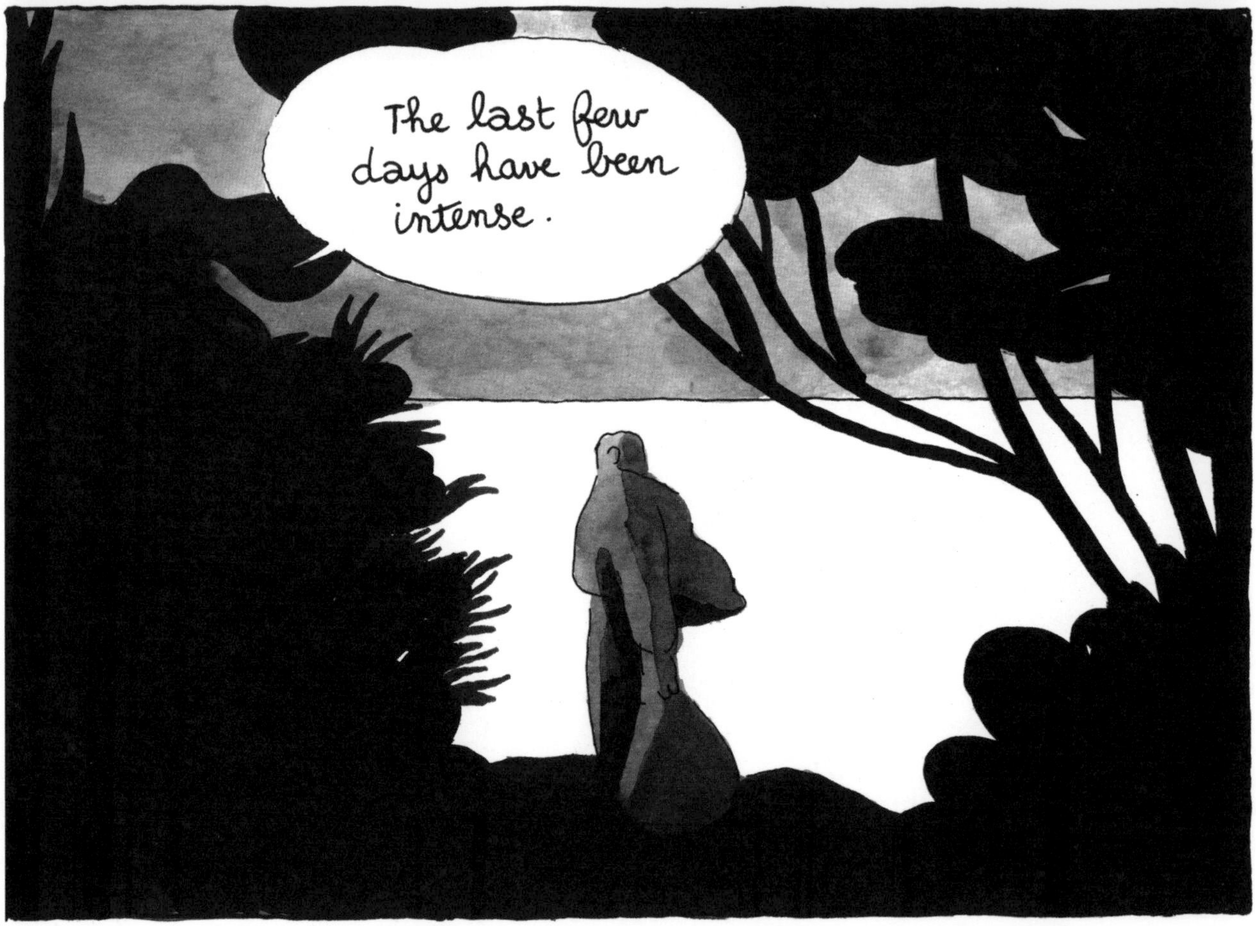
The last few days have been intense.

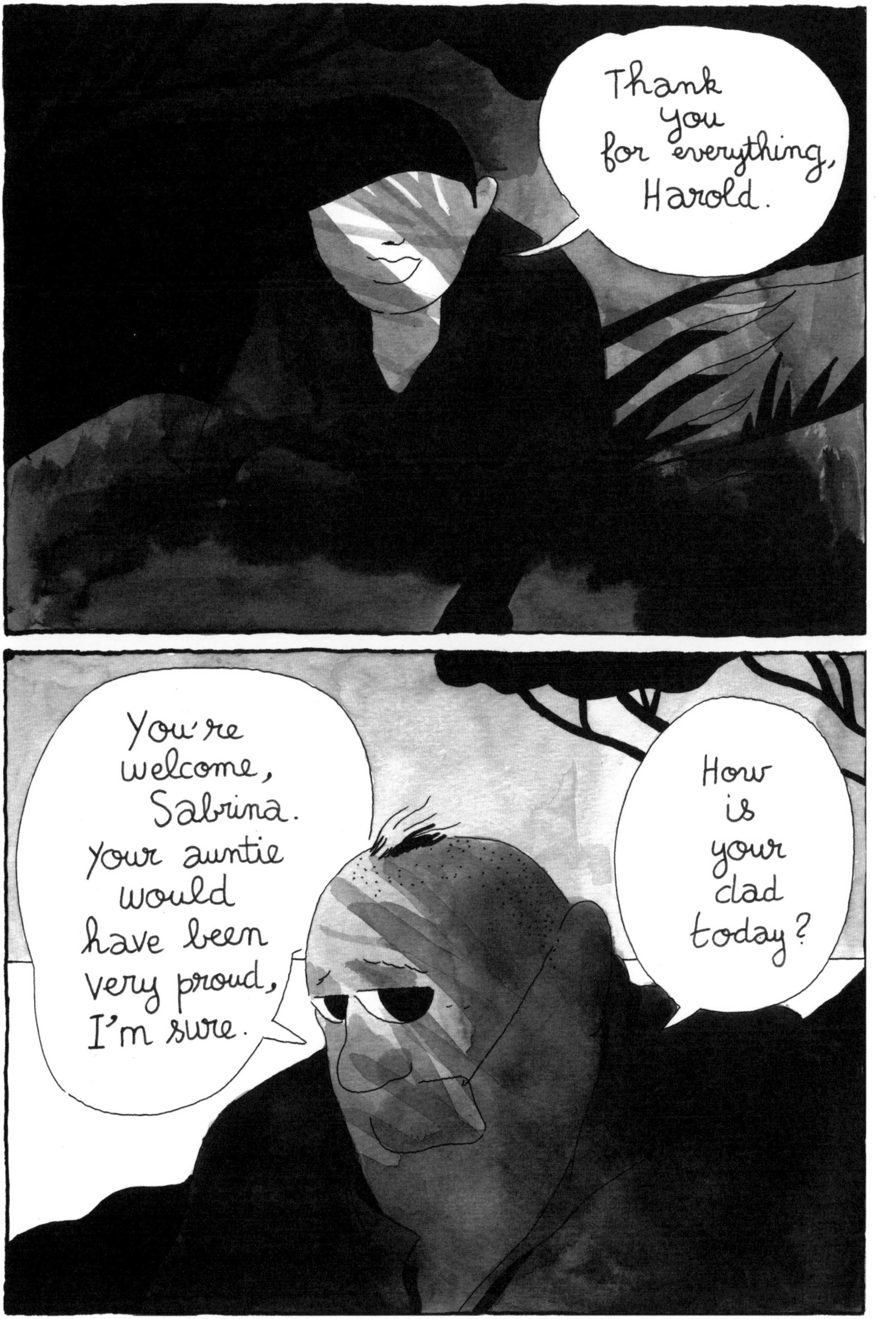
Thank you for everything, Harold.
You're welcome, Sabrina. Your auntie would have been very proud, I'm sure.
How is your dad today?

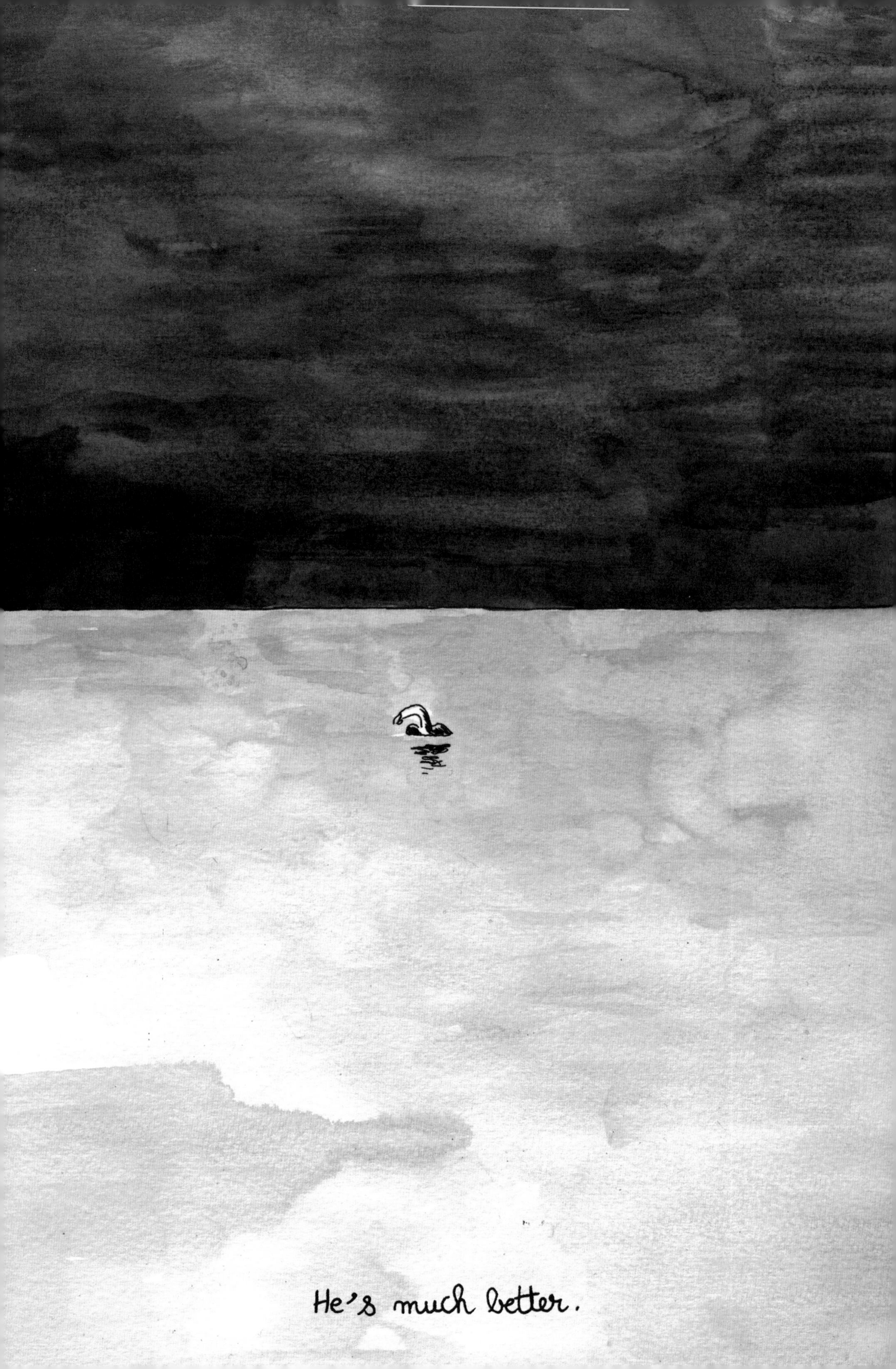
He's much better.

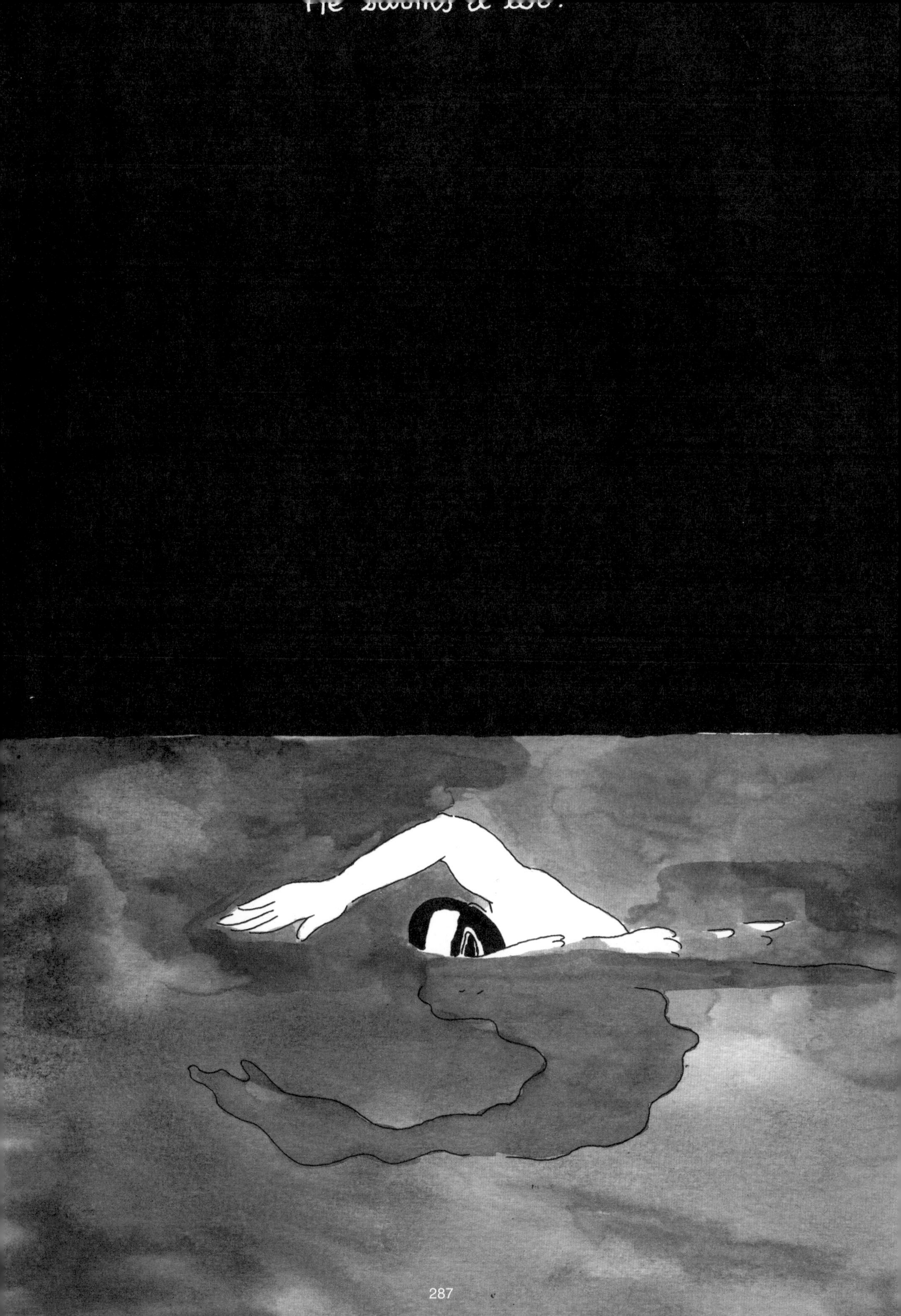

The stars in his eye
have disappeared.